38ᵘ

99BB

CONDITIONING
An Image Approach

CONDITIONING
An Image Approach

by

DONALD L. KING

Howard University

GARDNER PRESS, INC. • *New York*

DISTRIBUTED BY HALSTED PRESS,
DIVISION OF JOHN WILEY & SONS, INC.

New York   Toronto   London   Sydney

GARDNER PRESS, INC.
19 Union Square West
New York 10003

Distributed solely by the HALSTED PRESS
Division of John Wiley & Sons, Inc., New York

Library of Congress Cataloging in Publication Data

King, Donald L., 1941-
    Conditioning, an image approach.
    1. Conditioned response.   2. Imagery
(Psychology) I. Title.
BF319.K54   153.1'5   78-7268
ISBN 0-470-26386-5

THIS BOOK
IS DEDICATED TO MY PARENTS,

MARIE *and* RENO C. KING

Preface

This book was written for undergraduate and graduate students taking courses in the learning area. The major elementary and advanced topics in conditioning are covered. Elementary results and concepts are carefully described and discussed before considering more advanced ones.

In addition, the text uses an image theory to account for basic conditioning results. This theory is also used to interpret a relatively large number of more advanced topics in conditioning; it is importantly involved with findings in all of the text's chapters. The text's primary contribution is the quality of the integration of conditioning material achieved with the use of the image theory of conditioning, and in other ways as well. This integration should enhance students' understanding of and intellectual satisfaction with the conditioning area.

Naturally, the image theory of conditioning is somewhat related to other theoretical approaches. Many now consider it appropriate to discuss conditioning in terms of representations of stimuli, and an image of a stimulus involves the representation of a stimulus. Results obtained with humans that involve images of stimuli support the theory that brain events responsible for images of stimuli mediate conditioning outcomes. For this and additional reasons it is better to analyze conditioning in terms of images of stimuli than in terms of representations of stimuli. Image theory is intimately related to what is called an engram activation theory of learning. Both theories assume that an engram or permanent brain event that corresponds to a stimulus becomes activated under certain circumstances. This assumption has a long history, for example, it is an integral component of Hebb's theory of perceptual learning. Image theory's account of instrumental conditioning is also related in one respect to Mowrer's explanation of this conditioning.

Because of the new theoretical approach, the text will also be of interest to researchers in conditioning. In addition, this approach more readily relates to the language learning, human learning, memory, and perception areas than the traditional behavioristic orientation, and thus students and investigators in these areas should find this conditioning text of more than normal use.

A minor purpose of the text is to provide students with some appreciation for the position that conditioning principles help in understanding human social behavior. The idea that much of social behavior is acquired through conditioning is stressed, and systematic desensitization and instrumental conditioning therapies are touched on.

My wife, Barbara, provided emotional support through the many hours that I worked on the text. My young children, Christopher and Daniel, did likewise and at other times were not unduly difficult. Barbara prepared most of the figures, and Michael J. Miller and Kenneth D. Smith of Howard University prepared some of the figures and did the photography. I am also grateful to the large number of researchers whose findings and ideas are the basis for the text. My publisher helped to make it more readable.

I also wish to thank the organizations and authors who permitted publication of their materials. Their contribution is acknowledged in specific figures in the body of the text.

DONALD L. KING
Washington, D. C.

Contents

CHAPTER 1

Introduction to and Theories of Classical and Instrumental Conditioning

This text describes a type of learning called *conditioning*. There are two main types of conditioning, classical and instrumental conditioning. Two other important types of learning are verbal and language learning and perceptual learning, but they are not the focus of this text.

A learned response is a relatively permanent change in response to a stimulus that results, at least in part, from previous exposure to the same stimulus or one that is similar. In addition, for this change in response to be considered a learned one it ordinarily cannot be due to a factor that affects responses to a relatively wide variety of stimuli. A response refers to the behavior, that is, the overt action of an animal or a person, although response may be used more broadly, for example, to refer to a change in electrical potential of the skin or to a reaction by a nerve cell.

A stimulus involves a change in physical energy or chemical substance that may be responded to by a receptor. Examples of stimuli are the ringing of a bell, the termination of a light, and the appearance of food. Stimulation of a receptor generally results in a series of neural impulses. These neural impulses are at least partly responsible for the responses that certain stimuli elicit. Neural impulses produced by the stimulus of food in the mouth, for instance, are partly responsible for the salivation response that food in the mouth elicits. Neural impulses also contribute to our ability to describe the stimulus that results in stimulation of a receptor. For example, neural impulses produced by a visual stimulus of a certain wavelength are partly responsible for our ability to say that a particular color is being perceived.

Let us apply our definition of learning to typewriting. Practice ordinarily results in an increase in the accuracy and rate of typing, an increase that is a change in response to the stimulus complex of the typewriter, paper, and so on. Clearly, this change in response results from the practice correlated with previous exposure to this stimulus complex. Also, practice in typing results in a relatively permanent change in response, for the increase in accuracy and rate of typing will be retained from one day to the next. Moreover, the increase in accuracy and rate of typing is not due to a factor that affects responses to a relatively wide variety of stimuli, because practicing typewriting will not influence responding in general.

Injury, illness, and maturational development are examples of factors that affect responses to a relatively wide variety of stimuli, and therefore their effect on responding cannot ordinarily be considered to be due to learning. An injury to a limb and illness will impair performance of many skilled responses, and an increase in maturational development will improve performance of the same responses, but these effects are not due to learning. Of course, injury, illness, and maturational development may also affect responding through learning. A person may learn not to come too close to a fan if he catches a finger in it.

Much of our understanding of conditioning comes from research with nonhuman subjects. The main reason animals are usually studied is that their environment can be controlled in ways that the environment of humans cannot. However, humans become conditioned in much the same way as other mammals and birds, so that findings of animal conditioning studies can be applied to humans. In fact, conditioning findings will sometimes be applied to the areas of human psychopathology and development of human social behavior.

Classical Conditioning

I. P. Pavlov virtually discovered *classical conditioning* and was the first to investigate it extensively.

Examples of Classical Conditioning. A response that has been classically conditioned is the salivation response. Food is often used to establish salivary conditioning. Typically, a food-deprived animal is first presented with a stimulus such as a light or a bell. A few seconds later food is presented. Delivery of the food follows delivery of the first stimulus (the light or bell) independently of the animal's responding. The first stimulus is usually terminated at about the time the food occurs.

The sight and taste of food elicits a large increase in salivation. Classical conditioning of salivation is said to occur when it can be shown that the first stimulus has acquired the ability also to produce an increase in salivation as a consequence of the pairings between this stimulus and food. The increase in salivation elicited by food in the mouth is not an instance of learning. Animals automatically salivate when food is in the mouth; they do not learn to do so. However, the increase in salivation produced by the first stimulus is a learned response. The increase in salivation to this stimulus is a change in response to the same stimulus the animal was previously exposed to. In addition, this increase in salivation response is relatively permanent, because if the first stimulus is subsequently presented, say a day later, it will still produce an increase in salivation. Also, the procedure resulting in this increase in salivation response does not affect the responses to a wide variety of stimuli. Thus, the increase in salivation produced by the first stimulus is a learned response; it is called a classically conditioned response.

Figure 1-1 illustrates a typical setup for classical conditioning of salivation. Food is delivered in the cup directly in front of the dog. The straps keep the dog in the same position during training. The tube goes through the dog's cheek and terminates at the parotid gland, the gland responsible for salivation. Drops of saliva from this gland travel down the tube coming from the cheek and activate a transducer that translates changes in amount of saliva into changes in air pressure. Alteration in air pressure displaces a recording pen that writes on a moving roll of paper, an apparatus called a kymograph or polygraph. The change in salivation over time is indicated by the extent of deflection of the pen that occurs along the polygraph paper.

In one classical conditioning study (Zener, 1937), a bell was used as the first stimulus. The time separating the onset of the bell and the moment food was delivered was 15 seconds. The food was four to six pieces of dog biscuit, and it was placed in a pan directly under the dog's mouth. Sounding the bell came to produce a marked increase in salivation.

Another example is the classical conditioning of the galvanic skin response (GSR), measured by changes in skin conductance. Skin conductance is measured by placing electrodes at two points on the surface of skin and sending a current between the two electrodes that is sufficiently low in amperage that it is not responded to. The amount of current that passes by these electrodes increases as the skin conductance increases, that is, as the skin resistance reciprocally decreases, and this amount of current is measured by a galvanometer. Deflection of the galvanometer needle can be observed directly, or the current passing through the recording electrodes can be made to alter movement of a pen of a polygraph. Variations in the height of pen deflections along the polygraph paper correspond to changes in the GSR over time.

As in salivary conditioning, a first stimulus is followed by a second stimulus independently of a subject's responding, and the second stimulus automatically elicits the classically conditioned response. The first stimulus is usually a simple auditory or visual stimulus that precedes the onset

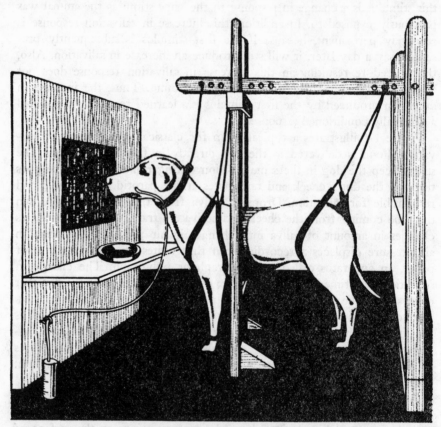

FIGURE 1-1. Set-up for classical conditioning of salivation. (Kendler, H. H., Basic Psychology, 2nd. ed. Copyright 1968. Adapted by permission of W. A. Benjamin, Inc.)

of the second stimulus by several seconds and terminates about the time the second stimulus is presented. Electric shock to a finger, for example, automatically increases the conductance of skin and is frequently employed as the second stimulus. The outcome of the pairing of the first stimulus and the shock is that the first stimulus comes to increase the conductance of the skin. This is a classically conditioned response because the increase in skin conductance is produced by the same stimulus that was previously paired with shock; this increase in skin conductance is a relatively permanent change in response; and the pairings between the first stimulus and shock do not affect responses to a wide variety of stimuli.

In classical conditioning of the GSR of humans, a subject typically sits at a table and GSR recording electrodes and electrodes for electrically shocking the subject are attached. A number of pairings of the first stimulus and shock (called trials) are presented, the shock following the first stimulus independently of how the subject responds. Figure 1-2 (Kimmel, 1965) shows the GSR classical conditioning records of six humans for the first ten pairings (ten trials) of the first stimulus, a red light, and shock. Onset of the red light preceded onset of the shock by 7.5 seconds. Durations of the red light and shock were 7.5 seconds, and 0.2 second, respectively. The left almost vertical black line of each trial record indicates the onset of the red light, and the right almost vertical black line of each trial record indicates the onset of shock. The thicker irregular line is the measured GSR. Downward movement of this line indicates an increase in skin conductance. Note that on the first trial an increase in skin conductance occurred only after shock onset. On most of the subsequent trials an increase in skin conductance also occurred after onset of the red light and before onset of the shock. This increase is the learned, classically conditioned response.

General Description of Classical Conditioning. The outcomes of salivary and galvanic skin response (GSR) classical conditioning illustrate the basic phenomenon of classical conditioning: the first stimulus acquires the ability to produce a response similar to the one elicited by the second stimulus. Presentation of food produces an increase in salivation, and so does a stimulus that has been presented just prior to food; electric shock produces an increase in the GSR, and so does a stimulus that has been presented just prior to shock; and so on.

Other classical conditioning results indicate that the learned response, that is the one produced by the first stimulus, usually resembles the one elicited by the second stimulus. For example, in the classical conditioning of mouth movement of water-deprived animals, the second stimulus, water, is placed directly into the oral cavity of the animal. This stimulus elicits mouth movements, and the stimulus that precedes it, for instance, a tone comes to produce similar mouth movements. For classical conditioning of leg movement, an electric shock to the leg elicits movement of the shocked limb, and the stimulus preceding shock to the leg acquires the ability to produce similar leg movement. For eyelid classical conditioning, a puff of air to the eye is often the second stimulus. This stimulus elicits eyelid closure, that is, a blink. The stimulus preceding the air puff comes to produce much the same response.

The second stimulus is called *unconditioned stimulus* (UCS). The UCS elicits a response not by conditioning (learning); it elicits a response

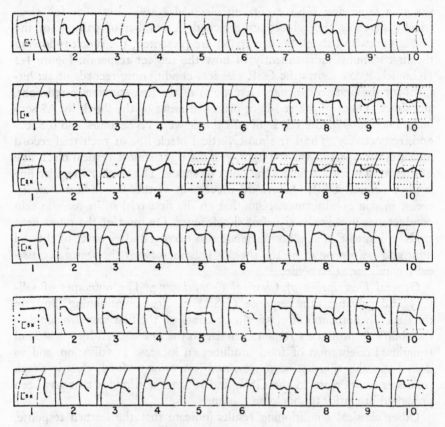

FIGURE 1-2. GSR classical conditioning records of six humans for the first ten trials. (W. F. Prokasy (Ed.), Classical Conditioning: A Symposium, Copyright 1965. Adapted by permission of Irvington Publishers, Inc.)

automatically. The first stimulus is called the *conditioned stimulus* (CS). The ability of the CS to produce a response is acquired through conditioning. The response elicited by the UCS is called the *unconditioned response* (UCR). The UCR does not occur because of conditioning; it occurs automatically. The response produced by the CS is a *conditioned response* (CR). The CR is the learned response.

Thus, the main characteristics of experiments in classical conditioning are: onset of the CS precedes onset of the UCS; the UCS follows the CS independently of an animal's responding; and the length of the time interval separating the onsets of the CS and UCS is relatively short. The CS is a stimulus such as a bell or light, and the UCS elicits a response automatically. The CS comes to produce a CR, a response usually similar to the UCR.

CR strength is a measure of the CR that is thought to be indicative of learning. The amplitude of the CR is the most frequently employed measure of CR strength. Examples of the amplitude of the CR are the amount of saliva the CS produces or the extent of the change in skin resistance in ohms that the CS produces. The strength of the CR generally increases over at least the first few pairings of the CS and UCS. This result is consistent with the idea that learning improves with practice. Another result is that the strength of the CR is usually less than the strength of the UCR (Hilgard, 1936; Kimmel, 1965). Figure 1-2, for example, shows that the strength of the CSR CR was less than the strength of the GSR UCR.

We are now able to define classical conditioning. It occurs when (a) one stimulus, S_1, predicts that a second stimulus, S_2, is relatively likely to occur in its presence or relatively soon thereafter; (b) S_2 is presented independently of responding; and (c) S_1 comes to produce a response because of the indicated relation between S_1 and S_2. Note that by this definition of classical conditioning, S_1 can come to produce a response even though the other stimulus does not automatically elicit a response. In the typical laboratory study, the CS predicts that the UCS will occur relatively soon, because CS onset precedes UCS onset by a relatively short time interval. But there are other ways in which S_1 can predict that S_2 is relatively likely to occur in its presence or relatively soon thereafter, and these will be discussed later, in Chapter 2.

Additional Terms. A few terms require definition.

A *neutral stimulus* is a stimulus that is automatically (not because of learning) relatively unlikely to be either approached and continued to be perceived or escaped from and avoided. An example of a neutral stimulus is a light. Most animals are not particularly likely to approach and continue to perceive, that is, go over and stay near, a light. They are also not particularly likely to escape from and avoid, that is, move away and stay back from, a light. A neutral stimulus previously involved in conditioning may be relatively likely to be either approached and continued to be perceived or escaped from and avoided. But if it is not relatively likely to elicit either type of response prior to conditioning, it is a neutral stimulus. Many neutral stimuli are approached and continued to be perceived or escaped from and avoided to a relatively small extent. For example, rats, which are nocturnal animals, tend to approach and continue to perceive darker stimulus areas. The CS typically is a neutral stimulus.

A *reinforcer* is a stimulus that establishes learning, that is responsible for learning occurring, that causes learning to take place. The reinforcer in a typical classical conditioning study is the UCS. This is because without the UCS following the CS a very large number of CSs would fail to produce a CR, and because with the UCS following the CS a very large number of CSs would produce a CR. Note that the ability of a stimulus to *establish* learning should be distinguished from the ability of a stimulus to *produce* a learned response. The UCS establishes classical conditioning, while the CS produces the learned response.

A *primary reinforcer* is a reinforcer that is automatically (not because of learning) relatively likely to be either approached and continued to be perceived or escaped from and avoided. Examples of primary reinforcers are food and shock. Both food and shock establish conditioning. In addition, a food-deprived animal automatically approaches and continues to perceive food, that is, moves closer to and stays right by it; and an animal automatically escapes from and avoids shock, that is, moves away and keeps away from it. Most UCSs are automatically approached and continued to be perceived or escaped from and avoided, and therefore are primary reinforcers.

A neutral stimulus may be automatically either approached and continued to be perceived or escaped from and avoided in special situations. If an animal is given a choice between exposure to shock all around the outside of a box and no shock inside the box, it will obviously approach and continue to perceive the stimulus of the shock-free box. But we defined a neutral stimulus in terms of its being relatively unlikely to be approached and continued to be perceived. Is the box a neutral stimulus? The box should still be considered a neutral stimulus, because the shock external to the box is responsible for the animal's approaching and continuing to perceive the stimulus of the shock-free box. This is because a similar choice between most other stimuli on the one hand and shock on the other will result in the animal's approaching and continuing to perceive the nonshock stimulus.

Similarly, in special situations a primary reinforcer may not automatically elicit the response it typically does. If an animal is given a choice between exposure to an intense shock outside of a box and a weak shock inside of a box, it will obviously approach and continue to perceive the weak shock inside the box. However, this outcome should not lead to the conclusion that the weak shock is not a primary reinforcer, due to its failing to be escaped from and avoided in this special situation. The intense shock is responsible for the animal's approaching and continuing to perceive the weak shock. The considerations of this and the previous paragraph indicate why it is important to define a neutral stimulus in terms of its being *relatively* unlikely to be either approached and continued to be perceived or escaped from and avoided, and why it is important to define a primary reinforcer in terms of its being *relatively* likely to be either approached and continued to be perceived or escaped from and avoided.

Food and water are relatively likely to be approached and continued to be perceived when an animal is deprived of food and water, respectively. But neither stimulus is particularly likely to be approached and continued to be perceived when an animal has free access to it. Therefore, food and water are primary reinforcers when an animal is deprived of food and water.

Extinction. If, after classical conditioning has occurred, the CS is presented alone, that is, without the UCS following it, then the strength of the CR, for example, the amplitude of the CR, decreases. If presentations of the CS alone continue, CR strength declines to at least the level present before classical conditioning was begun. The procedure of presenting the CS while omitting the UCS subsequent to establishing a CR is called *extinction*. The decline in CR strength in extinction is referred to as *extinction of the CR*.

Extinction of the CR meets the criteria for a learned response. The CS is presented in extinction; the change in response to the CS is a relatively permanent one; and extinction does not affect responses to a wide variety of stimuli.

The extinction procedure for classical conditioning is quite similar to the procedure for establishing classical conditioning. Both involve one stimulus, the CS, being followed independently of responding by a second stimulus; for extinction, the second stimulus may be thought of as *no particular event*. No particular event is a stimulus. For example, the offset of a stimulus, that is, the occurrence of no particular event, serves as a CS (Kamin, 1965; Logan & Wagner, 1962). According to the definition of classical conditioning, extinction of the CR is an instance of classical conditioning. S_1 (the CS) does predict the occurrence of S_2 (no particular event); S_2 does follow S_1 independently of responding; and S_1 does produce a change in response (a decrease in CR strength).

Everyday Analogue. One example of an analogue of classical conditioning in real life is the experience of seeing a door swing open, which is then followed by the sight of a person in the doorway. Another is seeing a phonograph needle being lowered onto a revolving record, which is then followed by sound from the record. Everyday analogues of classical conditioning are not instances of classical conditioning, because the stimulus occurring first does not come to produce a response that is similar to a CR.

Everyday analogues of classical conditioning are similar to typically investigated classical conditioning in that pairings of two stimuli, S_1 and S_2, occur; S_2 follows S_1 independently of responding; and a learned association involving S_1 and S_2 takes place. This learned association occurs: for example, pairings between the sight of a door opening and seeing a person in the doorway enable the sight of the door opening to produce the expectation of seeing a person in the doorway. In addition, everyday analogues of classical conditioning could be proven to result in learning in humans. Pairings of two neutral stimuli would be delivered to humans and subsequently, perhaps 24 hours later, they would be asked about what would happen if the first stimulus occurred. These pairings will certainly change humans' verbal reports about their expectation of the second stimulus occurring, given that the first stimulus is presented. Because a relatively permanent change in verbal behavior will occur when the first of two previously paired neutral stimuli is presented, everyday analogues of classical conditioning result in learning.

Instrumental Conditioning

Instrumental conditioning is another kind of conditioning. E. L. Thorndike was probably the first to investigate instrumental conditioning in the laboratory. B. F. Skinner has probably done the best-known laboratory research. A synonym for instrumental conditioning is *operant conditioning.*

Examples of Instrumental Conditioning. Figure 1-3 shows a rat exhibiting an instrumentally conditioned bar press response. In instrumental conditioning of bar pressing, a rat is typically placed in an enclosed

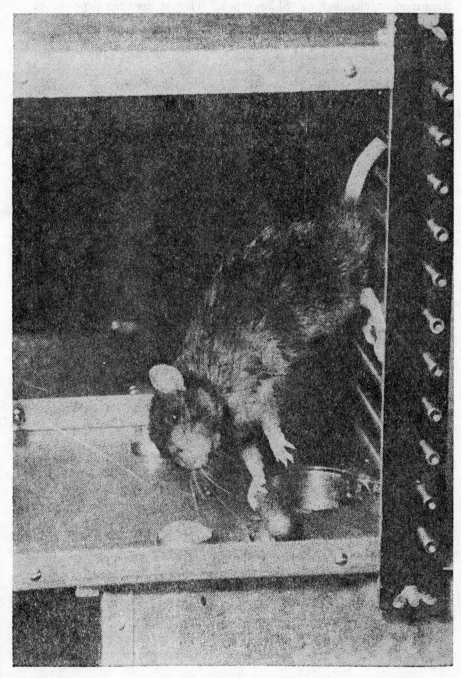

FIGURE 1-3. A rat exhibiting an instrumentally conditioned bar press response. (Will Rapport.)

compartment, chamber, or "Skinner box." The rat has been deprived of food or water for some time. Each downward movement of the bar by the rat results in the delivery of a small amount of food or water. When the rat is first placed in the chamber, it has no way of "knowing" that each press of the bar will deliver food or water. If it is left on its own from the onset of training, the rat will usually move around the chamber, sniff, rear on its hind legs, look around, and so on. Eventually it usually happens to press the bar, perhaps as it comes down from rearing on its hind legs. Directly after it presses the bar, a small amount of food or water appears; in Figure 1-3, food would appear in the circular receptacle on the same wall as the bar. The rat hears and sees the food or water arriving and consumes it. Each succeeding bar press is followed by a small amount of food or water. At the beginning of training, as the number of times the bar press is followed by food or water increases, the rate of bar pressing (the number of bar presses per unit of time) tends to increase. Because only a small amount of food or water follows each bar press, the rate of bar pressing is not apt to decrease due to satiation, unless training is prolonged.

Because the rate of the bar press response is greater after it has been followed by food or water than before the first time the bar press response was followed by food or water, a change in the response to the stimuli comprising the learning chamber occurs. This change in response to stimuli is a change in response to the same stimuli an animal was previously exposed to. In addition, this change in response is relatively permanent, because if an animal is placed in the learning chamber a day later, it will still bar press at a faster rate than before the initiation of training. Also, the pairings between the bar press response and food or water do not affect the response to a wide variety of stimuli. The increase in the rate of bar pressing is therefore a learned response. Instrumental conditioning has therefore occurred; the bar press response is referred to as having been instrumentally conditioned. The finding that the bar press rate tends to increase over pairings between the bar press response and food or water is in accord with the idea that learning improves with practice.

Figure 1-4 shows a pigeon exhibiting the response of pecking a circular illuminated disc called a response key or *key* for short. In instrumental conditioning of this response, each peck of the key causes food to appear. The pigeon then moves its head and obtains the food, as indicated in Figure 1-4. The pigeon has been previously deprived of food. Before the first key peck, it has no way of knowing that a key peck will result in food. Through chance or by other means the pigeon eventually

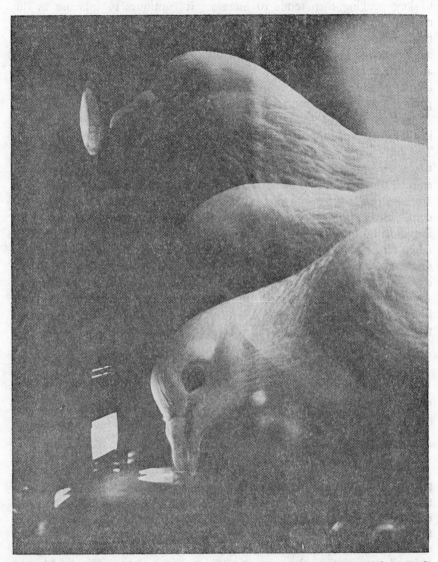

FIGURE 1-4. A pigeon exhibiting an instrumentally conditioned key peck response and then obtaining food. (Norman Guttman.)

pecks the key, and then it consumes the food that is delivered. The rate of key pecking then tends to increase; it continues to increase as the number of times a key peck is followed by food increases until, eventually, the rate of key pecking levels off. It is evident that the procedure and result for key pecking are analogous to those for bar pressing. Thus, an increase in the rate of the key peck response is evidence that instrumental conditioning has occurred; and when this increase occurs, the key peck response is referred to as having been instrumentally conditioned.

Another type of apparatus frequently employed in investigations of instrumental conditioning is the runway apparatus shown in Figure 1-5. The instrumental response is to traverse the runway from its beginning to its end. When food is used to establish the traversal response, an animal, usually a rat, is deprived of food prior to training. Discrete trials are usually used for runway learning; that is, an animal is not free to continue to make successive responses as it is in bar press and key peck instrumental conditioning. At the onset of each trial, the rat is typically taken from its home cage or a waiting cage and placed in the start area of the runway. After the rat traverses the runway and obtains food at the end (goal), it is lifted from the apparatus and returned to its home or waiting cage. On the first trial, the rat has no way of knowing that food is at the end of the runway, and therefore it is relatively slow to traverse the runway and obtain the food. However, the average rate

FIGURE 1-5. A typical runway. An animal is placed in the start box at the beginning of a trial. At this time the door for the start box is down and the door for the goal box is up. Raising the start box door permits the animal to traverse the runway, and the goal box door is lowered after the animal passes it. The lamps and photocells are for timing the animal's traversal of the runway. Raising the start box door could start two clocks. Passing the first photocell would stop one of these clocks, and passing the second photocell would stop the other one. (J. W. Kling and L. A. Riggs (Eds.), Woodworth & Schlosberg's Experimental Psychology (3rd ed., Vol. 2: Learning, Motivation, and Memory), Copyright 1971. Adapted by permission of Holt, Rinehart, and Winston, Inc.)

(speed) with which the runway is traversed increases over at least the next several trials. An increase in the rate of traversing the runway indicates that instrumental conditioning has occurred.

Instrumental conditioning may also employ electric shock. An animal, typically a rat, may be placed on a relatively small platform that is elevated a fairly short distance above the floor of the apparatus. The natural response of a rat on such a platform is to step down onto the floor. Upon contact with the floor, the rat is shocked. The rat is then removed from the floor of the apparatus. The second time—that is, in trial two—that the rat is placed on the platform it is less likely to step down. The instrumental response is stepping off the platform. The decrease in the rate of the step-down response indicates that instrumental conditioning has occurred.

Another way in which traversal of a runway is instrumentally conditioned involves delivering shock from the floor of all portions of the runway apparatus except the end area. For each trial, the animal, usually a rat, is placed in the start area of the runway, receives shock, and continues to receive shock until it reaches the end area of the runway. It is then removed from the apparatus and placed in the home or waiting cage until the next trial. On the first trial, the rate of traversing the runway is relatively slow. However, the average rate (speed) of moving from the start area to the end area of the runway decreases gradually over at least the first several trials. The runway traversal response is the instrumental response. The increase in the rate of this response indicates that instrumental conditioning has occurred.

General Description of Instrumental Conditioning. These examples of instrumental conditioning illustrate the statement that instrumental conditioning occurs when a response causes a stimulus to take place and this response changes in rate as a consequence of this response-stimulus pairing. In more general terms, instrumental conditioning occurs when a response predicts that a stimulus is relatively likely to occur relatively soon after the response is made, and this response changes in rate as a consequence of the indicated relation between the response and the predicted stimulus. The response causing a stimulus to occur is called the *instrumental response*. The instrumental response may either increase or decrease in rate.

When an increase in the rate of an instrumental response occurs, the instrumental response causes a stimulus to take place that is more likely to be approached and continued to be perceived than the stimuli present prior to the execution of the instrumental response, or the stimuli that would be present if the instrumental response were not made. This stimulus is a *goal stimulus*. When a decrease in the rate of an instrumental response occurs, the instrumental response causes a stimulus to take place that is more likely to be escaped from and avoided than the stimuli present prior to the execution of the instrumental response, or the stimuli that would be present if the instrumental response were not made. This stimulus is a *negative-goal stimulus*.

Consider the instrumental conditioning of the bar press response. The bar press response causes a stimulus, food or water, to occur. As a result of this response-stimulus pairing, the rate of the bar press response increases. Instrumental conditioning has therefore occurred. Food or water is more likely to be approached and continued to be perceived than the stimuli present prior to the execution of the bar press response; that is, food or water is a goal stimulus, which is consistent with an increase in, rather than no change or a decrease in, the rate of bar pressing occurring.

Consider the instrumental conditioning of the response of stepping off a platform. The stepping off response causes a stimulus, shock, to occur. As a result of this response-stimulus pairing, the rate of the stepping off response decreases. Instrumental conditioning has therefore occurred. Shock is more likely to be escaped from and avoided than the stimuli present prior to the execution of the stepping off response; that is, shock is a negative-goal stimulus, which is consistent with a decrease in the rate of the stepping off response occurring.

Traversing the runway causes a stimulus, the absence of shock, to occur. As a result of this response-stimulus pairing, the rate of traversing the runway increases. Instrumental conditioning has therefore occurred. The absence of shock is more likely to be approached and continued to be perceived than the stimuli present prior to execution of the runway traversal response. The absence of shock is therefore a goal stimulus, which is consistent with an increase in the rate of the runway traversal response occurring.

A reinforcer was defined above as a stimulus that establishes learning. For our example of bar pressing, food or water is the reinforcer. These stimuli clearly establish instrumental conditioning of bar pressing, because we know that the rate of many other responses of subjects deprived of food or water also increase if they cause food or water to occur. Thus, for the instrumental conditioning of bar pressing, the goal stimulus and the reinforcer are the same stimuli. The same thing is true of the instrumental conditioning of key pecking and traversal of a runway using food.

For stepping off a platform, shock is the reinforcer, because we know that the rate of many other responses would also decrease if they caused shock to occur. Thus, for instrumental conditioning of stepping off a descending platform, the negative-goal stimulus and the reinforcer are the same stimuli.

For traversing a runway using shock, shock is also the reinforcer. However, in this instance, the goal stimulus and the reinforcer are not identical. The goal stimulus is the absence of shock, and the reinforcer is shock.

Positive reinforcers can be distinguished from negative ones. A positive reinforcer is relatively likely to be approached and continued to be perceived, and a negative reinforcer is relatively likely to be escaped from and avoided. The positive reinforcers most frequently employed in the laboratory are food and water. The negative reinforcer most frequently employed in the laboratory is shock.

Extinction. Extinction in classical conditioning was defined in terms of presenting the CS while omitting the UCS, the reinforcer. Similarly, extinction in instrumental conditioning consists of not presenting the reinforcer subsequent to establishing instrumental conditioning. For example, extinction for the instrumental conditioning of bar pressing consists of omitting the positive reinforcer following each bar press response. Extinction in instrumental conditioning often results in a relatively rapid change in the rate of the instrumental response. For example, in extinction of the instrumental conditioning of bar pressing, a decrease in the bar pressing rate to about the level that occurred before initiating training results relatively quickly. The change in the rate of the instrumental response that results because of extinction is referred to as the extinction of the instrumentally conditioned response.

Extinction of the instrumentally conditioned response, like extinction of the CR, is a learned response. The change in response is to the stimuli of the instrumental conditioning apparatus, the stimuli present in extinction. In addition, the change in response is relatively permanent, and the extinction procedure does not affect responses to a wide variety of stimuli.

The extinction procedure for instrumental conditioning is often quite similar to the procedure for establishing instrumental conditioning. Take instrumental conditioning of bar pressing. The training and extinction procedures for the instrumentally conditioned bar press response both involve a response being followed by a stimulus. For extinction, the stimulus followed by a response is thought of as no particular event, and a change in response rate is thought of as a consequence. According to the definition of instrumental conditioning, extinction of the instrumentally conditioned bar press response is therefore an instance of instrumental conditioning. Recall that extinction of the CR is an instance of classical conditioning.

Everyday Occurrences and Analogues. Everyday occurrences of instrumental conditioning are plentiful. The probability (similar to rate) is high that a person in a dark room who wishes to read will push a light switch. In the past, pushing the switch has been followed by light in the room; therefore, the probability of pushing the light switch again was increased. Instrumental conditioning occurs when a response causes a stimulus to take place, and this response changes in rate as a consequence of this response-stimulus pairing—so by definition, instrumental conditioning of pushing the light switch in the dark room has occurred. Furthermore, an increase in the rate of an instrumental response occurs when it causes a goal stimulus to take place, and illumination of the room is a goal stimulus, since the person tends to remain in the room after it is lit.

An everyday analogue of instrumental conditioning occurs when one of our hands strikes a surface and thereby causes a sound. This situation differs from instrumental conditioning, because the response of a hand striking a surface would not normally change in rate as a consequence of its causing a sound. Nevertheless, the hand's hitting the surface does cause a stimulus, a sound. In general, in everyday analogues of instrumental conditioning, a response causes a stimulus to occur, but a change in the rate of this response does not take place as a consequence of this response-stimulus pairing. Everyday analogues of instrumental conditioning do not result in instrumental conditioning because the stimulus that the instrumental response causes to occur is neither a goal nor a negative-goal stimulus. The sound produced by striking a surface, for example, is neither a goal nor a negative-goal stimulus.

It is obvious that in these everyday analogues humans learn something about a relationship between a response and the stimulus the response causes, even though the response does not change in rate. Moreover, analogues of instrumental conditioning result in learning. A person might be asked to raise his right arm, for instance, after which response the experimenter turns on a light. The pairings between the arm-raise response and the light would not increase the rate of the arm-raise response, but they would undoubtedly alter the subject's response concerning the expectation of a light to go on after he or she raises the arm. Because a relatively permanent change in verbal response would occur with the indicated procedure, and because the other criteria for the occurrence of learning would be satisfied, the indicated procedure would result in learning.

Expectancy-Purpose Theory

A number of theories have been advanced to explain why classical and instrumental conditioning occur. Two of these theories, expectancy-purpose and stimulus-response theory, do not appear to be appropriate.

Description of Expectancy-Purpose Theory. An expectancy-purpose theory of instrumental conditioning makes intuitive sense. The instrumental response causes a goal or a negative-goal stimulus to occur; the natural conclusion is that an animal changes the rate of an instrumental response because its purpose is to obtain the expected goal stimulus or to avoid the expected negative-goal stimulus.

Tolman (1932) has advocated this expectancy-purpose approach. Details of his theories of conditioning have varied, but three interrelated ideas consistently appear. The first is that conditioning is a matter of an animal's learning to associate stimuli with the stimuli that follow them; that is, he maintains that animals acquire stimulus-stimulus connections. The second idea is that the stimulus-stimulus connection enables the occurrence of the first stimulus to result in the expectation that the second stimulus will occur. The third idea deals with the behavioral consequence of the expectation of the second stimulus; it is that an animal will exhibit the response that causes an expected goal stimulus to occur or will cease to exhibit the response that causes an expected negative-goal stimulus to occur. Furthermore, this response is viewed as being either the CR or the instrumental response. Thus, Tolman assumes that both the CR and the instrumental response have a purpose, which is to obtain the goal stimulus or avoid the negative-goal stimulus that the individual expects will occur.

Problem with Expectancy-Purpose Theory. A major problem with expectancy-purpose theory is that it does not account for the CR of classical conditioning. How can learned responses that are similar to UCRs always have a purpose? In addition, what can the purpose of the CR be if the occurrence of the UCS is independent of any response of the animal?

Tolman (1932, p. 331) took the approach that every CR does have a purpose. For example, in discussion of salivary classical conditioning he suggests that the purpose of the salivation CR is to enable the animal more quickly to digest the food that it expects to obtain as a result of the CS. However, whether or not digestion of food is hastened if salivation increases before the arrival of food remains speculative.

Many responses have been classically conditioned and in most cases the CR is similar to the UCR. It defies common sense to think that each CR that is similar to a UCR also has a purpose. The purpose of the GSR CR is not clear, for example, because an increase in skin conductance does not seem to lower the aversiveness of the shock UCS. It is not at all definite that the mouth movement CR enables an animal to drink a water UCS more quickly. The purpose of the leg movement CR is also in doubt, because this response does not seem to reduce the aversiveness of the UCS of a shock to the leg. Closure of the eyelid prior to the UCS of a puff of air to the eye may reduce the aversiveness of the puff of air; however, eyelid classical conditioning can be established with the UCS of electric shock delivered close to the eye (Leonard & Theios, 1967), this UCS also eliciting an eyelid closure UCR. It is problematical that a blink has a purpose in relation to shock to an area around the eye.

Stimulus-Response Theory

Reflexes and Conditioning. Stimulus-response theories are based on the idea that the processes that govern reflexes and conditioning are related. Reflexes are relatively simple responses that certain stimuli elicit automatically, not because they are learned. The hand withdrawal that occurs when a pain-producing stimulus is touched and the knee jerk produced when the tendon below the kneecap is hit are reflexes. Because UCSs elicit relatively simple responses automatically, UCRs are reflexes.

Limb reflexes have been investigated extensively in animals whose spinal cords have been severed from the brain. In such animals, stimulation of the skin by touch or electric shock automatically results in limb movements, that is, limb reflexes. Stimulation of the skin produces a nerve impulse, a momentary change in current, in the afferent nerve cells. This impulse travels down the length of the axons of these nerves, and then is transferred from afferent nerve cells to associative nerve cells by means of the synapses between these two types of nerve cells. Associative nerve cells for the limb reflex lie entirely within the spinal cord. The associative nerve cells also form synapses with efferent nerve cells. The nerve impulse is transferred through these synapses to efferent nerve cells, travels down the axons of the efferent nerve cells, and terminates at the muscles, producing a contraction that leads to overt movement—the reflexes. Stimulation of the skin automatically results in limb movements; therefore the connections involving afferent, associative, and efferent nerve cells do not exist because of learning.

Stimulus-response theories maintain that the process responsible for classical and instrumental conditioning is a learned connection between a stimulus and a response. Stimulus-response connections are believed to be closely related to the afferent-associative-efferent connections that produce reflexes; the only major difference between the neural events responsible for reflexes and those that are responsible for conditioning is that stimulus-response connections are established through learning, and the neural connections for reflexes are not established through learning. The CR and the instrumentally conditioned response theoretically occur like reflexes; that is, just as certain stimuli elicit reflexes, certain stimuli are assumed to produce the CR and the instrumentally conditioned response. Knowledge of the UCS, goal, and negative-goal stimulus is not assumed to mediate the conditioning process.

Hull's Stimulus-Response Theory. The most influential stimulus-response theory of conditioning is probably Hull's (for example, Hull, 1952). In his theory, motivational factors, such as hunger, thirst, and pain, are considered to produce drive stimuli. When a stimulus is followed by a response, and when reduction of drive stimuli is closely associated in time with this response, a connection is formed between this stimulus and response. The onset of a positive primary reinforcer is assumed to reduce drive stimuli, and the termination of a negative primary reinforcer is assumed to reduce drive stimuli. Therefore, he hypothesizes, if a stimulus is followed by a response and a positive primary reinforcer occurs, or if a stimulus is followed by a response and a negative primary reinforcer is terminated, the stimulus and response in question become connected. As is true of stimulus-response theories of conditioning in general, Hull assumes that once a stimulus-response connection is formed, the occurrence of the stimulus produces the learned response in much the same way that a reflex is elicited by a stimulus.

Hull accounts for both classical and instrumental conditioning with these assumptions about the stimulus-response connection and drive reduction. In classical conditioning, the CS, a neutral stimulus, is followed by the UCS, a primary reinforcer. The UCS is viewed as having two important functions: (a) it elicits a response, the UCR; and (b) it results in drive reduction, either by its onset (for positive primary reinforcers) or by its offset (for negative primary reinforcers). The CS is therefore followed by both a response and drive reduction. This combination of conditions should result in the formation of a stimulus-response connection. The CS should therefore become connected to the response following it, which is the UCR. As a consequence, each occurrence of the CS should produce in a reflex-like fashion a response similar to the UCR, thereby accounting for the CS's ability to produce the CR. Consider that in classical salivary conditioning, a CS is followed by the UCS of food and therefore by the UCR of salivation and drive reduction. A CS-salivation stimulus-response connection is therefore formed. As a result, each occurrence of the CS produces the salivation response in a reflex-like fashion, thereby accounting for the salivation CR.

For the instrumental conditioning of bar pressing, the bar press response is the response member of the stimulus-response connection. The stimuli of the walls, floors, and bar of the apparatus may constitute the stimulus member of the stimulus-response connection, but precisely which stimuli are part of the stimulus-response connection is not clear. Because an animal is exposed to the stimuli of the apparatus prior to pressing a bar, it is clear that some of the stimuli of the general learning situation are perceived prior to each bar press response. The bar press response is followed by a positive primary reinforcer such as food and therefore by drive reduction. It follows that some of the stimuli of the general learning situation should become connected to the bar press response. The acquired stimulus-response connection between some of the stimuli of the general learning situation and the bar press response should then function as connections for reflexes do. This means that some of the stimuli of the general learning situation should produce the bar press response in a reflex-like fashion, the occurrence of this response being the result to be explained.

Hull's accounts of classical and instrumental conditioning differ in that in classical conditioning the UCS, that is, the reinforcer, has two functions—to elicit the response member of the stimulus-response connection and to provide for drive reduction; while in instrumental conditioning, the reinforcer has only one function—to provide for drive reduction. Another difference is that in classical conditioning the stimulus member of the stimulus-response connection is denotable—it is the CS; in instrumental conditioning, the stimulus member of the stimulus-response connection is an unknown aspect of the general learning situation.

Stimulus-response explanations of classical and instrumental conditioning run counter to intuition, because a concept related to the knowledge of a stimulus is not employed. In respect to classical conditioning, the CS is not assumed to result in some kind of knowledge of the UCS. In other words, the ability of the CS to produce a CR is not assumed to be due to an expectation of the UCS, an image of the UCS, or some other construct that suggests in some sense knowledge of the UCS. According to Hull, the role of the UCS is only to produce a response and drive reduction. He assumes the CR occurs not because of knowledge of the UCS but because it is essentially a reflex produced by the CS. The CR occurs when the CS takes place, just like a hand is taken off a hot stove. Hull does not assume that an animal has some kind of knowledge of the positive primary reinforcer that follows the bar press response. The positive primary reinforcer only connects the stimuli of the learning situation with the bar press response. The bar press response is essentially a reflex produced by some of the stimuli of the learning situation.

Problems with Hull's Theory. Hull's stimulus-response theory does have trouble in accounting for learning findings. In the first place, the theory maintains that conditioning cannot occur unless a response is made. To account for extinction of the CR and the instrumentally conditioned response, Hull hypothesizes that a stimulus becomes associated with the response of cessation of activity. But it is clear that cessation of activity is not a specific response like salivation or a bar press. Everyday analogues of classical and instrumental conditioning do not involve the occurrence of learned nonverbal responses and yet they are learning results. If this learning is not due to classical and instrumental conditioning processes, it would appear incumbent for a stimulus-response theorist to discuss what processes are involved. Furthermore, in some situations learning takes place without a response occurring while the learning is being acquired. Presenting S_1-S_2 pairings in which S_2 does not produce a response can affect a subsequently acquired CR. In language learning, including that by chimpanzees, words become associated with the object or action they refer to without any clear response occurring. Also, in delayed imitation learning and other instances of observation learning, an observer acquires associations between the visual stimuli he views without his exhibiting any clear response. These results, too, must be accounted for.

A second problem with Hull's theory is that conditioning occurs even though drive reduction does not take place. Extinction of the CR and the instrumentally conditioned response are kinds of classical and instrumental conditioning. Drive reduction should not occur in extinction; drive reduction occurs when primary reinforcers are employed, which is not done in extinction. Hull (1952) hypothesized a source of drive reduction in extinction, but the hypothesis appears ad hoc. Everyday occurrences of instrumental conditioning, for example, a person's turning on a light in a dark room when he or she wishes to read, are instances of this conditioning, and are established by reinforcers that do not result in drive reduction. Classical conditioning also occurs without drive reduction. In one study (Fink, 1954), for instance, subjects were instructed to press a response key when S_2, a neutral stimulus, came on. Another stimulus, S_1, was consistently presented a short time prior to the onset of S_2. S_1 came to produce a response similar to the key press response produced by S_2. Everyday experience analogues of conditioning usually involve only neutral stimuli, so that this learning may occur without drive reduction. The CR and the instrumental response can be affected through pairings between stimuli or between a response and a stimulus, also without drive reduction.

A third problem with Hull's theory is that drive reduction is assumed to occur with the termination of a negative reinforcer. Consider touching a hot stove. It seems intuitively obvious that we "learn" the stove is hot the moment we touch it; that is, learning appears to occur with the onset of the negative reinforcer of the hot stove, rather than with the termination of this reinforcer. Because drive reduction is assumed to occur with the termination of a negative reinforcer, Hull would have to predict that better classical conditioning should result when a brief CS occurs just before the termination of a negative reinforcer than when a brief CS occurs just before the onset of a negative reinforcer. However, consideration of the stove example suggests we learn mainly about the onset of negative reinforcers, which leads to a prediction the opposite of Hull's—a prediction that has been confirmed (Davitz, 1955; Mowrer & Aiken, 1954).

A fourth problem with Hull's theory stems from the assumption that a response preceded by a CS and followed by drive reduction should be acquired. Hull would predict that if the CS itself elicited a response, and if this CS were followed by a UCS, then the response elicited by the CS would be strengthened. In one study (Davydova, 1967), a CS that elicited leg flexion was used and paired with a food UCS. During the course of conditioning, the leg flexion response grew weaker, a result that disconfirms Hull's prediction. Pavlov (1927, pp. 29-30) reported a similar result.

Engram Activation Theories

Engram Activation Theory of Classical Conditioning. An engram is a hypothetical permanent event contained within the brain that corresponds to a stimulus. Figure 1-6 helps explain how engram activation theory is related to classical conditioning. S_1 is a specific stimulus. When it stimulates a receptor, it produces a temporary event within the brain, T_1. As indicated in Figure 1-6A, T_1 has three consequences. It enables a relatively detailed and accurate description of S_1 to be made; it may produce a nonverbal response, R_1; and it results in a permanent brain event or engram, P_1, which corresponds to S_1. Obviously, considerations involving the description of S_1 apply to humans. However, T_1 should result in an experience of S_1 for nonhuman animals, even though they are not capable of describing S_1.

On logical grounds, the brain events responsible for relatively detailed and accurate descriptions of stimuli and nonverbal responses produced by stimuli must be temporary, because otherwise these descriptions and nonverbal responses would continue to occur after termination of the stimulus. In addition, because the initiation of a relatively detailed and accurate description of a stimulus and the nonverbal response it produces can occur at about the same time, it is parsimonious to assume that the same temporary brain event results in both these responses.

We said above that T_1 results in a permanent brain event or engram, P_1, that corresponds to S_1. This assumption is supported by a body of evidence that suggests that people can recall a stimulus just after it has terminated, but are much less likely to be able to recall it later on. Theoretically, they can remember the stimulus just after it is terminated be-

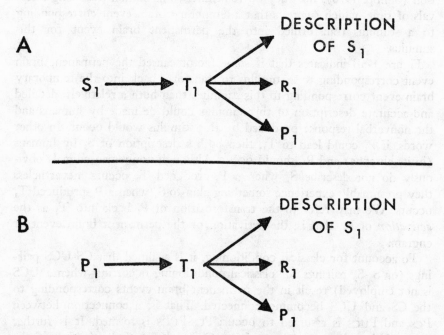

FIGURE 1-6. Summary of the effects of a stimulus and the effects of the activation of the permanent brain event corresponding to this stimulus.

cause the temporary brain event that corresponds to this stimulus temporarily continues to exist; they are less likely to remember the stimulus at a later time because the temporary brain event that corresponds to this stimulus has ceased to exist; and they are sometimes able to remember the stimulus at a later time, because the temporary brain event corresponding to it was transformed into its permanent brain event, and because this permanent brain event enables this memory.

One study showing that people can recall stimuli just after they terminate but cannot recall them later on was done by Sperling (1961). Subjects were presented with different 4-by-3 matrices of randomly selected letters. The duration of an exposure was 50 milliseconds. One of three tones immediately followed a presented matrix. The high-, medium-, and low-pitched tones indicated to the observer that he or she should report the top, middle, and bottom rows of letters, respectively. Observers were generally able to accurately report three or all four letters in the row indicated by a tone. In a second condition, the tones were delayed by 1 second. This led to fewer letters being accurately reported.

Nonhuman animals may also quickly forget stimuli after their termination (Shimp, 1976). But they do remember some stimuli over long intervals of time, which suggests that a temporary brain event corresponding to a stimulus transformed into the permanent brain event for this stimulus.

Figure 1-6B indicates that if some factor caused the permanent brain event corresponding to a stimulus to transform back into the temporary brain event corresponding to this stimulus, then both a relatively detailed and accurate description of this stimulus could be made by humans and the nonverbal response produced by this stimulus would occur. In other words, if P_1 could lead to T_1, then both a description of S_1 by humans (in its absence) and R_1 should occur. Although nonhuman animals obviously do not describe S_1 when a P_1-produced T_1 occurs, nevertheless they presumably experience something akin to S_1 when a P_1-produced T_1 occurs. We may refer to the transformation of P_1 back into T_1 as the *activation* of P_1, that is, the activation of the permanent brain event or engram.

To account for classical conditioning, it is assumed that CS-UCS pairings (or S_1-S_2 pairings for classical conditioning occurring when a UCS is not employed) result in the permanent brain events corresponding to the CS and UCS becoming connected. That is, a connection between Pcs and Pucs is assumed to occur; Pcs-Pucs is formed. It is further assumed that the occurrence of the CS results in the activation of the permanent brain event corresponding to the UCS. The temporary brain event produced by the CS "finds" the permanent brain event corresponding to the UCS through the connection of the permanent brain events corresponding to the CS and UCS, that is, by way of Pcs-Pucs.

Once the permanent brain event corresponding to the UCS is activated by the CS, a response similar to the UCR should occur. This statement follows from the meaning of activation, which is the transformation of a permanent brain event into the corresponding temporary brain event, and from the assumption that the temporary brain event corresponding to a stimulus results in the nonverbal response this stimulus elicits. In other words, we assume that the CS results in the activation of Pucs, and that Tucs therefore occurs; in addition, once Tucs occurs, much the same response is exhibited as elicited by the UCS itself. This accounts for the CS's ability to produce the CR.

Konorski's Theory of Classical Conditioning. Konorski (1967) proposed an engram activation theory of classical conditioning using the concept of gnostic unit. The gnostic unit is approximately equivalent in meaning to the permanent brain event, because it is a permanent representation of a specific stimulus.

Konorski explains classical conditioning by saying that the gnostic unit corresponding to the CS becomes connected to the gnostic unit corresponding to the UCS. He also assumes that the occurrence of the CS results in the activation of the gnostic unit corresponding to the UCS. He accounts for the occurrence of the CR by assuming that activation of the gnostic unit corresponding to the UCS results in much the same response that the real UCS elicits.

His assumption that there is an acquired connection between gnostic units corresponding to the CS and UCS is like the assumption of the engram theory that the permanent brain events corresponding to the CS and UCS become connected. Also, his assumption that the CS activates the gnostic unit corresponding to the UCS is analogous to the engram theory assumption that the CS activates the permanent brain event corresponding to the UCS. In both theories, the outcome of activation of the permanent brain event (gnostic unit) corresponding to the UCS by the CS is a response similar to the UCR, that is, the CR.

Hebb's Perceptual Learning Theory. Hebb (1949, 1968) proposed a perceptual learning theory that is essentially one of engram activation.

Hebb addresses the problem of how the meaning and wholeness of a figure or object is apprehended, that is, the problem of how "one perception is arrived at" and "separate visual impressions (are) integrated" (Hebb, 1968, p. 469), when a sub-portion of the figure or object is focused on. He discusses the learning that may be involved in the perception (recognition) of a figure of a triangle. For his purposes, he considers the triangle to consist of three parts, these parts being centered at the three points of a triangle. Corresponding to each part of the triangle is what Hebb refers to as the cell assembly. The cell assembly is thought of as a specific neural network that conducts relatively few nerve impulses when not activated and that temporarily conducts relatively many nerve impulses when activated. If the three parts of the figure of a triangle have been previously focused on repeatedly, it is assumed that the cell assemblies corresponding to these three parts become interconnected. Interconnected cell assemblies are called phase sequences.

Focusing on one part of the triangle is assumed to result in the activation of the cell assembly corresponding to that part of the triangle. In addition, if the phase sequence corresponding to the three parts of the triangle has been formed, focusing on one part of the triangle is assumed to result in the activation of the cell assembly corresponding to the other two parts of the triangle. The perception of a triangle as a single whole recognizable thing when only one part of the triangle is focused on is assumed to result from the near simultaneous activation of the three cell assemblies corresponding to the three parts of the triangle. In general, the verbal reports and perceptual data that indicate that a single, whole, meaningful experience of a figure or object occurs when a subportion of a figure or object is focused on are assumed to result from the near simultaneous activation of the cell assemblies making up the phase sequences corresponding to this complete figure or object.

Cell assemblies correspond to permanent brain events or engrams. Hebb assumes they become interconnected, much as the permanent brain events corresponding to the CS and UCS do. Focusing on one spot of a figure or object—for instance, on one corner of a triangle—can be thought of as perception of a stimulus that leads first to the activation of a cell assembly that corresponds to it and then to the activation of the cell assemblies that were previously connected to it, just as, in engram activation theory, the CS produces the temporary brain event corresponding to the CS, and then by way of the connected permanent brain events corresponding to the CS and UCS, to the temporary brain event corresponding to the UCS. That activation of cell assemblies corresponding to stimuli that are not focused on enables a description that includes reference to parts of the stimulus complex that are not focused on is in accord with the assumption of the engram activation theory that activation of a permanent brain event, P_1, enables a relatively detailed and accurate description of the stimulus, S_1, that P_1 and T_1 correspond to.

Image Theory of Classical Conditioning

An image of a stimulus is an experience of a stimulus not currently present such that humans are able to describe the stimulus, this description being similar to the one that would be made if the real stimulus were present. Nonhuman animals are thought to have images of stimuli, although they do not appear to communicate about them. An image theory of classical conditioning (King, 1973) will be discussed.

Main Hypothesis. The image theory of classical conditioning maintains that the CS produces an image of the UCS and that this image results in the CR. The idea that the CR is due to a CS-produced image of the UCS is supported by findings that suggest that images of stimuli result in responses similar to the ones produced by real stimuli. For example, when we have an image of how food tastes and smells, we salivate more, just as we salivate more when real food is in our mouths. The theory proposes that in classical conditioning of salivation, the CS acquires the ability to produce an image of food, and that the salivation CR is a result of this image, like the salivation that ensues when we imagine food. The GSR CR results, according to the theory, because the CS produces an image of electric shock, and because this image results in an increased GSR, much as imagining electric shock leads to heightened GSR activity. An image theory of classical conditioning is generally applicable to classical conditioning because the CR usually resembles the UCR and because images of stimuli appear to result in responses resembling those produced by real stimuli.

Image-Produced Responses Resemble Stimulus-Produced Ones. Images of stimuli (more correctly, requests to imagine stimuli or indications of having images of stimuli) do appear to result in responses similar to the ones produced by real stimuli (King, 1973). It is clear that we salivate both when we imagine food and when food actually occurs, and that the GSR increases both when we imagine an exciting event and when an exciting event actually occurs. In addition, Rowland (1936) found that requests to imagine exciting scenes resulted in greater changes in GSR, heart rate, and respiration. Presumably real exciting scenes would also produce greater changes in these responses.

Barber, Chauncey, and Winer (1964) requested subjects to either imagine that a sour solution tasted like tap water or that tap water tasted like a sour solution. They found that the former request produced a decrease in salivation and the latter request produced an increase in salivation. Because a real sour solution increases salivation, these results

support the statement that image-produced responses are similar to stimulus-produced ones.

Barber and Hahn (1964) requested subjects to imagine that their arm
was immersed in very cold water when in fact the water was at room
temperature. Imagining that the water was very cold resulted in increases
in heart rate and tension in the muscles of the forehead. Real very cold
water also resulted in increases in these responses. Craig (1969) replicated the heart rate result.

Extensive support for the statement that image-produced responses are
similar to stimulus-produced responses comes from studies in which subjects were asked to imagine stimuli that involve voluntary movement. The
request to imagine flexing one's arm, for instance, was followed by not
directly observable arm movement (Jacobsen, 1930a). Even though a
movement cannot be seen, an increase in electrical potential in relevant
muscles may occur—which is called a *covert response*. To obtain evidence of a covert response, recording electrodes are placed over or into
the muscle. The recording electrodes pick up the electrical potential of
the muscle, the potential is amplified, and the potential is observed either
with a polygraph or an oscilloscope. Electrical potentials recorded from
muscles are called *electromyograms* (EMGs). Thus, Jacobsen demonstrated that imagining flexing an arm results in covert arm movements by
comparing the EMGs that occurred prior to and just after the request
to imagine an arm-flexing movement. Jacobsen also requested subjects to
imagine flexing one arm, and found no increase in EMGs in the other
arm.

Jacobsen also requested his subjects to imagine other stimuli—for instance, to "imagine lifting a ten pound weight with your right forearm"
(Jacobsen, 1930b) and to "imagine the Eiffel Tower in Paris" (Jacobsen,
1930c). He found increased EMGs on a high percentage of trials in the
right forearm muscles and eye muscles, respectively.

Requests to imagine stimuli involving movement also result in overt
responses. For example, the request to imagine an extended arm is moving toward the floor is followed by actual arm lowering, and requests
to imagine that an extended arm is light or that the subject is leaning
forward are followed by overt arm raising and leaning forward responses
(Barber & Calverley, 1963; Weitzenhoffer & Hilgard, 1959).

Subjects exhibit image-produced responses similar to stimulus-produced
ones when they spontaneously imagine stimuli, as well as when they
imagine stimuli upon request. Jacobsen (1930a) asked subjects to indicate
when they were spontaneously imaging arm movement, and these indications were correlated in time with increased EMGs in a muscle of

the appropriate arm. In addition, it certainly appears that we salivate when we spontaneously think about food, and thinking about food probably involves images of food occurring.

The amplitudes of the responses following requests to imagine stimuli involving movement were frequently so small that amplification of electrical potentials were required. In general, image-produced responses are lower in amplitude than the ones produced by real stimuli.

Images in Thought and Memory. Covert responses in the muscles responsible for speech are also likely to occur when subjects are engaged in verbal thought and in recall of verbal material. Jacobsen (1931) asked subjects to engage in mental activities—"Imagine counting," "Multiply 19 by 19," and "Recall any poem." He found increased EMGs in the muscles of the tongue and lip on a high percentage of trials. McGuigan and Winstead (1974) asked subjects to read, view, memorize, or recall words with sounds either frequently involving movement of the lips or frequently involving movement of the tongue. While the subjects engaged in the requested activities, they were more likely to exhibit covert lip movements when the task material primarily involved sounds requiring lip movements, and they were more likely to exhibit covert tongue movements when the task material primarily involved sounds requiring tongue movements.

Images of stimuli resulting in finger movement responses probably occur when deaf people engage in various mental activities, because deaf people are likely to communicate by sign language. Max (1935) found that increased EMGs in the finger muscles occurred when deaf subjects dreamed. He (1937) also found that problem solving resulted in increased EMGs in the finger muscles. Max's results on problem solving were replicated by McGuigan (1971), who also found that leg muscle EMGs did not increase during verbal problem solving and finger muscle EMGs increased more for verbal than nonverbal problem solving.

Image-produced responses resemble stimulus-produced responses, which means that images of stimuli that occurred during thought and recall in the studies described above may have been responsible for the covert speech responses that occurred. For example, reading about words with sounds frequently involving lip movements may result in frequent images of the stimuli that are correlated with making these sounds, and these images may result in frequent covert lip movements.

In addition, thinking about and recalling nonverbal stimuli probably involves the occurrences of images of nonverbal stimuli. If we think about food or if we recall a tasty meal we had, we salivate, presumably because images of the nonverbal stimulus of food occur during thinking about and recalling food. Paivio (1971) found that words known to provoke relatively vivid images of nonverbal stimuli facilitated the solving of verbal learning tasks; other factors affecting verbal learning were controlled. This result suggests that thinking about words referring to nonverbal stimuli during the acquisition of verbal learning resulted in images of the nonverbal stimuli. Thus, it will be concluded that thinking about and recalling both verbal and nonverbal stimuli result in images of these kinds of stimuli.

An image of a stimulus, that is, the experience (awareness) of it in its absence, can vary in vividness. Vivid images result in descriptions of stimuli that are fairly similar to the descriptions of real stimuli, and faint images result in less complete descriptions of stimuli. Images may be so faint that we do not experience the stimuli to which they correspond. Whether or not an image of a stimulus occurs probably depends on the amount of brain event that corresponds to this stimulus. It should also depend on the extent of the "interference" occurring from brain events corresponding to other stimuli.

When we think about and recall stimuli we do not always experience these stimuli. Thus, to be precise, the conclusion involving thought, recall, and images should be modified: thinking about and recalling both verbal and nonverbal stimuli result in the brain events corresponding to these stimuli, these brain events possibly resulting in images.

Image Theory and Verbal Reports Involving Classical Conditioning. The main hypothesis of the image theory of classical conditioning, then, is that the CS produces an image of the UCS and the CR thereby results. This hypothesis makes sense, because the CR is usually similar to the UCR, and because image-produced responses are similar to stimulus-produced ones.

Humans frequently describe the effect of CS-UCS pairings by saying that the CS makes them "think" of the UCS; or that the CS results in an idea of the UCS; or that the CS leads to an expectation of the UCS. This suggests that the CS results in a faint image of the UCS, because it was concluded above that thinking about nonverbal stimuli results in images of these stimuli.

Evidence exists that the CS sometimes produces hallucinations, that is, very vivid images of the UCS. Both Cole (1939) and Ellson (1939) presented the CS but not the UCS after prior CS-UCS pairings and found that subjects spontaneously verbalized that the UCS was perceived. Following presentation of the CS in extinction, one subject reported that shock was "awfully weak" (Cole, p. 361). In another study (Scott, 1930), classical conditioning of finger movement was established, using shock to the finger. Both the UCR and CR are movement of the finger that is shocked. Subjects were given hypnotic-induction instructions either prior to classical conditioning or after classical conditioning. Subsequently, the CS was presented alone, that is, without the UCS. Subjects reported that the CS produced a sensation of shock, pain, or tingling. This result suggests that the CS produced relatively vivid images of the shock UCS. The hypnotic-induction instructions may have increased the vividness of the image of the UCS that the CS apparently produced.

Image Theory Explanations. An important aspect of the image theory of classical conditioning is that it explains why a CR occurs when CS-UCS pairings are presented and why a CR frequently does not occur when a stimulus is paired with a stimulus that is not a UCS. If the second of two paired stimuli is a UCS or otherwise produces a response, then the first stimulus should tend to produce a response (the CR), because (a) the first stimulus should produce an image of the second stimulus; and (b) image-produced responses are similar to stimulus-produced responses. However, if the second of two paired stimuli does not produce a response, then the first stimulus should tend to not produce a response, because (a) the first stimulus should produce an image of the second stimulus; and (b) an image of a stimulus that does not produce a response should not result in a response.

The image theory of classical conditioning also explains the result that the strength of the CR is usually less than the strength of the UCR, since the amplitude of image-produced responses is usually less than the amplitude of stimulus-produced responses, and since the CS is assumed to produce an image of the UCS.

Image theory also offers a straightforward explanation of extinction of the CR. In extinction, the CS is paired with the stimulus of no particular event, and therefore the CS should come to produce an image of no particular event. Because no particular event does not elicit a response, an image of no particular event should not result in a response. The consequence is a decrease in the strength of the CR in extinction.

For everyday analogues of classical conditioning, the result to be explained is that the first of two paired neutral stimuli results in the thought of the second stimulus. Thinking about a stimulus is probably mediated by the occurrence of an image of this stimulus. Thus, image theory assumes that the first of two paired neutral stimuli produces an image of the second stimulus, that is, the thought of this stimulus.

Image and Engram Activation Theories. A close relationship exists between the image theory of classical conditioning and the engram activation theory of classical conditioning. The basis for this is the conclusion that when the permanent brain event corresponding to a stimulus is transformed to the temporary brain event corresponding to the stimulus in the absence of the stimulus, an image of the stimulus results. That a P_1-produced T_1 results in an image of S_1 makes sense, because it was previously reasoned that when a temporary brain event corresponding to a stimulus occurs, this stimulus can be experienced and described, and because an image of a stimulus is an experience of a stimulus in its absence that enables humans to describe the stimulus.

Transformation of a permanent brain event into a temporary brain event, that is, occurrence of a P_1-produced T_1, should result in a response similar to the one produced by the stimulus, S_1, according to the engram activation theory. In addition, the same temporary brain event stemming from the same source has just been assumed to result in an image of S_1. Thus, an image of a stimulus, S_1, should be accompanied by a response that is similar to the one produced by S_1, which accounts for the result that image-produced responses resemble stimulus-produced responses.

The image theory, like the engram activation theory, assumes that CS-UCS pairings result in an association between the permanent brain events corresponding to the CS and UCS, that is, they result in Pcs-Pucs. In addition, the permanent brain events corresponding to two neutral stimuli become connected when these stimuli are paired through the process for straightforward classical conditioning. Consequently, the occurrence of the first member of a stimulus pair results in the temporary brain event corresponding to the second member of the stimulus pair, and therefore in an image of the second member of the stimulus pair—whether or not the second member is a UCS or a neutral stimulus.

Image theory assumes that nonhuman animals have images of stimuli. The process that transforms the permanent brain event corresponding to a stimulus into the temporary brain event corresponding to this stimulus, and hence into an image is one that very simple nervous systems should be capable of. Even for animals without nervous systems, the transformation from a permanent brain event into a temporary one might be possible; the process could be totally chemical, rather than being neural as well. It is therefore reasonable to maintain that nonhuman animals as well as humans have images. The big difference, of course, is that nonhuman animals do not communicate about their images. In addition, nonhuman animals are surely less capable than humans of producing images of stimuli voluntarily, that is, relatively independently of current stimuli.

One other important matter is that the temporary brain event produced by a stimulus and the temporary brain event produced from the transformation of the permanent brain event corresponding to this stimulus cannot be precisely identical. Descriptions indicative of images of stimuli are less detailed and accurate than descriptions of real stimuli. In addition, the amplitude of image-produced responses is less than the amplitude of stimulus-produced responses. Image theory therefore assumes that the temporary brain event occurring for an image of a stimulus is qualitatively identical to but quantitatively less than the temporary brain event produced by the real stimulus.

The amount of activated temporary brain event, that is, temporary brain event occurring through the transformation of a permanent brain event, may be sufficiently low that the experience and therefore image of the corresponding stimulus does not occur. Temporary brain events corresponding to other stimuli should also interfere with the experience of the stimulus corresponding to an activated temporary brain event. Probably, the more stimulus-produced and activated temporary brain events that occur at the same time as an activated temporary brain event corresponding to a certain stimulus; and the more attention-eliciting and meaningful are the stimuli to which these other temporary brain events correspond; the less likely it is for this stimulus to be experienced. Thinking about and recalling stimuli may occur without images of them taking place. This imageless thought should nevertheless be mediated by activated temporary brain events, because it was previously indicated that thinking about and recalling stimuli result in responses resembling image-produced responses. Similarly, it may be that sometimes the CS does not result in an experience and therefore image of the UCS; but if the CR occurs, image theory assumes that it is due to the CS's producing at least a small amount of temporary brain event corresponding to the UCS. Finally, we will continue to say that the CS produces an image of the UCS, even if we cannot be certain that the CS produces an experience of it.

The engram activation theories of Konorski (1967) and Hebb (1968) involve images in much the same way that the image theory of classical conditioning does. Activation of gnostic units and some kinds of cell assemblies contribute to the occurrence of images, according to Konorski and Hebb, respectively. In addition, Konorski did propose (p. 208) that the CS produces an image of the UCS. But neither Konorski (1967) nor Hebb (1968) discussed the relevance of the conclusion that image-produced responses are similar to stimulus-produced responses to either their theories of conditioning or their theories of images.

Image Theory of Instrumental Conditioning

An image theory of instrumental conditioning (King, 1974) will be discussed.

Response-Produced Stimuli. Responses refer to actions. By definition we cannot perceive our responses. What we perceive are the stimuli produced by our responses.

Stimuli produced by a response can be both internal (for example, kinesthetic) and external (for example, visual). Consider the bar press response. The act of reaching out and pressing down on the bar produces kinesthetic stimuli from muscle, tendon, and joint receptors. In addition, visual stimuli corresponding to, for example, the paw extending out toward the bar, the gradual reduction in the distance between the paw and the bar, and the position of the body in relation to the bar and the walls of the apparatus may be perceived. Most likely, all overt responses produce kinesthetic stimuli; usually overt responses also produce visual stimuli.

These response-produced stimuli must be distinguished from experimenter-delivered and experimenter-arranged stimuli. An experimenter-delivered stimulus is one that the experimenter presents following a response of an animal. For example, when a bar press is followed by food, the food is an experimenter-delivered stimulus; it is not response-produced. Experimenter-arranged stimuli are stimuli of the learning situation. Experimenter-arranged stimuli do affect the kind of response-produced stimuli that occur. If one wall of a chamber is orange, when an animal makes the response of orienting its head in the direction of this wall, the stimuli produced by this head response will include orange light.

Image of the Goal and Negative-Goal. When an increase in the rate of an instrumental response occurs, the instrumental response causes a goal stimulus to occur—that is, a stimulus that is more likely to be approached and continued to be perceived than are the stimuli present before the execution of the instrumental response or the stimuli that would be present if the instrumental response were not made. When a decrease in the rate of an instrumental response occurs, the instrumental response causes a negative-goal stimulus to occur—that is, a stimulus that is more likely to be escaped from and avoided than are the stimuli present before the execution of the instrumental response or the stimuli that would be present if the instrumental response were not made. Accounts of instrumental conditioning in which the instrumental response causes a goal stimulus or a negative-goal stimulus to occur are essentially identical; for brevity's sake, we will concentrate on instrumental conditioning in which the instrumental response causes a goal stimulus to occur.

It will be reasoned that an image of the goal stimulus for an instrumental response occurs before the execution of the instrumental response. Take, for example, instrumental conditioning of the bar press response. After the bar press response is made and the goal stimulus (food) is delivered, two acquired associations between stimuli should occur according to the image theory of classical conditioning. Because the stimuli of the general learning situation were followed by the bar press response, these stimuli should become associated through the classical conditioning process with the stimulus produced by the bar press response. The assumed association is between two neutral stimuli. In addition, because the bar press response was followed by the goal stimulus, the stimulus produced by the bar press response should become associated through the classical conditioning process with the goal stimulus. These two associations should result in an image of the goal stimulus while an animal is in the general learning situation but has not yet initiated another bar press response.

The reasons for this are: The stimuli of the general learning situation should result in an image of the stimulus produced by the bar press response. If the real stimulus produced by the bar press response were to occur, it should result in an image of the goal stimulus. However, the real stimulus produced by the bar press response does not occur before this response; only an image of the stimulus produced by the bar press occurs. But the effects of the real stimulus produced by the bar press response and the image of this stimulus are due to qualitatively identical temporary brain events. It follows that an image of the stimulus produced by the bar press response should result in an image of the goal stimulus. Thus, while an animal is in the general learning situation but has not yet initiated another bar press response, an image of the goal stimulus should occur. This reasoning applies to all instrumental responses that cause a goal stimulus to occur, which leads to the conclusion that while an animal is in the learning situation, but has not yet initiated another instrumental response, an image of the goal stimulus occurs.

In instrumental conditioning with a negative-goal stimulus, the stimuli of the general learning situation are followed by the stimulus produced by the instrumental response, and this stimulus is followed by the negative-goal stimulus. Therefore, associations acquired between the stimuli of the general learning situation and the stimulus produced by the instrumental response, and between the stimulus produced by the instrumental response and the negative-goal stimulus should occur. It follows from the above discussion that the stimuli of the general learning situation result in an image of the negative-goal stimulus.

We have yet to account for the performance of the instrumentally conditioned response.

Bringing about Images of Goals or Terminating Images of Negative-Goals. We will assume that during instrumental conditioning animals behave (including within-the-brain responding) so as to bring about and maintain images of goal stimuli and to terminate and avoid bringing about images of negative-goal stimuli.

Subjects deprived of food were relatively likely to include food-related themes in their responses to TAT-like pictures (Atkinson & Mc-Clelland, 1948; Sanford, 1937). (The TAT or Thematic Apperception Test is a projective test, in which people are asked to write stories about what they see in a set of deliberately ambiguous pictures.) Food-related themes involve thinking about food and therefore probably indicate occurrences of images of food. Food is a stimulus that is approached and continued to be perceived for food-deprived humans. Therefore, the obtained result suggests that humans bring about and maintain an image of a stimulus that would be approached and continued to be perceived.

Tondo and Cautela (1974) asked subjects to imagine a highly pleasant scene each time they overestimated the size of a circle. Subjects capable of vivid imagery, as measured by a self-report scale, increased their estimates of the size of circles, while subjects capable only of faint imagery did not. A real pleasant scene should be approached and continued to be perceived. The obtained result therefore suggests that the subjects overestimated the size of circles in order to bring about an image of a stimulus that is approached and continued to be perceived, providing that the image of this stimulus was sufficiently vivid.

In one study (King, unpublished) students received pairings between a tone and shock. Subsequently they were asked whether or not they attempted to alter the vividness of the image of the shock while the tone was on, and 18 of the 28 subjects indicated they did attempt to make this alteration. Open-ended responses that were also obtained suggest that humans tend to terminate and avoid bringing about an image of a stimulus that is escaped from and avoided. For example, one student wrote that he wanted to "prevent the sensation produced by the tone."

A goal stimulus is one that is more likely to be approached and continued to be perceived than the stimuli present prior to the execution of the instrumental response or the stimuli that would be present if the instrumental response were not made, and a similar definition applies to negative-goal stimulus. In addition, it appears that humans bring about and maintain images of stimuli that are approached and continued to be perceived and terminate and avoid bringing about images of stimuli that are escaped from and avoided. Consequently, the assumption that during instrumental conditioning animals behave so as to bring about and maintain images of goal stimuli and terminate and avoid bringing about images of negative-goal stimuli has been supported.

Images of Goals and Negative-Goals and Image Theory. Figure 1-7 relates to how the assumption that animals behave so as to bring about and maintain an image of a goal stimulus fits in with the image theory of conditioning. Figure 1-7A indicates that the temporary brain event, T_1, produced by a stimulus that is approached and continued to be perceived, S_1, is assumed to have four consequences: (a) a relatively detailed and accurate description of S_1 (and an experience of S_1 for human and nonhuman animals alike); (b) a nonverbal response, R_1; (c) a permanent brain event, P_1, corresponding to S_1; and (d) a tendency to behave (including within-the-brain responding) so as to bring about and maintain T_1.

Approaching and continuing to perceive a stimulus means that an animal behaves so as to bring about and maintain the temporary brain event corresponding to this stimulus. For example, when an animal remains close to (continues to perceive) food it is maintaining the tempo-

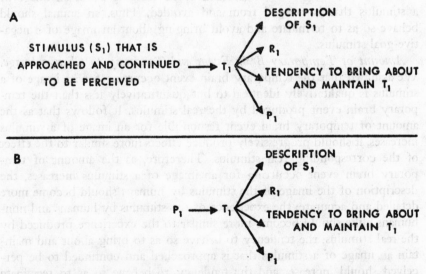

FIGURE 1-7. Summary of the effects of a stimulus that is approached and continued to be perceived and the effects of the activation of the permanent brain event corresponding to this stimulus.

rary brain event produced by food. Figure 1-7B indicates that an animal should behave so as to bring about and maintain (if it can) the temporary brain event corresponding to a stimulus that is approached and continued to be perceived when the source of this temporary brain event is the corresponding permanent brain event. In addition, an image of a stimulus is assumed to result from the transformation of a permanent brain event into a temporary brain event. It follows that an animal should behave so as to (attempt to) bring about an image of a stimulus that is approached and continued to be perceived. A goal stimulus is one that is more likely to be approached and continued to be perceived than the stimuli present prior to the execution of the instrumental response or the stimuli that would be present if the instrumental response were not made. Therefore, during instrumental conditioning an animal should behave so as to bring about and maintain an image of a goal stimulus, the assumption under consideration.

Analogous reasoning applies to negative-goal stimuli. Escaping from and avoiding a stimulus means that an animal behaves so as to terminate and avoid bringing about the temporary brain event produced by this stimulus. For example, when an animal escapes from shock it terminates the temporary brain event produced by shock. Therefore, an animal should behave so as to terminate and avoid bringing about an image of a stimulus that is escaped from and avoided. Thus, an animal should behave so as to terminate and avoid bringing about an image of a negative-goal stimulus.

Amount of Temporary Brain Event and Tendency to Change Image. We assumed that the temporary brain event occurring for an image of a stimulus is qualitatively identical to but quantitatively less than the temporary brain event produced by the real stimulus. It follows that as the amount of temporary brain event responsible for an image of a stimulus increases, it should progressively produce effects more similar to the effect of the corresponding real stimulus. Therefore, as the amount of temporary brain event occurring for an image of a stimulus increases, the description of the image of the stimulus by humans should become more detailed and accurate; the experience of the stimulus by humans and nonhumans alike should become more similar to the experience produced by the real stimulus; the tendency to behave so as to bring about and maintain an image of a stimulus that is approached and continued to be perceived should increase; and the tendency to behave so as to terminate and avoid an image of a stimulus that is escaped from and avoided should increase.

As the experience of a stimulus in its absence becomes more similar to the experience produced by the corresponding real stimulus, the vividness of the image of this stimulus is said to increase. Therefore, there should be a positive relationship among measures of the vividness of an image, the amplitude of an image-produced response; and the tendency to either bring about and maintain an image or terminate and avoid an image.

The expectation that a positive relation exists between the vividness of an image and the amplitude of an image-produced response makes sense. If a person hallucinates that there is food in the mouth, that is, if the person has a very vivid image of this stimulus, then he or she should salivate just as much as if the food were really there. This expectation is supported empirically by positive correlations between measures of vividness of images and measures of suggestibility (Palmer & Field, 1968; Shor, Orne, & O'Connell, 1966). An example of a suggestibility measure is the amount of responding that occurs after being asked to imagine that one's extended arm is heavy and that it is falling. Also, since sensory restriction is known to often increase the vividness of images people have, King and Lummis (1974) expected that the amount of arm lowering that occurred after being asked to imagine that an extended arm was getting heavy and that it was falling would be greater for subjects exposed to a sensory restriction condition than for subjects in control conditions. They used a visual sensory restriction procedure, placing translucent white patches over subjects' eyes, and confirmed the prediction.

A positive relation also seems to exist between the vividness of an image and the tendency to behave so as to either bring about and maintain or terminate and avoid this image. For example, suppose that it were possible for a hungry person to successfully (completely) hallucinate that food was in his or her mouth. Presumably the tendency to increase the vividness of the image of food to this high level would be very strong, since successfully hallucinating food would stop the discomfort correlated with hunger. Tondo and Cautela (1974) showed that only those subjects with high vividness of imagery scores tended to bring about the opportunity to imagine pleasant scenes by overestimating the size of circles. This suggests that subjects who have more vivid images of a stimulus that is approached and continued to be perceived are also more likely to bring about this image.

Recall that a goal stimulus is more likely to be approached and continued to be perceived than either the stimuli present before the instrumental response is made or the stimuli that would be present if the instrumental response were not made. It follows that during instrumental conditioning an animal should behave so as to increase the vividness of the image of the goal stimulus; any increase in the vividness of the image of the goal stimulus that the animal could bring about would be correlated with an increased tendency to maintain it, any further increase in the vividness of the image of the goal stimulus that the animal could bring about would be correlated with an even stronger tendency to maintain it, and so on. The parallel assumption for a negative-goal stimulus is that during instrumental conditioning an animal should behave so as to decrease the vividness of the image of a negative-goal stimulus.

How the Instrumental Response Is Made. How is the instrumental response executed?

We previously decided that while an animal is in the learning situation, an image of the goal stimulus for the instrumental response occurs. However, the amount of temporary brain event responsible for this image should be relatively small and therefore it should be relatively faint, because the real stimulus produced by the instrumental response has not yet occurred, and because it was this stimulus that was previously followed by the goal stimulus. If the real stimulus produced by the instrumental response were to occur, then the amount of temporary brain event resulting in an image of the goal stimulus should increase and this image should be more vivid. It was concluded above that an animal should behave so as to increase the vividness of an image of a goal stimulus. It follows that an animal should behave so as to (attempt to) bring about the actual stimulus produced by the instrumental response.

We will, in fact, assume that an animal is successful in its attempt to bring about the stimulus produced by the instrumental response. When an animal has brought about the stimulus produced by the instrumental response it has, of course, executed this response, the result to be accounted for.

Execution of the instrumental response is followed by the goal stimulus. This contributes to the further development of a classically conditioned association between the stimulus produced by the instrumental response and the goal stimulus, and thereby contributes to the subsequent execution of the instrumental response.

Essentially the same reasoning explains instrumental conditioning in which an instrumental response causes a negative-goal stimulus to occur. While an animal is in the learning situation, an image of the negative-goal stimulus should occur. The vividness of this image should be relatively small, because it is the real stimulus produced by the instrumental response that was previously followed by the negative-goal stimulus. If the real stimulus produced by the instrumental response were to occur, then the vividness of the image of the negative-goal stimulus should increase. But an animal should behave so as to decrease the vividness of the image of a negative-goal stimulus. It follows that it should behave so as to (attempt to) avoid bringing about the actual stimulus produced by the instrumental response. And we assume that an animal is successful in its attempt to avoid bringing about the stimulus produced by the instrumental response. A successful attempt to avoid bringing about the stimulus produced by the instrumental response means that the instrumental response will not be executed, the result to be accounted for.

How the Instrumental Response Is Made: Feedback Theory. A basic assumption of this explanation of instrumental conditioning is that an animal behaves so as to bring about or avoid bringing about the stimulus produced by the instrumental response. This response-produced stimulus is probably brought about or avoided by a feedback (closed-loop) process.

Consider a feedback account of the execution of a response that results in obtaining a perceived target stimulus—say, the response of extending an arm and picking up a cigar (Wiener, 1950/1967, p. 37). As the reaching out response is begun, the visual information provided by the relationship between the cigar and the hand indicates that the direction of the arm extension is not exactly correct. This visual information is called feedback; the result of responding is fed back to the source of responding. As a result of this visual information, the direction of the extending arm is altered slightly. If the new direction of the extending arm is still incorrect, either because too little or too much of a change in direction occurred, visual information about the extent of proximity between the cigar and hand will indicate this, and another change in the direction of arm extension will be made. The visual information provided by this new direction of arm extension will then indicate whether yet another change in direction of the extending arm is required. Thus, through a sequence of responding and obtaining visual information about the consequences of responding, the distance between the cigar and the hand is gradually reduced and the cigar is picked up.

This example indicates the basic elements of the feedback theory of response production. The information or feedback stemming from a response indicates that a disparity exists between the present condition and the condition of target attainment; this stimulates a response alteration, new feedback occurs as a result of this response alteration, and so on, until response alterations result in attainment of the target. Here the cigar is a perceived target stimulus; the feedback is the visual information indicating the physical proximity between the cigar and the hand; and response alterations are changes in the direction of the extending arm.

As we have said, an animal brings about the stimulus produced by the instrumental response, because by doing so it increases the vividness of the image of a goal stimulus. Bringing about the stimulus produced by the instrumental response is probably accomplished through the feedback process. The target of the feedback process should be a relatively vivid image of the goal stimulus. The feedback provided by responding should occur by way of response-produced stimuli. Because the stimulus produced by the instrumental response was previously followed by the goal stimulus, as the stimuli produced by responses become more similar to the stimulus produced by the instrumental response, the vividness of the image of the goal stimulus should increase. And the tendency to bring about and maintain an image of the goal stimulus should increase as this image becomes more vivid. An animal therefore adjusts its responses on the basis of the vividness of the image of the goal stimulus occurring at the moment, current responding becomes progressively more similar to the instrumental response and concurrently the vividness of the image of the goal stimulus becomes increasingly greater, and the execution of the instrumental response eventually occurs.

The stimuli produced by the response adjustments may so rapidly follow one another, and the amount of temporary brain event corresponding to the goal stimulus may so rapidly increase, that the images of the stimulus produced by the instrumental response and the goal stimulus that occur before the initiation of the instrumental response may not be experienced; much like a stimulus tends to be forgotten when it is followed by several somewhat similar rapidly occurring stimuli. Nevertheless, our account of instrumental conditioning applies—activated temporary brain events corresponding to the stimulus produced by the instrumental response and the goal stimulus should still mediate instrumental conditioning. Also, we will continue to say that the stimuli of the general learning situation result in an image of the stimulus produced by the instrumental response and an image of the goal stimulus, even if we cannot be certain that these stimuli are experienced.

Feedback theory accounts for a decrease in the rate of an instrumental response that causes a negative-goal stimulus to occur in essentially the same way. When the stimulus produced by the response occurring at the moment becomes somewhat similar to the stimulus produced by the instrumental response, an increase in the vividness of the negative-goal stimulus occurs. The animal therefore adjusts its responding; the outcome is a decrease in the vividness of the image of the negative-goal stimulus, due to a reduced similarity between the stimulus produced by the response that is occurring at the moment and the stimulus produced by the instrumental response. A reduction in the similarity between the stimulus produced by a response that is occurring at the moment and the stimulus produced by the instrumental response means that the instrumental response is not executed.

Feedback Theory and Machines. That animals behave so as to obtain a goal stimulus or avoid a negative-goal stimulus by adjusting their responding on the basis of information provided by this responding sounds anthropomorphic. However, it is known that machines function by the feedback process to attain specific outcomes. Because machines can operate in this way, it is clear that the brain is sufficiently complex to be capable of operating likewise.

The simple thermostat even operates by a feedback process. The target is a relatively constant specific temperature. The responses are to turn on or turn off the heat. After the heat is on for a while, the temperature of the room increases sufficiently so that the temperature sensitive component of the thermostat produces a current that results in the heater being turned off. Thus, feedback from the response of turning on the heat is provided by a change in the temperature sensitive component of the thermostat, and this feedback results in the response of turning off the heat. An analogous process occurs when the heat is off for a while, the result being that the target of a relatively constant specific temperature is obtained.

Novel Responding Appropriate to the Instrumental Contingency of Training. Consider the following prediction. The task is for an animal to move a slider along a straight path from a start point to an end point in 2 seconds. To establish this learning, the animal would be given food each time that it responded close to 2 seconds. Training would be carried out with the slider having a constant resistance to movement. Then, on a test trial, the resistance to movement of the slider would be changed, for example, made greater. At the start of the test trial the rate of responding should be slower than at the start of a training trial, due to the increased resistance to movement. But during the latter portion of the test trial the rate of responding should be faster than during the latter portion of a training trial. Speaking intuitively, an animal should "catch up" during the latter portion of the test trial. And an acceleration in the rate of responding during the latter portion of the test trial is the performance of a novel response that is appropriate to the instrumental contingency of training.

This catch-up prediction is made by closed-loop theory. Consider that the decrease in response rate on the test trial has just occurred. If a small increase in the rate of responding occurs at this moment, the similarity of the response-produced stimulus to the stimulus produced by the instrumental response will increase, and therefore the image of food should become more vivid. An animal should bring about and maintain a more vivid image of the food. Thus, this small increase in the rate of responding should take place. Moreover, any additional increase in the rate of responding that occurs at a slightly later moment in time will result in a further increase in the similarity of the response-produced stimulus to the stimulus produced by the instrumental response, and therefore the vividness of the image of food should increase some more. Thus, this additional increase in the rate of responding should also take place. Furthermore, this process should repeat itself, the outcome being that the animal will respond faster during the latter portion of the test trial than during the latter portion of a training trial, which is the catch-up prediction.

In general, many kinds of novel interference with the performance of an instrumental response should result in novel responding that is appropriate to the instrumental contingency of training. Just after the novel interference is applied, any response alteration that approximates the instrumental response more closely should result in a more vivid image of the goal stimulus. An animal should bring about and maintain a more vivid image of a goal stimulus. Thus, a response alteration that approximates the instrumental response more closely should occur. Moreover, additional response alterations that approximate the instrumental response still more closely should occur, because they should result in further increases in the vividness of the image of the goal stimulus, and so on. The closed-loop process accounts for the indicated response alterations. Machines that are governed by this process are known to exhibit novel responding that results in target attainment.

Novel but appropriate articulatory responses occur when speech is interfered with in a novel way. Halwes and Jenkins (1971) point out "the ability to modify articulatory behavior in order to talk while performing other acts with the mouth such as eating, chewing gum, holding a pencil in the mouth, or smoking; the ability to whisper, to shout, to speak rapidly or slowly" (p. 126). Similarly, MacNeilage (1970) wrote that "As tongue position is dependent on mandibular movement, speaking with a closed jaw requires modification of every tongue movement required for speech" (p. 189), and yet appropriate pronunciation occurs. Surely these and similar interferences with speech will be novel for some humans and yet appropriate articulatory responding will occur. Articulatory responses must be greatly influenced by instrumental conditioning. Therefore, the prediction that novel responding that is appropriate to the instrumental contingency of training occurs is supported.

Stimulus-response theory cannot make this prediction. For a stimulus-response connection to occur and therefore for an instrumentally conditioned response to take place, the instrumental response must have been previously executed. But a novel response cannot have been previously executed. Thus, stimulus-response theory predicts that novel responding that is appropriate to the instrumental contingency of training does not occur.

Central Response-Produced Stimulus. Response-produced stimuli play a critical role in image theory. It is probable that central (within-the-brain) response-produced stimuli are involved in instrumental conditioning.

Consider that Taub, Bacon, and Berman (1965), for example, instrumentally conditioned a response in monkeys in the likely absence of response-produced stimuli from receptors. The instrumental response was raising an arm. Kinesthetic and tactual response-produced stimuli from receptors were probably eliminated by a surgical operation on the spinal cord at the point where sensory nerves from the arm enter. Visual response-produced stimuli from the retina were removed by arranging the learning situation so that the monkeys could not see their arms move. Monkeys deprived of response-produced stimuli were instrumentally conditioned (albeit slowly) to raise their arms. How can instrumental conditioning occur when response-produced stimuli from receptors are eliminated, if, according to image theory, stimuli produced by the instrumental response are essential for the occurrence of this response?

A reasonable answer is that a response produces stimuli within the brain as well as produces stimuli that affect receptors. Figure 1-8 indicates one way to think of central response-produced stimuli as influencing instrumental conditioning. A "decision" neuron discharges into an efferent nueron. The efferent neuron discharges into both an afferent neuron and a neuron on a path to a muscle. The afferent neuron discharges into the decision neuron, that is, provides a central response-produced stimulus. If the afferent neuron's discharge is similar to a component of the temporary brain event corresponding to the stimulus produced by the instrumental response, the decision neuron continues to discharge into the efferent neuron and sufficient activity builds up for the efferent neuron to activate the neuron on a path to a muscle.

There are other reasons for maintaining that central response-produced stimuli necessarily mediate instrumental conditioning. The execution of an instrumental response often occurs without obvious response alterations, whereas response adjustments are called for by feedback theory. However, it does seem that discrete response alterations that tend to increasingly approximate the correct response do occur early in training. For example, early in training a rat may approach the bar, then temporarily stop responding (hesitate), and then move closer to the bar. As training progresses, inappropriate response adjustments are eliminated. Also, consider the instrumental response sequence of a child's learning to tie his or her shoelaces. The child often appears to wait in between the segments of the response sequence, possibly while he or she processes information about previous responses in relation to the goal of tied shoelaces. Early in training, then, response alterations may occur largely because of response-produced stimuli stemming from receptors; later on in training, the response alterations may be mainly due to central response-produced stimuli.

Execution of instrumental responses can occur so quickly that receptor stimulation produced by one response does not reach the brain quickly enough to function as a cue for the next response. For example, playing a piece on the piano very rapidly involves pressing a number of piano keys so quickly that the stimuli provided through receptor stimulation from pressing one piano key may not function as a cue for the next piano key press (Lashley, 1951). It is considered likely, therefore, that stimuli

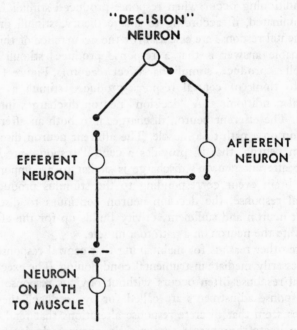

FIGURE 1-8. How central response-produced stimuli may influence instrumental conditioning.

produced within the brain by one response of a rapidly executed response sequence function as a cue for the next response.

Image Theory and Verbal Reports Involving Instrumental Conditioning. Let us consider the instrumental response of opening the door of a refrigerator. The goal for this response is food. Before initiating the door opening response, people might say that they have an idea of the "feel" of this response, which may be interpreted as the occurrence of an image of the stimulus produced by this response. They probably would also report that they have an idea of the desired item of food inside the refrigerator, similarly interpretable as the occurrence of an image of the stimulus of food. Such reports would be in accord with the hypotheses that before the execution of the instrumental response, an image of the stimulus produced by this response and an image of the goal stimulus for this response occur.

As the door opening response is begun, people probably would report to the effect that the idea of the desired item of food inside the refrigerator becomes clearer, in accord with the assumption that the vividness of an image of the goal stimulus increases as the response occurring at the moment increasingly approximates the instrumental response. In addition, people's reports might suggest that as the door opening response is continued, an increasingly more vivid image of the desired item of food inside the refrigerator "merges" with the sight of this item of food inside the refrigerator.

In one study (Hefferline & Perrera, 1963), a covert thumb press response was followed by a tone that could barely be heard. Subsequently, the tone was omitted. Even though the tone no longer followed the covert thumb press response, humans behaved as if the tone occurred. One subject even reported that it did occur. This result suggests, in accord with image theory, that execution of an instrumental response increases the vividness of the image of the stimulus this response causes to occur.

Image Theory Explanations. An advantage of the image theory of conditioning is that it accounts for the result that instrumental conditioning usually occurs when a response causes a goal or negative-goal stimulus to take place, and that instrumental conditioning ordinarily does not occur when a response causes a stimulus that is neither a goal nor a negative-goal to take place. An animal is relatively unlikely to approach and continue to perceive or escape from and avoid a stimulus that is neither a goal nor a negative-goal stimulus. It follows that an animal should not behave so as to increase or decrease the vividness of a stimulus that is neither a goal nor a negative-goal stimulus. But image theory maintains that instrumental conditioning occurs because an animal increases or decreases the vividness of the image of the stimulus the instrumental re-response causes to occur. Thus, when a response causes a stimulus that is neither a goal nor a negative-goal stimulus to occur, instrumental conditioning should not take place.

Even though instrumental conditioning usually does not result when the instrumental response causes a stimulus that is neither a goal nor a negative-goal stimulus to occur, the stimulus produced by the instrumental response should still become associated with this stimulus through the process for classical conditioning. This statement derives from the assumption that pairings between two stimuli, regardless of whether or not they are neutral stimuli, result in an association between these stimuli through the process for classical conditioning.

Image theory explains extinction of the instrumentally conditioned reponse of, for example, bar pressing. Recall that extinction of bar press learning consists of omitting the positive reinforcer (goal stimulus) for this response, whether or not the response is performed. In extinction the stimulus produced by the bar press response should therefore become associated through classical conditioning with the stimulus of no particular event. Because no particular event is not a goal stimulus, an animal should not increase the vividness of the image of it, and therefore the rate of the bar press response should decline in extinction.

Image theory maintains that instrumental conditioning will usually occur when a response causes a goal stimulus to take place. The basis for this is that a goal stimulus is more likely to be approached and continued to be perceived than are the stimuli present before the execution of the instrumental response or the stimuli that would be present if the instrumental response were not made. Thus, the goal stimulus need not be a special kind of stimulus such as a positive primary reinforcer for instrumental conditioning to occur. Everyday instances of instrumental conditioning involve the occurrence of instrumental conditioning with goal stimuli or negative-goal stimuli that are not the reinforcers typically employed in the laboratory. The relatively high probability of turning a light switch on in a dark room when one wishes to read is an example of an everyday instance of instrumental conditioning. Because image theory assumes that the goal stimulus need not be a special kind of stimulus, it accounts for everyday instances of instrumental conditioning.

Everyday analogues of instrumental conditioning involve a response causing a neutral stimulus to occur—for instance, a hand striking a surface and causing a sound. For everyday analogues of instrumental conditioning, execution of the response results in some kind of knowledge of the neutral stimulus this response causes to occur. A classically conditioned association should occur between the stimulus produced by this response and the neutral stimulus; therefore the stimulus produced by this response should result in an image of the neutral stimulus. This image of the neutral stimulus is probably the basis for the execution of the response resulting in some kind of knowledge of the neutral stimulus the response causes to occur.

Similarity of Image-Produced and Stimulus-Produced Effects. Image theory's explanations for classical and instrumental conditioning are based, in part, on the similarity of the effects of images of stimuli and real stimuli. Descriptions of images of stimuli and descriptions of real stimuli are by definition similar. Image-produced responses are similar to stimulus-produced responses. Humans tend to bring about and maintain images of certain stimuli, similar to approaching and continuing to perceive these stimuli; and humans tend to terminate and avoid images of other stimuli, similar to escaping from and avoiding these stimuli. These similarities between images of stimuli and real stimuli support the assumption that images of stimuli and the effects of real stimuli are due to qualitatively identical temporary brain events.

There are many other ways in which the effects of images of stimuli and real stimuli are similar (Moyer, 1973; Pressey & Wilson, 1974; Segal & Fusella, 1970; Shepard & Metzler, 1971; Yaremko, Glanville & Leckart, 1972). Segal and Fusella, for example, found that images of auditory stimuli (more correctly, requests to imagine such stimuli) interfered more with detection of auditory stimuli than did images of visual stimuli, and that images of visual stimuli interfered more with detection of visual stimuli than did images of auditory stimuli. Similarly, real auditory stimuli interfere more with detection of other auditory stimuli than do real visual stimuli, and real visual stimuli interfere more with detection of other visual stimuli than do real auditory stimuli. Yaremko et al. found that repeatedly imagining a tone resulted in a greater subsequent reduction in the strength of the GSR elicited by repeated presentation of a real tone than did repeatedly imagining a light. Similarly, prior repeated presentation of a real tone results in a greater subsequent reduction in the strength of the GSR elicited by the tone than does prior repeated presentation of a real light.

Related Theories of Instrumental Conditioning. Some theories of instrumental conditioning related to the image theory of instrumental conditioning will be discussed.

Konorski (1967) assumed that activation of the gnostic unit corresponding to some of the stimuli produced by an instrumental response results directly in the performance of the instrumental response. Greenwald (1970) made essentially the same assumption. He postulated an image of the stimulus produced by an instrumental response occurring through a central representation of this stimulus, and said that this image tended to result directly in performance of the instrumental response. In terms of permanent brain events, both Konorski and Greenwald hypothesized that activation of the permanent brain event corresponding to the stimulus produced by the instrumental response results directly in the execution of this response. Their hypothesis differs from image theory, which assumes that an animal increases or decreases the amount of temporary brain event corresponding to a goal or negative-goal stimulus; that an animal brings about or avoids bringing about the stimulus produced by the instrumental response; and that a feedback process mediates response production.

When people are requested to imagine a situation involving movement they are likely to exhibit the appropriate covert responses, as indicated by amplified potentials of muscles (EMGs) recorded from relevant muscles. Greenwald considered these observations to support his main hypothesis; however, it appears more parsimonious to think of these findings as examples of the more general finding that image-produced responses are similar to stimulus-produced responses.

Konorski also assumes that activation of the gnostic unit or permanent brain event corresponding to a UCS results in a response similar to the UCR elicited by the UCS (that is, the CR). But this assumption results in an inconsistency: a real UCS elicits a UCR, but the real stimulus produced by a response does not result in another execution of this response.

Konorski and Greenwald both predict that responses will occur in situations in which they do not take place. For example, we know that rats will learn to remain on a platform if they are shocked after stepping off it. Because the stimuli of the general learning situation precede the step-down response, the central representation, gnostic unit, or permanent brain event corresponding to the stimuli of the general learning situation should become associated with the central representation, gnostic unit, or permanent brain event corresponding to the stimulus produced by the step-down response. It would then appear that the stimuli of the general learning situation should result in the activation of the central representation, gnostic unit, or permanent brain event corresponding to the stimulus produced by this response. According to the main hypothesis of Konorski and Greenwald, the step-down response should therefore occur. However, the obtained result is that rats learn to remain on the platform.

Mowrer (1960a, 1960b) proposed a feedback theory of instrumental conditioning that is fairly similar to the image theory of instrumental conditioning. However, Mowrer conceived of the stimulus produced by the instrumental response as becoming associated with either positive or negative emotional responses rather than with brain events corresponding to specific stimuli. A major problem with Mowrer's theory is that it offers no explanation of the CR of classical conditioning. Conditioned emotional responses cannot account for the occurrence of the typical CR, because the typical CR is a specific response and emotions are not specific responses.

Summary

A learned response is defined. In typical classical conditioning, the CS (conditioned stimulus), a neutral stimulus, is followed independently of responding by the UCS (unconditioned stimulus), a stimulus that elicits a response automatically (not because of learning). The CS comes to produce a learned response, the CR (conditioned response), that is usually similar to the UCR (unconditioned response) elicited by the UCS. Classical conditioning also may include situations in which one stimulus predicts a second stimulus is relatively likely to occur in the presence of the first stimulus or relatively soon thereafter, and situations in which the second stimulus need not automatically elicit a response. A neutral stimulus is one that is automatically relatively unlikely to be either approached and continued to be perceived or escaped from and avoided. A reinforcer is a stimulus that establishes learning. A primary reinforcer is a reinforcer that is automatically relatively likely to be either approached and continued to be perceived or escaped from and avoided. Most UCSs are primary reinforcers. Consideration of choice situations involving the presence of two stimuli, e.g., a neutral stimulus and shock, clarified the meanings of neutral stimulus and primary reinforcer. Extinction consists of presenting the CS alone after classical conditioning has been established. It usually decreases the amplitude of the CR. This change in response is learned and an instance of classical conditioning. Everyday analogues of classical conditioning involve the first of two paired stimuli not producing a learned response, the second stimulus following the first stimulus independently of responding, and the first stimulus resulting in some kind of knowledge of the second stimulus.

Examples of instrumental conditioning were described. Instrumental conditioning occurs when a response causes a stimulus to take place and this response changes in rate as a consequence of this response-stimulus pairing. The response causing a stimulus to occur is called the instrumental response. A response usually increases in rate when it causes a goal stimulus to occur and usually decreases in rate when it causes a negative-goal stimulus to occur. A goal stimulus is one that is more likely to be approached and continued to be perceived than the stimuli present prior to the execution of the instrumental response or the stimuli that would be present if the instrumental response were not made. A similar definition applies to negative-goal stimulus. Three types of instrumental conditioning were identified on the basis of the sign of the reinforcer and on the basis of whether or not the goal stimulus and negative-goal stimulus were reinforcers. Extinction in instrumental conditioning consists of not presenting the reinforcer subsequent to establishing instrumental conditioning and often results in a relatively fast change in the rate of an instrumental response, a finding that is itself an instance of instrumental conditioning. Everyday occurrences of instrumental conditioning involve instrumental conditioning established with reinforcers not typically employed in the laboratory. Everyday analogues of instrumental conditioning are not instances of instrumental conditioning, but do entail a response causing a stimulus to occur and this response resulting in some kind of knowledge of this stimulus.

The expectancy-purpose theory of conditioning maintains that the CR and the instrumentally conditioned response are purposive behaviors resulting from the expectation of a stimulus. The purpose of the CR is not clear, however; it is not apparent why learned responses similar to the UCR should be those responses having a purpose, especially since the UCS arrives independently of an animal's responding.

According to stimulus-response theory, the CR and the instrumental response are produced in a reflex fashion by the stimulus connected to the UCR or the instrumental response. In Hull's stimulus-response theory, a stimulus and response become connected if the stimulus is followed by the response and drive reduction occurs. The onset of a positive primary reinforcer and the offset of a negative primary reinforcer result in drive reduction. The theory accounts for both the CR and the instrumental response. Hull's theory has difficulty in explaining why learning occurs without a response taking place; why learning occurs without drive reduction taking place; why better learning occurs when a stimulus is paired with the onset rather than the offset of a negative reinforcer; and why an increase in the strength of a CS-elicited response in classical conditioning does not occur.

Engram activation theories of learning are based on the ideas that (a) a stimulus produces a specific temporary brain event; (b) this temporary brain event enables humans to describe the stimulus and human and nonhuman animals alike to experience it, is responsible for the nonverbal response that the stimulus may produce, and results in a specific permanent brain event or engram; (c) learning consists of the development of connections between permanent brain events corresponding to paired stimuli; and (d) the permanent brain event corresponding to a stimulus can become activated, that is, transformed back into the temporary brain event corresponding to this stimulus, thereby permitting humans to describe this stimulus in its absence and producing a nonverbal response similar to the stimulus-produced one. For classical conditioning, the CS results in the activation of the permanent brain event corresponding to the UCS by way of a previously established connection between the permanent brain events corresponding to the CS and UCS; the result of this activation should be a UCR-like response, that is, the CR. Konorski's theory of classical conditioning and Hebb's perceptual learning theory are engram activation theories.

Image theory assumes that the CR results from a CS-produced image of the UCS. This theory makes sense because the CR is similar to the UCR, and because image-produced responses are similar to stimulus-produced ones. Images of both verbal and nonverbal stimuli occur in thinking about and recalling them. Image theory can therefore explain why the CS results in some kind of knowledge of the UCS. In addition, the theory explains why a CR occurs when a stimulus is paired with a UCS, and why a CR does not occur when a stimulus is paired with a second stimulus that does not produce a response. It also accounts for extinction of the CR and for everyday analogues of classical conditioning. The connection between image theory and the engram activation theory is based on the inference that an image of a stimulus occurs when the permanent brain event corresponding to this stimulus is transformed into the temporary brain event corresponding to this stimulus in the absence of the real stimulus. This assumption is tantamount to maintaining that the effects of real stimuli and images of stimuli are due to qualitatively identical temporary brain events; however, the amount of temporary brain event responsible for an image of a stimulus should be less than the amount of temporary brain event produced by a real stimulus.

To explain instrumental conditioning, image theory states that after the instrumental response has caused the goal stimulus to occur, stimuli of the general learning situation should become associated with the stimulus produced by the instrumental response through classical conditioning; and the stimulus produced by the instrumental response should become associated with the goal stimulus, also through classical conditioning. It follows that while an animal is in the learning situation a relatively faint image of the goal stimulus should occur. The idea that animals behave so as to bring about and maintain an image of a goal stimulus was supported with human data. In addition, the conclusion that the effects of real stimuli and images of stimuli are due to qualitatively identical temporary brain events leads to this assumption. An increase in the amount of temporary brain event corresponding to a goal stimulus should result in both a more vivid image of this stimulus and a stronger tendency to bring about and maintain it. Bringing about the stimulus produced by the instrumental response should increase the vividness of the image of the goal stimulus. It follows that animals should attempt to bring about the stimulus produced by the instrumental response. It is, in fact, assumed that animals are successful in bringing about the stimulus produced by the instrumental response, which accounts for its execution. Bringing about the stimulus produced by the instrumental response is probably accomplished through a feedback process. Machines attain specific outcomes through this process. Image theory predicts that novel responding that is appropriate to the instrumental contingency of training occurs, and there is support for this prediction. It is necessary to assume that central response-produced stimuli contribute to mediating instrumental conditioning. Image theory is in accord with verbal reports about instrumental conditioning; explains why a response should not be instrumentally conditioned when it causes a stimulus to occur that is neither a goal nor a negative-goal; and accounts for extinction of the instrumentally conditioned response, everyday occurrences of instrumental conditioning, and everyday analogues of instrumental conditioning. More evidence that image-produced and stimulus-produced effects are similar is indicated. Some related theories of instrumental conditioning are discussed.

REFERENCES

ATKINSON, J. W., & McCLELLAND, D. C. The projective expression of needs: II. The effect of different intensities of the hunger drive on thematic apperception. *J. Exp. Psychol.*, 1948, 38, 643-658.

BARBER, T. X., & CALVERLEY, D. S. "Hypnotic-like" suggestibility in children and adults. *J. Abnorm. Soc. Psychol.*, 1963, 66, 589-597.

BARBER, T. X., CHAUNCEY, H. H., & WINER, R. A. Effect of hypnotic and nonhypnotic suggestions on parotid gland response to gustatory stimuli. *Psychosom. Med.*, 1964, 26, 374-380.

BARBER, T. X., & HAHN, K. W., JR. Experimental studies in "hypnotic" behavior: Physiologic and subjective effects of imagined pain. *J. Nerv. Ment. Dis.*, 1964, 139, 416-425.

COLE, L. E. A comparison of the factors of practice and knowledge of experimental procedure in conditioning the eyelid response. *J. Gen. Psychol.*, 1939, 20, 349-373.

CRAIG, K. D. Physiological arousal as a function of imagined, vicarious, and direct stress experiences. *J. Abnorm. Psychol.*, 1969, 73, 513-520.

DAVITZ, J. R. Reinforcement of fear at the beginning and end of shock. *J. Comp. Physiol. Psychol.*, 1955, 48, 152-155.

DAVYDOVA, E. K. Changes in excitability of motor cortex during formation of conditioned reflex in response to stimulation. *Neuroscience Translations*, 1967, 1, 53-56.

ELLSON, D. G. Spontaneous recovery of the galvanic skin response as a function of the recovery interval. *J. Exp. Psychol.*, 1939, 25, 586-600.

FINK, J. B. Conditioning of muscle action potential increments accompanying an instructed movement. *J. Exp. Psychol.*, 1954, 47, 61-68.

GREENWALD, A. G. Sensory feedback mechanisms in performance control: With special reference to the ideo-motor mechanism. *Psychol. Rev.*, 1970, 77, 73-99.

HALWES, T., & JENKINS, J. J. Problem of serial order in behavior is not resolved by context-sensitive associative memory models. *Psychol. Rev.*, 1971, 78, 122-129.

HEBB, D. O. *The Organization of Behavior*. New York: Wiley, 1949.

HEBB, D. O. Concerning imagery. *Psychol. Rev.*, 1968, 75, 466-477.

HEFFERLINE, R. F., & PERERA, T. B. Proprioceptive discrimination of a covert operant without its observation by the subject. *Science*, 1963, 139, 834-835.

HILGARD, E. R. The nature of the conditioned response. I. The case for and against stimulus substitution. *Psychol. Rev.*, 1936, 43, 366-385.

HULL, C. L. *A Behavior System*. New Haven: Yale University Press, 1952.

JACOBSEN, E. Electrical measurements of neuromuscular states during mental activities: I. Imagination of movement involving skeletal muscle. *Am. J. Physiol.*, 1930, 91, 567-608. (a)

JACOBSEN, E. Electrical measurements of neuromuscular states during mental activities: II. Imagination and recollection of various muscular acts. *Am. J. Physiol.*, 1930, 94, 22-34. (b)

JACOBSEN, E. Electrical measurements of neuromuscular states during mental activities: III. Visual imagination and recollection. *Am. J. Physiol.*, 1930, 95, 694-702. (c)

JACOBSEN, E. Electrical measurements of neuromuscular states during mental activities: VII. Imagination, recollection and abstract thinking involving the speech musculature. *Am. J. Physiol.*, 1931, 97, 200-209.

KAMIN, L. J. Temporal and intensity characteristics of the conditioned stimulus. In W. F. Prokasy (Ed.), *Classical Conditioning: A Symposium*. New York: Appleton-Century-Crofts, 1965.

KIMMEL, H. D. Instrumental inhibitory factors in classical conditioning. In W. F. Prokasy (Ed.), *Classical Conditioning: A Symposium*. New York: Appleton-Century-Crofts, 1965.

KING, D. L. An image theory of classical conditioning. *Psychol. Rep.*, 1973, 33, 403-411.

KING, D. L. An image theory of instrumental conditioning. *Psychol. Rep.*, 1974, 35, 1115-1122.

KING, D. L., & LUMMIS, G. Effect of visual sensory-restriction and recent experience with the imagined stimulus on a suggestibility measure. *Int. J. Clin. Exp. Hypn.*, 1974, 22, 239-248.

KONORSKI, J. *Integrative Activity of the Brain.* Chicago: University of Chicago Press, 1967.

LASHLEY, K. S. The problem of serial order in behavior. In L. A. Jeffress (Ed.), *Cerebral Mechanisms in Behavior.* New York: Wiley, 1951.

LEONARD, D. W., & THEIOS, J. Effect of CS-US interval shift on classical conditioning of the nictitating membrane in the rabbit. *J. Comp. Physiol. Psychol.*, 1967, 63, 355-358.

LOGAN, F. A., & WAGNER, A. R. Supplementary report: Direction of change in CS in eyelid conditioning. *J. Exp. Psychol.*, 1962, 64, 325-326.

MACNEILAGE, P. F. Motor control of serial ordering of speech. *Psychol. Rev.*, 1970, 77, 182-196.

MAX, L. W. An experimental study of the motor theory of consciousness: III. Action-current responses in deaf-mutes during sleep, sensory stimulation and dreams. *J. Comp. Psychol.*, 1935, 19, 469-486.

MAX, L. W. Experimental study of the motor theory of consciousness: IV. Action-current responses in the deaf during awakening, kinesthetic imagery and abstract thinking. *J. Comp. Psychol.*, 1937, 24, 301-344.

MCGUIGAN, F. J. Covert linguistic behavior in deaf subjects during thinking. *J. Comp. Physiol. Psychol.*, 1971, 75, 417-420.

MCGUIGAN, F. J., & WINSTEAD, C. L., JR. Discriminative relationship between covert oral behavior and the phonemic system in internal information processing. *J. Exp. Psychol.*, 1974, 103, 885-890.

MOWRER, O. H. *Learning Theory and Behavior.* New York: Wiley, 1960. (a)

MOWRER, O. H. *Learning Theory and the Symbolic Processes.* New York: Wiley, 1960. (b)

MOWRER, O. H., & AIKEN, E. G. Contiguity vs. drive-reduction in conditioned fear: Temporal variations in conditioned and unconditioned stimulus. *Am. J. Psychol.*, 1954, 67, 26-38.

MOYER, R. S. Comparing objects in memory: Evidence suggesting an internal psychophysics. *Percept. Psychophys.*, 1973, 13, 180-184.

PAIVIO, A. *Imagery and Verbal Processes.* New York: Holt, Rinehart & Winston, 1971.

PALMER, R. D., & FIELD, P. B. Visual imagery and susceptibility to hypnosis. *J. Consult. Clin. Psychol.*, 1968, 32, 456-461.

PAVLOV, I. P. *Conditioned Reflexes* (G. V. Anrep, trans.). Oxford: Oxford University Press, 1927.

PRESSEY, A. W., & WILSON, A. E. The Poggendorff illusion in imagination. *Bull. Psychon. Soc.*, 1974, 3, 447-449.

ROWLAND, L. R. The somatic effects of stimuli graded in respect to their exciting character. *J. Exp. Psychol.*, 1936, 19, 547-560.

SANFORD, R. N. The effects of abstinence from food upon imaginal processes: A further experiment. *J. Psychol.*, 1937, 3, 145-159.

SCOTT, H. E. Hypnosis and the conditioned reflex. *J. Gen. Psychol.*, 1930, 4, 113-130.

SEGAL, S. J., & FUSELLA, V. Influence of imaged pictures and sounds on detection of auditory and visual signals. *J. Exp. Psychol.*, 1970, 83, 458-464.

SHEPARD, R. N., & METZLER, J. Mental rotation of three-dimensional objects. *Science*, 1971, 171, 701-703.

SHIMP, C. P. Short-term memory in the pigeon: Relative recency. *J. Exp. Anal. Behav.*, 1976, 25, 55-61.

SHOR, R. E., ORNE, M. T., & O'CONNELL, D. N. Psychological correlates of plateau hypnotizability in a special volunteer sample. *J. Pers. Soc. Psychol.*, 1966, 3, 80-95.

SPERLING, G. The information available in brief visual presentations. *Psychol. Monogr.*, 1960, 74 (Whole No. 498).

TAUB, E., BACON, R. C., & BERMAN, A. J. The acquisition of a trace-conditioned avoidance response after deafferentiation of the responding limb. *J. Comp. Physiol. Psychol.*, 1965, 59, 275-279.

TOLMAN, E. C. *Purposive Behavior in Animals and Men.* New York: Century, 1932.

TONDO, T. R., & CAUTELA, J. R. Assessment of imagery in covert reinforcement. *Psychol. Rep.*, 1974, 34, 1271-1280.

WEITZENHOFFER, A. M., & HILGARD, E. R. *Stanford Hypnotic Susceptibility Scale, Forms A and B.* Palo Alto, Calif.: Consulting Psychologists Press, 1959.

WIENER, N. *The Human Use of Human Beings: Cybernetics and Society.* New York: Avon Books, 1967. (Originally published, 1950.)

YAREMKO, R. M., GLANVILLE, B. B., & LECKART, B. I. Imagery-mediated habituation of the orienting reflex. *Psychon. Sci.*, 1972, 27, 1271-1280.

ZENER, K. The significance of behavior accompanying conditioned salivary secretion for theories of the conditioned response. *Am. J. Psychol.*, 1937, 50, 384-403.

CHAPTER 2

Classical Conditioning

Classically Conditioned Responses

Recall that the typical procedure for establishing classical conditioning consists of presenting a neutral stimulus (the conditioned stimulus or CS) and then a stimulus that elicits a response and is a primary reinforcer (the unconditioned stimulus or UCS). Delivery of the UCS is independent of an animal's responding. This procedure usually results in the CS producing a response (the conditioned response or CR) that is similar to the response elicited by the UCS (the unconditioned response or UCR). For example, a food-deprived dog is presented with a tone (CS) and several seconds later with a piece of food (UCS) (delivery of the food being independent of the dog's responding); these tone-food (CS-UCS) pairings are repeated; the tone comes to produce an increase in salivation (the CR), a response similar to the one elicited by food (the UCR). Let us now consider some of the responses that have been classically conditioned.

CS Followed by Positive UCS. Classical conditioning of salivation and mouth movement were previously described.

Classical conditioning of the pecking response of pigeons is another example of classical conditioning in which a CS is followed by a positive UCS. (Do not confuse this with the previously described instrumental conditioning of pecking.) In a study of Brown and Jenkins (1968), pigeons deprived of food were placed in a chamber in which a key was intermittently illuminated with white light during the course of the

63

experiment. Eight seconds after each onset of the white light, 4 seconds access to food was given independently of how the pigeons responded. Following repeated presentations of light and food, the pigeons pecked the key when it was lit but did not peck the key when it was dark. The pecking response was not an instrumentally conditioned response, because it did not cause food to occur. The peck CR is quite similar to the peck at actual food; that is, the forms of the peck CR and peck UCR are closely related (Jenkins & Moore, 1973).

Classical conditioning of licking and gnawing in food-deprived rats has also been demonstrated (Peterson, Ackil, Frommer, & Hearst, 1972; Stiers & Silterberg, 1974). The CS was the insertion of a retractable lever into the learning enclosure for 15 seconds. This CS was followed by delivery of food independently of the subjects' responding. The rats eventually licked and gnawed the lever, responses they exhibit when eating food.

In another study (Jenkins & Moore, 1973), the CS was illumination of a key, the UCS was water, and the subjects, pigeons, were deprived of water. CS-water pairings led to a peck CR, but the topography of this CR differed from the topography of the peck CR that resulted from CS-food pairings. The peck CR established with the UCS of water was longer in duration than the sharp and vigorous peck CR that occurred when the UCS of food was employed. Judges rated the peck CR that was established with the UCS of water as resembling the drinking response of pigeons to water rather than the eating response of pigeons to food.

Classical conditioning of courtship behavior has also been found (Rackham, 1971; cited by Moore, 1973). The CS was onset of a light, the UCS was access to a female pigeon, and the subjects were male pigeons. CS-UCS pairings resulted in the male pigeons exhibiting courtship dances, including strutting, pirouetting, and nest calling, in front of the CS.

The UCS of electrical stimulation of the hypothalamus has been used. This UCS resulted in sniffing and exploratory UCRs. A neutral stimulus preceding this UCS came to produce sniffing and exploratory responses (Peterson, Ackil, Frommer, & Hearst, 1972).

CS Followed by Negative UCS. We have already mentioned examples of classical conditioning using a negative UCS, including GSR, leg movement, eyelid closure, and finger movement.

Nictitating membrane classical conditioning resembles eyelid classical conditioning. The nictitating membrane is an inner eyelid. It moves laterally across the eye when the external eyelid closes. Rabbits possess this membrane, and they are used for classical conditioning of its response. A puff of air to an eye and shock around an eye both elicit the eyelid and nictitating membrane responses; neutral stimuli that precede these UCSs are able to produce the eyelid and nictitating membrane responses.

Electric shock elicits a variety of responses, and several of these responses have been classically conditioned. Rats (and probably other animals) often run and jump and exhibit increased activity when given inescapable shocks (Glazer & Weiss, 1976; Sheffield, 1948). Some classical conditioning of running, using shock, has been reported (Brodgen, Lipman, & Culler, 1938). When rats are given the opportunity to leave (escape from) a chamber in which they were shocked they do so by running (Bolles, 1970) and jumping (McAllister, McAllister, Brooks, & Goldman, 1972). The CS for the running and jump CRs should therefore be viewed as consisting of some of the stimuli of the chamber in which the rats were shocked.

Inescapable shocks have also been observed to elicit crouching and inactivity (Glazer & Weiss, 1976; Sheffield, 1948). In addition, when rats and pigeons were given CS-shock pairings without being allowed to escape from the chamber in which shock was received, the CS came to produce immobility, crouching, or some less extreme form of inactivity (Blanchard & Blanchard, 1969; Hunt & Brady, 1955; Stein, Hoffman, & Stitt, 1971).

A type of classical conditioning called *conditioned suppression* is used extensively in studies of classical conditioning. In conditioned suppression, a CS followed by shock acquires the ability to decrease the rate of many responses that are otherwise likely to occur. Most frequently, an animal is first instrumentally conditioned to bar press or key peck by following bar press or key peck responses with a positive reinforcer. After an animal performs the instrumental bar press or key peck response at a relatively high rate, classical conditioning is begun. While an animal is free to perform the acquired instrumental response, CS-shock pairings are presented. The CS comes to decrease the rate of the instrumental response; conditioned suppression is said to occur. The general result that a CS paired with shock comes to reduce the rate of many responses is probably at least partially due to the already indicated finding that a CS paired with shock comes to produce inactivity. CS-produced inactivity should effectively interfere with performing many responses.

The effect of a CS on the rate of an instrumental response is too complex to be pursued in detail here. A CS paired with a positive UCS usually also comes to suppress the rate of an instrumental response established by following this response with a positive reinforcer (Azrin & Hake, 1969; Meltzer & Brahlek, 1970). But a CS paired with a shock UCS will often increase rather than decrease the rate of an instrumental response in a type of instrumental conditioning called avoidance learning.

Aggressive biting and striking responses in rats and biting responses in monkeys have been classically conditioned using shock as a UCS (Hutchinson, Renfrew, & Young, 1971; Vernon & Ulrich, 1966). When animals are provided with an appropriate target, they frequently attack it just after being shocked. Aggression directed toward inanimate objects is also elicited by shock. In the Vernon and Ulrich study, a tone was followed by shock simultaneously delivered to pairs of rats in the same chamber. The shocks elicited striking and biting responses by both rats toward the other rat. Each eleventh presentation of the tone was not followed by shock. An observer rated whether or not striking and biting responses were made by either rat toward the other rat on the tone-alone trials. The tone-shock pairings resulted in an increase in the frequency of striking and biting responses occurring on tone-alone trials; that is, classical conditioning of striking and biting occurred.

Shock also elicits an increase in heart rate, so it is not surprising that a CS paired with shock comes to produce an increase in heart rate. However, classical conditioning of heart rate is a complicated matter, at least partly because often the heart rate response to the CS may decrease just before onset of the shock UCS, and because heart rate may be strongly affected by classically conditioned changes in activity and respiration (Black & Toledo, 1972; Zeaman & Smith, 1965).

Other physiological responses can be classically conditioned. For example, classical conditioning of decreased blood glucose using insulin as a UCS has been reported. Insulin decreases the concentration of blood glucose. In one study (Woods & Shogren, 1972), rats were injected with insulin. The injection procedure is a stimulus complex that can be thought of as a CS. After several pairings between the CS of the injection procedure and the stimulus of insulin within the body (the UCS), a saline solution rather than insulin was injected. A decrease in blood glucose still occurred, which indicates that the injection procedure functioned as a CS that produced the CR of a reduction in blood glucose. The obtained result raises the possibility that the responses to various drugs like aspirin and narcotics, may actually be, in part, CRs produced by the stimuli involved with taking the drug. Also, the general result that a number of physiological responses can be classically conditioned raises the possibility that some psychosomatic illnesses may result from the occurrence of classically conditioned illness-producing responses.

Similarity of CR to UCR. All these examples of classical conditioning are instances of the general result that the CR is similar in response topography to the UCR. This outcome contradicts the expectancy-purpose theory of conditioning, because it does not make sense to maintain that the CR has a purpose and is simultaneously almost always similar to the UCR, especially since the UCS is delivered independently of responding. Take, for example, classical conditioning of a decrease in blood glucose. It seems clear that the CR of a decrease in blood glucose should have a negative rather than a positive consequence for the health of animals.

Omission of UCS Studies. Studies dealing with the omission of the UCS involve the occurrence of the CR resulting in omission of a positive UCS or the withholding of the CR resulting in omission of a negative UCS.

In one such study (Sheffield, 1965), a CS was followed by food if a dog salivated to the CS below a criterion level, and this CS was followed by no particular event if the dog salivated to it above the criterion level. The finding was that the dog continued to salivate above the criterion level on roughly half the trials over the 800 trials of training. Note that the dog continued to salivate to the CS above the criterion level even though it was in effect "punished" by omission of food for doing so. In a similar study, Williams and Williams (1969) found that pigeons were relatively likely to continue to peck a key upon illumination of this key even though not pecking the illuminated key resulted in food occurring and pecking the illuminated key caused food to be omitted. Also, Stiers and Silberberg (1974) found that rats were relatively likely to make contact with a lever when it was inserted into the experimental chamber and followed by the delivery of food even though the only way that food could be omitted was to make contact with the lever.

In related research (Breland & Breland, 1961), apparent classical conditioning was obtained when animals performed instrumental responses with objects that were followed by food. Raccoons were deprived of food and given a piece of food after they deposited coins into a container. The raccoons were expected to make the coin dropping response reliably and quickly, much as rats bar press reliably and quickly when a bar press response is followed by food. However, as training progressed the raccoons became less rather than more likely to reliably and quickly deposit the coins. They spent seconds and even minutes handling and rubbing the coins before dropping them into the container. The natural response of raccoons to food is to manipulate it with their paws before eating it. Because a similar response was made to the coins, and because the coins were followed by food when they were deposited, it appears that the coins functioned as a CS and produced a food manipulation CR.

Similar results were found with pigs, who came to root coins instead of performing an instrumental response involving exchanging these coins for food; also, porpoises and whales swallowed objects instead of performing an instrumental response involving exchanging these objects for food. Note that, as in the omission studies, the raccoons, pigs, porpoises, and whales appear to have "punished" themselves by exhibiting a CR, because performance of the CR entailed either a delay in receiving food or omission of food.

Schlosberg (1934, 1936) obtained similar results using shock as a UCS. A CS was followed by shock if the subjects, rats, made a CR; but the CS was not followed by shock if these subjects did not make a CR. Execution of the CR continued during training. This result is similar to the results described above; subjects "punished" themselves by continuing to exhibit the CR, in this case receiving shock when the CR was made.

The omission of UCS results are theoretically important, in part because they contradict both the expectancy-purpose theory and Hull's stimulus-response theory. The CRs performed in these studies neither caused a goal stimulus to occur nor avoided the occurrence of a negative-goal stimulus. Therefore, there was no purpose to these CRs in the sense of the expectancy-purpose theory. As for Hull's stimulus-response theory, if exhibiting the CR is less likely to be followed by drive reduction than not exhibiting the CR, how can it be, then, that the CR is established?

CS Is Approached and Continued to Be Perceived. Evidence indicates that a CS that is paired with a positive UCS comes to be approached and continued to be perceived. Positive UCSs are also approached and continued to be perceived, so that the generalization that CRs are typically similar to UCRs remains valid.

Previously described findings indicate that a CS that is followed by a positive UCS comes to be approached and continued to be perceived. For example, pigeons approached (and then pecked) an illuminated key that was followed by food (Brown & Jenkins, 1968). Also, male pigeons approached and continued to perceive (while exhibiting a courtship dance) a light that was paired with the delivery of a female pigeon (Rackham, 1971; cited by Moore, 1973).

The stimuli of a receptacle containing a positive reinforcer can be viewed as a CS in many conditioning situations, because these stimuli are perceived just before obtaining the positive reinforcer. Zener (1937) found that dogs oriented to and approached the food tray prior to the arrival of food. Given that the tray can be viewed as a CS, the obtained result supports the conclusion that a CS paired with a positive UCS comes to be approached and continued to be perceived.

In another study (Haraway, Wirth, & Maples, 1974), onset of a light preceded delivery of food in the home cage of rats by 0.5 second. This light was on a funnel that served as a conduit for the delivery of food. Subsequently, each rat was placed at one end of an apparatus that was essentially a runway. The light that preceded delivery of food in the home cage was placed at the other end of the apparatus. The rats given light-food pairings in the home cage approached the light at the far end of the apparatus at a faster rate than a control group that perceived the light several hours prior to obtaining food.

In a somewhat similar study (Gonzalez & Diamond, 1960), rats were first placed at the start of a runway and were permitted to traverse it, but did not receive food in it. A box was present at the end of the runway. In a second stage, the rats were placed directly into this box or a similar one instead of traversing the runway to reach the box. In this stage, food was available during each placement into the box. In a third stage, the rats were again placed at the start of the runway and were again permitted to traverse the runway, but did not receive food in the apparatus at any time. Rats in three out of four conditions traversed the runway more quickly after they had received food in the box they were placed in than when they were first permitted to traverse the runway. This result suggests that the stimuli of the box the rats were placed in and where they received food constituted a CS that the rats subsequently approached.

Approach and continued perception of a CS paired with a positive UCS is likely to be facilitated by instrumental conditioning. For example, an approach response to a receptacle containing a positive reinforcer is likely to be instrumentally conditioned, because this approach response causes the goal of food to occur. However, it is clear that for at least some instances of approach and continued perception of a CS paired with a positive UCS the contribution of classical conditioning is relatively great. As noted earlier, pigeons and rats tended to approach a CS and then peck or make contact with it even though the peck and contact responses caused food to be omitted that would otherwise occur (Stiers & Silberberg, 1974; Williams & Williams, 1969). In addition, the finding that rats traversed a runway at a faster rate after being placed directly into and receiving food in a box that was either identical or similar to the box at the end of the runway could not have been due to the instrumental conditioning of the response of approaching the food box. The rats received food by being placed right into the box, which means that approaching the food box could not have been instrumentally conditioned.

CS Is Escaped from and Avoided. A CS paired with a negative UCS is escaped from and avoided. An example (McAllister, McAllister, Brooks, & Goldman, 1972) of this general result involved placing rats in a compartment that they could not get out of and shocking them. Subsequently, a door to the compartment was opened. As expected, rats left the compartment in which they had been previously shocked. In this study, the CS consists of the stimuli of the compartment in which shock was received, because these stimuli were perceived prior to shock onset, and because shock onset occurred independently of responding. Exiting from the box therefore was an escape from a CS response. Because the compartment in which shock was received was not returned to, it is also clear that the CS of the stimuli of the shock compartment was avoided. Odling-Smee (1975) also showed that the stimuli of a shock compartment were escaped from and avoided.

Animals must be restrained when they are classically conditioned using a shock UCS. This is because the CS and also the stimuli of the general learning situation would be escaped from if a subject were not restrained.

A currently active area of research involves the classical conditioning of escape and avoidance of taste CSs that are paired with the illness-producing stimuli of poisons or Xrays. In one study (Domjan & Wilson, 1972), a group of water-satiated rats received injections of a saccharin solution directly into the mouth. Immediately thereafter they were injected with a poison. Subsequently, the rats were deprived of water and given a preference test between drinking from a tube filled with tap water and a tube filled with the saccharin solution. The group that received pairings between the saccharin solution and poison was much less likely to drink from the tube containing the saccharin solution than a control group. This result suggests that pairings between the saccharin solution and the poison resulted in the saccharin solution being escaped from and avoided.

Escape from a CS paired with a negative UCS is not usually importantly influenced by instrumental conditioning. Consider the situation involving escape from a compartment in which shock was received. The acquired response of exiting from the shock compartment cannot have been instrumentally conditioned due to termination of shock, because the exiting response occurred subsequent to the termination of shock. In addition, the acquired exiting response cannot have been instrumentally conditioned by omission of shock (which involves a type of instrumental conditioning called avoidance learning that will be described later), because the exiting response did not cause the omission of shock.

The contribution of instrumental conditioning to escape from and avoidance of a CS paired with a negative UCS is minimal. In addition, pairings between a CS and a negative UCS and between a CS and a positive UCS most likely involve the same process. This supports the conclusion that a CS paired with a positive UCS is approached and continued to be perceived independently of instrumental conditioning.

CS Paired with Absence of UCS. A CS is said to be paired with the absence of a UCS when the time that the UCS is presented is relatively different from the time that the CS is presented. In addition, as is true for the more typical classical conditioning procedure, delivery of a UCS that occurs in the absence of a CS is independent of an animal's responding.

A CS paired with the absence of a UCS does not come to produce specific CRs. For example, a CS paired with the absence of food does not come to produce salivation. According to the image theory of conditioning, a CS paired with the absence of a UCS should not come to produce a specific CR, because such a CS should become associated with the stimulus that immediately follows it, which is no particular event; and because no particular event and therefore an image of no particular event should not result in a specific response.

Classical conditioning does occur when a CS is paired with the absence of a UCS, however. Such a CS comes to be either approached and continued to be perceived, or escaped from and avoided. In addition, it affects the performance of other responses.

A study by Wasserman, Franklin, and Hearst (1971) suggests that a CS paired with the absence of a positive UCS was escaped from and avoided. Food-deprived pigeons were given food intermittently as long as both keys in the chamber were dark. In addition, food was never delivered for a period of time before and a period of time after illumination of either of the two keys. More specifically, (a) food was delivered 40 times in an experimental session; (b) illumination of each key occurred 20 times in an experimental session; (c) food never preceded onset of illumination of a key by less than 20 seconds and never followed offset of illumination of a key by less than 33 seconds; and (d) the time separating illumination of a key from the next illumination of a key (either the same key or the other key) equalled 86 seconds on the average. The procedure indicated in (c) is the main reason for saying that the study under consideration involved pairing a CS with the absence of a UCS.

When a key was illuminated, the pigeons tended to stay on the side of the chamber containing the dark key. This behavior suggests that the pigeons escaped from and avoided the key that was illuminated. Because illumination of each key was paired with the absence of food, the obtained result suggests that pigeons escaped from and avoided CSs paired with the absence of the positive UCS of food. Results in Chapter 4 also indicate that a stimulus paired with the absence of a reinforcer is escaped from and avoided.

A stimulus paired with the absence of a negative UCS appears to come to be approached and continued to be perceived (Weisman & Litner, 1969). Rats were placed in a chamber in which they faced the possibility of intermittently receiving shocks that were 0.3 second long. In addition, in a different chamber the rats received pairings between a 5 second tone and the absence of a 0.3 second shock. The tone and shock were separated in time by 1.5 minutes on the average, with a range of 50 to 130 seconds. The time between adjacent shocks was 3.0 minutes. In a second stage, the rats were again placed in the chamber where they faced the possibility of being shocked intermittently. Now, however, they could produce the tone paired with the absence of shock in the first stage by making 10 wheel turning responses in a 5 second period. The rate of wheel turning increased as a result. When the tone was no longer delivered following 10 wheel turning responses, the rate of wheel turning decreased. The tone therefore served as a goal stimulus and reinforcer for the instrumental response of wheel turning. Because this tone is a goal stimulus for an instrumental response, it should be approached and continued to be perceived. The obtained result thus suggests that a CS paired with the absence of a negative UCS is approached and continued to be perceived.

Other procedures show that a CS paired with the absence of a UCS comes to affect responding. One approach is to show that a CS paired with the absence of a UCS retards subsequent classical conditioning in which the same CS and UCS are paired in the typical (CS-UCS) fashion. In an illustrative study (Rescorla, 1969), rats were first instrumentally conditioned to press a bar. One group then received pairings between a tone and the absence of shock in a different chamber. A control group received the same number of tones and almost the same number of shocks (actually, slightly more) in this chamber, but the tones and shocks were delivered randomly in respect to each other. The two groups were then returned to the chamber containing the bar, and bar pressing continued to be followed by food. While the rats were free to engage in bar pressing, on occasions pairings between the previously employed tone and shock were given. The tone-shock pairings led to the tone producing a conditioned suppression CR; that is, the occurrence of the tone came to decrease the rate of bar pressing. The result of interest is that the group that previously received the tone paired with the absence of shock decreased its rate of bar pressing more slowly than the control group. Therefore, pairing a CS with the absence of shock inhibited subsequent acquisition of a conditioned suppression CR resulting from the same CS and shock being paired in the typical (CS-UCS) fashion.

Another approach used to show that a CS paired with the absence of a UCS comes to affect responding is called the *summation procedure*. This approach essentially consists of presenting two CSs simultaneously, one of which was previously paired with the absence of the UCS, and the other of which was previously paired with this UCS. The idea is that the CS paired with the absence of the UCS should decrease the strength of the CR produced by the CS paired with the UCS; that is, a subtraction effect is expected, even though the procedure is called a summation one. (An additive effect is usually obtained when the simultaneously presented CSs were both previously paired with the occurrence of the same UCS.)

In an illustrative study (Rescorla, 1969), rats were first instrumentally conditioned to press a bar. Subsequently, one group received pairings between a tone and the absence of shock in a different chamber. A control group received the same number of tones in this chamber but did not receive shocks. The two groups were returned to the chamber containing the bar, and bar pressing continued to be followed by food. While the rats were free to engage in bar pressing, light-shock pairings were presented to both groups. This procedure was carried out so that the light would produce a conditioned suppression CR, that is, so that the light would decrease the rate of bar pressing. Finally, the tone and light were simultaneously presented to both groups. The rate of bar pressing by the group receiving pairings between the tone and absence of shock was greater than the rate of bar pressing by the control group. Thus, a CS paired with the absence of a UCS reduced the strength of a CR produced by another CS paired in the typical (CS-UCS) fashion with the same UCS.

A CS paired with the absence of a UCS is often called a *conditioned inhibitor,* and the resulting classical conditioning is often called *inhibitory classical conditioning.* These terms are used because, as has been indicated, a CS paired with the absence of a UCS impairs acquisition of typical classical conditioning between the same CS and UCS, and decreases the strength of a CR produced by another CS paired with the same UCS.

Typical (CS-UCS) classical conditioning is therefore frequently said to result in *excitatory classical conditioning*.

Physical and Temporal Proximity of Stimuli. Why should a CS paired with the absence of a positive UCS be escaped from and avoided, and a CS paired with the absence of a negative UCS be approached and continued to be perceived? The reason probably involves the effect of the physical and temporal proximity of the UCS (reinforcer) to a neutral stimulus on responding to this neutral stimulus.

A neutral stimulus occurring in sufficiently close physical and temporal proximity to a positive UCS is probably escaped from and continued to be avoided (as long as it is possible to make these responses). A study of Adelman and Maatsch (1956) supports this statement. Food-deprived rats were instrumentally conditioned to traverse a runway. At the beginning of a trial they were placed at the start of the runway, and food could be obtained at the end of the runway. After the runway was being quickly traversed, extinction was instituted. Unlike the typical extinction procedure, however, rats were permitted to jump out of the box at the end of the runway once extinction was initiated. They were able to do this by starting from the floor of the box and jumping to a ledge that ran around three sides at the top of the box. Another group did not traverse the runway. Instead, rats in this group were placed in the end box of the runway the same number of times that the first group traversed the runway. In addition, this group did not receive food in the end box. Subsequently, rats in this group were instrumentally conditioned to jump onto the ledge around the top of the end box by placing a piece of food on the ledge each time an animal was placed in the endbox. The group that traversed the runway was more likely to jump onto the ledge than the group that received explicit instrumental conditioning of the response of jumping onto the ledge. In addition, the group that traversed the runway continued to quickly jump onto the ledge for 100 trials, at which point the study was terminated; whereas the other group became much less likely to jump onto the ledge when food was no longer placed on the ledge.

In training, the stimuli of the end box were paired with food for the group that traversed the runway; however, in extinction, the stimuli of the end box were followed by the absence of food for this group. This group escaped from the stimuli of the end box at a faster rate than a second group that was explicitly instrumentally conditioned to exit from the end box. Also, the group that traversed the runway persisted in escaping from the stimuli of the end box. Food and the end box stimuli occurring in the absence of food obviously were in the same physical location for the group that traversed the runway. In addition, since extinction trials began the day after training, the time interval separating food and the end box stimuli occurring in the absence of food for this group was not very long. Therefore, the indicated results are in accord with the statement that when a neutral stimulus, in this case the end box stimulus complex, occurs in sufficiently close physical and temporal proximity to a positive UCS, in this case food, the neutral stimulus is escaped from and continued to be avoided.

A neutral stimulus occurring in sufficiently close physical and temporal proximity to a positive UCS also tends to elicit aggressive behavior (Azrin, Hutchinson, & Hake, 1966; Hutchinson, Azrin, & Hunt, 1968). In the former study, in one condition food-deprived pigeons were exposed to two different treatments that alternated in time while the pigeons remained in the same chamber. One of these conditions was delivery of food ten times independently of responding. The second condition was the occurrence of no particular event, neither food nor any other stimulus being presented during this period. A live pigeon was continuously available for subject pigeons to attack. A control condition was also employed—a prolonged time period in which no particular event occurred. It was found that the duration of attack against the target pigeon was much longer when food delivery alternated in time with brief durations of no particular event than when no particular event was in effect for a prolonged period of time.

The stimuli of the general learning situation in this study can be viewed as a neutral stimulus that occurred in relatively close physical and temporal proximity to food. The importance of temporal proximity is evident, because when the stimuli of the general learning situation were no longer preceded and followed by food relatively quickly, the stimuli of the general learning situation elicited much less attack behavior. Therefore, the described study supports the idea that when a neutral stimulus, in this study the stimuli of the general learning situation, occurs in sufficiently close physical and temporal proximity to a positive reinforcer, in this study food, the neutral stimulus tends to elicit aggressive behavior.

Shock is escaped from and avoided and elicits aggressive behavior. A neutral stimulus is also escaped from and avoided and elicits aggressive behavior when it occurs in relatively close physical and temporal proximity to a positive reinforcer. That a neutral stimulus can be made to affect responding in somewhat the same way that shock does, through the neutral stimulus occurring in relatively close physical and temporal proximity to a positive reinforcer, indicates the importance of the relationship between a neutral stimulus and a reinforcer on responding.

The effect of the physical and temporal proximity of two stimuli leads to an explanation of why a CS paired with the absence of a positive UCS is escaped from and avoided. A CS paired with the absence of a positive UCS can be viewed as equivalent to a CS paired with no particular event that occurs in relatively close physical and temporal proximity to a positive UCS. When no particular event—that is, the end box stimuli and the stimuli of the general learning situation—occurred in relatively close physical and temporal proximity to a positive UCS, no particular event was escaped from or elicited aggressive behavior. Therefore, a CS paired with no particular event that occurs in relatively close physical and temporal proximity to a positive UCS should be escaped from; that is, a CS paired with the absence of a positive UCS should be escaped from. Also, such a CS should tend to produce aggressive behavior, especially so if escape is not permitted and a suitable target for aggressive behavior is presented.

Presumably no particular event is approached and continued to be perceived when it occurs in sufficiently close physical and temporal proximity to a negative UCS (as long as it is possible to make these responses). Reasoning similar to that in the above paragraph explains why a CS paired with the absence of a negative UCS is approached and continued to be perceived.

The explanation of why a CS paired with the absence of a UCS comes to be approached and continued to be perceived or escaped from and avoided assumes that animals acquire an association between a CS and no particular event through classical conditioning. This assumption is in accord with the image theory of conditioning, which assumes that when one neutral stimulus is followed by a second neutral stimulus independently of responding, an association between the two stimuli is acquired through the classical conditioning process.

An explanation of why a CS paired with the absence of a UCS retards subsequent typical (CS-UCS) classical conditioning between the same CS and UCS is that CS-UCS pairings must replace (overcome) an acquired association between the CS and no particular event, as well as result in an acquired association between the CS and the UCS.

Recall that simultaneously presenting a CS previously paired with the absence of a UCS, and a CS previously paired with the same UCS results in a weaker CR than presenting only the CS previously paired with the UCS. The CS previously paired with the absence of a UCS should result in an image of no particular event. The CS previously paired with the same UCS should result in an image of the UCS. Perhaps the outcome of simultaneously occurring images of no particular event and a UCS is a less vivid image of the UCS than is produced by the CS previously paired with the UCS. Since a positive relation is taken to exist between the vividness of an image of a stimulus and the amplitude of the image-produced response that takes place, simultaneously presenting a CS previously paired with the absence of a UCS, and a CS previously paired with the same UCS should result in a weaker CR than presenting only the CS paired with the UCS.

CS Paired with Termination of UCS. Suppose that on the average of once every minute an animal is permitted access to food—let us say, for a variable length of time ranging from 5.0 to 10.0 seconds—and that a brief tone comes on just 0.5 second before the termination of each access to food, independently of how an animal responds. The tone would then be a CS paired with the termination of a UCS.

Pairing a CS with the termination of a UCS and pairing a CS with the absence of a UCS are similar procedures in that they both involve a CS being followed by the absence of a UCS for a relatively long time period. The major difference between the two procedures is, of course, that in one case but not the other onset of the CS is followed for a relatively brief time by the continued occurrence of the UCS.

This difference in procedure between pairing a CS with the termination of a UCS and pairing a CS with the absence of a UCS is probably not theoretically important. Research to be described shows that a classically conditioned association between a CS and UCS occurs when the CS predicts that the UCS is relatively likely to take place while the CS is on or relatively shortly after the CS terminates. Both a CS paired with the termination of a UCS, and a CS paired with the absence of a UCS predict a relatively long time period in which the UCS does not occur; in both these cases, therefore, a classically conditioned association between the CS and no particular event should take place.

We will assume, on the basis of these statements, that a CS paired with the termination of a positive UCS comes to be escaped from and avoided, and a CS paired with the termination of a negative UCS comes to be approached and continued to be perceived. In one relevant study (Maples, Tomporowski, & Haraway, 1975), one group of rats received a 30 second shock delivered through the grid floor of a chamber. This group also received a light that started 5 seconds before the termination of the shock and was delivered independently of responding. A control group received the same light and shock; for this group the light came on 100 seconds after termination of the shock. For both groups the time interval separating one presentation of the UCS and CS from the next was 1 hour. In a second stage, a subject was placed into the choice point of what were essentially two runways. This apparatus was similar to the chamber of the first stage in that both floors were grids. The light that was used in the first stage was presented in one of the two runways, the position (left or right) for different subjects being determined on a random basis. Only one trial in the apparatus was given. The group that received the tone paired with the termination of shock was more likely to enter the runway with the light on than the group receiving the tone following the termination of shock. Thus, a CS paired with the termination of shock was approached.

Another result (Segundo, Galeano, Sommer-Smith, & Roig, 1961) provides some support for the assumption under consideration. Cats received relatively long shocks that were terminated 2 to 5 seconds after onset of a tone. The tone came to produce responses suggestive of positive emotional behavior. The responses it produced, although variable, included "head elevation or rotation, ear movements, eye opening or blinking, body straightening (or general shift) and interruption of previous activities (mewing, licking)" (p. 273). These responses indicate a change from tense behavior to relaxed, natural behavior. If a stimulus produces responses suggestive of positive emotional behavior, it would appear likely that this stimulus would be relatively likely to be approached and continued to be perceived. This study therefore supports the possibility that a stimulus paired with the termination of shock is approached and continued to be perceived.

In another study (Moscovitch & LoLordo, 1968), dogs received shocks that were 4.0 to 6.0 seconds long. Onset of a tone occurred 1.0 second prior to the termination of these shocks. It was shown that this tone was a conditioned inhibitor. A CS paired with the absence of a UCS is also a conditioned inhibitor. In addition, it was concluded that a CS paired with the absence of a UCS is likely to be either approached and continued to be perceived or escaped from and avoided. The possibility that a CS paired with the termination of a negative UCS is approached and continued to be perceived therefore receives additional support.

CS Paired with Continuation of UCS. Suppose that on the average of once every minute an animal is permitted access to food for either 3 seconds or 9 seconds. In addition, suppose that when access is limited to 3 seconds, a neutral stimulus is not presented; when access to food is permitted for 9 seconds, a tone comes on 2.5 seconds after access to food is first permitted. The tone in this example would be a CS paired with the continuation of food.

A classically conditioned association between a CS and UCS occurs when a CS predicts that the UCS is relatively likely to take place while the CS is on or a relatively short time after the CS terminates. A CS paired with the continuation of a UCS predicts that the UCS is relatively likely to occur relatively soon after the CS takes place. A CS paired with the continuation of a UCS should therefore result in an acquired association between this CS and UCS, that is, to the same kind of acquired association resulting from CS-UCS pairings. A CS paired with the continuation of a UCS may therefore be assumed to result in a specific CR (for instance, salivation). We may also assume that a CS paired with the continuation of a positive UCS comes to be approached and continued to be perceived, and a CS paired with the continuation of a negative UCS comes to be escaped from and avoided.

Random Presentation of CS and UCS. Random presentations of a CS and UCS have been found to retard acquisition of a CR when CS-UCS pairings are subsequently presented (Kremer, 1971; Mackintosh, 1973). Research to be described shows that classical conditioning occurs when a CS predicts that a UCS is relatively likely to take place while the CS is on or relatively shortly after the CS terminates. In other words, animals respond on the basis of a comparison between the probability of the UCS occurring, given that the CS is on or has just terminated; and the probability of the UCS occurring, given that no particular event has been in effect for a while. It therefore appears that animals could in some sense learn that a CS is randomly associated with a UCS. Such an acquired association would appear to impair acquisition of an association based on the CS's predicting that the UCS is relatively likely to occur while the CS is on; that is, it would appear to impair acquisition of a CR when CS-UCS pairings are subsequently presented.

CR Not Similar to UCR. Classical conditioning in which the CR is not similar to the UCR is known to occur. In one study (Wasserman, 1973), chicks were placed in a cooled incubator. Illumination of a key was paired with onset of a heat lamp. Chicks in a relatively cool environment will normally approach a warmer area; in addition, wing extension frequently occurs when chicks are exposed to a relatively warm stimulus. As a result of the pairings between illumination of the key and increase in heat, the chicks came to approach, peck, and snuggle against the illuminated key. The approach response is not surprising, because chicks will approach a warmer area when they are placed in a cooler area. But the pecking and snuggling of the key are CRs dissimilar to the UCR of wing extension elicited by the UCS of a relatively warm stimulus.

Perhaps there is an automatic (not because of learning) tendency for chicks not to extend their wings when this response will cause the wings to bump into an object. A classically conditioned approach response to the key would, of course, bring the chicks into a position where wing extension would be likely to be followed by the wings bumping into the wall on which the key was placed. It therefore may be that the obtained pecking and snuggling CRs result from blocking of a CR that would otherwise occur, and from replacement of this CR by other responses that are in some sense relatively dominant in the repertoire of responses exhibited by young chicks.

Two other studies (Bindra & Palfai, 1967; Woodruff & Williams, 1976) involved CS-water pairings and the occurrence of CRs dissimilar to the UCR elicited by water. In the latter study, the CS of illumination of a key was paired with the UCS of water injected directly into the mandibles of pigeons. The UCR produced by this UCS was "mumbling" and swallowing. CRs that occurred included bowing in front of the illuminated key and "rooting" the surface of the key, responses not observed when the UCS was injected.

To account for these results, we may have to assume that innately formed connections exist between the permanent brain event corresponding to a UCS and the neural centers responsible for initiating behaviors not similar to the UCR. The obtained results may also be involved with bowing and rooting normally occurring before drinking water and conditioning thereby taking place.

Failure of CR to Occur Even Though UCR Takes Place. There have been instances of a CS failing to produce a CR even though the UCS it is paired with elicits a relatively strong UCR. Colavita (1965) arranged for an acidic solution to be delivered into the mouths of dogs and then evacuated by way of a fistula in the dogs' esophaguses. The procedure for delivering and then evacuating an acidic solution to the dogs elicited about as much salivation as delivering the acidic solution into the mouth and permitting it to reach the stomach. In other words, the two different procedures for presenting the acidic solution UCS resulted in UCRs of about equal strength. Nevertheless, a CS paired with the delivery of an acidic solution that was drained through the esophagus failed to produce a clear CR, even though good evidence of classical conditioning occurring was obtained when the same CS was paired with the delivery of the acidic solution that reached the stomach. Other reports (Bruner, 1965; Frey, Maisiak, & Dugue, 1976) employed a brief light as the UCS, eyelid movement as the CR and UCR, and rabbits as subjects. The light flash elicited a relatively strong eyelid closure response. However, pairings between a CS and the light flash contributed little to the classical conditioning of eyelid movement.

These above results raise the possibility that classical conditioning will not occur or will be relatively poor unless a UCS is employed that elicits a relatively strong arousal response. Unfortunately, there is little agreement on the precise meaning of arousal response. A stimulus that produces a relatively strong arousal response is often thought of as a stimulus with motivational consequences to the animal. Also, an arousal response may be thought of as closely related to the orienting and activation response that will be discussed later. An acidic solution is a negative stimulus, and when a negative stimulus remains in the body it may produce a stronger arousal response than it does when it leaves the body. Also, the negative motivational effect of a flash of light should be less than a puff of air to the eye and shock around the area of the eye; thus, a flash of light may elicit a weaker arousal response than the UCSs typically employed to establish classical conditioning of eyelid closure.

Many studies indicate or suggest that classical conditioning occurs with a UCS that elicits a relatively weak arousal response. It will be seen that classical conditioning and learning occurring through the classical conditioning process results when neutral stimuli are paired, and neutral stimuli elicit relatively weak arousal responses. In addition, in both the Bruner and Frey et al. studies, a light flash did contribute a little to eyelid movement classical conditioning. In the Bruner study a group that received the CS followed by a puff of air in half of the trials, and received the CS followed by a light flash in the other half of the trials exhibited a stronger CR than a group that received the CS followed by a puff of air in half of the trials, and received the CS followed by no particular event in the other half of the trials. Therefore, it cannot be concluded that classical conditioning fails to occur when a UCS is employed that does not elicit an arousal response.

It remains somewhat likely that UCSs that elicit relatively strong arousal responses establish better classical conditioning than UCSs that elicit relatively weak arousal responses. A stimulus that elicits a relatively strong arousal response may be viewed as a stimulus that is paid attention to to a relatively large extent. We will see in Chapter 4 that a CS paired with a UCS that is relatively strongly attended to should itself become more strongly attended to. Also, if under certain circumstances a CS paired with a UCS fails to come to produce a CR, then this failure can be viewed as a consequence of the CS not being attended to. Therefore, a CS paired with a UCS that is not relatively strongly attended to may not come to be more strongly atended to, and thereby may not come to produce a CR. This possibility agrees with the consideration that it is likely that UCSs that elicit relatively strong arousal responses establish better classical conditioning than UCSs that elicit relatively weak arousal responses.

Acquisition and Extinction

Attention will now be focused on factors affecting the most frequently studied kind of classical conditioning, the classical conditioning that results from CS-UCS pairings. In this section, measures of the CR and the effects of training (acquisition) and extinction on these measures will be discussed.

Measures of CR Strength. The strength of a learned response is a measure of responding that is thought to be indicative of learning. *CR strength* refers to a measure of the responding produced by a CS. The amplitude of the CR is a measure of CR strength, since it indicates how much responding occurs. Examples of amplitude measures are the number of drops of saliva that occur and the distance that a leg moves. The rate with which a CR occurs is also used as a measure of CR strength— for example, the rate of pecking the CS of an illuminated key. Actually, the distinction between amplitude and rate measures is not particularly clear. When a leg moves at a high rate over a period of time the amplitude of the leg movement is high.

The probability of a CR occurring is another measure of CR strength. When the amplitude of a CR is greater than an established criterion amplitude, a CR is said to occur; the probability of a CR occurring equals the proportion of a block of trials in which the CR occurred. A trial is one CS-UCS pairing or, in some cases, one presentation of a CS alone. Probability measures are often employed when a CR does not occur on some trials; otherwise, amplitude or rate measures are used.

Measures of CR strength are typically obtained in two ways: (a) responding produced by a CS before onset of the UCS is determined; (b) CR strength in the absence of the UCS is measured by inserting presentations of the CS alone between CS-UCS pairings.

Training and CR Strength. CR strength increases over trials. This result fits in with the idea that learning improves with practice. With continued training, CR strength eventually levels off, that is, reaches asymptote. Figure 2-1 illustrates the increase in the strength of a jaw movement CR in rabbits over trials. The "CS-UCS" group received pairings between the CS and the UCS of water. The control group received the same CS and UCS, but they were not presented close together in time.

Little is understood about why CR strength increases over trials. An increase in the strength of the acquired association between the CS and UCS occurring over trials may be responsible for an increase in CR strength over trials, but this is a vague notion.

One possible reason why CR strength increases as training continues is based on two ideas that will be subsequently supported: (a) better classical conditioning results in a CS that is more strongly attended to; and (b) a CS that is more strongly attended to results in better classical conditioning. At the start of training, a CS-UCS pairing should increase the extent to which the CS is attended to. This increase in attention should improve the classical conditioning that occurs when the next CS-UCS pairing is received. This improved classical conditioning should result in a further increase in attention to the CS. And this further increase in attention should lead to an additional improvement in the classical conditioning that occurs when the subsequent CS-UCS pairing is received. Thus, the increase in attention to the CS that should result

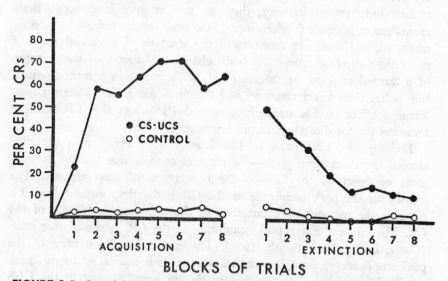

FIGURE 2-1. Acquisition and extinction of jaw movement in classical conditioning. For acquisition each block consisted of 40 trials, and for extinction each block consisted of 10 trials. (Adapted from Smith, DiLollo, and Gormezano, 1966.)

through classical conditioning is viewed as facilitating this classical conditioning, hence further increasing attention to the CS, thereby further facilitating this classical conditioning, and so on, the outcome being a gradual increase in CR strength.

Relatedness of CR Strength Measures. The amplitude, rate, and probability measures of CR strength are related, partly because they all increase over trials. That is, they are related because the same independent variable, the number of trials, influences them similarly.

The indicated measures of CR strength are not perfectly related, however, since they do not all increase at exactly the same rate as training continues. Nor do the correlations between two different measures obtained from the same animals indicate perfect relatedness. For example, Campbell and Hilgard (1936) obtained a correlation of .63 between amplitude and probability measures of eyelid movement CRs, a value that indicates good but by no means perfect relatedness between these two CR strength measures.

Given that they are considered to be measures of learning, the reader may expect that measures of CR strength should agree perfectly, because they should accurately measure the extent of classical conditioning occurring. But measures of response strength in learning situations at best only reflect learning; they do not measure it directly. Brain events are responsible for learning. These brain events cannot be directly measured, and therefore measures of the strength of a learned response can only indirectly reflect the brain changes. Measures of the strength of a learned response are measures of *performance* in a learning situation rather than direct measures of learning. Some variables exert a non-learning effect on CR strength, which also indicates that CR strength measures do not directly measure learning.

Training and CR Latency. The latency of a response is the time elapsed from a starting point—for classical conditioning usually the moment of onset of the CS—to the occurrence of this response. The latency of the peak amplitude of the CR is the time elapsed from CS onset to the moment of occurrence of the maximum amplitude of the CR. The latency of the peak amplitude of the CR increases over trials (Ost & Lauer, 1965; Smith, 1968). The result that the latency of the peak amplitude of the CR increases over trials is equivalent to this peak amplitude's moving closer in time to the moment of onset of the UCS over trials.

Another measure of the latency of the CR is the latency of the onset (beginning) of the CR. When the time duration between CS onset and

UCS onset is in the order of a couple of seconds or less, the latency of the onset of the CR decreases over trials (Ebel & Prokasy, 1963; Smith, 1968). The direction of this effect of training on latency is opposite to the effect on latency indicated above.

The latency of the peak amplitude of the CR increases over trials because (a) the CS can be thought of as a stimulus complex consisting of a beginning portion that is never immediately followed by the UCS and a later portion that immediately precedes the moment of onset of

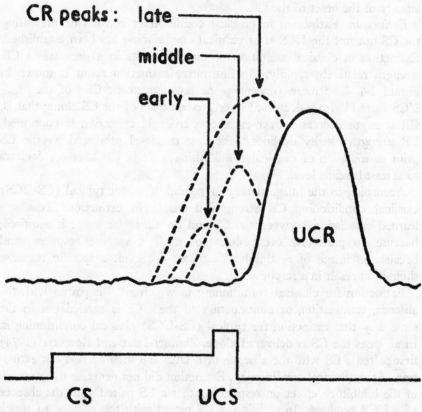

FIGURE 2-2. Shape of the CR during the early, middle, and late portions of acquisition of eyelid conditioning. The first upward excursion of the bottom line indicates CS onset, and the second UCS onset. The downward excursion indicates both CS and UCS offset. (Martin, I. and Levy, A. B., The Genesis of the Classical Conditioned Response, © 1969. Adapted by permission of Pergamon Press, Ltd.)

the UCS; and (b) as training continues, animals may learn that the beginning portion of the CS is never immediately followed by the UCS, the consequence being that the CR tends to not occur during the beginning portion of the CS.

Figure 2-2 indicates a way of understanding the result that the latency of the onset of the CR decreases over trials when the time separating CS onset from UCS onset is in the order of a couple of seconds or less. It shows that as training continues the CR "spreads out" in addition to its amplitude increasing, as found in humans by Martin and Levey (1969). The consequence of the CR spreading out is a decrease in the latency of the onset of the CR.

Extinction. Extinction in classical conditioning consists of presenting the CS but not the UCS after classical conditioning has been established. Extinction in classical conditioning usually results in a decrease in CR strength relatively rapidly. An illustrative extinction result is shown in Figure 2-1. The mean percentage of jaw movement CRs of the "CS-UCS Paired" group decreased over presentations of the CS alone; that is, CR strength decreased over extinction trials. If extinction is continued, CR strength usually declines to at least the level produced by the CS prior to initiation of classical conditioning; that is, CR strength declines to at least baseline level.

According to the image theory of conditioning, for typical (CS-UCS) classical conditioning CR strength decreases in extinction because a learned association between the CS and no particular event is acquired; because no particular event does not elicit a specific response; and because an image of a stimulus that does not elicit a specific response should not result in a response.

Extinction for classical conditioning in which a CS is paired with the absence, termination, or continuation of the UCS is carried out in the same way that extinction for typical (CS-UCS) classical conditioning is. In all cases the CS is delivered alone. Zimmer-Hart and Rescorla (1974) first paired a CS with the absence of a UCS and then carried out extinction of this classical conditioning. Extinction did not decrease the strength of the inhibitory effect on responding that a CS paired with the absence of a UCS produces. In addition, a CS paired with the absence of shock maintained performance of an instrumentally conditioned response for at least several hundred responses when this CS was presented in what was essentially an extinction procedure (Weisman & Litner, 1969). The obtained lack of an effect of extinction on classical conditioning in which a CS is paired with the absence of a UCS will be discussed later.

Time Relationships between CS and UCS

The most frequently employed time relationship between a CS and UCS is to present CS-UCS pairings in which the CS continues until at least the moment of onset of the UCS. However, before we can determine if any arrangement between a neutral stimulus and a UCS establishes classical conditioning, we have to use a *pseudoconditioning procedure.*

Pseudoconditioning Procedures. Pseudoconditioning procedures control for the possibility that the CS comes to produce an increase in CR strength because of factors not due to a relatively close temporal and predictive relationship between the CS and UCS—the kind of relationship between the CS and UCS that results in excitatory classical conditioning.

Pseudoconditioning procedures employ the same number of presentations of the CS (or, to be precise, neutral stimulus, because referring to a neutral stimulus as a CS implies that classical conditioning occurs) and UCS that other conditioning procedures employ. One pseudoconditioning procedure eliminates a relatively close temporal and predictive relationship between the CS and UCS by alternating occurrences of the CS and UCS, with relatively long time intervals separating occurrences of the CS from occurrences of the UCS. For all pseudoconditioning procedures the dependent variable of interest is the same as that for other time relationships between the CS and UCS; it is the strength of the response produced by the CS.

In the pseudoconditioning procedure described in the preceding paragraph, the CS never occurs relatively close in time to the UCS. The CS is therefore paired with the absence of the UCS. Because pairing a CS with the absence of a UCS results in classical conditioning, the above procedure is in a sense not a pseudoconditioning procedure at all, even though it is often referred to as such.

Another pseudoconditioning procedure consists of presenting the CS and UCS on a random basis. This procedure often results in the CS and UCS being separated by relatively long time intervals. However, this procedure will occasionally result in the CS preceding the UCS by a short time interval. Random presentations of the CS and UCS eliminate the problem that the strength of the CR for the control condition is underestimated because the CS is paired with the absence of the UCS.

One reason that classical conditioning cannot be concluded to occur without the use of a pseudoconditioning control is that presentation of the UCS can increase the strength of a CR-like response the CS produces, even though CS-UCS pairings have never occurred (Harris, 1941; Sheafor, 1975). In Harris's study, 8 out of 42 humans responded to the first presentation of a sound with finger movement. Ten of these subjects then received 80 consecutive presentations of shock alone. The first occurrence of the sound after these 80 shocks resulted in finger movement by all 10 subjects. Thus, unpaired shocks increased the probability of a neutral stimulus producing the same response the shocks did. Similarly, the Sheafor study found that presentations of water alone to water-deprived rabbits increased the strength of a jaw movement response to a tone. It was found that 48 presentations of water alone resulted in a relatively strong jaw movement response to a tone. These results raise the possibility that in general CS-UCS pairings elevate the strength of the CR because of the occurrence of the UCS, and not because of a relatively close temporal and predictive relationship between the CS and UCS. The pseudoconditioning procedure controls for the effect of UCSs presented alone on the response produced by a neutral stimulus, because it consists, in part, of presenting the same number of UCSs as in classical conditioning with CS-UCS pairings. The basis of the effect of unpaired presentations of a UCS on the CR-like response produced by a neutral stimulus is not clear.

Another reason for employing a pseudoconditioning control is that the CS itself may be responsible for producing a CR-like response. This possibility is certainly operative for the GSR, because it is well known that neutral stimuli will increase GSR activity, albeit to a lesser extent than does the shock UCS that is typically employed in GSR classical conditioning. A pseudoconditioning procedure controls for the response-eliciting effect of presentations of the CS alone, because the pseudoconditioning procedure consists, in part, of presentations of the CS alone.

Forward Conditioning. In *forward conditioning*, onset of the CS precedes onset of the UCS. Forward conditioning results in excitatory classical conditioning, because forward conditioning results in a stronger CS-produced specific response (for instance, salivation) than does a pseudoconditioning procedure. Actually, this outcome has been assumed all along.

Another essential aspect of classical conditioning is that CR strength increases as the onset of the CS occurs closer in time to the onset of the UCS. (A very small time delay between CS onset and UCS onset will impair classical conditioning, however; see below.) It is because of the facilitative effect of a relatively brief time delay between CS onset and UCS onset in forward conditioning that the pseudoconditioning procedure involves separating presentations of the CS and UCS with, at least on the average, relatively long time intervals.

An optimal time interval between CS onset and UCS onset exists. That is, both relatively long and quite short time intervals between CS onset and UCS onset result in weaker CRs than otherwise. The optimal time interval between CS onset and UCS onset is about 0.5 second for eyelid, nictitating membrane, and finger movement classical conditioning (Hall, 1966, pp. 196-199; Smith, Coleman, & Gormezano, 1969). The optimal time interval between CS onset and UCS onset is probably usually greater than 0.5 second for many other CRs (Boice & Denny, 1965; Gormezano, 1972). Krane and Wagner (1975) indicated that the optimal time interval between CS onset and UCS onset with a taste stimulus as the CS and shock as the UCS is surprisingly long. Factors affecting the duration of the optimal time interval between CS onset and UCS onset are not well understood.

Two types of forward conditioning are generally distinguished. Forward conditioning in which the CS terminates at the onset of the UCS or later is referred to as *delayed conditioning*. Figures 2-3A, 2-3B, and 2-3C indicate three possible arrangements of the CS and UCS in delayed conditioning. Forward conditioning in which the CS terminates prior to onset of the UCS is referred to as *trace conditioning*. The trace conditioning procedure is shown in Figure 2-3D. Trace conditioning results in a weaker CR than does delayed conditioning when the two conditioning procedures are identical in other respects, such as length of the time interval between CS onset and UCS onset and type of CS. For example, in one study (Kamin, 1965) the time interval between CS onset and UCS onset was 180.0 seconds and the duration of the CS was 179.5 seconds, leaving a gap of only 0.5 second between CS offset and UCS onset. This trace conditioning treatment nevertheless resulted in poorer conditioning than did corresponding delayed conditioning treatments.

Memory in Classical Conditioning. Classical conditioning is relatively poor if the time interval between CS onset and UCS onset is relatively long. Also, the trace conditioning procedure results in poorer conditioning than the delayed conditioning procedure. These results are probably involved with partial forgetting of the CS or a portion of the CS.

Let us first consider the superiority of delayed over trace conditioning. Suppose offset of a CS regularly preceded onset of a UCS by 1 hour. Even adult humans probably would have difficulty in acquiring an association between the CS and UCS with this time interval, because the CS should be largely forgotten by the moment the UCS occurs. But the problem of remembering a terminated CS does not exist for delayed conditioning, because by definition the CS is present at the moment the UCS occurs in delayed conditioning. It therefore appears that the inferiority of trace conditioning is due to partial forgetting of the previously terminated CS by the moment of UCS onset.

A memory problem is probably also involved in the poorer performance that results in delayed conditioning when the time interval between CS onset and UCS onset is relatively long. Components of the orienting or activation response include directing sense organs toward the position

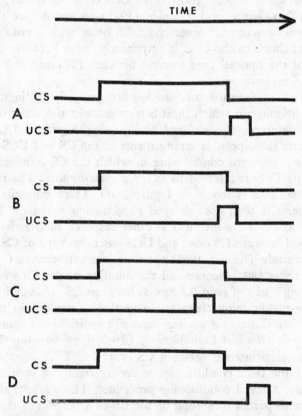

FIGURE 2-3. Possible time relations between CS and UCS in forward conditioning. The top line indicates the passage of time. For the CS and UCS lines, the upward excursion indicates stimulus onset and the downward excursion indicates stimulus offset.

of a stimulus in space, an increase in the GSR, an increase in muscle tension, and a tendency for synchronized high amplitude voltage changes recorded from the scalp or cortex to be replaced by desynchronized low amplitude voltage changes. Attention to a stimulus can be said to occur when it produces a relatively strong orienting or activation response. It is known that the onset of a neutral stimulus tends to produce a relatively strong orienting or activation response. It is also known that as a neutral stimulus continues to occur the strength of the orienting or activation response it produces decreases markedly. Suppose that in delayed conditioning CS onset precedes UCS onset by a relatively long time interval, say 1 hour. It follows from what we know about the orienting or activation response that the end portion of an hour-long CS should be attended to much less than the earliest portion of this CS. The likely result is that humans would report that they notice a neutral stimulus less after it has been on for an hour than when it first begins. As we will show subsequently, CR strength decreases with a decrease in the extent to which the CS is attended to. Therefore, if the CS is only weakly attended to at the end of 1 hour, the consequence should be poorer classical conditioning.

This argument implies that in delayed conditioning in which the time interval between CS onset and UCS onset is relatively long, the beginning portion of the CS is at least partially forgotten. The beginning portion of a CS should be relatively well attended to. If it could be remembered at the moment of UCS onset, then delayed classical conditioning should not be impaired by a relatively long time interval between CS onset and UCS onset. But, in fact, delayed conditioning in which the time interval between CS onset and UCS onset is relatively long is impaired. It therefore follows that in delayed conditioning in which the time interval between CS onset and UCS onset is relatively long, the attention-eliciting beginning portion of the CS should be at least partially forgotten by the moment of UCS onset. This memory loss is analogous to the forgetting of the CS after its termination that apparently occurs in trace conditioning.

It follows that factors known to affect forgetting should similarly affect forgetting of both the terminated CS in trace conditioning and the attention-eliciting beginning portion of the CS in delayed conditioning. Research on forgetting indicates that when subjects learn verbal material after learning relatively similar verbal material, it contributes to forgetting of the first-learned verbal material—that is, it results in retroactive inhibition. Therefore, introducing stimuli similar to a CS between CS onset and UCS onset should increase forgetting of the CS and thereby impair classical conditioning. This expectation has been confirmed (Kalat & Rozin, 1971; Revusky, 1971).

In the Kalat and Rozin study, drinking a sucrose solution by two groups of water-deprived rats was followed by injecting them with poison approximately half an hour later. One of these groups received no taste stimuli between drinking the sucrose solution and being poisoned. The second group was given access to and drank three solutions with different tastes—salt, casein hydrolysate, and coffee—in the interval between drinking the sucrose solution and being poisoned. After the rats recovered from the poisoning, a preference test which permitted access to both tap water and sucrose solution was carried out. Both groups should have acquired a classically conditioned escape and avoidance response to the sucrose solution. The group that received the three taste stimuli between the sucrose solution and the poison was more likely to drink the sucrose solution than was the group that had not received these three intervening stimuli. This result indicates that classical conditioning between the CS of the sucrose taste and the poison UCS was impaired by the intervening taste stimuli. In addition, it suggests that the intervening taste stimuli increased forgetting of the terminated sucrose-taste CS.

Another study in forgetting indicates that when sleep intervenes between learning verbal material and the test for recall of this material, forgetting of this material is reduced. Rozin and Ree (1972) supplied water-deprived rats with a solution with a distinctive taste, then anesthesized these rats, and afterward injected them with a poison. The anesthetization increased the tendency of the rats to escape from and continue to avoid the solution with a distinctive taste; that is, it facilitated classical conditioning. Anesthetization is obviously related to sleep. The obtained result therefore suggests that classical conditioning was facilitated by the anesthetization because it reduced forgetting of the terminated distinctive taste CS.

Classical Conditioning and CS Predicting UCS. Classical conditioning requires that one stimulus, S_1, predicts that a second stimulus, S_2, is relatively likely to occur in the presence of S_1 or relatively soon thereafter. It is not enough that one stimulus be followed by a second stimulus relatively soon, because the second stimulus may also occur at other times. The second stimulus must be *relatively* likely to occur in the presence of the first stimulus or fairly soon thereafter.

Two studies indicate the importance of the relative likelihood of the UCS occurring while the CS is on. In one study (Rescorla, 1968), classical conditioning of suppression in rats was investigated. The rats were first instrumentally conditioned to bar press. Then the bar in the apparatus was removed, and various arrangements of a tone and shock were given to independent groups. The durations of the tone and shock for these groups were always 2.0 minutes and 0.5 second, respectively. In addition, successive presentations of the tone were separated by a mean of 8 minutes. Also, the probability of shock occurring during presentation of the tone was .4. The groups differed in that they received unequal probabilities of shock occurring during each 2 minute interval the tone was not on. For one group the probability of shock occurring for each 2 minute interval the tone was not on was .4; for a second .2; for a third .1; and for a fourth .0. Subsequently, the bar was reintroduced into the apparatus, and instrumental conditioning of bar pressing was carried out once more. In addition, at times the tone was delivered. The result of greatest interest is that the group receiving shock with a probability of .4 in both the presence of the 2 minute tone and each 2 minute period of absence of the tone did not decrease its rate of bar pressing when the tone was delivered; that is, this group did not exhibit a suppression CR. The other groups did acquire the suppression CR; the strength of this response increased as the probability of receiving shock in each 2 minute interval of absence of the tone decreased.

In a second study (Gamzu & Williams, 1971), classical conditioning of pecking in pigeons was studied. A key was intermittently illuminated for 8.6 seconds, and food was delivered with a probability of .03 at the start of each second of key illumination in both experimental conditions. In one condition, the probability of receiving food when the key was not illuminated was zero. This condition resulted in relatively rapid pecking of the illuminated key by the pigeons. In the second condition, the probability of receiving food when the key was not illuminated was the same (.03 for each second) as when the key was illuminated. This condition resulted in very little pecking of the illuminated key.

In both studies, classical conditioning occurred when the CS predicted that the UCS was more likely to occur when the CS was on than when no particular event took place, and classical conditioning did not occur when the UCS was as likely to occur in the presence of no particular event as in the presence of the UCS. Thus, classical conditioning in which the CS produces a specific response, that is, excitatory classical conditioning, tends to be obtained when the UCS is relatively likely to occur in the presence of the CS. In trace conditioning, the CS predicts that the UCS is relatively likely to occur soon after termination of the CS. Therefore, excitatory classical conditioning tends to take place when a CS predicts that a UCS is relatively likely to occur in its presence or relatively soon thereafter. Analogously, inhibitory classical conditioning tends to take place when a CS predicts that no particular event is relatively likely to occur in the presence of the CS or relatively soon thereafter (and when the UCS occurs at other times).

The predictive nature of classical conditioning may be appreciated at an intuitive level. Suppose that a tone and the absence of the tone, that is, no particular event, alternated in time, and that the durations of the tone and no particular event were equal. In addition, suppose that in one condition a brief shock occurred at some point when the tone was on with a probability of 1.0, and shock occurred at some point when no particular event was in effect with a probability of .5. Also, suppose that in a second condition the same brief shock occurred at some point when the tone was on with a probability of .5, and shock occurred at some point when no particular event was in effect with a probability of 1.0. In the first condition, the tone should serve as a "signal" that shock is more likely to occur than otherwise, and therefore the tone should be expected to produce a negative emotional response. In the second condition, the tone should serve as a signal that shock is less likely to occur than otherwise, and therefore the tone should be expected to produce a positive emotional response. Thus, the nature of an established emotional response should be determined by the relative probabilities of a UCS occurring in the presence of a CS, and the UCS occurring in the presence of no particular event—that is, by the likelihood of a UCS occurring in the presence of a CS in relation to the likelihood of a UCS occurring at other times.

The predictive nature of classical conditioning indicates that the CS and UCS is in some sense compared to no particular event and the UCS. Such a comparison seems to require that classical conditioning involves representations of the CS, UCS, and no particular event within the brain, which is consistent with the image theory of conditioning.

The predictive nature of classical conditioning embarrasses Hull's stimulus-response theory. This theory predicts that classical conditioning will occur when a CS is followed by a UCS with a not very low probability, because the CS would then be followed by the response elicited by the UCS and drive reduction, the conditions necessary for formation of a stimulus-response connection. However, classical conditioning will not occur when a UCS is delivered in the presence of a CS with a not very low probability, if the UCS is equally likely to be delivered in the presence of no particular event.

Backward Conditioning. The backward conditioning procedure is one in which UCS onset precedes CS onset. Four possible arrangements of the CS and UCS in backward conditioning are indicated in Figure 2-4.

When CS onset occurs after UCS offset (Figure 2-4A) or simultaneously with UCS offset (Figure 2-4B), the CS has usually failed to produce specific CRs; that is, the procedures outlined in Figures 2-4A and 2-4B have generally not resulted in excitatory classical conditioning (Smith, Coleman, & Gormezano, 1969; Spooner & Kellogg, 1947).

The procedures outlined in Figures 2-4A, 2-4B, and 2-4C all indicate that the CS predicts that no particular event will occur while and/or soon after the CS occurs. A CS paired with the absence of a UCS also predicts that no particular event will occur while and soon after the CS

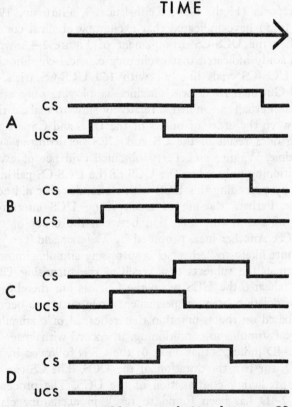

FIGURE 2-4. Possible time relations between CS and UCS in backward conditioning. The top line indicates the passage of time. For the CS and UCS lines, the upward excursion indicates stimulus onset and the downward excursion indicates stimulus offset.

occurs, and, in addition, results in inhibitory classical conditioning. Also, Siegel and Domjan (1971, 1974) used the procedure outlined in Figure 2-4B and obtained inhibitory classical conditioning. In Figure 2-4C a CS is paired with the termination of a UCS. Moscovitch and LoLordo (1968) found this procedure to result in inhibitory classical conditioning. It therefore appears that the backward conditioning procedures outlined in Figures 2-4A, 2-4B, and 2-4C all typically result in inhibitory classical conditioning, because inhibitory classical conditioning has been found using the procedures outlined in Figures 2-4B and 2-4C, and because for all three of these procedures the CS predicts that no particular event will occur while and/or soon after the CS occurs.

Three reports (Heth, 1976; Keith-Lucas & Guttman, 1975; Wagner & Terry, 1975) have indicated that excitatory classical conditioning occurred when the UCS-CS arrangement of Figure 2-4A was employed. The Heth study indicated that excitatory classical conditioning occurred with ten UCS-CS trials but not with 160 UCS-CS trials. The Keith-Lucas and Guttman result was obtained employing only a single conditioning trial. Perhaps an animal is relatively slow to make a time discrimination between the order of onsets of the UCS and CS; after all, a UCS-CS pairing does result in the CS and UCS occurring at approximately the same time. Wagner and Terry obtained evidence of excitatory classical conditioning only when the UCS of the UCS-CS pairings was made surprising by preceding this UCS with a stimulus that did not predict its occurrence. Perhaps the use of a surprising UCS interfered with the formation of a time discrimination between the order of onsets of the UCS and CS. Another idea, proposed by Wagner and Terry, is that animals are more likely to "rehearse" a surprising stimulus immediately after its occurrence; the subjects that received the surprising UCS therefore tended to rehearse the UCS when the CS was on; thereby permitting a CS-UCS association between permanent brain events to occur. This possibility is based on the assumption that rehearsal of a stimulus can function as a real stimulus in conditioning, in accord with image theory.

Figure 2-4D indicates that onset of the CS is followed by continuation of the UCS for half the duration of the UCS. The CS can therefore be viewed as predicting continuation of the UCS. The procedure outlined in Figure 2-4D has been found to result in excitatory classical conditioning (Heth, 1976; Heth & Rescorla, 1973). This result is in accord with the conclusion that excitatory classical conditioning tends to take place when the CS predicts that the UCS is relatively likely to occur while the CS is on or soon after the CS terminates. The Heth and Rescorla result also supports the assumption that a CS paired with the continuation of a UCS results in excitatory classical conditioning, because the procedure outlined in Figure 2-4D and the procedure for pairing a CS with the continuation of a UCS are obviously somewhat similar.

CS Effects

Type of CS. In laboratory investigations of classical conditioning, onset of a relatively specific stimulus, such as occurrence of a light or occurrence of a tone, is most frequently employed as a CS. Offset of a stimulus can also be a CS (Kamin, 1965; Logan & Wagner, 1962). This indicates that it makes sense to talk of a stimulus as being no particular event, as we have done.

A CS does not have to be a relatively specific stimulus. For example, at least some of the stimuli comprising an injection procedure have functioned as a CS in the classical conditioning of a decrease in blood glucose level, using insulin as a UCS. The stimuli of the general learning situation —the walls of the apparatus, the food receptacle, and so on—can be CSs. For example, an animal that is shocked in a compartment will escape from it even though shock no longer occurs, and thus some of the stimuli of the compartment constitute a CS that is escaped from and avoided.

CS and Topography of CR. In classical conditioning of pecking, illumination of a key is paired with food, and pecking the illuminated key is the CR that results. The CR of a peck of the key is similar to the peck that is made by pigeons to actual food. Illumination of a key is similar to a piece of food in that both stimuli are visual, small, and normally stationary. Also, raccoons handled and rubbed, pigs rooted, and porpoises and whales swallowed objects that could be exchanged for food. These apparent CRs closely resemble the responses made to real food, much as the peck CR closely resembles the peck to real food. In general, therefore, when the CS is relatively similar to the UCS, particularly strong CRs will occur; in addition, they will be directed at the CS.

Perhaps CRs so strong that they would be suggestive of hallucinations of the UCS could be obtained in the laboratory if CSs were employed that were highly similar to the UCSs that were used. For example, swallowing the CS by rats might be observed in the laboratory if CS-food pairings were employed in which the CS is an object resembling the shape of a food pellet. Perhaps copulatory responses to the CS might be observed in male pigeons given pairings between a CS and access to female pigeons in which the CS is made of cardboard and shaped and painted to resemble a real female pigeon. The CS-produced image of the UCS in these suggested studies would perhaps combine with the effects of perceiving the CS to alter the perception of the CS in the direction of its appearing more like the real UCS, much as stimulus-produced images of stimuli may combine with the effects of stimuli currently impinging on receptors to alter the perception of stimuli that are currently present (King, 1974).

It is clear that the topography of the CR can be affected by the nature of the stimuli of the general learning situation. For example, a CS previously paired with shock will probably result in the CR of escape, if escape from the stimuli of the general learning situation is possible, and will probably result in suppression of activity (crouching) if this escape is not possible. Also, a CS previously paired with shock is probably much more likely to produce aggressive behavior if the stimuli of the general learning situation include a suitable target stimulus for aggressive responding.

CS and Difference from Background Stimuli. More intense CSs generally result in stronger CRs. For example, Barnes (1956) found that a 80 decibel tone CS produced a stronger leg movement CR than did a 60 decibel tone CS.

Background stimuli are the stimuli of the general learning situation. Intense CSs differ from background stimuli more than weak CSs do. A relatively large reduction in the intensity of a stimulus is also a relatively large change from background stimuli. Kamin (1965) found that larger reductions in the intensity of a background stimulus resulted in stronger CRs. Part of the background stimuli was an ongoing 80 decibel tone. The CSs for independent groups of rats were different extents of reduction in the intensity of the tone, with the intensities of the tone used as CSs ranging from 0 to 70 decibels. It was found that the lower intensity tones produced the stronger conditioned suppression CRs. It therefore appears that the general finding that more intense CSs result in stronger CRs is at least partly due to more intense CSs differing from background stimuli to a greater extent than less intense CSs. The effect of the difference between the CS and background stimuli on CR strength probably involves discrimination learning (Chapter 4).

UCS Effects

Neutral Stimulus as S_2 and CR. S_1-S_2 pairings refer to pairings between two neutral stimuli, S_1 and S_2, in which S_1 onset precedes S_2 onset. Classical conditioning in which S_2 produces a response will be considered.

In one study (Fink, 1954), S_2 was a tone. Subjects were instructed to press a key when the tone occurred. Each delivery of the tone was preceded by a sound, S_1; in addition, the tone followed this sound independently of the subjects' responding. The pretone sound came to produce an increase in tension in a muscle responsible for the key press response that subjects made when the tone occurred, as indicated by amplification of the voltage recorded from this muscle. The pretone sound, S_1, therefore came to produce a CR.

In two studies, stimuli producing passive movement of an arm were employed as S_2s. S_1 came to produce a response similar to the one elicited by passive movement of the arm—increased tension from a muscle involved in the passive arm movement (Doehring, 1957) and desynchronized low amplitude voltage activity recorded from the brain (Sokolov, 1963, pp. 154-158).

As discussed previously, S_1-S_2 pairings should result in an acquired association between S_1 and S_2, and therefore S_1 should produce an image of S_2. Also, if S_2 produces a response, then an image of S_2 should result in a similar response. It is therefore expected that S_1-S_2 pairings in which S_2 produces a response should result in S_1's producing a similar response, as the results described above indicate.

Amount and Intensity of UCS and CR and UCR. Larger amounts of positive UCSs, for example, 5 pellets of food rather than 1 pellet, and more intense negative UCSs, such as more milliamperes of shock, result in stronger CRs.

More intense UCSs elicit stronger GSR and eyelid movement UCRs, as well as establish stronger GSR and eyelid movement CRs (Öhman, Björkstrand, & Ellström, 1973; Sheafor & Gormezano, 1972). Also, it seems clear that a larger amount of food will elicit a stronger salivation UCR. Therefore, both larger amounts of positive UCSs and more intense negative UCSs probably result in stronger UCRs as well as stronger CRs.

Because variation in the amount and intensity of the UCS appears to result in a positive relation between CR strength and UCR strength, it seems that the effect of amount and intensity of a UCS on CR strength is a special case of the generalization that CRs usually resemble UCRs. In other words, CRs resemble UCRs quantitatively as well as qualitatively.

Because CR strength and UCR strength appear to be quantitatively related, factors other than amount and intensity of the UCS that affect UCR strength should similarly affect CR strength. This expectation is supported. Repeated presentations of a puff of air to the eye decreased both the amplitude of the eyelid movement UCR and the number of eyelid movement CRs that occurred (Taylor, 1956). In other words, manipulation of UCR strength via repeated exposure to a UCS resulted in a change in CR strength in the same direction. In addition, Holland and Rescorla (1975) found that pairing food with rotation decreased food consumption, and also decreased the strength of an activity CR subsequently established with CS-food pairings.

Image theory accounts for the effect of amount and intensity of reinforcement on CR strength. We probably salivate more when we imagine a large piece of food than when we imagine a small piece of food, and a real large piece of food should produce more salivation than a real small piece of food. Similarly, we probably exhibit a stronger GSR when we imagine an intense shock than when we imagine a weak one, and a real intense shock will produce a stronger GSR than a real weak shock. In addition, Rowland (1936) had judges scale written descriptions of situations in respect to how exciting they were. When subjects imagined these situations, those situations judged as more exciting led to stronger GSRs. Real highly exciting situations should also result in relatively strong GSRs. The effect of amount and intensity of reinforcement on CR strength is explained: the CS is assumed to produce an image of the UCS, and imagining different amounts or intensities of food or shock result in responses that are quantitatively related to the responses produced by real differences in amount of food or shock.

In addition, image theory explains the conclusion that, in general, CRs resemble UCRs quantitatively as well as qualitatively. If the strength of image-produced responses is positively related to the strength of stimulus-produced responses, and if the CR is the outcome of a CS-produced image of the UCS, it follows that CR strength should be positively related to the strength of the UCS-produced response, that is, to UCR strength.

Furthermore, the finding that the strength of image-produced responses is positively related to the strength of stimulus-produced responses is also in accord with image theory. The effects of a real stimulus and an image of this stimulus are assumed to be due to qualitatively identical temporary brain events. If a stimulus produces a relatively strong response, then the temporary brain event corresponding to this stimulus should cause a relatively strong response to occur, regardless of whether the source of this temporary brain event is the real stimulus or the permanent brain event corresponding to the real stimulus.

Type of Response Elicited by UCS. Overt eyelid, nictitating membrane, and finger withdrawal CRs are relatively difficult to classically condition. When the interval between CS onset and UCS onset is 5 seconds or more, these CRs almost never occur (Hall, 1966, pp. 196-199). On the other hand, classical conditioning of salivation, GSR, and heart rate readily occurs with intervals between CS onset and UCS onset of more than 10 seconds.

Image theory accounts for the above results. Requests to imagine a puff of air to the eye and shock to the finger probably do not usually result in performance of overt blink and overt finger movement responses. On the other hand, the instrumentation typically employed in classical conditioning of salivation, GSR, and heart rate will yield evidence of changes in these responses following requests to imagine the UCSs employed for these kinds of conditioning (Barber, Chauncey, & Winer, 1964; Barber & Hahn, 1964; Craig, 1969). Because the CR is assumed to result from a CS-produced image of the UCS, it follows that responses unlikely to occur when UCSs are requested to be imagined should be relatively difficult to classically condition and that responses relativley likely to occur when UCSs are requested to be imagined should be relatively easy to classically condition, which is the obtained result.

Relationship between Type of CS and Type of UCS. The type of CS and type of UCS employed may interact to affect CR strength.

At least for rats, a taste CS and an illness-producing UCS frequently appear to result in particularly strong learning. For example, escape from and avoidance of taste CSs can be established using poison and X-ray illness-eliciting UCSs, even though an unusually long interval of time elapses between the occurrence of the CS and UCS onset (Revusky, 1968; Rozin & Ree, 1972). In Revusky's study, food-deprived rats were given a sucrose solution to drink. Depriving the rats of food assured that the rats would be exposed to the taste of the sucrose solution. The rats were irradiated 6.5 hours after drinking the sucrose solution. After recovery from the irradiation, the rats were given a choice between drinking a sucrose solution and drinking milk. A sham-irradiated control group was given the same preference test. The irradiated group was less likely to drink the sucrose solution than the control group. A 6.5 hours time interval between the occurrence of the CS and UCS onset is particularly long. Most demonstrations of classical conditioning employ intervals of no more than a couple of minutes between the occurrence of the CS and UCS onset.

It is also known that employing a taste stimulus and an illness-eliciting reinforcer results in better learning than employing a taste stimulus and a shock reinforcer, and that employing an auditory or audiovisual stimulus and a shock reinforcer results in better learning than employing an auditory or audiovisual stimulus and an illness-eliciting reinforcer (Domjan & Wilson, 1972; Garcia & Koelling, 1966). In the Domjan and Wilson study, one group of rats received pairings between two simultaneously presented stimuli and a poison. These stimuli were the taste of a saccharin solution, brought about by injecting the solution into the mouth, and a buzzer. Immediately after these stimuli were delivered, the rats were poisoned. Another group received pairings between the same two simultaneously presented stimuli and shock. In respect to the CR to the taste of saccharin, the group receiving the poison was much less likely to drink the saccharin solution than tap water, but the group receiving the shock was not less likely to drink the saccharin solution than tap water. For testing the response to the buzzer, two tubes of tap water were provided, and the buzzer sounded when one but not the other of these two tubes was drunk from. The group receiving poison exhibited no preference between the two tubes, but the group receiving shock hardly drank from the tube resulting in the buzzer sounding.

These findings cannot be explained by assuming that taste stimuli generally tend to result in particularly strong classical conditioning, because the taste CS led to little if any classical conditioning when it was paired with shock. But the saccharin taste CS and illness-eliciting UCS resulted in good classical conditioning, as did the buzzer CS and shock UCS. The relationship between type of CS and type of UCS therefore greatly affected classical conditioning.

An explanation based on biological specialization may best apply to the results involving type of CS and type of UCS. From a survival viewpoint it is advantageous for rats to be particularly able to associate taste stimuli with poisons; rats have poor vision, for one thing, and for another wild rats will be exposed to pairings between taste stimuli and poisons. Because taste stimuli are probably not particularly likely to be followed by pain-eliciting stimuli in the wild, rats (and presumably most other animals) should not be biologically prepared to acquire associations between taste CSs and pain-eliciting stimuli. In addition, consider that quail condition better with a visual CS and an illness-eliciting UCS than with a taste CS and an illness-eliciting UCS (Wilcoxon, Dragoin, & Kral, 1971). Birds generally have superior vision. A specialized ability to associate visual and illness-eliciting stimuli may therefore have developed in birds through survival pressures.

Another possibility is that biological specialization has led to the development of a process not closely akin to classical (or instrumental) conditioning. This possibility is supported by the result (Revusky & Bedarf, 1967) that a novel taste stimulus was escaped from and avoided more than a familiar taste stimulus when both the novel and familiar taste stimuli preceded the delivery of Xrays by the same interval of time. In addition, Mitchell, Kirschbaum, and Perry (1975) found that a relatively novel food receptacle was escaped from and avoided even though a familiar food receptacle immediately preceded poisoning. Perhaps escape and avoidance of a taste CS can only be brought about with a very long interval between CS onset and onset of an illness-eliciting UCS when the taste stimulus is relatively novel.

Another possibility is that established principles of learning and forgetting can at least partially account for the results involving type of CS and type of UCS. For example, it may be difficult to obtain classical conditioning in rats between a taste CS and a shock UCS because in the lives of laboratory rats taste stimuli are probably either paired with the absence of pain-eliciting stimuli or randomly paired with pain-eliciting stimuli. Either type of pairing might retard excitatory classical conditioning between a taste stimulus and a shock UCS. A traditional forgetting account of escape and avoidance of a taste CS established with a very long time interval between CS onset and UCS onset may also be appropriate. In such classical conditioning, other taste stimuli ordinarily do not occur between CS onset and UCS onset. Therefore, retroactive inhibition may be minimal, possibly thereby permitting classical conditioning with a very long interval between CS onset and UCS onset to occur. Introduction of other taste stimuli between the occurrence of a taste CS and delivery of the UCS would then be expected to reduce the strength of the escape and avoidance CR to the taste CS, which was the result obtained by Kalat & Rozin (1971) and Revusky (1971).

Learning and Nonlearning Effects on Performance

Three criteria must usually be satisfied for a change in response to a stimulus to be considered an instance of learning. (a) An animal must have been previously exposed to the stimulus producing the altered response or to a similar stimulus. (b) The change in response to the stimulus must be relatively permanent. (c) The factor establishing the change in response to the stimulus must not ordinarily be due to the same factor that affects responses to a relatively wide variety of stimuli.

Nonlearning factors as well as learning factors affect the strength of a learned response. The strength of a learned response is often referred to as a measure of the performance of a learned response. Thus, both learning and nonlearning factors affect performance of a learned response.

Deprivation of food and water are the most frequently studied factors to exert a nonlearning effect on performance of a CR or an instrumentally conditioned response. Deprivation of food and water leads to what we refer to as hunger motivation or thirst motivation, so sometimes the effects of deprivation of food and water on performance are referred to as motivational effects on performance. The effect of food and water deprivation on CR strength, that is, on performance of the CR, will be discussed next, and we will also see that at least most of the main influences on CR strength that have been mentioned thus far exert their effect through learning.

Nonlearning Effect of Deprivation. An increase in deprivation of food or water increases CR strength. For example, in one study rabbits were permitted 30, 90, or 180 ccs. of water per day or had continuous access to water on the days they were classically conditioned. An increase in deprivation of water resulted in stronger jaw movement CRs (Mitchell & Gormezano, 1970).

The effect of deprivation level on CR strength is a nonlearning one. CR strength can be increased or decreased by simply raising or lowering the level of deprivation. Thus, a change in deprivation level can bring about a change in response to a CS without an animal's being exposed to the CS. In addition, the effect of a change in deprivation level on CR strength is not relatively permanent. For example, satiating an animal only temporarily reduces CR strength; when the previous level of deprivation is reinstated, CR strength also returns to about its previous level. Also, a change in deprivation level affects the responses to a relatively wide variety of stimuli. For example, a change in deprivation level will affect the strength of most learned responses established with food.

Deprivation and Image Theory. Although deprivation of food and water exerts a nonlearning effect on CR strength, this effect can be explained by image theory.

Recall that an increase in the amount or intensity of the UCS usually increases both CR strength and UCR strength. Analogous results are obtained with an increase in deprivation level. The strength of both mouth licking and jaw movement CRs and UCRs increased with an increase in deprivation of water (DeBold, Miller, & Jensen, 1965; Mitchell & Gormezano, 1970). In addition, Finch (1938) found that an increase in deprivation of food increased the strength of both a salivation CR and UCR. Because variation in deprivation level apparently results in a positive relation between CR strength and UCR strength, the effect of deprivation level on CR strength is probably an instance of the conclusion that CRs resemble UCRs quantitatively as well as qualitatively.

Everyday experience suggests that humans salivate more when they imagine food as the extent to which they are deprived of food increases. In addition, depriving humans of food increased their salivation when words referring to food were read (Staats & Hammond, 1972). Reading words that refer to food is probably involved with thinking about food, and thinking about a stimulus involves the occurrence of an image of this stimulus. This result suggests, therefore, that depriving humans of food increases the strength of the salivation response produced by an image of food. Because an image of food probably produces a stronger salivation responses as the food deprivation increases, and because the CR is assumed to result from a CS-produced image of the UCS, it follows that the strength of a salivation CR should increase as deprivation of food increases, which it does.

It also seems clear that humans salivate more to real food as the extent to which they are deprived of food increases. This result and the likely result that imagining food produces a stronger salivation response as deprivation of food increases support the conclusion that the strength of image-produced responses is, in general, positively related to the strength of stimulus-produced responses. And as reasoned previously, this conclusion leads to the conclusion that CRs resemble UCRs quantitatively as well as qualitatively.

Learning Effect of Other Factors. The effects of training, extinction, and different time relationships between the CS and UCS are definitely due to learning. The change in response to the CS brought about by these factors is obviously produced by a stimulus, the CS, to which an animal was previously exposed. In addition, these factors result in a relatively permanent change in the CR. For example, Figure 2-1 indicates that a progressive increase in CR strength occurred over days of training. The effect of training on CR strength was therefore relatively permanent. Also, these factors do not affect the response to a relatively wide variety of stimuli. For example, CS-food pairings will at best only marginally facilitate classical conditioning between a CS in a different modality and food.

The idea that amount and intensity of the UCS temporarily affect CR strength through a nonlearning process has some appeal. It might be thought, for example, that an intense shock would temporarily "excite" or "sensitize" an animal to respond more to the next presentation of the CS. Nevertheless, amount and intensity of the UCS permanently affect CR strength. Differences in CR strength brought about by using different amounts or intensities of a UCS are maintained from one day of testing to the next (Sheafor & Gormezano, 1972), thereby indicating that the effect on different amounts and intensities of a UCS on CR strength is relatively permanent. In addition, Spence, Haggard, and Ross (1958) controlled for differences in the intensity of the UCS that immediately preceded a subsequent CS-UCS pairing and found that the pairing with the more intense UCS resulted in the stronger CR. One group of humans received pairings between a CS and a weak UCS and also received unpaired presentations of an intense UCS. A second group received pairings between the same CS and the intense UCS and also received unpaired presentations of the weak UCS. The CR for the group receiving pairings between the CS and the intense UCS was stronger.

The idea that the extent of the difference between a CS and background stimuli temporarily affects CR strength also has some appeal. It might be thought that a CS that is quite dissimilar to background stimuli would temporarily "excite" or "sensitize" an animal to exhibit a stronger CR. It cannot be directly determined that the extent of the difference between a CS and background stimuli affects CR strength relatively permanently. The CS precedes the CR and therefore may affect CR strength temporarily no matter how long ago the last CS-UCS pairing occurred. To determine if the extent of the difference between a CS and background stimuli permanently affects CR strength, complicated experimental designs have been employed. Let us say that the CSs employed are sounds of different intensity but otherwise identical. Each group receives a CS of one particular intensity in acquisition. The experimenter then attempts to equate CS intensity in extinction. One way to do this is to proceed with extinction using a CS intermediate in intensity to the CSs employed in acquisition. The logic of these designs is that if a performance difference occurs in extinction, then it must be due to differences in CS intensity that existed during acquisition, because in extinction CS intensity is equated. A performance difference due to a difference in CS intensity in acquisition would indicate a permanent effect of CS intensity.

Studies employing this type of design have often suggested that the extent of the difference between the CS and background stimuli exerts a temporary effect on CR strength (Grant & Schneider, 1949; Kamin & Schaub, 1963). One study (Nowlis, 1974), however, does indicate that the extent of the difference between a CS and background stimuli permanently affects CR strength. Another consideration indicates that the extent of the difference between a CS and background stimuli permanently affects CR strength (Chapter 4).

Pairings between Neutral Stimuli

Image theory assumes that when one neutral stimulus, S_1, is followed by a second neutral stimulus, S_2, independently of responding, that is, when S_1-S_2 pairings occur, an acquired association between S_1 and S_2 takes place through the classical conditioning process. Extinction and everyday analogues of classical conditioning involve acquiring an association between paired neutral stimuli. Pairings between a CS and the absence of a UCS and between a CS and the termination of a UCS also involve acquiring an association between paired neutral stimuli. These associations involve pairings between a CS and no particular event, except for the association occurring in everyday analogues of classical conditioning, which involves pairings between a CS and one of numerous other stimuli.

One finding, previously discussed, shows directly that pairing neutral stimuli results in classical conditioning. It is that S_1 produces a CR when S_2 elicits a response; for example, S_1 produces a covert key press response when S_2 elicits an overt key press response (Fink, 1954). Other evidence that pairing neutral stimuli results in their being associated through classical conditioning will be indicated.

Sensory Preconditioning. Table 2-1 outlines a three-stage procedure for demonstrating the sensory preconditioning result. In the first stage,

TABLE 2-1

Sensory Preconditioning

Stage	Sensory preconditioning	Control
1	S_1 followed by S_2	S_1 and S_2 but not paired
2	S_2 followed by UCS	S_2 followed by UCS
3	S_1	S_1

S_1-S_2 (light-tone) pairings are presented to the sensory preconditioning group. A control group is also run. It receives unpaired or random presentations of S_1 and S_2 in stage 1. In stage 2, both the sensory preconditioning and control groups receive S_2-UCS (tone-shock) pairings. In stage 3, both groups receive S_1 (the light of stage 1) presented alone.

Sensory preconditioning is defined as occurring if, in stage 3, S_1 produces a stronger CR in the sensory preconditioning group than in the control group. Starting with Brogden (1939), many investigators have obtained evidence of sensory preconditioning.

Because the stage 2 and stage 3 procedures for demonstrating sensory preconditioning are the same for the sensory preconditioning and control groups, the S_1-S_2 (sensory) pairings the former group receives in stage 1 (the pre-stage) must be responsible for sensory preconditioning occurring. The sensory preconditioning finding therefore indicates that S_1-S_2 pairings, that is, pairings between neutral stimuli, result in learning. This learning can be said to occur through the classical conditioning process, because S_1 follows S_2 independently of responding, and because S_1 affects the strength of a CR.

Image theory accounts for sensory preconditioning. The S_1-S_2 pairings in stage 1 should make S_1 result in an image of S_2 in stage 3. In addition, the real S_2 should result in an image of the UCS, due to the S_2-UCS pairings in stage 2. Because an image of S_2 and the effects of the real S_2 should be due to qualitatively identical temporary brain events, in stage 3, S_1 should result in an image of S_2 and this image should result in an image of the UCS, the latter image being responsible for S_1's producing a CR in stage 3.

In sensory preconditioning an acquired association involving S_1 and S_2 occurs even though S_2 does not produce an obvious response and does not result in drive reduction. The sensory preconditioning result is therefore at variance with Hull's stimulus-response theory.

S_1-S_2 Pairings and Vivid Image of S_2. Recall that a CS appears to sometimes produce very vivid images of the UCS with which it was paired. An analogous outcome apparently sometimes occurs for pairings between neutral stimuli.

In one study (Ellson, 1941), for each trial a light was followed by a tone that gradually increased in intensity. The intensity of the beginning portion of the tone was low enough so that it could not be detected. Subjects were instructed to press a key when they thought they heard the tone. On trials 20, 40, and 60, the tone followed the light with a delay of 15 seconds. On these trials subjects frequently indicated by pressing the key that they heard the tone before it was actually presented. Perhaps this result occurred because the light produced an image of the tone, and because differentiating between an image of a low-intensity tone and a genuine low-intensity tone is relatively difficult.

In another study (Leuba, 1940), subjects were given hypnotic induction instructions. When subjects appeared to be in a deep trance, S_1-S_2

pairings were presented. The hypnotist suggested posthypnotic amnesia for these pairings, after which the subjects were told to return to the waking state. Their responses in the waking state to the S_1s used while they were hypnotized and to other, control stimuli were observed. As an example of the findings, one subject was rubbed on the arm (S_1) and then given the odor of creosote (S_2) while hypnotized. After he was told to return to the waking state, he was rubbed on various parts of the body. He did not respond in any specific way until being rubbed on the arm, at which point "he sniffed the air and said that something smelled funny and that an odor had just entered the room" (p. 348). The subject's report does suggest that he vividly imagined the second of two paired neutral stimuli when the first of these stimuli was presented.

Verbal Effect on CR Strength. CR strength can be affected by verbal instructions (Grings, Schell, & Carey, 1973; Wilson, 1968). The verbal instructions in these studies involved descriptions of pairings between a neutral stimulus and the neutral stimulus of no particular event.

In the Wilson study, on some trials a blue light was presented. It was followed by shock on the average of 50 percent of the occasions it was presented, and it was followed by no particular event on the remaining occasions. In addition, on other trials a yellow light was presented. It was followed by no particular event each time it was presented. The blue light came to produce a relatively strong GSR CR, and the yellow light did not.

Subsequent to the acquisition of the GSR CR to the blue light, subjects were told that "By now you will have noticed that the shock occurs only after a blue light. From now on, the procedure is reversed; the shock will occur only after the yellow light" (p. 492). In actuality, after these instructions were given extinction was in effect; that is, shock was no longer presented after either light. Subjects probably did not "realize" this immediately, because in training the shock followed the blue light only 50 percent of the time. Over the first few extinction trials, the strengths of the GSR produced by the blue and yellow lights were reversed, the yellow light producing a stronger GSR than the blue one. The fact that verbal instructions increased the strength of the response produced by one stimulus and decreased the strength of the response produced by a second stimulus rules out the possibility that the verbal instructions simply changed the general responsivity of subjects.

The obtained effect of the verbal instructions on the strength of the GSR may have been mediated by images of shock and absence of shock. The instruction that shock would follow the yellow light may have resulted in the yellow light producing an image of shock and therefore a stronger GSR; the instruction that no shock would follow the blue light may have led to the blue light producing an image of the absence of shock and therefore a weaker GSR. That a verbally produced change in the image that a CS produces affects CR strength supports the theory that the CR results from the CS-produced image of the UCS.

Repeated S_1-S_2 Pairings and the GSR. A novel neutral stimulus that differs sufficiently from background stimuli produces a moderately strong GSR, and with repeated presentations of this stimulus the strength of the GSR decreases. Badia and Defran (1970) presented a number of tone-light pairings to humans. With repeated presentations of these S_1-S_2 pairings, the strength of the GSR decreased, as expected. Then the tone was presented alone. It resulted in an increase in the strength of the GSR. Sokolov (1963, pp. 150-152) obtained a similar result.

The tone that was presented alone had previously been repeatedly presented as a component of the tone-light pairings. Because the tone presented alone increased the strength of the GSR, it functioned as a novel stimulus. But if the tone presented alone functioned as a novel stimulus, an association involving the tone and light must have been acquired when the tone was paired with the light. The process for classical conditioning was presumably responsible for acquisition of the association between the tone and light.

Configural Conditioning. Configural conditioning involves the simultaneous presentation of two neutral stimuli prior to delivery of a UCS. Configural conditioning is said to occur when the two simultaneously presented neutral stimuli produce a progressively stronger CR relative to the CR strengths produced by each individual neutral stimulus as training continues. The two simultaneously presented neutral stimuli are referred to as a *compound,* and each of these stimuli presented individually is called an *element.* Configural conditioning appears to involve an acquired association between the elements of the compound stimulus. How else could the compound stimulus come to produce a progressively stronger CR relative to the strength of the CRs produced by either element? Presumably the acquired association between the elements of the compound stimulus occurs through the classical conditioning process.

Booth and Hammond (1971) and Wickens, Nield, Tuber, and Wickens (1970) obtained evidence of configural conditioning. In the first study, classical conditioning of suppression with rats was established by presenting a light and tone simultaneously and following this compound stimulus with shock. Three independent groups received 4, 12, or 20 pairings between the compound stimulus and shock. The strength of the suppression CR increased for the compound stimulus, leveled off for the light element, and increased slightly and then decreased for the tone element as the number of pairings between the compound stimulus and shock that a group received increased.

Humans tend to group stimuli they perceive; they tend to perceive wholes rather than component parts. The configural conditioning result appears to be of particular interest, because the increasing effectiveness of the compound stimulus relative to its elements as training continues is similar to the tendency to perceive wholes rather than their component parts.

Systematic Desensitization Therapy

Systematic desensitization therapy is a type of psychotherapy based on classical conditioning that has been used, most notably by J. Wolpe, to treat psychological disorders, particularly phobias.

Description and Theory. Phobic disorders are characterized by an excessive irrational fear of or anxiety about at least one type of stimulus. Theoretically, systematic desensitization therapy is used to treat phobic disorders by establishing classical conditioning in which the fear-producing stimulus is a CS that comes to produce a response different from fear. The procedure is similar to pairing the fear-producing stimulus with a stimulus that produces relaxation.

Systematic desensitization therapy is usually carried out in three stages. In the first stage the client is trained to relax, that is, to reduce muscle tension on cue. During this training, the therapist directs the client to become more aware of muscle tone.

In the second stage the therapist sets up an anxiety hierarchy. A particular stimulus evokes a very great amount of fear in a phobic person, and as the similarity of other stimuli to this stimulus decreases so does the fear they produce. In one anxiety hierarchy (Freeman & Kendrick, 1960), for example, the stimulus that produced the greatest fear was "sight of a cat." A stimulus that produced an intermediate amount of fear was "the thought of going out by herself at night in case she should meet a cat in the dark." A stimulus that produced relatively low fear was "cat-like fur." Anxiety hierarchies are established from the case history, from responses to self-report questionnaires, and from the conversations between therapist and client.

In the third stage of therapy, the client imagines the stimuli of the anxiety hierarchy, starting with the least anxiety-producing stimulus. As the client imagines the stimuli of the anxiety hierarchy, he or she attempts to remain relaxed with the help of the relaxation training procedures received in the first stage of therapy. When the client is able to imagine an entry in the hierarchy with little or no anxiety, the stimulus that is next higher on the list is imagined, always with as strong a relaxation response as possible. In many instances the client is eventually able to imagine the most anxiety-producing member of the anxiety hierarchy while remaining relaxed. After this point is reached, it is often reported that clients have little or no fear of the real stimuli to which they had previously been phobic. Sometimes, instead of the client's imagining the stimuli comprising the anxiety hierarchy, real stimuli corresponding to members of the anxiety hierarchy are employed.

The rationale for systematic desensitization therapy rests mainly on the assumption that in the third stage of the therapy, the fear-producing stimuli function as CSs that come to produce a relaxation response. This classical conditioning should be established because the imagined fear-producing stimuli are being paired with stimuli (presumably self-instructional) resulting in a relaxation response. Some theorists also stress the importance of the relaxation response being antagonistic to the fear response. If imagining the stimulus originally producing the greatest fear can come to produce little or no fear, the outcome of systematic desensitization therapy should be fairly successful.

It is evident that this rationale involves two assumptions: (a) that imagined stimuli function as real stimuli in classical conditioning, and (b) that classical conditioning involving imagined stimuli in therapy transfers to the corresponding real stimuli encountered outside of therapy. These assumptions follow from the hypothesis that images of stimuli and the effects of real stimuli are due to qualitatively identical temporary brain events.

Fear-producing stimuli low in the anxiety hierarchy are imagined in conjunction with relaxation first to avoid the overwhelming fear produced by imagining stimuli at the top of the hierarchy. The relaxation response that is the result of imagining stimuli low on the anxiety hierarchy while relaxing should then also carry over to some extent to similar more fear-provoking stimuli, which permits them to be imagined without undue anxiety. Eventually the stimulus at the top of the anxiety hierarchy will thus produce relaxation instead of fear.

An experimental study of Davison (1968) suggests that the third stage of imagining fear-producing stimuli simultaneously with relaxation is the most important component of systematic desensitization therapy which supports the idea that its efficacy lies in classical conditioning. Subjects were college student volunteers who reported they were highly fearful of nonpoisonous snakes. One group was treated with a typical systematic desensitization procedure. Subjects in a second group received the same treatment, except that they imagined snake-irrelevant stimuli while relaxing in stage 3. Subjects in a third group were also treated with systematic desensitization, except that they imagined the snake-related fear-producing stimuli of the anxiety hierarchy but did not simultaneously engage in relaxation in stage 3. The measure of change was the subjects' capacity to come close to a live snake. The group that received the typical systematic desensitization procedure approached the live snake after treatment more than did members of the other two groups.

Outcome of Systematic Desensitization Therapy. Systematic desensitization therapy was reported to result in improvement rates of 78 and 90 percent (Hain, Butcher, & Stevenson, 1966; Wolpe, 1958). Many case histories also attest to the effectiveness of systematic desensitization therapy. An illustrative case history (Clark, 1965) is that of a woman, Mrs. B., with a longstanding phobic fear of feathers and birds. She could not go for walks outdoors, since she was afraid of encountering birds. Mrs. B. otherwise seemed normal; she ran her home well, and in a personality inventory test scored fairly low in neuroticism. She underwent systematic desensitization therapy in which real stimuli—real feathers, a stuffed blackbird—were used rather than imagined stimuli. The therapy was successful enough so that she was able to walk outside, go close to a flock of pigeons, and sleep on pillows stuffed with feathers.

Systematic desensitization therapy may not be effective with a client who has more than one phobia and exhibits other neurotic tendencies (Meyer & Gelder, 1963). In one of several case histories described by these authors, the client was a housewife who was extremely afraid to go out of the house. She also feared closed spaces and had obsessional fears about hurting others and about death. Her fear of leaving the house and walking to work had kept her unemployed. She was also unable to visit friends. The systematic desensitization program was aimed at reducing her phobia about walking outside the house. Fear of several walking routes was thereby reduced, but little transfer of fear reduction to other routes occurred. She took a job, now being able to work, and she also began to visit friends. But the authors reported that the client's anxiety and depression remained, and she became dependent on the therapist.

Classical Conditioning, Development of Social Behavior, and Contact Comfort

Parents may classically condition their children to respond to parental interpersonal behaviors. The CSs are certain interpersonal behaviors exhibited by parents (and other people), and the UCS frequently is contact comfort initiated by the parents. In general, important aspects of children's social behavior may be the outcome of both classical and instrumental conditioning.

Effect of Contact Comfort. Contact comfort is soft, pleasurable tactual stimulation. It occurs when a child is being held in a relaxed manner, when a child clings to another person, when a child and another person hold hands, when a child encircles the leg of an adult with an arm, and so on.

Observations suggest that contact comfort for children is a stimulus that is approached and continued to be perceived and that reduces fear. Young children frequently try to get contact comfort from other people, in our society most usually the mother. They climb onto laps, hold onto legs, and hold hands. Contact comfort appears to reduce fear and other behaviors indicative of emotional distress. Holding a child will often stop its crying. The frequency of lap climbing, leg holding, hand holding, and the like all seem to increase when children are hurt, afraid, or otherwise emotionally distressed. Stimuli producing emotional distress probably also affect the nature of the contact comfort the young child tries for; he or she is probably more likely to seek extensive ventral to ventral contact when a fear-producing stimulus is present than when it is not.

Coates, Anderson, and Hartup (1972) found that during separation from the mother 10-, 14-, and 18-month-old infants cried more, and that after the mother returned they were more likely to touch the mother than before separation. These results may mean that contact comfort with the mother upon her return helped to reduce the child's emotional distress. It is known that the presence of the mother reduces fear-related behavior in the child (Arsenian, 1943; Rheingold & Eckerman, 1970). But to what extent contact comfort and other attributes of the mother such as seeing or hearing her contributed to fear reduction in these studies is not clear.

Contact comfort is a primary reinforcer that is approached and continued to be perceived and that reduces fear in children; in other words, it is a positive reinforcer that automatically (not because of learning) establishes learning and reduces fear in children. This statement is supported by Harlow and Zimmerman's (1959) research on the responses of young monkeys to artificial cloth and wire mothers. They showed that (a) young monkeys spent more time in physical contact with a cloth mother than a wire mother; (b) young monkeys were more likely to run to and hold on to a cloth mother than a wire mother when they were afraid; (c) physical contact with a cloth mother was more likely to reduce young monkeys' fear than physical contact with a wire mother; and (d) the opportunity to obtain contact comfort with a cloth mother established a much stronger instrumentally conditioned response than the opportunity to make physical contact with a wire mother. Their research also showed that the attracting and fear-reducing property of contact comfort with a cloth mother was not due to acquired associations of contact comfort with other primary reinforcers. Another finding was that food was much less likely than contact comfort to be approached and continued to be perceived and to reduce fear. The Harlow and Zimmerman work therefore indicates that, for young monkeys, contact comfort is a positive primary reinforcer that reduces fear. Observations of young monkeys and other primates in natural settings also indicate that the young often approach and continue to hold onto an older member of the species, particularly when a fear-producing stimulus occurs (Rheingold, 1963). Since contact comfort results in the same behaviors in children as it does in monkeys, and since humans and other primates are phylogenetically related, we may assume that for children contact comfort is a positive primary reinforcer that reduces fear.

Attention Behaviors as CSs. Attention behaviors include smiling, talking in a pleasant tone of voice, turning toward or facing, and physical proximity. The child probably acquires a classically conditioned association between a familiar person's attention behaviors and his or her delivery of contact comfort (Gewirtz, 1961; Skinner, 1953).

Observations indicate that attention behaviors exhibited by a familiar person to a child are relatively likely to be accompanied or followed by this person's initiating contact comfort with the child. In one study, Ou (1977) videotaped the interactions of children (mean age, 4.7 years) with their mothers while the children worked on tasks. Every 3-second interval that a child and a mother were involved with a task was rated for whether or not the mother smiled and initiated contact comfort with the child. It was found that if mothers smiled in a 3 second interval they were relatively likely to initiate contact comfort in the next 3 second interval, and that if mothers initiated contact comfort in a 3-second interval they were relatively likely to smile in the next 3-second interval.

In other words, mothers were relatively likely to smile and initiate contact comfort about the same time.

In another study (King, 1973; King & Marcus, 1974), mothers and college students completed paragraphs in which a two (and in some cases seven) year-old child was described as approaching his or her mother (or, in some cases, father). The parent was described as exhibiting specific facial expression, tone of voice, direction of turning, and physical proximity behaviors. Subjects indicated by their completions what the parent would do as the child approached. Instructions to subjects emphasized that they should indicate how the parent in the paragraph would actually behave. The paragraph completions were scored for initiation of contact comfort by the parent. The obtained results indicated that subjects expected that when parents smiled, talked in a pleasant tone of voice, and turned toward the child, these behaviors were relatively likely to be followed by their initiating contact comfort with the child. When parents approached, looked, and talked in a normal tone of voice to the child, these behaviors were expected to be followed by their initiating contact comfort with the child less frequently. When parents grimaced, turned away from, and talked in a harsh tone of voice to the child, these behaviors were expected to be followed by their initiating contact comfort with the child least frequently.

We will assume that attention behaviors are neutral stimuli, because there is little evidence to suggest that these behaviors are particularly likely to be approached and continued to be perceived automatically (not because of learning). (Certain stimuli automatically elicit smiling in the human infant and young child but this is a different matter.) Contact comfort is also assumed to be a primary reinforcer and therefore a UCS. If a UCS is likely to occur when the CS is on and not likely to occur at other times, excitatory classical conditioning takes place. Therefore, if parents' attention behaviors are relatively likely to be accompanied by or briefly precede their initiating contact comfort with the child, then classical conditioning in the child between these attention behaviors (CSs) and contact comfort (UCS) should occur. Contact comfort is a positive reinforcer that reduces fear. Consequently, parental attention behaviors should be approached and continued to be perceived by the child and should reduce the child's fear.

This outcome appears to occur. Children tend to approach and continue to stay close to familiar people, probably partly because the attention behaviors of these people are approached and continued to be perceived. In addition, when children are afraid they approach and stay close to familiar people even more than they do when unafraid, probably partly because the attention behaviors of familiar people help to reduce the fear.

Gewirtz (1961) and Skinner (1953) maintained that other reinforcers were effective in establishing the properties of attention behaviors. Although this position is undoubtedly valid, it is thought that contact comfort is especially important in relation to classical conditioning and attention behaviors. Attention behaviors most likely reduce fear, but the positive reinforcers of food and water are not known to effectively reduce fear. Harlow and Zimmerman (1959) showed, for monkeys, that contact comfort was more likely to be approached and continued to be perceived and to reduce fear than food. Certain stimuli of the mother are approached and continued to be perceived and reduce fear in a large number of mammals and birds (King, 1966); it may be that, in general, the positive social interactions among members of a species are for the most part established with these stimuli. The nature of these stimuli vary; it is probably contact comfort for primates but is the sight of a moving object for other animals. It may turn out that peoples' attention behaviors are more highly correlated with their delivering contact comfort to children than they are with their delivering other positive primary reinforcers to children.

Summary

Examples of classical conditioning established with positive and negative UCSs indicate that the CR is usually similar to the UCR. The CR will be acquired even if it causes a goal stimulus to be omitted or a negative-goal stimulus to occur. CSs paired with positive UCSs are approached and continued to be perceived, and CSs paired with negative UCSs are escaped from and avoided. Neither result is due to instrumental conditioning. A CS paired with the absence of a positive UCS is escaped from and avoided, and a CS paired with the absence of a negative UCS is approached and continued to be perceived. A CS paired with the absence of a UCS is called a conditioned inhibitor, because it impairs the establishment of subsequent typical (CS-UCS) classical conditioning with the same CS and UCS, and because it reduces the strength of the CR produced by another CS paired with the same UCS. When no particular event occurs in sufficiently close physical and temporal proximity to a positive reinforcer, it is escaped from and avoided; when it occurs in sufficiently close physical and temporal proximity to a negative reinforcer, it is approached and continued to be perceived. This explains why a CS paired with the absence of a positive UCS is escaped from and avoided, and why a CS paired with the absence of a negative UCS is approached and continued to be perceived. A CS paired with the termination of a UCS functions as a CS paired with the absence of a UCS. A CS paired with the continuation of a UCS probably produces specific CRs; in addition, it should be approached and continued to be perceived when paired with the continuation of a positive UCS, and it should be escaped from and avoided when paired with the continuation of a negative UCS. Random presentations of a CS and UCS inhibit subsequently introduced typical (CS-UCS) classical conditioning between the same CS and UCS. Not all CRs are similar to UCRs. It appears that UCSs that elicit relatively strong arousal responses establish better classical conditioning than UCSs that elicit relatively weak arousal responses.

The amplitude, rate, and probability of the CR—measures of CR strength—increase over trials. A reason for this involves attention to the CS. The measures of CR strength are not perfectly related, which is one indication that learning cannot be directly measured. The effects of training on the latency of the CR are discussed. Extinction usually decreases the strength of a CR established with CS-UCS pairings relatively rapidly, but classical conditioning in which a CS is paired with the absence of a UCS is probably relatively resistant to extinction.

Pseudoconditioning control procedures are used because, in part, unpaired presentations of a UCS may elevate the strength of a response produced by a neutral stimulus. A basic conditioning result is that CR strength increases as CS onset occurs closer in time to UCS onset up to a point where an optimal time interval between CS onset and UCS onset is reached. The superiority of delayed conditioning to trace conditioning and of shorter to longer time intervals between CS onset and UCS onset in delayed conditioning probably arises from partial forgetting of the CS after it has terminated, and from partial forgetting of the attention-eliciting beginning portion of the CS. Excitatory classical conditioning occurs when the CS predicts that the UCS is more likely to occur in the presence of or shortly after termination of the CS than a relatively long time after termination of the CS. Backward conditioning results are analyzed in terms of whether or not the CS predicts the absence or continuation of the UCS.

A CS can be the offset of a stimulus, and it need not be a relatively specific stimulus. The CS and the stimuli of the general learning situation affect the topography of the CR. CR strength increases as the difference between the CS and background stimuli increases.

A neutral stimulus that produces a response can establish a CR. An increase in the amount or intensity of a UCS increases both CR and UCR strength. This result supports the conclusion that CRs resemble UCRs quantitatively as well as qualitatively. Image theory accounts for the effects of amount and intensity of the UCS on CR strength and for the conclusion that CRs resemble UCRs quantitatively as well as qualitatively, in that the strengths of image-produced responses are probably generally positively related to the strengths of stimulus-produced responses. Those responses that are relatively difficult to classically condition are elicited by stimuli that lead to little or no responding when they are requested to be imagined. Particularly good classical conditioning appears to occur in rats when a taste CS and an illness-producing UCS are paired. This result may be the outcome of a biological specialization that facilitates classical conditioning between taste and illness-producing stimuli, but there are also other ways to interpret it.

Deprivation of food and water exerts a nonlearning effect on CR strength. An increase in deprivation level increases UCR as well as CR strength. In addition, at least the strength of the salivation response produced by imagining food increases with an increase in deprivation level. Analysis of the effect of deprivation on CR strength is therefore analogous to the analysis of the effect of amount and intensity of the UCS on CR strength. Training, extinction, time relationships between the CS and the UCS, and amount and intensity of the UCS all affect CR strength through learning.

Image theory assumes that acquired associations between paired neutral stimuli occur. Several types of results support this conclusion. These findings include the occurrence of classical conditioning in which the second of two paired neutral stimuli produces a response; the sensory preconditioning outcome; findings that suggest the second of two paired neutral stimuli was vividly imagined when the first member of the pair occurred; the fact that verbal instructions involving paired neutral stimuli affect CR strength; the fact that pairings between neutral stimuli decrease the strength of the GSR to these paired stimuli, but an equivalent decrease in the strength of the GSR elicited by one of the neutral stimuli presented alone does not occur; and the configural conditioning outcome.

The rationale for systematic desensitization therapy is that imagining fear-producing stimuli while relaxing enables these stimuli to produce a relaxation response through classical conditioning. Outcomes of systematic desensitization therapy are described.

Contact comfort for children probably is a positive primary reinforcer that reduces fear. Parents appear to accompany or follow attention behaviors with their initiating contact comfort with children. Attention behaviors should therefore be CSs that are approached and continued to be perceived by children and that reduce their fear.

REFERENCES

ADELMAN, H. M., & MAATSCH, J. L. Learning and extinction based upon frustration, food reward, and exploratory tendency. *J. Exp. Psychol.*, 1956, 52, 311-315.

ARSENIAN, J. M. Young children in an insecure situation. *J. Abnorm. Soc. Psychol.*, 1943, 38, 225-249.

AZRIN, N. H., & HAKE, D. F. Positive conditioned suppression: Conditioned suppression using positive reinforcers as the unconditioned stimuli. *J. Exp. Anal. Behav.*, 1969, 12, 167-173.

AZRIN, N. H., HUTCHINSON, R. R., & HAKE, D. F. Extinction-induced aggression. *J. Exp. Anal. Behav.*, 1966, 9, 191-204.

BADIA, P., & DEFRAN, R. H. Orienting responses and GSR conditioning: A dilemma. *Psychol. Rev.*, 1970, 77, 171-181.

BARBER, T. X., CHAUNCEY, H. H., & WINER, R. A. Effect of hypnotic and nonhypnotic suggestions on parotid gland response to gustatory stimuli. *Psychosom. Med.*, 1964, 26, 374-380.

BARBER, T. X., & HAHN, K. W., JR. Experimental studies in "hypnotic" behavior: Physiologic and subjective effects of imagined pain. *J. Nerv. Ment. Dis.*, 1964, 139, 416-425.

BARNES, G. W. Conditioned stimulus intensity and temporal factors in spaced-trial classical conditioning. *J. Exp. Psychol.*, 1956, 51, 192-198.

BINDRA, D., & PALFAI, T. Nature of positive and negative incentive-motivational effects on general activity. *J. Comp. Physiol. Psychol.*, 1967, 63, 288-297.

BLACK, A. H., & DE TOLEDO, L. The relationship among classically conditioned responses: Heart rate and skeletal behavior. In A. H. Black and W. F. Prokasy (Eds.), *Classical Conditioning II: Current Theory and Research.* New York: Appleton-Century-Crofts, 1972.

BLANCHARD, R. J., & BLANCHARD, D. C. Passive and active reactions to fear-eliciting stimuli. *J. Comp. Physiol. Psychol.*, 1969, 68, 129-135.

BOICE, R., & DENNY, M. R. The conditioned licking response in rats as a function of the CS-UCS interval. *Psychon. Sci.*, 1965, 3, 93-94.

BOLLES, R. C. Species-specific defense reactions and avoidance learning. *Psychol. Rev.*, 1970, 77, 32-48.

BOOTH, J. H., & HAMMOND, L. J. Configural conditioning: Greater fear in rats to compound than component through overtraining of the compound. *J. Exp. Psychol.*, 1971, 87, 255-262.

BRELAND, K., & BRELAND, M. The misbehavior of organisms. *Am. Psychol.*, 1961, 16, 681-684.

BROGDEN, W. J. Sensory pre-conditioning. *J. Exp. Psychol.*, 1939, 25, 323-332.

BROGDEN, W. J., LIPMAN, E. A., & CULLER, E. The role of incentive in conditioning and extinction. *Am. J. Psychol.*, 1938, 51, 109-117.

BROWN, P. L., & JENKINS, H. M. Auto-shaping of the pigeon's key peck. *J. Exp. Anal. Behav.*, 1968, 11, 1-8.

BRUNER, A. UCS properties in classical conditioning of the albino rabbit's nictitating membrane response. *J. Exp. Psychol.*, 1965, 69, 186-192.

CAMPBELL, A. A., & HILGARD, E. R. Individual differences in ease of conditioning. *J. Exp. Psychol.*, 1936, 19, 561-571.

CLARK, D. F. The treatment of monosymptomatic phobia by systematic desensitization. *Behav. Res. Ther.*, 1963, 1, 63-68.

COATES, B., ANDERSON, E. P., & HARTUP, W. W. Interrelations in the attachment behavior of human infants. *Dev. Psychol.*, 1972, 6, 218-230.

COLAVITA, F. B. Dual function of the US in classical salivary conditioning. *J. Comp. Physiol. Psychol.*, 1965, 60, 218-222.

CRAIG, K. D. Psychological arousal as a function of imagined, vicarious, and direct stress experiences. *J. Abnorm. Psychol.*, 1969, 73, 513-520.

DAVISON, G. C. Systematic desensitization as a counterconditioning process. *J. Abnorm. Psychol.*, 1968, 73, 91-99.

DeBOLD, R. C., MILLER, N. E., & JENSEN, D. D. Effect of strength of drive determined by a new technique for appetitive classical conditioning of rats. *J. Comp. Physiol. Psychol.*, 1965, 59, 102-108.

DOEHRING, D. G. Conditioning of muscle action potential responses resulting from passive hand movement. *J. Exp. Psychol.*, 1957, 54, 292-296.

DOMJAN, M., & WILSON, N. E. Specificity of cue to consequence in aversion learning in the rat. *Psychon. Sci.*, 1972, 26, 143-145.

EBEL, H. C., & PROKASY, W. F. Classical eyelid conditioning as a function of sustained and shifted interstimulus intervals. *J. Exp. Psychol.*, 1963, 65, 52-58.

ELLSON, D. G. Hallucinations produced by sensory conditioning. *J. Exp. Psychol.*, 1941, 28, 1-20.

FINCH, G. Hunger as a determinant of conditional and unconditional salivary response magnitude. *Am. J. Physiol.*, 1938, 123, 379-382.

FINK, J. B. Conditioning of muscle action potential increments accompanying an instructed movement. *J. Exp. Psychol.*, 1954, 47, 61-68.

FREEMAN, H. L., & KENDRICK, D. C. A case of cat phobia: Treatment by a method derived from experimental psychology. *Br. Med. J.*, 1960, 2, 497-502.

FREY, P. W., MAISIAK, R., & DUGUE, G. Unconditional stimulus characteristics in rabbit eyelid conditioning. *J. Exp. Psychol.: Anim. Behav. Processes*, 1976, 2, 175-190.

GAMZU, E., & WILLIAMS, D. R. Classical conditioning of a complex skeletal act. *Science*, 1971, 171, 923-925.

GARCIA, J., & KOELLING, R. A. Relation of cue to consequence in avoidance learning. *Psychon. Sci.*, 1966, 4, 123-124.

GEWIRTZ, J. L. A learning analysis of the effects of normal stimulation, privation and deprivation on the acquisition of social motivation and attachment. In B. M. Foss (Ed.), *Determinants of Infant Behaviour*. London: Methuen, 1961.

GLAZER, H. I., & WEISS, J. M. Long-term and transitory interference effects. *J. Exp. Psychol.: Anim. Behav. Processes*, 1976, 2, 191-201.

GONZALEZ, R. C., & DIAMOND, L. A test of Spence's theory of incentive motivation. *Am. J. Psychol.*, 1960, 73, 396-403.

GORMEZANO, I. Investigations of defense and reward conditioning in the rabbit. In A. H. Black and W. F. Prokasy (Eds.), *Classical Conditioning II: Current Theory and Research*. New York: Appleton-Century-Crofts, 1972.

GRANT, D. A., & SCHNEIDER, D. E. Intensity of the conditioned stimulus and strength of conditioning: II. The conditioned galvanic skin response to an auditory stimulus. *J. Exp. Psychol.*, 1949, 39, 35-40.

GRINGS, W. W., SCHELL, A. M., & CAREY, C. A. Verbal control of an autonomic response in a cue reversal situation. *J. Exp. Psychol.*, 1973, 99, 215-221.

HAIN, J. D., BUTCHER, R. H. G., & STEVENSON, I. Systematic desensitization therapy: An analysis of results in twenty-seven patients. *Br. J. Psychiatry*, 1966, 112, 295-307.

HALL, J. F. *The Psychology of Learning*. Philadelphia: Lippincott, 1966.

HARAWAY, M. M., WIRTH, P. W., & MAPLES, E. G. Contiguous approach conditioning: A model for positive reinforcement. *Psychol. Rep.*, 1974, 34, 127-130.

HARLOW, H. F., & ZIMMERMAN, R. R. Affectional responses in the infant monkey. *Science*, 1959, 130, 421-432.

HARRIS, J. D. Forward conditioning, backward conditioning, pseudo-conditioning, and adaptation to the conditioned stimulus. *J. Exp. Psychol.*, 1941, 28, 491-502.

HETH, C. D. Simultaneous and backward fear conditioning as a function of number of CS-UCS pairings. *J. Exp. Psychol.: Anim. Behav. Processes*, 1976, 2, 117-129.

HETH, C. D., & RESCORLA, R. A. Simultaneous and backward fear conditioning in the rat. *J. Comp. Physiol. Psychol.*, 1973, 82, 434-443.

HOLLAND, P. C., & RESCORLA, R. A. The effect of two ways of devaluing the unconditioned stimulus after first- and second-order appetitive conditioning. *J. Exp. Psychol.: Anim. Behav. Processes*, 1975, 1, 355-363.

HUNT, H. F., & BRADY, J. V. Some effects of punishment and intercurrent "anxiety" on a simple operant. *J. Comp. Physiol. Psychol.*, 1955, 48, 305-310.

HUTCHINSON, R. R., AZRIN, N. H., & HUNT, G. M. Attack produced by intermittent reinforcement of a concurrent operant response. *J. Exp. Anal. Behav.*, 1968, 11, 489-495.

HUTCHINSON, R. R., RENFREW, J. W., & YOUNG, G. A. Effects of long-term shock and associated stimuli on aggressive and manual responses. *J. Exp. Anal. Behav.*, 1971, 15, 141-166.

JENKINS, H. M., & MOORE, B. R. The form of the auto-shaped response with food or water reinforcers. *J. Exp. Anal. Behav.*, 1973, 20, 163-181.

KALAT, J. W., & ROZIN, P. Role of interference in taste-aversion learning. *J. Comp. Physiol. Psychol.*, 1971, 77, 53-58.

KAMIN, L. J. Temporal and intensity characteristics of the conditioned stimulus. In W. F. Prokasy (Ed.), *Classical Conditioning: A Symposium*. New York: Appleton-Century-Crofts, 1965.

KAMIN, L. J., & SCHAUB, R. E. Effects of conditioned stimulus intensity on the conditioned emotional response. *J. Comp. Physiol. Psychol.*, 1963, 56, 502-507.

KEITH-LUCAS, T., & GUTTMAN, N. Robust-single-trial delayed backward conditioning. *J. Comp. Physiol. Psychol.*, 1975, 88, 468-476.

KING, D. L. A review and interpretation of some aspects of infant-mother relationships in mammals and birds. *Psychol. Bull.*, 1966, 65, 143-155.

KING, D. L. Expectations of behaviors of mothers preceding initiation of contact comfort with their children. *Psychol. Rep.*, 1973, 33, 131-137.

KING, D. L. Perception, binocular fusion, and an image theory of classical conditioning. *Percept. Mot. Skills*, 1974, 39, 531-537.

KING, D. L., & MARCUS, M. Expectations of parents' behaviors preceding initiation of contact comfort with children: An extension. *Psychol. Rep.*, 1974, 35, 795-801.

KRANE, R. V., & WAGNER, A. R. Taste aversion learning with a delayed shock US: Implications for the "generality of the laws of learning." *J. Comp. Physiol. Psychol.*, 1975, 88, 882-889.

KREMER, E. F. Truly random and traditional control procedures in CER conditioning in the rat. *J. Comp. Physiol. Psychol.*, 1971, 76, 441-448.

LEUBA, C. Images as conditioned sensations. *J. Exp. Psychol.*, 1940, 26, 345-351.

LOGAN, F. A., & WAGNER, A. R. Supplementary report: Direction of change in CS in eyelid conditioning. *J. Exp. Psychol.*, 1962, 64, 325-326.

MACKINTOSH, N. J. Stimulus selection: Learning to ignore stimuli that predict no change in reinforcement. In R. A. Hinde and J. Stevenson-Hinde (Eds.), *Constraints on Learning*. London: Academic Press, 1973.

MAPLES, E. G., TOMPOROWSKI, P. D., & HARAWAY, M. M. Contiguous approach conditioning: A model for negative reinforcement. *Psychol. Rep.*, 1975, 37, 851-856.

MARTIN, I., & LEVEY, A. B. *The Genesis of the Classical Conditioned Response*. London: Pergamon Press, 1969.

McALLISTER, D. E., McALLISTER, W. R., BROOKS, C. I., & GOLDMAN, J. A. Magnitude and shift of reward in instrumental aversive learning in rats. *J. Comp. Physiol. Psychol.*, 1972, 80, 490-501.

MELTZER, D., & BRAHLEK, J. A. Conditioned suppression and conditioned enhancement with the same positive UCS: An effect of CS duration. *J. Exp. Anal. Behav.*, 1970, 13, 67-73.

MEYER, V., & GELDER, M. G. Behaviour therapy and phobic disorders. *Br. J. Psychiatry*, 1963, 109, 19-28.

MITCHELL, D., KIRSCHBAUM, E. H., & PERRY, R. L. Effects of neophobia and habituation on the poison-induced avoidance of exteroceptive stimuli in the rat. *J. Exp. Psychol.: Anim. Behav. Processes*, 1975, 1, 47-55.

MITCHELL, D. S., & GORMEZANO, I. Effects of water deprivation on classical appetitive conditioning of the rabbit's jaw movement response. *Learn. Motiv.*, 1970, 1, 199-206.

MOORE, B. R. The role of directed Pavlovian reactions in simple instrumental learning in the pigeon. In R. A. Hinde and J. Stevenson-Hinde (Eds.), *Constraints on Learning*. London: Academic Press, 1973.

MOSCOVITCH, A., & LoLORDO, V. M. Role of safety in the Pavlovian backward fear conditioning procedure. *J. Comp. Physiol. Psychol.*, 1968, 66, 673-678.

NOWLIS, G. H. Conditioned stimulus intensity and acquired alimentary aversions in the rat. *J. Comp. Physiol. Psychol.*, 1974, 86, 1173-1184.

ODLING-SMEE, F. J. The role of background stimuli during Pavlovian conditioning. *Q. J. Exp. Psychol.*, 1975, 27, 201-209.

ÖHMAN, A., BJÖRKSTRAND, P., & ELLSTRÖM, P. Effect of explicit trial-by-trial information about shock probability in long interstimulus interval GSR conditioning. *J. Exp. Psychol.*, 1973, 98, 145-151.

OST, J. W. P., & LAUER, D. W. Some investigations of classical salivary conditioning in the dog. In W. F. Prokasy (Ed.), *Classical Conditioning: A Symposium*. New York: Appleton-Century-Crofts, 1965.

Ou, Y. *Mothers' Contact Comfort and Other Behaviors while Children Work on Tasks.* Unpublished Ph.D. dissertation, Howard University, 1977.

PETERSON, G. B., ACKIL, J. E., FROMMER, G. P., & HEARST, E. S. Conditioned approach and contact behavior toward signals for food or brain-stimulation reinforcement. *Science,* 1972, 177, 1009-1011.

RACKHAM, D. W. *Conditioning of the Pigeon's Courtship and Aggressive Behavior.* Unpublished master's thesis, Dalhousie University, 1971.

RESCORLA, R. A. Probability of shock in the presence and absence of CS in fear conditioning. *J. Comp. Physiol. Psychol.,* 1968, 66, 1-5.

RESCORLA, R. A. Conditioned inhibition of fear resulting from negative CS-UCS contingencies. *J. Comp. Physiol. Psychol.,* 1969, 67, 504-509.

REVUSKY, S. H. Aversion to sucrose produced by contingent X-irradiation: Temporal and dosage parameters. *J. Comp. Physiol. Psychol.,* 1968, 65, 17-22.

REVUSKY, S. H. The role of interference in association over a delay. In W. K. Honig and P. H. R. James (Eds.), *Animal Memory.* New York: Academic Press, 1971.

REVUSKY, S. H., & BEDARF, E. W. Association of illness with prior ingestion of novel foods. *Science,* 1967, 155, 219-220.

RHEINGOLD, H. L. (Ed.) *Maternal Behavior in Mammals.* New York: Wiley, 1963.

RHEINGOLD, H. L., & ECKERMAN, C. O. The infant separates himself from his mother. *Science,* 1970, 168, 78-83.

ROWLAND, L. R. The somatic effects of stimuli graded in respect to their exciting character. *J. Exp. Psychol.,* 1936, 19, 547-560.

ROZIN, P., & REE, P. Long extension of effective CS-UCS interval by anesthesia between CS and US. *J. Comp. Physiol. Psychol.,* 1972, 80, 43-48.

SCHLOSBERG, H. Conditioned responses in the white rat. *J. Genet. Psychol.,* 1934, 45, 303-305.

SCHLOSBERG, H. Conditioned responses in the white rat: II. Conditioned responses based upon shock to the foreleg. *J. Genet. Psychol.,* 1936, 49, 107-138.

SEGUNDO, J. P., GALEANO, C., SOMMER-SMITH, J. A., & ROIG, J. A. Behavioural and EEG effects of tones 'reinforced' by cessation of painful stimuli. In J. F. Delafresnaye (Ed.), *Brain Mechanisms and Learning.* Oxford: Blackwells Scientific Publications, 1961.

SHEAFOR, P. J. "Pseudoconditioned" jaw movements of the rabbit reflect associations conditioned to contextual background cues. *J. Exp. Psychol.: Anim. Behav. Processes,* 1975, 1, 245-260.

SHEAFOR, P. J., & GORMEZANO, I. Conditioning the rabbit's (Oryctolagus cuniculus) jaw-movement response: US magnitude effects on URs, CRS, and pseudo-CRs. *J. Comp. Physiol. Psychol.,* 1972, 81, 449-456.

SHEFFIELD, F. D. Avoidance training and the contiguity principle. *J. Comp. Physiol. Psychol.,* 1948, 41, 165-177.

SHEFFIELD, F. D. Relation between classical conditioning and instrumental learning. In W. F. Prokasy (Ed.), *Classical Conditioning: A Symposium.* New York: Appleton-Century-Crofts, 1965.

SIEGEL, S., & DOMJAN, M. Backward conditioning as an inhibitory procedure. *Learn. Motiv.,* 1971, 2, 1-11.

SIEGEL, S., & DOMJAN, M. The inhibitory effect of backward conditioning as a function of the number of backward pairings. *Bull. Psychon. Soc.,* 1974, 4, 122-124.

SKINNER, B. F. *Science and Human Behavior*. New York: Macmillan, 1953.

SMITH, M. C. CS-US interval and US intensity in classical conditioning of the rabbit's nictitating membrane response. *J. Comp. Physiol. Psychol.*, 1968, 66, 679-687.

SMITH, M. C., COLEMAN, S. R., & GORMEZANO, I. Classical conditioning of the rabbit's nictitating membrane response at backward, simultaneous, and forward CS-US intervals. *J. Comp. Physiol. Psychol.*, 1969, 69, 226-231.

SOKOLOV, Y. N. *Perception and the Conditioned Reflex*. New York: Pergamon Press, 1963.

SPENCE, K. W., HAGGARD, D. F., & ROSS, L. E. UCS intensity and the associative (habit) strength of the eyelid CR. *J. Exp. Psychol.*, 1958, 55, 404-411.

SPOONER, A., & KELLOG, W. N. The backward conditioning curve. *Am. J. Psychol.*, 1947, 60, 321-334.

STAATS, A. W., & HAMMOND, O. W. Natural words as physiological conditioned stimuli: Food-word-elicited salivation and deprivation effects. *J. Exp. Psychol.*, 1972, 96, 206-208.

STEIN, N., HOFFMAN, H. S., & STITT, C. Collateral behavior of the pigeon during conditioned suppression of key pecking. *J. Exp. Anal. Behav.*, 1971, 15, 83-93.

STIERS, M., & SILBERBERG, A. Lever-contact responses in rats: Automaintenance with and without a negative response-reinforcer dependency. *J. Exp. Anal. Behav.*, 1974, 22, 497-506.

TAYLOR, J. A. Level of conditioning and intensity of the adaptation stimulus. *J. Exp. Psychol.*, 1956, 51, 127-130.

VERNON, W., & ULRICH, R. Classical conditioning of pain-elicited aggression. *Science*, 1966, 152, 668-669.

WAGNER, A. R., & TERRY, W. S. Backward conditioning to a CS following an expected vs. a surprising UCS. *Anim. Learn. & Behav.*, 1975, 3, 370-374.

WASSERMAN, E. A. Pavlovian conditioning with heat reinforcement produces stimulus-directed pecking in chicks. *Science*, 1973, 181, 875-877.

WASSERMAN, E. A., FRANKLIN, S. R., & HEARST, E. Pavlovian appetitive contingencies and approach versus withdrawal to conditioned stimuli in pigeons. *J. Comp. Physiol. Psychol.*, 1974, 86, 616-627.

WEISMAN, R. G., & LITNER, J. S. Positive conditioned reinforcement of Sidman avoidance behavior in rats. *J. Comp. Physiol. Psychol.*, 1969, 68, 597-603.

WICKENS, D. D., NIELD, A. F., TUBER, D. S., & WICKENS, C. Classical conditioned compound-element discrimination as a function of length of training, amount of testing, and CS-US interval. *Learn. Motiv.*, 1970, 1, 95-109.

WILCOXON, H. C., DRAGOIN, W. B., & KRAL, P. A. Illness-induced aversions in rat and quail: Relative salience of visual and gustatory cues. *Science*, 1971, 171, 826-828.

WILLIAMS, D. R., & WILLIAMS, H. Auto-maintenance in the pigeon: Sustained pecking despite contingent non-reinforcement. *J. Exp. Anal. Behav.*, 1969, 12, 511-520.

WILSON, G. D. Reversal of differential GSR conditioning by instructions. *J. Exp. Psychol.*, 1968, 76, 491-493.

WOLPE, J. *Psychotherapy by Reciprocal Inhibition*. Stanford: Stanford University Press, 1958.

WOODRUFF, G., & WILLIAMS, D. R. The associative relation underlying autoshaping in the pigeon. *J. Exp. Anal. Behav.*, 1976, 26, 1-13.

Woods, S. C., & Shogren, R. E., Jr. Glycemic responses following conditioning with different doses of insulin in rats. *J. Comp. Physiol. Psychol.*, 1972, 81, 220-225.

Zeaman, D., & Smith, R. W. Review of some recent findings in human cardiac conditioning. In W. F. Prokasy (Ed.), *Classical Conditioning: A Symposium.* New York: Appleton-Century-Crofts, 1965.

Zener, K. The significance of behavior accompanying conditioned salivary secretion for theories of the conditioned response. *Am. J. Psychol.*, 1937, 50, 384-403.

Zimmer-Hart, C. L., & Rescorla, R. A. Extinction of Pavlovian conditioned inhibition. *J. Comp. Physiol. Psychol.*, 1974, 86, 837-845.

CHAPTER 3

Instrumental Conditioning

Instrumental conditioning occurs when an instrumental response causes a stimulus to take place, and as a result of this response-stimulus pairing the response increases or decreases in rate. When an instrumental response causes a goal stimulus to occur, an increase in the rate of the instrumental response is likely to take place. When an instrumental response causes a negative-goal stimulus to occur, a decrease in the rate of the instrumental response is likely to take place. A goal stimulus is a stimulus that is more likely to be approached and continued to be perceived than either the stimuli present prior to the execution of the instrumental response or the stimuli that would be present if the instrumental response were not made. A negative-goal stimulus is a stimulus that is more likely to be escaped from and avoided than either the stimuli present prior to the execution of the instrumental response or the stimuli that would be present if the instrumental response were not made.

Instrumentally Conditioned Responses

Several examples of instrumental conditioning have already been de-scribed, including the instrumental conditioning of bar pressing, key pecking, traversal of a runway established with a positive reinforcer,

127

remaining on a platform, and traversal of a runway established with a negative reinforcer. They represent more than one type of instrumental conditioning, and the different types of instrumental conditioning will now be described and discussed.

Reward Learning. In reward learning the instrumental response causes a positive reinforcer to occur. This response usually increases in rate as a result of the pairings between it and the positive reinforcer. The goal stimulus is the positive reinforcer, because the positive reinforcer is more likely to be approached and continued to be perceived than are the stimuli present before the execution of the instrumental response. Bar pressing, key pecking, and runway learning established with a positive reinforcer are instances of reward learning.

Consider, for example, the instrumental conditioning of bar pressing. A bar press response by a food-deprived rat brings food. As a result of the pairing between the bar press response and food, an increase in the rate of bar pressing occurs. Food is the reinforcer for the instrumentally conditioned bar press response; food increases the rate of a very large number of responses that cause it to occur, and a high rate of the bar press response would not occur if the bar press response were followed by no particular event rather than by food. Food is also the goal stimulus, because a food-deprived animal is more likely to approach and continue to perceive food than it is to approach and continue to perceive the stimuli preceding the bar press response.

A nonlaboratory example of reward learning is a child's increasing the time spent on school work following praise from parents for completing homework. The praise may be a positive reinforcer and goal stimulus, and the increase in time spent on school work may be a reward-trained response.

In reward learning, the stimuli of the general learning situation are present; then the instrumental response occurs; and then the goal stimulus takes place. Therefore, there should be classically conditioned associations between the stimuli of the general learning situation and the stimulus produced by the instrumental response, and between the stimulus produced by the instrumental response and the goal stimulus. As a result of these classically conditioned associations, an image of the goal stimulus should occur while an animal is in the learning situation; that is, a temporary brain event corresponding to the goal stimulus should arise while an animal is in the learning situation.

The amount of temporary brain event corresponding to the goal stimulus and the vividness of the image of the goal stimulus should be increased by bringing about the stimulus produced by the instrumental response. This is because the stimulus produced by the instrumental response has previously been followed by the goal stimulus. Furthermore, an animal should behave so as to bring about and maintain a more vivid image of the goal stimulus. It follows that an animal should attempt to bring about the stimulus produced by the instrumental response, and it is assumed that it is successful in doing so. To bring about the stimulus produced by the instrumental response, the instrumental response itself must occur, which is the result to be explained.

A feedback process is assumed to be responsible for an animal's ability to bring about the stimulus produced by the instrumental response. Response adjustments affect the similarity between the vividness of the image of the goal stimulus occurring at the moment and a relatively vivid image of the goal stimulus through the feedback provided by the stimuli produced by these response adjustments. The instrumental response thereby eventuates.

The assumption that an animal attempts to either bring about or not bring about the stimulus produced by the instrumental response can be supported for each type of instrumental conditioning. In respect to reward learning, this assumption is supported by the finding that a CS paired with a positive UCS comes to be approached and continued to be perceived. Reward learning is analogous to classical conditioning in which a CS is paired with a positive UCS: the stimulus produced by the instrumental response in reward learning corresponds to a CS; the positive reinforcer in reward learning corresponds to the UCS; and for both types of conditioning a neutral stimulus is followed by a positive reinforcer. The fact that a stimulus is approached and continued to be perceived means that an animal behaves so as to bring about and maintain the temporary brain event corresponding to this stimulus. Because of the analogy between reward learning and classical conditioning in which a CS is paired with a positive UCS, and because a CS paired with a positive UCS comes to be approached and continued to be perceived, an animal should attempt to bring about the temporary brain event corresponding to the stimulus produced by the instrumental response. Bringing about the stimulus produced by the instrumental response is equivalent to bringing about the temporary brain event corresponding to the stimulus produced by the instrumental response. Therefore, an animal should attempt to bring about the stimulus produced by the instrumental response.

Punishment Learning. Punishment learning is a second type of instrumental conditioning. In punishment learning the instrumental response causes a negative reinforcer to occur. This response usually decreases in rate as a result. The negative reinforcer is the negative-goal stimulus, because the negative reinforcer is more likely to be escaped from and avoided than are the stimuli present prior to the execution of the instrumental response. Instrumental conditioning of remaining on a platform is an example of punishment learning. The naturally occurring response of stepping off a platform causes a shock. As a result there is a decrease in the rate of the stepping off response. Shock is the reinforcer for the decrease in the rate of stepping off the platform, because shock decreases the rate of a very large number of responses that cause it to occur, and because the rate of stepping off does not decrease if stepping off is followed by no particular event rather than by shock. Shock is also the negative-goal stimulus, because an animal is more likely to escape from and avoid shock than it is apt to escape from and avoid the stimuli preceding the stepping off response.

A nonlaboratory example of punishment learning is a child's decreasing the rate of a response because this response has previously caused the negative reinforcer of having a parent yell at him.

In punishment learning, the stimulus produced by the instrumental response is followed by a negative-goal stmulus. The stimuli of the general learning situation should therefore become associated through classical conditioning with the stimulus produced by the instrumental response; and the stimulus produced by this response should therefore become associated through classical conditioning with the negative-goal stimulus. As a result, while an animal is in the learning situation an image of the negative-goal stimulus should occur; that is, a temporary brain event corresponding to the negative-goal stimulus should take place.

If an animal begins to initiate the instrumental response, both the amount of temporary brain event corresponding to the negative-goal stimulus and the vividness of the image of the negative-goal stimulus should increase. This is because the stimulus produced by the instrumental response has previously been followed by the negative-goal stimulus. In addition, an animal should behave so as to terminate and avoid a more vivid image of a negative-goal stimulus. It follows that an animal should attempt to avoid bringing about the stimulus produced by the instrumental response. The animal is assumed to be successful in this attempt, which means that the instrumental response will not occur, the result to be accounted for. A feedback process is responsible for an animal's ability to avoid bringing about the stimulus produced by the instrumental response.

The assumption that in punishment learning an animal should attempt to avoid bringing about the stimulus produced by the instrumental response is supported by the classical conditioning finding that a CS paired with a negative UCS comes to be escaped from and avoided. Punishment learning is analogous to classical conditioning in which a CS is paired with a negative UCS: the stimulus produced by the instrumental response in punishment learning corresponds to a CS, the negative reinforcer in punishment learning corresponds to the UCS, and for both types of conditioning a neutral stimulus is followed by a negative reinforcer. The fact that a stimulus is escaped from and avoided means that an animal behaves so as to terminate and avoid the temporary brain event corresponding to this stimulus. The analogy between punishment learning and classical conditioning in which a CS is paired with a negative UCS, and the fact that a CS paired with a negative UCS comes to be escaped from and avoided, together mean that an animal should attempt to avoid bringing about the temporary brain event corresponding to the stimulus produced by the instrumental response. Thus an animal should attempt to avoid bringing about this stimulus.

Escape Learning. Escape learning is a third type of instrumental conditioning. In escape learning the instrumental response causes a negative reinforcer to terminate. This response usually increases in rate as a result. The absence of the negative reinforcer is the goal stimulus, because an animal is more likely to approach and continue to perceive the absence of the negative reinforcer—that is, no particular event—than the stimuli present prior to the execution of the instrumental response. Instrumental conditioning of runway learning in which the reinforcer is shock is an example of escape learning. The instrumental response is a traversal of the runway, because this response causes shock, the negative reinforcer, to terminate. As a result, there is an increase in the rate of traversing the runway. The absence of shock is the goal stimulus, because an animal is more likely to approach and continue to perceive the absence of shock— that is, no particular event—than it is to approach and continue to perceive the stimuli occurring prior to the completion of the instrumental response.

A nonlaboratory example of escape learning is a child who learns to promise to do better while the mother is criticizing him or her. This response of the child should become escape-trained, because it is relatively likely to cause the mother to stop criticizing the child.

Image theory explains escape learning in the same way as for reward learning, because in both these types of instrumental conditioning the instrumental response causes a goal stimulus to occur. Thus, for escape learning an animal is assumed to bring about the stimulus produced by the instrumental response and thereby execute this response. The related assumption that an animal should attempt to bring about the stimulus produced by the instrumental response in escape learning is supported by the conclusion that a CS paired with the termination of a negative UCS is approached and continued to be perceived. The stimulus produced by an instrumental response in escape learning is analogous to a CS paired with the termination of a negative UCS. An animal in escape learning should therefore attempt to bring about the temporary brain event corresponding to the stimulus produced by the instrumental response—that is, it should attempt to bring about the stimulus produced by the instrumental response.

Types of Instrumental Conditioning. Reward learning, punishment learning, and escape learning illustrate three different ways to classify instrumental conditioning. The first is by the type of reinforcer employed. This can be positive, as in reward learning, or negative, as in punishment and escape learning. A second way is by whether the occurrence of a response causes either a goal stimulus to occur, as it does in reward and escape learning, or a negative-goal stimulus to occur, as it does in punishment learning. The third way is by whether the reinforcer

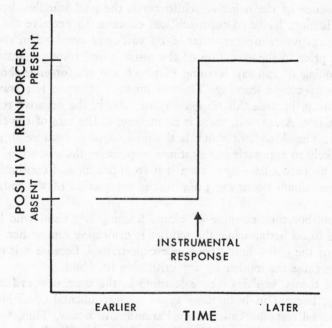

FIGURE 3-1. Outline of procedure for reward
learning.

is not present before the execution of the instrumental response, as in reward and punishment learning, or whether the reinforcer is present prior to the execution of the instrumental response, as in escape learning.

The combination of these classifications makes a total of 8 (2x2x2) types of instrumental conditioning. (Woods (1974) presents a related classification.) Table 3-1 shows these classifications, with their names. For each type of instrumental conditioning there is an analogous type of classical conditioning; these are also shown in Table 3-1.

Figures 3-1, 3-2, and 3-3 outline the procedures for reward, punishment, and escape learning. The ordinate indicates the presence or ab-

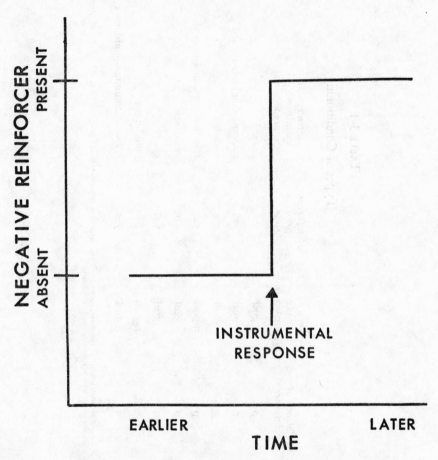

FIGURE 3-2. Outline of procedure for punishment learning.

TABLE 3-1
Types of Conditioning

Valence of reinforcer	Type of stimulus following ir	Reinforcer prior to ir	Instrumental conditioning type	Classical conditioning type
p	goal	no	reward	CS, onset of p UCS
p	goal	yes	response-continues-reward	CS, continuation of p UCS
p	n-goal	no	omission	CS, absence of p UCS
p	n-goal	yes	response-terminates-reward	CS, termination of p UCS
n	goal	no	avoidance	CS, absence of n UCS
n	goal	yes	escape	CS, termination of n UCS
n	n-goal	no	punishment	CS, onset of n UCS
n	n-goal	yes	response-continues-punishment	CS, continuation of n UCS

Note: ir = instrumental response, p = positive, n-goal = negative goal, n = negative. The type of instrumental and classical conditioning that are on the same row are analogous to each other.

sence of the positive or negative reinforcer. The abcissa indicates the passage of time. The arrow shows when the instrumental response is made.

Avoidance Learning: Description. In avoidance learning, the instrumental response, often called the *avoidance response*, causes a negative reinforcer to not occur; that is, the instrumental response omits (avoids) the occurrence of a negative reinforcer that would otherwise take place. The instrumental response usually increases in rate as a result. Figure 3-4 outlines the basic avoidance learning procedure. The dotted line indicates that the negative reinforcer will occur if the instrumental response is not made.

A simple avoidance learning procedure (Sidman, 1962) involves sched-

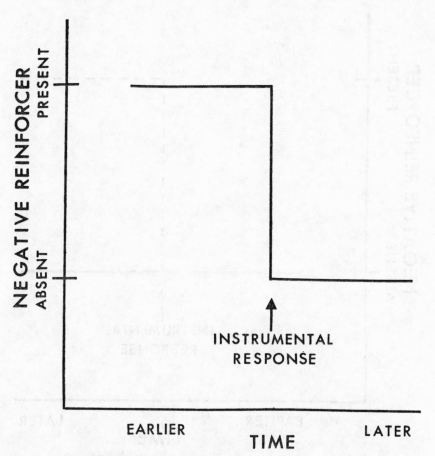

FIGURE 3-3. Outline of procedure for escape learning.

uling brief shocks to occur at constant intervals of time. If a single instrumental response is not made, the brief shock is delivered at the termination of the constant time interval. A single occurrence of the instrumental response within each constant time interval causes the next scheduled shock to be omitted, and has no other consequences. In addition, other responses made within the same constant time interval have no consequences. Rats responding on the indicated schedule with the constant time interval equaling 15 seconds came to make about two responses per constant time interval.

A nonlaboratory example of avoidance learning is putting suntan lotion on before going out on the beach. Applying the lotion is the instrumental

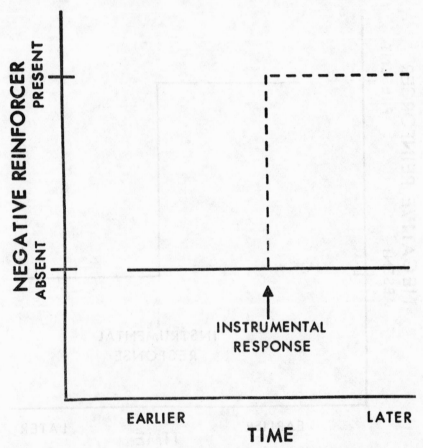

FIGURE 3-4. Outline of procedure for avoidance learning.

response, because this response causes sunburn not to occur. If the instrumental response were not made, sunburn would occur.

In the classification scheme for instrumental conditioning outlined in Table 3-1, avoidance learning is established with a negative reinforcer, the instrumental response causes a goal stimulus to occur, and the reinforcer is not present before the execution of the instrumental response. Absence of the negative reinforcer, that is, no particular event, is the goal stimulus. This stimulus is more likely to be approached and continued to be perceived than the negative reinforcer that would occur if the instrumental response were not made.

In avoidance learning the instrumental response increases in rate, which supports the conclusion that instrumental responses tend to increase in rate when they cause goal stimuli to occur. The explanation of avoidance learning by image theory is essentially identical with the explanation of other types of instrumental conditioning in which the instrumental response causes a goal stimulus to occur.

Because execution of the avoidance response results in the absence of a negative reinforcer, and because failure to perform the avoidance response results in the occurrence of a negative reinforcer, it is clear that the stimulus produced by the avoidance response is paired with the absence of a negative reinforcer. Avoidance learning is therefore analogous to the type of classical conditioning in which a CS is paired with the absence of a negative UCS. Such a CS should be approached and continued to be perceived. Therefore, an animal should bring about and maintain the temporary brain event corresponding to this CS. Because the stimulus produced by the avoidance response is analogous to a CS paired with the absence of a negative UCS, it follows that an animal should attempt to bring about the temporary brain event produced by the instrumental response; that is, it should try to bring about the stimulus produced by this response. (And if an animal were successful in bringing about the stimulus produced by the instrumental response, as image theory assumes, this response would occur, the result to be explained.)

Unsignalled and Signalled Avoidance Learning. Two kinds of avoidance learning, unsignalled and signalled, are frequently studied. In unsignalled avoidance learning, shock is delivered only on the basis of time and response considerations, as follows: (a) If the last event to occur was a shock rather than the instrumental response, the next shock is scheduled to be delivered after a constant time interval since the previous shock occurred, for example, 5 seconds. This time interval is called the *shock-shock interval;* (b) If the last event to occur was a shock, and the instrumental response occurs prior to the elapsing of the shock-shock interval, the shock next scheduled to occur is omitted (avoided); (c) If the last event to occur was the instrumental response rather than a shock, the next shock is scheduled to be delivered after a constant time interval since the previous instrumental response occurred, for example, 10 seconds. This time interval is the *response-shock interval;* and (d) If the last event to occur was an instrumental response, and if the next instrumental response occurs prior to the elapsing of the response-shock interval, the shock next scheduled to occur is omitted (avoided). Theoretically, therefore, all shocks could be omitted by always making an avoidance response prior to the termination of the response-shock interval.

An avoidance response often employed is the bar-press response. An animal, frequently a rat, is placed in a chamber. It receives the next shock scheduled to be delivered by the shock-shock and response-shock schedules in effect unless it responds sufficiently soon after the last shock or the last response. The free responding procedure is employed, and the animal is continuously permitted to respond, as in the typical procedure for the instrumental conditioning of bar pressing and key pecking. This procedure usually results in an increase in the rate of the instrumental response. In addition, as training continues the proportion of shocks received decreases (Sidman, 1966).

A signalled avoidance learning procedure is also frequently employed. In signalled avoidance learning, a neutral stimulus is delivered shortly before a negative reinforcer is scheduled to occur, and therefore may function as a signal that the negative reinforcer is forthcoming unless the instrumental response is made.

A signalled avoidance learning procedure is fairly complex. We can illustrate it using a wheel-turning response as the instrumental response. An animal, usually a rat, is placed inside a wheel that is in an upright position, as in Figure 3-5. The animal cannot climb the inside walls of the wheel, so it remains at or close to the bottom of the wheel. By walking or running (at or close to the bottom of the wheel) the animal can make the wheel rotate. The instrumental response is defined as a turn of the wheel to a certain extent, for example, one complete revolution of the wheel. While the animal is in the wheel, the stimulus that signals shock, called the *warning stimulus,* is presented. Onset of the shock is scheduled to occur at a constant time interval past onset of the warning stimulus, say, 10 seconds. Execution of the instrumental response while the warning stimulus is on omits the shock that would otherwise occur at this constant time interval. In addition, making the instrumental response while the warning stimulus is on terminates the warning stimulus, which typically otherwise remains on until at least the moment of shock onset. Sometimes the shock employed is brief and/or cannot be escaped from. Each presentation of the warning stimulus constitutes a trial, and the subject remains in the wheel over trials.

This procedure results in an increase in the rate of the instrumental response. For example, Bolles, Stokes, and Younger (1966) found that rats avoided shock on about 90 percent of trials 80 to 100.

Avoidance Learning: Analysis. It has not always been clear that the instrumental response in avoidance learning increases in rate because it causes the omission of the negative reinforcer to occur, partly because

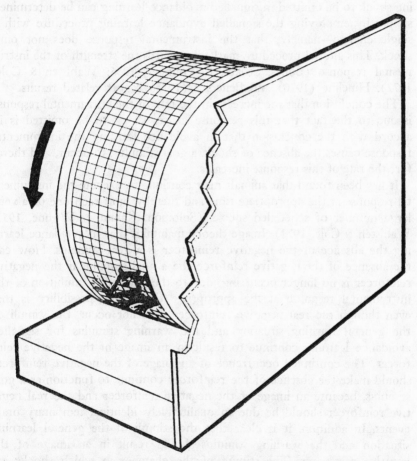

FIGURE 3-5. Wheel-turning apparatus. (Millenson, J. .R., Principles of Behavioral Analysis, Copyright 1967. Adapted by permission of The Macmillan Co.)

termination of the warning stimulus by the instrumental response has been considered to be mostly responsible for this increase. Termination of the warning stimulus by the instrumental response does contribute to signalled avoidance learning (Chapter 5). But we can also say that the instrumental response in avoidance learning increases in rate because this response causes the omission of shock that would otherwise occur.

In unsignalled avoidance learning, there is no warning stimulus. Therefore, an increase in the rate of the instrumental response in unsignalled avoidance learning probably occurs because the instrumental response causes shock to be omitted. The effect of the instrumental response causing shock to be omitted in signalled avoidance learning can be determined simply by employing the signalled avoidance learning procedure with a single change—namely, that the instrumental response does not omit shock. This altered procedure markedly retards the strength of the instrumental response (Bolles, Stokes, & Younger, 1966; Wahlsten & Cole, 1972). Hineline (1970) and Benedict (1975) report related results.

The conclusion that the increase in the rate of the instrumental response is due to the fact that this response causes shock to be omitted is in accord with the conclusion that in avoidance learning the instrumental response causes the absence of shock, a goal stimulus, to occur, and therefore the rate of this response increases.

It has been found that animals may continue to execute the instrumental response at the appropriate time and thereby omit each one of a very large number of scheduled shocks (Solomon, Kamin, & Wynne, 1953; Wahlsten & Cole, 1972). Image theory maintains that in avoidance learning the absence of the negative reinforcer is a goal stimulus. How can the absence of the negative reinforcer be a goal stimulus if the negative reinforcer is no longer occurring, due to the continued exhibition of the instrumental response at the appropriate time? One possibility is that even though the real negative reinforcer does not occur, the stimuli of the general learning situation and the warning stimulus for signalled avoidance learning continue to result in an image of the negative reinforcer. The continued occurrence of an image of the negative reinforcer should make the absence of the reinforcer continue to function as a goal stimulus, because an image of the negative reinforcer and the real negative reinforcer should be due to qualitatively identical temporary brain events. In addition, it is clear that the stimuli of the general learning situation and the warning stimulus should result in an image of the negative reinforcer. The stimuli of the chamber in which shocks are delivered are CSs, and therefore presumably result in an image of shock. Also, at least early in training, the warning stimulus often precedes the delivery of shock and should therefore also result in an image of shock. In addition, in respect to unsignalled avoidance learning, stimuli correlated with the shock-shock and response-shock time intervals should result in images of the shock; therefore, stimuli correlated with similar, briefer time durations probably also result in images of shock.

The stimulus of the absence of shock, that is, no particular event, in avoidance learning should be a stronger goal stimulus when the negative reinforcer is occurring than when only an image of the negative reinforcer is occurring. A stronger goal stimulus means a stimulus that is more likely to be approached and continued to be perceived. In addition, a stronger goal stimulus should establish a stronger instrumental response, an assumption we will discuss later. A relatively vivid image of a stimulus is due to a temporary brain event that should be quantitatively more similar to the temporary brain event produced by the corresponding real stimulus than the temporary brain event for a relatively faint image of a stimulus. It follows that if, in avoidance learning, the vividness of the image of the negative reinforcer is increased, the rate of the instrumental response should also increase.

Experimental results support this expectation. In one study (Rescorla & LoLordo, 1965), animals were initially given unsignalled avoidance learning training. Then a CS that was paired with shock was presented while the unsignalled avoidance learning procedure remained in effect. They found that the CS for shock increased the rate of the avoidance-trained response. It was indicated above that an increase in the vividness of the image of shock should increase the rate of the avoidance-trained response. Presenting a CS paired with shock should increase the vividness of the image of shock, and therefore such a CS should increase the rate of the avoidance-trained response, which explains the obtained result.

A CS paired with the absence of shock should result in an image of the absence of shock. Such a CS presented while an animal responds on an unsignalled avoidance learning schedule therefore probably decreases the vividness of the image of shock. A decrease in the rate of the avoidance-trained response should therefore occur, a result that has, in fact, been obtained (Rescorla, 1966; Weisman & Litner, 1969).

The stimulus produced by the instrumental response in avoidance learning is paired with the absence of shock. Since a CS paired with the absence of shock decreases the rate of the instrumental response in unsignalled avoidance learning, the stimulus produced by the instrumental response in unsignalled avoidance learning—that is, execution of the instrumental response itself—should also decrease the rate of the instrumental response in unsignalled avoidance learning. The expectation is, in other words, that a single instrumental response in unsignalled avoidance learning should be relatively unlikely to be quickly followed by subsequent avoidance-trained responses. This result is frequently obtained, particularly with extended training (Sidman, 1966).

One other study (Rescorla, 1968) shows that the role of the stimulus produced by the instrumental response is involved with an understanding of avoidance learning. A typical unsignalled avoidance learning procedure was used, except that the instrumental response caused a brief neutral stimulus to occur as well as a scheduled shock to be omitted. Subsequently, the brief neutral stimulus was no longer regularly presented directly after execution of the instrumental response; instead, it was presented at various times while animals continued to perform on the unsignalled avoidance learning task. The finding of this subsequent stage was that the brief neutral stimulus decreased the rate of the instrumental response when it was on and shortly after its termination. The brief neutral stimulus in the first stage of this study was paired with the absence of shock, because it came on when the instrumental response was made, and because the instrumental response itself is, in general, paired with the absence of shock. A CS paired with the absence of shock decreases the rate of the instrumental response in unsignalled avoidance learning; therefore, the reason that the brief neutral stimulus decreased the rate of the instrumental response when it was on and shortly after its termination was probably that the brief neutral stimulus functioned as a CS paired with the absence of shock. Because in the first stage this brief neutral stimulus occurred at the same time that the instrumental response did, it follows that the stimulus produced by the instrumental response should have also functioned like a CS paired with the absence of shock, as has been assumed all along.

Response-Continues-Reward Learning. Another type of instrumental conditioning is *response-continues-reward learning*. In this type of instrumental conditioning, the instrumental response causes a positive reinforcer to be continued; otherwise the positive reinforcer terminates. The rate of the instrumental response should increase in response-continues-reward learning; this was found by D'Andrea (1971). Figure 3-6 outlines the basic procedure for response-continues-reward learning. The dotted line indicates that the positive reinforcer will be terminated if the instrumental response is not made.

A nonlaboratory example of response-continues-reward learning would be an actor learning to milk an audience for additional applause by behaving as if he appreciates the applause he initially receives. This response my be acquired because it causes the continuation of applause to occur, the applause otherwise being terminated.

The classification scheme for instrumental conditioning outlined in Table 3-1 shows that response-continues-reward learning is established with a positive reinforcer; the instrumental response causes a goal stimulus to occur; and the reinforcer is present prior to execution of the instrumental response. Presence of the positive reinforcer is the goal stimulus. This stimulus is more likely to be approached and continued to be perceived than the stimulus of no particular event that would be present if the instrumental response were not made.

The fact that in response-continues-reward learning, the instrumental

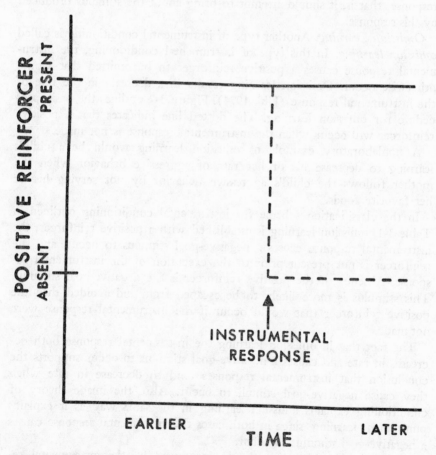

FIGURE 3-6. Outline of procedure for response-continues-reward learning.

response both increases in rate and causes a goal stimulus to occur supports the conclusion that instrumental responses tend to increase in rate when they cause goal stimuli to occur. Also, the explanation of instrumental conditioning in which the instrumental response causes a goal stimulus to occur applies to response-continues-reward learning.

The stimulus produced by a response that causes a positive reinforcer to be continued is paired with the continuation of a positive reinforcer. This stimulus is therefore analogous to a CS that is paired with the continuation of a positive UCS. A CS paired with the continuation of a positive UCS is probably approached and continued to be perceived, so an animal should attempt to bring about and maintain the temporary brain event corresponding to the stimulus produced by the instrumental response; that is, it should attempt to bring about the stimulus produced by this response.

Omission Learning. Another type of instrumental conditioning is called *omission learning.* In this type of instrumental conditioning, the instrumental response causes a positive reinforcer to be omitted that would otherwise occur. Omission learning results in a decrease in the rate of the instrumental response (Uhl, 1974). Figure 3-7 outlines the basic procedure for omission learning. The dotted line indicates that a positive reinforcer will occur when the instrumental response is not made.

A nonlaboratory example of omission learning would be a child's learning to decrease his or her rate of aggressive behavior when the mother follows the child's aggressive behavior by not serving his or her favorite foods.

In the classification scheme for instrumental conditioning outlined in Table 3-1, omission learning is established with a positive reinforcer; the instrumental response causes a negative-goal stimulus to occur; and the reinforcer is not present prior to the execution of the instrumental response. Absence of the positive reinforcer is the negative-goal stimulus. This stimulus is more likely to be escaped from and avoided than the positive reinforcer that would occur if the instrumental response were not made.

The fact that in omission learning the instrumental response both decreases in rate and causes a negative-goal stimulus to occur supports the conclusion that instrumental responses tend to decrease in rate when they cause negative-goal stimuli to occur. Also, the image theory of conditioning explains omission learning in the same way as it explains punishment learning, since in both cases the instrumental response causes a negative-goal stimulus to occur.

In omission learning the stimulus produced by the instrumental response is paired with the absence of a positive reinforcer. The stimulus produced by this response is therefore analogous to a CS paired with the absence of a positive reinforcer. Such a CS is escaped from and avoided. Therefore, an animal should attempt to terminate and avoid the brain event corresponding to the stimulus produced by the instrumental response in omission learning. Therefore, it should attempt to avoid bringing about the stimulus produced by this instrumental response, as assumed by image theory. (And if an animal were successful in avoiding bringing about the stimulus produced by this instrumental response, as also assumed by image theory, this response would not occur, the result to be accounted for.)

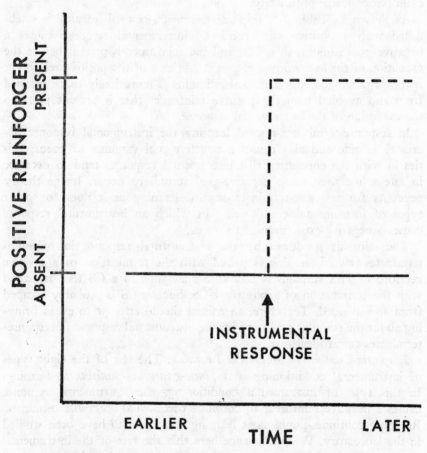

FIGURE 3-7. Outline of procedure for omission learning.

Response-Terminates-Reward Learning. Another type of instrumental conditioning is *response-terminates-reward* learning. In this type of instrumental conditioning, the instrumental response causes a positive reinforcer to be terminated that would otherwise continue to occur. Response-terminates-reward learning seems not to have been studied in the laboratory. We will assume here that the rate of the instrumental response decreases in response-terminates-reward learning; an animal would be relatively unlikely to exhibit the response that terminates access to a positive reinforcer. Figure 3-8 outlines the basic procedure for response-terminates-reward learning. A nonlaboratory example is a mother's decreasing the rate of an undesired response by her child through taking away a toy the child has been playing with after the child responds inappropriately.

As shown in Table 3-1, response-terminates-reward learning is established with a positive reinforcer; the instrumental response causes a negative-goal stimulus to occur; and the reinforcer is present before the execution of the instrumental response. Absence of the positive reinforcer is the negative-goal stimulus. This stimulus is more likely to be escaped from and avoided than the positive reinforcer that is present prior to the execution of the instrumental response.

In response-terminates-reward learning the instrumental response decreases in rate and also causes a negative-goal stimulus to occur; this ties in with the conclusion that instrumental responses tend to decrease in rate when they cause negative-goal stimuli to occur. Image theory accounts for response-terminates-reward learning as it does for other types of instrumental conditioning in which an instrumental response causes a negative-goal stimulus to occur.

The stimulus produced by the instrumental response in response-terminates-reward learning is paired with the termination of a positive reinforcer. This stimulus is therefore analogous to a CS that is paired with the termination of a positive UCS. Such a CS is probably escaped from and avoided. Therefore, an animal should attempt to avoid bringing about the stimulus produced by the instrumental response in response-terminates-reward learning.

Response-Continues-Punishment Learning. The last of the eight types of instrumental conditioning is *response-continues-punishment* learning. In this type of instrumental conditioning, the instrumental response causes a negative reinforcer to continue that would otherwise terminate. Response-continues-punishment learning seems not to have been studied in the laboratory. We will assume here that the rate of the instrumental response decreases in response-continues-punishment learning; an animal would be relatively unlikely to exhibit the response that prolonged the occurrence of a negative reinforcer. Figure 3-9 outlines the basic procedure for response-continues-punishment learning. The dotted line indicates that the negative reinforcer is terminated if the instrumental response is not made. A nonlaboratory example of response-continues-punishment learning would be a person's learning not to argue with someone who is criticizing him or her. When criticism terminates relatively quickly if the person does not argue back, response-continues-punishment learning should be relatively likely to occur; that is, the person will be apt to acquire the response of not arguing back.

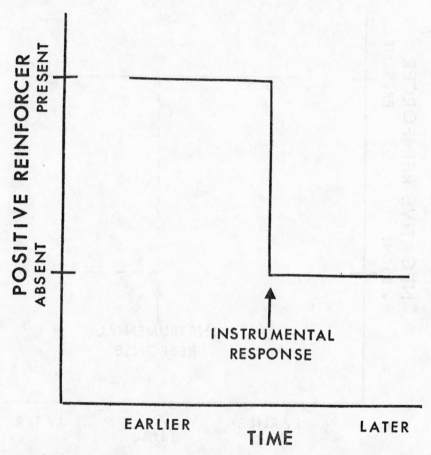

FIGURE 3-8. Outline of procedure for response-terminates-reward learning.

As shown in Table 3-1, response-continues-punishment learning is established with a negative reinforcer; the instrumental response causes a negative-goal stimulus to occur; and the reinforcer is present prior to the execution of the instrumental response. Presence of the negative reinforcer is the negative-goal stimulus. This stimulus is more likely to be escaped from and avoided than the stimulus of no particular event that would occur if the instrumental response were not made.

The instrumental response in response-continues-punishment learning causes a negative-goal-stimulus to occur, and therefore it decreases in rate. Explanation of this learning is essentially identical to the accounts

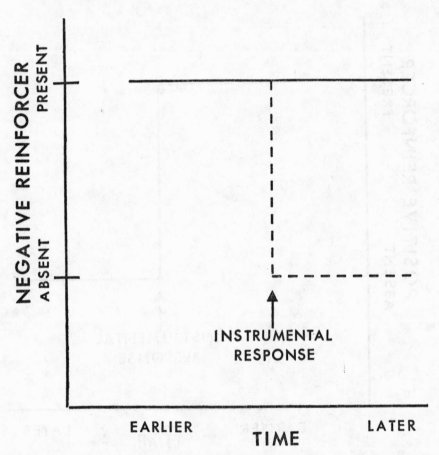

FIGURE 3-9. Outline of procedure for response-continues-punishment learning.

of the other types of instrumental conditioning in which the instrumental response causes a negative-goal stimulus to occur.

The stimulus produced by the instrumental response in response-continues-punishment learning is paired with the continuation of a negative reinforcer. The stimulus produced by the instrumental response is therefore analogous to a CS that is paired with the continuation of a negative UCS. We assume that such a CS is escaped from and avoided. Therefore, an animal should attempt to avoid bringing about the stimulus produced by the instrumental response in response-continues-punishment learning.

Physical and Temporal Proximity of Stimuli. The outcome of a reinforcer and no particular event occurring in relatively close physical and temporal proximity on the response to no particular event is of critical importance for instrumental conditioning. In instrumental conditioning the reinforcer and no particular event alternate in time in the same apparatus, that is, in relatively close physical and temporal proximity. If a positive reinforcer (UCS) occurs in sufficiently close physical and temporal proximity to no particular event, then no particular event tends to be escaped from and avoided. The evidence for this is that animals escape from no particular event when it occurs in relatively close physical and temporal proximity to a positive reinforcer, when escape is possible; and also that no particular event elicits aggressive behavior when it occurs in relatively close physical and temporal proximity to a positive reinforcer, when escape is not possible, and when a target for aggressive behavior is provided. Analogously, if a negative reinforcer (UCS) occurs in sufficiently close physical and temporal proximity to no particular event, then no particular event tends to be approached and continued to be perceived. It follows that in instrumental conditioning no particular event should tend to be either approached and continued to be perceived or escaped from and avoided, depending on the sign of the reinforcer.

The inference that in instrumental conditioning no particular event tends to be either approached and continued to be perceived or escaped from and avoided is critically involved with the analysis of the avoidance, escape, omission, and response-terminates-reward types of instrumental conditioning. In these types of instrumental conditioning, the stimulus produced by the instrumental response is followed by the stimulus of no particular event. The image theory of conditioning assumes that an animal should attempt to bring about or attempt to avoid bringing about the stimulus produced by the instrumental response. This assumption is supported by the finding that a CS that is analogous to the stimulus produced by the instrumental response is approached and continued to be perceived or escaped from and avoided. But the stimulus produced by the instrumental response for the avoidance, escape, omission, and response-terminates-reward learning types of instrumental conditioning can only be analogous to a CS that is approached and continued to be perceived or escaped from and avoided, if no particular event is approached and continued to be perceived or escaped from and avoided.

Specific Response versus Responses Other than the Specific Response. It is possible to account for all eight types of instrumental conditioning in terms of pairings between the stimuli produced by the set of responses that is not the instrumental response and a second stimulus. For example, in respect to reward learning, the stimuli produced by responses other than the instrumental response are all paired with the absence of the positive reinforcer, that is, no particular event. It is possible that the stimuli produced by many of these responses would become associated through classical conditioning with the absence of the positive reinforcer; these responses are thereby not exhibited, so that the rate with which the instrumental response is exhibited will be raised.

This explanation accounts for the result that the instrumental response in reward learning increases in rate, but nonetheless does not seem to be adequate. It leads to the prediction that in reward learning the rates of responses that are not similar in topography to the instrumental response will also increase, these responses being the ones that have not yet been exhibited and followed by the absence of the positive reinforcer. It also leads to the prediction that the rate of acquisition of reward learning should be relatively slow, because execution of the instrumental response would be dependent on the acquisition of associations between numerous responses and the absence of the positive reinforcer. Neither of these predictions is correct. These or analogous considerations apply to all the previously described types of instrumental conditioning.

Empirical evidence also does not support the idea that instrumental conditioning is due to a change in rate in the set of responses that is not the instrumental response. Dunham (1971) measured the proportion of time several responses were likely to occur. When one of these responses was followed by shock, that is, when punishment learning of this response was carried out, the probability of this response decreased; but the probability of the other responses increased only some time later. This finding shows that the decrease in the probability of the punished response was not due to an increase in the probability of the other responses that were measured. In a second study (Dunham, 1972), drinking was followed by shock. The probability of drinking decreased, and the probability of running in a wheel increased. But an equivalent increase in the probability of running in the wheel was produced when access to water was blocked by removing the water tube. Therefore, it does not appear that the increase in the probability of running in the wheel was responsible for decreasing the probability of drinking.

In respect to omission learning, Uhl (1974) observed that omission-trained rats performed much the same responses during periods in which food was not occurring. These responses included being positioned at the dipper housing for delivery of food, bobbing the head back and forth, and frequently licking and gnawing at the dipper housing. Therefore, the rats did not acquire a wide and idiosyncratic variety of responses, as would be expected if a decrease in the rate of the instrumental response occurred as a result of the set of other responses being followed by food.

Reinforcer Randomly Presented in Relation to Instrumental Response. Each of the eight types of instrumental conditioning described above corresponds to a different type of classical conditioning. Randomly presenting a UCS in relation to a CS retards acquisition of a CR when typical (CS-UCS) pairings between the same CS and UCS are subsequently delivered. We might expect that if a reinforcer were randomly presented in relation to the occurrence of a single clearly defined response, then subsequent straightforward instrumental conditioning involving this reinforcer and response would be retarded. This prediction makes sense because the reinforcer is analogous to a UCS; the stimulus produced by a single clearly defined response is analogous to a CS; and randomly presenting a reinforcer in relation to the occurrence of the response is analogous to the UCS being randomly presented in relation to a CS. However, this prediction may not have been tested.

Other studies (for example, Seligman & Maier, 1967) involve a large number of undefined responses that do not predict the occurrence of a reinforcer. Thus, they should not always yield results similar to the expected effect of a single clearly defined response occurring in a random relation to a reinforcer, which is what is found (Glazer & Weiss, 1976a, 1976b).

Acquisition and Extinction

We will now consider the effects of various factors on instrumental conditioning. Since reward learning has been most frequently studied, much of the following material will be concerned with this type of instrumental conditioning.

Measures of Instrumental Response Strength. The strength of a learned response is a measure of responding that is thought to be indicative of learning. For instrumental conditioning of bar pressing and key pecking, the instrumental response strength measure usually employed is rate of responding. A frequency count of the number of responses occurring in a certain time period is divided by the duration of this time period. The rate (speed) of responding is also frequently obtained for both reward-trained and escape-trained runway learning, although often the results are reported in terms of the time taken (inverse of rate) to traverse the runway. Rate measures are essentially probability measures, because as response rate increases, the probability of the response occurring per unit of time also increases.

The latency of an instrumental response is usually taken as the length of time elapsing before the start of the response. Latency measures are frequently employed in studies of runway learning. Runways are often constructed with a door blocking the start area—the place where an animal is set at the beginning of a trial—from the remainder of the apparatus. The latency of the runway response is often considered the time elapsed between opening the door that permits entrance into the rest of the runway, and the moment an animal moves past this door.

Training and Instrumental Response Strength. As training continues, instrumental response strength increases. With additional training, instrumental response strength levels off, that is, becomes asymptotic. Figure 3-10 shows the mean speeds in a runway of two groups of rats increasing and then leveling off in acquisition. The "high deprivation" group was more deprived of food than the "low deprivation" group. The data of Figure 3-10 support the conclusion that asymptotic performance is not generally due to animals reaching their physical capacity to respond at maximum strength. The low deprivation group exhibited a lower asymptotic running speed than the high deprivation group, but physically it would have been capable of responding about as quickly as the high deprivation group since animals were randomly assigned to these two groups.

Acquisition may be measured with a record of responding and reinforcement occurrence called the *cumulative curve*. Skinner (1938) kept food-deprived rats in a chamber. A bar was present, and each bar press response caused food to occur. The first bar press "happened" to occur, and subsequent bar presses were probably influenced by prior pairings between the bar press response and food. Figure 3-11 depicts acquisition of bar pressing for five rats in the form of cumulative curves.

The abcissa for a cumulative curve indicates the time elapsed while an animal is in a conditioning situation. The ordinate indicates the total number of responses made in the time interval shown by the abcissa. Consider the cumulative curve at the top right of Figure 3-11. The rat made its first bar press at about 13 minutes after being placed in the chamber and its second bar press at about 24 minutes; thereafter, it responded at a faster rate. At the end of 30 minutes it had made about 13 responses. The cumulative curves all indicate that the rate of bar pressing increased with an increase in the number of pairings between the bar press response and food.

Cumulative curves are typically used to measure reward learning of bar pressing and key pecking. Automated equipment transforms each response into an increment along the ordinate of the cumulative curve at the moment it occurs.

The basic effect of training in instrumental conditioning is to increase the strength of the instrumental response. However, little is understood about why instrumental conditioning improves with practice, which is also true for classical conditioning. In instrumental conditioning, continued training may increase the strength of the acquired associations between the stimuli preceding the instrumental response and the stimulus

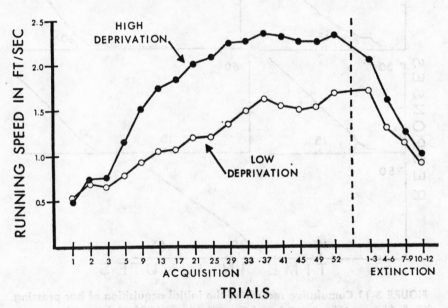

FIGURE 3-10. Acquisition and extinction of runway learning. (Adapted from Barry, 1958.)

produced by this response, and between the stimulus produced by this response and the goal or negative-goal stimulus; but this is a vague notion. CR strength may increase as training continues, because the increase in attention to the CS that should result from classical conditioning may facilitate this conditioning, hence further increase attention to the CS, thereby further facilitate this conditioning, and so on. The outcome thus is a gradual increase in CR strength. According to image theory, instrumental conditioning involves the occurrence of a classically conditioned association between the stimulus produced by the instrumental response and the goal or negative-goal stimulus it causes to occur. It follows that an increase in attention to the stimulus produced by the instrumental response may similarly result in an increase in the strength of the instrumentally conditioned response as training continues.

Another consideration involves the well-known result that a decrease in the delay of a goal or negative-goal stimulus increases the strength of an instrumental response. Performing instrumental responses at a

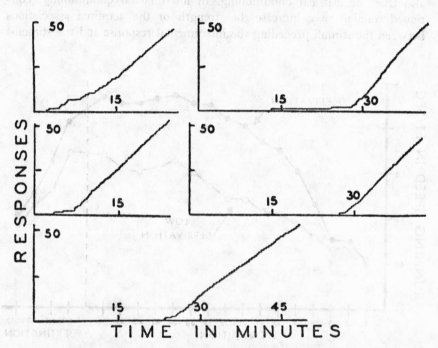

FIGURE 3-11.Cumulative records of the initial acquisition of bar pressing. (B. F. Skinner, The Behavior of Organisms, © 1938. Adapted by permission of Prentice-Hall, Inc., Englewood Cliffs, New Jersey.)

slightly faster rate will necessarily decrease the average delay of a goal or negative-goal stimulus. For example, traversing a runway at a faster rate will result in less of a delay in time between initiation of the traversal response and receipt of the goal stimulus at the end of the runway. Thus, performing instrumental responses at a faster rate should result in a stronger instrumental response; that is, the faster rate of responding should be acquired. Once an instrumental response is performed at a faster rate, it may happen by chance to be subsequently performed at a still faster rate, the consequence being that this still faster rate of responding is acquired; the outcome would thus be a progressive increase in the rate of the instrumental response as training continues, the result to be explained.

The components of the instrumental response as a function of training have also been analyzed. Cicala (1961) and Kintsch (1961) systematically observed the frequency with which competing responses—for example, rearing, sniffing, grooming, and exploratory movement—occurred during acquisition of a reward-trained traversal response by rats. They found that frequency decreased over trials. Reduction in the frequency of competing responses will normally result in an increase in the rate of an instrumental response. Both Cicala and Kintsch also found that with continued training the forward locomotor aspect of the runway response was executed more quickly as well.

Relatedness of Instrumental Response Strength Measures. Rate and latency measures of instrumental response strength are related partly because they are similarly affected by extent of training. These measures are not perfectly related, however. For example, the correlation between the speed and latency measures of a reward-trained runway response was only .45 (Hall & Kobrick, 1952). The fact that measures of instrumental response strength are not perfectly related is one indication that learning cannot be measured directly.

The latency of the instrumental response is generally negatively related to the rate of the instrumental response and to all subportions of the instrumental response. The latency of the instrumental response should therefore be regarded as a measure of the strength of the instrumental response. But the latency of the peak amplitude CR is positively related to the amplitude and probability measures of CR strength, in the sense that all three measures increase with continued classical conditioning. In addition, the latency of the peak amplitude CR may vary independently of the amplitude of the CR. These considerations indicate that the latency of the peak amplitude CR should not be regarded as a measure of CR strength.

Extinction. Extinction in instrumental conditioning will be defined here as not presenting the reinforcer for an instrumental response after this response has been conditioned. Extinction generally decreases the strength of reward-trained and escape-trained responses relatively rapidly. Figure 3-10 indicates the effect of extinction on the speed of a reward-trained runway response. Extinction—that is, omitting the positive reinforcer at the end of the runway on all trials—resulted in a gradual decline in the speed of the runway response.

According to image theory, in extinction of reward learning the stimulus produced by the instrumental response becomes associated through classical conditioning with the stimulus of the absence of the positive reinforcer, that is, no particular event. Becasue an animal should not behave so as to increase the vividness of the image of no particular event, an acquired association between the stimulus produced by a reward-trained response and no particular event should result in a decline in the strength of this response.

It is clear that extinction of punishment- and avoidance-trained responses is not always relatively rapid. Extinction of a punishment-trained response did not occur when a relatively intense shock was employed in acquisition (Appel, 1961; Azrin, 1960). For example, in Appel's study the rate of the punishment-trained response did not increase over 400 hours of extinction. Extinction of an avoidance-trained response resulted in the avoidance response continuing to be made hundreds of times (Solomon, Kamin, & Wynne, 1953; Wahlsten & Cole, 1972).

Equivalent of Extinction Approach. The term, *equivalent of extinction approach,* will refer to a theory of why learned responses are relatively resistant to extinction, including the responses just mentioned.

The equivalent of extinction approach assumes that a decrease in the strength of a learned response will usually not occur unless the S_1-reinforcer or S_1-S_2 (S_2 equals a neutral stimulus) pairings that result in conditioning are in extinction followed by pairings between S_1 and a stimulus relatively different from the reinforcer or S_2. Each time this condition is met in extinction, an equivalent of extinction occurs. Also, the rate of decrease in the strength of the learned response in extinction is usually determined by the number of equivalents of extinction that occur; the greater the number of equivalents of extinction taking place, the greater the decline in the strength of the learned response.

Let us discuss first the equivalent of extinction approach in respect to extinction of reward learning. The S_1-reinforcer pairings resulting in conditioning are pairings between the stimulus produced by the instrumental response and the positive reinforcer that the instrumental response causes to occur. In extinction of reward learning, the stimulus produced by the instrumental response, S_1, is followed by the absence of the positive reinforcer, that is, no particular event, a stimulus relatively different from the reinforcer that occurred in training. An equivalent of extinction therefore occurs. Pairings between the stimulus produced by the instrumental response and no particular event should result in a decrease in the strength of the instrumental response. Thus, an equivalent of extinction should result in a decrease in the strength of the instrumental response, as the equivalent of extinction approach assumes.

The equivalent of extinction approach predicts that extinction of reward learning will occur relatively quickly. In extinction of reward learning, each execution of the instrumental response is followed by no particular event. Therefore, each instrumental response made in extinction results in an equivalent of extinction. The equivalent of extinction approach assumes that the rate of decrease in the strength of the learned response in extinction is usually determined by the number of equivalents of extinction that occur. The greater the number of equivalents of extinction taking place, the greater the decline in the strength of the learned response. Because each execution of the instrumental response made in extinction results in an equivalent of extinction, it follows that extinction of reward learning will occur relatively quickly, which it does.

The equivalent of extinction approach explains why punishment learning established with an intense shock is relatively resistant to extinction. Punishment learning is assumed to occur because, in part, the stimulus produced by the instrumental response (S_1) becomes associated through classical conditioning with the negative reinforcer following it. When a sufficiently intense shock is employed in establishing punishment learning, the instrumental response is not likely to occur early in extinction for even a few times, as Appel (1961) and Azrin (1960) found. Because the instrumental response is hardly exhibited at all early in extinction, the stimulus produced by the instrumental response (S_1) cannot be followed by the absence of shock early in extinction. That is, the S_1-reinforcer pairings of acquisition are not replaced by pairings between S_1 and a different kind of stimulus early in extinction. Therefore, equivalents of extinction should not occur early in extinction. Because the rate of decrease in the strength of a learned response in extinction should usually be determined by the number of equivalents of extinction that occur, and because equivalents of extinction will sometimes hardly take place early in extinction of punishment learning, it follows that sometimes little decrease in the strength of a punishment-trained response should ensue as extinction continues, the result to be explained.

The equivalent of extinction approach also helps to explain why avoidance learning can be relatively resistant to extinction. Avoidance learning occurs because, in part, the stimulus produced by the instrumental response (S_1) becomes associated through classical conditioning with the absence of shock (S_2). Because in extinction of avoidance learning the instrumental response, and therefore the stimulus produced by the instrumental response, continues to be followed by the absence of shock, equivalents of extinction should not occur. Because the rate of decrease in the strength of a learned response in extinction should usually be determined by the number of equivalents of extinction that occur, it follows that avoidance learning should be relatively resistant to extinction.

Classical conditioning in which a CS is paired with the absence of a UCS is relatively resistant to extinction. Pairing a CS with the absence of a UCS should result in classical conditioning through an acquired S_1-S_2 association in which S_1 is the CS and S_2 is the absence of the UCS, that is, no particular event. In extinction, the absence of the UCS occurs by definition. Therefore, a CS paired with the absence of the UCS in acquisition continues to be paired with the absence of the UCS in extinction; that is, the S_1-S_2 pairings of acquisition continue in extinction. Thus, equivalents of extinction do not occur. Consequently, classical conditioning in which a CS is paired with the absence of a UCS should be relatively resistant to extinction, which it is.

The similarity in the explanations of the relatively strong resistance to extinction of avoidance learning and classical conditioning in which a CS is paired with the absence of a UCS stems from the fact that both types of learning involve an acquired association between a neutral stimulus and the absence of a reinforcer.

Ratio and Interval Schedules

Ratio and interval schedules of reinforcement are frequently employed in conditioning research. They result in reward learning. However, they do not deliver the positive reinforcer following each performance of the instrumental response. Because the positive reinforcer is delivered only after more than a single response is made, they are called *partial reinforcement schedules*. They are frequently used with the bar press and key peck instrumental responses. A *continuous reinforcement schedule* delivers the reinforcer after each instrumental response is made. It is the type of reinforcement schedule that has been discussed up until now.

Ratio and Interval Schedules. The fixed-ratio (FR) schedule of reinforcement requires that a constant number of responses be made since the previous delivery of the positive reinforcer for the next delivery of the positive reinforcer to occur. First, usually bar pressing or key pecking is established with a continuous reinforcement schedule. Then the number of responses the animal must make to cause the reinforcer to occur is gradually increased, from 1 response per reinforcement, let us say, to 2 responses per reinforcement to 5 responses per reinforcement, and so on. In this manner an animal can be trained to execute a relatively large number of responses per reinforcement.

The animal usually remains in the apparatus and is free to respond on an FR schedule over a fairly long time period, for example, 20 minutes. As an animal continues to respond on an FR schedule, it comes to exhibit a fairly typical pattern of responding. For much of the time between adjacent deliveries of the reinforcer, it responds at a relatively fast and steady rate; however, it tends not to respond immediately after receiving the reinforcer. This pause, which is called the *post-reinforcement pause*, is not due to time taken to consume the reinforcer or to a temporary satiation effect (Chapter 6).

Variable-ratio (VR) schedules are similar to FR schedules in that making a certain number of responses since the previous reinforcement occurred causes the next reinforcement to take place. Unlike FR schedules, however, the number of responses required since the previous reinforcement occurred for the next reinforcement to be delivered varies. For a VR X schedule, the mean number of responses required for a reinforcement equals X.

Like FR schedules, VR schedules tend to result in a relatively fast rate of responding. Unlike FR schedules, the rate of responding on VR schedules is normally steady; a post-reinforcement pause does not usually occur.

Both FR and VR schedules are partial reinforcement schedules because the reinforcer occurs after only a proportion of the responses made.

Interval Schedules. The fixed-interval (FI) schedule of reinforcement delivers the reinforcer following the first response made after a constant (fixed) interval of time has elapsed since the last delivery of the reinforcer. For example, a FI 1 (minute) schedule delivers the reinforcer following the first response made after 1 minute past the time the last delivery of the reinforcer occurred. Responses made before the elapsing of the fixed interval of time since the last reinforcement occurred do not alter the probability or the time of subsequent reinforcements in any way. Suppose an animal responding on a FI 1 schedule waits 2 minutes to make its first response after receiving the last reinforcement. Another reinforcement will then be delivered, and the next reinforcement will not be delivered until the first response made after 1 minute since this last reinforcement. As with ratio schedules, FI schedules are generally introduced after preliminary training with a continuous reinforcement schedule. Animals typically remain in the apparatus and are free to respond.

As an animal continues to respond on a FI schedule, it comes to exhibit a relatively typical pattern of responding. Responding tends not to occur immediately after receiving a reinforcement. Then, as the FI interval elapses, the rate of responding tends to gradually accelerate. Close in time to the complete elapsing of the FI interval, the rate of responding tends to be relatively fast. Thus, usually a number of responses are made before the elapsing of the FI interval, even though these responses have no scheduled consequences.

For a variable-interval X (VI X) schedule, the first response made after a variable length of time has elapsed since the last reinforcement causes the next reinforcement to take place; the mean of these variable time intervals equals X. Otherwise VI X schedules are identical to FI schedules. A typical VI schedule results in responding at a moderate and fairly constant rate between reinforcements.

The FI and VI schedules are partial reinforcement schedules because the reinforcer occurs after only a proportion of the responses made.

Time Relationships between Instrumental Response and Stimulus It Causes to Occur

Pseudoconditioning. It is possible that the strength of an instrumental response is affected by the reinforcer independently of response-stimulus pairings. Moreover, this possibility is not always remote. Consider punishment learning in which a rat learns to remain on a platform. We know that response-independent shock can result in a crouching or less severe form of suppression CR by the stimuli of the general learning situation. If instrumental conditioning is responsible for the learned response of remaining on a platform, then this response must result from the stepping off response that causes shock to occur. However, an animal's remaining on a platform may be the result of a crouching or suppression CR which effectively interferes with stepping off the platform. The learned response of remaining on a platform indicates that a pseudoconditioning control is required to determine that instrumental conditioning has occurred, that is, to determine that an effect on a response is due to this response causing a stimulus to occur. One pseudoconditioning procedure for instrumental conditioning consists of delivering the reinforcer independently of responding the same number of times and in the same temporal pattern as the reinforcer was delivered in the instrumental conditioning procedure. Another procedure that functions as a pseudoconditioning control is to arrange for the instrumental response to cause a stimulus to occur, but to deliver this stimulus a relatively long time after the instrumental response is made. Delaying the stimulus that the instrumental response causes to occur impairs acquisition of this response, while permitting effects of the reinforcer to operate that are independent of the effect of response-stimulus pairings. Instrumental conditioning is said to occur when the standard instrumental conditioning treatment results in a stronger instrumental response than a pseudoconditioning treatment. For example, we may say that punishment learning occurs when an instrumental response is stronger when it is immediately followed by shock than when it is followed by shock some time later (Barcik, 1972; Camp, Raymond, & Church, 1967).

Delay of the Stimulus that a Response Causes to Occur. An essential aspect of instrumental conditioning is that the strength of the instrumental response tends to decrease as the time interval separating the execution of the instrumental response from the occurrence of the stimulus this response causes to occur increases. The Barcik and Camp et al. studies, for example, obtained this result. For reward learning, a delay between the instrumental response and the stimulus it causes to occur is referred to as *delay of reinforcement*. Grice (1948) obtained a marked effect of delay of reinforcement. A 0.5 second delay between an instrumental response and the occurrence of a positive reinforcer resulted in twice as many trials being required for rats to attain a criterion of good performance than no delay did. Also, instrumental conditioning of the same response did not occur at all over 700 training trials when the delay of reinforcement was 10.0 seconds.

S_1 will refer to the stimulus produced by an instrumental response and S_2 will refer to the stimulus that this response causes to occur. An increase in the time interval separating the execution of the instrumental response from the onset of the stimulus this response causes to occur is equivalent to an increase in the time interval separating onset of S_1 from onset of S_2. Because an increase in the time interval separating onset of S_1 from onset of S_2 is analogous to an increase in the time interval between CS onset and UCS onset; because an increase in the time interval between CS onset and UCS onset retards trace classical conditioning; and because instrumental conditioning is assumed to result, in part, from a classically conditioned association between S_1 and S_2, it follows that the strength of the instrumental response should decrease as the time interval separating performance of the instrumental response from the occurrence of the stimulus this response causes to occur increases, which it does.

Memory in Instrumental Conditioning. The detrimental effect of an increase in the length of time separating CS onset from UCS onset is interpreted as being due to forgetting of either a CS that has terminated, or the beginning attention-eliciting portion of a CS. Because of the analogue between CS-UCS pairings, and pairings between a stimulus produced by an instrumental response and the stimulus this response causes to occur, it is reasonable to assume that an increase in the length of time separating the stimulus produced by the instrumental response (and therefore the instrumental response itself) from onset of the stimulus this response causes to occur results in greater forgetting of the stimulus produced by this response. This greater forgetting should impair the acquisition of an association between the stimulus produced by the instrumental response and the stimulus this response causes to occur, and thereby should retard the strength of the instrumental response.

The memory approach to the effect of the time interval between CS onset and UCS onset on classical conditioning was supported by the result that the occurrence of stimuli similar to the CS between CS onset and UCS onset decreases the strength of the CR produced by the CS. The inference is that these similar stimuli resulted in greater forgetting of the CS and thereby decreased CR strength, since in other situations the occurrence of similar stimuli during a delay interval is well-known to increase forgetting of the stimuli that occur first. Therefore, the occurrence of response-produced stimuli that are similar to the stimulus produced by the instrumental response during the time interval separating the instrumental response from the stimulus this response causes to occur should decrease the strength of the instrumental response. Results of Lett (1975) and Spence (1956, Ch. 5) support this expectation.

Lett employed the apparatus illustrated in Figure 3-12. At the beginning of a trial, a rat was placed into the start area of the apparatus through the front door. The response of entering the "correct" chamber, either the white left chamber or the black right chamber, caused food to occur, although not immediately. Half the rats received food if they entered the white left chamber and half received food if they entered the black right chamber. A subject was forced to remain in the chamber it entered by a door, as indicated in Figure 3-12, that dropped after the animal moved into the chamber. Two minutes after the subject entered the chamber, it was returned to the start box. At this time, it received food if it had entered the correct chamber 2 minutes before. Thus, choice of the correct chamber caused food to occur with a delay of reinforcement interval of 2 minutes. Receipt of food or no particular event in the start box terminated a trial. One trial was run per day. Three independent groups of rats were run. One group was immediately removed from the chamber it had entered and spent the entire 2 minutes of the delay interval in the home cage. A second group remained in the chamber it had entered for the first 15 seconds of the 2 minute delay interval, and spent the remaining 105 seconds in the home cage. A third group remained in the chamber it had entered for the first 60 seconds of the 2 minute delay interval, and spent the remaining 60 seconds in the home cage. As the amount of time a group remained in the chamber it had entered increased, the percentage of choices of the correct chamber decreased.

Choosing the correct chamber more frequently than would be expected by chance is a reward-trained response. Remaining in the chosen chamber resulted in response-produced stimuli similar to those occurring when this chamber was entered; for instance, the visual stimuli were much the same when the animal remained in the chamber as when it entered, such as the visual stimuli provided by the chamber walls. Therefore,

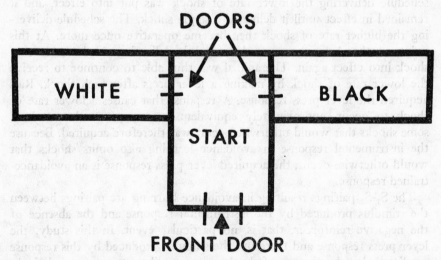

FIGURE 3-12. Apparatus employed by Lett. (Adapted from Lett, 1975.)

longer durations of stimuli similar to the stimuli produced by the instrumental response of entering the correct chamber occurred as the strength of the instrumental response decreased. As previously indicated, this result supports the assumption that a time delay between the instrumental response and the stimulus this response causes to occur impairs instrumental conditioning through increasing forgetting of the stimulus produced by the instrumental response.

Lett (1975) also showed that if rats were removed from the chosen chamber immediately after it was entered they tended to enter the correct chamber when the unusually long delay of reinforcement interval of 1 hour was employed.

Instrumental Response Predicts Stimulus Is Relatively Likely to Occur. Excitatory classical conditioning tends to occur when a CS predicts that the UCS is relatively likely to occur in the presence of the CS or relatively soon thereafter. Herrnstein and Hineline (1966) reported an analogous result for instrumental conditioning.

They showed that rats acquired a response that caused a lower rate of randomly occurring shock to take place. Two different deliveries or schedules of shocks were employed. Both schedules delivered shock of the same intensity and duration (0.3 second) independently of responding. However, the rate of shock delivered by the two schedules differed. A lever was present. When the lever was not pressed after the last shock occurred, the schedule delivering the higher rate of shock remained in effect. When the lever was pressed after the last shock occurred, the schedule delivering the lower rate of shock was put into effect, and it remained in effect until it delivered a single shock. The schedule delivering the higher rate of shock then became operative once more. At this point, another lever press put the schedule delivering the lower rate of shock into effect again. The animal was thus able to continue to receive the lower rate of shock by making a lever press after each shock. Rats acquired the lever press response. A response that causes a lower rate of shock to occur, approximately equivalent to a response that omitted some shocks that would otherwise occur, was therefore acquired. Because the instrumental response in avoidance learning also omits shocks that would otherwise occur, the acquired lever press response is an avoidance-trained response.

The S_1-S_2 pairings resulting in avoidance learning are pairings between the stimulus produced by the instrumental response and the absence of the negative reinforcer, that is, no particular event. In this study, the lever press response and therefore the stimulus produced by this response predicted that the absence of shock was more likely to occur a relatively short time after the stimulus produced by this response took place than otherwise. It was previously indicated that an acquired association between a CS and UCS occurs when the CS predicts that the UCS is relatively likely to occur relatively shortly after the CS is terminated. Therefore, an acquired association between the stimulus produced by the lever press response and the absence of shock should have occurred. This acquired association should result in avoidance learning and thus the execution of the lever press response, which was the obtained result.

Role of Stimuli Preceding Instrumental Response

CR-Like Response Prior to Instrumental Response. According to image theory, a stimulus present just prior to the execution of an instrumentally conditioned response should result in an image of the stimulus produced by the instrumental response, and an image of the stimulus that the instrumental response causes to occur. It follows that when the stimulus that the instrumental response causes to occur is a primary reinforcer, the stimulus preceding an instrumentally conditioned response should produce a CR. This expectation has been supported (Gamzu & Williams, 1975; Shapiro, 1962).

In the former study, in the first stage pigeons were reward-trained to step on a treadle, a response that caused food to appear. In addition, a tone was employed as a cue for performing the treadle response. That is, when the tone was presented, a treadle response was followed by food; and when the tone was not presented, the treadle response was not followed by food. In a second stage, on occasion a key was illuminated 6 seconds prior to tone onset. Otherwise the procedures were identical to those of the first stage. The finding of interest is that the pigeons came to peck the key when it was illuminated.

The peck response was not instrumentally conditioned, because the tone came on whether or not a pigeon pecked the illuminated key. The peck response therefore resembles a classically conditioned peck response established with food. In addition, the peck response occurred before the instrumental treadle response. The idea that the stimulus preceding an instrumentally conditioned response produces a CR when the stimulus that the instrumental response causes to occur is a primary reinforcer is therefore supported. According to image theory, illumination of the key resulted in an image of the tone, thereby an image of the stimulus produced by the treadle response, and thereby an image of food, the image of food leading to the CR-like peck response.

Image theory assumes that an image of the stimulus that an instrumental response causes to occur is due to an image of the stimulus produced by the instrumental response taking place. If the stimulus preceding the instrumentally conditioned response failed to result in an image of the stimulus produced by the instrumental response, then an image of the stimulus that the instrumental response causes to occur should not take place. We will discuss a result in accord with this possibility in Chapter 5.

CS-UCS Pairing and Subsequent Instrumental Conditioning. If a stimulus preceding an instrumentally conditioned response results in an image of the stimulus the instrumental response causes to occur, it would seem that arranging beforehand for the stimulus that precedes an instrumental response to produce an image of the stimulus the instrumental response causes to occur will facilitate acquisition of this instrumental response. Arranging beforehand for a stimulus that precedes an instrumental response to produce an image of a reinforcer this instrumental response causes to occur may be done by (a) presenting CS-reinforcer pairings prior to instrumental conditioning; and (b) using this CS as a cue for performing an instrumental response that causes the reinforcer that the CS was paired with to occur. Trapold and Overmier (1972) summarize results that employed essentially this procedure.

In an illustrative study (Trapold, 1972), in stage 1, one group of rats received pairings between a tone and a food pellet, and pairings between a clicker and sucrose. In stage 2, two bars were made available. When the tone of the first stage was presented, pressing bar A caused a food pellet to appear, and pressing bar B resulted in no particular event. When the clicker of the first stage was presented, pressing bar A caused no particular event to occur, and pressing bar B resulted in sucrose. A second group of rats received pairings between the clicker and a food pellet and pairings between the tone and sucrose in stage 1. This group received the same treatment as the first group in stage 2. Note that the first group received tone-pellet pairings and then was required to press bar A when the tone occurred to obtain a pellet. However, the second group received tone-sucrose pairings and then was required to press bar A when the tone occurred to obtain a pellet. That is, for the first group the cue for performing the instrumental response was also a CS previously paired with the reinforcer that was used to establish instrumental conditioning; but for the second group the cue for performing the instrumental response was a CS previously paired with a reinforcer that was not used to establish instrumental conditioning. The same difference between the two groups holds for the requirement that bar B be pressed when the clicker was presented for sucrose to be obtained. The percentage of correct responses was measured. When the tone was on, pressing bar A was the correct response in the sense that pressing bar A at this time caused a pellet to appear. Also, when the clicker was on, pressing bar B was the correct response in the sense that pressing bar B at this time caused sucrose to appear. The first group made a higher percentage of correct responses than the second group. This result probably means that a CS paired with a reinforcer facilitates instrumental conditioning in which this CS is a cue for performing the instrumental response, and in which the instrumental response causes the same reinforcer to occur.

Let the stimulus preceding an instrumental response be called A; the stimulus produced by an instrumental response be called B; and the stimulus the instrumental response causes to occur be called C. Arranging for the stimulus preceding an instrumental response to be paired with the stimulus the instrumental response causes to occur should therefore result in an acquired A-C association. When instrumental conditioning is carried out, the stimulus produced by the instrumental response should become associated with the stimulus that the instrumental response causes to occur; that is, a B-C connection should be acquired. The difficult part of the learning task in the Trapold study was for a rat to in some sense associate the tone (A) with the stimulus produced by making one instrumental response (B); and to associate the clicker (A') with the stimulus produced by making the second instrumental response (B'). Studies of human verbal learning indicate that acquisition of both an A-C and a B-C connection facilitates acquisition of an A-B connection. Therefore, a prior acquired association between the tone (A) and food (C), and between the stimulus produced by one instrumental response (B) and food (C), may have facilitated formation of an association between the tone (A) and the stimulus produced by one instrumental response (B); and a prior acquired association between the clicker (A') and sucrose (C'), and between the stimulus produced by the second instrumental response (B') and sucrose (C'), may have facilitated formation of an association between the clicker (A') and the stimulus produced by the second instrumental response (B').

Role of Instrumental Response

Shaping. Responses exhibited with a very low rate prior to the initiation of training cannot be directly instrumentally conditioned, because in instrumental conditioning the response in question must first be exhibited before its rate can be changed by its causing a stimulus to occur. Instrumental conditioning of low probability responses is accomplished by a procedure called *shaping*. This procedure essentially involves instrumentally conditioning a series of responses, each response in the sequence being progressively more similar to the desired response than the one before it. By this gradual approximation procedure, a response initially exhibited at a very low rate can come to be instrumentally conditioned.

Skinner (1951) described a shaping procedure to instrumentally condition a food-deprived pigeon to peck the keys of a toy piano as if it were playing a tune. First, a clear sound, such as a clicking sound, is followed by food several times. Then shaping is begun. Initially, any movement in the direction of the piano is followed by the sound and then food. (The sound should be effective because it can be presented immediately after the desired response occurs.) As a result of receiving the sound-food presentation, the pigeon is instrumentally conditioned to move in the direction of the piano. Subsequently, the sound-food pairings are delivered only when the pigeon pecks a piano key, the outcome being that this response becomes instrumentally conditioned. Then, sound-food pairings are delivered only when the pigeon strikes two piano keys in succession, which results in the instrumental conditioning of a two-key pecking sequence, and so on.

Shaping procedures are used to develop fairly elaborate sequences of responding. For example, shaping was used to instrumentally condition pigs to perform for a show, "Priscilla the Fastidious Pig." In this show a sow ate breakfast at a table, deposited clothes in a hamper, ran a vacuum cleaner, picked out her favorite brand of food, and answered questions from the audience by lighting up "yes" and "no" signs (Breland & Breland, 1951).

Experimenters are not apt to wait until an animal "happens" to make bar press or key peck responses to instrumentally condition these responses. Instead, they frequently establish these responses through shaping. For the instrumental conditioning of bar pressing by a rat through shaping, pairings between the sound produced by the food delivery apparatus and food are often initially presented. The bar press response is then gradually developed by shaping. An effective procedure is to first present sound-food pairings only after the rat moves close to the bar, then only after it rears on its hind legs, then only after it raises a front paw toward the bar, and so on until the rat presses the bar. Of course, each time the rat hears the sound of the food being delivered, it moves quickly to the food dish and consumes the pellet before returning to the vicinity of the bar.

The importance of the initial rate of performing the response to be instrumentally conditioned is apparent from the following technique for developing bar pressing quickly. A small amount of wet food is spread on the bar. This assures that the initial probability of pressing the bar will be very high. The usual practice of following each bar press with food obtained from the food dish is also carried out. After making a bar press response, the animal consumes the food in the dish. After several bar presses, food is left off the bar; the result is that the animal continues bar pressing.

Shaping is an integral part of the socialization of humans. There are thousands of responses with essentially a zero probability of occurrence that young humans come increasingly to approximate through shaping.

CR and Instrumental Response. Recall that the stimuli preceding the performance of an instrumentally conditioned response tend to produce CRs. Also, the stimuli of the general learning situation precede a reinforcer that an instrumental response causes to occur, and thus may come to produce CRs through classical conditioning. When the topography (form) of these CRs is opposite to or mutually exclusive with the topography of the instrumental response, instrumental conditioning appears to be impaired; and when the topography of these CRs is similar to the topography of the instrumental response, instrumental conditioning appears to be facilitated.

Examples of CRs impairing instrumental conditioning include animals rooting, manipulating, and swallowing objects instead of exchanging the objects for food. The difficulty in instrumentally conditioning the food exchange response could not have been due to its occurring at a very low rate, because rooting, manipulating, and swallowing objects would have occurred only after the objects were exchanged for food. Also, omission studies (Chapter 2) indicate that salivation and pecking CRs continue to occur even though they cause food to be omitted. Thus, salivation and pecking CRs impair omission learning.

CRs also interfere with instrumental conditioning established with negative reinforcers. Other omission studies show that CRs continue to occur even though they cause shock to take place; therefore CRs impair punishment learning. As another example, when escape and avoidance learning of bar pressing are carried out with rats using shock, the rats tend to continue to press down on the bar when shock is not on and when it is not about to occur (Davis, Hirschorn, & Hurwitz, 1973; Keehn, 1967). Continuing to press down on the bar does not result in escape from or avoidance of shock; the bar must be released and then pressed again. Continuing to press down on the bar probably is a suppression CR; rats probably learn to "freeze" on the bar. The possibility that rats continue to press down on the bar to "be ready" for the next bar press response does not appear to be valid. Keehn (1967) trained rats to first press bar A and then press bar B to escape from and avoid shock. Pressing the two bars in the reverse order did not result in termination and avoidance of shock. If rats prepared to bar press in order to escape from or avoid shock, they should have continued to press down on bar A. Instead, they continued to press down on bar B. Therefore, a suppression CR interfered with escape and avoidance learning.

When the topography of the CR is similar to the topography of the instrumental response, instrumental conditioning appears to be facilitated. Classical conditioning of pecking can be established with food. The relative ease with which instrumental conditioning of pecking is established with food is probably partly due to the stimuli of the general learning situation tending to produce a pecking CR. Classical conditioning with a food UCS results in a rearing (animal on hind legs) CR in hamsters; and reward learning of rearing with food as the reinforcer occurs much more readily than the reward learning of several other responses with food as the reinforcer (Shettleworth, 1975). Classical conditioning of approach to the CS of a box placed at the end of a runway increases the rate with which the runway is subsequently traversed. Reward learning of traversing a runway should therefore be facilitated by the CR of approaching the box at the end of the runway.

Classical conditioning also facilitates instrumental conditioning established with negative reinforcers. An example of this general statement is that a suppression CR often contributes to the strength of a punishment-trained response. The suppression CR successfully competes with performance of the response that causes shock to occur, and thereby contributes to a decrease in the rate of this response. A CR facilitates signalled avoidance learning in which the instrumental response is to leave one compartment and enter a second compartment. At the start of each trial, an animal is placed into the same compartment. Entrance into the second compartment is blocked at this time. A warning stimulus is then presented at the same time the door separating the two compartments is opened. The instrumental response is to move into the second compartment before shock is delivered in the first compartment. This one-way avoidance response may be acquired very quickly (Page, 1955; Theios, Lynch, & Lowe, 1966), probably at least partly because the compartment in which shock is received produces the CR of escape from it.

Difference between Response-Produced and Background Stimuli. It is likely that if the stimulus produced by a response differs only minimally from background stimuli, then the response will be relatively difficult to instrumentally condition. Perhaps the best evidence to support this statement is a study (Hefferline & Keenan, 1963) that suggests it is relatively difficult to instrumentally condition a voluntary covert response. The voluntary covert response tested was tensing the muscles that move a finger without actually moving the finger. Evidence that the voluntary covert response occurred was obtained by amplifying the voltage changes produced by the muscles governing the response in question; the record of amplified voltage changes is called an electromyogram (EMG). Subjects were told they would earn money if they responded correctly, but they were not informed of the identity of the instrumental response that increased the amount of money earned. The instrumental response was a covert finger movement of an increase in voltage to only a certain range and then an immediate decrease in voltage, as determined by EMG recordings from the appropriate muscle. Each occurrence of this response caused the amount of money earned to increase; this was indicated visually by a counter, in front of which the subjects were seated. An increase in the rate of the covert finger movement response occurred with training; that is, instrumental conditioning of a covert finger response took place. However, the increase in the rate of the covert finger movement response was relatively small. For example, between the 20th and 30th minute of training, all four subjects made less than 25 covert finger movement responses. It seems certain that subjects would have acquired an overt finger movement response much more quickly than a covert one.

The stimulus produced by the covert finger movement response differed minimally from background stimuli. By definition, covert responses do not produce visual and auditory stimuli. In addition, subjects could not describe what response caused an increase in the amount of money, when they were asked to do so at the end of the study. The fact that subjects were not aware of the stimulus produced by the covert finger movement response clearly suggests that the stimulus produced by this response differed very little from background stimuli.

The probable difficulty in instrumentally conditioning responses producing stimuli that differ minimally from background stimuli relates to the finding that CR strength decreases as the similarity between the CS and background stimuli increases. What accounts for the difficulty in instrumentally conditioning responses that produce stimuli differing minimally from background stimuli is that: (a) classical conditioning between a S_1, the stimulus produced by the instrumental response, and S_2, the stimulus this response causes to occur, is essential to instrumental conditioning; (b) S_1 is analogous to a CS that is paired with a UCS; and (c) CR strength is low when a CS differs minimally from background stimuli.

Instrumental Conditioning of Autonomic Responses. Examples of autonomic responses are heart rate, GSR, and salivation responses. Autonomic responses are not easily controlled by naive humans, and are primarily innervated by the autonomic nervous system. In contrast, voluntary responses such as arm and leg movements are easily controlled by naive adults, and are primarily innervated by the central nervous system.

Some learning theorists once thought that autonomic responses are classically but not instrumentally conditioned, and that voluntary responses are instrumentally but not classically conditioned. This idea is no longer viable. We have already discussed many examples of classical conditioning of voluntary responses, such as classical conditioning of gnawing and approach responses. We also know that instrumental conditioning of autonomic responses does occur. The fact that both classical conditioning of voluntary responses and instrumental conditioning of autonomic responses do occur is in accord with the view of image theory that classical and instrumental conditioning processes are intimately related.

Miller (1969) established instrumental conditioning of the autonomic responses of salivation, heart rate, intestinal contractions, urine formation, blood distribution, blood pressure, and the GSR in nonhumans. In one study (Miller & Carmona, 1967), one group of water-deprived dogs was reward-trained to increase its rate of salivation by following a burst of salivation with water. A second group was omission-trained to decrease its rate of salivation, by delivering water following a relatively long time period without the occurrence of salivation. Both these results could not have been due to a CR, since a CR should have been capable of affecting the salivation response in only one direction.

Miller and his associates also controlled for the possibility that instrumental conditioning of overt voluntary responses was responsible for the obtained effects on autonomic responses. This possibility makes some sense, for perhaps an animal can increase its rate of salivation by mouth movements, or increase its heart rate by increasing its locomotor activity. This possibility was controlled for by establishing instrumental conditioning of an autonomic response while animals were paralyzed with a drug (DiCara & Miller, 1969).

Nevertheless, autonomic responses remain relatively difficult to instrumentally condition. It is possible that one reason is that the stimuli produced by most autonomic responses differ little from background stimuli.

It does seem that humans are much less aware of stimuli produced by autonomic responses such as salivation, heart rate, and the GSR than they are of stimuli produced by overt voluntary responses. As we have seen, when a response-produced stimulus differs relatively little from background stimuli, the response in question should be relatively difficult to instrumentally condition. It follows that autonomic responses should be relatively difficult to instrumentally condition.

Role of Stimulus Instrumental Response Causes to Occur

A goal stimulus was defined as a stimulus that is more likely to be approached and continued to be perceived than the stimuli present before the execution of the instrumental response, or the stimuli that would be present if the instrumental response were not made. A negative-goal stimulus was defined as a stimulus that is more likely to be escaped from and avoided than the stimuli present before the execution of the instrumental response, or the stimuli that would be present if the instrumental response were not made. An instrumental response tends to increase in rate when it causes a goal stimulus to occur, and it tends to decrease in rate when it causes a negative-goal stimulus to occur. Thus, the instrumental response increases in rate for the four types of instrumental conditioning in which the instrumental response causes a goal stimulus to occur, and it decreases in rate for the four types of instrumental conditioning in which it causes a negative-goal stimulus to occur.

Response to Perceived Goal Stimulus. The importance of the goal stimulus is also shown by determining the strength of the response to the perception of it.

Premack (1963a) measured the number of times monkeys manipulated each of four different objects (manipulanda)—a lever, a plunger, a hinged flap, and a horizontally, rather than the usual vertically operated lever—in a certain time period. A single manipulandum was made available at a time, and a subject was free to operate it. Manipulating, that is, operating, responding on, or exploring a manipulandum, is, of course, perceiving the tactual stimuli provided by the manipulandum. The number of times monkeys perceived (manipulated, operated) the four manipulanda in the time period varied. In other words, the extent to which the four manipulanda were approached and continued to be tactually perceived varied.

In a second stage, the opportunity to tactually perceive (manipulate, operate) one manipulandum occurred, providing another manipulandum was responded on. Suppose that the rate of approach to and continued perception of manipulandum A was less than the rate of approach to and continued tactual perception of manipulandum B. Suppose also that the opportunity to tactually perceive (manipulate, operate) manipulandum B occurred only if manipulandum A was responded on. Would the rate of responding on the less-likely-to-be-perceived manipulandum be increased by this responding being followed by the opportunity to tactually perceive the more-likely-to-be-perceived manipulandum? The answer to this question was yes. In other words, the rate of response on manipulandum A increased as a result of this response's causing the opportunity to perceive manipulandum B to occur. Thus, instrumental conditioning took place.

It was determined in the first stage that approaching and continuing to tactually perceive manipulandum B was more likely to occur than approaching and continuing to tactually perceive manipulandum A. In the second stage responding on manipulandum A caused the opportunity to tactually perceive manipulandum B to occur. It follows that tactual perception of manipulandum B was a goal stimulus. Thus, the result described in the previous paragraph indicates that a response that caused a goal stimulus to occur did increase in rate, as had been assumed.

Another second stage experiment was carried out. Again suppose that the rate of approach to and continued tactual perception of manipulandum A was less than the rate of approach to and continued tactual perception of manipulandum B. In addition, also suppose that the opportunity to tactually perceive manipulandum A occurred only if manipulandum B was responded on. Would the rate of responding on the more-likely-to-be-perceived manipulandum be increased by this responding's causing the opportunity to perceive the less-likely-to-be-perceived manipulandum to occur? The answer to this question was no. This result supports the conclusion that if a response causes a stimulus to occur, but this stimulus is not a goal stimulus, then the rate of this response tends not to increase.

Response to Perceived Negative-Goal Stimulus. A study (Premack, 1971), in which the strength of the response to the perception of a negative-goal stimulus was determined, is also informative. In the first stage, the proportion of time water-deprived rats drank water, and the proportion of time these rats ran in a wheel were measured. Drinking water is equivalent to perceiving the taste stimuli provided by water, and running in a wheel to perceiving various tactual, kinesthetic, and vestibular stimuli. The proportion of time measures are therefore measures of the strength of approaching and continuing to perceive a stimulus. Obviously, the water-deprived rats were more likely to approach and continue to perceive the stimuli provided by the water than the stimuli provided by the wheel.

In the second stage, drinking water caused the opportunity to run in the wheel to occur. In addition, drinking water could not occur while running in the wheel took place. This procedure resulted in a decrease in the rate of drinking water.

The stimuli provided by running in the wheel were less likely to be approached and continued to be perceived than the stimuli provided by drinking water; this is about equivalent to the stimuli provided by running in the wheel being more likely to be escaped from and avoided than the stimuli provided by drinking water. Thus, drinking water caused a negative-goal stimulus to occur. The obtained decrease in the rate of drinking therefore supports the assumption that a response that causes a negative-goal stimulus to occur usually decreases in rate.

Strength of Response to Perceived Goal Stimulus. Does the strength of an instrumental response increase with an increase in the strength of the response of approaching and continuing to perceive the goal stimulus for this instrumental response? The answer appears to be yes (Premack, 1963b).

In stage 1 of this study, he determined the proportion of time that rats which were not deprived of food spent drinking sucrose solutions of three different concentrations. Also he determined in stage 1, the proportion of time these rats spent turning a wheel requiring two different amounts of force to turn it. Exposure to only one concentration or to only one force occurred at a time. The proportions of time spent drinking and time spent turning a wheel are measures of the strength of approaching and continuing to perceive a stimulus.

In stage 2, Premack carried out a reward learning procedure. The goal stimulus for a bar press response was one of the three concentrations of sucrose solution, or one of the two wheel turning conditions of stage 1. The obtained result was that the strength of the bar press response increased with an increase in the proportion of time a particular sucrose solution was drunk, or an increase in the proportion of time a particular wheel was turned. Thus, the strength of the bar press response increased with an increase in the strength of approaching and continuing to perceive the goal stimulus. This result is in accord with other results to be described. In addition, it will also be assumed that the strength of an instrumental response increases with an increase in the strength of the response of escaping from and avoiding a negative-goal stimulus.

Response and Strength of Response to Perceived Goal and Image Theory. The way image theory explains instrumental conditioning is based, in part, on the assumption that the response to the perceived goal and negative-goal stimulus is critically related to whether or not instrumental conditioning occurs. This theory assumes that an animal behaves so as to increase the amount of temporary brain event corresponding to a goal stimulus, correlated with an increase in the vividness of the image of the goal stimulus; and assumes that an animal behaves so as to decrease the amount of temporary brain event corresponding to a negative-goal stimulus, correlated with a decrease in the vividness of the image of the negative-goal stimulus. By definition, an animal is relatively likely to approach and continue to perceive a goal stimulus. Furthermore, an animal that approaches and continues to perceive a goal stimulus actually behaves so as to bring about and maintain the temporary brain event corresponding to a goal stimulus; therefore, an animal should behave so as to increase the amount of temporary brain event corresponding to a goal stimulus by some other means, this means being by increasing the extent of the transformation of the permanent brain event corresponding to the goal stimulus into the temporary brain event corresponding to the goal stimulus. By analogous reasoning, we may assume that an animal attempts to decrease the amount of temporary brain event corresponding to a negative-goal stimulus. On the basis of this reasoning, image theory predicts that instrumental conditioning usually occurs when a response causes a goal or negative-goal stimulus to take place—which it does.

The strength of an instrumental response, as we said above, is positively related to the strength of the response to the perceived goal stimulus or negative-goal stimulus. This finding is also in accord with image theory. If an animal approaches a goal stimulus with relatively little delay in time, for instance, by moving immediately toward it when it sees it from a distance and by drinking it at a fast rate, the animal is in effect causing the temporary brain event produced by this goal stimulus to come into existence with relatively little delay in time. Therefore, an animal should attempt to increase the amount of temporary brain event corresponding to a goal stimulus with relatively little delay in time by another means, which it can do by executing the instrumental response at a relatively fast rate. Thus, the goal stimulus that is approached with relatively little delay in time should result in an instrumental response occurring at a relatively fast rate, and this essentially is the obtained result. Analogous reasoning applies to the conclusion about the strength of an instrumental response and the strength of the response to a perceived negative-goal stimulus.

Amount and Intensity of Reinforcer. An increase in the amount of the positive reinforcer in reward learning, and an increase in the intensity of the negative reinforcer in punishment and escape learning usually increases the strength of these types of instrumental responses (Azrin, 1960; Campbell & Kraeling, 1953; Zeaman, 1949). Zeaman's finding, for example, was that the latency to leave the start area of a runway decreased as the amount of food rats received at the end of the runway on each trial increased from .05 gram to 2.4 grams.

The strength of an instrumental response is positively related to the strength of the response to the perceived goal or negative-goal stimulus this response causes to occur. The just described effect of amount and intensity of reinforcement on the strength of an instrumental response is most likely an instance of this conclusion. Consider reward learning. The strength of a response to a perceived positive reinforcer (goal stimulus), that is, the extent to which a positive reinforcer is approached and continued to be perceived, most likely increases with an increase in the amount of the reinforcer. For example, many animals are probably likely to approach a large piece of food at a faster rate than a small piece of food when they see the food from a distance. Because the strength of response to a perceived positive reinforcer (goal stimulus) probably increases with an increase in the amount of this reinforcer, and because the strength of an instrumental response is positively related to the strength of the response to the perceived goal stimulus for this response, the result that the strength of a reward-trained response usually increases with an increase in the amount of the positive reinforcer used to establish it is acounted for.

Learning and Nonlearning Effects on Performance

Recall that the strength of a learned response is affected by nonlearning as well as by learning factors, and that the strength of a learned response is often referred to as a measure of the performance of a learned response. Deprivation of food and water exerts a nonlearning effect on the strength of the instrumental response. Most of the previously discussed factors that affect the strength of the instrumental response do so through learning.

Nonlearning Effect of Deprivation. It is intuitively obvious and has been empirically proved that after reward learning has been established with food or water, satiation of the subjects markedly decreases the strength of the instrumental response. In addition, an increase in the deprivation of food or water usually increases the strength of an instrumental response established with food or water. Figure 3-10 indicates the speed of traversing a runway for food by rats deprived of food for 2½ hours or 26½ hours. Greater deprivation resulted in faster running speeds.

The effect of deprivation level on the strength of the instrumental response is a nonlearning one. A change in deprivation level alters the strength of an instrumental response occurring in the presence of a stimulus even though the animal is not exposed to this stimulus while the deprivation level is being changed. In addition, the effect of a change in deprivation level on the strength of an instrumental response is not relatively permanent. Furthermore, the fact that a change in deprivation level affects the responses to a relatively wide variety of stimuli also suggests that the effect of deprivation on performance is a nonlearning one. A change in deprivation level does affect the responses to a relatively wide variety of stimuli, for example, CRs established with the reinforcer an animal is deprived of.

One study (Hillman, Hunter, & Kimble, 1953) that indicates a temporary effect of deprivation level on the strength of an instrumental response will be described. Water-deprived rats were reward-trained on a task resembling the runway task. The time to move from the start to the end of the apparatus was measured. One group of rats was deprived of water for 2 hours before each trial for all 15 trials. A second group was deprived of water for 22 hours before each trial for all 15 trials. For a third group, the deprivation level was switched from 2 hours to 22 hours before a trial between the 10th and 11th trials. For a fourth group, the deprivation level was switched from 22 hours to 2 hours before a trial between the 10th and 11th trials. Figure 3-13 indicates that 2 hours of deprivation did not permanently increase the time the rats took to reach the end of the apparatus, and that 22 hours of deprivation did not permanently decrease the time the rats took to reach the end of the apparatus. Two hours of deprivation did not permanently affect responding, because as soon as the switch from 2 to 22 hours of deprivation was made, the group performed as quickly as the group tested at 22 hours of deprivation for all 15 trials. The time taken to reach the end of the apparatus by the group switched from 22 to 2 hours of deprivation changed following this switch almost as quickly. Extent of deprivation probably produces at best only a slight permanent effect on rate measures of performance of relatively simple instrumental responses (Barry, 1958; Leach, 1971).

Deprivation and Strength of Response to Perceived Goal Stimulus. As extent of deprivation of food and water increases, the strength of the response to perceived food and water as measured, for example, by the proportion of time food or water is consumed, probably increases. Since the strength of an instrumental response is positively related to the strength of the response to the perceived goal stimulus or negative-goal stimulus for this response, it follows that the strength of a reward-trained response established with food or water should increase with an increase in deprivation of food or water, which is the result described above.

A study by Premack (1965) supports this analysis of the effect of deprivation of food and water on the strength of an instrumental response. It suggests that water established reward learning because deprivation of water resulted in a relatively strong response of approaching and continuing to perceive water. In one condition, rats were not deprived of water, but were permitted only limited access to an activity wheel.

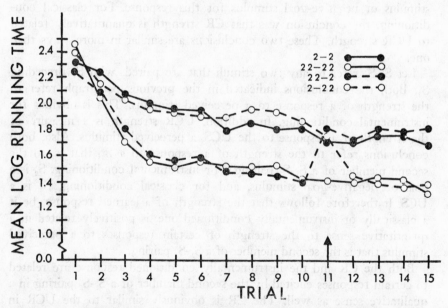

FIGURE 3-13. Effect of a change in deprivation level on performance. (Adapted from Hillman, Hunter, and Kimble, 1953.)

It was found for this condition that the proportion of time rats spent drinking was less than the proportion of time rats spent running in the wheel. In addition, in a second stage, running in the wheel caused water to occur, that is, brought about the opportunity to drink water. This response-stimulus pairing did not result in an increase in the strength of running in the wheel. In a second condition, rats were deprived of water. Naturally, this condition resulted in rats spending a greater proportion of time drinking than running in the wheel. In addition, in a second stage, running in the wheel caused water to occur. This response-stimulus pairing led to an increase in the strength of running in the wheel. It was also found that when drinking water caused the opportunity to run in the wheel to occur, the strength of drinking did not increase. The obtained results indicate that water established reward learning when it was a goal stimulus, and did not establish reward learning when it was not a goal stimulus; and that deprivation and satiation of water resulted in water being and not being a goal stimulus, respectively.

Learned Responses and Responses to Perceived Stimuli. These results support the conclusion that the strength of an instrumental response is positively related to the strength of the response to the perceived goal stimulus or negative-goal stimulus for this response. For classical conditioning, the conclusion was that CR strength is quantitatively related to UCR strength. These two conclusions are similar in more ways than one.

Let S_1-S_2 refer to any two stimuli that are paired, with S_1 preceding S_2. Both the conclusions indicated in the previous paragraph refer to the strength of a response to a perceived stimulus. This is obvious for instrumental conditioning. In addition, UCR strength is a measure of the strength of a response to the UCS, a perceived stimulus. Also, both conclusions refer to the strength of a response to a S_2, that is, to the second member of a S_1-S_2 pairing. For instrumental conditioning, S_2 is a goal or negative-goal stimulus, and for classical conditioning, S_2 is a UCS. It therefore follows that the strength of a learned response, be it a classically or instrumentally conditioned one, is positively related in a quantitative sense to the strength of certain responses to a perceived stimulus that is the second member of a S_1-S_2 pairing.

Both the CR and the instrumentally conditioned response are related to certain responses elicited by the second member of a S_1-S_2 pairing in a qualitative sense as well. The CR is obviously similar to the UCR in respect to response topography. The instrumentally conditioned response is qualitatively related to the response to a perceived goal or negative-goal stimulus it causes to occur: the instrumentally conditioned response changes the rate an animal is permitted to approach and continue to perceive a goal stimulus or escape from and avoid a negative-goal stimulus, and measures of the strength of response to a perceived stimulus relevant to instrumental conditioning—for example, the proportion of time a stimulus is perceived—also involve permitting an animal to affect the rate it approaches and continues to perceive a stimulus or escapes from and avoids a stimulus.

Therefore, both classically and instrumentally conditioned responses are quantitatively and qualitatively related to certain responses to a perceived stimulus that is the second member of the S_1-S_2 pairing resulting in conditioning.

Quantitative and Qualitative Relation and Image Theory. An analogous conclusion is that the effects of images of stimuli on responding are quantitatively and qualitatively related to the effects of perceived stimuli on responding. They are analogous in three respects. The first is that for both conclusions a quantitative and qualitative relation exists between two factors. The second respect is that they both involve responses to perceived stimuli. The third respect is that they both involve responses that are not elicited by perceived stimuli: by definition, learned responding excludes any contribution to this responding by the UCS or by the stimulus that the instrumental response causes to occur, and by definition the effect of an image of a stimulus on responding is distinguished from the effect of the corresponding real stimulus on responding.

These analogies suggest that an image of the UCS (S_2) or the stimulus (S_2) that the instrumental response causes to occur is responsible, at least in part, for the performance of the learned response. The reason that the learned response is quantitatively and qualitatively related to the response to the perceived stimulus that is the second member of a S_1-S_2 pairing, is that (a) the effects of an image of a stimulus on responding are quantitatively and qualitatively related to the effects of a perceived stimulus on responding, and (b) an image of the second member of a S_1-S_2 pairing mediates learned responding (King, 1976). Thus, the effects of the amount and intensity of a reinforcer and deprivation of a reinforcer on the two types of conditioning and on image-produced responses support image theory.

Learning Effect on Instrumental Response. Most of the previously described factors affecting the strength of the instrumental response do so through learning. The effects of these factors are due to stimuli an animal was previously exposed to in the learning situation, they are relatively permanent, and they do not affect the responses to a relatively wide variety of stimuli. Consider the effect of delay of reinforcement. The same stimulus complex is present both when a delay of reinforcement is employed and when its effect is subsequently determined. The effect of delay of reinforcement on performance is relatively permanent, as evidenced, for example, by a divergence in the performance of groups receiving different delays of reinforcement over days of training (Grice, 1948). The effect of delay of reinforcement is obviously not widespread; for example, delay of reinforcement of a bar press response should not noticeably affect acquisition of a runway traversal response established with the same reinforcer.

Pairings between Neutral Stimuli

Image theory assumes that acquired associations between paired neutral stimuli occur as part of the instrumental conditioning process. Some of the stimuli of the general learning situation become associated with the stimulus produced by the instrumental response. Both everyday instances and everyday analogues of instrumental conditioning (Chapter 1) should result from pairings between a response-produced stimulus and a neutral stimulus. For the avoidance, escape, omission, and response-terminates-reward types of instrumental conditioning, the stimulus produced by the instrumental response should become associated with no particular event. Finally, extinction of reward learning should result from pairings between the stimulus produced by the instrumental response and no particular event. The present section discusses evidence that supports the assumption that acquired associations between neutral stimuli influence instrumental conditioning.

Strong support for this assumption has already been cited. For instance, tactual perception of a manipulandum, a neutral stimulus, established reward learning. Also, the stimuli provided by running in a wheel, a neutral stimulus complex, established punishment learning. Stimuli such as tactual perception of a manipulandum and running in a wheel should be viewed as neutral stimuli. Both these stimuli are not relatively likely to be approached and continued to be perceived or escaped from and avoided. Whether a particular manipulandum was a goal stimulus depended on the nature of a second manipulandum monkeys responded on. Also, running in a wheel was both a goal stimulus and a negative-goal stimulus depending on other conditions.

Response Causes Neutral Stimulus and Instrumental Conditioning. Khavari and Eisman (1971) reported another way of showing that a response that causes a neutral stimulus to occur can become instrumentally conditioned. In this study, evidence of the instrumental conditioning was obtained subsequent to the pairings between the instrumental response and the neutral stimulus.

In stage 1, water-deprived rats were reward-trained to bar press using physiological saline, a solution of salt in water, as the reinforcer. The positive reinforcer for the bar press response in this stage was water, since the rats were deprived of water. In stage 2, one group was injected with formalin, a substance that depletes the body's sodium ion. The control group was injected with a solution not affecting the concentration of sodium ion. Subjects were then returned to the learning apparatus, and the amount of bar pressing in extinction, that is, in the absence of physiological saline, was determined. The group receiving formalin exhibited more bar presses during 1 hour of extinction than the control group did. When saline is dissolved in water, sodium (and chloride) ions are formed. Therefore, it appears that in stage 1 an association was acquired between the stimulus produced by the bar press response and sodium ion, a neutral stimulus in stage 1. This inference is reasonable, because the group subsequently deprived of sodium ion bar pressed more in extinction than the control group did.

This kind of finding is sometimes referred to as a *latent learning* result. The learning that was involved with the bar-press response and sodium ion was not apparent, that is, it was latent, until a relevant biological change was produced through injection of formalin.

Responses causing neutral stimuli to occur probably contribute to the strength of most instrumental responses, including those established with a primary reinforcer. Consider, for example, that in the reward learning of bar pressing an animal may acquire an association between the stimulus produced by turning in a certain direction and the stimulus of the sight of the food receptacle. An acquired association between these two stimuli should reduce the time it takes for an animal to obtain food after making a bar press response, thereby increasing the strength of this response. Similarly, the stimulus produced by traversing the beginning portion of a runway may become associated with the stimuli provided by the middle portion of the runway, thereby resulting in a rat's traversing the runway more quickly.

Vivid Image of a Neutral Stimulus a Response Causes to Occur. Image theory assumes that the stimulus produced by an instrumental response results in an image of the stimulus this response causes to occur. One study (Hefferline and Perrera, 1963) supports this assumption. In addition, the stimulus that the instrumental response caused to occur was a neutral stimulus. Thus, this study also supports the assumption that instrumental conditioning can be mediated by an acquired association between neutral stimuli.

In stage 1, each occurrence of a covert thumb response caused a tone to sound. Occurrences of a covert thumb response were determined by EMG recordings from an appropriate muscle. In addition, subjects were instructed to press a key with the index finger of the other hand whenever the tone occurred. Subjects were not informed of the connection between the covert thumb response and the tone, however. Also, each occurrence of the tone was followed by an advance in score, as indicated by a digital display. The subjects were told at the outset that any advance in score would result in their receiving more money at the end of the experiment. In stage 2, the procedures were the same as for stage 1, except that the tone that followed the covert thumb response was delayed by 2 seconds. In stage 3, the procedures were the same as for stage 2 except that the intensity of the tone was gradually reduced to zero over 20 presentations of the tone. In stage 4, the procedures were the same as for stage 3 except that the intensity of the tone was zero.

One stage 4 finding was that subjects remained relatively likely to follow the occurrence of a covert thumb response by performing the overt finger response. This outcome was obtained even though the tone no longer occurred in stage 4, and subjects had been told at the outset that the tone was the cue for making the overt index finger response. This outcome therefore suggests that subjects had very vivid images or hallucinations of the tone in stage 4. In addition, at the end of the experiment one subject reported that he still heard the tone occurring in stage 4 when in fact it was no longer being presented. These results suggest that an acquired association between the neutral stimulus produced by the covert thumb response and the tone had occurred, and that the stimulus produced by the covert thumb response resulted in an image of the tone.

Observation Learning Involving Neutral Stimuli. Acquired associations between neutral stimuli not involving the stimulus produced by the instrumental response probably affect the strength of this response.

Consider, for example, reward learning of bar pressing. Suppose that the food receptacle is 6 inches from the bar. While an animal is engaged in reward learning of bar pressing, it will probably alternately look at (observe) the bar and then the food receptacle. That is, pairing between the sight, including position, of the bar and the sight, including position, of the food receptacle will probably take place. An acquired association between the stimuli indicating the position of the bar and the stimuli indicating the position of the food receptacle should therefore be acquired, and this acquired association should increase the strength of the bar press response. For example, when an animal is at the food receptacle, the food receptacle may produce an image of the bar in its position in the conditioning apparatus, and this image may contribute to executing that portion of the instrumental response involving approaching the bar and moving in front of it, thereby increasing the rate of the bar press response. Acquired associations between other stimuli when an animal observes these stimuli may arise, and it is possible that these acquired associations also contribute to the strength of the bar press response. In general, it is clear that observation learning occurs, that is, learning through viewing stimuli takes place (Chapter 8); observation learning may thus contribute to the strength of most instrumentally conditioned responses.

Forgetting and Recall in Conditioning

Let us now consider material related to forgetting and recall in conditioning.

Forgetting in Conditioning. The strength of a classically or instrumentally conditioned response generally decreases with an increase in the time interval between acquisition of a response and the test for recall of this response. That is, the strength of a learned response generally decreases with an increase in the retention interval. For example, rats reward-trained to traverse a runway performed worse on this task 60 days after the last day of training than 1 day after the last day of training (Gleitman & Steinman, 1963). Thus, forgetting of classically and instrumentally conditioned responses does occur, and forgetting tends to increase with an increase in the retention interval.

Although an acquired response is frequently fairly well retained over a period of a couple of months, extensive forgetting of components of the learning situation over this time period can occur (McAllister & McAllister, 1971; Steinman, 1967). In Steinman's study, rats were reward-trained to traverse a runway that was either white (for some rats) or black (for others). Four groups of rats were then formed. One group was tested on the runway used in training one day after training terminated; a second group was tested on the runway used in training 66 days after training terminated. A third group was tested on the runway of the color not used in training one day after training terminated; a fourth group was tested on the runway of the color not used in training 66 days after training terminated. The two groups that received the 66 day retention interval performed almost identically on the recall test on the runway. In addition, they performed worse than the group that received a one-day retention interval and was tested on the runway used in training, and they performed better than the group that received a one-day retention interval and was tested on the runway not used in training. Because a switch from the color of the runway used in training to a different color did not affect the performance of the groups receiving the recall test after 66 days, but did affect the performance of the groups receiving the recall test after 1 day, we may infer that the 66-day retention interval resulted in forgetting of the color of the runway used in training.

Reminder for Reinforcer. A *reminder stimulus* is a component or a subset of the stimuli of a conditioning situation. Studies suggest that presenting reminder stimuli during the retention interval facilitates recall of the reinforcer employed in acquisition.

In one study (Greenfield & Riccio, 1972), training consisted of shocking rats several times in an enclosed compartment. The retention interval was 14 days. Some groups were placed in the compartment in which shock was previously delivered for brief periods of time during the retention interval without shock occurring. One group was not exposed to the shock compartment during the retention interval. The test for recall of the effects of the shocks in the enclosed compartment was given 14 days after the shocks were given. It consisted of measuring the extent to which the shock compartment was escaped from and avoided. That is, the strength of the CR of escaping from and avoiding the shock compartment was determined. This measurement was accomplished by placing a rat in the shock compartment, providing an open door to a second compartment, and obtaining the cumulative time spent in the second compartment. The groups that were placed in the shock compartment during the retention interval were more likely to remain in the second compartment on test trials than the group not exposed to the shock compartment during the retention interval. Exposure to the shock compartment therefore probably facilitated recall of the shock that occurred in training. Exposure to the shock compartment during the retention interval is equivalent to the presentation of a reminder stimulus, because this exposure is a component of the original learning situation. Note that presenting this reminder stimulus is also an extinction procedure. The effect of the reminder stimulus on recall was therefore greater than the effect of extinction.

In another study (Quartermain, McEwen, & Azmitia, 1972), forgetting was produced by employing an electroconvulsive shock rather than by events correlated with the passage of time. An electroconvulsive shock is intense and usually brief; it causes a subject to convulse. Presentation of a convulsive shock directly after acquisition of a learned response markedly impairs subsequent performance of the learned response. Quartermain et al. first established punishment learning in rats, using footshock. They found, as expected, that delivering electroconvulsive shock 1 second after termination of the footshock decreased the strength of the punishment-trained response. In other words, the electroconvulsive shock resulted in forgetting of the punishment learning. However, it was also found that re-exposing rats to the apparatus in which footshock was delivered during the retention interval reduced the effect of electroconvulsive shock to some extent. This re-exposure to the conditioning apparatus is a reminder stimulus. Because presentation of the reminder stimulus during the retention interval facilitated performance of the punishment-trained response on the recall test, it can be said to have resulted in recall of punishment learning.

A reminder stimulus also affected performance in a study (Gordon & Spear, 1973) that employed a customary design for the study of memory —a proactive inhibition study. In this procedure, task A is acquired first; task B is then acquired; and finally a test for recall of task B is carried out. Proactive inhibition is said to occur if task A can be shown to be responsible for a decrease in memory for task B, as evidenced by a proactive inhibition group performing worse than a control group on the test for recall. Gordon and Spear thought that if the memory for task A could be strengthened, then more forgetting of task B should occur. They expected that memory of task A could be strengthened by presenting a reminder stimulus for this task just prior to the acquisition of task B. Therefore, they predicted that presenting a reminder stimulus for task A just prior to acquisition of task B would impair the performance of task B on the test for recall. Task A was a punishment learning task in which the response of leaving compartment 1 and entering compartment 2 caused shock to occur. Task B was an avoidance learning task in which scheduled shock was omitted by leaving compartment 1 and entering compartment 2. The reminder stimulus was, for different groups, a brief exposure to compartment 1 or compartment 2 in the absence of shock. The reminder stimulus was presented just before acquisition of task B. Both reminder stimuli impaired performance on the test for recall of task B that was given 1 hour after acquisition of task B.

In all three studies just described, the reminder stimulus consisted of the stimuli of a conditioning chamber. Also, the reminder stimulus apparently resulted in recall of other components of the previously acquired learning. Greenfield and Riccio essentially carried out classical conditioning, so presumably the reminder stimulus in their study led to recall of the UCS. The other two studies investigated the recall of instrumental conditioning, so the reminder stimulus in these studies may have resulted in recall of both the stimulus produced by the instrumentally conditioned response and the reinforcer employed for this learning.

These findings suggest that memory of a stimulus is appropriately viewed as mediated by the occurrence of an image of this stimulus. Take the Greenfield and Riccio study. According to image theory, the reminder stimulus, the CS of the stimuli of the chamber in which shock was received, should result in an image of the UCS. This image of a stimulus could well have been responsible for the improved recall of the previously acquired classical conditioning.

The idea that memory of stimuli is mediated by the occurrence of images of stimuli has already been discussed in connection with covert responses from the muscles responsible for speech that were observed when humans were asked to recall verbal material. We said there that these covert responses probably result from images of the stimuli produced by speech responses that occur when humans are asked to recall various material. The idea that recall of a stimulus is mediated by the occurrence of an image of this stimulus also makes sense on an intuitive basis. If we imagine a stimulus, we can describe it. And a description of a stimulus that occurred in the past is the recall of this stimulus.

The described studies also support the idea that animals have memories for reinforcers and for the stimuli produced by instrumental responses. If animals have these memories, it seems obvious that permanent brain events corresponding to these stimuli exist, as image theory assumes.

Reminder for Stimuli Preceding Learned Response. In one study (Lewis, Miller, & Misanin, 1968), the response of stepping off a platform by rats was punishment-trained by following this response with footshock. One group received an electroconvulsive shock immediately after receiving the footshock. On the following day, the rats were returned to the platform. They exhibited very little memory for the punishment learning that had been carried out; they performed much worse than another group that had received footshock following stepping off the platform, but had not received electroconvulsive shock. Four hours after this test for recall of the punishment learning, the group that received the electroconvulsive shock received a reminder footshock in another apparatus in another room. This group was then tested for recall of punishment learning once more, 24 hours after being given the reminder footshock. On this second recall test, they were much more likely to remain on the platform than on the first recall test. This finding suggests that the reminder stimulus facilitated recall of the stimuli of the punishment learning situation and of the stimulus produced by stepping off the platform.

Another study (Lyon & Ozolins, 1970) successfully employed unpaired presentations of the UCS for a previously acquired CR during a retention interval to increase the strength of this CR. This result suggests that the unpaired presentations of the UCS functioned as a reminder stimulus that increased recall of the CS.

The described studies suggest that reminder stimuli can increase the recall of the stimuli of the general learning situation and the CS. The recall of the stimuli of the general learning situation and the CS may be mediated by the occurrence of images of these stimuli, for much the same reason that recall of the reinforcer and the stimulus produced by the instrumental response may be based on the occurrence of images of these stimuli. In addition, if animals can recall the stimuli of the general learning situation and the CS, it seems necessary that permanent brain events exist that correspond to these stimuli.

Reminder Stimuli Immediately Followed by Electroconvulsive Shock. An electroconvulsive shock interferes with recall of previously acquired learning when it is delivered immediately after the presentation of a reminder stimulus for this learning (Misanin, Miller, & Lewis, 1968; Schneider & Sherman, 1968).

In the Misanin et al. study, a classically conditioned suppression CR was established in rats. The next day the CS for this classical conditioning was presented alone, that is, without the UCS. Immediately afterward electroconvulsive shock was delivered. A second group was not presented with the CS, but received the electroconvulsive shock. Performance of the previously acquired suppression CR was measured 24 hours later. The group that received the CS and then the electroconvulsive shock exhibited a weaker suppression CR than the group that received only the electroconvulsive shock. Studies described above suggest that the CS presented alone may have functioned as a reminder stimulus for the UCS. Thus, an electroconvulsive shock interfered with previously acquired classical conditioning when it was delivered immediately after a reminder stimulus for this learning.

The ability of the electroconvulsive shock to impair previously acquired classical conditioning even though only a reminder CS was presented just before the electroconvulsive shock was delivered is explained by image theory. The reminder stimulus should have resulted in an image of the UCS. Thus, the real CS and an image of the UCS occurred at about the same time. When the CS and UCS are paired, the CS and the UCS occur at about the same time, by definition. Following a CS-UCS pairing immediately by electroconvulsive shock almost certainly impairs classical conditioning resulting from this CS-UCS pairing. An image of a stimulus and the effects of a real stimulus are assumed to be due to qualitatively identical temporary brain events. It follows that delivering electroconvulsive shock immediately after the occurrence of a real CS and an image of the UCS should result in much the same outcome as delivering electroconvulsive shock immediately after the occurrence of a CS-UCS pairing. In both cases, therefore, classical conditioning should be impaired.

Unpaired Presentations of UCS. Unpaired presentations of a UCS similar to the UCS employed in CS-UCS pairings have been found to affect CR strength. This result will be discussed in relation to forgetting.

In a study by Rescorla (1974), one group of rats received unpaired shocks of low intensity prior to classical conditioning; a second group received unpaired shocks of moderate intensity; and a third group received unpaired shocks of high intensity. Subsequently, all groups were given classical conditioning of suppression training. The result was that the strength of the suppression CR increased with an increase in the intensity of the unpaired shocks that the different groups received prior to classical conditioning. The same result was obtained by first establishing the suppression CR, then presenting different groups with unpaired shocks of low, moderate, or high intensity, and then testing for the strength of the suppression CR.

A similar result was obtained with classical conditioning of an increase in activity brought about by presenting CS-food pairings to food-deprived rats (Holland & Rescorla, 1975). After this classical conditioning was established, rats in one group were permitted to eat food in the home cage and were immediately thereafter rotated at 120 revolutions per minute. This rotation was probably a negative reinforcer; it resulted in a decrease in food consumption. A control group received the same rotation but was not given access to food beforehand. The group receiving pairings between food and rotation exhibited less activity than the control group when both these groups were presented with the CS used in carrying out classical conditioning of an increase in activity.

In the 1974 study, Rescorla found that CR strength was affected by presentations of a shock that was similar to the shock UCS employed in classical conditioning. In the 1975 study, CR strength was affected by presentations of food previously paired with rotation, the food being identical to the food UCS employed in classical conditioning. Thus, it appears possible that the UCS employed in conditioning may become "confused" with similar UCSs, or occurrences of the same UCS in different situations. In addition, it appears to be difficult to account for these results without in some way assuming that a representation of the UCS employed in classical conditioning becomes partially replaced by a representation of a similar UCS, or by a representation of the same UCS occurring in a different situation. In image theory terms, it may be that the permanent brain event corresponding to the UCS employed to establish the CR becomes partially replaced with the permanent brain event corresponding to a shock of different intensity (the 1974 study); or becomes partially replaced with a permanent brain event that has become connected to a permanent brain event corresponding to the negative reinforcer of rotation (the 1975 study).

That the UCS employed in classical conditioning becomes in some sense confused with similar UCSs that are not paired with the CS is probably related to forgetting. Remember that forgetting of aspects of the stimuli of the learning situation increases as the length of the retention interval increases. This suggests that the UCS employed in classical conditioning tends to be increasingly forgotten as the time since it last occurred increases. Perhaps the UCS employed in classical conditioning becomes confused with similar UCSs, since aspects of the UCS employed in classical conditioning become forgotten. It is also known that the magnitude of proactive and retroactive inhibition usually increases with an increase in the similarity of different sets of verbal material that are acquired. It might prove profitable to try to show that CR strength is less affected by unpaired presentations of a similar UCS when the unpaired presentations of the similar UCS are delivered very soon after the CS-UCS pairings are delivered rather than at a later time.

Psychotherapy Based on Instrumental Conditioning

Instrumental conditioning has been used to treat a wide variety of psychological disorders, both through establishing desired behaviors and eliminating undesired behaviors.

Examples of Instrumental Conditioning Therapy. The reward-learning type of instrumental conditioning was used by Bachrach, Erwin, & Mohr (1965) to treat a 37-year-old woman who weighed only 47 pounds. The patient's life was in danger because of her low weight, the result of not eating. Instrumental conditioning of eating was begun. The patient was removed from her attractive hospital room and placed in a barren "experimental" room without a TV set or a record player. In addition, hospital employees were instructed not to talk to her or otherwise socially interact. At meal times, the therapists delivered positive reinforcers whenever she responded by eating. The reinforcer used was attention; for instance, they talked to the woman about something that interested her. At first the preliminary components of the feeding sequence, such as picking up a piece of food with a fork, were followed by an increase in attention. As time went on, an increase in attention was not delivered until she lifted the food to her mouth, then until she put food in her mouth, and so on. In other words, shaping was employed to get her to approach the desired response of eating. Other reinforcers such as a TV set and a record player were eventually permitted when she ate a portion of a meal, and finally a complete meal. The patient's food consumption did increase markedly, and she did gain weight. Once discharged from the hospital, she continued to maintain her weight above a level dangerous to health, got a job, and interacted reasonably well with other people.

Punishment learning was used to reduce the frequency of head banging in a 9-year-old boy diagnosed as psychotic (Tate & Baroff, 1966). The boy's head banging gave him detached retinas; punishment learning was started to save his eyesight. Head-banging and other self-injurious behaviors were followed by delivering electric shock to the right leg. The rate of exhibiting self-injurious behaviors declined. The last self-injurious behavior occurred on the 147th day after shock was first used; after that he was observed for another twenty days.

A 3½-year-old boy who had been diagnosed as autistic started throwing his glasses away. To eliminate this behavior, after each such action he was put in his room for 10 minutes, which led to his almost completely stopping this undesired response (Wolf, Risley, & Mees, 1964). Isolating the boy probably terminated the positive reinforcer of attention, an instance of the response-terminates-reward type of instrumental conditioning.

Temper tantrums were eliminated in a 21-month-old boy with an extinction procedure (Williams, 1959). The boy exhibited temper tantrums when he was put to bed, so that the parents remained with the child until he went to sleep. The temper tantrums were thus reward-trained, since the parents delivered attention when they took place. The parents were instructed to put the boy to bed in a relaxed and friendly fashion, but then to leave the room, close the door, and not re-enter the room. Starting with the time the parents first behaved as instructed, the duration of crying decreased gradually as the number of times the child was put to bed increased. Removing the positive reinforcer of attention thus resulted in extinction of the reward-trained temper tantrum response.

Often a combination of types of instrumental conditioning are employed to obtain a desired outcome. For example, Burchard and Tyler (1965) followed the delinquent responses of a 13-year-old boy with social isolation, and followed his exhibition of appropriate behavior with tokens that were used by the boy to pay for things he wanted. The social isolation probably resulted in response-terminates-reward learning, and the token procedure in reward learning. Yet both types of instrumental conditioning probably contributed to the obtained outcome, an increased frequency of appropriate behavior.

Considerations Involving Instrumental Conditioning Therapy. The types of reinforcers used in psychotherapy obviously must differ from one person to the next. Food reinforcement has been used to establish certain responses (Hewett, 1965; Whitney & Barnard, 1966), but another type of reinforcer clearly was required for the woman who was starving herself to death. Social reinforcers are frequently found to be ineffective with children who are diagnosed as psychotic or autistic. These children are relatively likely to play with inanimate objects. Not surprisingly, therefore, inanimate stimuli, such as rotation of a motorized chair, have been used as reinforcers to establish reward learning of desired behaviors in a child diagnosed as autistic (Hewett, 1965). The effectiveness of a therapist as a source of social reinforcement does seem to increase when the therapist delivers nonsocial reinforcers. For example, the child whose responses were instrumentally conditioned with a motorized chair subsequently acquired instrumentally conditioned responses established with social reinforcers that were provided by the therapist. When social reinforcers are employed with children, they may frequently involve the occurrence of contact comfort. The reinforcer used in one study to establish peer interaction behavior in a child consisted of the words, "Good," "Fine," "spoken with an encouraging tone of voice and a touch with the hand or a brief embrace with the arm" (Jensen & Womack, 1967, p. 31).

Children diagnosed as psychotic and autistic frequently require a great deal of shaping of behavior, because these children tend to be deficient in a large variety of interpersonal and skill behaviors. Hewett's (1965) goal was to establish speech in a 2-year-old child whose vocal behavior was extremely limited. Early in training, food was delivered to the child only when he established eye contact with the therapist. As a result, the frequency of the child's making eye contact with the therapist increased. Later on, the therapist trained the child to imitate a variety of nonverbal behaviors. The child learned to imitate the teacher's touching parts of her head; the reinforcer for this imitated behavior was rotation of a chair the child sat in. This learning was probably made possible by the child's having been trained to look at the teacher's face. Subsequently, the child's first word, "Go," was established. This word was chosen because it resembled a nonspeech sound the child emitted. The therapist first made sounds similar to both the child's vocalization and the word "go," and delivered candy to the child when he imitated. The therapist then spoke progressively closer approximations to "Go," the child continued to imitate, and the candy continued to be delivered following the imitations. After "Go" was spoken by the child, other words were similarly established, using a variety of reinforcers. At the same time, the teacher began to teach the meaning of words. To enter the schoolroom door, for instance, the child had to say, "Go." Later on, he was trained on the meaning of two-word sentences. To get water, for example, he was required to say, "I want." The child finally came to spontaneously exhibit meaningful speech, and by the end of training, he "demonstrated an insatiable desire to learn new words and phrases" (p. 934).

The success of instrumental conditioning can be demonstrated by showing that extinction results in the reappearance of the undesired behavior, and that the previously acquired appropriate behavior returns when the original instrumental conditioning procedure is employed once more. In one case history (Whitney & Barnard, 1966), a 14-year-old girl diagnosed as mentally retarded was taught to use a spoon to eat, the positive reinforcer employed being food. Subsequently, the therapist left the girl for five days to be treated by the staff as she had been before teaching. When the therapist returned, the girl was no longer spoon feeding herself, but the therapist re-established this behavior with the same training procedure.

Appropriate behavior may also be acquired through instrumental conditioning in traditional psychotherapy. The therapist, perhaps without clearly understanding what he is doing, may establish reward learning of appropriate responses by following them with attention. He may also employ other types of instrumental conditioning to increase the frequency of appropriate responses and to decrease the frequency of inappropriate responses, using his interpersonal behaviors as positive and negative reinforcers.

Instrumental Conditioning, Development of Social Behavior, and Contact Comfort

Contact comfort, as we previously indicated, is a positive primary reinforcer for children. Everyday observation suggests that infants and young children are more likely to receive contact comfort from familiar people if they exhibit appropriate responses of various kinds than if they do not exhibit these responses. A mother is probably relatively likely to initiate contact comfort with a young child, for example, with a hug, arm-around-shoulder, or pat, after the child acquires skills, helps the mother, behaves independently, or exhibits interpersonal responses with positive affect, such as smiling and being cute.

In Ou's (1977) study, the interactions of children and their mothers were videotaped while the children worked on tasks, for example, completing a puzzle and answered questions. Every 3-second interval that a mother and child were involved with a task or question was rated for whether or not the child completed the task or answered the question, and for whether or not the mother initiated contact comfort with the child. It was found that maternal contact comfort was more likely to occur if a task completion or a correct answer had occurred in the previous 3-second interval than at other times; but that maternal contact comfort was not more likely to occur if an incorrect answer had been given in the previous 3-second interval than at other times. It appears reasonable to consider task completion and answering correctly as relatively appropriate behaviors, and behavior at other times and answering incorrectly as relatively neutral behaviors. The obtained result therefore supports the conclusion that familiar people are relatively likely to deliver contact comfort following the child's appropriate behavior.

In another study (King & Beatty, 1975), it was found that college students expect parents are relatively likely to follow the child's behaving appropriately with contact comfort. College students completed paragraphs in which a 4-, 7-, or 10-year-old child was described as either behaving or not behaving as requested by the father or mother. Three requested behaviors were used: clean up room; play on own; and work on a puzzle the child previously had trouble doing. The completions were to indicate what a parent would do following a child's either exhibiting or not exhibiting the requested behavior. For a given paragraph, only one combination of independent variables appeared, for example, mother, 7-year-old, clean up room, not exhibiting requested behavior. The completions were scored for initiation of contact comfort by a parent. It was found that subjects expected parents are more likely to initiate contact comfort with the child if the child behaves as requested, that is, appropriately, than if the child does not. This outcome was obtained for each of the behaviors the child was requested to perform.

If it is true that the child is relatively likely to receive contact comfort following his or her behaving appropriately, the child should then acquire appropriate behavior through reward learning. Socialization essentially means the acquisition of appropriate behavior, so it is possible that the indicated reward learning may importantly contribute to socialization of the child. Moreover, it will be suggested (Chapter 6) that the indicated reward learning is difficult to extinguish.

There is no doubt that children's responses are readily instrumentally conditioned. Some examples of this were described when psychotherapy based on instrumental conditioning was discussed. Of course, reinforcers other than contact comfort contribute to the instrumental conditioning of appropriate behavior in children (Gewirtz, 1961; Skinner, 1953).

Summary

In reward learning, the instrumental response causes a positive reinforcer to occur, a goal stimulus, and an increase in the rate of the instrumental response usually takes place. Image theory's account of this increase includes making the following assumptions: (a) An association between the stimulus produced by the instrumental response and the goal stimulus occurs through classical conditioning; (b) An image of the goal stimulus occurs prior to the execution of the instrumental response; (c) An animal behaves so as to increase the vividness of the image of the goal stimulus; and (d) An animal attempts to and does bring about the stimulus produced by the instrumental response. This last statement is supported by the finding that a CS paired with a positive UCS is approached and continued to be perceived. In punishment learning, the instrumental response causes a negative reinforcer to occur, a negative-goal stimulus, and a decrease in the rate of the instrumental response usually takes place. The way that image theory accounts for instrumental conditioning in which the instrumental response tends to decrease in rate is essentially identical with its explanation for instrumental conditioning in which the instrumental response tends to increase in rate—namely, that an animal should behave so as to decrease the vividness of the image of the negative-goal stimulus, and therefore an animal should attempt to avoid bringing about the stimulus produced by the instrumental response. The explanation for punishment learning is supported by the observation that a CS paired with a negative reinforcer is escaped from and avoided. Eight types of instrumental conditioning are generated by factorially combining three binary classifications—whether the reinforcer is positive or negative, whether the instrumental response causes a goal or negative-goal stimulus to occur, and whether the reinforcer is present or not present prior to the execution of the instrumental response. In escape learning, avoidance learning, and response-continues-reward learning, the instrumental response causes a goal stimulus to occur. Image theory explains these types of instrumental conditioning in essentially the same way as it does reward learning, because for all four of these types of instrumental conditioning, the instrumental response causes a goal stimulus to occur and thereby usually increases in rate. In omission, response-terminates-reward, and response-continues-punishment learning, the instrumental response causes a negative-goal stimulus to occur, and the instrumental response usually decreases in rate. Thus, image theory accounts for these types of instrumental conditioning as it does punishment learning. A particular type of classical conditioning is analogous to a particular type of instrumental conditioning. Image theory's account of each type of instrumental conditioning is supported by the known or likely result that the CS that is analogous to the stimulus produced by the instrumental response for each type of instrumental conditioning is either approached and continued to be perceived or escaped from and avoided. Unsignalled and signalled avoidance learning procedures were described. In avoidance learning, the instrumental response causes scheduled shock to be omitted, and this does contribute to avoidance learning. The effects of CSs paired with the onset or absence of negative reinforcers on unsignalled avoidance learning are discussed. When a reinforcer and no particular event occur in sufficiently close physical and temporal proximity, a stimulus paired with no particular event tends either to be approached and continued to be perceived or escaped from and avoided, and this supports image theory's explanation of avoidance, escape, omission, and response-terminates-reward learning. The instrumental response, rather than the set of responses that is not the instrumental response, is most likely responsible for instrumental conditioning occurring for all eight types of instrumental conditioning. If a reinforcer were randomly presented in relation to the occurrence of a single clearly defined response, then subsequent straightforward instrumental conditioning involving this reinforcer and response would probably be retarded.

Measures of the strength of instrumental responses are indicated, and the result that the strength of an instrumental response increases as training continues is discussed. Extinction results in a relatively rapid decrease in the strength of reward-trained responses, but punishment- and avoidance-trained responses are relatively resistant to extinction. An equivalent of extinction theory explains these findings. Consider, for example, extinction of punishment learning. A reduction in the strength of a punishment-trained response in extinction should occur only when the stimulus produced by the instrumental response is no longer followed by the negative reinforcer. However, this pairing between stimuli will not occur early in extinction if the instrumental response is not made at this time, and therefore punishment learning should sometimes be relatively resistant to extinction. In other words, equivalents of extinction may not occur early in extinction, the consequence being that punishment learning will be relatively resistant to extinction.

FR, VR, and VI schedules of reinforcement and their effects on re- sponding are described.

Delivery of the reinforcer independently of the execution of the instrumental response can affect the strength of this response, which indicates it is often advisable to employ a pseudoconditioning control. An increase in the time interval separating the execution of the instru- mental response from the occurrence of the stimulus this response causes to take place impairs instrumental conditioning. This result is analogous to the detrimental effect that an increase in the time interval between CS onset and UCS onset has on trace conditioning, which supports image theory's assumption that the instrumental conditioning process is, in part, a classical conditioning one. The possibility that an increase in the length of the indicated time interval increases forgetting of the stimulus pro- duced by the instrumental response is supported. Rats acquire a response that causes a lower rate of randomly occurring shock to occur. This result is analogous to the finding that excitatory classical conditioning tends to occur when a CS predicts that the UCS is relatively likely to occur while the CS is present or relatively shortly after the CS terminates, and it therefore supports image theory's assumption that the instrumental conditioning process is, in part, a classical conditioning one.

A stimulus present prior to the execution of an instrumentally condi- tioned response produces a CR-like response before this response is executed. This result supports the assumption that an image of the stimu- lus the instrumental response causes to occur takes place before the execution of the instrumentally conditioned response. CS-UCS pairings facilitate subsequently established instrumental conditioning in which the CS previously employed in classical conditioning precedes an instrumental response that causes the UCS previously employed in classical conditioning to occur.

Shaping is a procedure in which instrumentally conditioned responses are established that increasingly approximate a desired instrumentally conditioned response, thereby eventually establishing the desired instrumentally conditioned response. Stimuli present in the instrumental conditioning situation tend to produce CRs, and instrumental conditioning is impaired or facilitated depending on the similarity of the topography of the CR to the instrumental response. When the stimulus produced by a response differs only minimally from background stimuli, for example, the stimulus produced by a covert response, instrumental conditioning of this response is relatively poor. This finding is analogous to the poor classical conditioning that results when a CS differs only minimally from background stimuli. Instrumental conditioning of autonomic responses is discussed.

Instrumental responses that cause goal stimuli to occur usually increase in rate, and instrumental responses that cause negative-goal stimuli to occur usually decrease in rate—a finding supported by studies that measure the extent to which stimuli are approached and continued to be perceived. In addition, the strength of an instrumental response is positively related to the strength of the response to the perceived goal or negative-goal stimulus for the instrumental response. These studies are in accord with image theory's assumption that an animal behaves so as to increase the vividness of the image of the goal stimulus and to decrease the vividness of the image of the negative-goal stimulus. An increase in the amount or intensity of a reinforcer tends to increase the strength of an instrumental response, probably because the strength of the response to the perceived goal or negative-goal stimulus for the instrumental response is also increased.

Extent of deprivation of food and water exerts a nonlearning effect on the strength (performance) of the instrumental response. The effect of deprivation level on the strength of an instrumental response is most likely due to factors related to its effect on the strength of the response to the perceived goal stimulus for the instrumental response. Both the CR and the instrumentally conditioned response are quantitatively related to the response to the perceived second member of the S_1-S_2 pairing resulting in conditioning. In addition, the CR is obviously qualitatively related to the UCR in terms of response topography; also, the instrumental response is qualitatively related to measures of the strength of approaching and continuing to perceive a goal stimulus or escaping from and avoiding a negative-goal stimulus in the sense that an increase or decrease in the rate of an instrumental response affects the extent to which an animal approaches and continues to perceive a goal stimulus or escapes from and avoids a negative-goal stimulus. Thus, the conclusion is that classically and instrumentally conditioned responses are quantitatively and qualitatively related to certain responses to a perceived stimulus that is the second member of the S_1-S_2 pairing resulting in conditioning. This is analogous to the conclusion that the effects of images of stimuli on responding are quantitatively and qualitatively related to the effects of perceived stimuli on responding. This analogy supports image theory's assumption that the learned response is, in part, the outcome of an image of the UCS or the stimulus that the instrumental response causes to occur. Training, extinction, and delay of reinforcement affect the strength of the instrumental response through learning.

Image theory assumes that pairings between neutral stimuli mediate the instrumental conditioning process. This assumption is supported, because it is clear that instrumental conditioning occurs when a goal or negative-goal stimulus is a neutral stimulus. In addition, a study was described that showed an acquired association between some aspect of an instrumental response and a neutral stimulus this response caused to occur; the occurrence of this association was revealed when a relevant biological change was induced. Subjects of another study had very vivid images of a neutral stimulus that a response caused to occur. Observation learning involving neutral stimuli most likely contributes to instrumental conditioning.

Relatively extensive forgetting of components of the learning situation can occur over a retention interval of about two months. A reminder stimulus, a component of the original learning situation, appears to increase recall of the reinforcer and the stimulus produced by the instrumental response, when presented during a retention interval, following an electroconvulsive shock, and prior to acquisition of a second, similar task. These results support the assumption that recall of a stimulus should be viewed as mediated by the occurrence of an image of this stimulus, and the assumption that permanent brain events exist that correspond to reinforcers and to the stimuli produced by instrumental responses. A reminder stimulus also appears to increase recall of both the stimuli present before the execution of an instrumental response, and the CS; this supports the idea that permanent brain events exist that correspond to the stimuli of the general learning situation and the CS. The result that an electroconvulsive shock reduces recall of conditioning when it is delivered immediately after a reminder stimulus is presented is accounted for by image theory. UCSs employed in classical conditioning can in some sense become confused with similar unpaired UCSs, perhaps because aspects of the UCSs employed in classical conditioning become forgotten.

Different types of instrumental conditioning are used to establish desired and eliminate undesired responses of humans. Considerations in using instrumental conditioning procedures in psychotherapy include the type of reinforcer to employ; the use of shaping; the importance of demonstrating extinction and re-acquisition of responses; and what role instrumental conditioning plays in traditional psychotherapy.

Children are probably instrumentally conditioned to behave appropriately, since their appropriate behavior is relatively likely to cause a familiar person to initiate contact comfort with them.

REFERENCES

APPEL, J. B. Punishment in the squirrel monkey Saimiri sciurea. *Science,* 1961, 133, 36.

AZRIN, N. H. Effects of punishment intensity during variable-interval reinforcement. *J. Exp. Anal. Behav.,* 1960, 3, 123-142.

BACHRACH, A. J., ERWIN, W. J., & MOHR, J. P. The control of eating behavior in an anorexic by operant conditioning techniques. In L. P. Ullman & L. Krasner (Eds.), *Case Studies in Behavior Modification.* New York: Holt, Rinehart, and Winston, 1965.

BARCIK, J. D. Step-down passive avoidance: CER or specific avoidance? *Psychon. Sci.,* 1972, 27, 27-28.

BARRY, H., III. Effects of strength of drive on learning and extinction. *J. Exp. Psychol.,* 1958, 55, 473-481.

BENEDICT, J. O. Response-shock delay as a reinforcer in avoidance behavior. *J. Exp. Anal. Behav.,* 1975, 24, 323-332.

BOLLES, R. C., STOKES, L. W., & YOUNGER, M. S. Does CS termination reinforce avoidance behavior? *J. Comp. Physiol. Psychol.,* 1966, 62, 201-207.

BRELAND, K., & BRELAND, M. A field of applied psychology. *Am. Psychol.,* 1951, 6, 202-204.

BURCHARD, J., & TYLER, V., JR. The modification of delinquent behaviour through operant conditioning. *Behav. Res. Ther.,* 1965, 2, 245-260.

CAMP, D. S., RAYMOND, G. A., & CHURCH, R. M. Temporal relationship between response and punishment. *J. Exp. Psychol.,* 1967, 74, 114-123.

CAMPBELL, B. A., & KRAELING, D. Response strength as a function of drive level and amount of drive reduction. *J. Exp. Psychol.,* 1953, 45, 97-101.

CICALA, G. S. Running speed in rats as a function of drive level and presence or absence of competing response trials. *J. Exp. Psychol.,* 1961, 62, 329-334.

D'ANDREA, T. Avoidance of timeout from response-independent reinforcement. *J. Exp. Anal. Behav.,* 1971, 15, 319-325.

DAVIS, H., HIRSCHORN, P., & HURWITZ, H. M. B. Lever holding behavior during a lever-lift shock escape procedure. *Anim. Learn. Behav.,* 1973, 1, 215-218.

DICARA, L. V., & MILLER, N. E. Transfer of instrumentally learned heart-rate changes from curarized to noncurarized state: Implications for a mediation hypothesis. *J. Comp. Physiol. Psychol.,* 1969, 68, 159-162.

DUNHAM, P. J. Punishment: Method and theory. *Psychol. Rev.*, 1971, 78, 58-70.

DUNHAM, P. J. Some effects of punishment upon unpunished responding. *J. Exp. Anal. Behav.*, 1972, 17, 443-450.

GAMZU, E., & WILLIAMS, D. R. The source of keypecking in autoshaping. *Anim. Learn. Behav.*, 1975, 3, 37-42.

GEWIRTZ, J. L. A learning analysis of the effects of normal stimulation, privation and deprivation on the acquisition of social motivation and attachment. In B. M. Foss (Ed.), *Determinants of Infant Behaviour*. London: Methuen, 1961.

GLAZER, H. I., & WEISS, J. M. Long-term and transitory interference effects. *J. Exp. Psychol.: Anim. Behav. Processes*, 1976, 2, 191-201. (a)

GLAZER, H. I., & WEISS, J. M. Long-term interference effect: An alternative to "learned helplessness." *J. Exp. Psychol.: Anim. Behav. Processes*, 1976, 2, 202-213. (b)

GLEITMAN, H., & STEINMAN, F. Retention of runway performance as a function of proactive interference. *J. Comp. Physiol. Psychol.*, 1963, 56, 834-838.

GORDON, W. C., & SPEAR, N. E. Effect of reactivation of a previously acquired memory on the interaction between memories in the rat. *J. Exp. Psychol.*, 1973, 99, 349-355.

GREENFIELD, H., & RICCIO, D. C. Conditioned reinstatement in rats: Effects of exposure distribution and type of cue. *Psychol. Rep.*, 1972, 31, 79-83.

GRICE, G. R. The relation of secondary reinforcement to delayed reward in visual discrimination learning. *J. Exp. Psychol.*, 1948, 38, 1-16.

HALL, J. F., & KOBRICK, J. L. The relationships among three measures of response strength. *J. Comp. Physiol. Psychol.*, 1952, 45, 280-282.

HEFFERLINE, R. F., & KEENAN, B. Amplitude-induction gradient of a small-scale (covert) operant. *J. Exp. Anal. Behav.*, 1963, 6, 307-315.

HEFFERLINE, R. F., & PERERA, T. B. Proprioceptive discrimination of a covert operant without its observation by the subject. *Science*, 1963, 139, 834-835.

HERRNSTEIN, R. J., & HINELINE, P. N. Negative reinforcement as shock-frequency reduction. *J. Exp. Anal. Behav.*, 1966, 9, 421-430.

HEWETT, F. M. Teaching speech to an autistic child through operant conditioning. *Am. J. Orthopsychiatry*, 1965, 35, 927-936.

HILLMAN, B., HUNTER, W. S., & KIMBLE, G. A. The effect of drive level on the maze performance of the white rat. *J. Comp. Physiol. Psychol.*, 1953, 46, 87-89.

HINELINE, P. N. Negative reinforcement without shock reduction. *J. Exp. Anal. Behav.*, 1970, 14, 259-268.

HOLLAND, P. C., & RESCORLA, R. A. The effect of two ways of devaluing the unconditioned stimulus after first- and second-order appetitive conditioning. *J. Exp. Psychol.: Anim. Behav. Processes*, 1975, 1, 355-363.

JENSEN, G. D., & WOMACK, M. G. Operant conditioning techniques applied in the treatment of an autistic child. *Am. J. Orthopsychiatry*, 1967, 37, 30-34.

KEEHN, J. D. Is bar-holding with negative reinforcement preparatory or preservative? *J. Exp. Anal. Behav.*, 1967, 10, 461-465.

KHAVARI, K. A., & EISMAN, E. H. Some parameters of latent learning and generalized drives. *J. Comp. Physiol. Psychol.*, 1971, 77, 463-469.

KING, D. L. Learned and perceived reinforcer response strengths and image theory. *Bull. Psychon. Soc.*, 1976, 7, 438-441.

KING, D. L., & BEATTY, L. A. Students' expectations of parents' behavior following children's appropriate and inappropriate behavior. *Psychol. Rep.*, 1975, 36, 875-881.

KINTSCH, W. Runway performance as a function of drive strength and magnitude of reinforcement. *J. Comp. Physiol. Psychol.*, 1962, 55, 882-887.

LEACH, D. A. Rats' extinction performance as a function of deprivation level during training and partial reinforcement. *J. Comp. Physiol. Psychol.*, 1971, 75, 317-323.

LETT, B. T. Long delay learning in the T-maze. *Learn. Motiv.*, 1975, 6, 80-90.

LEWIS, D. J., MILLER, R. R., & MISANIN, J. R. Recovery of memory following amnesia. *Nature*, 1968, 220, 704-705.

LYON, D. O. & OZOLINS, D. Pavlovian conditioning of shock-elicited aggression: A discrimination procedure. *J. Exp. Anal. Behav.*, 1970, 13, 325-331.

MCALLISTER, W. R., & MCALLISTER, D. E. Behavioral measurement of conditioned fear. In F. R. Brush (Ed.), *Aversive Conditioning and Learning*. New York: Academic Press, 1971.

MILLER, N. E. Learning of visceral and glandular responses. *Science*, 1969, 163, 434-435.

MILLER, N. E. & CARMONA, A. Modification of a visceral response, salivation in thirsty dogs, by instrumental training with water reward. *J. Comp. Physiol. Psychol.*, 1967, 63, 1-6.

MISANIN, J. R., MILLER, R. R., & LEWIS, D. J. Retrograde amnesia produced by electroconvulsive shock after reactivation of a consolidated memory. *Science*, 1968, 160, 554-555.

OU, Y. *Mothers' Contact Comfort and Other Behaviors while Children Work on Tasks*. Unpublished Ph.D. dissertation, Howard University, 1977.

PAGE, H. A. The facilitation of experimental extinction by response prevention as a function of the acquisition of a new response. *J. Comp. Physiol. Psychol.*, 1955, 48, 14-16.

PREMACK, D. Rate differential reinforcement in monkey manipulation. *J. Exp. Anal. Behav.*, 1963, 6, 81-89. (a)

PREMACK, D. Prediction of the comparative reinforcement values of running and drinking. *Science*, 1963, 139, 1062-1063. (b)

PREMACK, D. Reinforcement theory. In D. Levine (Ed.), *Nebraska Symposium on Motivation*. Lincoln: University of Nebraska Press, 1965.

PREMACK, D. Catching up with common sense or two sides of a generalization: Reinforcement and punishment. In R. Glaser (Ed.), *The Nature of Reinforcement*. New York: Academic Press, 1971.

QUARTERMAIN, D., MCEWEN, B. S., & AZMITIA, E. C., JR. Recovery of memory following amnesia in the rat and mouse. *J. Comp. Physiol. Psychol.*, 1972, 79, 360-370.

RESCORLA, R. A. Predictability and number of pairings in Pavlovian fear conditioning. *Psychon. Sci.*, 1966, 4, 383-384.

RESCORLA, R. A. Pavlovian conditioned fear in Sidman avoidance learning. *J. Comp. Physiol. Psychol.*, 1968, 65, 55-60.

RESCORLA, R. A. Effect of inflation of the unconditioned stimulus value following conditioning. *J. Comp. Physiol. Psychol.*, 1974, 86, 101-106.

RESCORLA, R. A., & LOLORDO, V. M. Inhibition of avoidance behavior. *J. Comp. Physiol. Psychol.*, 1965, 59, 406-412.

SCHNEIDER, A. M., & SHERMAN, W. Amnesia: A function of the temporal relation of footshock to electroconvulsive shock. *Science*, 1968, 159, 219-221.

SELIGMAN, M. E. P., & MAIER, S. F. Failure to escape traumatic shock. *J. Exp. Psychol.*, 1967, 74, 1-9.

SHAPIRO, M. M. Temporal relationship between salivation and lever pressing with differential reinforcement of low rates. *J. Comp. Physiol. Psychol.*, 1962, 55, 567-571.

SHETTLEWORTH, S. J. Reinforcement and the organization of behavior in golden hamsters: Hunger, environment, and food reinforcement. *J. Exp. Psychol.: Anim. Behav. Processes*, 1975, 1, 56-87.

SIDMAN, M. Classical avoidance without a warning stimulus. *J. Exp. Anal. Behav.*, 1962, 5, 97-104.

SIDMAN, M. Avoidance behavior. In W. K. Honig (Ed.), *Operant Behavior: Areas of Research and Application*. New York: Appleton-Century-Crofts, 1966.

SKINNER, B. F. *The Behavior of Organisms*. New York: Appleton-Century-Crofts, 1938.

SKINNER, B. F. How to teach animals. *Sci. Am.*, 1951, 185, 26-29.

SKINNER, B. F. *Science and Human Behavior*. New York: Macmillan, 1953.

SOLOMON, R. L., KAMIN, L. J., & WYNNE, L. C. Traumatic avoidance learning: The outcomes of several extinction procedures with dogs. *J. Abnorm. Soc. Psychol.*, 1953, 48, 291-302.

SPENCE, K. W. *Behavior Theory and Conditioning*. New Haven, Conn.: Yale University Press, 1956.

STEINMAN, F. Retention of alley brightness in the rat. *J. Comp. Physiol. Psychol.*, 1967, 64, 105-109.

TATE, B. G., & BAROFF, G. S. Aversive control of self-injurious behavior in a psychotic boy. *Behav. Res. Ther.*, 1966, 4, 281-287.

THEIOS, J., LYNCH, A. D., & LOWE, W. F., JR. Differential effects of shock intensity on one-way and shuttle avoidance conditioning. *J. Exp. Psychol.*, 1966, 72, 294-299.

TRAPOLD, M. A. Are expectancies based upon different positive reinforcing events discriminably different? *Learn. Motiv.*, 1970, 1, 129-140.

TRAPOLD, M. A., & OVERMIER, J. B. The second learning process in instrumental conditioning. In A. H. Black and W. F. Prokasy (Eds.), *Classical Conditioning II: Current Theory and Research*. New York: Appleton-Century-Crofts, 1972.

UHL, C. N. Response elimination in rats with schedules of omission training, including yoked and response-independent reinforcement comparisons. *Learn. Motiv.*, 1974, 5, 511-531.

WAHLSTEN, D. L., & COLE, M. Classical and avoidance training of leg flexion in the dog. In A. H. Black and W. F. Prokasy (Eds.), *Classical Conditioning II: Current Research and Theory*. New York: Appleton-Century-Crofts, 1972.

WEISMAN, R. G., & LITNER, J. S. Positive conditioned reinforcement of Sidman avoidance behavior in rats. *J. Comp. Physiol. Psychol.*, 1969, 68, 597-603.

WHITNEY, L. R., & BARNARD, K. E. Implications of operant learning theory for nursing care of the retarded child. *Ment. Retard.*, 1966, 4, 26-29.

WILLIAMS, C. D. The elimination of tantrum behavior by extinction procedures: Case report. *J. Abnorm. Soc. Psychol.*, 1959, 59, 269.

WOLF, M., RISLEY, T., & MEES, H. Application of operant conditioning procedures to the behaviour problems of an autistic child. *Behav. Res. Ther.*, 1964, 1, 305-312.

WOODS, P. J. A taxonomy of instrumental conditioning. *Am. Psychol.*, 1974, 29, 584-597.

ZEAMAN, D. Response latency as a function of the amount of reinforcement. *J. Exp. Psychol.*, 1949, 39, 466-483.

CHAPTER 4

Stimulus Generalization and Discrimination Learning

Stimulus Generalization

After a learned response has been established in the presence of certain stimuli, it continues to be exhibited if these stimuli are altered to some extent. This is referred to as *stimulus generalization*.

Procedures and Results. Hoffman and Fleshler (1961) investigated stimulus generalization of classically conditioned suppression. Pigeons were first reward-trained to peck a key. Subsequently, response-independent pairings between a tone with a frequency of 1000 cycles per second—that is, a 1000 Hz. tone—and shock were given, while the reward learning procedure remained in effect. Classical conditioning of suppression was acquired; the 1000 Hz. tone came to suppress the rate of key pecking almost completely. Then stimulus generalization was demonstrated by altering the stimuli of the learning situation and showing that classical conditioning of suppression continued to occur. Shock was discontinued—the test for stimulus generalization occurred in extinction—and pigeons were presented at different times with tones of 300, 450, 670, 1500, 2250, and 3500 Hz. as well as with the 1000 Hz. tone employed in acquisition. (Auditory stimuli varying along the frequency dimension are perceived as differing mainly in pitch.) All the tones presented in extinction were of the same intensity and duration as the 1000 Hz. tone. The order in which the tones were presented in extinction was randomized.

Figure 4-1 indicates the result obtained for a single bird. If no pecking occurred while the tone was on, the score was 1.00; if the pecking rate while a tone was on equaled the pecking rate occurring just before the tone went on, the score was 0.00. Figure 4-1 indicates that stimulus generalization occurred, because it shows that the learned response of a suppression of pecking took place in the presence of stimuli not identical to those present during acquisition. The curve in Figure 4-1 is called a *stimulus generalization gradient*, and it is typical for stimulus generalization results. It shows that learned response strength decreases as nontraining stimuli move away from a stimulus present during training along a dimension of this stimulus. In other words, the amount of stimulus

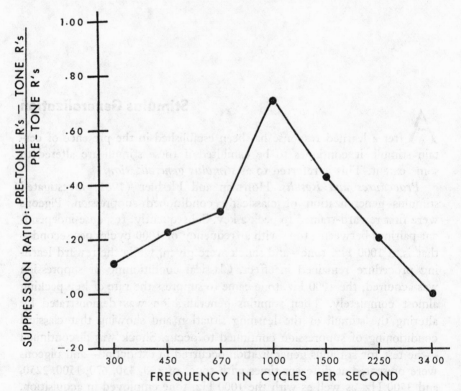

FIGURE 4-1. Stimulus generalization gradient for a classically conditioned response. (Adapted from Hoffman and Fleshler, 1961.)

generalization occurring decreases as the nontraining stimuli move away from a stimulus present during training along a dimension of this stimulus.

In one study investigating stimulus generalization of instrumentally conditioned responses (Hanson, 1959), pigeons were first reward-trained to peck using a VI (variable-interval) 1 minute food reinforcement schedule. The VI schedule is frequently used in studies of both stimulus generalization and discrimination learning. The response key—the circular area the pigeons pecked—was illuminated with light with a wavelength of 550 nanometers. (Lights of different wavelength are perceived as differing mainly in hue.) After the reward-trained response was well established, the amount of stimulus generalization occurring to different nontrained stimuli was determined. The 550 nanometer training stimulus and also nontraining lights of 480, 500, 510, 520, 530, 540, 560, 570, 580, 590, 600, and 620 nanometers were projected on the key one at a time in extinction. Each stimulus was presented 10 times in extinction, each time for 30 seconds. All stimuli were presented n times before any one of them was presented $n+1$ times. The order in which the stimuli were presented within each block of 13 stimuli was randomized.

Figure 4-2 shows the stimulus generalization gradients obtained from three pigeons. The measure of response strength was the total number of responses made in the presence of a stimulus employed in the stimulus generalization determination. Responding occurred to stimuli not present during acquisition, so by definition stimulus generalization took place. Each gradient also indicates that response strength decreased, that is, the amount of stimulus generalization occurring decreased, as the nontraining stimuli moved away from the stimulus present during training along a dimension of this stimulus.

Stimulus generalization of the effect of extinction also occurs in classical and instrumental conditioning (Hovland, 1937; Kling, 1952). In the Hovland study, GSR CRs to each of four different tones that varied only in frequency were established. The GSR CR to either the highest or lowest frequency CS was then extinguished. Subsequently, the effect of extinction on the other tones was determined. It was found that GSR CR strength increased as the distance between the tone presented in extinction and the remaining tones increased along the frequency dimension; that is, the effect of extinction spread to the remaining tones, more so to those tones closer in frequency to the one presented in extinction.

Discussion of Procedures and Results. Investigation of the stimulus generalization of a learned response naturally involves first establishing this response and then determining the strength of responding produced by the stimuli present during training and somewhat similar stimuli. The Hoffman and Fleshler and Hanson studies illustrate the most frequently employed procedure in the measurement of stimulus generalization. The nontraining stimuli vary along a dimension of a stimulus present during training, the CS for classical conditioning and a stimulus that is highly likely to be perceived for instrumental conditioning. The nontraining stimuli employed in a stimulus generalization determination are called *test stimuli*. The stimulus present during training and the test stimuli are presented individually in extinction. The order of presentation of the training and test stimuli is controlled so as to make sure that extinction of responding to each stimulus employed in the stimulus generalization determination is approximately equivalent.

An alternative procedure to presenting the training and test stimuli in extinction is to present them with delivery of the reinforcer. The purpose of both the extinction procedure and this nondifferential reinforcement procedure is to equate learning opportunities in the stimulus generalization determination.

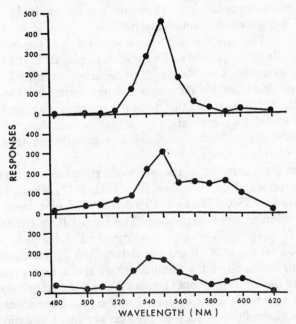

FIGURE 4-2. Stimulus generalization gradients for an instrumentally conditioned response. (Adapted from Hanson, 1959.)

The typically obtained stimulus generalization result is that response strength decreases, that is, the amount of stimulus generalization occurring decreases, as the distance along a dimension between a training stimulus and a test stimulus increases.

There has been one exception to this typical result: Blackwell and Schlosberg (1943) found that the strength of an instrumental response was greater to a test stimulus one octave lower than the stimulus present during training than to a tone of an intermediate frequency. The stimulus employed in training was a 10,000 Hz. tone, and more stimulus generalization occurred to a 5,000 Hz. tone than to a 7,000 Hz. tone, the 5,000 Hz. tone being exactly one octave lower than the 10,000 Hz. tone.

Two stimuli that differ relatively little along a dimension are apt to be reported as similar. Furthermore, two tones exactly one octave apart art apt to be reported as more similar than some tone pairs closer together in frequency. Consequently, the amount of stimulus generalization occurring between two stimuli is related to reports about similarity of stimuli. So, the amount of stimulus generalization that occurs is often described in terms of the similarity of the stimuli involved.

The usual procedure for measuring stimulus generalization of an instrumentally conditioned response leads to clear results for two reasons. One is that the use of a VI schedule in acquisition helps to maintain responding in extinction, when stimulus generalization is usually measured, because the VI schedule (and other partial reinforcement schedules) increase the resistance to extinction of learned responses. The second is that placing the visual stimuli on the key that is pecked almost guarantees that pigeons orient toward the stimuli of interest just before the execution of the instrumental response.

Stimulus Generalization and Image Theory. We continue to speak of an image of a stimulus occurring, even though we cannot be sure that an animal experiences a stimulus when the temporary brain event that corresponds to it takes place.

Humans would probably report that as test stimuli became less similar to a stimulus present during training along a dimension of this stimulus, the vividness of the image of the UCS or positive reinforcer (for reward learning) employed in acquisition decreases. For example, if the CS were a white circle, humans might report that a light gray circle leads to a clearer idea, that is, a more vivid image, of the UCS than a black circle does. The vividness of the image of a UCS or goal or negative-goal stimulus is correlated (positively) with the strength of the image-produced response, and the strength of the tendency to behave so as to bring about and maintain or terminate and avoid the image of the goal or negative-goal stimulus. We assume the CR results from an image-produced response, and that the instrumentally conditioned response results from an animal's behaving so as to either increase or decrease the vividness of an image of a goal or negative-goal stimulus. A decrease in the vividness of the image of a UCS or goal or negative-goal stimulus should therefore be accompanied by a decrease in CR strength or the strength of the instrumental response. It follows that as test stimuli become less similar to a stimulus present during training along a dimension of this stimulus, the strength of the learned response should decrease, which it does.

Stimulus generalization also contributes to image theory's explanation of instrumental conditioning. It maintains that the vividness of the image of a goal or negative-goal stimulus increases as the response-produced stimulus occurring at the moment becomes more similar to the stimulus produced by the instrumental response. The stimulus produced by the instrumental response can be viewed as analogous to the stimulus present during training; response-produced stimuli occurring at different moments in time are analogous to test stimuli that vary in similarity to the stimulus present during training. Also, vividness of the image of a goal or negative-goal stimulus should increase as the response-produced stimuli occurring at different moments in time become more similar to the stimulus produced by the instrumental response, just as the vividness of the image of a goal or negative-goal stimulus probably increases as the test stimuli become more similar to the training stimulus. Stimulus generalization therefore is a basic, integral component of the instrumental conditioning process.

Another matter involving stimulus generalization and image theory is that it appears that some sort of comparison process occurs between a test stimulus presented in a stimulus generalization determination and the training stimulus. If each test stimulus is not in some sense compared to the training stimulus, how else can an orderly decrease in the strength of responding occur as the test stimuli move away from the training stimulus along a dimension of the training stimulus? It is suggested that a test stimulus in a stimulus generalization determination results in an image of the training stimulus, and the test stimulus is in some sense compared to this image. If a stimulus that is paired with a second, dissimilar stimulus is capable of producing an image of this dissimilar stimulus, it would seem that a test stimulus would result in an image of a similar training stimulus. Note that the assumption that a test stimulus results in an image of the training stimulus implies that a permanent brain event corresponding to the training stimulus exists. This inference is in accord with image theory's assumption that the permanent brain events corresponding to the CS and the stimuli of the general learning situation are involved with the processes for classical and instrumental conditioning.

Stimulus Generalization and Substimuli. Guthrie (1935) pointed out the advantages of viewing a stimulus as composed of substimuli or stimulus elements. Even a simple stimulus such as a light is composed of substimuli that correspond to the light's hue, saturation, intensity, area, position, and duration.

Substimuli should become associated with other substimuli through the classical conditioning process just as more molar stimuli are. Learned response strength is assumed to be positively related to (number of conditioned substimuli perceived)/(number of conditioned sub-stimuli perceived plus number of unconditioned substimuli perceived). *Perceived* here means "attended to," or "noticed." In addition, as the distance between two stimuli along a dimension increases, the number of perceived substimuli that the two stimuli possess in common normally decreases, and the number of perceived substimuli that the two stimuli do not possess in common normally increases.

These substimuli considerations are consistent with the typical stimulus generalization result, because: (a) as the test stimuli move away from a training stimulus along a dimension of this stimulus, the proportion of substimuli a test stimulus and the training stimulus possess in common decreases; (b) the substimuli of a test stimulus that are not also possessed by the training stimulus are unconditioned substimuli, since they were not present during acquisition; (c) therefore, as the test stimuli move away from a training stimulus along a dimension of this stimulus, the proportion of perceived conditioned substimuli decreases; and (d) thus, the strength of the learned response also decreases.

Substimuli and Relation between Training Stimulus and Receptor. A study by Richardson and Evans (1975) is discussed in terms of substimuli. Two keys were placed close to each other in a chamber; they were separated by a short horizontal distance. One key was illuminated with white light, and a second key was illuminated with 555 nanometer light. One group of pigeons was reward-trained to peck the white key. The other illuminated key was present, but pecking it had no scheduled consequences. A second group was reward-trained to peck the key illuminated with 555 nanometer light. The other illuminated key was present, but pecking it had no scheduled consequences. Stimulus generalization along the wavelength dimension was then measured. For both groups the training and test stimuli were placed on the key that had been illuminated with 555 nanometer light during acquisition. Figure 4-3 indicates that the amount of stimulus generalization occurring along the wavelength dimension decreased markedly as the test stimuli moved away from the training stimulus for the group that pecked the key illuminated with 555 nanometer light to obtain food. In other words, a steep stimulus generalization gradient was obtained for this group. However, the amount of stimulus generalization occurring along the wavelength dimension barely decreased as the test stimuli moved away from the training stimulus for the group that pecked the white light to obtain food. In other words, a flat stimulus generalization gradient was obtained for this group.

The results may be explained as follows. Because the pigeons' eyes were most likely pointed directly at the 555 nanometer light stimulus when pecking occurred for the group yielding the steep stimulus gen-

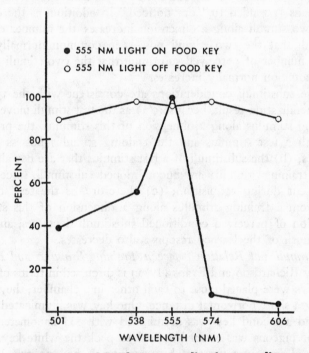

FIGURE 4-3. Stimulus generalization gradients obtained after a 555 nanometer light was either on the food key or off the food key. Percent equals the number of responses made in the presence of a stimulus divided by the number of responses made to the modal stimulus multiplied by 100. (Adapted from Richardson and Evans, 1975.)

eralization gradient, the number of conditioned substimuli perceived that were part of this light stimulus was probably relatively large. Introducing test stimuli varying along the wavelength dimension on the response key for this group would therefore result in a relatively large decrease in the number of conditioned substimuli perceived, and a relatively large increase in the number of unconditioned substimuli perceived. A relatively large decrease in the proportion of conditioned substimuli perceived would therefore occur, thus producing a relatively large decrease in the amount of stimulus generalization occurring along the wavelength dimension. For the group pecking the white key during acquisition, the number of conditioned substimuli perceived that were part of the 555 nanometer light stimulus was probably relatively low, because the pigeons' eyes were most likely primarily not directed at the 555 nanometer light. Introducing test stimuli varying along the wavelength dimension on the key not responded on for this group would therefore result in a relatively small decrease in the number of conditioned substimuli perceived, and a relatively small increase in the number of unconditioned substimuli perceived, thus leading to a relatively small decrease in the amount of stimulus generalization occurring along the wavelength dimension.

Discrimination Learning

Discrimination learning occurs when an animal learns to make one response (R_1) in the presence of one stimulus, and a second response (R_2) in the presence of a somewhat similar stimulus.

Procedures. A study by Ellison (1964) illustrates the procedure generally used to establish discrimination learning in classical conditioning. Some dogs received a 510 Hz. tone paired with food independently of responding. These dogs also received a 1700 Hz. tone, otherwise identical to the 510 Hz. tone, followed by the absence of food, that is, no particular event. For other dogs, the stimuli following these two tones were reversed. The tone paired with food is called the CS+ tone, and the tone paired with no particular event is called the CS— tone. Each day 13 CS+ trials and 13 CS— trials were run. Figure 4-4 indicates the amplitude of salivation produced by CS+ and CS— in acquisition. Discrimination learning occurred, because CS+ came to produce an increase in salivation (R_1), while CS—, similar to CS+, resulted in no increase in salivation (R_2).

This procedure is typical of discrimination learning procedures in general in that the absence of a reinforcer, that is, no particular event, is used to establish a different response (R_2) to a similar stimulus. The CS— would have produced a much stronger salivation response if it had not been paired with the absence of the UCS, because it was sufficiently similar to CS+ to have produced a sizable salivation response through stimulus generalization. In general, in discrimination learning an animal learns not to respond to one of two similar stimuli; a tendency to respond in the same way to both stimuli operates through stimulus generalization.

In discrimination learning in classical conditioning, the stimulus paired with the UCS, whether the UCS is positive or negative, is referred to as CS+, and the stimulus presented without the UCS, that is, alone, is

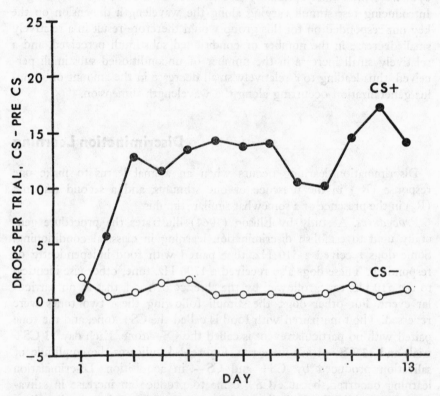

FIGURE 4-4. Discrimination learning in classical conditioning. The level of salivation occurring just before a trial was subtracted from the salivation that occurred when the CS+ or CS— was presented. (Adapted from Ellison, 1964.)

referred to as CS—. CS+ and CS— are spoken of as being discriminated between, and each of them is called a *discriminative stimulus*.

There are several standard procedures for establishing discrimination learning with the reward learning type of instrumental conditioning. The T-maze is frequently employed in establishing reward learning discriminations. The T-maze apparatus (Figure 4-5) has the shape of the letter "T". It is similar to the runway, except that a subject is presented with a choice at the end of the runway (stem) portion of the apparatus. As in runway learning studies, discrete trials are usually employed in T-maze discrimination learning. At the start of a trial, an animal, usually a rat, is placed in the start area of the T-maze. It is permitted to move down the stem portion of the T-maze and enter an arm. A positive reinforcer, for instance, a piece of food, is placed at the end of one of two arms. A subject is not allowed to perceive which arm of the T-maze contains the positive reinforcer before it chooses, that is, enters, one of the two arms of the T-maze, usually by placing a door at some point in both arms. When an animal enters an arm, the door in this arm is either opened by the experimenter or is pushed aside by the animal. In one procedural

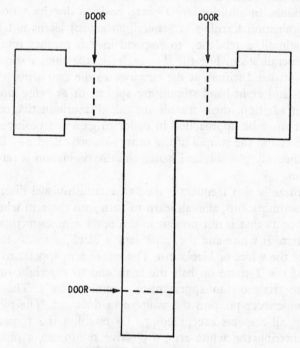

FIGURE 4-5. A T-maze.

variation, the subject is taken out of the maze after it reaches the end of the arm of the T-maze it first entered, after being permitted to obtain the reinforcer in this arm if it made a correct choice. This practice is called the *noncorrection procedure*. Alternatively, the animal is allowed to retrace its steps and enter the correct arm, if it first entered the incorrect arm. This practice is called the *correction procedure*.

The T-maze is frequently used to establish left-right position discriminations. Training a rat to turn, let us say, right is accomplished by putting the positive reinforcer at the end of the right arm on all trials and never placing a reinforcer at the end of the left arm. When position discriminations are taught, the two arms of the T-maze are identical, except spatially. When a rat learns to enter the right arm more than would be expected by chance, we may conclude that discrimination learning has occurred; the rat is likely to approach the stimuli to the right of the choice point (R_1), and is not likely to approach the stimuli to the left of the choice point (R_2).

The procedure described above is typical of discrimination learning procedures in general in that the absence of the reinforcer (in either the left or right arm) can be used to establish a different response (R_2) to a similar stimulus. In addition, in T-maze position discrimination learning, as in discrimination learning in general, an animal learns not to respond to similar stimuli, a tendency to respond in this manner resulting from stimulus generalization. For the T-maze task, the similar stimuli are the right- and left-hand stimuli at the entrance to the two arms.

The left- and right-hand stimuli are spoken of as being discriminated between. In addition, these stimuli are called discriminative stimuli. The stimuli that must be approached in order to gain the positive reinforcer are called S+, and the stimuli of the other side are called S—. S+ and S— are simultaneously present, and hence the discrimination is referred to as simultaneous.

The T-maze is also frequently used to establish visual discriminations. In these discriminations, animals learn to turn into the arm where a visual stimulus appears that is not present in the other arm. Sometimes one arm of the T-maze is white and the other arm is black; animals are trained to enter either the white or black arm. The white arm appears to the left of the stem of the T-maze on half the trials and to the right on the other half of the trials on an approximately random basis. The black arm occupies whichever position the white arm does not. The two arms are identical in all respects except color. To establish the response of, for example, entering the white arm, a positive reinforcer, a piece of food, is placed at the end of the white arm on all trials and a reinforcer never appears at the end of the black arm. If an animal eventually tends to enter the white arm, there has been discrimination learning. The tendency to enter the white arm (R_1) appears to be made to the white arm stimulus, and the tendency to not enter the black arm (R_2) appears to be made to the black arm stimulus.

As is true of discrimination learning in general, absence of the reinforcer is used to establish a different response (R_2) to a similar stimulus. As is also true of discrimination learning in general, the effect of stimulus generalization must be overcome in visual discrimination learning in a T-maze. In the described example, stimulus generalization from the white arm to the similar black arm must be overcome. The white color is S+, the positive discriminative stimulus, and the black color is S—, the negative discriminative stimulus. These two colors are simultaneously present, and therefore the discrimination is simultaneous.

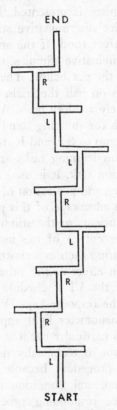

FIGURE 4-6. A multiunit T-maze.

More complex mazes, usually multiples of a single T-maze, are also used. An outline of a typical multiunit T-maze appears in Figure 4-6. Multiunit T-mazes usually require the rat to make left-right position discriminations at each choice point, where the openings to the two arms of each of the component T-mazes occur. At the start of a trial, a subject is placed into the start area of the maze. It is permitted to retrace its steps after entering incorrect arms—that is, the correction procedure is used—and the subject is not removed from the maze until it gets the reinforcer at the maze's end. With training, the tendency to enter the incorrect arms of the component T-mazes decreases.

Another apparatus frequently used in discrimination learning research is the jumping stand (Figure 4-7). This apparatus is often used to establish simultaneous visual discriminations, and the procedures employed are similar to those used for establishing simultaneous visual discriminations with the T-maze. In Figure 4-7 a choice between a triangle and what appears to be a square is presented. If the animal jumps to the square, the S+ or positive discriminative stimulus, the door is pushed aside and the animal receives food. If the animal jumps to the triangle, the S— or negative discriminative stimulus, the door is not pushed aside and the animal falls into the net below. The square and triangle appear on the left and right sides on half the trials, and are switched from side to side on an approximately random basis. Animals acquire simultaneous visual discriminations with the jumping stand apparatus; they do learn to jump to the S+. R_1 is a jump to S+, and R_2 is not jumping to S—.

Successive discrimination learning tasks are also used. One such task is a go/no-go discrimination task. It is used most frequently with birds, reward learning of pecking, and projection of visual discriminative stimuli on the response key. The advantage of this practice is that it practically guarantees that the bird orients to the stimuli of interest to the experimenter just before the execution of the instrumental response. In one study (Hanson, 1959), during each experimental session a VI 1 (minute) schedule was sometimes in effect and at other times no particular event was operative. Whenever the VI 1 schedule was in effect, a 550 nanometer light appeared on the response key. Whenever no particular event was programmed, a 560 nanometer light appeared on the response key. (The programming of no particular event is often referred to as extinction being operative, although technically no particular event being in effect is not an extinction procedure, because extinction does not involve the occurrence of instrumental conditioning in the presence of another stimulus.) The free responding procedure was employed; the pigeons were free to peck or not peck while the VI 1 schedule and extinction and their correlated stimuli alternated in time. At first, the pigeons pecked at a not very low rate when extinction was in effect because of stimulus generalization from the 550 nanometer to the 560 nanometer stimulus. With continued training, the pigeons came to respond hardly at all when extinction was in effect, and pecked at a moderately fast rate when the VI 1 schedule was operative. Discrimination learning therefore took place, because pecking at a moderately fast rate

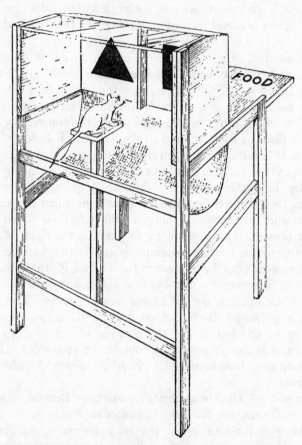

FIGURE 4-7. A jumping stand. (Lashley, K. S. The mechanism of vision: XV. Preliminary studies of the rat's capacity for detail vision. Journal of General Psychology, 1938, 18, 123-193, Copyright 1938. Adapted by permission of The Journal Press.)

(R_1) occurred when the VI 1 schedule was in effect and a 550 nanometer light appeared on the key, and pecking at a very low rate (R_2) occurred when extinction was in effect and another light appeared on the key.

The 550 nanometer light stimulus is S+, the positive discriminative stimulus, and the 560 nanometer light stimulus is S—, the negative discriminative stimulus. The discrimination learning procedure is successive, because S+ and S— were not simultaneously present. In addition, the discrimination is go/no-go, because the pigeons learned to respond (go) in the presence of S+, and learned not to respond (no-go) in the presence of S—.

There is another type of successive discrimination learning task, and an example will be described. On some trials a black square appears on each of the two doors of the jumping stand; on other trials a white square appears on each of the two doors. When the black squares are present, one response, say a jump to the right door, is followed by a positive reinforcer, a piece of food; a jump to the left door is followed by falling into the net. When the white squares are present, a jump to the left door is followed by the positive reinforcer and a jump to the right door is followed by falling into the net. Animals acquire the described discrimination; they come to jump to the right door when the black squares are present, and they come to jump to the left door when the white squares are present. R_1 is a tendency to jump to the right, R_2 is a tendency to jump to the left, and stimulus generalization between the black and white squares must be overcome for R_1 and R_2 to occur. The discrimination is a successive one because the discriminative stimuli, the white and black squares, do not appear simultaneously. The discrimination is not a go/no-go discrimination because R_2 is not the absence of R_1; jumping to the left is not the absence of jumping to the right. Furthermore, it is always possible to obtain the reinforcer. This type of discrimination may best be called a *reinforcer-always-possible successive discrimination.*

Measurement of Discrimination Performance. Because discrimination learning involves making different responses to discriminative stimuli that would otherwise produce much the same responses, measures of discrimination learning performance reflect the comparative strengths of responding to the discriminative stimuli. For discrimination learning in classical conditioning, the difference in CR strength produced by CS+ and CS— is compared. Simultaneous discriminations typically involve a choice between approaching S+ and approaching S—. Approach to S+ is referred to as a correct response, and approach to S— is referred to as an error. Performance on simultaneous discriminations is usually measured by counting the number of errors made. For go/no-go successive discriminations established with the free responding procedure, the rates of responding in the presence of S+ and S— are usually compared, for example, by computing the ratio of these rates. As discrimination training continues, the difference in response strengths produced by CS+ and CS— usually increases, the frequency of errors on a simultaneous discrimination usually decreases, and the ratio of the rate of responding in the presence of the S+ to the rate of responding in the presence of the S— for a go/no-go successive discrimination usually increases. With continued training, these measures of discrimination performance reach asymptote.

Discrimination Learning in Classical Conditioning. Discrimination learning occurs in straightforward classical conditioning in more ways than one.

Discrimination learning occurs between the CS and the stimuli of the general learning situation, that is, background stimuli, every time classical conditioning with a CS takes place. If X equals the background stimuli and A equals the nominal CS, then presentation of the CS in the learning situation means that A + X occurs. Because A + X produces a stronger response than the similar stimulus, X, discrimination learning between A + X, the positive discriminative stimulus, and X, the negative discriminative stimulus, occurs.

The idea that discrimination learning between A + X and X occurs in straightforward classical conditioning is supported by a study done by Kremer (1974). In his work the background stimuli X probably produced the CR to some extent, as evidenced by the strength of the CR produced by background stimuli alone being greater after CS-UCS pairings were presented than before these pairings occurred. Also supportive is the result that the strength of responding in the presence of background stimuli alone decreases as training continues (Annau & Kamin, 1961; Sheffield, 1965).

The result that the latency of the peak amplitude of the CR increases during training is probably also the outcome of discrimination learning. The CS can be thought of as composed of various substimuli. One substimulus occurs directly before the UCS, and therefore should definitely function as a CS+. Earlier occurring substimuli of the CS are not directly followed by the UCS. Therefore, with continued training they may be increasingly discriminated from the substimulus of the CS that is immediately followed by UCS onset. In other words, earlier substimuli of the CS may move with continued training in the direction of functioning as CS—s. If so, then the peak amplitude of the CR should occur increasingly closer to the time of UCS onset as training continues, which is the result to be explained.

Discrimination Learning in Instrumental Conditioning. Image theory assumes that straightforward instrumental conditioning always involves a discrimination learning process. Take reward learning for example. The stimulus produced by the instrumental response is always followed by a positive reinforcer; and the background stimuli and the stimuli produced by other responses are never followed by the reinforcer. Therefore, the stimulus produced by the instrumental response is analogous to the CS+ of a classical conditioning discrimination: the background stimuli and the stimuli produced by other responses are analogous to the CS— of this discrimination.

Discrimination Learning to Show Stimuli Control Responding. If stimuli of a certain type can be discriminated between, the type can affect, that is, control learned responses. Discrimination learning may therefore be used to show that certain types of stimuli control learned responses.

Image theory assumes that the stimulus produced by the instrumental response mediates the execution of this response. This hypothesis is supported by discrimination learning studies that show that the stimuli produced by instrumental responses control learned responses. In one such study (Hobson, 1975), pigeons could discriminate at an above-chance level between two different numbers of consecutive pecks on a single key when the two numbers differed by only 10 percent. Because no external stimulus signalling whether the larger or smaller number of consecutive pecks occurred was present, the pigeons must have discriminated between the two different numbers of consecutive pecks on the basis of response-produced stimuli.

Hobson's apparatus contained three keys. At the start of a trial the center key was illuminated and the two side keys were dark. The pigeons were trained to continue pecking the center key until it became dark and the two side keys were illuminated. The experimenter sometimes arranged for the center key to become dark and the two side keys to become illuminated after the smaller number of consecutive responses were made on the center key. On other occasions the experimenter waited until the larger number of consecutive responses were made on the center key before darkening the center key and illuminating the two side keys.

When the center key was dark and the two side keys were illuminated, a peck on the left key was followed by food, provided that the smaller number of consecutive responses had been made on the center key; and a peck on the right key was followed by food, provided that the larger number of consecutive responses had been made on the center key. In both cases, a peck on the other (incorrect) side key was not followed by food. After a single peck on the correct or incorrect side key, and after food was obtained when a correct response was made, a new trial was begun by again illuminating the center key, and so on. No experimenter-delivered stimulus signalled whether the smaller or larger number of consecutive responses had been made on the center key. Nevertheless, pigeons pecked the correct side key at an above-chance level even when there was only a 10 percent difference between the smaller and larger number of consecutive responses that were made on the center key. The stimuli controlling choice of the correct side key must therefore have been produced by responding on the center key, that is, they must have been response-produced.

Animals also discriminate quite well between time-correlated stimuli. For example, in a study by Kinchla (1970), occurrence of a tone of 3 seconds duration and a peck on the left key was followed by food; occurrence of a 5 second tone and a peck on the right key was also followed by food. If a pigeon pecked the wrong key, that is, the right-hand key when the 3-second tone was on or the left-hand key when the 5-second tone was on, food was not delivered. The pigeons performed well on this reinforcer-always-possible successive discrimination.

Time-correlated stimuli that control learned responses are usually response-produced. For example, in Kinchla's study, no experimenter-provided stimulus signalled which key to peck, and therefore the time-correlated stimuli that controlled performance on the discrimination must have been response-produced. Although on some occasions time-correlated stimuli are produced at least in part by overt responses, on other occasions they are produced by unobserved responses, most likely including response-produced stimuli within the brain. This possibility supports the assumption that the stimuli that responses produce that contribute to the execution of the instrumental response include stimuli produced within the brain.

It is also known that the stimuli corresponding to the time elapsed between two responses, for instance, two bar presses, can be discriminated between (Wilkie & Pear, 1972; Wilson & Keller, 1953). Such stimuli are clearly response-produced.

Various types of relations among stimuli are capable of controlling learned responses. One study (Lashley, 1938) used the jumping stand apparatus to successfully teach rats a discrimination in which (a) a jump in the direction of an erect triangle was followed by the positive reinforcer and a jump in the direction of a simultaneously present inverted triangle was not followed by the positive reinforcer when these triangles appeared against a black background; and (b) a jump in the direction of the inverted triangle was followed by the positive reinforcer and a jump in the direction of the simultaneously present erect triangle was not followed by the positive reinforcer when these triangles appeared against a striped background. The relationship between the triangular stimuli and the background stimuli obviously controlled performance. Discriminations in which the sign (+ or —) of a discriminative stimulus is dependent on the presence or absence of another stimulus are called *conditional discriminations*. Acquisition of conditional discriminations indicates that the relation between stimuli can acquire control over responding. Conditional discriminations can be acquired without undue difficulty, and therefore relations among stimuli are apt to control learned responses.

The nature of the stimuli controlling learned responding is not always clear. Consider two discriminative stimuli that differ in only one dimension—two squares, say, one white and one black, that are otherwise identical. There are two possible ways in which stimuli that vary along a single dimension may come to be discriminated between. One, absolute control, is that one discriminative stimulus has a specific identity, that the other discriminative stimulus has a different, specific identity, and that these independent identities affect discrimination performance. The other, relational control, is that discrimination learning occurs on the basis of one discriminative stimulus being more or less than the other discriminative stimulus along the dimension in question—one square being more or less dark, for example, than the other square.

What are called transposition studies try to determine whether absolute or relational stimulus control occurs when a discrimination between stimuli differing along a single dimension is acquired. No one seriously doubts that absolute control contributes to acquisition of a discrimination between stimuli that differ along a single dimension. Many transposition studies (Baker & Lawrence, 1951; Gentry, Overall, & Brown, 1959; Lawrence & DeRivera, 1954; Riley, Goggin, & Wright, 1963) indicate that relational control also contributes to acquisition of a discrimination between stimuli differing along a single dimension. This should not be surprising, since we know from research with conditional discriminations that other types of relations between stimuli can control learned responses. We may conclude that whatever signals or cues there are to the solution of a discrimination task will tend to acquire at least some control over responding.

Factors that Influence Discrimination Learning

Effect of Previously Discussed Independent Variables. In discrimination learning in classical conditioning, a stimulus (CS+) is followed by a UCS independently of responding, just as in straightforward classical conditioning a stimulus (CS) is followed by a UCS independently of responding. In discrimination learning in reward learning and in straightforward reward learning, a response made in the presence of certain stimuli causes a positive reinforcer to occur. Therefore, the independent variables that affect straightforward conditioning should similarly affect discrimination performance.

Two illustrative findings that support this expectation will be mentioned. One is that as training continues, discrimination performance improves, just as the strength of the CR and the instrumental response increases with continued training. The second (Ellison, 1964) is that discrimination learning using a trace conditioning procedure has been found to be inferior to discrimination learning using a delayed conditioning procedure. CS+ terminated before UCS onset for the trace conditioning procedure, and CS+ did not terminate before UCS onset for the delayed conditioning procedure. This result is similar to the result that straightforward trace conditioning is inferior to straightforward delayed conditioning.

Effect of Amount of Reinforcement and Deprivation Level. Amount of reinforcement and level of deprivation only inconsistently affect performance on reward learning discriminations (Hall, 1966, pp. 166-169, 182-183). For example, Hill, Cotton, and Clayton (1962) found that a larger amount of reinforcement resulted in less errors on a simultaneous position discrimination in a T-maze, while Maher and Wickens (1954) found that a larger amount of reinforcement did not lead to fewer errors on a multiunit T-maze task. Also, Eisman, Asimow, and Maltzman (1965) found that an increase in deprivation of food decreased errors on a simultaneous black-white discrimination in an apparatus similar to a T-maze, while Dinsmoor (1952) found that a greater deprivation level did not increase the ratio of the rate of responding to S+ to the rate of responding to S— in a go/no-go successive discrimination between visual stimuli.

An increase in the amount of reinforcement and deprivation level usually increases the rate of reward-trained responses. An analogous result is typical for reward learning discriminations. For example, Maher and Wickens found that a larger amount of reinforcement resulted in faster traversal of the multiunit T-maze; and Dinsmoor found that an increase in deprivation level led to faster rates of responding in the presence of both S+ and S—.

Why is it that amount of reinforcement and level of deprivation affect the rate measure of instrumentally conditioned response strength in a relatively consistent way, but affect measures of performance on discriminations only inconsistently? The effects of amount of reinforcement and deprivation level on the rate of a reward-trained response are related to the effects of these factors on measures of the strength of response to the perceived positive reinforcer establishing a reward-trained response. An analogous interpretation appears appropriate for the finding that amount of reinforcement and level of deprivation fail to affect performance on a reward learning discrimination.

It is considered likely that food-deprived animals given a choice between a perceived large amount of food and a perceived neutral stimulus, and food-deprived animals given a choice between a perceived small amount of food and a perceived neutral stimulus would both almost always approach the food rather than the neutral stimulus. Similarly, it is considered likely that animals given a choice between perceived food and a perceived neutral stimulus would almost always approach the food regardless of deprivation level, unless the deprivation level were quite low. The discrimination learning result under consideration is that often amount of reinforcement and deprivation level do not affect performance on a reward learning discrimination. Measures of performance on discriminations also involve a comparison between the strengths of two responses. Therefore, both a measure of the relative strengths of learned responses and a measure of the relative strengths of responding to perceived stimuli should often be unaffected by considerable variation in amount of reinforcement and deprivation level.

Classically and instrumentally conditioned responses are quantitatively and qualitatively related to certain responses to a perceived stimulus that is the second member of the S_1-S_2 pairing resulting in conditioning. The CR is obviously qualitatively related to the UCR, the response produced by the second member of the S_1-S_2 pairing that results in conditioning, in respect to response topography. The instrumentally conditioned response is qualitatively related to the response produced by the second member of the S_1-S_2 pairing that results in conditioning. The instrumentally conditioned response changes the rate an animal is permitted to approach and continue to perceive a goal stimulus or escape from and avoid a negative-goal stimulus, and measures of the strength of a response to a perceived stimulus relevant to instrumental conditioning—

for example, the proportion of time a stimulus is perceived—also involve permitting an animal to affect the rate it approaches and continues to perceive a stimulus or escapes from and avoids a stimulus. It follows that the failure of amount of reinforcement and deprivation level to affect performance on a reward learning discrimination that is often found supports the idea that classically and instrumentally conditioned responses are quantitatively and qualitatively related to responses to a perceived stimulus that is the second member of the S_1-S_2 pairing resulting in conditioning. The qualitative relation between a reward learning discrimination and the responses to perceived stimuli entails a comparison between responses occurring in a choice situation involving a positive reinforcer and a neutral stimulus; the learned responses might be entering one or the other arm of a T-maze, and the responses to perceived stimuli might be approaching and continuing to perceive food or a neutral stimulus. Quantitatively, in neither the discrimination learning situation nor the situation involving a choice between the perceived positive reinforcer and a neutral stimulus does amount of reinforcement and deprivation level consistently affect a measure reflecting the relative strengths of two responses.

Theoretically, these considerations support image theory. This theory assumes for a reward learning discrimination that S+ results in an image of the positive reinforcer and that S— results in an image of the absence of the reinforcer, that is, no particular event. It may be assumed that an image of the reinforcer and an image of no particular event occur simultaneously, even in successive discriminations (see below). The simultaneous occurrence of an image of a reinforcer and an image of no particular event (a neutral stimulus) should affect learned responding in much the same way that the simultaneous occurrence of a perceived reinforcer and a perceived neutral stimulus does, since images of stimuli and the effects of real stimuli are due to qualitatively identical temporary brain events. Amount of reinforcement and level of deprivation tend not to affect performance in a choice situation between a perceived reinforcer and a perceived neutral stimulus. It follows that amount of reinforcement and deprivation level should not affect performance on a reward learning discrimination.

One other consideration: the finding that, on occasion, a larger amount of reinforcement and an increase in deprivation level improve performance on a reward learning discrimination may be due to the fact that a larger amount of reinforcement and an increase in deprivation level increase the rate of responding, thereby reducing delay of reinforcement, and thus improving discrimination learning performance.

Effect of Stimulus Generalization between Discriminative Stimuli. As the amount of stimulus generalization that occurs between discriminative stimuli prior to discrimination learning increases, performance on a discrimination between these stimuli deteriorates. The amount of stimulus generalization between two stimuli is relatively large if the strengths of responding they produce in a stimulus generalization determination are relatively similar.

When two stimuli are relatively close together along a dimension and are otherwise identical, performance on a discrimination between these stimuli is relatively poor. For example, Pavlov (1927, p. 122) found it relatively easy to establish a discrimination between a white circle and a dark gray circle, but failed to establish a discrimination between a white circle and a light gray circle. In addition, stimulus generalization results indicate that the amount of stimulus generalization occuring between two stimuli is relatively large when these two stimuli are relatively close together along a dimension. The relatively poor performance on a discrimination between two stimuli that occurs when these stimuli are relatively close together along a dimension may therefore be due to a relatively large amount of stimulus generalization occurring between these two stimuli. This inference leads to the conclusion that as the amount of stimulus generalization which occurs between discriminative stimuli before discrimination learning increases, performance on a discrimination between these stimuli deteriorates.

This conclusion is supported by somewhat different findings. Butter (1963) trained pigeons to peck a key while it was illuminated with a vertical line of 550 nanometer light. The test stimuli for the subsequent stimulus generalization determination often varied along both the wavelength and orientation dimensions; that is to say, the test stimuli often differed simultaneously from both 550 nanometer light and the vertical. Less stimulus generalization between a test stimulus and the training stimulus occurred when the test stimulus differed from the training stimulus along two dimensions rather than along one dimension. Discriminative stimuli that differ in two dimensions should therefore result in better discrimination learning than discriminative stimuli that differ in one dimension. This finding has been repeatedly confirmed. For example, Warren (1953) required monkeys to discriminate between stimuli varying in size, or shape, or along both of these dimensions; he found that the last condition resulted in the best discrimination performance.

Two stimuli obviously increase in similarity as the distance between them along a single dimension decreases. In addition, two stimuli that differ from each other along two dimensions are less similar to each other than two stimuli that differ from each other to the same extent, but along only a single dimension. Thus, a corollary conclusion is that as the extent of the similarity between discriminative stimuli increases, performance on a discrimination between these stimuli deteriorates.

Results (Haber & Kalish, 1963; Kalish & Haber, 1965) have been obtained that indicate an especially close relation between the amount of stimulus generalization that occurs between discriminative stimuli, and performance on a subsequent discrimination between these stimuli. Haber & Kalish, in their first experiment, reward-trained three groups of pigeons to peck a key illuminated with 550 nanometer light. Pecking by one group was followed by reinforcement delivered on a VI .25 (minute) schedule, a second on a VI 1 (minute) schedule, and a third on a VI 4 (minute) schedule. The least amount of stimulus generalization occurred for the group on the VI .25 schedule, and the largest amount of stimulus generalization occurred for the group on the VI 4 schedule.

In the second experiment, three new groups of pigeons first received the same training as in the first experiment; that is, they received positive reinforcement following pecking a key illuminated with 550 nanometer light on a VI .25; VI 1; or VI 4 schedule. These groups were then subdivided. One subgroup received a go/no-go successive discrimination between 550 nanometer (S+) and 540 nanometer (S—) lights projected on the response key, and the other received a go/no-go successive discrimination between 540 nanometer (S+) and 530 nanometer (S—) lights projected on the response key. Pecking in the presence of S+ during this stage was followed by reinforcement delivered on a VI 1 schedule for all groups. The pigeons that responded on the VI .25 schedule in the prediscrimination stage of this second study reached a criterion of good discrimination performance in the fewest number of sessions; pigeons that responded on the VI 4 schedule reached the same criterion in the greatest number of sessions. The first experiment found that the VI .25 schedule resulted in the least and the VI 4 schedule resulted in the most stimulus generalization between the discriminative stimuli used in the second experiment. Thus, the VI schedule that resulted in the least amount of stimulus generalization between stimuli led to the most rapid discrimination learning between these stimuli. Note that the obtained result also indicates that the amount of stimulus generalization occurring between discriminative stimuli can affect subsequent discrimination learning independently of the extent of the formal similarity of the discriminative stimuli.

The finding that the amount of stimulus generalization occurring between stimuli affects performance on a subsequent discrimination between these stimuli implies some sort of comparison process between these stimuli during acquisition of the discrimination. But in a successive discrimination, the two discriminative stimuli are not simultaneously perceived. How then can the amount of stimulus generalization that occurs between discriminative stimuli before discrimination learning similarly affect both simultaneous and successive discrimination learning? It is thought that during successive discrimination learning, an image of the discriminative stimulus currently not being perceived occurs, and this image is in some sense compared to the discriminative stimulus being perceived. The amount of stimulus generalization that occurs between discriminative stimuli before discrimination learning should therefore affect performance on successive discriminations in much the same way that it affects performance on simultaneous discriminations. If the assumption that an image of the discriminative stimulus not currently being perceived affects discrimination performance is justified, this image would have to come from a permanent brain event corresponding to the discriminative stimulus currently not being perceived. This consideration is consistent with the assumption that the permanent brain events corresponding to the CS and the stimuli of the general learning situation are involved in the processes for classical and instrumental conditioning.

Effects of Stimulus Generalization: Other Results. Some other findings are interpreted as due to the result that the amount of stimulus generalization that occurs between discriminative stimuli is negatively related to subsequent performance on a discrimination between these stimuli.

The fact that CR strength increases as the similarity between the CS and background stimuli decreases can be explained in terms of stimulus generalization and discrimination learning. The CS must be discriminated from background stimuli for classical conditioning to occur. Less stimulus generalization between the CS and background stimuli should occur as the CS becomes less similar to background stimuli. It follows that as the CS becomes less similar to background stimuli, discrimination learning between the CS and background stimuli should improve; that is, straightforward classical conditioning should improve, and therefore CR strength should increase.

It is clear that the amount of stimulus generalization that occurs between discriminative stimuli affects performance on a subsequent discrimination between these stimuli through learning. It follows that the effect of the similarity between the CS and background stimuli affects CR strength also through learning.

The stimulus produced by the instrumental response must be discriminated from both background stimuli and other response-produced stimuli. If the similarity of the stimulus produced by an instrumental response and background stimuli is large, then instrumental conditioning should be impaired. The relative difficulty in instrumentally conditioning voluntary covert responses is an example of such impairment, since the stimuli produced by voluntary covert responses differ minimally from background stimuli.

The stimulus produced by the instrumental response probably must also be discriminated from other response-produced stimuli. A high degree of similarity between the stimulus produced by an instrumental response and other response-produced stimuli should therefore seriously retard acquisition of this response. There are many instrumental responses that humans find very difficult to acquire; the difficulty does not appear to be due either to a very low probability of the initial occurrence of the response, or to CRs that are incompatible with the topography of the instrumental response. Skilled responses in sports are examples of such instrumental responses. The reason it is difficult to consistently execute these instrumental responses is the high degree of similarity between the stimulus produced by the desired instrumental response and the stimuli produced by other responses. Consider acquisition of the instrumental response of swinging a tennis racquet while running so as to cause the goal of a well hit tennis ball to occur. The probability of this instrumental response is not very low; even beginners can occasionally execute it. This instrumental response requires that the ball be hit neither too far in front nor too far behind the body with the racquet head at the correct angle. The stimuli produced by this response should be very similar to the stimuli produced by fractionally earlier or later responses, as well as those involving slightly different racquet tilts. These similarities account for the difficulty in being able to consistently hit a tennis ball appropriately while on the run.

Images of Discriminative Stimuli. In a study by John and Killam (1960), cats received a go/no-go successive discrimination between a 10 cycles per second (cps) on-off flicker (S+), and a 6 cps on-off light flicker (S—). A 10 cps flicker and a 6 cps flicker normally produce 10 cps and 6 cps voltage changes in certain brain structures. The occurrence of the 10 cps flicker produced 10 cps voltage changes in several brain structures, as revealed by brain recording techniques, when the correct response, a lever press, was made. However, the 10 cps flicker produced 10 cps voltage changes from these brain structures less frequently when the incorrect response, no lever press, was made. In fact, 6 cps voltage changes were sometimes observed from some brain structures when the

10 cps flicker was on and an incorrect response was made. The 6 cps flicker produced 6 cps voltage changes when a correct response, no lever press, was made; and the 6 cps flicker was less likely to produce 6 cps voltage changes when an incorrect response, a lever press was made. Sometimes 10 cps voltage changes occurred when an incorrect response was made.

The occurrence of 6 cps voltage changes in brain structures when a 10 cps flicker was on suggests that the presence of the 10 cps flicker was accompanied by what humans would describe as a very vivid image of the 6 cps flicker. A very vivid image of the 6 cps flicker should result in the same response that the real 6 cps flicker tends to produce, a response that is incorrect when the 10 cps flicker is actually present; this fits in with the obtained result that occurrence of 6 cps voltage changes was correlated with incorrect responding when the 10 cps flicker was on. The same argument suggests that when the 6 cps flicker was actually present, incorrect responding was due, at least in part, to what humans might describe as a very vivid image of the 10 cps flicker.

This and related findings (John, 1967) provide neurophysiological evidence that images of stimuli result in learned responses.

In addition, the described study supports the idea that an image of the discriminative stimulus that is not currently present occurs in successive discrimination learning. This idea was also supported when the effect of the amount of stimulus generalization occurring between stimuli on performance on a subsequent discrimination between these stimuli was discussed.

The described study also suggests that the permanent brain events corresponding to the 6 and 10 cps flicker stimuli become confused. Why else should the real 10 cps flicker stimulus result in 6 cps voltage activity and vice versa? A similar suggestion was made; it seems that the permanent brain event that corresponds to the UCS of a CS-UCS pairing becomes confused with the permanent brain event that corresponds to a similar unpaired UCS.

Good performance on discriminations frequently does not occur early in training. Part of this difficulty in discrimination learning may be due to confusion between the permanent brain events corresponding to the two discriminative stimuli, just as the permanent brain events corresponding to the 6 and 10 cps flicker stimuli became confused, which led to an increase in errors on the discrimination.

The John and Killam study supports the idea that an image of the discriminative stimulus that is not currently present occurs in successive discrimination learning. A study done by Thomas and Burr (1969) adds further support. Their results indicate that a go/no-go successive discrimination was forgotten to some extent with the passage of time. In addition, their results suggest that recall of the go/no-go successive discrimination was improved by presenting subjects with a reminder stimulus. The reminder stimulus consisted of a 3 minute exposure to S+, with the reinforcement schedule used in training on the discrimination being in effect during this 3-minute interval. It is likely that this reminder stimulus increased recall of the go/no-go successive discrimination by facilitating recall of S—. Recall of a stimulus involves the occurrence of an image of this stimulus. Thus, the reminder stimulus treatment in which S+ occurred may have resulted in an image of S—, which suggests that, in general, during successive discrimination learning an image of the discriminative stimulus not currently present takes place.

Effects of Discrimination Learning

Some effects of discrimination learning are in accord with previously described conditioning results. However, some results cannot be thus accounted for.

Control of Responding: Positive Discriminative Stimuli. Performance of the CR in discrimination learning in classical conditioning is controlled by CS+, because no other stimulus (outside of background stimuli) is present when CS+ occurs. For the same reason, performance of the instrumental response in go/no-go successive discrimination learning is controlled by S+. These two conclusions are quite predictable. In straightforward classical conditioning, the CS is paired with the UCS and controls performance of the CR. CS+ is also paired with a UCS, and therefore it should control performance of the CR. In straightforward reward learning, the stimuli of the general learning situation are present when the instrumental response is made and when the positive reinforcer occurs, and the stimuli of the general learning situation lead to the performance of the instrumental response. The S+ of a go/no-go successive discrimination is also present when the instrumental response is made and when the positive reinforcer occurs, and therefore the S+ should lead to the performance of the instrumental response.

It is not so obvious that in simultaneous discrimination learning S+ controls the typically reward-trained response of approaching it, for example, moving toward it, as in entering the S+ arm of a T-maze, or jumping to it, as with the jumping stand apparatus. One reason that the S+ of a simultaneous discrimination may not control the reward-trained response of approaching it is that related instrumental responses would occur if the simultaneously present S— was escaped from.

Figure 4-8 helps to indicate another reason why the S+ of a simultaneous discrimination may not control the reward-trained response of approaching it. It reminds us that in a simultaneous discrimination, two stimulus configurations are present to an animal. An animal may learn to approach the left member of a stimulus pair when configuration 1 is present, and it may learn to approach the right member of the stimulus pair when configuration 2 is present. Acquiring the simultaneous discrimination on this basis would mean that a reinforcer-always-possible successive discrimination was learned.

Experimental evidence (Mandler, 1968; Nissen, 1950; Sutherland, 1969; Webb, 1950) does indicate, however, that animals usually solve simultaneous discriminations by, in part, acquiring an approach response to S+. There are at least three ways in which evidence supporting this statement has been gathered. On test trials: (a) only S+ is presented; (b) S+ and a novel (new) stimulus are presented; and (c) S+ and S— are both presented in a new configuration, for instance, in a vertical line rather than in a horizontal line. Each of these three procedures can rule out at least one of the two indicated alternatives to the hypothesis that in a simultaneous discrimination S+ controls the execution of an approach response to it.

The result that in a simultaneous discrimination S+ controls the execution of an approach response to it is certainly in accord with conditioning results previously described. Approach to S+ should be instrumentally conditioned, because this response causes the positive reinforcer to occur. In addition, S+ is perceived directly before receiving a positive reinforcer and therefore an approach CR should be made to it.

All the simultaneous discrimination learning procedures that have been typically used facilitate discrimination learning by arranging that the instrumentally conditioned approach response to S+ is contributed to by an approach CR. An alternative procedure is to require that responses to one or the other of two identical stimuli, placed, say, 90 degrees to the left and right of the simultaneously presented discriminative stimuli, be made for the positive reinforcer to be received.

Stimulus Generalization along Dimension of CS+ or S+. After straightforward classical and instrumental conditioning is established, the amount of stimulus generalization occurring between the training stimulus and test stimuli tends to decrease as the test stimuli move away from the training stimulus along a dimension of this stimulus; that is, stimulus generalization gradients with shapes such as those in Figures 4-1 and 4-2

CONFIGURATION 1

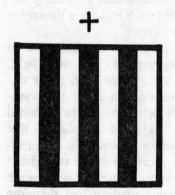

CONFIGURATION 2

FIGURE 4-8. Two configurations in a simultaneous discrimination.

are frequently obtained. Because both the CS and CS+ control CRs, and because both the stimuli of the general learning situation and S+ control instrumentally conditioned responses, after discrimination learning is established the amount of stimulus generalization should frequently decrease as the test stimuli move away from CS+ or S+ along a dimension of CS+ or S+. This prediction has been confirmed.

Marsh (1972) gave pigeons a go/no-go successive discrimination in which S+ was illumination of a response key with 555 nanometer light, and S— was illumination of the same key with white light. After discrimination learning occurred, stimulus generalization along the wavelength dimension, a dimension of S+, was determined. The obtained stimulus generalization gradient, shown in Figure 4-9, indicates that the amount of stimulus generalization occurring between the 550 nanometer training stimulus and the test stimuli decreased as the test stimuli moved away from the 550 nanometer stimulus along the wavelength dimension. The obtained stimulus generalization gradient was therefore similar to those typically obtained after straightforward classical and instrumental conditioning, as illustrated in Figures 4-1 and 4-2. The stimulus generalization gradients obtained after straightforward classical

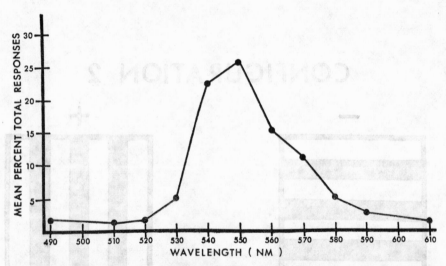

FIGURE 4-9. Stimulus generalization along a dimension of a positive discriminative stimulus when the negative discriminative stimulus is not on the same dimension. Percent equals the number of responses made to a stimulus divided by the total number of responses made multiplied by 100. (Adapted from Marsh, 1972.)

and instrumental conditioning and along a dimension of S+ are called *excitatory stimulus generalization gradients.*

Control of Responding: Negative Discriminative Stimuli. In discrimination learning in classical conditioning, CS— comes to not produce the CR. It can be concluded that the nonperformance of the CR in the presence of CS— is controlled by CS—, because no other stimulus (outside of background stimuli) is present when CS— occurs. For the same reason it can be concluded that the nonexecution of the instrumental response in the presence of the S— of a go/no-go successive discrimination is controlled by S—.

These two conclusions are clearly to be expected. Both CS— and the S— of a go/no-go successive discrimination are paired with the absence of the reinforcer; the reinforcer occurs at other times, when CS+ or the S+ of a go/no-go successive discrimination is present. A stimulus paired with the absence of a UCS or reinforcer does not come to produce a specific CR, such as salivation; a stimulus paired with the absence of a reinforcer will not produce instrumental-like responses either. It follows that CS— and the S— of a go/no-go successive discrimination should not produce a CR or an instrumental-like response.

A CS paired with the absence of a UCS comes to be either escaped from and avoided or approached and continued to be perceived, depending on whether the UCS is positive or negative. A CS paired with the absence of a UCS also results in inhibitory classical conditioning; that is, a CS paired with the absence of a UCS acquires the ability to impair subsequent forward classical conditioning between the same CS and UCS, and to reduce CR strength when simultaneously presented with the same UCS in a summation procedure. It follows that both CS— and the S— of a go/no-go successive discrimination should be either escaped from and avoided or approached and continued to be perceived, and should be conditioned inhibitors.

The S— of a go/no-go successive discrimination is escaped from (Rilling, Kramer, & Richards, 1973). A typical go/no-go successive discrimination was in effect for the pecking responses of pigeons on the right key. A left key was also present in the chamber. A single peck on the left key terminated the S— that appeared on the right key. Pigeons did come to peck the left key when S— was present on the right key.

CS— and the S— of a go/no-go successive discrimination are also conditioned inhibitors. A CS— did inhibit subsequent classical conditioning in which the identical stimulus was paired wth the same UCS (Hammond, 1968). In addition, a CS— simultaneously presented with the CS+ for the same discrimination in a summation procedure reduced the strength of the CR (Hammond, 1967; Hoffman, 1969). Also, the S— of a go/no-go successive discrimination reduced the rate of an instrumental response when presented simultaneously with the S+ for the same discrimination in a summation procedure (Cornell & Strub, 1965).

It is not obviously clear that in simultaneous discrimination learning S— controls the response of avoiding it. One reason that the S— of a simultaneous discrimination may not control the response of avoiding it is that related instrumental responses would occur if the simultaneously present S+ controls the response of approaching it, as it does. Nevertheless, experimental evidence similar to that indicating that the S+ of a simultaneous discrimination controls an approach response to it, shows that the S— of a simultaneous discrimination controls the response of avoiding it (Derdzinski & Warren, 1969; Mandler, 1968; Sutherland, Carr, & Mackintosh, 1962).

Physical and Temporal Proximity of Stimuli. The finding that a CS paired with the absence of a UCS comes to be either escaped from and avoided or approached and continued to be perceived, depending on the sign of the UCS, was explained by pointing out that when no particular event occurs in sufficiently close physical and temporal proximity to a UCS, the response to no particular event is affected. If the UCS is positive, no particular event occurring in sufficiently close physical and temporal proximity to this UCS is escaped from and avoided (as long as it is possible to make these responses); if the UCS is negative, no particular event occurring in sufficiently close physical and temporal proximity to this UCS should be approached and continued to be perceived (as long as it is possible to make these responses). A CS paired with the absence of a UCS is equivalent to a CS paired with no particular event occurring in relatively close physical and temporal proximity to a UCS. A CS paired with no particular event occurring in sufficiently close physical and temporal proximity to a UCS should therefore tend to produce the same response that this no particular event elicits; that is, such a CS should come to be either escaped from and avoided or approached and continued to be perceived. This analysis is of critical importance in interpreting instrumental conditioning, because the avoidance, escape, omission, and response-terminates-reward types of instrumental conditioning occur, in part, through a classical conditioning process in which the stimulus produced by the instrumental response becomes associated with no particular event that should be either approached and continued to be perceived or escaped from and avoided, due to its occurring in relatively close physical and temporal proximity to the reinforcer.

In respect to discrimination learning, it is clear that the no particular event that ensues after CS—; that follows making the instrumental response in the presence of the S— of a go/no-go successive discrimination; and that takes place after the S— of a simultaneous discrimination is approached occurs in relatively close physical proximity to the reinforcer and often in relatively close temporal proximity as well. Therefore, no particular event in these discrimination learning situations should tend to be either approached and continued to be perceived or escaped from and avoided. A stimulus paired with no particular event when no particular event is either approached and continued to be perceived or escaped from and avoided should come to produce much the same response that no particular event elicits. In a reward-learning discrimination, no particular event occurs in relatively close physical and temporal proximity to the positive reinforcer. Therefore, the stimulus paired with this no particular event, that is, S—, should come to be escaped from and avoided, as it is.

Other results support this analysis of the role of the physical and temporal proximity of no particular event to a reinforcer in straightforward classical and instrumental conditioning and in discrimination learning. No particular event occurring in relatively close physical and temporal proximity to food elicits aggressive behavior. No particular event occurring in the extinction part of a go/no-go successive discrimination takes place in relatively close physical and temporal proximity to food. Therefore, aggressive behavior should occur relatively frequently when the extinction part of a go/no-go successive discrimination is in effect and an appropriate target for aggression is provided. This result has been obtained (Azrin, Hutchinson, & Hake, 1966; Rilling & Caplan, 1973). In addition, some evidence suggests that the S— of a go/no-go successive discrimination comes to produce aggressive behavior through conditioning (Cohen & Looney, 1973; Cole & Litchfield, 1969).

A last point is that it is imprecise to state that the S— of a simultaneous discrimination is paired with the absence of the positive reinforcer. A better way to put it is to say that the stimulus produced by approaching this S— is paired with the absence of a reinforcer, since this S— is present just before receiving a positive reinforcer when the correct response is made. In addition, this S— can function as a cue to approach the S+ of the same discrimination (Hall, 1973).

Stimulus Generalization along Dimension of CS— or S—. The effect of extinction generalizes to other stimuli along a dimension of the stimulus presented in extinction in both classical and instrumental conditioning. In addition, CS— and S— inhibit performance of the CR and the instrumentally conditioned response. Therefore, it is to be expected that stimulus generalization of the inhibitory effect on responding produced by CS— and S— will occur.

A finding by Marsh (1972) confirms this expectation. He gave pigeons a go/no-go successive discrimination in which S+ was illumination of the response key with white light, and S— was illumination of the same key with 560 nanometer light. The stimulus generalization gradient that was obtained after acquisition of this discrimination is shown in Figure 4-10. The strength of responding was least to S—, and tended to gradually increase as the test stimuli moved away from S— along the wavelength dimension. The inhibitory effect of the S— therefore generalized to other stimuli in a way fairly similar to other instances of stimulus generalization.

Stimulus generalization along a dimension of a CS— or S— is often referred to as inhibitory stimulus generalization. Inhibitory stimulus generalization gradients tend to be relatively flat, as the one in Figure 4-10 is, probably at least partially because of a floor effect. The inhibitory effect on responding by a negative discriminative stimulus may often be so strong that relatively little increase in responding occurs to test

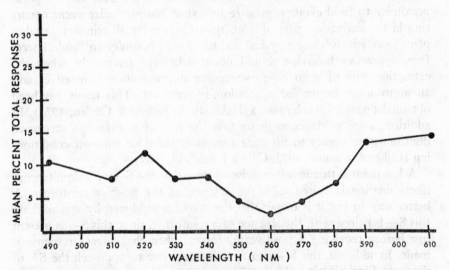

FIGURE 4-10. Stimulus generalization along a dimension of a negative discriminative stimulus when the positive discriminative stimulus is not on the same dimension. Percent equals the number of responses made to a stimulus divided by the total number of responses made multiplied by 100. (Adapted from Marsh, 1972.)

stimuli that are even relatively far away from the CS— or S— along a dimension of the CS— or S—.

Generalization along Dimension in Common to Discriminative Stimuli. In one part of Marsh's (1972) study S+ was a light of a specific wavelength; S—, a white light; and an excitatory stimulus generalization gradient along a dimension of S+ was obtained. In another part, S+ was a white light; S— a light of a specific wavelength; and an inhibitory stimulus generalization gradient along a dimension of S— was obtained. White light is not on the wavelength dimension because it is composed of lights of a number of different wavelengths. Thus, these results do not indicate the effect of discrimination learning on stimulus generalization along a dimension in common with the discriminative stimuli. Let us now consider this effect.

We may again use Marsh's work as an illustration. Pigeons received a go/no-go successive discrimination in which S+ was illumination of the response key with 550 nanometer light, and S— was illumination of the same key with 560 nanometer light. After discrimination learning occurred, stimulus generalization along the wavelength dimension, a dimension in common with S+ and S—, was determined. The obtained stimulus generalization gradient, shown in Figure 4-11, shows that a moderate percentage of responses was made in the presence of S+ (550 nanometers); even greater percentages of responses were made in the presence of the 540, 530, and 520 nanometer test stimuli; the maximum (peak) responding occurred in the presence of the 540 nanometer test stimulus; and very little responding occurred in the presence of S— (560 nanometers) and test stimuli with wavelengths greater than 560 nanometers.

The finding that the maximum strength of responding in the stimulus generalization determination occurred, not to the positive discriminative stimulus, but to a test stimulus on the side of the positive discriminative stimulus in the direction opposite to the negative discriminative stimulus is an instance of what is called the *peak shift* result. A post-discrimination stimulus generalization determination along a dimension in common with the discriminative stimuli frequently results in the peak shift result.

Marsh gave one group of pigeons a go/no-go successive discrimination between a 550 nanometer S+ and a white light S—; he gave a second group of pigeons a go/no-go successive discrimination between a white light S+ and a 560 nanometer S—. In addition, he obtained an excitatory post-discrimination stimulus generalization gradient along the wavelength dimension of the 550 nanometer S+, and an inhibitory post-discrimination stimulus generalization gradient along the wavelength dimension of the 560 nanometer S— (Figures 4-9 and 4-10). Marsh showed that the stimulus generalization gradient obtained after discrimination learning between the 550 nanometer (S+) and 560 nanometer (S—) stimuli was approximately predicted by combining the excitatory stimulus generalization gradient along the wavelength dimension centered at the 550 nanometer S+ with the inhibitory stimulus generalization gradient along the wavelength dimension centered at the 560 nanometer S—. These two gradients were combined by assigning increasingly more positive values to response strengths as they increased for the excitatory stimulus generalization gradient, and by assigning increasingly more negative values to response strengths as they decreased for the inhibitory stimulus generalization gradient. In particular, the peak shift result was predicted. It was due to the inhibitory effect that was maximal at 560 nanometers (the S— wavelength) being fairly large at 550 nanometers (the S+ wavelength), and then tapering off sufficiently so that the predicted response strength produced by the 540 nanometer test stimulus was maximal. Marsh's results replicate those of Hearst (1968), and Spence (1937) was the first to explain the post-discrimination stimulus generalization gradient along a dimension in common with the discriminative stimuli in terms of a summation of excitatory and inhibitory stimulus generalization gradients.

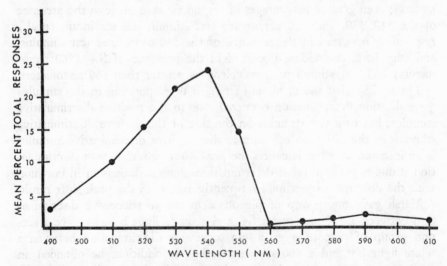

FIGURE 4-11. Stimulus generalization along a dimension in common with the positive and negative discriminative stimuli. Percent equals the number of responses made to a stimulus divided by the total number of responses made multiplied by 100. (Adapted from Marsh, 1972.)

It is somewhat likely that relational stimulus control also contributes to the peak shift result. Considering the Marsh study, the 550 nanometer S+ has a lower wavelength than the 560 nanometer S—. If the pigeons undergoing discrimination learning between the 550 nanometer S+ and the 560 nanometer S— acquired, in part, a tendency to peck the stimulus of the lower wavelength, they may have tended to respond maximally to the 540 nanometer test stimulus in the stimulus generalization determination because its wavelength is less than that of the 550 nanometer S+.

The post-discrimination stimulus generalization gradient along a dimension in common with the discriminative stimuli is also affected by what is called a contrast effect (Chapter 7).

Discrimination Learning Facilitates Subsequent Discrimination Learning. Discrimination learning between two stimuli that differ along a common dimension facilitates subsequent discrimination learning in which the discriminative stimuli differ along the same common dimension. For example, acquisition of a relatively easy discrimination between stimuli that differ along a common dimension facilitates acquisition of a more difficult discrimination between stimuli that differ along the same dimension (Lawrence, 1952; Pavlov, 1927, p. 122). A similar but more dramatic result was obtained by Mackintosh & Little (1970).

They first trained one group of pigeons on an easy discrimination between stimuli that differed along a common dimension. The discriminative stimuli were lights of 501 and 576 nanometers that were otherwise identical. In a second stage, this group received a difficult discrimination between stimuli that differed along the same common dimension as the first pair of discriminative stimuli did. The stage 2 discriminative stimuli were lights of 531 and 542 nanometers that were otherwise identical. In addition, the stage 2 discrimination was a reversal of the stage 1 discrimination. The longer wavelength stimulus was S+ in stage 1, and the shorter wavelength stimulus was S+ in stage 2. A second group received the difficult discrimination throughout training, this discrimination being the same as the one received by the first group in stage 2. By the end of training in stage 2, the group switched from the easy discrimination to the difficult reversed discrimination performed better than the group trained on the difficult discrimination throughout (Figure 4-12). Sweller (1972) reported somewhat similar findings.

First acquiring an easy discrimination should result in a smaller amount of stimulus generalization occurring between the discriminative stimuli for the difficult discrimination than an equivalent amount of training on the difficult discrimination. This is because the outcome of the acquisition of a discrimination between stimuli that differ along a common dimension is a precipitous decrease in the amount of stimulus generalization occurring between the discriminative stimuli (Figure 4-11). As the amount of stimulus generalization occurring between stimuli decreases, performance on a subsequent discrimination between these stimuli improves. Therefore, first acquiring an easy discrimination should facilitate acquisition of a subsequent difficult discrimination. Apparently, the facilitative effect of the reduction in the amount of stimulus generalization for a group receiving an initial easy discrimination is greater than the conflicting effect that is due to the fact that the difficult discrimination for this group is the reverse of the easy discrimination.

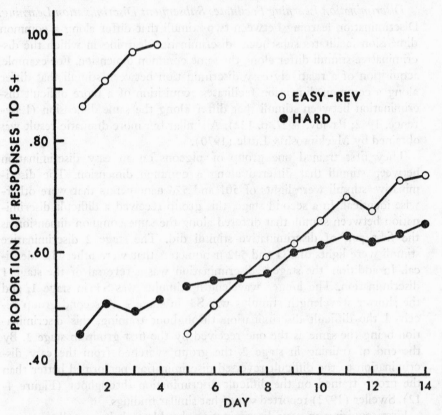

FIGURE 4-12. Facilitation of discrimination learning by prior training on an easier reversed discrimination. Proportion equals the number of responses made to S+ divided by the total number of responses made. For each day, there were 12 S+ and 12 S— periods. (Adapted from Mackintosh and Little, 1970.)

Other studies (Lawrence, 1949; Shepp & Eimas, 1964) show that discrimination learning facilitates subsequent discrimination learning in which the discriminative stimuli differ along the same common dimension as the discriminative stimuli of the initial task. These other results are probably also due to the fact that the initial discrimination reduces the amount of stimulus generalization occurring between the discriminative stimuli for the subsequent discrimination.

Effect of Nonlearning-Apparatus Discrimination Learning. Discrimination learning occurs in situations outside the learning apparatus. For example, a bird may learn to discriminate between a surface of one color, where it is relatively warm, from a surface of a second color, where it is relatively cold. Discrimination learning between stimuli that differ along a common dimension will greatly reduce the amount of stimulus generalization occurring between these stimuli. Suppose that a large number of nonlearning-apparatus discriminations between many pairs of stimuli that differ along a common dimension are acquired. Suppose also that the individual discriminative stimuli come from all portions of the dimension— for instance, that discriminations involving what humans describe as red, yellow, green, and blue stimuli occur. Because a single discrimination between stimuli that differ along a common dimension greatly reduces the amount of stimulus generalization occurring between these stimuli, it appears reasonable to expect that acquisition of a large number of the just described nonlearning-apparatus discriminations would reduce the amount of stimulus generalization occurring along the entire dimension in question.

In one study (Tees, 1972), rats that were reared in the dark were poorer at discriminating between visual patterns ("N" versus "X") than rats that were reared in the light. After this discrimination learning, the dark-reared rats exhibited more stimulus generalization when the N and X figures were rotated than did the light-reared rats. Rearing rats in the dark eliminated the possibility that nonlearning-apparatus discriminations between visual forms occurred. Therefore, nonlearning-apparatus visual discriminations involving form stimuli that were acquired by the light-reared rats may have been responsible for the obtained differences between the light- and dark-reared rats.

Mednick and Lehtinen (1957) found that the amount of stimulus generalization that occurred along the dimension of spatial distance was less for older children than for younger children. This finding supports the idea that as children grow older they acquire an increasing number of nonlearning-apparatus discriminations between stimuli that differ along a number of different common dimensions; and as a result, as children grow older the amount of stimulus generalization that occurs along a number of dimensions decreases. Suppose that the amount of stimulus generalization occurring along a number of dimensions does decrease as children grow older. Recall that a decrease in the amount of stimulus generalization occurring between two stimuli facilitates acquisition of a subsequent discrimination between these two stimuli. It follows that older children should acquire discriminations more readily than younger children for stimuli that differ along at least one of these common dimensions. Younger children are, in fact, poorer than older children and adults on a whole host of discriminations between stimuli that differ along common dimensions (Gibson, 1969). For example, they are poorer than older children at acquiring a discrimination between lines of different orientations.

Lack of Effect of Nonlearning-Apparatus Discrimination Learning. Work with the wavelength dimension and chickens shows that sensory restriction does not increase the amount of stimulus generalization that occurs (Malott, 1968; Riley & Leuin, 1971).

In the Malott study, chicks were kept in the dark until they were 21 days of age. At this age, one group was left in the dark at all times, and a second group was exposed to white light from a bulb, usually for 30 hours per week. White light permits different objects to reflect light with wavelengths in restricted ranges. The group exposed to white light therefore had an opportunity to acquire nonlearning-apparatus discriminations between stimuli of different wavelengths. Straightforward reward learning of pecking with the response key illuminated with 589 nanometer light was eventually carried out. Stimulus generalization along the wavelength dimension was subsequently determined. For both groups, the amount of stimulus generalization occurring between the 589 nanometer light and the test stimuli decreased at the same rate and relatively quickly as the test stimuli moved away from the 589 nanometer light along the wavelength dimension.

Both the Malott and Riley and Leuin studies indicate that the decrease in the amount of stimulus generalization occurring between training and test stimuli as the test stimuli move away from the training stimulus along the wavelength dimension is not due to nonlearning-apparatus discriminations between stimuli that differ along the wavelength dimension. Image theory assumes that the amount of stimulus generalization occurring between the stimulus produced by the instrumental response and other response-produced stimuli increases as these response-produced stimuli become more similar to the stimulus produced by the instrumental response. Therefore, it would not be expected that the amount of stimulus generalization occurring between the stimulus produced by the instrumental response and the stimuli produced by similar responses would entirely depend on previously acquired nonlearning-apparatus discriminations, in accord with the Malott and Riley and Leuin results.

Decrease in Stimulus Generalization along a Dimension of CS+ or S+. Discrimination learning reduces the amount of stimulus generalization occurring along a dimension of a positive discriminative stimulus that is not also a dimension of a negative discriminative stimulus (Jenkins & Harrison, 1960; Liu, 1971).

In the first of these studies, one group of pigeons received a go/no-go successive discrimination between a 1000 Hz tone (S+) and no sound (S—). In addition, a group that received training in straightforward instrumental conditioning, often called a *single stimulus training group*, was exposed to only the 1000 Hz tone. For both groups, responding on a key was followed by food delivered on the same VI schedule whenever the 1000 Hz tone was on. In a second stage, the amount of stimulus generalization occurring along the frequency dimension was measured. The group receiving the discrimination between the 1000 Hz tone and no sound exhibited much less stimulus generalization along the frequency dimension than did the group that received straightforward instrumental conditioning in the presence of the 1000 Hz tone, as indicated in Figure 4-13.

Note that the frequency dimension, a dimension of the 1000 Hz S+, is obviously not also a dimension of the S— of no sound. We cannot account for the general result that discrimination learning reduces the amount of stimulus generalization occurring along a dimension of a positive discriminative stimulus that is not also a dimension of a negative discriminative stimulus by application of straightforward conditioning results, as we have done with other effects of discrimination learning on stimulus generalization. In particular, we cannot account for it by hypothesizing an appropriate interaction between an excitatory stimulus generalization gradient along a dimension of S+, and an inhibitory stimulus generalization gradient along a dimension of S—; this is because there is no way to predict the interaction of these two stimulus generalization gradients when they are along different dimensions. Recall that the postdiscrimination stimulus generalization gradient obtained along a dimension in common to S+ and S— can be approximately predicted by subtracting the inhibitory stimulus generalization gradient along this dimension from the excitatory generalization gradient along the same dimension.

Discrimination Learning: Impairment by Irrelevant Stimuli. An *irrele-*

vant stimulus is one that is as likely to occur when the positive discriminative stimulus is present as when the negative discriminative stimulus is present; in addition, the two discriminative stimuli must be equally likely to take place. Background stimuli are usually irrelevant stimuli in discrimination learning, because they are present when both the positive and negative discriminative stimulus occur. A specific irrelevant stimulus in a go/no-go successive discrimination is the shape of the response key. This stimulus is always present when both S+ and S— are present. A specific irrelevant stimulus in a simultaneous visual T-maze discrimination is the stimulus complex indicating the right-hand position. This stimulus complex is always present when S+ is on the right and is also always present when S— is on the right, and S+ and S— are equally likely to be on the right.

Because irrelevant stimuli in discrimination learning are present when CS+ or S+ occurs, they are present when (or just before) the reinforcer occurs. Because irrelevant stimuli are also present when the reinforcer

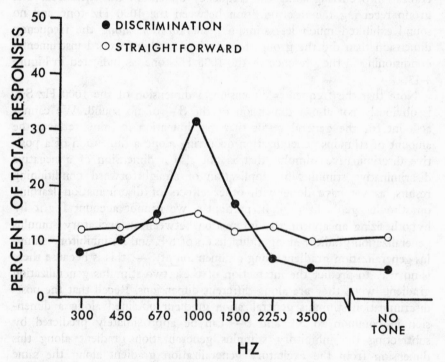

FIGURE 4-13. Discrimination learning decreases stimulus generalization. (Adapted from Jenkins and Harrison, 1960.)

does not occur, what is referred to as a *partial reinforcement schedule* must necessarily be in effect for such irrelevant stimuli. Partial reinforcement schedules can establish strong responding. Irrelevant stimuli are present when CS— or S— occurs. Irrelevant stimuli will therefore tend to result in the execution of the learned response in the presence of CS— or S—, as well as in the presence of CS+ or S+. The former tendency will obviously impair performance on a discrimination. Thus, irrelevant stimuli impair discrimination learning.

The *position habit* is an example of an irrelevant stimulus exercising strong control over a learned response and thereby markedly impairing discrimination learning. Animals receiving a simultaneous visual discrimination in a T-maze or jumping stand apparatus frequently consistently move toward or jump in one direction, either left or right, before they acquire the visual discrimination. The responding in one direction, either left or right, is called a position habit. Recall that in such a simultaneous visual discrimination, S+ appears on the left for half the trials and on the right for half the trials. The partial reinforcement of responding that results when an animal consistently approaches one position appears sufficient to maintain responding to this position over a long period of training. In fact, sometimes the position habit is exhibited indefinitely and the discrimination is never acquired.

Reduction of Control of Responding by Irrelevant Stimuli. Since irrelevant stimuli tend to result in the learned response when CS— or S— is present, and thereby impair performance on a discrimination, it follows that to get relatively good discrimination learning, control of the learned response by irrelevant stimuli must be reduced.

Wagner, Logan, Haberlandt, and Price (1968) trained one group of rats on a discrimination involving classical conditioning of the suppression CR. CS+ was an auditory stimulus. Present simultaneously, that is, in compound, with CS+ was a flashing light. CS— was an auditory stimulus of a different frequency than CS+ and otherwise identical to it. The same flashing light that occurred in compound with CS+ also occurred in compound with CS—. Therefore, the flashing light was an experimenter-delivered irrelevant stimulus; it was present whenever CS+ occurred and whenever CS— occurred, and CS+ and CS— occurred equally often. CS+ was paired with shock, and CS— was followed by no particular event. A second group received the same two auditory-visual compounds. For this group each auditory-visual compound was followed by shock half the time it was presented, and each auditory-visual compound was followed by no particular event the other half of the time it was presented. Therefore, the flashing light was followed by shock half the time it occurred for both groups. But the first group could and did acquire a discrimination between the two auditory stimuli. After the auditory discrimination was acquired by this group, both groups received the flashing light presented alone, without an auditory stmiulus. The flashing light produced a weaker suppression CR in the group acquiring the discrimination than in the second group. Because (a) the flashing light was followed by shock to the same extent for both groups; (b) the flashing light was an irrelevant stimulus for the group acquiring the discrimination; and (c) the flashing light produced a weaker CR in this group, the conclusion that discrimination learning reduces control of learned responding by irrelevant stimuli is supported.

Another study (Miles, Mackintosh, & Westbrook, 1970) demonstrates reduction of control of responding by an irrelevant stimulus as a consequence of discrimination learning. Pigeons received a discrimination in which S+ was a tone and S— was a noise. Present simultaneously in compound with both S+ and S— was a light (C) of a specific wavelength projected on the response key. This light was therefore an experimenter-delivered irrelevant stimulus. A go/no-go successive discrimination learning procedure was used, but discrete trials were employed. A trial was initiated with the onset of the light (C) on the response key, and was terminated with the offset of this light. One group received two sessions of training on the indicated discrimination; a second received four sessions; and a third received nine sessions. After discrimination training was terminated for a group, a stimulus generalization determination along the wavelength dimension was carried out. Two stimuli were used for this determination—the color (C) used in training (red or green), and a second color (green if red had been used, red if green had been used). Half the time each of the two colors was simultaneously presented with the tone (S+), and half the time with the noise (S—). The percentage of responses to the color (C) presented in training decreased as the number of training sessions a group received increased. When changing a stimulus present during training does not reduce the strength of the learned response, it can be said that this stimulus exerted little control over the learned response. The obtained result therefore indicates that as discrimination training continued, the control over responding by the irrelevant color stimulus present during training decreased. Performance on the auditory discrimination improved as training continued. This improvement should have been due, at least in part, to the progressive decrease in the control over responding by the irrelevant color stimulus that occurred as discrimination training continued.

Because successful discrimination learning reduces control of learned responding by irrelevant stimuli, irrelevant stimuli must be discriminated from discriminative stimuli. Therefore, every discrimination involves both a discrimination between discriminative stimuli, and discrimination between each of these discriminative stimuli and irrelevant stimuli. Effects of discrimination between a discriminative stimulus and an irrelevant stimulus have received very little attention.

Some findings (Bresnahan, 1970; Thomas, Freeman, Svinicki, Burr, & Lyon, 1970) may seem to conflict with the conclusion that discrimination learning decreases control of learned responding by irrelevant stimuli. They appear to be due to discrimination learning resulting in a decrease in control of responding by other "prepotent" irrelevant stimuli (Turner & Mackintosh, 1972). This interpretation is supported by other results that indicate that the amount of stimulus generalization occurring along a dimension can be affected even when stimuli on this dimension are not present in training (Honig, 1969, 1974).

Attention

Attention means the extent to which stimuli are noticed as being different from one another. Attention to a single stimulus means that it is noticed as being relatively different from background stimuli. Attention directed at two specific stimuli means that the two stimuli are noticed as being relatively different from each other. Attention in reference to conditioning usually refers to changes in the extent to which stimuli are noticed as being different from one another due to central nervous system factors, rather than to changes in stimulation on a receptor—for example, changes brought about by eye movement. The *orienting* or *activation response* is a measure of the extent of attention occurring between two stimuli.

Orienting or Activation Response and Attention. Major components of the orienting or activation response include the direction of sense organs in relation to the location of a stimulus in space; muscle tension; GSR; and electroencephalogram (EEG) responses. These responses tend to covary, which is why they are referred to as "the" orienting or activation response. They are similarly influenced by waking and sleeping, primary reinforcers, and neutral stimuli.

The statement that the orienting or activation response is a measure of attention is supported by the fact that the orienting or activation response has as one of its components the response of directing sense organs to the location of a stimulus in space. Directing sense organs toward a stimulus in space clearly means that this stimulus is noticed as being different from other stimuli. In addition, when people work on tasks that require full attention to certain stimuli, their muscle tension increases (Surwillo, 1956). Also, in sleep, when attention to most stimuli is minimal, the strength of the orienting response is low.

The types of stimuli that produce a relatively strong orienting or activation response also suggest that the strength of this response is a measure of attention. Primary reinforcers and novel stimuli increase the strength of the orienting response, and people tend to notice these stimuli as different from background stimuli. Consequently, if a stimulus produces a relatively strong orienting or activation response, it is relatively likely to be attended to, that is, relatively likely to be noticed as being different from other stimuli that are present.

Habituation. Habituation is a decrease in the strength of the orienting or activation response that results from repeated presentations of a stimulus. Repeated presentations of a neutral stimulus result in a marked decrease in the strength of the orienting or activation response; in other words, they result in extensive habituation. Much less reduction in the strength of the orienting or activation response occurs when a primary reinforcer is repeatedly presented.

The habituation finding supports the conclusion that the orienting or activation response is a measure of attention, because habituation is a decrease in the strength of the orienting or activation response brought about by repeated presentations of a stimulus, and because humans would probably report they are less likely to attend to a repeatedly presented stimulus than to the same stimulus when it initially occurs. Moreover, the result that habituation occurs much more slowly when a primary reinforcer rather than a neutral stimulus is repeatedly presented is consistent with the likely result that humans would report that they are more likely to attend to a repeatedly presented primary reinforcer than to a repeatedly presented neutral stimulus.

It is not necessary for a change in receptor stimulation to occur for habituation to take place. Habituation will occur when a sensory nerve is stimulated directly.

Habituation is obviously different from classical and instrumental conditioning but it does qualify as a type of learning. The stimulus that produces a change in response is one that an animal was previously exposed to. Habituation to a stimulus is relatively permanent (File, 1973; Leaton & Buck, 1971). The change in response to stimuli is not widespread; the effect of repeatedly presenting a stimulus is limited to the effect that this and similar stimuli have on the orienting or activation response (Sharpless & Jasper, 1956).

Increase in Attention to CS. In straightforward classical conditioning, the CS must be discriminated from background stimuli. Classical conditioning provides an especially good starting point for a discussion of attention in conditioning, partly because analysis of a discrimination between the CS and background stimuli is not complicated by the presence of irrelevant stimuli.

It probably seems obvious that after classical conditioning has been established, the CS is attended to more than before conditioning. In addition, suppose, for example, that pairings between a very slight increase in the intensity of a diffuse light and a UCS were delivered. The increase in intensity of the diffuse light could be small enough so that adult humans would initially not notice the change in intensity. Let us suppose that classical conditioning between the increase in the intensity of the diffuse light and the UCS eventually occurred, with acquisition being slow because the CS differs minimally from background stimuli. Finally, suppose that classical conditioning between the same CS and a different UCS was subsequently carried out. Would not acquisition of the second CR occur relatively quickly? And does it not make sense to conclude that acquisition of the second CR would occur relatively quickly because the prior classical conditioning increased attention to the CS of a slight increase in the intensity of a diffuse light? Moreover, the assumed increase in attention to this CS would not be due to a change in stimulation of a receptor; a change in the intensity of a diffuse light should stimulate the retina independently of changes in the positions of the eyes in space.

CS-UCS pairings result in the CS producing a relatively strong orienting or activation response. Zener (1937) gave bell-food pairings to dogs whose movement was restricted. The bell was on a wall. The dogs eventually often looked at the bell when it came on. Wessels (1974) gave pigeons light-food pairings in which the light was illumination of a key. The pigeons came to look at the key, even when they did not approach and peck it. Classical conditioning of the GSR component of the orienting or activation response is commonplace. Classical conditioning of an increase in muscle tension with a negative UCS has frequently been reported. CS-food pairings have resulted in the CS producing a change in the EEG response, indicating an increase in the strength in the orienting or activation response (Yoshii, Matsumoto, Maeno, Hasegawa, Yamagushi, Shimokochi, Hori, & Yamazaki, 1958). Because classical conditioning results in the CS producing a relatively strong orienting or activation response, and because a stimulus that produces a relatively strong orienting or activation response should be relatively strongly attended to, it follows that classical conditioning results in an increase in attention to the CS; that is, it results in the CS being noticed as being more different from background stimuli than beforehand. In addition, because CSs that are unlikely to result in a change in receptor stimulation—diffuse lights, sounds from an overhead speaker that is reflected well from the walls of the learning apparatus, or tactual stimuli—are able to produce an increase in the strength of the orienting or activation response, it appears that classical conditioning results in an increase in attention to a CS independently of a change in receptor stimulation.

Attention to CS Aids Subsequent Conditioning. The outcome of classical conditioning, therefore, is increased attention to the CS, that is to say, an increase in the extent to which the CS is noticed as being different from background stimuli. It follows that if the CS and background stimuli were noticed as being relatively different from each other before classical conditioning, classical conditioning should be facilitated. This expectation is supported by the following three considerations.

Recall that as the similarity between the CS and background stimuli decreases, CR strength increases. In addition, it is well known that as the similarity between the CS and background stimuli decreases, the strength of the orienting or activation response that the CS produces prior to conditioning increases. Also, recall that the strength of the orienting or activation response which a stimulus produces is taken as a measure of the extent to which this stimulus is noticed as being different from background stimuli. Therefore, CR strength increases as the extent to which the CS is noticed as being different from background stimuli prior to conditioning increases.

Latent inhibition involves exposing two groups to a learning situation for equivalent time durations. During this period one, but not the other, group is repeatedly presented with a neutral stimulus that is subsequently used as a CS. Pre-exposure to the CS retards subsequent classical conditioning (Lubow & Moore, 1959; Schnur, 1971); that is, latent inhibition occurs. Repeated presentations of the CS should result in habituation; that is, it should result in a decrease in the strength of the orienting or activation response. Pre-exposure to the CS should therefore decrease the extent to which the CS is noticed as being different from background stimuli. Thus, it appears that pre-exposure to the CS reduces the extent to which the CS is noticed as being different from background stimuli before the initiation of classical conditioning, and thereby decreases CR strength.

Consider the situation in which the background stimuli are novel, arranged by exposing an animal to a new learning situation, and in which the stimulus to be used as a CS has been previously repeatedly presented to the animal. In this situation the background stimuli should produce a relatively strong orienting or activation response, and the stimulus to be used as a CS should not. Therefore, the background stimuli and the CS should be noticed as being relatively different from each other. It follows that classical conditioning should be better when the background stimuli are novel and the CS has been previously repeatedly presented, than when both the background stimuli and the CS are new stimuli. A related result has been obtained by Lubow, Rifkin, & Alek (1976).

Reduction in Attention: Blocking. Learning can result in an increase in attention. Now it will be indicated that it also results in a decrease in attention.

Kamin (1969) reported a phenomenon that has come to be called *blocking.* In stage 1, one group of rats received 16 pairings between a noise and shock. In stage 2, the noise of stage 1 and a simultaneously present light—that is, a compound stimulus consisting of the stage 1 noise and a light—were paired with shock 8 different times. In stage 3, the stage 2 light was presented alone. Classical conditioning of suppression was measured. The result of importance was that the light failed to produce a suppression CR. A control group also received 8 pairings between the compound CS of the noise and light, but these pairings were received in stage 1. In stage 2, the control group received the 16 pairings between the noise CS and shock that the first group received in stage 1. In stage 3, the light alone was presented to the control group, and it produced a suppression CR. Note that the light did not produce a suppression CR for the first group even though in stage 2 the light (along with the noise) was paired with shock. The noise-shock pairings that the first group received in stage 1 must therefore have reduced (blocked) classical conditioning between the light and shock. Blocking also occurs in instrumental conditioning (Mackintosh & Honig, 1970).

Classical conditioning results in increased attention to the CS. Increased attention to the noise CS therefore should have occurred in stage 1 for the group receiving noise-shock pairings in this stage. This increased attention to the noise CS may have been responsible for impairing classical conditioning to the light in this group. Furthermore, the process by which increased attention to the noise CS was responsible for impairing classical conditioning to the light may have involved reduced attention to the light. If relatively little attention to a CS occurs prior to classical conditioning, then classical conditioning will be impaired. Therefore, it makes sense to assume that classical conditioning to the light was impaired by reduced attention to the light.

Reduction in Attention: Overshadowing. A finding by Pavlov (1927, p. 141) illustrates what is known as *overshadowing*. Tactile and thermal stimuli were simultaneously presented, and this stimulus compound was followed by the UCS of an acidic solution. After the subject, a dog, salivated to this compound stimulus, Pavlov presented the tactile and thermal stimuli individually. The tactile but not the thermal stimulus produced salivation. In addition, he found that the same thermal stimulus was an effective CS when it was presented individually and paired with the same UCS. Because the thermal stimulus did not come to produce salivation when it was presented simultaneously with the tactile stimulus and followed by the UCS of an acidic solution, the tactile stimulus is said to have overshadowed the thermal stimulus. Overshadowing also occurs in instrumental conditioning (Lovejoy & Russel, 1967).

Because the tactile stimulus occurred simultaneously with the thermal stimulus, it appears that the tactile stimulus was responsible for impairing classical conditioning with the thermal stimulus. The dog should have paid increased attention to the tactile stimulus, because it was paired with a UCS and did lead to classical conditioning. Probably the increased attention to the tactile stimulus reduced attention to the thermal stimulus, and thereby impaired classical conditioning with the thermal stimulus. This interpretation is analogous to the one of blocking. Increased attention to the noise CS (for the blocking study) and the tactile CS (for the overshadowing study) is assumed to occur, and to decrease attention to the light CS (for blocking) and the thermal CS (for overshadowing); and decreased attention to a CS should impair classical conditioning with that CS. Thus, the overshadowing result supports the conclusion that relatively strong attention to one stimulus tends to reduce attention to other stimuli. Also, note that it is quite unlikely that attention to the thermal stimulus could have been reduced through a change in receptor stimulation.

The reason why the tactile stimulus apparently reduced attention to the thermal stimulus and not vice versa may be that the tactile stimulus initially was more likely to be noticed as being different from background stimuli than was the thermal stimulus. Classical conditioning should therefore have occurred more rapidly with the tactile stimulus than with the thermal stimulus, thereby widening the difference in attention to the tactile and thermal stimuli, with the outcome being that the tactile stimulus reduced attention to the thermal stimulus. This reasoning is supported by results (Mackintosh, 1975a; Miles & Jenkins, 1973) indicating that the stimulus that should be noticed as being more different from background stimuli before classical conditioning reduces attention to the other stimulus of interest. For example, Mackintosh found that when an intense noise was presented in compound with a light, the light was overshadowed. He also found that when a low intensity noise was presented in compound with the light, the noise was overshadowed. A more intense stimulus should produce a stronger orienting or activation response than a weaker one and therefore should be noticed as being more different from background stimuli than a less intense stimulus. Mackintosh's findings therefore support the idea that, in overshadowing, the stimulus initially noticed as being more different from background stimuli is additionally attended to as a consequence of classical conditioning, and thereby reduces attention to the other stimulus of the compound. In addition, simultaneously presenting a more strongly attended to stimulus with a less strongly attended to stimulus probably tends to widen the difference in the strengths of attending to each stimulus, independently of conditioning.

Decrease in Attention to Irrelevant Stimulus. Discrimination learning results in a reduction in control of learned responding by irrelevant stimuli. It is likely that this reduction in control occurs, at least in part, through a decrease in attention.

Wagner et al. (1968) carried out a classical conditioning discrimination between two auditory stimuli. In addition, a light was presented in compound with each auditory discriminative stimulus, the light therefore being an irrelevant stimulus. After the discrimination was acquired, the light was presented alone (individually). It was found that the light produced a weaker CR than it did in a control condition. Increased attention to the CS+ auditory stimulus should have occurred as a consequence of classical conditioning. Therefore, it is considered likely that the relatively weak CR which the irrelevant light stimulus produced was due, in part, to the CS+ auditory stimulus reducing attention to it during the course of discrimination learning.

The stimuli preceding a reward-trained response result in CRs (Chapter 3). They therefore can be expected to produce an increase in the strength of the orienting or activation response, and thus they should be relatively strongly attended to. Consequently, reward learning discriminations should also result in a decrease in control of responding by irrelevant stimuli through, in part, a decrease in attention.

One problem with attributing the reduction in control of responding by irrelevant stimuli in discrimination learning to a decrease in attention is that an irrelevant stimulus will frequently differ more from background stimuli than the positive discriminative stimulus. Why, then, doesn't an irrelevant stimulus reduce attention to discriminative stimuli rather than vice versa? The answer to this question probably is that with continued discrimination training, the positive discriminative stimulus comes to be attended to more than the irrelevant stimulus. This should occur because the positive discriminative stimulus is always followed by the reinforcer, while the irrelevant stimulus is not. When the same animal is exposed to two stimuli, one of which is followed by the reinforcer more frequently than the other, the stimulus followed by the reinforcer more frequently produces a much stronger CR or instrumental response (Chapter 7).

Changes in Attention Processes in the Absence of Conditioning. Do essentially identical increases in attention and decreases in attention processes operate in the absence of conditioning as well as in conditioning?

A stimulus that is relatively different from background stimuli is relatively strongly attended to in the absence of conditioning. Such a stimulus probably increases the strength of the orienting or activation response in much the same way that a stimulus does as a result of learning. In other words, it appears parsimonious to assume that similar processes are responsible for strongly attending to a stimulus that is relatively different from background stimuli in the absence of conditioning, and strongly attending to a CS that was paired with a UCS.

The decrease in attention process probably operates in the absence of conditioning. Moreover, an increase in attention to one stimulus is probably responsible for a decrease in attention to other stimuli in the absence of conditioning, in the same way that an increase in attention to CSs brought about through conditioning presumably results in a decrease in attention to other CSs in blocking and overshadowing. For example, suppose that a person has a headache during a thunderstorm, and hears very loud thunder. The very loud thunder should be strongly attended to, because it is quite different from background stimuli. The person would probably also report that during the loud thunder he or she momentarily "forgot" about the headache. Which is to say, that the pain stimulus from the head was momentarily no longer attended to. In addition, it is obvious that thunder does not change the receptor stimulation responsible for the headache. Similarly, an increase in attention to a "distracting" auditory stimulus is probably responsible for a decrease in attention to visual stimuli—for instance, a book being read.

Stimulus Generalization Measures Attention. As the amount of stimulus generalization occurring between two stimuli decreases, the extent to which they are noticed as being different from each other increases. This statement seems to be intuitively acceptable. If the outcome of a stimulus generalization determination is that one stimulus produces a strong learned response, and a second stimulus produces a weak learned response, it is obvious that at least in some sense the two stimuli are noticed to be relatively different from each other.

The CS comes to produce the CR of a relatively strong orienting or activation response, which means that it comes to be noticed as being relatively different from background stimuli. Because CR strength typically decreases as the test stimuli move away from the CS along a dimension of the CS, it follows that test stimuli should be noticed as being different from background stimuli to increasingly smaller extents as they move away from the CS along a dimension of the CS. Consider that if stimulus A is noticed as being different from background stimuli to a large extent, and if stimulus B is noticed as being different from background stimuli to a small extent, stimulus A and stimulus B will then be noticed as being relatively different from each other. Therefore, the CS should usually be noticed as being different from the test stimuli of a stimulus generalization determination, more so as the test stimuli move away from the CS along a dimension of the CS. Furthermore, two test stimuli, both to the right or both to the left of the CS along a dimension of the CS, should be noticed as being relatively different from each other when the strengths of the CRs they produce are relatively different. Thus, as the amount of stimulus generalization between two stimuli decreases, the extent to which they are noticed as being different from each other should increase. This argument also applies to stimulus generalization occurring along a dimension of an S+ for a reward-trained response, because such an S+ probably produces a relatively strong orienting or activation response, given that it tends to produce CRs in general.

Richardson and Evans (1975) did a study, previously described, in which a stimulus of a specific wavelength appeared on a key adjacent to the white response key during acquisition of straightforward reward learning. A stimulus generalization determination along the wavelength dimension was subsequently carried out, in which both the training and the test stimuli appeared on the key adjacent to the response key. The obtained result was that the amount of stimulus generalization occurring along the wavelength dimension hardly decreased at all. The stimuli on a key adjacent to the response key should not be noticed as being relatively different from each other, because they are relatively unlikely to impinge on the retina. Consequently a large amount of stimulus generalization along a dimension of a stimulus occurred together with unnoticed differences in training and test stimuli.

It is concluded that as the amount of stimulus generalization occurring between two stimuli decreases, the extent to which they are noticed as being different from each other increases.

Stimulus Generalization and Increase and Decrease in Attention. The amount of stimulus generalization occurring along a dimension, and therefore the extent to which the stimuli employed for the stimulus generalization determination are noticed as being different from each other, can be affected by both increase in attention and decrease in attention processes.

Learned response strength is positively related to the number of conditioned substimuli perceived divided by the number of conditioned substimuli perceived plus the number of unconditioned substimuli perceived. A perceived substimulus is one that is relatively strongly attended to. Suppose that a stimulus was strongly attended to through an increase in attention resulting from conditioning. The contribution of this stimulus to the number of conditioned substimuli that are percevied would be relatively large. Presenting test stimuli that vary along a dimension of this stimulus should then result in the perception of a relatively large number of unconditioned substimuli. It follows from the formula for learned response strength that a stimulus generalization determination along a dimension of the stimulus in question would result in a relatively small amount of stimulus generalization occurring.

A decrease in attention process can also affect the amount of stimulus generalization that occurs along a dimension. Suppose that prior to conditioning, 10 percent of the perceived substimuli stemmed from one stimulus, and that all 10 percent of these substimuli became conditioned when learning was carried out. Also, suppose that as a result of learning, a decrease in attention process was responsible for eliminating attention to the other 90 percent of the substimuli that were perceived prior to conditioning. This would mean that the stimulus once providing 10 percent of the perceived substimuli would, after learning, provide 100 percent of the perceived substimuli. Furthermore, they would all be conditioned substimuli. Introduction of test stimuli that varied along a dimension of the stimulus originally supplying 10 percent of the perceived substimuli should then result in a relatively large reduction in the proportion of perceived substimuli that were conditioned. Therefore, a relatively small amount of stimulus generalization along a dimension of this stimulus should occur. In this way a decrease in attention to one stimulus should affect the amount of stimulus generalization occurring along a dimension of a different stimulus.

The occurrence of a relatively small amount of stimulus generalization along a dimension means that the stimuli along this dimension are noticed as being relatively different from each other. It follows that an increase in attention to a stimulus can increase the extent to which stimuli along a dimension of it are noticed as being different from each other; and a decrease in attention to one stimulus can increase the extent to which the stimuli along a dimension of a second stimulus are noticed as being different from each other.

Noticing Discriminative Stimuli as Different. Discrimination learning between two explicit discriminative stimuli, that is, between CS+ and CS—, or between S+ and S—, increases the extent to which the discriminative stimuli are noticed as being different from each other. This intuitively acceptable idea will be supported below.

Discrimination learning markedly reduces the amount of stimulus generalization occurring between discriminative stimuli that differ along the dimension the stimulus generalization determination is carried out on. A decrease in the amount of stimulus generalization occurring between two stimuli is accompanied by an increase in the extent to which they are noticed as being different from each other. It follows that discrimination learning between stimuli that differ along a common dimension increases the extent to which these stimuli are noticed as being different. Discriminative stimuli will usually differ along at least one common dimension; for example, a tone and no sound differ in intensity.

Discrimination learning reduces the amount of stimulus generalization occurring along a dimension of CS+ or S+ that is not also a dimension of CS— or S—. For example, discrimination learning between a 550-nanometer S+, and a white light S—, that were otherwise identical, reduced the amount of stimulus generalization occurring along the wavelength dimension (Marsh, 1972). We may infer from this finding that discrimination learning should reduce the amount of stimulus generalization occurring between positive and negative discriminative stimuli when they have no dimensions in common, for example, when they are a tone and a light. (However, these stimuli might vary along a spatial dimension.) As the amount of stimulus generalization occurring between two stimuli decreases, the extent to which they are noticed as being different from each other increases. It follows that discrimination learning increases the extent to which discriminative stimuli are noticed as being different, when the discriminative stimuli have no dimensions in common.

Noticing Discriminative Stimuli as Different: Increase in Attention.

Evidence exists to support the idea that an increase in attention process contributes to making discriminative stimuli noticed as being relatively different from each other.

A decrease in attention to one stimulus can increase the extent to which the stimuli along a second dimension are noticed as being different from each other. The increase in the extent to which discriminative stimuli are noticed as being different that occurs as a result of discrimination learning may therefore be due to a decrease in attention to other stimuli. Furthermore, there is a decrease in attention to the irrelevant stimuli that are present during discrimination learning. Moreover, irrelevant stimuli are present in any discrimination. Consider, for example, any discrimination between two stimuli that differ along the wavelength dimension: the two stimuli will possess identical substimuli, and these identical substimuli are irrelevant stimuli, because they are always present when either the positive or negative discriminative stimulus occurs. It is, therefore, by no means obvious that an increase in attention process contributes to making discriminative stimuli noticed as being relatively different from each other.

Behavior that appears to be the outcome of an increase in attention process operating on discriminative stimuli can often be observed when animals respond on simultaneous discriminations. When animals are at the choice point of a T-maze, they often look to and move slightly in the direction of the discriminative stimulus on the right, and then look to and move slightly in the direction of the discriminative stimulus on the left; often they do so repeatedly (Munn, 1950, p. 253). This behavior is called *vicarious trial-and-error*. It usually occurs just before the animal solves the simultaneous discrimination task. A similar result is reported by Hamlin (1975). He found that pigeons availed themselves of the opportunity to have discriminative stimuli of a very brief duration re-presented before making a choice point response fairly soon before they solved a discrimination task. Although these behaviors appear to suggest that animals actively increase their attention to simultaneously presented discriminative stimuli, instead it may be that they actively decrease attention to the substimuli that the discriminative stimuli share in common.

If the outcome of discrimination learning is an increase in the extent to which the discriminative stimuli are noticed as being different from each other that is contributed to by an increase in attention process, then discrimination learning should be facilitated by an increase in the extent to which the stimuli to be discriminated between are noticed as being different prior to the initiation of discrimination learning. There is support for this idea.

As the amount of stimulus generalization occurring between two stimuli decreases, the extent to which these stimuli are noticed as being different from each other increases. And as the amount of stimulus generalization occurring between two stimuli decreases, performance on a subsequent discrimination between these two stimuli improves. It follows that as the extent to which two stimuli are noticed as being different before discrimination learning increases, discrimination learning improves.

The extent to which two stimuli are noticed as being different from each other prior to discrimination learning may also be increased by pre-exposing animals to one, but not the other, discriminative stimulus. The novel discriminative stimulus should produce a relatively strong orienting or activation response, but the pre-exposed stimulus should not; this means that the two stimuli should be noticed as being relatively different from each other prior to discrimination learning. Both Porter and Treadway (1974) and Chantrey (1972) found that pre-exposing animals to one but not the other discriminative stimulus resulted in better discrimination learning than not pre-exposing animals to either discriminative stimulus. In addition, pre-exposing animals to both discriminative stimuli impaired discrimination learning (Chantrey, 1972). Thus, the idea that an increase in attention process contributes to the increase in the extent to which discriminative stimuli are noticed as being different is supported.

A factor that probably contributes to the difficulty of discrimination learning is that the permanent brain events corresponding to discriminative stimuli become confused. Perhaps an increase in attention process that operates on the substimuli that the discriminative stimuli do not possess in common, and a decrease in attention process that operates on the substimuli that the discriminative stimuli possess in common, together aid in reducing the extent to which the permanent brain events corresponding to these discriminative stimuli become confused.

It was indicated earlier that discrimination learning decreases the amount of stimulus generalization occurring along a dimension of a CS+ or S+ that is not also a dimension of a CS— or S—. This outcome is probably contributed to by an increase in attention to discriminative stimuli and a decrease in attention to irrelevant stimuli.

Blocking and Unpredictable Stimuli. The effect of unpredictable stimuli on blocking is of importance.

Presenting an unpredictable stimulus at about the same time or shortly after the UCS occurred in stage 2 of the blocking procedure reduces the magnitude of the blocking effect (Feldman, 1971; Gray & Appig-nanesi, 1973). In the latter study, in stage 1 rats received noise-shock pairings. In stage 2 the noise of stage 1 and a light were simultaneously presented, and each occurrence of this compound stimulus was followed by the previously employed shock. For the group of primary interest, in stage 2 each pairing between the compound stimulus and shock was also followed 3 seconds later by a flash of light and a click. These stimuli could not be predicted on the basis of the stage 1 procedures. The obtained result was that the group receiving the unpredictable stimulus after pairings between the noise-and-light compound stimulus and shock in stage 2 exhibited a stronger suppression CR to light than did groups either not receiving the unpredictable stimuli after pairings between the compound stimulus and shock in stage 2, or receiving it at a later time following the pairings between the compound stimulus and shock in stage 2. That is, presenting the unpredictable stimulus relatively soon after the pairings between the compound stimulus and shock in stage 2 reduced the magnitude of the blocking effect.

An unpredictable stimulus may initiate a scanning of the temporary brain events corresponding to the stimuli involved in conditioning that just precede the unpredictable stimulus, resulting in "recognition" of the CS that would otherwise not be attended to, thereby facilitating classical conditioning between it and the UCS. Another idea is that a surprising UCS increases the extent to which the temporary brain event corresponding to it exists; if the temporary brain event corresponding to a CS is present when the amount of temporary brain event corresponding to the UCS is increased by the presentation of a surprising UCS, classical conditioning between the CS and UCS may be facilitated (Terry & Wagner, 1975; Wagner & Terry, 1975).

Theories of Attention. The theory of attention advanced here assumes that an increase in attention process operates on a stimulus; that a decrease in attention process simultaneously operates on other stimuli; and that the increase in attention process is responsible for the decrease in attention process operating on other stimuli. An increase in attention process is assumed to operate on a stimulus as a consequence of its being paired with a reinforcer that elicits a relatively strong orienting or activation response CR. The stimuli that the decrease in attention process operates on may be other conditioned stimuli that produce weaker orienting or activation responses, or stimuli not involved in conditioning. What is not assumed is a relatively small limit to the number of stimuli on which the increase in attention process can operate. For example, if a compound stimulus composed of two stimuli is more likely to be followed by a UCS than is either member of the compound, it is assumed that an increase in attention to both members of the compound occurs.

Another theory of attention maintains that in conditioning only a limited amount of information about stimuli can be handled or stored; therefore, if one stimulus is strongly attended to, a second stimulus must be weakly attended to (Sutherland & Mackintosh, 1971; Zeaman & House, 1963). Rescorla and Wagner (1972) maintain that there is a limit to the amount of conditioning that can be established by a reinforcer. If two stimuli are followed by the same reinforcer, and one is relatively strongly conditioned to, then the second is predicted to be relatively weakly conditioned to, due to the limited amount of conditioning that the reinforcer can support. Both these theories predict that an increase in conditioning to one stimulus will be accompanied by a decrease in conditioning to a second stimulus. But this expectation is not always supported (Miles & Jenkins, 1973; Mackintosh, 1975a). The finding that an unpredictable stimulus decreases the magnitude of the blocking effect conflicts with both theories, because it is not clear why an unpredictable stimulus should increase handling or storage ability. Also, because Rescorla and Wagner stress the role of the reinforcer, they have difficulty in accounting for the changes in attention that occur in the absence of conditioning. It is also difficult for them to explain the likely result that once a CS produces a relatively strong orienting or activation response, it relatively quickly comes to produce a different CR when paried with a different reinforcer. There is additional negative evidence (Feldman, 1975; Mackintosh, 1975b).

Mackintosh (1975a) proposed that attention to redundant stimuli tends to be reduced. Blocking and overshadowing support this idea, because for both these results two stimuli predict the reinforcer will occur; redundancy therefore exists, and attention to one of the predicting stimuli is apparently reduced. But irrelevant stimuli are not redundant stimuli, yet it was concluded that a decrease in attention process acts on them.

Increase and Decrease in Attention and Image Theory. Increase in attention and decrease in attention are probably essential to an animal's rapid, skilled execution of instrumental responses. According to image theory, the instrumental response occurs or is withheld because, in part, the stimulus produced by this response is analogous to a CS, due to its becoming associated with a goal or negative-goal stimulus through classical conditioning. But it should be impossible for some instrumental responses to be executed quickly and accurately unless the stimulus produced by the instrumental response were clearly discriminated from similar response-produced stimuli and background stimuli. An increase in attention to the stimulus produced by the instrumental response, and a decrease in attention to similar response-produced stimuli and background stimuli are probably essential to establishing a clear discrimination between the stimulus produced by the instrumental response, on the one hand, and similar response-produced stimuli and background stimuli on the other.

Image theory explains those instrumental responses that increase in rate by supposing that an animal brings about the stimulus produced by the instrumental response. A stimulus produced within the brain necessarily functions as a response-produced stimulus mediating the execution of the instrumental response (Chapter 1). An increase in attention to a perceived stimulus may mean that the temporary brain event produced by the stimulus is increased. But if an animal can increase the amount of temporary brain event produced by a stimulus impinging on a receptor, it is more likely that it can bring about a stimulus produced within the brain, which the theory assumes does happen. For instrumental responses that decrease in rate, the theory states that an animal avoids bringing about a stimulus produced within the brain, similar to a decrease in attention to a stimulus.

Stimulus Generalization, Discrimination Learning, Development of Social Behavior, and Contact Comfort

Stimulus generalization pervades human interactions, because in these interactions precisely the same stimuli will usually not be repeated. Classical conditioning in children between a mother's attention behaviors, which include smiling, talking in a pleasant tone of voice, turning toward or facing, and physical proximity, and contact comfort was indicated to occur. An example of stimulus generalization of this learning is a mother's attention behaviors reducing her child's fear when they are in a strange building. Reward learning of appropriate behavior in children with contact comfort as the reinforcer also occurs. An example of stimulus generalization of this learning is a child's behaving appropriately when the mother has a new dress on.

Discrimination learning also pervades human social behavior. Subtle differences in interpersonal behavior often predict whether one adult will deliver a reinforcer to a second person. For children, consider that the probability of the child's being permitted to obtain contact comfort from the mother is relatively high when the mother is exhibiting attention behaviors; certainly, she is less likely to permit contact comfort when she is frowning or yelling at the child. In other words, a mother's attention behavior should be an S+, and her negative interpersonal behavior should be an S— for the instrumental response of a child's obtaining contact comfort.

This possibility has support. Arrington and King (1974) found that college students expected children to be more likely to initiate obtaining contact comfort with their mother or father if the parent exhibits attention rather than "neutral" interpersonal behaviors, and if the parent exhibits neutral rather than negative interpersonal behaviors. Completions to incomplete paragraphs describing a mother or father exhibiting attention, neutral, or negative interpersonal behaviors to a child were used to determine subjects' expectations. The written completions were scored for the extent to which the child attempted to obtain contact comfort from a parent.

Summary

Procedures for stimulus generalization determinations are discussed. The amount of stimulus generalization that occurs between a training and test stimulus typically decreases as the test stimuli move away from the training stimulus along a dimension of this stimulus. Relations between image theory and stimulus generalization are involved with the vividness of the image of the UCS or goal or negative-goal stimulus a test stimulus produces, the theory's account of straightforward instrumental conditioning, and the possibility that test stimuli produce an image of the training stimulus. Learned response strength is positively related to the proportion of perceived substimuli that are conditioned, and how this relates to stimulus generalization is indicated. The result that a large amount of stimulus generalization occurs along a dimension of a stimulus that is relatively unlikely to impinge on a receptor is related to considerations involving conditioned and unconditioned stimuli.

Discrimination learning in classical conditioning, position discrimination learning with the T-maze, multiunit T-maze discrimination learning, visual discrimination learning with the T-maze and jumping stand, go/no-go successive discrimination learning, and reinforcer-always-possible successive discrimination learning are described. Measures of discrimination performance involve a comparison between the strengths of a learned response produced by each discriminative stimulus. Straightforward classical conditioning involves the acquisition of a discrimination between the CS and background stimuli. In straightforward instrumental conditioning, the stimulus produced by the instrumental response must be discriminated from background stimuli and from other response-produced stimuli. Discrimination learning can be used to show which types of stimuli control responding. Response-produced stimuli can control learned responding.

Factors affecting straightforward classical and instrumental conditioning usually also affect performance on a discrimination. However, amount of reinforcement and deprivation level do not consistently affect performance on a reward-learning discrimination. The direction of choice between a perceived reinforcer and a perceived neutral stimulus is probably not importantly affected by the amount of the reinforcer, or the extent of deprivation of it; this accords with the conclusion that the learned response is quantitatively and qualitatively related to certain responses to the perceived stimulus that is the second member of the S_1-S_2 pairing that results in conditioning; it also accords with image theory. As the amount of stimulus generalization that occurs between stimuli decreases, performance on a subsequent discrimination between these stimuli improves. This finding is obtained for successive as well as simultaneous discriminations, and therefore implies that during successive discrimination learning, an image of the discriminative stimulus not currently present occurs. This suggests that the permanent brain events corresponding to the CS and the stimuli of the general learning situation are involved with the processes for straightforward classical and instrumental conditioning. The result that as the amount of stimulus generalization occurring between stimuli increases, discrimination learning between these stimuli worsens explains the finding that as the similarity between the CS and background stimuli increases, CR strength decreases. Neurophysiological evidence suggests that images of discriminative stimuli control the execution of learned responses.

CS+ controls performance of the CR; the S+ of both the go/no-go successive discrimination and the simultaneous discrimination control performance of the instrumental response, although other sources of control have to be considered for the simultaneous discrimination. The amount of stimulus generalization typically decreases as test stimuli move away from a CS+ or S+ along a dimension of these stimuli, when CS— or S— is not on the same dimension. CS— controls the nonperformance of the CR; both the S— of the go/no-go successive discrimination and the simultaneous discrimination control the nonperformance of the instrumental response, although for the simultaneous discrimination other sources of control have to be considered. Evidence suggests that the relatively close physical and temporal proximity of no particular event to reinforcer that occurs in discrimination learning affects the nature of the responses produced by negative discriminative stimuli; this is in accord with interpretations of classical conditioning in which a CS is paired with the occurrence of no particular event, and of instrumental conditioning in which the instrumental response is followed by the occurrence of no particular event. The amount of stimulus generalization of the inhibitory effect of a CS— or S— typically decreases as test stimuli move away from the CS— or S— along a dimension of these stimuli when CS+ or S+ is not on the same dimension. The stimulus generalization gradient obtained along a dimension in common with CS+ and CS— or S+ and S— can be approximately predicted by combining empirically obtained excitatory and inhibitory stimulus generalization gradients. Discrimination learning between two stimuli that differ along a common dimension often facilitates subsequent discrimination learning in which the discriminative stimuli differ along the same common dimension. This result probably occurs because the acquisition of the first discrimination reduces the amount of stimulus generalization occurring between the discriminative stimuli of the subsequent discrimination. Nonlearning apparatus discriminations between a number of stimuli that differ along a common dimension typically occur, and most likely thereby result in a decrease in the amount of stimulus generalization occurring along at least some dimensions. A relatively large decrease in the amount of stimulus generalization along the wavelength dimension occurred in pigeons in the absence of the opportunity to acquire nonlearning apparatus discriminations between stimuli differing along this dimension. Discrimination learning results in less stimulus generalization occurring along a dimension of a positive discriminative stimulus than does straightforward conditioning along a dimension of the same stimulus. Discrimination learning is necessarily impaired by control of responding by irrelevant stimuli, and this control decreases as a result of discrimination learning.

The orienting or activation response is a measure of attention to a stimulus, that is, a measure of the extent to which one stimulus is noticed as being different from a second stimulus. Habituation is a type of learning. In addition, habituation results support the idea that the orienting or activation response measures attention. The result that the CS produces a strong orienting or activation response supports the conclusion that classical conditioning results in an increase in attention to the CS. Noticing the CS as relatively different from background stimuli before conditioning probably facilitates this conditioning, which supports this conclusion. Both blocking and overshadowing suggest that when an increase in attention process operates on one CS, it results in a decrease in attention toward a second CS. It is likely that the reduction in control of responding by irrelevant stimuli that occurs in discrimination learning is due, in part, to a decrease in attention toward these stimuli. It is also likely that relatively strong attention to one stimulus tends to result in a decrease in attention toward a second stimulus in the absence of conditioning. Support for the conclusion that the extent to which stimuli are noticed as being different from each other increases as the amount of stimulus generalization occurring between them decreases comes from the result that test stimuli usually produce weaker orienting or activation responses than does the training stimulus, and the result involving stimulus generalization and the extent to which stimuli impinge on a receptor. The amount of stimulus generalization occurring along a dimension can be affected by both increase in attention and decrease in attention processes. The extent to which discriminative stimuli are noticed as being different from each other should be increased as a consequence of discrimination learning, because discrimination learning markedly decreases the amount of stimulus generalization that occurs between discriminative stimuli. Both a decrease in attention to irrelevant stimuli and an increase in attention to discriminative stimuli probably contribute to the increase in the extent to which discriminative stimuli are noticed as being different from each other as a consequence of discrimination learning. An unpredictable stimulus delivered at the appropriate time decreases the magnitude of blocking. Theories of attention are discussed. An increase in attention to the stimulus produced by the instrumental response, and a decrease in attention to similar response-produced stimuli and background stimuli are probably essential to the rapid accurate execution of the instrumental response. Attention results indicate that the effects of stimuli within the brain can be modified, which supports the hypothesis that in instrumental conditioning an animal brings about or avoids bringing about response-produced stimuli within the brain.

Stimulus generalization and discrimination learning are pervasive in social behavior. Attention behaviors are probably S+s for the instrumental response of a child's obtaining contact comfort from familiar people.

REFERENCES

ANNAU, Z., & KAMIN, L. J. The conditioned emotional response as a function of the intensity of the US. *J. Comp. Physiol. Psychol.*, 1961, 54, 428-432.
ARRINGTON, B. V., & KING, D. L. Expectations concerning children's obtaining con-

tact comfort following parents' interpersonal behaviors. *Psychol. Rep.*, 1974, 34, 455-460.

AZRIN, N. H., HUTCHINSON, R. R., & HAKE, D. F. Extinction-induced aggression. *J. Exp. Anal. Behav.*, 1966, 9, 191-204.

BAKER, R. A., & LAWRENCE, D. H. The differential effects of simultaneous and successive stimuli presentation on transposition. *J. Comp. Physiol. Psychol.*, 1951, 44, 378-382.

BLACKWELL, H. R., & SCHLOSBERG, H. Octave generalization, pitch discrimination, and loudness thresholds in the white rat. *J. Exp. Psychol.*, 1943, 33, 407-419.

BRESNAHAN, E. L. Effects of extradimensional pseudodiscrimination and discrimination training upon stimulus control. *J. Exp. Psychol.*, 1970, 85, 155-156.

BUTTER, C. M. Stimulus generalization along one and two dimensions in pigeons. *J. Exp. Psychol.*, 1963, 65, 339-346.

CHANTREY, D. F. Enhancement and retardation of discrimination learning in chicks after exposure to the discriminanda. *J. Comp. Physiol. Psychol.*, 1972, 81, 256-261.

CORNELL, J. M., & STRUB, H. A technique for demonstrating the inhibitory function of SΔ. *Psychon. Sci.*, 1965, 3, 25-26.

COHEN, P. S., & LOONEY, T. A. Schedule-induced mirror responding in the pigeon. *J. Exp. Anal. Behav.*, 1973, 19, 395-408.

COLE, J. M., & LITCHFIELD, P. M. Stimulus control of schedule-induced aggression in the pigeon. *Psychon. Sci.*, 1969, 17, 152-153.

DERDZINSKI, D., & WARREN, J. M. Perimeter, complexity, and form discrimination learning by cats. *J. Comp. Physiol. Psychol.*, 1969, 68, 407-411.

DINSMOOR, J. A. The effect of hunger on discriminated responding. *J. Abnorm. Soc. Psychol.*, 1952, 47, 67-72.

EISMAN, E., ASIMOW, A., & MALTZMAN, I. Habit strength as a function of drive in a brightness discrimination problem. *J. Exp. Psychol.*, 1956, 52, 58-64.

ELLISON, G. D. Differential salivary conditioning to traces. *J. Comp. Physiol. Psychol.*, 1964, 57, 373-380.

FELDMAN, J. M. Added cue control as a function of reinforcement predictability. *J. Exp. Psychol.*, 1971, 91, 318-325.

FELDMAN, J. M. Blocking as a function of added cue intensity. *Anim. Learn. Behav.*, 1975, 3, 98-102.

FILE, S. E. Long-term retention of behavioural habituation in the rat. *Anim. Behav.*, 1973, 21, 585-589.

GENTRY, G. V., OVERALL, J. E., & BROWN, W. L. Transpositional responses of rhesus monkeys to stimulus objects of intermediate size. *Am. J. Psychol.*, 1959, 72, 453-455.

GIBSON, E. J. *Principles of Perceptual Learning and Development.* New York: Appleton-Century-Crofts, 1969.

GRAY, T., & APPIGNANESI, A. A. Compound conditioning: Elimination of the blocking effect. *Learn. Motiv.*, 1973, 4, 374-380.

GUTHRIE, E. R. *The Psychology of Learning.* New York: Harper, 1935.

HABER, A., & KALISH, H. I. Prediction of discrimination from generalization after variations in schedule of reinforcement. *Science*, 1963, 142, 412-413.

HALL, G. Response strategies after overtraining in the jumping stand. *Anim. Learn. Behav.*, 1973, 1, 157-160.

HALL, J. F. *The Psychology of Learning.* Philadelphia: Lippincott, 1966.

HAMLIN, P. H. Observing responses as an index of attention in chickens. *J. Exp. Psychol.: Anim. Behav. Processes*, 1975, 1, 221-234.

HAMMOND, L. J. A traditional demonstration of the properties of Pavlovian inhibition using differential CER. *Psychon. Sci.*, 1967, 9, 65-66.

HAMMOND, L. J. Retardation of fear acquisition by a previously inhibitory CS. *J. Comp. Physiol. Psychol.*, 1968, 66, 756-759.

HANSON, H. M. Effects of discrimination training on stimulus generalization. *J. Exp. Psychol.*, 1959, 58, 321-334.

HEARST, E. Discrimination learning as the summation of excitation and inhibition. *Science*, 1968, 162, 1303-1306.

HILL, W. F., COTTON, J. W., & CLAYTON, K. N. Effects of reward magnitude, percentage of reinforcement, and training method on acquisition and reversal in a T-maze. *J. Exp. Psychol.*, 1962, 64, 81-86.

HOBSON, S. L. Discriminability of fixed-ratio schedules for pigeons: Effects of absolute ratio size. *J. Exp. Anal. Behav.*, 1975, 23, 25-35.

HOFFMAN, H. S. Stimulus factors in conditioned suppression. In B. A. Campbell and R. M. Church (Eds.), *Punishment and Aversive Behavior*. New York: Appleton-Century-Crofts, 1969.

HOFFMAN, H. S., & FLESHLER, M. Stimulus factors in aversive controls: The generalization of conditioned suppression. *J. Exp. Anal. Behav.*, 1961, 4, 371-378.

HONIG, W. K. Effects of extradimensional discrimination training upon previously acquired stimulus control. *Learn. Motiv.*, 1974, 5, 1-15.

HONIG, W. K. Attentional factors governing the slope of the generalization gradient. In N. S. Sutherland and R. M. Gilbert (Eds.), *Animal Discrimination Learning*. London: Academic Press, 1969.

HOVLAND, C. I. The generalization of conditioned responses: I. The sensory generalization of conditioned responses with varying frequencies of tone. *J. Gen. Psychol.*, 1937, 17, 125-148.

JENKINS, H. M., & HARRISON, R. H. Effect of discrimination training on auditory generalization. *J. Exp. Psychol.*, 1960, 59, 246-253.

JOHN, E. R. *Mechanisms of Memory*. New York: Academic Press, 1967.

JOHN, E. R., & KILLAM, K. F. Electrophysiological correlates of differential approach-avoidance conditioning in the cat. *J. Nerv. Ment. Dis.*, 1960, 131, 183-201.

KALISH, H. I., & HABER, A. Prediction of discrimination from generalization following variations in deprivation level. *J. Comp. Physiol. Psychol.*, 1965, 60, 125-128.

KAMIN, L. J. Predictability, surprise, attention, and conditioning. In B. A. Campbell and R. M. Church (Eds.), *Punishment and Aversive Behavior*. New York: Appleton-Century-Crofts, 1969.

KINCHLA, J. Discrimination of two auditory durations by pigeons. *Percept. Psychophys.*, 1970, 8, 299-307.

KLING, J. W. Generalization of extinction of an instrumental response to stimuli varying in the size dimension. *J. Exp. Psychol.*, 1952, 44, 339-346.

KREMER, E. F. The truly random control procedure: Conditioning to the static cues. *J. Comp. Physiol. Psychol.*, 1974, 86, 700-707.

LASHLEY, K. S. Conditional reactions in the rat. *J. Psychol.*, 1938, 6, 311-324.

LAWRENCE, D. H. Acquired distinctiveness of cues: I. Transfer between discriminations on the basis of familiarity with the stimulus. *J. Exp. Psychol.*, 1949, 39, 770-784.

LAWRENCE, D. H. The transfer of a discrimination along a continuum. *J. Comp. Physiol. Psychol.*, 1952, 45, 511-516.

LAWRENCE, D. H., & DeRIVERA, J. Evidence for relational transposition. *J. Comp. Physiol. Psychol.*, 1954, 47, 465-471.

LEATON, R. N. & BUCK, R. L. Habituation of the arousal response in rats. *J. Comp. Physiol. Psychol.*, 1971, 75, 430-434.

LIU, S. S. Differential conditioning and stimulus generalization of the rabbit's nictitating membrane response. *J. Comp. Physiol. Psychol.*, 1971, 77, 136-142.

LOVEJOY, E., & RUSSELL, D. G. Suppression of learning about a hard cue by the presence of an easy cue. *Psychon. Sci.*, 1967, 8, 365-366.

LUBOW, R. E., & MOORE, A. U. Latent inhibition: The effect of nonreinforced preexposure to the conditioned stimulus. *J. Comp. Physiol. Psychol.*, 1959, 52, 415-419.

LUBOW, R. E., RIFKIN, B., & ALEK, M. The context effect: The relationship between stimulus preexposure and environmental preexposure determines subsequent learning. *J. Exp. Psychol.: Anim. Behav. Processes*, 1976, 2, 38-47.

MACKINTOSH, N. J. A theory of attention: Variations in the associability of stimuli with reinforcement. *Psychol. Rev.*, 1975, 82, 276-298. (a)

MACKINTOSH, N. J. Blocking of conditioned suppression: Role of the first compound trial. *J. Exp. Psychol.: Anim. Behav. Processes*, 1975, 1, 335-345. (b)

MACKINTOSH, N. J., & HONIG, W. K. Blocking and attentional enhancement in the pigeon. *J. Comp. Physiol. Psychol.*, 1970, 73, 78-85.

MACKINTOSH, N. J., & LITTLE, L. An analysis of transfer along a continuum. *Can. J. Psychol.*, 1970, 24, 362-369.

MAHER, W. B., & WICKENS, D. D. Effect of differential quantity of reward on acquisition and performance of a maze habit. *J. Comp. Physiol. Psychol.*, 1954, 47, 44-46.

MALOTT, M. K. Stimulus control in stimulus-deprived chickens. *J. Comp. Physiol. Psychol.*, 1968, 66, 276-282.

MANDLER, J. M. The effect of overtraining on the use of positive and negative stimuli in reversal and transfer. *J. Comp. Physiol. Psychol.*, 1968, 66, 110-115.

MARSH, G. Prediction of the peak shift in pigeons from gradients of excitation and inhibition. *J. Comp. Physiol. Psychol.*, 1972, 81, 262-266.

MEDNICK, S. A., & LEHTINEN, L. E. Stimulus generalization as a function of age in children. *J. Exp. Psychol.*, 1957, 53, 180-183.

MILES, C. G., & JENKINS, H. M. Overshadowing in operant conditioning as a function of discriminability. *Learn. Motiv.*, 1973, 4, 11-27.

MILES, C. G., MACKINTOSH, N. J., & WESTBROOK, R. F. Redistributing control between the elements of a compound stimulus. *Q. J. Exp. Psychol.*, 1970, 22, 478-483.

MUNN, N. L. *Handbook of Psychological Research on the Rat.* Boston: Houghton Mifflin, 1950.

NISSEN, H. W. Description of the learned response in discrimination behavior. *Psychol. Rev.*, 1950, 59, 121-137.

PAVLOV, I. P. *Conditioned Reflexes* (G. V. Anrep, trans.). London: Oxford University Press, 1927.

PORTER, R. H., & TREADWAY, J. T. Effects of previous exposure on olfactory discrimination in Acomys cahirinus. *Nature*, 1974, 249, 157-158.

RESCORLA, R. A., & WAGNER, A. R. A theory of Pavlovian conditioning: Variations in the effectiveness of reinforcement and nonreinforcement. In A. H. Black and W. F. Prokasy (Eds.), *Classical Conditioning ll: Current Theory and Research*. New York: Appleton-Century-Crofts, 1972.

RICHARDSON, W. K., & EVANS, M. S. The effect of localizing the stimulus at the response key on generalization along the hue dimension in the pigeon. *Anim. Learn. Behav.*, 1975, 3, 119-122.

RILEY, D. A., GOGGIN, J. P., & WRIGHT, D. C. Training level and cue separation as determiners of transposition and retention in rats. *J. Comp. Physiol. Psychol.*, 1963, 56, 1044-1049.

RILEY, D. A., & LEUIN, T. C. Stimulus-generalization gradients in chickens reared in monochromatic light and tested with a single wavelength value. *J. Comp. Physiol. Psychol.*, 1971, 75, 399-402.

RILLING, M., & CAPLAN, H. J. Extinction-induced aggression during errorless discrimination learning. *J. Exp. Anal. Behav.*, 1973, 20, 85-92.

RILLING, M., KRAMER, T. J., & RICHARDS, R. W. Aversive properties of the negative stimulus during learning with and without errors. *Learn. Motiv.*, 1973, 4, 1-10.

SCHNUR, P. Selective attention: Effects of element preexposure on compound conditioning in rats. *J. Comp. Physiol. Psychol.*, 1971, 76, 123-130.

SHARPLESS, S., & JASPER, H. Habituation of the arousal reaction. *Brain*, 1956, 79, 655-680.

SHEFFIELD, F. D. Relation between classical conditioning and instrumental learning. In W. F. Prokasy (Ed.), *Classical Conditioning: A Symposium*. New York: Appleton-Century-Crofts, 1965.

SHEPP, B. E., & EIMAS, P. D. Intradimensional and extradimensional shifts in the rat. *J. Comp. Physiol. Psychol.*, 1964, 57, 357-361.

SPENCE, K. W. The differential response in animals to stimuli varying within a single dimension. *Psychol. Rev.*, 1937, 44, 430-444.

SURWILLO, W. W. Psychological factors in muscle-action potentials: EMG gradients. *J. Exp. Psychol.*, 1956, 52, 263-272.

SUTHERLAND, N. S. Shape discrimination in rat, octopus, and goldfish: A comparative study. *J. Comp. Physiol. Psychol.*, 1969, 67, 160-176.

SUTHERLAND, N. S., CARR, A. E., & MACKINTOSH, J. A. Visual discrimination of open and closed shapes by rats. I. Training. *Q. J. Exp. Psychol.*, 1962, 14, 129-139.

SUTHERLAND, N. S., & MACKINTOSH, N. J. *Mechanisms of Animal Discrimination Learning*. New York: Academic Press, 1971.

SWELLER, J. A test between selective attention and stimulus generalization interpretations of the easy-to-hard effect. *Q. J. Exp. Psychol.*, 1972, 24, 352-355.

TEES, R. C. Effects of visual restriction in rats on generalization along the dimension of angular orientation. *J. Comp. Physiol. Psychol.*, 1972, 79, 494-502.

TERRY, W. S., & WAGNER, A. R. Short-term memory for "surprising" vs. "expected" unconditioned stimuli in Pavlovian conditioning. *J. Exp. Psychol.: Anim. Behav. Processes*, 1975, 1, 122-133.

THOMAS, D. R., & BURR, D. E. S. Stimulus generalization as a function of the delay between training and testing procedures: A reevaluation. *J. Exp. Anal. Behav.*, 1969, 12, 105-109.

THOMAS, D. R., FREEMAN, F., SVINICKI, J. G., BURR, D. E. S., & LYONS, J. Effects of extradimensional training on stimulus generalization. *J. Exp. Psychol. Monogr.*, 1970, 83, (1, Pt. 2).

TURNER, C., & MACKINTOSH, N. J. Stimulus selection and irrelevant stimuli in discrimination learning by pigeons. *J. Comp. Physiol. Psychol.*, 1972, 78, 1-9.

WAGNER, A. R., & TERRY, W. S. Backward conditioning to a CS following an expected vs. a surprising UCS. *Anim. Learn. Behav.*, 1975, 3, 370-374.

WAGNER, A. R., LOGAN, F. A., HABERLANDT, K., & PRICE, T. Stimulus selection in animal discrimination learning. *J. Exp. Psychol.*, 1968, 76, 171-180.

WARREN, J. M. Additivity of cues in visual pattern discriminations by monkeys. *J. Comp. Physiol. Psychol.*, 1953, 46, 484-486.

WEBB, W. B. A test of "relational" vs. "specific stimulus" learning in discrimination problems. *J. Comp. Physiol. Psychol.*, 1950, 43, 70-72.

WESSELLS, M. G. The effects of reinforcement upon the prepecking behaviors of pigeons in the autoshaping experiment. *J. Exp. Anal. Behav.*, 1974, 21, 125-144.

WILKIE, D. M., & PEAR, J. J. Intermittent reinforcement of an interresponse time. *J. Exp. Anal. Behav.*, 1972, 17, 67-74.

WILSON, M. P., & KELLER, F. S. On the selective reinforcement of spaced responses. *J. Comp. Physiol. Psychol.*, 1953, 46, 190-193.

YOSHII, N., MATSUMOTO, J., MAENO, S., HASEGAWA, Y., YAMAGUSHI, Y., SHIMOKOCHI, M., HORI, Y., & YAMAZAKI, H. Conditioned reflex and electroencephalography. *Med. J. Osaka Univer.*, 1958, 9, 353-375.

ZEAMAN, D., & HOUSE, B. J. The role of attention in retardate discrimination learning. In N. R. Ellis (Ed.), *Handbook of Mental Deficiency: Psychological Theory and Research*. New York: McGraw-Hill, 1963.

ZENER, K. The significance of behavior accompanying conditioned salivary secretion for theories of the conditioned response. *Am. J. Psychol.*, 1937, 50, 384-403.

CHAPTER 5

Conditioned Reinforcement

A conditioned reinforcer is a stimulus that establishes conditioning through being involved in prior conditioning. Conditioned reinforcers are usually neutral stimuli. A neutral stimulus is automatically (not because of learning) relatively unlikely to be either approached and continued to be perceived or escaped from and avoided. The counterpart of conditioned reinforcement is primary reinforcement. A primary reinforcer is a stimulus that establishes conditioning that is automatically (not because of learning) relatively likely to be either approached and continued to be perceived or escaped from and avoided. The term *secondary reinforcer* is similar in meaning to conditioned reinforcer.

Neutral stimuli establish conditioning. However, those examples of neutral stimuli that establish conditioning discussed so far did not employ the same procedures as those used in investigating conditioned reinforcers. The procedures for investigating conditioned reinforcers usually include an initial stage in which a neutral stimulus is involved in prior conditioning, and a second stage in which it is demonstrated that this neutral stimulus can establish new conditioning on its own.

CS Establishes Classical Conditioning

CS Establishes Classical Conditioning: Results. The CS establishes classical conditioning, and in addition, is a neutral stimulus that is obviously involved in prior conditioning. The CS is therefore a conditioned reinforcer.

Pavlov (1927, pp. 33-34) was probably the first investigator to show that a CS establishes classical conditioning. In stage 1 a sound of a metronome was followed by food independently of the responses of the food-deprived subjects, dogs. As expected, the metronome came to produce salivation. In stage 2 a black square was held in front of a subject and 25 seconds later the metronome was presented independently of responding. These square-metronome pairings did not involve in any way the delivery of food or the occurrence of another primary reinforcer. The result was that the square came to produce salivation. Food was the reinforcer for the classical conditioning of stage 1. Analogously, the metronome established the salivation response produced by the square in stage 2; that is, the metronome was responsible for the square coming to produce salivation in stage 2. Because the metronome was a neutral stimulus that established a learned response (in stage 2) through being involved in prior conditioning (in stage 1), it was a conditioned reinforcer.

Rizley and Rescorla (1972) showed that a CS establishes classical conditioning with the use of appropriate control groups. Classical conditioning of suppression was studied. Initially the subjects, rats, were trained to bar press. While the rats continued to receive food following their bar pressing, a two-stage procedure was carried out. In stage 1 the experimental group received pairings between a tone and shock independently of responding. In stage 2 the experimental group received pairings between a light and the tone of stage 1 independently of responding. One control group received the same number of tones and shocks as the experimental group did in stage 1, but these tones and shocks were explicitly unpaired (a pseudoconditioning control procedure). It received the same treatment as the experimental group in stage 2. A second control group received the same treatment as the experimental group in stage 1. In stage 2 it received the same number of lights and tones as the experimental group did in stage 2, but these lights and tones were explicitly unpaired. Figure 5-1 indicates that the strength of the suppression response produced by the light in stage 2 was greater for the experimental group than the two control groups and increased with continued training.

Pairings between the light and tone in stage 2 were necessary for the light to produce a relatively strong suppression response, because when the light and tone were unpaired in stage 2, the light produced very little suppression of responding. Therefore, the tone established the suppression response. In addition, pairings between the tone and shock in stage 1 were necessary for the light to come to suppress responding in stage 2; when the tone and shock were unpaired in stage 1, the light did not come to suppress responding in stage 2. Therefore, it was necessary for the tone to be a CS for it to establish the suppression response. Also, the CS established classical conditioning, because the light came to produce the suppression response through being paired with the tone CS independently of responding. Thus, the tone both established classical

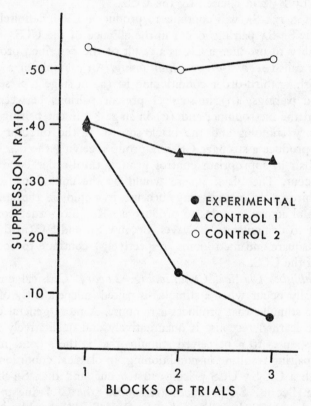

FIGURE 5-1. Acquisition of a classically conditioned suppression CR established with a CS. The suppression ratio equals A/(A+B); A is the rate of bar pressing in the presence of the CS, and B is the rate of bar pressing for a comparable period before CS onset. Each block consisted of two trials. (Adapted from Rizley and Rescorla, 1972.)

conditioning, and was necessarily involved in prior conditioning; hence it was a conditioned reinforcer.

The tone of the Rizley and Rescorla study and the metronome of the Pavlov study will be called S_A, and the light and black square of these two studies will be called S_B. In general, that a CS is a conditioned reinforcer that establishes classical conditioning is demonstrated by pairing S_A with a UCS in stage 1; pairing S_B with S_A in stage 2; and showing that S_B comes to produce a response, usually one similar to that produced by S_A and elicited by the UCS.

Neither S_B nor S_A will continue to produce a CR indefinitely. This is because the S_B-S_A pairings occur in the absence of the UCS.

S_B's ability to produce a CR as a result of the described procedures is sometimes called *second-order conditioning*. An example of a procedure for establishing third-order conditioning is: (a) in stage 1 present metronome-food pairings; (b) in stage 2 present pairings between a black square and the metronome; and (c) in stage 3 present pairings between an olfactory stimulus and the black square. If the olfactory stimulus comes to produce a stronger CR in a group receiving the described procedures than in appropriate control groups, third-order conditioning is said to occur. The black square would be the conditioned reinforcer for the third-order conditioning, because it would be the stimulus enabling the olfactory stimulus to produce a CR. Third-order conditioning is difficult to demonstrate, however, because S_B and S_A (in the example the black square and metronome, respectively) continue to occur in the absence of the UCS.

CS Establishes Classical Conditioning: Theory. Classical conditioning will normally occur when a stimulus is paired independently of responding with a stimulus that produces a response. A more general conclusion is that the learned response is quantitatively and qualitatively related to certain responses to a perceived stimulus that is the second member of the S_1-S_2 pairing resulting in conditioning. In classical conditioning established with a CS, S_A-UCS pairings first occur, and then S_B-S_A pairings take place. Because S_A produces a response (the CR) due to its being paired with a UCS, it follows that S_B-S_A pairings should result in S_B producing a similar response, the result to be accounted for.

The conclusion that the learned response is quantitatively and qualitatively related to certain responses to the perceived stimulus that is a second member of the S_1-S_2 pairing resulting in conditioning supports image theory. In respect to classical conditioning established with a CS, the S_B-S_A pairings should result in S_B producing an image of S_A. Because images of stimuli and the effects of real stimuli should be due to qualitatively identical temporary brain events, it follows that SB should produce an image of the UCS and thereby the CR, the result to be explained.

The finding that a CS establishes classical conditioning supports image theory's account of straightforward instrumental conditioning. The stimuli of the general learning situation should result in an image of the goal or negative-goal stimulus through pairings between the stimuli of the general learning situation and the stimulus produced by the instrumental response; through pairings between the stimulus produced by the instrumental response and the goal or negative-goal stimulus; and because an image of the stimulus produced by the instrumental response and the effects of the real stimulus produced by the instrumental response should be due to qualitatively identical temporary brain events. Recall that SA-UCS pairings in stage 1 and SB-SA pairings in stage 2 are used to obtain classical conditioning established with a CS. Both straightforward instrumental conditioning and classical conditioning established with a CS involve a three-member sequence of stimuli: the first is the stimulus of the general learning situation and SB; the second, the stimulus produced by the instrumental response and SA; and the third, the goal or negative-goal stimulus and the UCS. It was reasoned that if SB produces the CR, then it results in an image of the UCS. SB is the first member and the UCS is the third member of the sequence for classical conditioning. The stimuli of the general learning situation is the first member and the goal or negative-goal stimulus is the third member of the stimulus sequence for instrumental conditioning. It follows that SB's producing the CR supports image theory's assumption that prior to the performance of the instrumental response, the stimuli of the general learning situation result in an image of the goal or negative-goal stimulus.

The result that SB-SA pairings lead to classical conditioning is one more indication that acquired associations between paired neutral stimuli occur, which also supports image theory.

CS Establishes Classical Conditioning: UCS and S_1 Treatments. Rescorla and his associates have reported several findings that indicate that UCS-related and S_1-related treatments fail to affect the strength of the CR established with a CS. These results will be described, but the interpretation of their meaning will differ from Rescorla's.

In stage 1 of a study by Rescorla (1973), rats received food from bar pressing while presented with pairings between SA and a UCS, an intense noise. SA came to decrease the rate of bar pressing; that is, classical conditioning of suppression occurred. In stage 2 the rats continued to receive food for bar pressing, and on occasion SB-SA pairings were presented. S$_B$ did come to produce a decrease in the rate of bar pressing; that is, S$_A$ (a CS) established classical conditioning of suppression. In stage 3, one-half of the sample was given unpaired (individual) presentations of the noise UCS a total of 72 times in a different chamber with no bar present. The purpose of this manipulation was to decrease (habituate) the reinforcing strength of the noise, much as continued presentations of a neutral stimulus result in habituation, that is, a decrease in the strength of the orienting or activation response. In stage 4, all subjects were in the original apparatus, received food for bar pressing, and on occasion received unpaired (individual) presentations of S$_A$ and S$_B$. The stage 4 results indicated that the unpaired presentations of the noise in stage 3 decreased the strength of the suppression CR produced by S$_A$, but did not affect the strength of the suppression CR produced by S$_B$.

Recall that manipulations involving the UCS that occur both prior to and subsequent to CS-UCS pairings affect CR strength. The effect of the unpaired presentations of the noise in stage 3 on S$_A$-produced CR strength in stage 4 is therefore not new.

The failure of the unpaired presentations of the noise to noticeably affect the strength of the suppression CR produced by S$_B$ is new, however. Manipulations involving the UCS may affect CR strength, because the UCS of the CS-UCS pairings may in some sense become confused with similar UCSs or occurrences of the same UCS in different situations. Let us call the UCS following S$_A$ situation X; and the occurrence of a similar UCS or the same UCS in a different situation, situation Y. Manipulations involving the UCS may affect CR strength because situations X and Y are related, and thereby may in some sense become confused. In classical conditioning established with a CS in stage 2, S$_B$ is followed by S$_A$, and S$_A$ is followed by no particular event. Let us call the stimulus following S$_A$ in stage 2, that is, no particular event, stimulus X; and the occurrence of a UCS similar to the one used in stage 1, or the occurrence of the stage 1 UCS in a different situation, stimulus Y. Therefore, in classical conditioning established with a CS, situations X and Y are not similar, and they should not in some sense become confused. It follows that manipulations involving the UCS should not affect classical conditioning established with a CS, which was the actual result.

Rizley and Rescorla (1972) and Holland and Rescorla (1975) established S$_A$- and S$_B$-produced CRs, and then presented S$_A$ in extinction. Presenting S$_A$ (the CS) in extinction naturally reduced the strength of the S$_A$-produced CR. However, presenting S$_A$ in extinction failed to affect the strength of the S$_B$-produced CR. These two results make sense in terms of the equivalent of extinction approach (Chapter 3). A decrease in the strength of a learned response in extinction, that is, an equivalent of extinction, will usually not occur unless the S_1-reinforcer or S_1-S_2 pairings resulting in conditioning are in extinction, followed by pairings between S_1 and a stimulus relatively different from the reinforcer or S_2. Presenting SA-UCS pairings, and then presenting SA in extinction means that it is followed by a different kind of stimulus than it was in acquisition. SB-SA pairings can be viewed as consisting of two pairings between stimuli; SB is paired with SA, and, in addition, SA is paired with no particular event. Presenting SB-SA pairings and then presenting SA in extinction should not greatly decrease the strength of the SB-produced CR, because equivalents of extinction should not occur. They should not occur because when SB-SA pairings occur, SA is paired with no particular event; and when SA is presented in extinction it continues to be paired with no particular event.

CS Establishes Instrumental Conditioning

The CS establishes instrumental conditioning as well as classical conditioning.

CS Establishes Reward Learning. In a study by Jenkins (1950), in stage 1 food-deprived rats received response-independent pairings between a buzz sound of 3 seconds duration and food in a chamber. For different groups, the times between termination of the buzz and delivery of food were 1, 3, 9, 27, and 81 seconds. In stage 2, the primary reinforcer, food, was not employed. The rats remained deprived of food, and a bar was present in the chamber. In this stage, each bar press response caused the buzz sound that preceded food in stage 1 to occur. The number of bar presses made in 6 hours was determined. Figure 5-2 indicates that as the interval between buzz offset and receipt of food in stage 1 increased, the number of bar presses made in stage 2 decreased.

Jenkins' result suggests fairly strongly that a CS will establish instrumental conditioning. The instrumental response was bar pressing, and the goal for this response was the buzz sound, a CS formed in stage 1 through being paired with food. Pseudoconditioning in classical conditioning was controlled for, because all groups received the same number of presentations of the CS and UCS in stage 1. The buzz should have been a goal stimulus, because it was paired with a positive UCS, and because a CS paired with a positive UCS comes to be approached nad continued to be perceived. A CS previously paired with a positive UCS will be referred to as a *positive conditioned reinforcer,* because it establishes conditioning, and because it tends to be approached and continued to be perceived, much as a positive primary reinforcer is. The type of instrumental conditioning established with the CS was reward learning, because the instrumental response caused a stimulus to occur that was both a positive reinforcer and a goal.

There is control problem in this study, however. It is known that CS-food pairings may result in the CS producing an increase in locomotor activity. Animals exposed to briefer intervals between the buzz and food might have pressed the bar more frequently, because the buzz made them more active than animals exposed to longer intervals between the buzz and food. This is a CR effect of the buzz, rather than a goal effect. In order to rule out CR-related explanations of a CS's effect on what appears to be instrumental conditioning, a modified procedure is required.

One such procedure involves treating two groups identically in stage 1. In stage 2, one group receives the CS immediately after performing the instrumental response, and a second group receives the CS some time later (at least on the average) after performing the instrumental response. The treatment the second group receives controls for pseudoconditioning effects on the strength of an instrumental response. Crowder, Gill, Hodge,

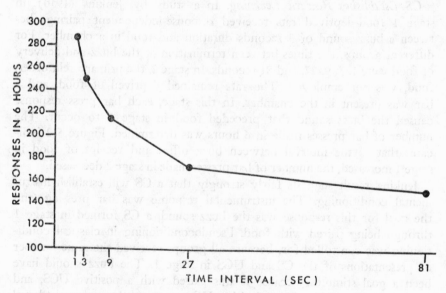

FIGURE 5-2. Reward learning established with a CS. (Adapted from Jenkins, 1950.)

and Nash (1959) did find that immediate delivery of a CS previously paired with a positive UCS following execution of the instrumental response in stage 2 resulted in a stronger instrumental response than delayed delivery of this CS after execution of the instrumental response.

A second procedure involves employing an instrumental response that should not be affected by CRs like the CR of an increase in activity. In one study (Saltzman, 1949), a CS previously paired with a positive UCS was received if the correct choice response was made in a T-maze. Because the CS was not perceived prior to making a choice point response, CR effects of the CS could not be expected to affect the choice-point response. Rats did acquire the choice-point response that caused the CS previously paired with a positive UCS to occur. Thus, both Salzman's and Crowder et al.'s studies indicate that a CS previously paired with a positive UCS establishes instrumental conditioning.

The ability of a CS previously paired with a positive UCS to maintain performance of a reward-trained response usually declines as the CS continues to be presented without the positive UCS also occurring. An analogous finding was mentioned for classical conditioning established with a CS.

CS Establishes Reward Learning: Theory. A response that causes a goal stimulus to occur tends to increase in rate. A more general conclusion is that the learned response is quantitatively and qualitatively related to certain responses to a perceived stimulus that is the second member of the S_1-S_2 pairing resulting in conditioning. A CS previously paired with a positive UCS is approached and continued to be perceived. It follows that a response that causes a CS previously paired with a positive UCS to occur should tend to increase in rate, which it does.

It appears that reward learning established with a CS previously paired with a positive UCS is the outcome of an animal's behaving so as to increase the vividness of the image of the positive UCS that the CS was previously paired with. While an animal is in the reward learning situation, the stimuli of this situation should result in an image of the stimulus produced by the instrumental response, which should result in an image of the CS that was previously paired with a positive UCS. The real CS should result in a relatively vivid image of the UCS. The image of the CS that the stimuli of the reward learning situation is assumed to produce should result in a less vivid image of the UCS. Therefore, an animal should behave so as to cause the real CS to occur, which, in fact, it does by executing the instrumental response at an increased rate.

The finding that a CS establishes reward learning suggests that the stimulus produced by the instrumental response that causes this CS to occur becomes associated with this CS. This finding is one more indication that the stimulus produced by the instrumental response can become associated with a neutral stimulus.

Maintained Strength of Conditioned Reinforcer. If a CS previously paired with a UCS continues to be presented in the absence of this UCS, its conditioned reinforcing strength decreases. However, if a CS continues to be paired with a UCS, its conditioned reinforcing strength does not decrease, as evidenced by continued performance of the response the CS establishes (Thomas, 1969; Zimmerman & Hanford, 1966).

In the Zimmerman and Hanford study, food was delivered to pigeons independently of responding. Each presentation of food was preceded by a simultaneously presented auditory and visual stimulus. A single key was available. Pecking it was followed by the auditory-visual compound stimulus that preceded the response-independent deliveries of food, but not by food itself. The pigeons came to peck this key, and, more importantly, pecking the key was maintained over six months of testing without a decrease in rate. Leaving all stimuli unchanged following pecking on the key, and replacing the compound stimulus paired with the response-independent delivery of food with novel stimuli following pecking the key both resulted in a marked decrease in the rate of pecking.

In this study the compound stimulus preceding response-independent delivery of food was a CS. Because pecking the key caused the compound CS to occur, and because this response was acquired, the compound CS established reward learning. Also, the compound CS continued to be paired with food throughout the experiment. This procedure was responsible for the pecking response being maintained throughout the experiment. That the compound CS maintained the pecking response is evident, because when the pecking response no longer caused the compound CS to occur, the rate of pecking decreased markedly.

The described result may be surprising. Why should a pigeon continue to peck the key when it should "know" that the CS that it thereby causes to occur is not followed by food? In actuality, a peck on the key delayed delivery of food when the food was scheduled to be presented within 6 seconds of this peck. Why should a pigeon peck to obtain a CS when this peck may even delay the occurrence of food? The peck response should be due to an animal's behaving so as to increase the vividness of the image of food. The obtained result therefore suggests that animals continue to behave so as to increase the vividness of an image of a goal stimulus for an indefinite length of time, even though doing so does not increase the probability of receiving actual food;

an increase in the vividness of the image of a goal stimulus may exert a powerful long lasting effect.

CS Establishes Punishment, Escape, and Avoidance Learning. A CS previously paired with a negative UCS establishes punishment, escape, and avoidance learning.

Hake and Azrin (1965) first reward-trained pigeons to peck a key. Subsequently, while this reward learning remained in effect, pairings between a compound visual and auditory stimulus and a brief shock were presented. In the next stage, reward learning remained in effect, shock was no longer presented at any time, and each key peck caused the compound stimulus that was paired with shock in the previous stage to occur. This procedure led to a noticeable decline in the rate of pecking. The compound CS previously paired with shock therefore established instrumental conditioning. A CS previously paired with shock is escaped from and avoided, and therefore the compound CS should have been a negative-goal stimulus. Punishment learning tends to occur when a response causes the onset of a stimulus to take place that is both a reinforcer and a negative-goal stimulus. Thus, the compound CS established punishment learning. A CS previously paired with a negative UCS is often called a *negative conditioned reinforcer.*

Walters and Glazer (1971) showed that a CS previously paired with shock establishes both escape and avoidance learning in gerbils. In stage 1, a 10-second tone was followed by a brief inescapable shock independently of responding. In stage 2, shock was no longer delivered at any time, a lever was introduced into the chamber that the gerbils received tone-shock pairings in, and a signalled avoidance learning procedure was carried out. In this procedure: (a) onset of three small lights preceded onset of the tone of stage 1 by 10 seconds; (b) if the lever was not pressed, the tone continued for 10 seconds, the duration of the tone in stage 1; (c) if a lever press was made while the tone was on, both the lights and tone were terminated; (d) if a lever press was made while the lights were on but tone onset had not yet occurred, two events took place—the tone that was scheduled to be presented 10 seconds after onset of the lights was omitted, and the lights were terminated; and (e) if a lever press was not made within 20 seconds after onset of the lights, the lights and tone were simultaneously terminated. The gerbils remained in the chamber between presentations of the lights. This complex procedure involves both escape and avoidance learning.

Figure 5-3 shows the median length of time elapsed (latency) from the onset of the lights to the first occurrence of a lever press over days of training in stage 2 for five gerbils. Lever presses between 10 and 20 seconds past the onset of the lights terminated the tone (and also the lights). It is evident from Figure 5-3 that the gerbils did come to press the lever during this time interval. The increased tendency to press the lever during this time interval indicates that a negative conditioned reinforcer, the tone, established escape learning. In escape learning, the instrumental response terminates a negative reinforcer. Analogously, in stage 2 the acquired response terminated the tone, a negative conditioned reinforcer established by virtue of its being a CS paired with shock in stage 1.

Figure 5-3 also shows that in stage 2 lever presses came to be frequently made in the presence of the lights while the tone had not yet come on. This result suggests that the tone, a negative conditioned reinforcer, established avoidance learning. In avoidance learning, the

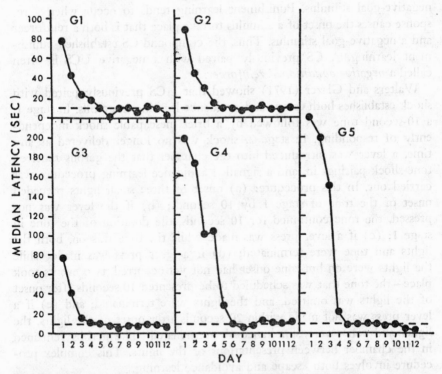

FIGURE 5-3. Acquisition of escape and avoidance learning established with a CS. Data points below the dotted line indicate a lever press latency that omitted a scheduled tone. There were five trials per day. (Adapted from Walters and Glazer, 1971.)

acquired response omits the scheduled occurrence of the negative reinforcer. A lever press in the presence of the lights omitted the scheduled occurrence of the tone, a negative conditioned reinforcer. Thus, a CS previously paired with shock probably established avoidance learning.

CS Establishes Punishment, Escape, and Avoidance Learning: Theory. Theoretical implications of the result that a CS previously paired with shock establishes punishment, escape, and avoidance learning are analogous to the theoretical implications of the result that a CS previously paired with a positive UCS establishes reward learning. The result that a CS previously paired with shock establishes punishment learning is considered.

This result is in accord with the conclusion that a response that causes a negative-goal stimulus to occur decreases in probability, because a CS paired with shock is escaped from and avoided. According to image theory, a CS previously paired with shock will result in a relatively vivid image of shock, and therefore an animal will behave so as to not cause this CS to occur, thereby decreasing the rate of the instrumental response, the result to be explained. The result that a CS paired with shock establishes punishment learning also supports the assumption that the stimulus produced by the instrumental response can become associated with a neutral stimulus.

Stimulus Paired with Absence of UCS Establishes Conditioning. A CS paired with the absence of a positive UCS comes to be escaped from and avoided, and a CS paired with the absence of a negative UCS probably comes to be approached and continued to be perceived. In addition, Adelman and Maatsch (1956) found that a stimulus previously paired with a positive UCS was escaped from when it occurred in extinction, and extinction involves pairings between a stimulus and the absence of a UCS. Results indicating that a CS paired with the absence of a UCS establishes instrumental conditioning, and a CS presented in extinction does likewise will be described.

In a study illustrating the latter result (Daly & McCroskery, 1973), a CS previously paired with food was presented in extinction and established instrumental conditioning. In stage 1 the experimental group of rats received 15 pellets of food independently of responding in a chamber. A control group did not receive food in stage 1. In stage 2 both groups were treated identically. They continued to be placed in the chamber, a bar was now available, but food was no longer delivered. A press of the bar caused the rat to be taken out of the chamber. If the bar was not pressed within 60 seconds from the time an animal was placed in the chamber, the animal was removed. The obtained results in stage 2 were that the experimental group pressed the bar with shorter latencies than the control group, and that the bar pressing latencies decreased over trials for the experimental group but increased over trials for the control group.

In stage 1, the stimuli of the chamber were a CS for the experimental group, because these stimuli were perceived prior to the response-independent delivery of food. In stage 2 this CS was presented in extinction for the experimental group. The bar press response was instrumentally conditioned for the experimental group, because the latency to bar press decreased over trials for this group. The CS presented in extinction was the reinforcer for this learning. A CS presented in extinction that was previously paired with a positive UCS should be escaped from and avoided. Therefore, the stimuli of the chamber should have been a negative conditioned reinforcer for the experimental group. Because removal from the chamber in stage 2 terminated the negative conditioned reinforcer for the experimental group, and because escape learning usually occurs when a response terminates a negative reinforcer, it follows that a CS presented in extinction established escape learning.

The S— of a typical go/no-go successive discrimination is a stimulus paired with the absence of a positive reinforcer. Recall that pigeons acquire a response that causes S— to terminate. S— is the reinforcer for this learning. In addition, because S— is paired with the absence of a positive reinforcer, it should be escaped from and avoided. It follows that the S— of a typical go/no-go successive discrimination establishes escape learning.

A study by Weisman and Litner (1969) showed that a CS paired with the absence of shock established both reward and omission learning. The unsignalled avoidance learning procedure was used to establish avoidance learning of a wheel turning response in rats. In addition, in a different chamber the same rats received pairings between a 5-second tone and the absence of shock. Each occurrence of the tone was separated from each occurrence of a shock by 1.5 minutes on the average, with a range of 50 to 130 seconds. The time between adjacent shocks was 3 minutes. Shock duration was 0.3 seconds. Subsequently, the rats were exposed again to the unsignalled avoidance learning procedure. Now, however, they could cause the tone that was previously paired with the absence of shock to occur by making 10 wheel turning responses in a 5-second period. The rate of wheel turning increased as a result. When the tone was no longer delivered following wheel turning responses, the rate of wheel turning decreased. The tone therefore established instrumental conditioning of wheel turning. A stimulus paired with the absence of a negative UCS probably tends to be approached and continued to be perceived. Therefore, the tone probably was a positive conditioned reinforcer, and most likely established reward learning of wheel turning.

In a later stage of this study, the rats continued to be exposed to the unsignalled avoidance learning procedure. In addition, the tone was presented after 0 or 1 wheel turning responses were made in a 5-second interval. This procedure reduced the rate of wheel turning below the rate occurring before the initiation of instrumental conditioning of wheel turning. Omission learning established by the tone therefore occurred.

Stimulus Paired with Absence of UCS Establishes Conditioning: Theory. Theoretical implications of the result that a CS paired with the absence of a UCS establishes instrumental conditioning are analogous to the theoretical implications of the results that a CS paired with a positive UCS establishes reward learning, and that a CS paired with a negative UCS establishes punishment, escape, and avoidance learning.

In addition, the finding that a CS paired with the absence of a UCS is capable of being a reinforcer agrees with the assumption that when no particular event and a reinforcer occur in sufficiently close physical and temporal proximity this affects the extent of approaching and continuing to perceive or escaping from and avoiding no particular event. For example, it is assumed that no particular event is approached and continued to be perceived when it is paired with the absence of shock; a CS paired with no particular event should therefore come to be approached and continued to be perceived; and thus a CS paired with the absence of shock should be a positive conditioned reinforcer, as, in fact, it is.

CS Establishes Instrumental Conditioning and Central Assumption. A central assumption of image theory is (a) that an animal brings about the stimulus produced by the instrumental response, and thereby executes this response for instrumental responses that increase in rate; and (b) that an animal avoids bringing about the stimulus produced by the instrumental response, and thereby withholds this response for instrumental responses that decrease in rate. The finding that CSs establish instrumental conditioning supports this assumption.

Perhaps the clearest supporting evidence available for the first half of the assumption is that a CS which is analogous to the stimulus produced by the instrumental response establishes reward and omission learning. A CS establishing reward and omission learning literally involves an animal responding so as to bring about this CS (causing it, including its onset, to occur). The possibility that an animal brings about a stimulus produced by its own response is obviously strengthened if an animal brings about a CS that is analogous to the stimulus produced by this response.

Perhaps the clearest supporting evidence available for the second half of the assumption is that a CS that is analogous to the stimulus produced by the instrumental response establishes avoidance and punishment learning. A CS establishing avoidance and punishment learning literally involves an animal responding so as to avoid bringing about this CS (causing it, including its onset, to not occur). The possibility that an animal avoids bringing about a stimulus produced by its own response is obviously strengthened if an animal avoids bringing about the CS that is analogous to the stimulus produced by this response.

Table 3-1 summarizes the eight types of instrumental conditioning and the analogous types of classical conditioning. The types of instrumental responses causing a goal stimulus to occur probably all increase in rate. Therefore, the types of CSs that correspond to the stimuli produced by these responses should all be capable of establishing reward and omission learning. The types of instrumental responses causing a negative-goal stimulus to occur all decrease in rate. Therefore, the types of CSs that correspond to the stimuli produced by these responses should all be capable of establishing avoidance and punishment learning.

Types of Instrumental Responses and Instrumental Conditioning Established with a CS. Table 3-1 indicates that a CS paired with the onset of a positive UCS corresponds to the stimulus produced by the instrumental response in reward learning, an instrumental response that increases in rate. According to the above discussion, this CS should establish reward and omission learning. It does establish reward learning. In addition, because a positive primary reinforcer establishes reward and omission learning, and because another type of CS establishes these two types of learning (see below), it is likely that a CS paired with the onset of a positive UCS will also establish omission learning.

Table 3-1 indicates that a CS paired with the continuation of a positive UCS corresponds to the stimulus produced by the instrumental response in response-continues-reward learning, an instrumental response that increases in rate. This CS should therefore establish reward and omission learning. A CS paired with the continuation of a positive UCS predicts that the positive UCS is relatively likely to occur in its presence or shortly thereafter, just as a CS paired with the onset of a positive UCS does. Thus, a CS paired with the continuation of a positive UCS probably does establish reward and omission learning.

Table 3-1 indicates that a CS paired with the absence of a negative UCS corresponds to the stimulus produced by the instrumental response in avoidance learning, an instrumental response that increases in rate. This CS should therefore establish reward and omission learning, and it does.

Table 3-1 indicates that a CS paired with termination of a negative UCS corresponds to the stimulus produced by the instrumental response in escape learning, an instrumental response that increases in rate. This CS should therefore establish reward and omission learning. There is reasonably good evidence that it establishes reward learning (Bellingham, Storlien, & Stebulis, 1975; Murray & Strandberg, 1965).

Table 3-1 indicates that a CS paired with the absence of a positive UCS corresponds to the stimulus produced by the instrumental response in omission learning, an instrumental response that decreases in rate. This CS should therefore establish avoidance and punishment learning. A CS paired with no particular event by virtue of being presented in extinction, and a stimulus paired with the absence of a positive reinforcer because it is a S— of a typical go/no-go successive discrimination establishes escape learning. A CS paired with the absence of a positive reinforcer should establish avoidance and punishment learning as well as escape learning, because negative primary reinforcers establish both escape learning and avoidance and punishment learning, and also because another type of CS establishes both escape learning and avoidance and punishment learning (see below).

Table 3-1 indicates that a CS paired with the termination of a positive UCS corresponds to the stimulus produced by the instrumental response in response-terminates-reward learning, an instrumental response that decreases in rate. This CS should therefore establish avoidance and punishment learning. A CS paired with the absence of a positive UCS probably establishes both avoidance and punishment learning. Both a CS paired with the absence of a positive UCS, and a CS paired with the termination of a positive UCS predict that the positive UCS is relatively unlikely to occur shortly after the onset of these CSs. Therefore, a CS paired with the termination of a positive UCS probably also establishes avoidance and punishment learning.

Table 3-1 indicates that a CS paired with the onset of a negative UCS corresponds to the stimulus produced by the instrumental response in punishment learning, an instrumental response that decreases in rate. Therefore, this CS should establish avoidance and punishment learning, and it does.

Table 3-1 indicates that a CS paired with the continuation of a negative UCS corresponds to the stimulus produced by the instrumental response in response-continues-punishment learning, an instrumental response that decreases in rate. This CS should therefore establish avoidance and punishment learning. A CS paired with the onset of a negative UCS establishes avoidance and punishment learning; in addition, both a CS paired with the onset of a negative UCS and a CS paired with the continuation of a negative UCS predict that the UCS is relatively likely to occur in the presence of the CS or shortly thereafter. It follows that a CS paired with the continuation of a negative UCS establishes avoidance and punishment learning.

All these findings support the central assumption of the image theory of conditioning, namely that an animal brings about or avoids bringing about the stimulus produced by an instrumental response depending on whether or not the instrumental response increases or decreases in rate.

Stimulus Present Prior to Instrumental Response Establishes Conditioning

A stimulus present prior to the execution of a reward-trained response is known to establish instrumental conditioning. Because this stimulus is a neutral one, establishes conditioning, and is involved in prior conditioning, it is a conditioned reinforcer. Such a stimulus probably also establishes classical conditioning as well, because it produces a CR, although this result has apparently not been reported. Neutral stimuli present prior to the execution of other types of instrumental conditioning most likely also establish conditioning.

Stimulus for Instrumental Response Establishes Conditioning. A study (Keehn, 1962) indicating that a stimulus present prior to the execution of a reward-trained response establishes instrumental conditioning will be described. Keehn used a two-compartment apparatus with a translucent partition that could be either raised or lowered to separate the two compartments. Water-deprived rats were placed in one of the two compartments, and entrance into the second compartment was blocked by the partition. After the rats were in the compartment they had been placed in for 30 seconds, a 2-second tone was presented. At the termination of the tone, the partition was either raised (for some rats) or lowered (for other rats). Water was available in the second compartment on a majority of trials. As a result, the rats in the raised-partition condition acquired the instrumental response of running under the partition and reaching the water delivery area as soon as the partition was raised; rats in the lowered-partition condition acquired the instrumental response of climbing over the partition and reaching the water-delivery area as soon as the partition was lowered. A trial was terminated by the rat's being removed from the compartment it had entered.

In stage 2 the tone and movement of the partition of stage 1 was shown to establish instrumental conditioning. A bar was introduced into the compartment where rats were placed at the start of a trial in stage 1, and the rats were again placed in this compartment at the start of a trial. Each press of the bar resulted in the 2-second tone of stage 1 and then the raising of the partition, for rats receiving this treatment in stage 1, or the lowering of the partition, for rats receiving this treatment in stage 1. Rats remained deprived of water, but neither water nor any other primary reinforcer was received in stage 2. Upon making a bar press, the rats did move into the other compartment. The result of interest was that the mean latencies to bar press decreased over the nine trials of stage 2.

Because the latency to bar press decreased over trials, the bar press response was instrumentally conditioned. The conditioned reinforcer for this response was the tone and movement of the partition. The tone and movement of the partition were stimuli present prior to the execution of the instrumental response in stage 1 of moving over or under the partition and reaching the water delivery area, and this response was established with water. The tone and movement of the partition were therefore stimuli present prior to the execution of an instrumental response (R_1) established with a primary reinforcer; moreover, the tone and movement of the partition established a second instrumental response (R_2). Recall that a stimulus present before the execution of a reward-trained response produces a CR. Because the tone and movement of the partition preceded R_1, these stimuli should have produced a CR including a tendency for these stimuli to be approached and continued to be perceived (Grastyan & Vereczkei, 1974). Therefore, the tone and movement of the partition were positive conditioned reinforcers, and established reward learning of the bar press response (R_2).

Stimulus for Instrumental Response: Role of This Response. The conditioned reinforcing strength of stimuli preceding the execution of the reward-trained response established with the primary reinforcer in the study just described was dependent on permitting the rats to perform this response. Not mentioned was that the lowered-partition and raised-partition groups of stage 1 were subdivided in stage 2. Some of the rats that ran under the raised partition in stage 1 received the tone and a lowered partition following each bar press in stage 2; that is, some of these rats were permitted only to climb over the lowered partition in stage 2. Also, some of the rats that climbed over the lowered partition in stage 1 received the tone and a raised partition following each bar press in stage 2; that is, some of these rats were permitted only to run under the raised partition in stage 2. Thus, there were two main groups in stage 2, rats permitted to make the same response as in stage 1 following tone onset, and rats not permitted to make the same response as in stage 1 following tone onset.

Figure 5-4 shows that when the response of crossing over into the second compartment in stage 2 was not permitted to occur in the same way as in stage 1, the latencies to press the bar increased rather than decreased over trials. Thus, the conditioned reinforcing strength of stimuli that preceded a reward-trained response established with a

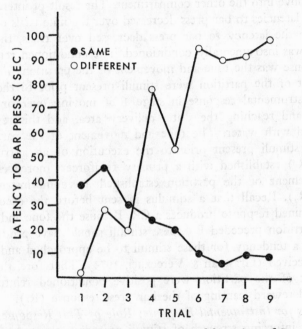

FIGURE 5-4. Acquisition of reward learning of R_2 established with a stimulus that was present before the execution of R_1, the reward-trained response established with a primary reinforcer. Reward learning of R_2 occurred when R_2 was followed by the same (R_1) response that occurred in the reward learning established with the primary reinforcer, but it did not occur when R_2 was followed by a different response. (Adapted from Keehn, 1962.)

primary reinforcer was nonexistent when this instrumental response was not permitted.

This finding argues against the possibility that a stimulus present prior to the execution of a reward-trained response established with a primary reinforcer is a conditioned reinforcer because it functions as a CS. This argument makes some sense, since a stimulus present before the execution of a reward-trained response established with a primary reinforcer produces a CR. The conclusion is questionable, however, because the conditioned reinforcing strength of a CS should not be affected by whether or not performance of an instrumental response established with a primary reinforcer occurs. Similarly, a stimulus present before the execution of a reward-trained response established with a primary reinforcer should produce a much weaker CR when the instrumental response is not permitted to be performed.

Stimulus for Instrumental Response: Theory. Why is it that a stimulus present prior to the execution of a reward-trained response (R_1) established with a primary reinforcer can establish another reward-trained response (R_2)? According to image theory, a stimulus present prior to the execution of R_1 results in an image of the positive primary reinforcer; an animal then behaves so as to increase the vividness of the image of the positive reinforcer, and therefore brings about the stimulus produced by R_1, and thereby R_1 itself. Because the positive conditioned reinforcer under discussion precedes R_1, it should result in an image of the positive primary reinforcer. A stimulus present before the execution of R_2 should result in an image of the stimulus that R_2 causes to occur, which is the positive conditioned reinforcer. But an image of the positive conditioned reinforcer should result in a less vivid image of the primary reinforcer than the real positive conditioned reinforcer does. An animal should therefore behave so as to cause the real positive conditioned reinforcer to occur. Bringing about the stimulus produced by R_2 does result in the real positive conditioned reinforcer, and thus R_2 occurs.

It was also found that if R_1 is not permitted, then the reinforcing strength of a stimulus present prior to the execution of R_1 markedly decreases. R_2 is made so as to increase the vividness of the image of the positive primary reinforcer. However, if R_1 is not permitted, the stimulus present prior to R_1 will not be followed by the stimulus produced by R_1. Therefore, while an animal is in the learning situation in which R_2 may be acquired (the stage 2 learning situation), an image of the stimulus present prior to R_1 should occur; but an image of the stimulus produced by R_1 should not occur, and thus an image of the positive primary reinforcer should not occur. Consequently, the occurrence of the stimulus produced by R_2 should not increase the vividness of the image of the positive primary reinforcer, which means that R_2 itself should not take place, the result to be explained.

Maintained Strength of Conditioned Reinforcer. The reinforcing strength of a stimulus present before the execution of a reward-trained response established with a primary reinforcer will typically decrease as extinction of the reward learning established with the primary reinforcer is carried out. A CS previously paired with a UCS will also lose its reinforcing strength as extinction of the classical conditioning established with the UCS is carried out. However, a CS can maintain a learned response almost indefinitely when it continues to be paired with a UCS. An analogous result is obtained with a stimulus present prior to the execution of a reward-trained response established with a primary reinforcer (Dinsmoor, Browne, & Lawrence, 1972).

The procedures for the Dinsmoor et al. study are outlined in Figure 5-5. Two keys are used. Pecking by food-deprived pigeons on the right-hand key, called the food key, was sometimes followed by food delivered on a VI schedule. At other times, pecking the food key resulted in no particular event occurring. Therefore, VI food reinforcement and extinction schedules for responding on the food key alternated as in a go/ no-go successive discrimination. When extinction was in effect for pecking the food key, the two keys were illuminated with white light no matter how a pigeon responded. But when the VI food reinforcement schedule was in effect for responding on the food key, pecking the second, left-hand key caused both keys to be illuminated with green light. Usually the green illumination of the keys was delivered on a second (nonfood) VI schedule; that is, the keys were illuminated with

EXTINCTION FOR RIGHT KEY

(W) (W)   AND PECKING LEFT KEY ⟶   (W) (W)

VI FOR RIGHT KEY

(W) (W)   AND PECKING LEFT KEY ⟶   (G) (G)

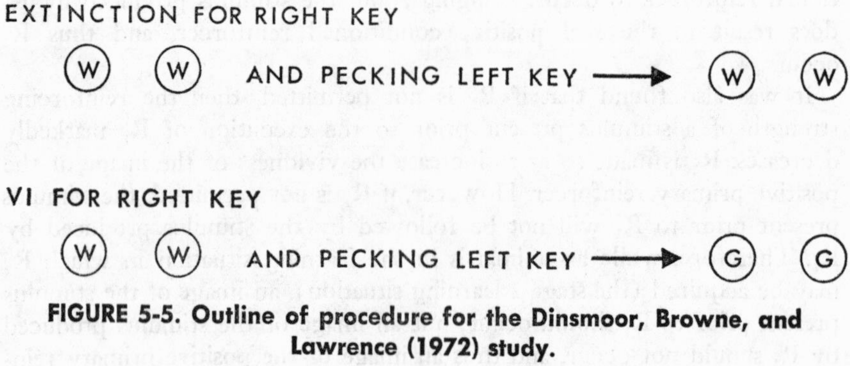

FIGURE 5-5. Outline of procedure for the Dinsmoor, Browne, and Lawrence (1972) study.

green light following the first response made on the second, left-hand key occurring after a variable interval of time since the keys were last illuminated with green light. Each time the green lights occurred they remained on for 30 seconds, unless the schedule in effect for the food key switched from VI to extinction, at which moment the green lights were replaced with white lights. The reason that an interval schedule was in effect for the food key was that responding at a fast rate on an interval schedule does not greatly affect the rate at which a positive reinforcer is received, because the positive reinforcer is delivered only when the first response made after a certain interval of time since the last reinforcer was delivered has elapsed. Therefore, responses on the second, left-hand key could be made without noticeably decreasing the rate of food received by responding on the food key. The result of interest is that the pigeons came to peck the second, left-hand key when the two keys were illuminated with white light. About 10 responses per minute were made on the second, left-hand key when the two keys were illuminated with white light. In addition, this responding continued for as long as the described procedures remained in effect. Very little pecking of the second, left-hand key occurred when both keys were illuminated with green light.

The green lights were stimuli that were present prior to the execution of a reward-trained response established with food, because responding on the food key in the presence of the green lights was always followed by food (delivered on a VI schedule). Responding on the second, left-hand key in the presence of the white lights caused the green lights to occur. It therefore is appropriate to view responding on the second, left-hand key as a reward-trained response established by the green lights, a positive conditioned reinforcer. Probably the reason the green lights maintained pecking of the second, left-hand key for the duration of the experiment is that the green lights continued to be a positive conditioned reinforcer, because the instrumental response of pecking the right-hand key in the presence of the green lights kept on causing food to occur.

The evidence that a CS can maintain instrumental conditioning almost indefinitely is potentially of great importance to the analysis of human interpersonal behavior. Our social behavior may, in part, be learned behavior that is maintained by conditioned reinforcers almost indefinitely, if they are paired with primary reinforcers often enough.

One final comment on this study: the green lights were a conditioned reinforcer, and they closely resemble the S+ of a typical go/no-go successive discrimination. Positive and negative discriminative stimuli control learned responding much as do a CS and the stimuli of the general learning situation in straightforward classical and instrumental conditioning. Therefore, it is to be expected that discriminative stimuli are also conditioned reinforcers.

Conditioned Reinforcers Function Like Primary Reinforcers

Similarity of Conditioned and Primary Reinforcers: Evidence. Previous results indicate that both primary and conditioned reinforcers establish both classical and instrumental conditioning. In addition, both types of reinforcers establish the reward, punishment, escape, avoidance, and omission learning types of instrumental conditioning.

Another similarity between conditioned and primary reinforcers is that the strengths of learned responses they establish increase with continued training. Figures 5-1 through 5-4 support this statement for learning established with conditioned reinforcers. Studies described earlier used controls in which the conditioned reinforcer was replaced with no particular event or with a novel stimulus. This procedure constitutes extinction of learning established with a conditioned reinforcer, and does result in a marked decrease in the strength of the responses established with conditioned reinforcers. The strength of responses established with primary reinforcers also decreases in extinction.

Increased deprivation of a primary reinforcer increases the strength of a learned response established with that primary reinforcer. Increased deprivation of a primary reinforcer should therefore also increase the strength of a learned response established with a conditioned reinforcer formed through learning established with that primary reinforcer. This expectation has been supported (Brown, 1956). Brown presented a compound stimulus of a light and buzzer to food-deprived rats, and followed it with food independently of responding in stage 1. A bar was introduced into the learning chamber in stage 2. Each bar press caused the compound stimulus of stage 1 to occur, but food was at no time delivered. One-half the rats were tested under high food deprivation, and one-half were tested under low food deprivation. The time to make 20 bar presses was measured. The group tested under high food deprivation took less time to make 20 bar presses than the group tested under low food deprivation.

Deprivation of the primary reinforcer used to establish a learned response results in better performance of this response than deprivation of another primary reinforcer. Therefore, deprivation of the primary reinforcer used to establish a conditioned reinforcer should lead to better performance of a learned response established with this conditioned reinforcer than deprivation of another primary reinforcer, the result obtained by Estes (1949).

Similarity of Conditioned and Primary Reinforcers: Theory. The general finding that conditioned reinforcers function like primary reinforcers follows from the conclusion that primary reinforcers establish classical and instrumental conditioning through factors related to the responses they elicit, and the result that conditioned reinforcers produce much the same responses. For example, in respect to reward learning established with food and with a CS paired with food, it was maintained that food establishes reward learning because of factors related to the food being more likely to be approached and continued to be perceived than stimuli present prior to the execution of the instrumental response; similarly, it was maintained that a CS paired with food establishes reward learning because of factors related to its being more likely to be approached and continued to be perceived than stimuli present prior to the execution of the instrumental response. Because conditioned reinforcers establish conditioning through much the same factors as primary reinforcers, it follows that conditioned reinforcers should function like primary reinforcers, which they do.

At a more theoretical level, the general finding that conditioned reinforcers function like primary reinforcers follows from the following assumptions of image theory: (a) conditioning established with primary reinforcers is mediated by an image of the UCS or goal or negative-goal stimulus occurring; (b) conditioning established with conditioned reinforcers is analogously mediated; and (c) conditioned reinforcers result in an image of the UCS or goal or negative-goal stimulus that occurred in the conditioning established with primary reinforcers in which the conditioned reinforcers were formed. In respect to reward learning established with food, and reward learning established with a CS previously paired with food, for example, because in both cases an animal is assumed to behave so as to increase the vividness of the image of food, it follows that learning established with a CS paired with food should function like learning established with food itself.

Factors that Affect the Reinforcing Strength of Conditioned Reinforcers

The factors affecting the reinforcing strength of conditioned reinforcers are usually the ones affecting the strength of responses established with primary reinforcers.

Effect on Conditioned Reinforcer Strength: Evidence. Conditioning established with a primary reinforcer improves as training continues. Similarly, as training with a primary reinforcer continues, the reinforcing strength of the resulting conditioned reinforcer increases. In a study by Hall (1951), in stage 1 different groups of water-deprived rats were reward-trained to traverse a runway using water as a reinforcer. Independent groups of rats received water a total of 25, 50, or 75 times in a box at the end of the runway. The color of the box at the end of the runway was black for some animals of each group, and white for other animals. In stage 2 the apparatus employed was a T-maze. The end box in which water was received in stage 1 (black or white) was placed at the end of the arm of the T-maze in the same position (left or right) on each trial for an individual subject. At the end of the arm in the other position (left or right), a box of the opposite color (black or white) was present on each trial. No primary reinforcers were received in stage 2. All groups learned to turn in the direction of the end box in which water was received in stage 1. This end box should have become a conditioned reinforcer, because it was perceived prior to obtaining water in stage 1. Because the rats learned to turn in the direction of this end box, this end box established a left-right position discrimination; it was a conditioned reinforcer. The result of interest is that the group that received water 75 times in stage 1 was most likely to turn in the direction of the end box in which water was previously received, and the group that received water 25 times in stage 1 was least likely to turn in the direction of this end box. Therefore, an increase in training with the primary reinforcer resulted in a stronger conditioned reinforcer, similar to an increase in training with the primary reinforcer resulting in a stronger learned response.

The strength of a response established with a primary reinforcer frequently decreases relatively rapidly in extinction. Similarly, the reinforcing strength of a conditioned reinforcer frequently decreases relatively rapidly as it is presented in the absence of the primary reinforcer that established it as a conditioned reinforcer.

CR strength decreases as the length of the time interval between CS onset and UCS onset increases. Similarly, the reinforcing strength of a CS decreases as the length of the time interval between its onset and onset of the UCS that established it as a conditioned reinforcer increases (Jenkins, 1950).

Learned response strength increases as the amount of the positive primary reinforcer that establishes the learned response increases. Similarly, the reinforcing strength of a conditioned reinforcer increases with an increase in the amount of the positive reinforcer that established the conditioned reinforcer (Butter & Thomas, 1958; D'Amato, 1955).

Extent of deprivation of a positive primary reinforcer frequently exerts only a temporary effect on the strength of a response established with the positive primary reinforcer. Similarly, the deprivation level existing when a conditioned reinforcer was established with a primary reinforcer did not affect the conditioned reinforcer's subsequent reinforcing strength (Brown, 1956).

Effect on Conditioned Reinforcer Strength: Theory. The general finding that the factors affecting the reinforcing strength of conditioned reinforcers are usually the ones affecting the strength of responses established with primary reinforcers can be explained. The learned response is quantitatively and qualitatively related to certain responses to a perceived stimulus that is the second member of the S_1-S_2 pairing resulting in conditioning. This means that the strength of the response established with a conditioned reinforcer should be quantitatively related to the strength of the response produced by the perceived conditioned reinforcer, But the factors affecting the strength of a response produced by a perceived conditioned reinforcer are precisely those factors affecting the strength of a learned response established with a primary reinforcer. The strength of the response established with a conditioned reinforcer, and hence the reinforcing strength of a conditioned reinforcer, should therefore be affected by the same factors that affect the strength of a response established with a primary reinforcer, which it is.

Conditioned Reinforcers Contribute to Reward Learning Established with Primary Reinforcers

Contribution of Conditioned Reinforcers. Conditioned reinforcers contribute importantly to learning established with primary reinforcers. Consider reward learning of the bar press response established with a primary reinforcer. Typically, a bar press is followed by the sound of the food or water delivery apparatus, and slightly later by the positive primary reinforcer. The sound of the food or water delivery apparatus should therefore be a CS, because its occurrence is followed by food or water independently of responding. It is known, in fact, that the sound of the apparatus that delivers a positive primary reinforcer can establish reward learning in the absence of this primary reinforcer, and therefore it is a positive conditioned reinforcer (Kelleher, 1961). Because the bar press causes the sound of the food or water delivery apparatus to occur, and because this sound should be a positive conditioned reinforcer, this sound should contribute to the reward learning of bar pressing.

Similarly, conditioned reinforcers must contribute to reward-trained runway learning. The stimuli at the end of the runway, for instance, the stimuli provided by the walls, floor, and top of the end of the runway, are most likely conditioned reinforcers, because they are perceived just before an animal obtains the positive primary reinforcer at the end of the runway. Because traversing the runway causes these stimuli to occur, and because these stimuli are conditioned reinforcers, these stimuli should contribute to reward learning of traversing the runway.

Contribution of Conditioned Reinforcers: Delay of Reinforcement. Delay of positive primary reinforcement, that is, a delay in time between the occurrence of a response and the occurrence of a positive primary reinforcer, can seriously retard acquisition of reward leaning. It is also known that providing a conditioned reinforcer during the delay of primary reinforcement interval facilitates acquisition of a reward-trained response (Perkins, 1947; Tombaugh & Tombaugh, 1971). This result is, of course, in accord with the conclusion that a conditioned reinforcer frequently contributes to reward learning established with very little delay of positive primary reinforcement.

In the Tombaugh and Tombaugh study, food-deprived rats received food 7.5 seconds after each bar press response. For one group, each bar press was immediately followed by onset of a light. This light remained on until food was delivered. A second group was treated identically, except that the light was omitted. Discrete trials were arranged by inserting the bar to mark the beginning of a trial, and retracting the bar after either a bar press was made or 60 seconds elapsed, whichever came first. The obtained result was that the group that received the light during the 7.5 second delay of positive primary reinforcement interval took less time to press the bar than the second group. The bar press response caused the light to occur; the light should have been a positive conditioned reinforcer, due to its being followed by food independently of responding. The obtained result therefore suggests that the light was a conditioned reinforcer that facilitated acquisition of the bar press response.

Note that although delay of positive primary reinforcement occurred, there was no delay of positive conditioned reinforcement. Evidence does exist that reward learning can be acquired with even very long delays of positive primary reinforcement when a positive conditioned reinforcer quickly follows the instrumental response.

In one study (Wolfe, 1936), chimpanzees were trained to exchange poker chips for food by inserting the poker chips into a vending machine. The poker chips were then used to instrumentally condition a number of responses. Correct responding on these tasks was quickly followed by delivery of the poker chips. The opportunity to exchange the poker chips for food only occurred more than an hour later. Because the poker chips were perceived just prior to obtaining food, they probably were positive conditioned reinforcers. Therefore, it appears that reward learning was established with a delay of positive primary reinforcement of more than an hour due to responding being quickly followed by the positive conditioned reinforcers of poker chips.

Another study (Ferster & Hammar, 1965) suggests that a positive conditioned reinforcer can maintain responding by monkeys on a FR 50 reinforcement schedule in which food was delayed 24 hours after the response requirement of the FR schedule was fulfilled. In one portion of this study, when a red light was on, making a total of 50 lever presses had two consequences. It caused food to be delivered 24 hours later; in addition, it immediately changed the red light to white, the white light then remaining on for 24 hours. At the end of the 24 hours and the delivery of food, the white light changed to red. The monkeys were then free to make an additional 50 responses in the presence of the red light, and so on, the monkeys living continuously in the learning situation. The described procedure resulted in 50 responses continuing to be made in the presence of the red light in a pattern similar to the pattern of responding typical for FR schedules.

How is it that 50 responses could be made when the food that these responses caused to occur was delayed for 24 hours? The white light was followed by food independently of responding, and therefore it should have been a CS and a positive conditioned reinforcer. Thus, completing the 50 responses that were required in the presence of the red light was immediately followed by a positive conditioned reinforcer that remained on throughout the delay of positive primary reinforcement interval. Given that the delay of primary reinforcement interval was so long, it is likely that the white light contributed greatly to completing the 50 responses, most likely because it was a positive conditioned reinforcer.

Extinction of Reinforcing Strength of Long Duration CS. Another question. Why doesn't a long duration CS such as the white light in the above study lose its conditioned reinforcing strength when the delay of positive primary reinforcement is quite long?

In general, a CS should retain its conditioned reinforcing strength even though its duration is quite long, if it continues to be followed by a UCS at about the time of its offset. A decrease in the strength of a learned response in extinction, that is, an equivalent of extinction, will usually not occur unless the S_1-reinforcer or S_1-S_2 (where S_2 is a neutral stimulus) pairings responsible for acquisition of the learned response are replaced in extinction by pairings between S_1 and a kind of stimulus that is different from the reinforcer or S_2 occurring in acquisition. A long duration CS corresponds to S_1, and the UCS for this CS corresponds to the reinforcer. An equivalent of extinction should therefore not occur unless pairings between a long duration CS and a UCS are replaced by pairings between a long duration CS and no particular event. Therefore, even though the duration of a CS is relatively long, it should maintain its conditioned reinforcing strength as long as it continues to be followed at its end by the UCS.

Conditioned Reinforcers Contribute to Avoidance Learning Established with Primary Reinforcers

Conditioned reinforcers also contribute to signalled avoidance learning. In signalled avoidance learning, a neutral stimulus, called the warning stimulus, precedes each shock that is scheduled to occur by a constant time interval. Performance of the instrumental response, often called the avoidance response, while the warning stimulus is on omits the next shock that is scheduled to occur. In addition, performing this response terminates the warning stimulus, which otherwise ordinarily remains on until at least the moment of shock onset. This procedure results in an increase in the rate of the instrumental response. It is due, in part, to the instrumental response omitting scheduled shock.

Contribution of Negative Conditioned Reinforcement. At least early in acquisition of signalled avoidance learning, the warning stimulus is followed by shock. Therefore, the warning stimulus should function as a CS, and should be a negative conditioned reinforcer. Moreover, the instrumental response terminates the warning stimulus. Termination of a negative conditioned reinforcer by a response establishes escape learning of this response. Termination of the warning stimulus by the instrumental response should therefore contribute to the strength of the instrumental response. That is, the instrumental response should be, in part, an escape-trained response established with the negative conditioned reinforcer of the warning stimulus. Of course, the primary reinforcer, shock, also contributes to the strength of the instrumental response, because the instrumental response's omitting shock increases the strength of this response. Reward learning is also contributed to by both primary and conditioned reinforcement.

It has, in fact, been found that termination of the warning stimulus by the instrumental response facilitates signalled avoidance learning (Bolles & Grossen, 1969; Bolles, Stokes, & Younger, 1966). The typical signalled avoidance learning procedure used in the second study resulted in a median of 70 instrumental responses (omissions of shock) in 100 trials. A procedure in which the instrumental response did not terminate the warning stimulus but which was otherwise identical to the typical signalled avoidance learning procedure resulted in a median of 40 instrumental responses in 100 trials.

Suppose that a brief neutral stimulus is presented immediately following each execution of an instrumental response in avoidance learning. Because the instrumental response omits scheduled shock, such a stimulus would occur in the absence of shock, that is, it would be a CS paired with the absence of shock. A CS paired with the absence of shock should be a positive conditioned reinforcer. Because a brief neutral stimulus presented immediately following execution of an instrumental response should be a positive conditioned reinforcer, and because such a stimulus is caused to occur by the instrumental response, it should contribute to the strength of the instrumental response through reward learning. It has, in fact, been found that presentation of a brief neutral stimulus immediately following the execution of the instrumental response in signalled avoidance learning does facilitate acquisition of this response (D'Amato, Fazzaro, & Etkin, 1968; Morris, 1975).

Resistance to Extinction and Warning Stimulus. Avoidance learning may be strongly resistant to extinction, with the instrumental response sometimes continuing to occur in the absence of shock hundreds of times. The instrumental response's omitting shock contributes to the relatively strong resistance to extinction of avoidance learning (Chapter 3). The warning stimulus and negative conditioned reinforcement are also involved with the relatively strong resistance to extinction of signalled avoidance learning.

Early in extinction of signalled avoidance learning, the instrumental response is made prior to the termination of the warning stimulus. Therefore, early in extinction the full duration of the warning stimulus is not followed by the absence of shock. A CS should retain its conditioned reinforcing strength unless the UCS fails to occur at the time it did in acquisition, even if the duration of the CS is very long. Thus, the conditioned reinforcing strength of the warning stimulus should be maintained early in extinction. It follows that the warning stimulus should continue to maintain performance of the instrumental response early in extinction through establishing escape learning. This means that later on in extinction the instrumental response should continue to occur and at the time it previously occurred (that is, prior to the termination of the warning stimulus). If the instrumental response continues to occur and at the time it previously occurred later on in extinction, the conditioned reinforcing strength of the warning stimulus should be maintained later on in extinction, which means that the instrumental response should continue to occur and at the time it previously occurred much later on in extinction, and so on. Thus, escape learning established with the negative conditioned reinforcer of the warning stimulus should contribute to the relatively strong resistance to extinction of signalled avoidance learning.

Now, consider extinction of escape learning established with a negative conditioned reinforcer without avoidance learning simultaneously occurring. Because the escape-trained response terminates the negative conditioned reinforcer, the reinforcing strength of the negative conditioned reinforcer should be maintained in extinction. Escape learning established with a negative conditioned reinforcer should therefore be relatively resistant to extinction. This result has, in fact, been obtained (Miller, 1948; Walters & Glazer, 1971). For example, the latter study found that a CS paired with shock in a prior stage maintained an escape-trained bar press response for 120 trials with no sign that the strength of this response decreased.

Response Prevention. Presenting the warning stimulus while preventing the instrumental response from occurring in the absence of shock decreases the resistance to extinction of avoidance learning (Baum & Myron, 1971; Coulter, Riccio, & Page, 1969).

In the Coulter et al. study, one-way signalled avoidance learning was first established. One-way signalled avoidance learning entails the use of a two compartment apparatus. At the start of each trial, an animal is placed into the same compartment. Entrance into the second compartment is blocked. A warning stimulus is then presented and at the same time the door separating the two compartments is opened. The instrumental response is movement into the second compartment before shock is delivered in the first compartment. The animal is removed from the apparatus between trials. One-way avoidance learning is said to occur because movement from one to the other compartment occurs in only one direction. As in the typical signalled avoidance learning procedure, in one-way signalled avoidance learning the instrumental response omits scheduled shock and terminates the warning stimulus. In addition, in one-way signalled avoidance learning the instrumental response also terminates the stimuli of the shock compartment, which additionally contribute to the strength of this avoidance learning (Masterson, 1970; McAllister, McAllister, Brooks, & Goldman, 1972).

Coulter et al. scheduled shock to occur 2 seconds after onset of the warning stimulus. Also, the warning stimulus was 2 seconds long; that is, it terminated at the time shock was scheduled to occur. After the subjects, rats, satisfied a criterion of performance of one-way signalled avoidance learning, two groups were formed. One group received a typical extinction of signalled avoidance learning procedure; that is, the procedure for signalled avoidance learning was carried out except that shock was no longer delivered at any time. The second group received five response-prevention trials before receiving the typical extinction of signalled avoidance learning procedure. A response-prevention trial consisted of placing a rat in the compartment in which shock could occur with the door to the second, shock-free compartment closed; presenting the warning stimulus; leaving the rat in the shock compartment for 15 seconds; and then removing the rat from the apparatus. The obtained result was that the strength of the instrumental response during typical extinction of one-way signalled avoidance learning was much less for the group receiving the five response-prevention trials beforehand than for the group not receiving response prevention trials beforehand.

The response-prevention procedure appears to reduce resistance to extinction of avoidance learning for at least two reasons. One is involved with omission of scheduled shock facilitating acquisition of avoidance learning, and the second is involved with termination of the warning stimulus facilitating acquisition of avoidance learning. In respect to the first reason, the response-prevention procedure forces a response other than the instrumental response to occur. Because absence of shock facilitates acquisition of the instrumental response in avoidance learning, and because absence of shock occurs in the response-prevention procedure, absence of shock may strengthen a noninstrumental response that takes place during response prevention. (Note that a noninstrumental response does not cause the absence of shock to occur. This absence of shock is adventitious, and thus a noninstrumental response that occurs during response prevention may be acquired through adventitious reinforcement, which is a concept that will be discussed in Chapter 7.) The acquired noninstrumental response may then effectively compete against performance of the instrumental response during typical extinction of avoidance learning, thereby reducing the resistance to extinction of this learning.

In respect to the second reason, the response-prevention procedure makes certain that the full duration of the warning stimulus is followed by the absence of shock. Equivalents of extinction of the conditioned reinforcing strength of the warning stimulus should therefore occur. As a consequence, the strength of the instrumental response in subsequent typical extinction of signalled avoidance learning should be reduced.

If the response-prevention procedure reduces the conditioned reinforcing strength of the warning stimulus, it should also reduce the extent to which the warning stimulus is avoided. Avoidance of the warning stimulus, as measured by the tendency to not enter the shock compartment when the warning stimulus is on, was found to decrease as a result of the response-prevention procedure (Bersh & Miller, 1975; Shipley, Mock, & Levis, 1971).

Conditioned Reinforcement, Development of Social Behavior, and Contact Comfort

Attention behaviors—smiling, talking in a pleasant tone of voice, turning toward or facing, and close physical proximity—may contribute to the classical and instrumental conditioning of social behavior because they are conditioned reinforcers.

Attention Behaviors and Classical Conditioning. A familiar person's attention behaviors are likely to be CSs for initiating contact comfort with a child (Chapter 2). Because attention behaviors are probably CSs paired with the positive UCS of contact comfort, they should be positive conditioned reinforcers. In addition, at least some attention behaviors of a familiar person are probably S+s for the child's performing the instrumental response of obtaining contact comfort (Chapter 4). Such an S+ should also be a positive conditioned reinforcer. Therefore, attention behaviors should be positive conditioned reinforcers partly through classical conditioning with contact comfort, and partly through instrumental conditioning with contact comfort.

Probably a familiar person's affectionate words, for example, "You're a good boy," tend to be followed relatively independently of the child's responding by the person's delivering attention behaviors to the child, for example, smiling at him. A person's attention behaviors should come to reduce fear and be approached and continued to be perceived through classical conditioning between the attention behaviors and contact comfort, which is a primary reinforcer. Affectionate words should then come to reduce fear and be approached and continued to be perceived through classical conditioning between these words and attention behaviors, which should be conditioned reinforcers. This prediction is supported by observations that children do tend to approach and continue to perceive familiar people when they say affectionate things. A person's saying affectionate words may also reduce a child's fear. Thus, attention behaviors may be conditioned reinforcers that result in affectionate words reducing fear and being approached and continued to be perceived through classical conditioning.

In the laboratory a CS can be shown to establish conditioning in the absence of primary reinforcement. With human interactions, however, the possibility of primary and conditioned reinforcers both contributing to acquisition of the same response is always present. For example, affectionate words spoken by a familiar person are probably fairly likely to be followed relatively independently of the child's responding by the familiar person initiating contact comfort with the child. Therefore, words with an affectionate meaning apparently reduce the child's fear and are approached and continued to be perceived by the child at least partly because of classical conditioning established with attention behaviors (conditioned reinforcers), and at least partly because of classical conditioning established with contact comfort (a primary reinforcer).

Attention Behaviors and Instrumental Conditioning. People are probably relatively likely to follow a child's appropriate behavior with at least some attention behaviors. Because attention behaviors should be positive conditioned reinforcers, they should contribute to the reward learning of appropriate behaviors by the child (Gewirtz, 1961; Skinner, 1953).

Ou's (1977) study shows that familiar people are relatively likely to deliver the attention behavior of smiling when the child behaves appropriately. The interactions of children with their mothers were videotaped while children worked on tasks—for example, completing a puzzle—and answered questions. It was found that the mother was more likely to smile in a 3-second interval if the child had completed a task in the previous 3-second interval than at other times; that the mother was more likely to smile in a 3-second interval if the child had answered a question correctly in the previous 3-second interval than at other times; but that the mother was not more likely to smile in a 3-second interval if the child had answered a question incorrectly in the previous 3-second interval than at other times. Task completion and answering correctly are relatively appropriate behaviors; responding at other times and answering incorrectly are relatively neutral behaviors. A mother's smiling was therefore relatively likely to follow a child's exhibiting appropriate behaviors.

In addition, college students expected parents are relatively likely to follow a child's behaving appropriately with the attention behaviors of smiling and pleasant tone of voice (King & Beatty, 1975). Each college student completed a single paragraph in which a 4-, 7-, or 10-year-old child was described as either behaving or not behaving as requested. One of the three types of requested behaviors appeared in a paragraph— clean up room, play on own, or work on a puzzle the child previously had trouble doing. The paragraph completions were to indicate what a parent would do after a child's exhibiting or not exhibiting the requested behavior. The completions were rated for occurrence of attention behaviors exhibited by a parent. It was found for the three behaviors requested that parents were expected to be more likely to smile and talk in a pleasant tone of voice after the child performed the requested task, that is, behaved appropriately, than after the child did not perform the requested task, that is, did not behave appropriately.

Most or even all types of appropriate behavior of the child are probably relatively likely to be followed by other people's smiling and pleasant tone of voice and perhaps by other attention behaviors. Types of appropriate behavior of the child include independent, skill, and task behavior, and certain interpersonal behaviors like smiling or talking in a pleasant tone of voice. Therefore, other people's smiling and pleasant tone of voice and perhaps other attention behaviors may contribute extensively to the socialization of the child by establishing most types of appropriate behavior in the child through reward learning.

It is possible that primary reinforcers other than contact comfort importantly contribute to the reinforcing strength of attention behaviors. Another idea is that additional responses of a person, for example, affectionate words, frequently accompany attention behaviors and thereby contribute to the reward learning of appropriate behavior.

Maintenance of Conditioning Established with Attention Behaviors. If the conditioned reinforcing strength of attention behaviors is due, in part, to their being followed by contact comfort either independently of responding or through the child's obtaining contact comfort instrumentally, how might contact comfort be involved with maintaining the conditioned reinforcing strength of attention behaviors, since the frequency with which the child receives contact comfort declines as the child grows older?

Conditioned reinforcers will retain their reinforcing strength if at approximately the same time they continue to be appropriately involved in conditioning established with a primary reinforcer. Therefore, occasional pairings between attention behaviors and contact comfort in later childhood, adolescence, and adulthood may importantly contribute to attention behaviors maintaining their reinforcing strength as the child grows older.

Attention behaviors do appear to be occasionally paired with contact comfort as the child moves into adulthood. Attention behaviors exhibited by close friends and relatives are apt to be followed by their initiating a limited form of contact comfort, such as an arm around a shoulder; this is certainly more apt to happen than when neutral or negative interpersonal behaviors occur. Similarly, smiling and pleasant tones of voice are more likely to be followed by contact comfort occurring in sexual behavior than are frowning and harsh tones. Therefore, attention behaviors may retain their conditioned reinforcing strength as the child becomes an adult.

Recall that a long duration CS probably maintains its conditioned reinforcing strength as long as it is eventually followed by the UCS. The child's appropriate behavior is relatively likely to be followed by attention behaviors and by contact comfort, although the frequency of contact comfort decreases as the child grows older. Attention behaviors correspond to a CS occurring during a delay of primary reinforcement interval; the decrease in frequency of contact comfort as the child grows older corresponds to a progressive lengthening of the delay of primary reinforcement interval; and the child's appropriate behavior corresponds to an instrumental response that is maintained by a CS (conditioned reinforcer) in the face of a delay of primary reinforcement. Therefore, one reason a person continues to exhibit appropriate behavior in adulthood may be that this behavior has been instrumentally conditioned by the conditioned reinforcers of attention behaviors occurring during an increasingly longer delay of primary reinforcement interval, the reinforcing strength of these conditioned reinforcers being maintained because a long duration CS does not lose its conditioned reinforcing strength until it is followed by the absence of the primary reinforcer.

Summary

A CS establishes classical conditioning. This finding follows from the fact that a CS produces a CR; more theoretically, it is explained by assuming that the stimulus paired with the CS results in an image of the UCS. This finding supports the assumption that in straightforward instrumental conditioning the stimuli of the general learning situation result in an image of the goal or negative-goal stimulus, and indicates once more that conditioning between paired neutral stimuli occurs. Manipulations involving the UCS and presenting the CS in extinction do not affect the strength of a CR established with a CS.

A CS previously paired with a positive UCS establishes reward learning. This finding is in accord with the result that a CS paired with a positive UCS is approached and continued to be perceived. It is viewed as the outcome of an animal's behaving so as to increase the vividness of the image of the positive UCS. It once more suggests that conditioning between the stimulus produced by the instrumental response and a neutral stimulus that the instrumental response causes to occur can take place. The reinforcing strength of a CS continues almost indefinitely when it is paired on occasion with the UCS. A CS previously paired with a negative UCS establishes punishment, escape, and avoidance learning, much as a CS previously paired with a positive UCS establishes reward learning. A CS paired with the absence of a UCS also establishes instrumental conditioning, in accord with the assumption that when no particular event and a reinforcer occur in sufficiently close physical and temporal proximity, the extent of either approaching and continuing to perceive or escaping from and avoiding no particular event is affected. Image theory's assumption that an animal brings about the stimulus produced by the instrumental response, and thereby executes this response for instrumental responses that increase in rate, was supported by evidence indicating that CSs analogous to the stimuli produced by the types of instrumental responses that increase in rate establish reward and omission learning. The corresponding assumption for instrumental responses that decrease in rate was supported in an analogous fashion.

A stimulus present before the execution of a reward-trained response (R_1) established with a primary reinforcer can establish another reward-trained response (R_2). The reinforcing strength of a stimulus present prior to the execution of R_1 is dependent on permitting R_1 to occur. It was reasoned that the stimulus present prior to the execution of R_1 can establish R_2 because an animal behaves so as to increase the vividness of the image of the positive primary reinforcer; but that R_2 does not result in a more vivid image of the positive primary reinforcer unless the stimulus produced by R_1 can occur. The reinforcing strength of a stimulus present prior to the execution of R_1 can be continued almost indefinitely by arranging for R_1 to cause the positive primary reinforcer to occur on occasion.

Conditioned reinforcers function like primary reinforcers. For example, both types of reinforcers can establish both classical and instrumental conditioning, and the strength of reward-trained responses estab-

lished with both types of reinforcers can be decreased by no longer
delivering the reinforcer, that is, by carrying out extinction. That conditioned reinforcers function like primary reinforcers follows from the
conclusion that primary reinforcers establish classical and instrumental
conditioning through factors related to the responses they elicit, and the
result that conditioned reinforcers produce much the same responses;
and is in accord with the assumption that conditioning established with
both primary and conditioned reinforcers is mediated by the occurrence
of an image of a UCS or goal or negative-goal stimulus.

Factors affecting the reinforcing strength of conditioned reinforcers
are usually the ones affecting the strength of responses established with
primary reinforcers. For example, as training with a primary reinforcer
continues, the strength of the response established with the primary
reinforcer and the strength of the conditioned reinforcer that was
formed as a result of training with the primary reinforcer both increase.
This general finding follows from the consideration that the strength of
the learned response established with a conditioned reinforcer is quantitatively related to the strength of the response produced by the perceived
conditioned reinforcer.

Conditioned reinforcement contributes to reward learning established
with a primary reinforcer. The occurrence of a CS during a very long
delay of primary reinforcement interval enables reward learning to occur.
A long duration CS followed at its end by a primary reinforcer should
retain its conditioned reinforcing strength.

Escape learning established with the negative conditioned reinforcer of
the warning stimulus contributes to the strength of the instrumental response in signalled avoidance learning. The finding that signalled avoidance learning is impaired when the instrumental response does not terminate the warning stimulus supports this inference. In extinction, the
warning stimulus is terminated prior to the time shock occurred in
acquisition, which should contribute to the relatively strong resistance to
extinction of signalled avoidance learning. Response prevention decreases
the resistance to extinction of signalled avoidance learning, probably
partly because the reinforcing strength of the warning stimulus is decreased due to the full duration of the warning stimulus being followed
by the absence of shock.

Other people's attention behaviors are probably followed by the child
receiving contact comfort both independently of the child's responding
and through the child performing an instrumental response to obtain
contact comfort. Therefore, other people's attention behaviors should be
conditioned reinforcers. Other interpersonal behaviors of people are

probably paired with their delivering attention behaviors to children. Thus, classical conditioning established with the conditioned reinforcers of attention behaviors should ensue, and these other interpersonal behaviors should come to reduce fear and be approached and continued to be perceived. The child's appropriate behavior tends to be followed by other people directing attention behaviors at the child. It follows that the child is reward-trained to behave appropriately with the conditioned reinforcers of attention behaviors. The conditioned reinforcing strength of attention behaviors may be maintained into adulthood because, in part, attention behaviors continue to be correlated with contact comfort in adulthood. In addition, attention behaviors for older children and adults may be viewed as a long duration CS that does not lose its conditioned reinforcing strength because it is eventually paired with contact comfort.

REFERENCES

ADELMAN, H. M., & MAATSCH, J. L. Learning and extinction based upon frustration, food reward and exploratory tendency. *J. Exp. Psychol.*, 1956, 52, 311-315.

BAUM, M., & MYRAN, D. D. Response prevention (flooding) in rats: The effects of restricting exploration during flooding and of massed vs distributed flooding. *Can. J. Psychol.*, 1971, 25, 138-146.

BELLINGHAM, W. P., STORLIEN, L. H., & STEBULIS, R. J. Discrimination learning in the T-maze based on the secondary reinforcing effects of shock termination. *Bull. Psychon. Soc.*, 1975, 5, 327-328.

BERSH, P. J., & MILLER, S. K. The influence of shock during response prevention upon resistance to extinction of an avoidance response. *Anim. Learn. Behav.*, 1975, 3, 140-142.

BOLLES, R. C., & GROSSEN, N. E. Effects of an informational stimulus on the acquisition of avoidance behavior in rats. *J. Comp. Physiol. Psychol.*, 1969, 68, 90-99.

BOLLES, R. C., STOKES, L. W., & YOUNGER, M. S. Does CS termination reinforce avoidance behavior? *J. Comp. Physiol. Psychol.*, 1966, 62, 201-207.

BROWN, J. L. The effect of drive on learning with secondary reinforcement. *J. Comp. Physiol. Psychol.*, 1956, 49, 254-260.

BUTTER, C. M., & THOMAS, D. R. Secondary reinforcement as a function of the amount of primary reinforcement. *J. Comp. Physiol. Psychol.*, 1958, 51, 346-348.

COULTER, X., RICCIO, D. C., & PAGE, H. A. Effects of blocking an instrumental avoidance response: Facilitated extinction but persistence of "fear." *J. Comp. Physiol. Psychol.*, 1969, 68, 377-381.

CROWDER, W. F., GILL, K., JR., HODGE, C. C., & NASH, F. A., JR. Secondary reinforcement or response facilitation? II. Response acquisition. *J. Psychol.*, 1959, 48, 303-306.

DALY, H. B., & McCROSKERY, J. H. Acquisition of a bar-press response to escape frustrative nonreward and reduce reward. *J. Exp. Psychol.*, 1973, 98, 109-112.

D'AMATO, M. R. Secondary reinforcement and magnitude of primary reinforcement. *J. Comp. Physiol. Psychol.*, 1955, 48, 378-380.

D'AMATO, M. R., FAZZARO, J., & ETKIN, M. Anticipatory responding and avoidance discrimination as factors in avoidance conditioning. *J. Exp. Psychol.*, 1968, 77, 41-47.

DINSMOOR, J. A., BROWNE, M. P., & LAWRENCE, C. E. A test of the negative discriminative stimulus as a reinforcer of observing. *J. Exp. Anal. Behav.*, 1972, 18, 79-85.

ESTES, W. K. Generalization of secondary reinforcement from the primary drive. *J. Comp. Physiol. Psychol.*, 1949, 42, 286-295.

FERSTER, C. B., & HAMMER, C. Variables determining the effects of delay in reinforcement. *J. Exp. Anal. Behav.*, 1965, 8, 243-254.

GEWIRTZ, J. L. A learning analysis of the effects of normal stimulation, privation and deprivation on the acquisition of social motivation and attachment. In B. M. Foss (Ed.), *Determinants of Infant Behaviour*. London: Methuen, 1961.

GRASTYAN, E., & VERECZKEI, L. Effects of spatial separation of the conditioned signal from the reinforcement: A demonstration of the conditioned character of the orienting response or the orientational character of conditioning. *Behav. Biol.*, 1974, 10, 121-146.

HAKE, D. F., & AZRIN, N. H. Conditioned punishment. *J. Exp. Anal. Behav.*, 1965, 8, 279-293.

HALL, J. F. Studies in secondary reinforcement: I. Secondary reinforcement as a function of the frequency of primary reinforcement. *J. Comp. Physiol. Psychol.*, 1951, 44, 246-251.

HOLLAND, P. C., & RESCORLA, R. A. Second-order conditioning with food unconditioned stimulus. *J. Comp. Physiol. Psychol.*, 1975, 88, 459-467.

JENKINS, W. O. A temporal gradient of derived reinforcement. *Am. J. Psychol.*, 1950, 63, 237-243.

KEEHN, J. D. The effect of post-stimulus conditions on the secondary reinforcing power of a stimulus. *J. Comp. Physiol. Psychol.*, 1962, 55, 22-26.

KELLEHER, R. T., Schedules of conditioned reinforcement during experimental extinction. *J. Exp. Anal. Behav.*, 1961, 4, 1-5.

KING, D. L., & BEATTY, L. A. Students' expectations of parents' behavior following children's appropriate and inappropriate behavior. *Psychol. Rep.*, 1975, 36, 875-881.

MASTERSON, J. L. Is termination of a warning signal an effective reward for the rat? *J. Comp. Physiol. Psychol.*, 1970, 72, 471-475.

McALLISTER, D. E., McALLISTER, W. R., BROOKS, C. I., & GOLDMAN, J. A. Magnitude and shift of reward in instrumental aversive learning in rats. *J. Comp. Physiol. Psychol.*, 1972, 80, 490-501.

MILLER, N. E. Studies of fear as an acquirable drive: I. Fear as motivation and fear-reduction as reinforcement in the learning of new responses. *J. Exp. Psychol.*, 1948, 38, 89-101.

MORRIS, R. G. M. Preconditioning of reinforcing properties to an exteroceptive feedback stimulus. *Learn. Motiv.*, 1975, 6, 289-298.

MURRAY, A. K., & STRANDBERG, J. M. Development of a conditioned positive reinforcer through removal of an aversive stimulus. *J. Comp. Physiol. Psychol.*, 1965, 60, 281-285.

OU, Y. *Mother's Contact Comfort and Other Behaviors While Children Work on Tasks.* Unpublished doctoral dissertation, Howard University, 1977.

318   Conditioned Reinforcement

PAVLOV, I. P. *Conditioned Reflexes* (G. V. Anrep, trans.). London: Oxford University Press, 1927.

PERKINS, C. C., JR. The relation of secondary reward to gradients of reinforcement. *J. Exp. Psychol.*, 1947, 37, 377-392.

RESCORLA, R. A., Effect of US habituation following conditioning. *J. Comp. Physiol. Psychol.*, 1973, 82, 137-143.

RIZLEY, R. C., & RESCORLA, R. A. Associations in second-order conditioning and sensory preconditioning. *J. Comp. Physiol. Psychol.*, 1972, 81, 1-11.

SALTZMAN, I. J. Maze learning in the absence of primary reinforcement: A study of secondary reinforcement. *J. Comp. Physiol. Psychol.*, 1949, 42, 161-173.

SHIPLEY, R. H., MOCK, L. A., & LEVIS, D. J. Effects of several response prevention procedures on activity, avoidance responding, and conditioned fear in rats. *J. Comp. Physiol. Psychol.*, 1971, 77, 256-270.

SKINNER, B. F. *Science and human behavior.* New York: Macmillan, 1953.

THOMAS, J. R. Maintenance of behavior by conditioned reinforcement in the signaled absence of primary reinforcement. In D. P. Hendry (Ed.), *Conditioned Reinforcement.* Homewood, Ill.: Dorsey Press, 1969.

TOMBAUGH, J. W., & TOMBAUGH, T. N. Effects on performance of placing a visual cue at different temporal locations within a constant delay interval. *J. Exp. Psychol.*, 1971, 87, 220-224.

WALTERS, G. C., & GLAZER, R. D. Punishment of instinctive behavior in the Mongolian gerbil. *J. Comp. Physiol. Psychol.*, 1971, 75, 331-340.

WEISMAN, R. G., & LITNER, J. S. Positive conditioned reinforcement of Sidman avoidance behavior in rats. *J. Comp. Physiol. Psychol.*, 1969, 68, 597-603.

WOLFE, J. B. Effectiveness of token-rewards for chimpanzees. *Comp. Psychol. Monogr.*, 1936, 12, (5, Serial No. 60).

ZIMMERMAN, J., & HANFORD, P. V. Sustaining behavior with conditioned reinforcement as the only response-produced consequence. *Psychol. Rep.*, 1966, 19, 391-401.

CHAPTER 6

Partial Reinforcement

Partial reinforcement of reward learning entails delivering the positive reinforcer after only some of the instrumental responses that are made rather than after every instrumental response. Ratio and interval schedules of reinforcement, which were briefly described earlier, are partial reinforcement schedules, because more responses occur on these schedules than are followed by the reinforcer. Partial reinforcement of a reward-trained response established with a discrete trial procedure, for instance, the runway traversal response, consists of following this response by the reinforcer on only some of the total number of trials. Most of the research on partial reinforcement in instrumental conditioning has employed reward learning; therefore we will limit our discussion to this type of instrumental conditioning.

Ratio and Interval Schedules

Ratio and interval schedules include fixed-ratio (FR); variable-ratio (VR); fixed-interval (FI); and variable-interval (VI) schedules of reinforcement. Responding on ratio and interval schedules is controlled by events corresponding to stimuli that are not currently present. This conclusion supports the assumption that images of stimuli control responding on ratio and interval schedules. A similar conclusion and inference is drawn about the control of responding in discrete trial reward learning established with partial reinforcement. An important finding is that ratio and interval schedules of reinforcement result in responding that is relatively resistant to extinction. The equivalent of extinction approach explains this finding. A similar result and explanation pertain to partial reinforcement of discrete trial reward learning.

Responding on Ratio and Interval Schedules. FR schedules require that a constant (fixed) number of responses be made since delivery of the previous reinforcement for the next reinforcement to occur. That is, execution of the last of the number of responses that are required to be made since delivery of the last reinforcement results in the next reinforcement occurring. This reinforcement is usually delivered immediately after the last of the required responses is made. VR schedules are similar to FR schedules in that a certain number of responses must be made since a reinforcement was delivered for the next reinforcement to be delivered, usually immediately. For VR schedules, however, the number of responses required since delivery of the previous reinforcement for the next reinforcement to occur varies. In a FR X schedule, X responses are required since delivery of the previous reinforcement for the next reinforcement to come. In a VR X schedule, X equals the mean number of responses required since delivery of the previous reinforcement for the next reinforcement to come.

For FI schedules, the first response made after a constant (fixed) interval of time has elapsed since delivery of the previous reinforcement causes the next reinforcement to occur, usually immediately. Responses made before the time interval of the FI schedule has elapsed have no scheduled consequences; they do not alter the probability, rate, or time of delivery of the next reinforcement. A FI X schedule delivers a reinforcement following the first response made after X seconds or minutes since delivery of the previous reinforcement. VI schedules are similar to FI schedules in the way that VR schedules are similar to FR schedules. For a VI X schedule, the first response made after a variable interval of time has elapsed since delivery of the previous reinforcement causes the next reinforcement to occur, usually immediately, and X equals the mean of the variable intervals of time.

To obtain responding on ratio and interval schedules, an animal is usually first reward-trained by following each response with the reinforcer. This was the procedure indicated when reward learning was first discussed, and it is called a *continuous reinforcement* (CRF) schedule. After reward learning is established with a CRF schedule, the ratio or interval schedule is introduced. Responding on ratio schedules is accomplished by gradually increasing the response requirement for reinforcement; for example, by moving from CRF to FR 5, then from FR 5 to FR 10, and so on.

Ratio and interval schedules are normally employed in conjunction with the free responding procedure. The free responding procedure consists of permitting an animal to remain in the learning situation for a period of time, usually a number of minutes, with the opportunity to respond being made available continuously during this time period. Typically, many responses are made, and the reinforcer is received more than a few times in a single session.

A record of responding on ratio and interval schedules called a cumulative curve is generally obtained. The cumulative curve was introduced when the initial acquisition of bar pressing was discussed (Figure 3-11). Figure 6-1 is a record obtained from a pigeon that responded on a FR 120 food reinforcement schedule. The ordinate of Figure 6-1 indicates the accumulated number of pecks that occurred in an interval of time during which the pigeon was free to respond. The duration of this time interval is indicated by the abcissa. The insert at the bottom right of the Figure indicates the number of responses and amount of time elapsed for distances along the ordinate and abcissa, respectively. Because this insert indicates the number of responses occurring over time, the pigeon's rate of responding can be determined from the cumulative curve. The jags on the cumulative curve indicate deliveries of the reinforcer. The vertical distance between jags therefore indicates the number of responses occurring between two adjacent deliveries of the reinforcer, these distances being equal because a FR schedule was in effect. Note the pauses in responding that occurred after deliveries of the reinforcer, as indicated by the horizontal lines following the jags. Also, note that once responding began it continued, this responding occurring at a rate of about 3 pecks per second. Figure 6-1 illustrates the typical effect of a FR schedule on responding, which is that a pause in responding occurs after a reinforcement, and that once responding begins it continues at a relatively fast rate until the next reinforcement is delivered, whereupon another post-reinforcement pause takes place, and so on.

Figure 6-2 shows a cumulative record obtained from a pigeon that responded on a VR 110 food reinforcement schedule. The unequal vertical distances between adjacent jags, which indicate reinforcements, reveal that a VR rather than a FR schedule was in effect. Relatively rapid responding usually occurred between reinforcements. The rate of responding did, however, decrease noticeably on two occasions when the sizes of the FR components of the VR 110 schedule were relatively large. Post-reinforcement pauses hardly ever occurred. The depicted effect of the VR 110 schedule on responding is typical. VR schedules do generally produce a relatively fast and steady rate of responding.

Figure 6-3 presents a cumulative curve obtained from a pigeon that responded on a FI 1 (minute) food reinforcement schedule. The cumulative curve indicates that usually a pause of about 15 seconds occurred after delivery of a reinforcement; then the rate of responding accelerated, with the rate of responding being quite fast just before delivery of the next reinforcement. This pattern of responding between reinforcements often occurs on FI schedules and is called a *scallop pattern.* Note that a large number of responses are made during the inter-reinforcement interval of a FI schedule, even though responding during an interval has no scheduled consequences.

Figure 6-4 indicates a cumulative record obtained from a pigeon that responded on a VI 3 (minute) food reinforcement schedule. The unequal horizontal distances between two adjacent jags indicate that a VI rather than a FI schedule was in effect. This Figure shows the generally obtained finding that VI schedules result in a relatively steady rate of responding, the same result obtained with VR schedules. However, the rate of responding occurring on VI schedules is usually less than the rate of responding occurring on ratio schedules. For example, Figure 6-4

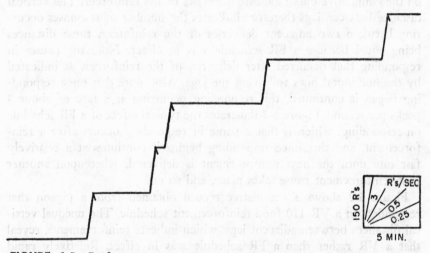

FIGURE 6-1. Performance on FR 120 after extensive training. (C. B. Ferster, B. F. Skinner, Schedules of Reinforcement, © **1957. Adapted by permission of Prentice-Hall, Inc., Englewood Cliffs, New Jersey.)**

indicates that the rate of responding on the VI 3 schedule was about 1 peck per second, a rate lower than that normally obtained with FR and and VR schedules with the same species and response.

Ratio Schedules and Responding in Acquisition. For FR schedules, we will assume that a stimulus produced by making the number of responses that causes the reinforcer to occur becomes associated through classical conditioning with this reinforcer. In other words, we assume that there is a distinctive stimulus produced by making a specific number of the same responses, and that this stimulus functions as do other stimuli, including becoming associated with the reinforcer that follows it. This assumption explains the animal's ability to exhibit the required number of responses. An animal that responds on a FR schedule brings about the stimulus produced by the required number of responses, in the same way that an animal brings about the stimulus produced by a single instrumental response. By bringing about the stimulus produced by the required number of responses, an animal will, of course, execute the required number of responses.

One problem involved in assuming that the stimulus produced by making the number of responses required for a reinforcement by a FR

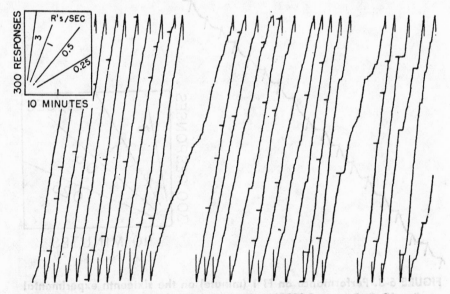

FIGURE 6-2. Performance on FR 110 on the twelfth experimental session. (C. B. Ferster, B. F. Skinner, Schedules of Reinforcement, © **1957. Adapted by permission of Prentice-Hall, Inc., Englewood Cliffs, New Jersey.)**

schedule becomes associated with the reinforcer is that an animal may simply learn to respond repetitively until an experimenter-provided stimulus paired with the delivery of food occurs; the sound of the food delivery apparatus and the sound of food dropping into the food receptacle may be such stimuli. They could serve as cues for the instrumental response of approaching the food receptacle. Therefore, it is possible that an animal does not associate the stimulus produced by a specific number of consecutive responses with the reinforcer.

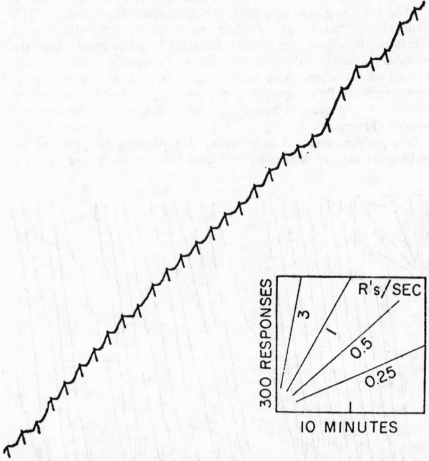

FIGURE 6-3. Performance on FI 1 (minute) on the sixteenth experimental session. (C. B. Ferster, B. F. Skinner, Schedules of Reinforcement, © 1957. Adapted by permission of Prentice-Hall, Inc., Englewood Cliffs, New Jersey.)

One way to deal with this question involves determining when the food receptacle is approached. In one study (Platt & Johnson, 1971), rats were required to make a certain number of lever press responses for food to be delivered. To obtain food, the rats had to move their heads through a hole in the wall of the chamber beyond which the food tray was placed. This hole was positioned immediately above the lever. Entries into the hole were recorded automatically. Approaching the food tray, that is, entering the hole, before executing the required minimal number of lever press responses did not have any programmed consequences. In addition, making more than the required number of lever press responses for a reinforcement before approaching the food tray did not "count"

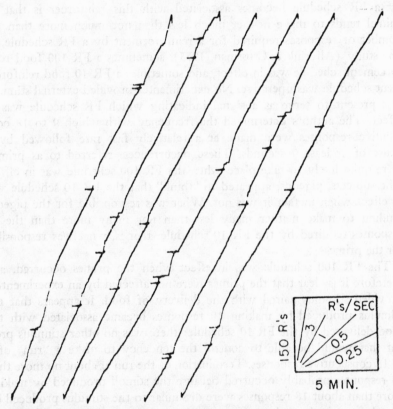

FIGURE 6-4. Performance on VI 3 (minutes) on the twenty-seventh experimental session. (C. B. Ferster, B. F. Skinner, Schedules of Reinforcement, © 1957. Adapted by permission of Prentice-Hall, Inc., Englewood Cliffs, New Jersey.)

toward satisfying the response requirement for the next reinforcement. Figure 6-5 shows the performance of a typical rat. It was most likely to approach the food tray slightly before completing the response requirement. No experimenter-provided stimuli had occurred at this time. Response-produced stimuli therefore must have controlled the approach response to the food tray. Thus, it appears that the stimulus produced by making the number of responses required for a reinforcement became associated with the reinforcer, and that when the response-produced stimulus that occurred at the moment became sufficiently similar to this response-produced stimulus, the rat approached the food tray.

Another finding that supports the assumption that the stimulus produced by making the number of responses required for a reinforcement by a FR schedule becomes associated with this reinforcer is that an animal tends to make neither much less than nor much more than the number of responses required for a reinforcement by a FR schedule. In one study (Alferink & Crossman, 1975), sometimes a FR 100 food reinforcement schedule was in effect, and sometimes a FR 10 food reinforcement schedule was operative. No experimenter-provided external stimulus was present to serve as a signal indicating which FR schedule was in effect. The authors determined the frequency with which 9 to 18 consecutive responses were made at a relatively fast rate followed by a pause of at least 9 seconds. These occurrences, referred to as primes, were quite likely to take place when the FR 100 schedule was in effect. The subjects, pigeons, appeared to "think" that the FR 10 schedule was in effect when in fact it was not. What was responsible for the pigeons tending to make neither many less than nor many more than the 10 responses required by the FR 10 schedule; that is, what was responsible for the primes?

The FR 100 schedule was in effect when the primes occurred, and therefore it is clear that the primes were not affected by an experimenter-provided stimulus paired with the delivery of food. It appears that the stimulus produced by making 10 responses became associated with the food delivered by the FR 10 schedule: there was no other stimulus present that would be able to control the tendency to make a "run" of 9 to 18 consecutive responses. Termination of the run at about no more than 18 responses probably occurred because the stimuli produced by making more than about 18 responses were dissimilar to the stimulus produced by 10 (the required number of) responses.

Animals are able to discriminate between different numbers of consecutive responses in the absence of experimenter-provided stimuli signalling the completion of the different numbers of responses (Chapter

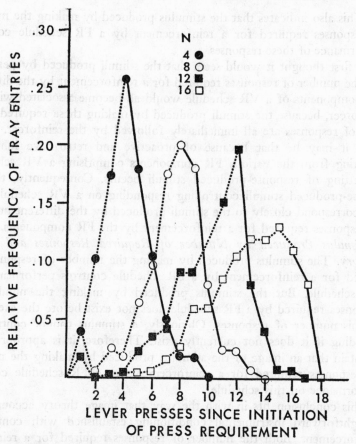

FIGURE 6-5. Tendency to approach food tray as functions of the minimal number of responses required for a reinforcement (N) and the number of responses made since receiving the last reinforcement (the abcissa). Relative frequency equals the frequency of making one number of responses before a tray entry divided by the total number of tray entries made. The dotted lines are for numbers of responses made before satisfying the minimal response requirement, and the solid lines are for numbers of responses that equalled or exceeded this requirement. The animal responded under all four values of N, and responded for a number of sessions under each value before responding under another such value. The data is taken from the last four sessions of responding under each value of N. (Adapted from Platt and Johnson, 1971.)

4). This also indicates that the stimulus produced by making the number of responses required for a reinforcement by a FR schedule controls performance of these responses.

At first thought it would seem that the stimuli produced by performing the number of responses required for a reinforcement by the different FR components of a VR schedule would all become associated with the reinforcer, because the stimuli produced by making these required numbers of responses are all immediately followed by the reinforcer. However, it may be that because of proactive and retroactive inhibition resulting from the various FR components comprising a VR schedule, forgetting of response-produced stimuli occurs. Consequently, the response-produced stimuli controlling responding on a VR schedule may not correspond closely to the stimuli produced by the different numbers of responses required for a reinforcement by the FR components.

Stimulus Produced by Number of Required Responses and Image Theory. The stimulus produced by making the number of responses required for a reinforcement by a FR schedule controls performance on this schedule. But the stimulus produced by making the number of responses required by a FR schedule does not exist before the execution of this number of responses. Obviously, a stimulus cannot control responding if it does not currently exist. Therefore, it is appropriate to maintain that an image of the stimulus produced by making the number of responses required for a reinforcement by a FR schedule controls performance on this schedule.

This conclusion fits in with the way that image theory accounts for straightforward instrumental conditioning established with continuous reinforcement. Both the number of responses required for a reinforcement by a FR schedule and a single response that causes a reinforcement to occur are instrumental responses; they both cause a stimulus to occur. If performance of the instrumental response required for a reinforcement by a FR schedule is controlled by an image of the stimulus produced by this response, then performance of an instrumental response that is a single response should also be mediated by an image of the stimulus produced by this response, as image theory assumes.

Ratio Schedules and Responding in Extinction. Ratio schedules increase the resistance to extinction of responding. For example, a pigeon that responded on a FR 60 food reinforcement schedule in acquisition made about 7,000 responses in about 3½ hours of extinction (Ferster & Skinner, 1957, p. 58). Nowhere near that many responses would have been made over the same time period of extinction if a pigeon had been trained on a continuous reinforcement (CRF) schedule.

The equivalent of extinction approach was previously employed to account for the relatively strong resistance to extinction of punishment learning, avoidance learning, and classical conditioning in which a CS is paired with the absence of a UCS; the lack of an effect of presenting a CS in extinction on the strength of the CR established with this CS; and the relatively strong resistance to extinction of the conditioned reinforcing strength of a long duration CS. The equivalent of extinction approach, together with the assumption that the stimulus produced by making the number of responses required for a reinforcement by a ratio schedule becomes associated with the reinforcer, appear to account for the finding that a ratio schedule results in more resistance to extinction of responding than a CRF schedule. A decrease in the strength of a learned response in extinction, that is, an equivalent of extinction, will usually not occur unless the S_1-reinforcer or S_1-S_2 (where S_2 is a neutral stimulus) pairings responsible for exhibition of the acquired response are replaced in extinction by pairings between S_1 and a stimulus different in kind from the reinforcer or S_2 occurring in acquisition. Because the stimulus produced by making the number of responses required for a reinforcement by a FR schedule should become associated with the reinforcer, equivalents of extinction should take place only when this response-produced stimulus is no longer followed by the reinforcer. To bring about the stimulus produced by making the number of responses required for a reinforcement by a FR schedule, this number of responses must be exhibited. It follows that the number of responses required for a reinforcement by a FR schedule should occur for an equivalent of extinction to take place. Because the rate of decrease in the strength of a learned response in extinction usually should be determined by the number of equivalents of extinction that occur, and because a FR schedule results in more responses being made for each equivalent of extinction that occurs than a CRF schedule does, it follows that a FR schedule should result in more responses in extinction than a CRF schedule, which it does.

Resistance to extinction increases as the size of the ratio increases (Boren, 1951; Mowrer & Jones, 1945). For example, Boren had independent groups of rats responding on CRF, FR 3, FR 6, FR 10, FR 15, and FR 20 food reinforcement schedules. Each group received a total of 500 food reinforcements on their respective schedules. The mean number of bar presses made by the independent groups in extinction sessions of identical duration increased monotonically with an increase in the size of the ratio.

The equivalent of extinction approach also accounts for the result that resistance to extinction of responding increases with an increase in the size of the ratio of a FR schedule. Consider two FR schedules, one with a larger number of required responses than the other. The stimulus produced by both these numbers of responses should become associated with the reinforcer. Also, the stimulus produced by both these numbers of responses should be followed by the absence of the reinforcer for an equivalent of extinction to occur. But a greater number of responses must be made for the stimulus produced by the greater number of responses to be followed by the absence of the reinforcer, that is, for an equivalent of extinction to occur. Because the rate of decrease in the strength of a learned response in extinction usually should be determined by the number of equivalents of extinction that occur, and because more responses must be made for equivalents of extinction to take place for the FR schedule with the larger response requirement, it follows that this FR schedule should result in more responses in extinction, which it does.

Measurement of Equivalents of Extinction for Ratio Schedules. Findings by Denny, Wells, and Maatsch (1957) and Overmann and Denny (1974) support the hypothesis that the rate of decrease in the strength of a learned response in extinction usually should be determined by the number of equivalents of extinction that occur. In the Overmann and Denny study, the experimental chamber contained a bar, a food cup, and a door to the food cup; the bar was separated from the entrance to the food cup by 9 centimeters. One group of rats responded in acquisition on a CRF food reinforcement schedule, and a second on a FR 10 food reinforcement schedule. After each bar press response for the CRF group, and after each tenth bar press response since delivery of the last reinforcer for the FR 10 group, the apparatus that delivered food clicked, and food was made available. As training progressed, approaches to the food cup when the click had not occurred ceased to take place, and approaches to the food cup after the click occurred became more rapid. Thus, a learned response sequence was acquired, the members of which consisted of either 1 or 10 bar presses, approach to the door, and pushing the door open. The result of interest is that the CRF and FR 10 groups made almost the same number of doorway opening responses prior to reaching a 10 minute extinction criterion of no bar pressing.

An equivalent of extinction should have occurred each time the empty food cup was perceived in extinction, because the response of pushing the door open was eventually consistently followed by obtaining food in acquisition, and because this response-food pairing should support the other member of the response sequence, that is, bar pressing either 1 or 10 times (as will be discussed subsequently). Measurement of the number of doorway opening responses in extinction should therefore have provided a measure of the number of equivalents of extinction occurring for the CRF and FR 10 groups. Because the CRF and FR 10 groups made the same number of doorway openings prior to reaching the same criterion of extinction of bar pressing, the same number of equivalents of extinction occurred prior to reaching the same criterion of extinction of a learned response. This supports the assumption that the rate of decrease in the strength of a learned response in extinction usually is determined by the number of equivalents of extinction that occur.

Stimuli Controlling Responding in Acquisition and Extinction. Explanation of the effect of ratio schedules of reinforcement on resistance to extinction of responding was possible because of evidence that the stimulus produced by the number of responses required for a reinforcement by a FR schedule becomes associated with the reinforcer, and thereby controls responding on the FR schedule. Similarly, the analysis of the effect of the warning stimulus on signalled avoidance learning relied on knowledge of how the warning stimulus contributes to control of the instrumental response in this type of learning. Application of the equivalent of extinction approach requires that the stimuli that control responding in extinction be known with a fair degree of certainty. If these stimuli are not known, equivalents of extinction cannot be identified.

Another result of Overmann and Denny illustrates that knowledge of the stimuli which control responding in extinction is essential to be able to explain the effect of extinction on responding. Not previously indicated was that they divided the group that responded on a FR 10 schedule in acquisition into three subgroups in extinction. One subgroup received the click of the food delivery apparatus in extinction following every 6th bar press; a second after every 10th bar press; and a third after every 14th bar press. The click controlled the response of opening the door to the food cup in extinction, because when extinction was first begun the rats in each subgroup opened the door after the click occurred, rather than after an average of ten responses since the previous opening of the door. Thus, the stimulus produced by the number of responses required for a reinforcement by a FR schedule was replaced as a source of control of responding in extinction by a stronger source of control, the click. Each opening of the door should have resulted in an equivalent of extinction. In extinction the click occurred after different numbers of bar presses. It follows that different numbers of bar presses preceded occurrences of equivalents of extinction. Because the rate of decrease in the strength of a learned response in extinction usually should be determined by the number of equivalents of extinction that occur, it follows that the number of bar presses made in extinction should have increased as the number of bar presses followed by a click in extinction increased, which was the obtained result.

Note the similarity between the above explanation and the explanation of the result that an increase in the size of the ratio of a FR schedule results in an increase in the resistance to extinction of responding. Experimenter-provided stimuli paired with the delivery of the reinforcer in acquisition, such as the click in the Overmann and Denny study, are not typically presented in extinction. Control of responding in extinction is therefore exercised by the stimulus produced by the number of responses required for a reinforcement by the FR schedule in acquisition. In both cases, greater resistance to extinction of responding results when more responses precede equivalents of extinction; and the stimuli controlling responding in extinction determine the number of responses preceding equivalents of extinction.

Interval Schedules and Responding in Acquisition. For FI schedules it appears that a stimulus corresponding to the duration of the FI interval functions as a positive discriminative stimulus (S+) for a single response, for instance, a bar press. An animal responding on a FI schedule typically executes an instrumental response almost directly after the FI interval has elapsed and thereby receives the reinforcer; and we know that a stimulus corresponding to a specific time duration can control responding (Chapter 4).

The assumption that a stimulus corresponding to the duration of the interval of a FI schedule functions as a S+ for a single instrumental response appears to account for the increase in response rate that often occurs between two adjacent deliveries of the reinforcer by a FI schedule, that is, for the scallop pattern of responding that often occurs on a FI schedule. As the length of time since delivery of the last reinforcement increases, an increasing amount of stimulus generalization should occur between the time-correlated stimuli taking place at the moment and the time-correlated stimulus corresponding to the duration of the entire FI interval. Therefore, as the length of time since delivery of the last reinforcement increases, so should the strength of the instrumental response; that is, an increase in response rate should occur between two adjacent deliveries of the reinforcer.

The stronger responding that occurs as the FI interval elapses does not appear to be due to the fact that responding that occurs closer in time to the termination of the FI interval is followed by the next reinforcement with a shorter time delay. For one reason, this explanation does not account for why responses are made during much of the FI interval; also, an experimental result (Morgan, 1970) argues against it.

For VI schedules, the time-correlated stimuli corresponding to the different intervals of the FI components of a VI schedule may all function as S+s for a single instrumental response. However, it may be that forgetting of these time-correlated stimuli occurs because of proactive and retroactive inhibition involved with the different intervals of the various FI components. Consequently, the time-correlated stimuli controlling responding on VI schedules may not closely resemble the time-correlated stimuli corresponding to the different intervals of the FI components of a VI schedule.

Stimulus Corresponding to Length of FI Interval and Image Theory. It was reasoned that a time-correlated stimulus corresponding to the duration of a FI interval controls responding that occurs while the FI interval elapses. But the time-correlated stimulus corresponding to the duration of a FI interval does not exist prior to the moment the FI interval has completely elapsed. Strictly speaking, a stimulus cannot control responding if it does not currently exist. Therefore, an image of the time-correlated stimulus corresponding to the duration of a FI interval probably controls responding that occurs while the FI interval elapses. Since temporal discriminations involve discriminations between response-produced stimuli, the image of the stimulus that apparently controls responding while the FI interval elapses should be an image of a response-produced stimulus. The responding that occurs while the FI interval elapses is probably due to stimulus generalization of the instrumental conditioning of a single response. It follows that an image of a response-produced stimulus mediates the performance of an instrumentally conditioned response, as image theory assumes.

A finding known as *temporal conditioning* is similarly interpreted. In a study by Zamble (1969), food was delivered to rats every 2 minutes independently of responding. A CS, such as a bell or light, paired with food produces an increase in activity in rats. Zamble found that the strength of the activity CR increased during the 2-minute period between response-independent deliveries of food. This result is an example of temporal conditioning. The CS can be viewed as a response-produced time-correlated stimulus corresponding to a 2-minute time period. The increase in the strength of the activity CR that occurred between deliveries of the food probably resulted from stimulus generalization from the time-correlated stimulus corresponding to 2 minutes to time-correlated stimuli corresponding to less than 2 minutes. But by definition the response-produced time-correlated stimulus corresponding to 2 minutes could not have occurred while the 2 minute interval was elapsing. It therefore appears reasonable to assume that performance of the activity CR prior to the elapsing of the 2-minute interval was mediated by an image of the response-produced time-correlated stimulus corresponding to 2 minutes, that is, was mediated by the occurrence of an image of the CS.

Interval Schedules and Responding in Extinction. Interval schedules increase the resistance to extinction of responding. For example, a pigeon that responded on a VI 7 (minute) food reinforcement schedule in acquisition made about 5500 responses in the first 1½ hours of extinction (Ferster & Skinner, 1957, p. 348). It is certain that nowhere near that many responses would have been made over the same time period of extinction if a pigeon had been trained on a CRF schedule.

We may explain the result that interval schedules result in more resistance to extinction of responding than a CRF schedule on the basis that the time-correlated stimulus corresponding to the length of the FI interval functions as a S+ for a single instrumental response, together with the equivalent of extinction approach. An equivalent of extinction should occur only when the single instrumental response, for instance, a bar press, is made in the presence of the time-correlated stimulus corresponding to the length of the FI interval, and is followed by the absence of the reinforcer. However, a number of responses are made while the FI interval elapses, which means that a number of responses should be made in extinction before each equivalent of extinction occurs. Because the rate of decrease in the strength of a learned response in extinction usually should be determined by the number of equivalents of extinction that occur, it follows that interval schedules should result in more responses in extinction than a CRF schedule, which they do.

Response Rates on Ratio and Interval Schedules. The over-all response rate on ratio schedules is usually greater than the over-all response rate on interval schedules. Over-all response rate refers to the number of responses occurring during the time period a reinforcement schedule is in effect, that is, to the number of responses occurring in a time period in which both the post-reinforcement pause and responding may occur, divided by the length of this time period. Ferster and Skinner (1957) presented a large number of cumulative curves of pigeons responding on ratio and interval schedules. The over-all response rates on ratio schedules were usually above 2 responses per second, and sometimes were as high as 5 responses per second. Over-all response rate on interval schedules tended to be about 1 response per second.

Faster responding on ratio schedules than interval schedules probably occurs because faster responding on ratio schedules decreases delay of primary reinforcement, but faster responding while the intervals of FI and VI schedules are elapsing does not decrease delay of primary reinforcement. Because ratio schedules deliver the reinforcer directly after the number of required responses are made, it follows that when the required number of responses are exhibited at a faster rate, that is, in a shorter time period, delay of primary reinforcement will be decreased. Shorter delays of primary reinforcement result in better reward learning. Exhibiting the required number of responses at a faster rate should therefore be better learned than exhibiting the required number of responses at a slower rate. That is why exhibiting the required number of responses at a relatively fast rate should tend to occur. Note that we are not saying that an animal "chooses" to respond at a relatively fast rate on a ratio schedule "in order to" receive the reinforcer more quickly. Instead, we are saying that a relatively fast rate of responding on a ratio schedule occurs because such responding is better learned than responding at a slower rate. In respect to interval schedules, responding while the intervals of FI and VI schedules are elapsing cannot decrease delay of primary reinforcement, because responding during this time period has no scheduled consequences.

It is clear that animals are able to respond at a relatively fast rate when this responding decreases delay of positive reinforcement. An illustrative study by Ferster and Skinner (1957, p. 495) involved the use of a modified VI 1 (minute) food reinforcement schedule. Food was delivered on a VI schedule providing that a certain number of responses were made within a prescribed time period. By increasing the number of responses to be made within such a time period, the over-all response rate on the modified VI 1 schedule was increased to about 4 responses per second. By responding at a faster rate within the prescribed time period the reinforcer was more likely to occur, that is, it was delivered with a briefer average delay of reinforcement. The obtained result therefore supports the conclusion that the rate of responding that results in a briefer delay of primary reinforcement tends to be acquired.

Faster responding on ratio schedules increases the over-all rate of reinforcement (reinforcements per hour) as well as decreases delay of reinforcement. But delay of reinforcement is most likely the factor that establishes faster responding on ratio schedules, because in a discrimination learning situation involving a choice between two responses, the response that results in the briefer delay of reinforcement is established even though the over-all rate of reinforcement for the two responses is equated (Anderson, 1932; Hursh & Fantino, 1973; Killeen, 1968; Yoshioka, 1929).

A ratio schedule with a relatively large response requirement results in a lower over-all response rate than does an interval schedule with a relatively long FI interval (Ferster & Skinner, 1957). In addition, a ratio schedule with a very large response requirement has the result that responding just about ceases. As the size of the ratio continues to increase, the post-reinforcement pause becomes progressively longer. In addition, as the size of the ratio continues to increase, the length of time separating the initiation of responding from the time the response requirement is completed also progressively lengthens. Perhaps this increased delay of reinforcement is responsible for responding just about ceasing when a ratio schedule with a very large response requirement is in effect. In respect to an interval schedule, an increase in the length of the minimum time interval between reinforcements does not necessarily result in an increase in delay of reinforcement of responding. For this schedule, the longer a single response is not performed the more likely it is that a single response will be immediately followed by the reinforcer. A single response that is followed by little or no delay of reinforcement should contribute greatly to maintaining responding on an interval schedule with relatively long minimum time intervals between reinforcements.

Post-Reinforcement Pause. Recall that FR and FI schedules frequently result in a post-reinforcement pause, a period of time occurring directly after delivery of a reinforcement in which no responding occurs.

Responding on FR and FI schedules occurring immediately after delivery of a reinforcement is never directly followed by a reinforcement. The stimuli present directly after a reinforcement are therefore paired with the absence of a positive reinforcer. Thus, they should function like the S— of a typical go/no-go successive discrimination. Such a S— tends to inhibit performing the reward-trained response. The post-reinforcement pause therefore appears to be the outcome of responding being inhibited in the presence of a stimulus functioning like the S— of a go/no-go successive discrimination.

Evidence exists that supports the assumption that the post-reinforcement pause is due to stimuli functioning as the S— of a go/no-go successive discrimination and thereby inhibiting responding after a reinforcement is delivered. Wilkie (1974) had pigeons respond on FI schedules with a vertical white line superimposed on the response key. Subsequently, while a FI schedule remained in effect, different orientations of the white line were presented for brief time periods throughout the FI interval. An inhibitory stimulus generalization gradient along the line orientation dimension was obtained when the different line orientations occurred during the first third of the FI interval, that is, during the time period occurring relatively soon after a reinforcement. This result is direct evidence that post-reinforcement stimuli inhibit performing the reward-trained response. In addition, the S— of a go/no-go successive discrimination also results in an inhibitory stimulus generalization gradient along a dimension.

Brown and Flory (1972) and Dardano (1973) found that post-reinforcement stimuli occurring during responding on FR and FI schedules, respectively, establish escape learning. The S— of a go/no-go successive discrimination also establishes escape learning.

The post-reinforcement stimuli occurring during responding on FR and FI schedules produce aggressive behavior (Hutchinson, Azrin, & Hunt, 1968; Richards & Rilling, 1972). The S— of a go/no-go successive discrimination probably also produces aggressive behavior, since the S— of a similar successive discrimination produces this behavior (Cohen & Looney, 1973; Cole & Litchfield, 1969).

The post-reinforcement pause does not occur when a typical VR schedule is employed. Typical VR schedules employ FR components with very small ratios as well as FR components with much larger ratios. For example, the smallest FR component of a VR schedule used by Ferster and Skinner (1957, p. 392) was 1, and the largest components were over 700. FR schedules with relatively small ratios do not result in a post-reinforcement pause, which helps explain the absence of a post-reinforcement pause when typical VR schedules are used. Analogous reasoning applies to the absence of a post-reinforcement pause on typical VI schedules, because typical VI schedules normally contain some FI components with very short intervals. When a VI schedule consisting of only relatively long FI components was employed, post-reinforcement pauses frequently occurred (Dews, 1962).

Post-Reinforcement Pause, Size of Ratio, and Length of Interval. The stimulus produced by making the number of responses required for a reinforcement by a FR schedule is followed by the reinforcer, and therefore is related to a positive discriminative stimulus. The post-reinforcement stimuli function as a negative discriminative stimulus. An increase in the size of the ratio decreases the similarity between the stimulus produced by the number of responses required for a reinforcement by a FR schedule and the post-reinforcement stimuli, like a decrease in similarity between positive and negative discriminative stimuli. A decrease in the similarity between positive and negative discriminatve stimuli should result in better discrimination learning as evidenced by a greater tendency to not respond in the presence of the negative discriminative stimulus. An increase in the size of the ratio should therefore result in a greater tendency to not respond to post-reinforcement stimuli. This result is, in fact, obtained. When the size of the ratio is relatively small, the post-reinforcement pause usually does not occur at all (Ferster & Skinner, 1957). As the size of the ratio increases, so does the length of the post-reinforcement pause (Felton & Lyon, 1966).

Analogous reasoning in respect to the post-reinforcement pause and FI schedules leads to the expectation that as the length of the FI interval increases, so does the length of the post-reinforcement pause, an outcome which is, in fact, obtained (Catania & Reynolds, 1968; Ferster & Skinner, 1957).

One final matter involving the post-reinforcement pause remains to be discussed. We have assumed that the stimulus produced by the number of responses required for a reinforcement by a FR schedule becomes associated with the reinforcer. The nature of this stimulus is, of course, in doubt, but there are two possibilities. The first is that this stimulus corresponds in a straightforward fashion to the number of responses required for a reinforcement by a FR schedule. The second is more complex. Because an animal comes to respond on a FR schedule at a relatively constant rate over sessions, it follows that the average time elapsed between adjacent reinforcements comes to be approximately constant. A stimulus corresponding to the length of the time interval between adjacent reinforcements may therefore be the stimulus that becomes associated with the reinforcer. Both possibilities have received support (Crossman, Heaps, Nunes, & Alferink, 1974; Lyderson & Crossman, 1974; Neuringer & Schneider, 1968; Rilling, 1967). An experimental approach used in some of these studies was either to manipulate the number of responses occurring between adjacent reinforcements while keeping the length of the time interval between these reinforcements constant, or to manipulate the length of the time interval between adjacent reinforcements while keeping the number of responses required for a reinforcement constant; and determine whether the duration of the post-reinforcement pause was affected.

Post-Reinforcement Pause and Image Theory. It was reasoned that the length of the post-reinforcement pause is affected by the stimulus produced by the number of responses required for a reinforcement by a FR schedule. But when post-reinforcement stimuli are occurring, the stimulus produced by the number of responses required for a reinforcement by a FR schedule is obviously not present. Clearly, the real stimulus produced by the required number of responses does not affect the length of the post-reinforcement pause. However, the event that does affect the length of the post-reinforcement pause appears to possess the properties of a stimulus produced by the number of responses required for a reinforcement by a FR schedule. Therefore, it seems appropriate to assume that an image of the stimulus produced by the number of repsonses required for a reinforcement by a FR schedule affects the length of the post-reinforcement pause. In respect to the FI schedule, similar reasoning leads to the assumption that an image of the time-correlated stimulus corresponding to the duration of the FI interval affects the length of the post-reinforcement pause. These conclusions are obviously in accord with image theory.

Image theory assumes that instrumental conditioning is mediated by the image of the stimulus produced by the response that will be performed next. A study done by Crossman (1971) supports this assumption. He presented pigeons with single alternations of two FR schedules. One FR schedule was in effect until it delivered a single reinforcement, then the other FR schedule was in effect until it delivered a single reinforcement, then the first FR schedule was in effect until it delivered a single reinforcement, and so on. The sizes of the ratios of the FR schedules were unequal. A white light illuminated the response key at all times. It was found that the length of the post-reinforcement pause was greater when the larger number of responses had to be made following termination of the post-reinforcement pause for the next reinforcement to be obtained; in other words, the longer post-reinforcement pause occurred when the size of the upcoming ratio was the larger one.

The length of the post-reinforcement pause is increased by an increase in the size of the ratio of a FR schedule. Therefore, the length of a post-reinforcement pause in Crossman's study was affected by the size of the ratio that had to be completed next, that is, in the immediate future. The event correlated with the size of a ratio responsible for affecting the length of the post-reinforcement pause should be an image of the stimulus produced by the number of responses required for a reinforcement. Thus, the lengths of the post-reinforcement pauses may have been affected by an image of the stimulus produced by the number of responses required for the next reinforcement, that is, by an image of the stimulus produced by the number of responses required for a reinforcement in the immediate future. The number of responses required for a reinforcement is an instrumental response. Therefore, the length of the post-reinforcement pause may have been affected by an image of the stimulus produced by the instrumental response that was performed next. Because post-reinforcement stimuli by definition precede the required number of responses, that is, the instrumental response, that will occur next, it follows that prior to the execution of the instrumental response that was performed next, an image of the stimulus produced by this instrumental response occurred, as assumed by image theory.

Homogeneous Response Sequences. A *homogeneous response sequence* is a series of consecutive homogeneous responses, the last response of which causes a reinforcer to occur. Homogeneous responses are those with nearly identical topographies exhibited at the same position in space with the same operandum. Homogeneous response sequences occur when animals respond on ratio and interval schedules. For FR, VR, and VI schedules, the rate with which a homogeneous response sequence is performed is usually fairly constant and not particularly low. For FR schedules, the homogeneous response sequence is preceded by a post-reinforcement pause. The finding that once responding begins on FR, VR, and VI schedules it continues at a not particularly low rate until the reinforcer is delivered suggests that the homogeneous response sequences occurring on these reinforcement schedules function as a unit; the members, that is, the individual responses, of these homogeneous response sequences do not appear to function independently of one another. Other findings lead to the conclusion that homogeneous response sequences tend to function as a unit.

Sidman and Stebbins (1954) permitted animals to continue responding on a FR schedule and thereby obtain food for a sufficiently long period of time that the over-all response rate decreased markedly through partial satiation. The result of interest is that the decline in over-all response rate was due solely to an increase in the duration of the post-reinforcement pause. The rate with which the homogeneous response sequence occurred, that is, the rate based on the time elapsed from making the first response after a reinforcement to the response causing delivery of the next reinforcement, was not affected by a decrease in deprivation level. The result that the rate of executing the homogeneous response sequence was independent of deprivation level indicates that the homogeneous response sequence tended to function as a unit.

Dardano (1970, 1972) had pigeons respond on FR schedules. Some of the key pecks caused shock to occur, in addition to contributing to satisfying the response requirement of the FR schedules. This punishment of responding on a FR schedule tended to increase the duration of the post-reinforcement pause more than it decreased the rate with which the homogeneous response sequence occurred. The relative imperviousness of the rate of exhibiting the homogeneous response sequence to the punishment condition indicates that the homogeneous response sequence tended to function as a unit.

Finally, homogeneous response sequences sometimes occur at a steady and not particularly low rate on FI schedules (Schneider, 1969). The post-reinforcement pause still occurs; it precedes the steady rate of responding. The occurrence of a pause and run, rather than a scallop pattern of responding on FI schedules is one more indication that homogeneous response sequences tend to function as a unit.

Homogeneous Response Sequences: Analysis. Why do homogeneous response sequences tend to function as a unit?

The stimulus produced by each member of a homogeneous response sequence should be a positive conditioned reinforcer. The stimulus present prior to the occurrence of a reward-trained response (R_1) established with a primary reinforcer is a positive conditioned reinforcer (Chapter 5). However, the reinforcing strength of the stimulus present before R_1 is exhibited is much decreased when R_1 is not permitted to occur after this stimulus is used as a goal for establishing a second instrumental response (R_2). Because R_2 is not established unless R_1 and therefore the stimulus produced by R_1 occurs, it is reasonable to suppose that the stimulus produced by R_1 is also a positive conditioned reinforcer. Such a hypothesis is supported by the finding that a CS paired with a positive UCS is a positive conditioned reinforcer, because both the stimulus produced by R_1 and this type of CS are followed by a positive primary reinforcer.

If the stimulus produced by a reward-trained response established with a primary reinforcer is a positive conditioned reinforcer, then the stimulus produced by the member of the homogeneous response sequence that causes the primary reinforcer to occur should also be a positive conditioned reinforcer. Because the members of a homogeneous response sequence are nearly identical in topography, position of the operandum, and nature of the operandum, it follows that through stimulus generalization the stimuli produced by all the members of the homogeneous response sequence should be positive conditioned reinforcers. If each member of a homogeneous response sequence is a positive conditioned reinforcer, each should help to establish reward learning of the preceding member of the homogeneous response sequence. If each member of a homogeneous response sequence tends to establish reward learning of the preceding member, a homogeneous response sequence should tend to function as a unit.

This analysis of homogeneous response sequences helps us understand why homogeneous response sequences tend to be exhibited at not a particularly low rate. If each member of the homogeneous response sequence is executed relatively soon after performing the preceding member, there will be relatively little delay of the conditioned reinforcer of the stimulus produced by the next member. An animal acquires the response that results in a lesser delay of positive primary reinforcement. Therefore, it should also acquire the response that results in a lesser delay of positive conditioned reinforcement. Each member of the homogeneous response sequence should thus tend to be executed relatively soon after performing the preceding member; in other words, a homogeneous response sequence should tend to be exhibited at a not particularly low rate.

An additional factor contributes to a homogeneous response sequence functioning as a unit, including a homogeneous response sequence being exhibited at a not particularly low rate. Because the members of a homogeneous response sequence are by definition homogeneous responses, it follows that nearly identical conditioned reinforcers contribute to the reward learning of nearly identical responses. That much the same conditioned reinforcer repeatedly tends to establish much the same response should surely operate in the direction of making a homogeneous response sequence function as a unit.

Partial Reinforcement with Discrete Trials

In discrete trial reward learning procedures, a subject is not free to respond continuously over time. Partial reinforcement with a discrete trial procedure is most frequently studied by using reward learning of the runway traversal response. Partial reinforcement of this learning is carried out by presenting the positive reinforcer at the end of the runway on only a proportion of trials, rather than on all trials. An event corresponding to a stimulus that is not currently present controls responding in discrete trial reward learning established with partial reinforcement. Partial reinforcement of discrete trial reward learning results in responding that is more resistant to extinction than responding established with continuous reinforcement of discrete trial reward learning. The analyses of the effects of partial reinforcement of discrete trial reward learning on acquisition and extinction of responding are fairly similar to the analyses of the effects of ratio and interval schedules on acquisition and extinction of responding made above.

Partial Reinforcement, Extinction, and Equivalents of Extinction. A typical study indicating the effect of partial reinforcement on resistance to extinction of discrete trial reward learning was done by Weinstock (1958). One group of water-deprived rats received water at the end of a runway on 50 percent of the trials in acquisition. A second group received water at the end of the runway on every trial in acquisition. The group that received water on 50 percent of the trials is said to have been on a partial reinforcement schedule; the group that received water on 100 percent of the trials is said to have been on a continuous reinforcement schedule. The total number of trials in acquisition was the same for both groups. One trial per day was given. Extinction of reward learning was then carried out for both groups. The group that received partial reinforcement of runway learning traversed the runway at a faster speed in extinction than the group that received continuous reinforcement of runway learning.

Trials on which the reinforcer is not present are called *N trials*, and trials on which the reinforcer is present are called *R trials*. In general, it has been found that an irregular series of N and R trials results in greater resistance to extinction of reward learning than does continuous reinforcement. This outcome is obtained when the partial and continuous reinforcement groups receive the same number of trials in acquisition, that is, when the partial reinforcement group receives fewer R trials than the continuous reinforcement group in acquisition.

Capaldi (1966) proposed (in terms of stimulus-stimulus theory) that during acquisition of discrete trial reward learning, stimuli stemming from consecutive N trials become associated with the reinforcer occurring on the R trial following these N trials. We will discuss the empirical support for this proposal below. First let us see how this proposal fits in with the equivalent of extinction approach to understanding resistance to extinction of learning.

Equivalents of extinction should not occur until the S_1-reinforcer or S_1-S_2 pairings responsible for acquisition of a response are replaced in extinction by pairings between S_1 and a stimulus different in kind from the reinforcer or S_2 occurring in acquisition. In acquisition, stimuli stemming from consecutive N trials become associated with the reinforcer occurring on the R trial following these N trials. An equivalent of extinction should therefore occur each time that the stimuli stemming from consecutive N trials are followed by the absence of the reinforcer. Extinction trials are by definition N trials. Because the stimuli stemming from N trials must be followed by the absence of the reinforcer for equivalents of extinction to occur, and because the instrumental response is made for each N trial that is completed, it follows that in extinction more than a single instrumental response will be made for each equivalent of extinction that occurs. In respect to continuous reinforcement of discrete trial reward learning, in acquisition only the stimuli stemming from R trials can become associated with the reinforcer occurring on the next R trial. Each N trial of extinction should therefore result in an equivalent of extinction. A single response should therefore be made for each equivalent of extinction that occurs. However, for partial reinforcement of discrete trial reward learning more than a single response should be made for each equivalent of extinction that occurs. Because the rate of decrease in the strength of a learned response in extinction usually should be determined by the number of equivalents of extinction that occur, it follows that partial reinforcement of discrete trial reward learning should result in more responses occurring in extinction, that is, a greater resistance to extinction of learning, than continuous reinforcement of discrete trial reward learning.

The equivalent of extinction approach explains the resistance to extinction of discrete trial reward learning with partial reinforcement in essentially the same way that it explains the resistance to extinction of responding on ratio schedules of reinforcement. In both cases stimuli that result from responding that is not immediately followed by the primary reinforcer are assumed to become associated with the reinforcer following these stimuli. Therefore, more than a single response should occur for each equivalent of extinction that takes place, thereby increasing resistance to extinction of responding.

Acquisition of N-R Sequences. As far as the discrete trial procedure is concerned, it is certainly not obvious that the stimuli stemming from consecutive N trials become associated with the reinforcer occurring on the R trial following these N trials. A typical discrete trial procedure involves the passage of time and the fact that the animal is out of the learning situation between trials. Can the animal recall the stimuli stemming from consecutive N trials on the next R trial? Also, it is true that these recalled stimuli become associated with the reinforcer occurring on the next R trial? Evidence exists to indicate that the answer to both these questions is yes.

Procedures which favor recall of the stimuli stemming from consecutive N trials on the R trial following these N trials should result in a stronger association between the stimuli stemming from consecutive N trials and the reinforcer occurring on the following R trial, that is, they should facilitate formation of N-R sequences. A stronger association between the stimuli stemming from consecutive N trials and the reinforcer occurring on the following R trial, that is, a better learned N-R sequence, should increase resistance to extinction of learning. Procedures which favor recall of the stimuli stemming from consecutive N trials on the R trial following these N trials should therefore result in stronger resistance to extinction of learning. This prediction has been supported (Mackintosh, 1970; Spivey & Hess, 1968).

In the Spivey & Hess study, two groups of rats both received four trials per day in acquisition. One group, the N-R group, received two N trials followed by two R trials, a NNRR sequence, each day. The second group, the R-N group, received two R trials and then two N trials, a RRNN sequence, each day. The time interval between trials on the runway occurring on the same day, the intertrial interval, was 15 seconds. The obtained result was that the N-R group ran faster in extinction than the R-N group.

This finding supports the assumption that an association is acquired between the stimuli stemming from N trials and the reinforcer occurring on the following R trial, and is at least partly responsible for the effect of partial reinforcement on resistance to extinction of discrete trial reward learning. The time delay between the last N trial and the next R trial was only 15 seconds for the N-R group, but was about 24 hours for the R-N group. Much more forgetting of the stimuli stemming from the two N trials should have occurred by the time the R trial following the N trials took place for the R-N group, than for the N-R group. Therefore, a stronger learned association between the stimuli stemming from the two N trials and the reinforcer occurring on the next R trial should have occurred for the N-R group than for the R-N group; this should have resulted in responding by the N-R group being more resistant to extinction than responding by the R-N group, which it was.

Suppose that in acquisition of runway learning, the stimuli stemming from N trials were followed by a large amount of a reinforcer (reward) for one group, and by a small amount of a reinforcer (reward) for a second group. Remember that a larger reward results in faster traversal of a runway in acquisition, and that extinction trials are N trials. If the first group acquires an association between the stimuli stemming from consecutive N trials and a large reward, and if the second group acquires an association between the stimuli stemming from consecutive N trials and a small reward, then in extinction the first group should traverse the runway faster than the second group. Thus, a group given an opportunity to acquire an association between the stimuli stemming from consecutive N trials and a large reward will traverse a runway faster in extinction than a group given the opportunity to acquire an association between the stimuli stemming from consecutive N trials and a small reward. This prediction is based on the assumption that the stimuli stemming from consecutive N trials become associated with the reinforcer that follows these stimuli.

This prediction and one quite similar have been supported (Capaldi, 1970; Leonard, 1969). Capaldi employed two groups, both of which received 22 acquisition trials on a runway. One trial was given each day. The small reward (S) was two .045 gram food pellets; the large reward (L) was twenty-two .045 gram food pellets. Group SNL received the following sequence of N, S, and L trials in the order indicated: SSSNNNLNNLNNNLSSSLNNLL. Group LNS received the following sequence of N, S, and L trials in the order indicated: LLLNNNSNN-SNNNSSLLLLNNSS. Note that for group SNL, consecutive N trials were always followed by a large reward; and that for group LNS consecutive N trials were always followed by a small reward. The obtained result was that the resistance to extinction of responding was greater for group SNL than for group LNS (Figure 6-6), a finding that supports the assumption that an acquired association between the stimuli stemming from consecutive N trials and the reinforcer occurring on the next R trial is at least partly responsible for the effect of partial reinforcement on resistance to extinction of discrete trial reward learning. This result also suggests that the stimuli stemming from consecutive N trials became associated with the reinforcer after these trials when the time intervening between the last N trial and the next R trial is 24 hours.

Other studies have demonstrated that the stimuli stemming from N trials become associated with the reinforcer occurring on the next R trial (Homzie, 1974; Wolach, Latta, Manshio, & Aderman, 1972). In addition, the stimuli stemming from N trials apparently become associated with stimuli other than the reinforcer occurring on the next R trial. For example, the stimuli stemming from N trials appear to become associated with stimulus consequences of other subsequently occurring N trials (Leonard & Capaldi, 1971), and with the stimuli produced by a slow rate of responding (Rashotte & Amsel, 1968).

Number of Consecutive N Trials. Capaldi (1966) essentially proposed that the stimuli stemming from different numbers of consecutive N trials can frequently be discriminated between, and that they come to be associated with the reinforcer occurring on the R trial following these N trials. This assumption leads to the prediction that resistance to extinction of discrete trial reward learning will increase as the number of consecutive N trials that are followed by a R trial increases.

Suppose that several times in acquisition ten consecutive N trials are followed by a R trial. The stimuli stemming from ten consecutive N trials should then become associated with the reinforcer occurring on the next R trial. In extinction, an animal should then have to make eleven consecutive responses for each equivalent of extinction to occur. Another animal receiving a maximum of, for example, two consecutive N trials followed by a R trial in acquisition, would have to make only three consecutive responses in extinction for each equivalent of extinction to occur. Generalizing from the above, we may say that as the number of consecutive N trials followed by a R trial increases, the number of responses occurring in extinction for each equivalent of extinction that takes place should increase. Because the rate of decrease in the strength of a learned response in extinction usually should be determined by the number of equivalents of extinction that occur, it follows that as the number of consecutive N trials followed by a R trial increases, so will the resistance to extinction of responding.

Similar reasoning led us to predict that as the number of responses

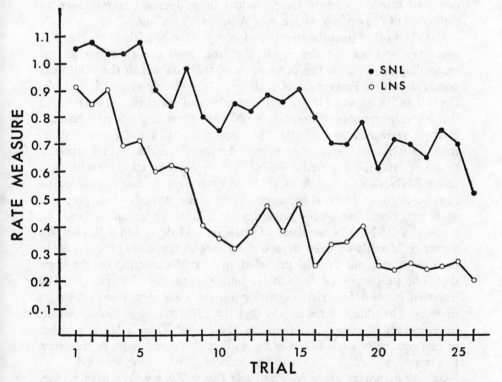

FIGURE 6-6. Responding in extinction by groups SNL and LNS. The rate measure equals the time (seconds) to traverse the runway. (Adapted from Capaldi, 1970.)

required for a reinforcement by a ratio schedule increases, so does the resistance to extinction of the acquired responding.

The expectation that an increase in the number of consecutive N trials followed by a R trial results in an increase in resistance to extinction of responding agrees with the finding that resistance to extinction of responding increases with a decrease in the percentage of responses followed by the primary reinforcer. Weinstock's (1958) study illustrates this. Independent groups of rats received the reinforcer following traversal of a runway on 100, 83, 67, 50, 33, and 17 percent of the total number of trials. As the percentage of trials on which the reinforcer was delivered decreased, the resistance to extinction of responding increased. Because the distribution of N and R trials was approximately random, the percentage of total trials on which the reinforcer occurred decreased with an increase in the number of consecutive N trials preceding a R trial. A decrease in the percentage of total trials on which the reinforcer occurred should therefore have resulted in an increase in resistance to extinction of responding, which was Weinstock's finding.

Variables other than the number of consecutive N trials preceding a R trial may account for the result that the resistance to extinction of responding increases as the percentage of trials on which the reinforcer occurs decreases. Percentage of such trials is obviously one such variable. Capaldi and Kassover (1970) and Gonzalez and Bitterman (1964) found that a greater number of consecutive N trials preceding a R trial resulted in more resistance to extinction of responding with the percentage of trials on which the reinforcer occurred equated. In the former study, a group of rats, 3N, received a RRNNNR sequence of trials on odd days, and a RNNNRR sequence of trials on even days during acquisition of runway learning. In both sequences, three consecutive N trials preceded an R trial occurring on the same day. In addition, a group of rats, 1N, received a RRNRRN sequence of trials on odd days, and a RNRRNN sequence of trials on even days with otherwise the same procedures. In both sequences, one N trial preceded an R trial occurring on the same day. The proportion of R trials for both groups was identical, .50. The intertrial interval for trials occurring on the same day was at least 20 minutes. The obtained result was that the 3N group was more resistant to extinction of responding than the 1N group. Thus, a larger number of consecutive N trials followed by an R trial resulted in more resistance to extinction of responding with the percentage of R trials equated.

Stimuli Stemming from N Trials and Image Theory. We have spoken of the stimuli stemming from consecutive N trials as becoming associated with the reinforcer occurring on the next R trial. But the stimuli stemming from consecutive N trials are obviously not present when the next R trial occurs. Nevertheless, some factor corresponding to these stimuli is present on the R trial following consecutive N trials; if some factor were not present, the indicated evidence for the establishment of N-R sequences should not have been obtained. Since the factor present on the R trial following consecutive N trials functions like a stimulus, although it is not a present stimulus, we may consider it to be an image of a stimulus, just as we assumed that an image of a response-produced stimulus controls responding on ratio and interval schedules. That an image of a stimulus controls responding obviously supports image theory.

The stimuli stemming from consecutive N trials occur prior to the R trial that follows the consecutive N trials. It therefore appears that the stimuli stemming from consecutive N trials are recalled on the R trial that follows the consecutive N trials. We know that stimuli of the general learning situation can result in recall of components of what has been learned, and we concluded that recall of a stimulus is mediated by the occurrence of an image of this stimulus. Therefore, the assumption that an image of the stimuli stemming from consecutive N trials occurs on the following R trial ties in with the conclusion that recall of a stimulus is mediated by the occurrence of an image of the stimulus that is recalled.

One other question requires discussion. If an image of the stimuli stemming from consecutive N trials occurs on the next R trial, we must then assume that an image of a stimulus can become associated with the reinforcer occurring on the R trial following consecutive N trials. This assumption is reasonable. An image of a stimulus should be able to become associated with a stimulus that follows it because images of stimuli and the effects of real stimuli are due to qualitatively identical temporary brain events.

Intertrial Interval. The length of the time interval between trials, that is, the intertrial interval, influences the effect of partial reinforcement on resistance to extinction of discrete trial reward learning.

Long intertrial intervals decrease the resistance to extinction of discrete trial reward learning established with partial reinforcement (Gonzalez & Bitterman, 1969; Mackintosh, 1970). In the latter study, the group that received long intertrial intervals, called the "spaced trials" group, received trials both in acquisition and extinction that were separated by an interval of 40-50 minutes. The group that was given short intertrial intervals, the "massed trials" group, received trials both in acquisition and extinction separated by 30 seconds. Ten trials were given per day in both acquisition and extinction. The massed trials group was more resistant to extinction of responding than the spaced trials group.

Suppose that some of the stimuli stemming from X consecutive N trials are forgotten. The "functional" stimuli stemming from X consecutive N trials would then correspond to less than X consecutive N trials. Therefore, forgetting some of the stimuli stemming from X consecutive N trials should be equivalent to the effect of reducing the number of consecutive N trials. A reduction in the number of consecutive N trials results in less resistance to extinction of responding. Also, forgetting the stimuli stemming from X consecutive N trials should increase as the length of the intertrial interval for these N trials increases. It follows that resistance to extinction of responding should decrease with an increase in the length of the intertrial interval, the result to be explained. An increase in the length of the intertrial interval may also increase the extent to which different numbers of consecutive N trials are confused, a possible outcome of which is that the average number of consecutive N trials comes to control responding, the consequence again being a decrease in resistance to extinction of responding.

The work of Spivey and Hess (1968) and similar studies suggest that the stimuli stemming from consecutive N trials are more likely to be forgotten as the length of the intertrial interval increases. In the Spivey and Hess study, the second of two consecutive N trials was followed by an R trial with a time delay of either 15 seconds or 24 hours. Formation of an association between the stimuli stemming from the consecutive N trials and the reinforcer occurring on the next R trial should have increased resistance to extinction of responding. The 15-second intertrial interval condition resulted in the greater resistance to extinction of responding. This result suggests that the briefer intertrial interval resulted in less forgetting of the stimuli stemming from consecutive N trials by the time the next R trial occurred.

Additional support for the assumption that the stimuli stemming from consecutive N trials are more likely to be forgotten as the length of the intertrial interval increases comes from studies in which single alternation of N and R trials, a RNRNRN . . . sequence of trials, occurs in acquisition. If the stimuli stemming from a preceding trial are recalled on the next trial, single alternation of N and R trials should result in a discrimination between N and R trials, with the rate of responding being greater on R trials than on N trials. This discrimination between N and R trials is, in fact, acquired. In addition, an increase in the length of the intertrial interval reduces or eliminates this discrimination between N and R trials (Katz, Woods, & Carrithers, 1966; Surridge & Amsel, 1966). The failure to acquire a discrimination between N and R trials with the single alternation training procedure indicates that the stimuli stemming from a previous trial are forgotten. The obtained result therefore supports the assumption that forgetting stimuli stemming from consecutive N trials increases with an increase in the length of the intertrial interval.

A related study (Johnson & Platt, 1973) involved introducing a time-out while rats were engaged in making the number of responses required for delivery of a primary reinforcer by a FR-like schedule. The time-out appears to have increased forgetting of the stimuli produced by responding that occurred prior to the introduction of the time-out.

Recall that a relatively long time interval between acquisition of a learned response and a test for its recall can result in relatively extensive forgetting of aspects of the learned response. This conclusion supports the possibility that an increase in the length of the intertrial interval results in more forgetting of the stimuli stemming from consecutive N trials by the time the R trial following these consecutive N trials occurs.

Predictions based on the assumptions involving N-R sequences and the number of consecutive N trials that precede an R trial have not always been supported (Haggbloom & Williams, 1971; Mackintosh, 1970). These results may be the outcome of fairly extensive forgetting of the stimuli stemming from consecutive N trials that precede an R trial.

Although an increase in the intertrial interval increases forgetting of the stimuli stemming from consecutive N trials, Capaldi's (1970) study that was described above suggests that the stimuli stemming from consecutive N trials can be partially recalled after as long as twenty-four hours. In addition, the single alternation training procedure may result in a discrimination between N and R trials even though the intertrial interval is twenty-four hours (Capaldi & Spivey, 1964; Davis & Brown, 1974).

Acquisition and Homogeneous Response Sequence Analysis. Partial reinforcement retards performance of the reward-trained runway response early in acquisition, but it has on occasion even resulted in asymptotic performance superior to that established with continuous reinforcement (Goodrich, 1959; Weinstock, 1958). The result that partial reinforcement does not consistently retard asymptotic performance of runway learning is probably best viewed as due to the formation of a homogeneous response sequence. The last member of a homogeneous response sequence causes a positive primary reinforcer to occur. The earlier analysis of homogeneous response sequences was based on the assumption that the stimulus produced by the last member of a homogeneous response sequence is a positive conditioned reinforcer. In partial reinforcement of discrete trial reward learning, it is clear that the response on a R trial does cause the reinforcer to occur; therefore the stimulus produced by this response should function as a positive conditioned reinforcer.

Usually much the same response occurs on N and R trials in partial reinforcement of discrete trial reward learning. Therefore, the stimulus produced by the response occurring on a N trial should also be a positive conditioned reinforcer.

If the stimuli stemming from consecutive N trials become associated with the reinforcer occurring on the next R trial, as was inferred, then the stimuli stemming from a N trial should be recalled on the next N trial. Also, the stimuli stemming from a N trial should include the stimulus produced by responding on that trial. Therefore, the stimulus produced by responding on the previous N trial should be recalled on the next N trial, and should be followed by the positive conditioned reinforcer resulting from responding on the next N trial. An association between an image of the stimulus produced by responding on the previous N trial and the positive conditioned reinforcer produced by responding on the next N trial should therefore be acquired, the consequence being that responding on the previous N trial should be strengthened through reward learning established with a conditioned reinforcer. This argument applies to responding on all N trials that are followed by a N trial. Therefore, responses occurring on consecutive N trials in partial reinforcement of discrete trial reward learning should function as a unit, and tend to be exhibited at not a particularly low rate. This last consideration is in accord with the finding that partial reinforcement does not consistently retard asymptotic performance of a runway response.

Partial Reinforcement and Extinction in Classical Conditioning. Partial reinforcement in typical (CS-UCS) classical conditioning consists of presenting the CS but not the UCS on some trials, while on other trials CS-UCS pairings are presented. Partial reinforcement in classical conditioning tends to increase the resistance to extinction of the CR. However, the effect of partial reinforcement on resistance to extinction of the CR is less consistent and of lower magnitude than the effect of partial reinforcement on resistance to extinction of reward learning (Thomas & Wagner, 1964; Wagner, Siegel, Thomas, & Ellison, 1964).

To account for the effect of partial reinforcement on the resistance to extinction of the CR, we will assume that stimulus consequences of consecutive UCS-absent (N) trials exist on the next UCS-present (R) trial. The stimulus consequences stemming from consecutive N trials should become associated with the UCS occurring on the next R trial. These assumptions are analogous to those made to account for the effect of partial reinforcement on the resistance to extinction of discrete trial reward learning. Because the stimuli stemming from consecutive N trials should become associated with the UCS, each N trial in extinction should not result in an equivalent of extinction. Because the rate of decrease in the strength of a learned response in extinction usually should be determined by the number of equivalents of extinction that occur, it follows that partial reinforcement in classical conditioning should increase the resistance to extinction of the CR.

The single alternation of N and R trials, that is, a RNRNRN . . . sequence of trials, in classical conditioning has been found to result in a discrimination between N and R trials (Longenecker, Krauskopf, & Bitterman, 1952; Poulas, Sheafor, & Gormezano, 1971). This finding indicates that in classical conditioning the stimuli stemming from a preceding trial can be recalled at the time the next trial occurs. The assumption that the stimuli stemming from consecutive N trials become associated with the UCS occurring on the R trial following these N trials therefore has some support.

Single alternation of N and R trials in classical conditioning sometimes results in little or no discrimination learning (Hoehler & Leonard, 1973; Leonard & Theios, 1967). This result suggests that it is typically less likely for animals to recall the stimuli stemming from consecutive N trials at the time a R trial occurs in classical conditioning than in instrumental conditioning. This result accords with the finding that the effect of partial reinforcement on the resistance to extinction of the CR is relatively inconsistent and low in magnitude.

Partial Reinforcement and Acquisition in Classical Conditioning. What is the effect of partial reinforcement on acquisition of the CR? Partial reinforcement in classical conditioning usually retards acquisition of the CR, including decreasing CR strength relatively late in training (Gormezano & Coleman, 1975; Thomas & Wagner, 1964). On the other hand, partial reinforcement in instrumental conditioning does not tend to impair performance relatively late in training. In fact, responding is faster on ratio schedules than on a CRF schedule, and the speed of the reward-trained runway response has sometimes been found to be greater when partial rather than continuous reinforcement is employed.

The explanation of the not particularly slow rate of performing a homogeneous response sequence that occurs on FR, VR, and VI schedules, that sometimes occurs on FI schedules, and that occurs in partial reinforcement of discrete trial reward learning is based on the conclusion that the stimulus produced by a member of a homogeneous response sequence is a positive conditioned reinforcer. But the stimulus produced by a CR should not be a positive conditioned reinforcer because the CR does not cause the UCS to occur. In addition, the stimulus produced by a CR will obviously not be a positive conditioned reinforcer when a negative UCS is employed. Therefore, the presumed failure of the stimulus produced by the CR to be a positive conditioned reinforcer explains why partial reinforcement usually results in a weaker CR than continuous reinforcement.

Heterogeneous Response Sequences

Heterogeneous responses are responses with dissimilar topographies and/or exhibited at different positions in space and/or with different operanda. A heterogeneous response sequence is a sequence of consecutive heterogeneous responses that occur in the same order over successive occurrences of a group of heterogeneous responses, the last member of which may cause a primary reinforcer to occur. What is meant by "same order" is that R_N must occur before R_{N-1}, that R_{N-1} must occur before R_{N-2}, and so on, where R_N, R_{N-1}, R_{N-2} are the members of the heterogeneous response sequence. Situations will be considered in which it is necessary that all members of the sequence be executed in the order defining the sequence for the last member of the sequence to cause a primary reinforcer to occur.

Much or perhaps all instrumentally conditioned behavior, when examined in sufficiently fine detail, can be viewed as a sequence of heterogeneous responses. For example, the instrumental response of a bar press can be thought of as part of a learned heterogeneous response sequence, the last member of which is movement from the bar to the reinforcer receptacle, and the first member of which is movement from the reinforcer receptacle to the bar.

Examples of Heterogeneous Response Sequences. A sequence of seven heterogeneous responses was learned by pigeons. The last member of the sequence, that is, the one causing the reinforcer to occur, was acquired first, the second to last response was acquired second, and so on (Napalkov, 1959; cited in Kelleher and Gollub, 1962). Table 6-1 summarizes the heterogeneous response sequence that was acquired. The first response taught was a peck of a lever. This response was reward-trained using food. Afterward, discrimination learning involving this response was carried out. A peck of the lever was followed by food in the presence of a white light, and was not followed by food in the absence of this light. The white light thus was a positive discriminative stimulus. The second to last response was a jump on platform. This response was acquired next by following its occurrence with the white light, which was then followed by a peck of the lever due to the previously established discrimination learning, and delivering food after the peck of the lever. After the jump-on-platform response was acquired, discrimination learning involving this response was developed by following it with the white light when a rotating black air vane was present, and by not following it with the white light when the rotating black air vane was not present. In addition, a peck of the lever in the presence of the white light continued to cause food to occur, but a peck of the lever in the presence of no particular event was not followed by food. Analogous procedures were carried out for the rest of the responses; acquisition of the jump onto floor of apparatus response, jump down onto a plaftorm response, and so on, occurring in that order.

Multiunit maze learning is also an example of a learned heterogeneous response sequence. The typical multiunit maze learning procedure resembles Napalkov's just described procedure in that a number of correct responses occurring in a set order must be made for the primary reinforcer to be delivered. It differs from Napalkov's procedure in several respects, however. In multiunit maze learning, the required responses are usually left and right turns at choice points. At least partly because it is relatively easy for rats (and other species as well) to acquire left-right position discriminations, and at least partly because an animal is permitted to retrace its steps after responding incorrectly at the choice

TABLE 6-1

Summary of Heterogeneous Response Sequence

Response	Discriminative Stimulus
1. peck lever	white light
1. jump on platform	rotating black air vane
3. jump on floor of apparatus	whistle
4. jump down onto a platform	blue light
5. jump onto rod	horn
6. jump into right section of apparatus	bell
7. jump into left section of apparatus and up onto a shelf	large white air vane

point in the multiunit maze learning procedure, it is not necessary that the response causing the reinforcer to occur be taught first, the response next closest to the reinforcer be taught second, and so on, as in Napalkov's procedure. Also, in multiunit maze learning the occurrence of each member of the required heterogeneous response sequence is not followed by the onset of a specific stimulus, such as the white light and rotating black air vane in Napalkov's procedure. Instead, stimulus changes occur because of an animal's movement through the maze.

Acquisition of complex motor skills by humans can be viewed as heterogeneous response sequences. Consider a jump shot in basketball. The responses leading up to release of the basketball differ in topography; in addition, these responses will tend to be made in the same order; and making these responses in the same order probably raises the probability that a jump shot will be successful.

Extinction and Equivalents of Extinction. Learned heterogeneous response sequences are not particularly resistant to extinction. For example, after perfect performance on a multiunit maze task, errors will often begin to occur after a few extinction trials.

However, there is a sense in which learned heterogeneous response sequences are relatively resistant to extinction. Consider extinction of the learning of a ten-unit maze task. An equivalent of extinction should not occur until the last choice point response is made. In acquisition, the stimulus produced by the last response of a heterogeneous response sequence should become associated with the positive primary reinforcer. Thus, an equivalent of extinction for the last response should occur when the last response is made, and is followed by the absence of the positive primary reinforcer. In addition, an equivalent of extinction occurring for the last response of the heterogeneous response sequence should then work backward to reduce the strength of the other members of the heterogeneous response sequence. We make the statement that this equivalent of extinction should work backward to affect responding because: (a) the association between the stimulus produced by the last member of a heterogeneous response sequence and the positive primary reinforcer helps to establish acquisition of the entire heterogeneous response sequence; and (b) the heterogeneous response sequence tends to function as a unit much as the homogeneous response sequence does (see below).

Given that an equivalent of extinction for responding on a ten-unit maze does not occur until the last response is followed by the absence of the primary reinforcer, and considering each choice point response as a separate response, it follows that ten responses should be exhibited prior to each equivalent of extinction that takes place. Because the rate of decrease in the strength of a heterogeneous response sequence usually should be determined by the number of equivalents of extinction that occur, it follows that the number of individual responses made in extinction should be about ten times greater when a ten-unit maze is learned than when a single unit maze is learned.

Explanations of the resistance to extinction of responding on ratio and interval schedules, and the resistance to extinction of discrete trial reward learning established with partial reinforcement are siimlar. In each of these cases, more than a single response should occur for each equivalent of extinction that should take place, and resistance to extinction of responding is thereby increased.

Analysis of Heterogeneous Response Sequences. How is a heterogeneous response sequence acquired?

The stimulus produced by the last member of a heterogeneous response sequence is followed by a positive primary reinforcer. According to discussion of homogeneous response sequences, the stimulus produced by the last member of a heterogeneous response sequence should therefore be a positive conditioned reinforcer. The next to last member of a heterogeneous response sequence is followed by the stimulus produced by the last member of a heterogeneous response sequence, a stimulus that should be a positive conditioned reinforcer. It follows that the next to last member of a heterogeneous response sequence should be acquired through reward learning established with a positive conditioned reinforcer. Because conditioned reinforcers function like primary reinforcers, just as the stimulus produced by a reward-trained response established with a primary reinforcer presumably is a conditioned reinforcer, the stimulus produced by a reward-trained response established with a conditioned reinforcer should also be a conditioned reinforcer. The stimulus produced by the next to last member of a heterogeneous response sequence should therefore establish reward learning of the next to next to last member of the heterogeneous response sequence, and so on.

The third-order classical conditioning result is also an instance of a sequence of acquired responses in which a learned response is established with a primary reinforcer, the next learned response is established with a conditioned reinforcer resulting from the learning established with a primary reinforcer, and the next to next learned response is established with a conditioned reinforcer resulting from the learning established with the primary reinforcer. For second-order classical conditioning, S_A is followed by the UCS in stage 1 and S_B is followed by S_A in stage 2. The result that S_B produces the CR in stage 2 is referred to as second-order conditioning, and this indicates that S_A is a conditioned reinforcer. In third-order classical conditioning, S_C is followed by S_B in stage 3; the result that S_C produces the CR is referred to as third-order conditioning, and this indicates that S_B is a conditioned reinforcer. The stimulus produced by the last member of a heterogeneous response sequence corresponds to S_A, the stimulus produced by the second to last member of a heterogeneous response sequence corresponds to S_B, and the stimulus produced by the third to last member of a heterogeneous response sequence corresponds to S_C.

In second- and third-order classical conditioning, S_B-S_A pairings occur in the absence of the UCS, and S_C-S_B pairings occur in the absence of S_A. Therefore, a tendency should develop for S_B and S_C to not produce the CR. This tendency should compete with the tendency for S_B and S_C to produce the CR through second- and third-order conditioning, respectively. An outcome of this competition probably would be that it would be quite difficult to demonstrate that S_D-S_C pairings, then S_E-S_D pairings, and so on, result in classical conditioning. An important point is that the corresponding learning occurring for heterogenous response sequences should not be similarly impaired. For a heterogeneous response sequence, each member of the sequence is followed by the reinforcer helping to establish it each time the entire sequence is performed. Occurrence of the primary reinforcer after execution of the last member should maintain the conditioned reinforcing strength of the stimulus produced by the last member of the sequence, occurrence of the last member of the sequence should maintain the conditioned reinforcing strength of the stimulus produced by the next to last member of the sequence, and so on.

Experimenter-delivered stimuli that follow a member of a heterogeneous response sequence should also be conditioned reinforcers for this member. For example, the white light in Napalkov's study was a positive discriminative stimulus in a reward-learning discrimination, therefore it probably was a positive conditioned reinforcer, and therefore it probably contributed to the reward learning of the response that caused it to occur. Because conditioned reinforcers function like primary reinforcers, a stimulus that is present just prior to the execution of an instrumental response established with a conditioned reinforcer should also be a conditioned reinforcer. In Napalkov's study, the rotating black air vane was present just prior to the execution of the instrumental response that caused the positive conditioned reinforcer of the white light to occur; thus the rotating black air vane should also be a conditioned reinforcer. A stimulus present just prior to the execution of an instrumental response established with a conditioned reinforcer should then contribute to establishing the instrumental response causing it to occur, and so on. For example, the rotating black air vane should have contributed to establishing the instrumental response that caused it to occur.

Heterogeneous Response Sequence Functions as a Unit. Homogeneous response sequences tend to be exhibited at a moderate rate at least, and tend to function as a unit in other respects. These tendencies were reasoned to be due to the fact that each member produces a stimulus that should be a positive conditioned reinforcer that establishes reward learning of the previous member of the homogeneous response sequence. Each member of a heterogeneous response sequence produces a stimulus that probably is a positive conditioned reinforcer establishing reward learning of the previous member of the heterogeneous response sequence. In addition, heterogeneous response sequences are usually executed at a relatively fast rate; typically there is little pause between performing members of a heterogeneous response sequence. Therefore, it is expected that heterogeneous response sequences should tend to function as a unit in respects other than tending to be exhibited at at least a moderate rate. Results support this prediction; they indicate that heterogeneous response sequences tend to function as a unit, since they show that members of heterogeneous response sequences are not affected to different extents by satiation and shock.

In a study by Mansfield and Rachlin (1970), in stage 1 a peck by pigeons on the right-hand of two keys resulted in illumination of the left-hand key for 10 seconds. If the left key was pecked during this 10-second interval, food was delivered and the left key was again made dark. Then another peck on the right key illuminated the left key again, and so on. The left key could not be illuminated unless the right key was pecked, and food could not be obtained unless the left key was pecked when it was illuminated. The heterogeneous response sequence that resulted in the delivery of food therefore consisted of a single peck on the right key, and then a single peck on the illuminated left key. In a second stage, the procedures were identical, except that the level of food deprivation was much reduced.

An abortive response was defined as a peck on the right key followed by a peck on the right key. It might be expected that the number of abortive responses would increase in stage 2, because an animal might not be sufficiently "motivated by hunger" to complete the heterogeneous response sequence of a single right key peck and then a single left key peck on the illuminated key. However, the obtained result was that the rate of abortive responses in stage 2 was actually less than it was in stage 1. Also, the rate of initiating the indicated heterogeneous response sequence was noticeably lower in stage 2 than it was in stage 1. Thus, reducing the extent of food deprivation decreased the rate of performing the indicated heterogeneous response sequence as a whole, but did not decrease the probability of one member being followed by a second member. Similarly, Sidman and Stebbins (1954) found that a decrease in deprivation level decreased the over-all rate of a homogeneous response sequence, but did not markedly affect the rates with which the members of the homogeneous response sequence were executed.

A related finding is that following the member of a heterogeneous response sequence occurring closer in time to receipt of the positive primary reinforcer with shock decreased the rate of performing the heterogeneous response sequence as a whole, rather than decreasing the rate with which this particular member of the heterogeneous response sequence was executed (Mansfield & Rachlin, 1970; Myer, 1973). In a later portion of Mansfield and Rachlin's study, the extent of food deprivation was increased, and pigeons were again exposed to the stage 1 (now stage 3) procedure. In a fourth stage, the procedure was identical, except that shock as well as food followed a peck on the illuminated left key.

An abortive response was again defined as a peck on the right key followed by a peck on the right key. It might be expected that the number of abortive responses would be greater in stage 4 than in stage 3, because in stage 4, but not in stage 3, a peck on the illuminated left key was followed by shock. In stage 4 a pigeon might peck the right key, then "remember" that shock would occur following a peck on the illuminated left key, and therefore be relatively unlikely to peck this key. However, the rate of abortive responses was somewhat less in stage 4 than in stage 3. In addition, the shock did decrease the rate of initiating the heterogeneous response sequence. Similarly, Dardano (1970, 1972) found that following a member of a homogeneous response sequence by shock tended to increase the length of the post-reinforcement pause more than it tended to decrease the rate at which the members of the homogeneous response sequence preceding shock occurred.

The complex motor skills of humans can be thought of as heterogeneous response sequences. These skills are sequences of smoothly integrated different component responses; they function as a unit.

Closeness in Position to Primary Reinforcer. Although heterogeneous response sequences tend to function as a unit, the strengths of all members of the sequence are not equal. The strengths of members of a heterogeneous response sequence tend to increase as the position of a response in the sequence moves closer to the position of the primary reinforcer. For example, a frequently obtained result is that errors at the choice points of multiunit mazes gradually decrease as the choice points become closer to the goal box where the primary reinforcer is received (Gardner & Gamboni, 1971; Kimble, 1961, pp. 145-149). The response closest, next closest, and so on, in time to the occurrence of the primary reinforcer may be referred to as the position 1, position 2, and so on, response. Catania (1971) showed that the strength of a member of a response sequence decreased as the position of that member moved from position 2 to position 12.

The response strengths of the earlier members of a homogeneous response sequence are also frequently somewhat weaker than the response strengths of the members occurring closer in position to the primary reinforcer. This statement is obviously valid for responding on FI schedules. In respect to FR schedules, Platt and Senkowski (1970) and Weiss (1961) found that the rate at which the earlier members of a homogeneous response sequence occurred was less than the rate at which later members of the sequence occurred.

Responses closer in position to the primary reinforcer should be better learned, because the primary reinforcer should establish stronger learning than conditioned reinforcers that are the stimuli produced by the members of a learned response sequence; and also because the strength of these conditioned reinforcers may decrease progressively as the members of a learned response sequence are further away in position from the primary reinforcer. In addition, it is possible that different delays of primary reinforcement may act directly on the members of a learned response sequence to affect their strengths.

Partial Reinforcement and Strength of Conditioned Reinforcer

Effect of Partial Primary Reinforcement. Partial primary reinforcement has been found to increase the reinforcing strength of a conditioned reinforcer (Armus & Garlich, 1961; D'Amato, Lachman, & Kivy, 1958). In the former study, in stage 1, one group of rats was trained to bar press on a FR 5 food reinforcement schedule. The sound of the food delivery apparatus and a flash of light close to the food receptacle area immediately preceded each delivery of food by the FR 5 schedule, and did not occur at other times. A second group received food following bar pressing on a continuous reinforcement schedule. Each press produced the sound of the food delivery apparatus, the flash of light, and then food. In stage 2, two new levers were introduced into the chamber. In this stage, for both groups, each press of the left lever was followed by the sound of the food delivery apparatus and the flash of light of stage 1. The group responding on the FR 5 food reinforcement schedule during stage 1 responded proportionately more on the left lever in stage 2 than the group responding on a continuous reinforcement schedule in stage 1. This result indicates that a partial primary reinforcement schedule resulted in a stronger conditioned reinforcer than a continuous primary reinforcement schedule. Note that for the group responding on the FR 5 schedule in stage 1, although the primary reinforcer was delivered on a partial reinforcement schedule, the conditioned reinforcer was always followed by the primary reinforcer.

Maintained Conditioned Reinforcer Strength. Studies to be described suggest that the reinforcing strength of a conditioned reinforcer established by being paired with a primary reinforcer delivered on a partial reinforcement schedule may be unusually resistant to extinction. Such results are of interest at least in part because they support the possibility that conditioned reinforcers establish and maintain human behavior in the long-term absence of primary reinforcement.

Kelleher (1961) showed that a conditioned reinforcer previously paired with food deliveries on a FI 5 (minute) schedule maintained reward learning for about 3½ hours in the absence of primary reinforcement, with no sign that the reinforcing strength of the conditioned reinforcer diminished. In addition, conditioned reinforcers have been shown to maintain responding in the absence of primary reinforcement for time intervals much longer than 3½ hours (Thomas, 1969; Zimmerman, 1969).

At one point in Thomas's study, pigeons responded on a combined (multiple) FR 80 food reinforcement FR 10 conditioned reinforcement schedule. The FR 80 food reinforcement component schedule and the FR 10 conditioned reinforcement component schedule were alternated, each component schedule being in effect for 4 minutes, and then followed by the other component schedule. When the FR 80 food reinforcement component schedule was in effect, a triangle was present on the response key. When the FR 10 conditioned reinforcement component schedule was in effect, the same response key was illuminated with green light. The sound of the food delivery apparatus and illumination of the food receptacle area with white light preceded each delivery of food by the FR 80 food reinforcement component schedule. The same auditory and visual compound stimulus was used as the conditioned reinforcer delivered by the FR 10 component reinforcement schedule; that is, the auditory and visual compound stimulus was delivered immediately after each block of ten pecks on the key when it was green. The response rate in the presence of the green light was moderate, which points to the auditory and visual compound stimulus being a conditioned reinforcer.

In the next stage of the study, the FR 80 food reinforcement component schedule was eliminated. Now the FR 10 conditioned reinforcement component schedule alternated with a 5-minute period of extinction in which all lights in the apparatus were off. This combined (multiple) FR 10 conditioned reinforcement extinction schedule remained in effect for 20 consecutive experimental sessions. The pattern of responding occurring on the FR 10 conditioned reinforcement component schedule often resembled the pattern that occurred on the same component schedule when it alternated with the FR 80 food reinforcement component schedule in the previous stage. Figure 6-7 shows a typical cumulative record for a single pigeon for a period of responding on the FR 10 conditioned reinforcement component schedule when it alternated with the extinction component schedule. The jags indicate occurrences of the conditioned reinforcer. At other times responding on the FR 10 conditioned reinforcement component schedule almost did not occur. Thus, responding on the FR 10 conditioned reinforcement component schedule was variable. But pigeons did continue to respond on the FR 10 conditioned reinforcement component schedule when it alternated with extinction over the 20 experimental sessions without any noticeable decline in over-all response rate occurring.

Zimmerman (1969) reported an even more dramatic instance of the maintenance of the reinforcing strength of a conditioned reinforcer. A conditioned reinforcer delivered on a FR 5 schedule usually maintained responding at a rate of 3.8 responses per minute or more, even though primary reinforcement had been terminated from 77 to 105 experimental sessions previously. The pause and run pattern of responding typical of FR schedules was often exhibited while the FR 5 conditioned reinforcement schedule was in effect. In addition, the over-all response rate on the FR 5 conditioned reinforcement schedule was greater than on a conditioned reinforcement schedule that typically results in a relatively low rate of responding.

Partial Reinforcement, Development of Social Behavior, and Contact Comfort

Appropriate behavior by children appears to be followed by contact comfort delivered by familiar adults on a VR schedule in which the sizes of the FR components of the VR schedule increase as the child grows older. This possibility has implications for understanding how appropriate adult behavior is maintained.

Age, VR Schedule, and Size of Ratio. It was previously concluded that a familiar person is relatively likely to follow a child's behaving appropriately with contact comfort, and thereby contribute to the instrumental conditioning of appropriate behavior by the child. As the child grows older, he probably must on the average exhibit longer sequences of appropriate behavior for contact comfort to be delivered by another person. In other words, as the child grows older other people are probably on the average increasingly unlikely to deliver contact comfort to the child after the child exhibits only a few individual appropriate responses. If it is true that on the average the maturing child must exhibit longer sequences of appropriate behavior, that is, a greater number of individual appropriate behavior responses, in order to receive contact comfort from other people, then contact comfort is being delivered contingent on the child's appropriate behavior on a VR schedule in which the sizes of the FR components comprising the VR schedule are gradually increasing.

College students do expect that as a child grows older, parents are increasingly likely to deliver contact comfort only after the child exhibits progressively longer sequences of appropriate behavior (Beatty & King, 1977). A parent was described in a paragraph as requesting a 4-, 7-, or 10-year-old son or daughter to engage in an activity—cleaning up his or her room, playing on his or her own, or working on a puzzle he or she previously had trouble doing. The paragraph then indicated that the child started on and continued to do what the parent requested, and that the parent eventually came over and hugged the child. Subjects were requested to indicate the time duration between the child's starting on the activity the parent requested, and the moment the parent hugged the child.

College students expected that the time elapsed between the child's initiating an activity requested by a parent and the parent's hugging the child would increase as the age of the child increased. The children were described in the paragraphs as engaging in the requested activity throughout the interval in question, and therefore can be thought of as exhibiting a greater number of individual appropriate behavior responses as the expected length of time preceding hugging increased. The result therefore supports the idea that the number of individual appropriate behavior responses required for delivery of contact comfort increases as the child grows older; in other words, it supports the idea that the child is instrumentally conditioned to behave appropriately with contact comfort delivered on a VR schedule in which the size of the FR components comprising the VR schedule gradually increases as the child grows older.

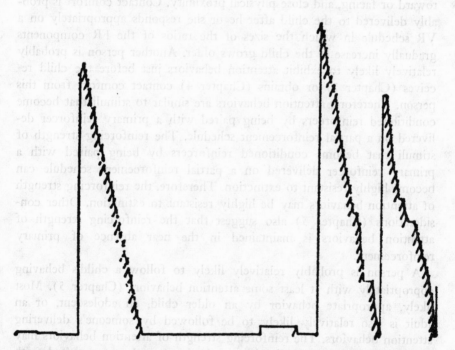

FIGURE 6-7. Responding on a FR 10 conditioned reinforcement component schedule when it alternated with an extinction component schedule. (Hendry, D. P., Conditioned Reinforcement **(Homewood, IL: The Dorsey Press, 1969 C.) p. 86. Reproduced with permission of the publisher.)**

The resistance to extinction of responding on a ratio schedule with a large ratio is quite strong. In addition, gradually increasing the size of a ratio is a good way to establish responding on a ratio schedule in which the response requirement is large. Therefore, a changing VR schedule in which the average response requirement for delivery of the reinforcer increases is a very good procedure for maintaining responding during long periods of absence of the reinforcer or in extinction. The child appears to be instrumentally conditioned for responding appropriately with contact comfort with the changing VR schedule. It follows that as the child grows older, possibly even when the child becomes an adult, his or her appropriate behavior is maintained because, in part, it was instrumentally conditioned in childhood on the changing VR schedule under consideration.

Age, VR Schedule, Size of Ratio, and Attention Behaviors. Attention behaviors include smiling, talking in a pleasant tone of voice, turning toward or facing, and close physical proximity. Contact comfort is probably delivered to the child after he or she responds appropriately on a VR schedule in which the sizes of the ratios of the FR components gradually increase as the child grows older. Another person is probably relatively likely to exhibit attention behaviors just before the child receives (Chapter 2) or obtains (Chapter 4) contact comfort from this person. Therefore, attention behaviors are similar to stimuli that become conditioned reinforcers by being paired with a primary reinforcer delivered on a partial reinforcement schedule. The reinforcing strength of stimuli that become conditioned reinforcers by being paired with a primary reinforcer delivered on a partial reinforcement schedule can become highly resistant to extinction. Therefore, the reinforcing strength of attention behaviors may be highly resistant to extinction. Other considerations (Chapter 5) also suggest that the reinforcing strength of attention behaviors is maintained in the near absence of primary reinforcement.

A person is probably relatively likely to follow a child's behaving appropriately with at least some attention behaviors (Chapter 5). Most likely, appropriate behavior by an older child, an adolescent, or an adult is also relatively likely to be followed by someone's delivering attention behaviors. The reinforcing strength of attention behaviors may be highly resistant to extinction partly because they are paired with contact comfort delivered on a VR schedule in which the sizes of the ratios of the FR components gradually increase as the child grows older. It follows that the older child, adolescent, or adult may behave appropriately in the near absence of primary reinforcement because, in part, behaving appropriately is the outcome of reward learning established with attention behaviors.

Summary

FR and FI schedules tend to result in a pause-and-run and scallop pattern of responding, respectively. Both VR and VI schedules typically result in responding at a steady rate. The assumption that the stimulus produced by making the number of responses required for a reinforcement by a FR schedule becomes associated with the reinforcer is supported. It is reasoned that an image of the stimulus produced by the number of responses required for a reinforcement by a FR schedule controls responding on a FR schedule, which supports image theory's assumption that an image of the stimulus produced by an instrumental response mediates performance of this response. Equivalents of extinction should occur only when the stimulus produced by the number of responses required for a reinforcement by a FR schedule is followed by the absence of the reinforcer, which accounts for the result that responding on FR schedules is relatively resistant to extinction. The assumption that the strength of a learned response in extinction usually should be determined by the number of equivalents of extinction that occur is supported. It is necessary to know the stimuli that control responding in applying the equivalent of extinction approach. The assumption that a time-correlated response-produced stimulus corresponding to the length of an FI interval functions as a positive discriminative stimulus for an instrumental response that is a single response is supported. It is reasoned that an image of the time-correlated response-produced stimulus corresponding to the duration of an FI interval controls responding while the FI interval elapses. Equivalents of extinction should occur only when the time-correlated response-produced stimulus corresponding to the length of an FI interval occurs, the single instrumental response occurs, and the absence of the reinforcer follows, which accounts for the result that responding on FI schedules is relatively resistant to extinction. The over-all response rate on ratio schedules is usually greater than on interval schedules, probably because responding at a relatively fast rate on ratio schedules is acquired due to the reduced delay of primary reinforcement that ensues. The post-reinforcement pause is due to post-reinforcement stimuli functioning as the S— of a go/no-go successive discrimination. The post-reinforcement pause increases with an increase in the size of the ratio or length of the interval of a FR or FI schedule, a result viewed in terms of the effect of the similarity between discriminative stimuli on discrimination learning. A post-reinforcement pause result supports the assumption that an image of the stimulus produced by an instrumental response occurs immediately prior to the execution of this response. Homogeneous response sequences occur on ratio and interval schedules, tend to be exhibited at a not particularly low rate, and tend to function as a unit in other respects. Homogeneous response sequences tend to function as a unit, probably mostly because the stimulus produced by each member of the sequence is a positive conditioned reinforcer establishing reward learning of the preceding member of the sequence.

The assumption that stimuli stemming from consecutive N trials become associated with the reinforcer occurring on the next R trial, together with the equivalent of extinction approach, explain the effect of partial reinforcement on the resistance to extinction of discrete trial reward learning. The assumption pertaining to the stimuli stemming from consecutive N trials is supported. The assumption that stimuli stemming from a specific number of consecutive N trials become associated with the reinforcer occurring on the R trial following the consecutive N trials, together with the equivalent of extinction approach, explain the result that resistance to extinction of discrete trial reward learning increases with a decrease in the percentage of trials on which the reinforcer is obtained. It is reasoned that an image of the stimuli stemming from consecutive N trials occurs on the R trial following these N trials. This means that an image of a stimulus can become associated with the stimulus that follows it, an assumption that follows from image theory. Resistance to extinction of discrete trial reward learning established with partial reinforcement decreases with an increase in the length of the intertrial interval, probably at least partly because an increase in the intertrial interval increases forgetting of the stimuli stemming from X consecutive N trials; the "functional" stimuli that result correspond to less than X consecutive N trials. Asymptotic performance of a discrete trial reward-trained response established with partial reinforcement does not tend to be impaired, probably because the stimulus stemming from each execution of the reward-trained response is a positive conditioned reinforcer that establishes reward learning of the previous response. Partial reinforcement in classical conditioning tends to increase the resistance to extinction of the CR, which can be explained in essentially the same way that partial reinforcement's effect on resistance to extinction of discrete trial reward learning is explained. Partial reinforcement in classical conditioning usually decreases CR strength relatively late in training (as well as earlier), probably because the CR does not produce a stimulus that is a conditioned reinforcer.

Heterogeneous response sequences are described. An increase in the resistance to extinction of responding will occur with an increase in the number of members of a heterogeneous response sequence, if the unit for a response is taken as the occurrence of a single member of the heterogeneous response sequence; this increase is accounted for by the equivalent of extinction approach. The stimulus produced by a member of a heterogeneous response sequence should be a positive conditioned reinforcer that contributes to the reward learning of the preceding member. It follows that heterogeneous response sequences should be executed relatively quickly, which they are, and they should function as a unit in other respects, which they do. The strengths of members of heterogeneous and homogeneous response sequences tend to increase as the position of a member of the sequence moves closer to the position of the primary reinforcer.

Partial primary reinforcement has been found to increase the reinforcing strength of a conditioned reinforcer. Partial primary reinforcement schedules have established conditioned reinforcers that maintained their reinforcing strength over very long periods of absence of the primary reinforcer.

Appropriate behavior in later childhood, adolescence, and adulthood may be maintained, in part, because (a) appropriate behavior is followed by contact comfort delivered on a VR schedule in which the sizes of the ratios of the FR components increase with an increase in the age of the child; and (b) appropriate behavior causes attention behaviors to occur, the reinforcing strength of which is sustained, in part, because they precede contact comfort delivered on a VR schedule in which the sizes of the ratios of the FR components increase with an increase in the age of the child.

REFERENCES

ALFERINK, L. A., & CROSSMAN, E. K. Mixed fixed-ratio schedules: Priming and the pre-ratio pause. *Psychol. Rec.*, 1975, 25, 123-130.

ANDERSON, A. C. Time discrimination in the white rat. *J. Comp. Psychol.*, 1932, 13, 27-55.

ARMUS, H. L., & GARLICH, M. M. Secondary reinforcing strength as a function of schedule of primary reinforcement. *J. Comp. Physiol. Psychol.*, 1961, 54, 56-58.

BEATTY, L. A., & KING, D. L. Students' expectations involving parents' contact comfort, duration of child's appropriate behavior, and child's age. *Psychol. Rep.*, 1977, 41, 175-178.

BOREN, J. J. Resistance to extinction as a function of the fixed ratio. *J. Exp. Psychol.*, 1961, 61, 304-308.

BROWN, T. G., & FLORY, R. K. Schedule-induced escape from fixed-interval reinforcement. *J. Exp. Anal. Behav.*, 1972, 17, 395-403.

CAPALDI, E. J. Partial reinforcement: A hypothesis of sequential effects. *Psychol. Rev.*, 1966, 73, 459-477.

CAPALDI, E. J. An analysis of the role of reward and reward magnitude in instrumental learning. In J. H. Reynierse (Ed.), *Current Issues in Animal Learning*. Lincoln: University of Nebraska Press, 1970.

CAPALDI, E. J., & KASSOVER, K. Sequence, number of nonrewards, anticipation, and intertrial interval in extinction. *J. Exp. Psychol.*, 1970, 84, 470-476.

CAPALDI, E. J., & SPIVEY, J. E. Stimulus consequences of reinforcement and nonreinforcement: Stimulus traces or memory. *Psychon. Sci.*, 1964, 1, 403-404.

CATANIA, A. C. Reinforcement schedules: The role of responses preceding the one that produces the reinforcer. *J. Exp. Anal. Behav.*, 1971, 15, 271-287.

CATANIA, A. C., & REYNOLDS, G. S. A quantitative analysis of the responding maintained by interval schedules of reinforcement. *J. Exp. Anal. Behav.*, 1968, 11, 327-383.

COHEN, P. S., & LOONEY, T. A. Schedule-induced mirror responding in the pigeon. *J. Exp. Anal. Behav.*, 1973, 19, 395-408.

COLE, J. M., & LITCHFIELD, P. M. Stimulus control of schedule-induced aggression in the pigeon. *Psychon. Sci.*, 1969, 17, 152-153.

CROSSMAN, E. K. The effects of fixed-ratio size in multiple and mixed fixed-ratio schedules. *Psychol. Rec.*, 1971, 21, 535-544.

CROSSMAN, E. K., HEAPS, R. S., NUNES, D. L., & ALFERINK, L. A. The effects of number of responses on pause length with temporal variables controlled. *J. Exp. Anal. Behav.*, 1974, 22, 115-120.

D'AMATO, M. R., LACHMAN, R., & KIVY, P. Secondary reinforcement as affected by reward schedule and the testing situation. *J. Comp. Physiol. Psychol.*, 1958, 51, 734-741.

DARDANO, J. F. Fractional punishment of fixed-ratio performance. *J. Exp. Anal. Behav.*, 1970, 14, 185-198.

DARDANO, J. F. Self-imposed timeouts under increasing response requirements. *J. Exp. Anal. Behav.*, 1972, 17, 433-441.

DARDANO, J. F., Self-imposed timeouts under increasing response requirements. *J. Exp. Anal. Behav.*, 1973, 19, 269-287.

DAVIS, S. F., & BROWN, B. R. Response patterning in the operant-conditioning situation with twenty-four hour intertrial interval. *Percept. Mot. Skills*, 1974, 38, 231-234.

DENNY, M. R., WELLS, R. H., & MAATSCH, J. L. Resistance to extinction as a function of the discrimination habit established during fixed-ratio reinforcement. *J. Exp. Psychol.*, 1957, 54, 451-456.

DEWS, P. B. A behavioral output enhancing effect of imipramine in pigeons. *Inter. J. Neuropharm*, 1962, 1, 265e-272.

FELTON, M., & LYON, D. O. The post-reinforcement pause. *J. Exp. Anal. Behav.*, 1966, 9, 131-134.

FERSTER, C. B., & SKINNER, B. F. *Schedules of Reinforcement.* New York: Appleton-Century-Crofts, 1957.

GARDNER, R. A., & GAMBONI, W. R. Anticipatory responses in a linear maze. *Psychon. Sci.*, 1971, 25, 277-278.

GONZALEZ, R. C., & BITTERMAN, M. E. Resistance to extinction in the rat as a function of percentage and distribution of reinforcement. *J. Comp. Physiol. Psychol.*, 1964, 58, 258-263.

GONZALEZ, R. C., & BITTERMAN, M. E. Spaced-trials partial reinforcement effect as a function of contrast. *J. Comp. Physiol. Psychol.*, 1969, 67, 94-103.

GOODRICH, K. P. Performance in different segments of an instrumental response chain as a function of reinforcement schedule. *J. Exp. Psychol.*, 1959, 57, 57-63.

GORMEZANO, I., & COLEMAN, S. R. Effects of partial reinforcement on conditioning, conditional probabilities, asymptotic performance, and extinction of the rabbit's nictitating membrane response. *Pavlov. J. Biol. Sci.*, 1975, 10, 13-22.

HAGGBLOOM, S. J., & WILLIAMS, D. T. Increased resistance to extinction following partial reinforcement: A function of N-length or percentage of reinforcement? *Psychon. Sci.*, 1971, 24, 16-18.

HOEHLER, F. K., & LEONARD, D. W. Classical nictitating membrane conditioning in the rabbit (Oryctolagus cuniculus): Single alternation with differential intertrial intervals. *J. Comp. Physiol. Psychol.*, 1973, 85, 277-288.

HOMZIE, M. J. Nonreward anticipated: Effects on extinction runway performance in the rat. *Anim. Learn. Behav.*, 1974, 2, 77-79.

HURSH, S. R., & FANTINO, E. Relative delay of reinforcement and choice. *J. Exp. Anal. Behav.*, 1973, 19, 437-450.

HUTCHINSON, R. R., AZRIN, N. H., & HUNT, G. M. Attack produced by intermittent reinforcement of a concurrent operant response. *J. Exp. Anal. Behav.*, 1968, 11, 489-495.

JOHNSON, D. M., & PLATT, J. R. Short-term retention of location within a homogeneous behavior sequence in rats. *J. Comp. Physiol. Psychol.*, 1973, 84, 111-117.

KATZ, S., WOODS, G. T., & CARRITHERS, J. H. Reinforcement aftereffects and intertrial interval. *J. Exp. Psychol.*, 1966, 72, 624-626.

KELLEHER, R. T. Schedules of conditioned reinforcement during experimental extinction. *J. Exp. Anal. Behav.*, 1961, 4, 1-5.

KELLEHER, R. T., & GOLLUB, L. R. A review of positive conditioned reinforcement. *J. Exp. Anal. Behav.*, 1962, 5, 543-597.

KILLEEN, P. On the measurement of reinforcement frequency in the study of preference. *J. Exp. Anal. Behav.*, 1968, 11, 263-269.

KIMBLE, G. A. *Hilgard and Marquis' Conditioning and Learning* (2nd ed.). New York: Appleton-Century-Crofts, 1961.

LEONARD, D. W. Amount and sequence of reward in partial and continuous reinforcement. *J. Comp. Physiol. Psychol.*, 1969, 67, 204-211.

LEONARD, D. W., & CAPALDI, E. J. Successive acquisitions and extinctions in the rat as a function of number of nonrewards in each extinction session. *J. Comp. Physiol. Psychol.*, 1971, 74, 102-107.

LEONARD, D. W., & THEIOS, J. Classical eyelid conditioning in rabbits under prolonged single alternation conditions of reinforcement. *J. Comp. Physiol. Psychol.*, 1967, 64, 273-276.

LONGENECKER, E. D., KRAUSKOPF, J., & BITTERMAN, M. E. Extinction following alternating and random reinforcement. *Am. J. Psychol.*, 1952, 65, 580-587.

LYDERSEN, T., & CROSSMAN, E. K. Fixed-ratio discrimination: Effects of response-produced blackouts. *J. Exp. Anal. Behav.*, 1974, 22, 547-551.

MACKINTOSH, N. J. Distribution of trials and the partial reinforcement effect in the rat. *J. Comp. Physiol. Psychol.*, 1970, 73, 341-348.

MANSFIELD, R. J. W., & RACHLIN, H. C. The effect of punishment, extinction, and satiation on response chains. *Learn. Motiv.*, 1970, 1, 27-35.

MORGAN, M. J. Fixed interval schedules and delay of reinforcement. *Q. J. Exp. Psychol.*, 1970, 22, 663-673.

MOWRER, O. H., & JONES, H. M. Habit strength as a function of the pattern of reinforcement. *J. Exp. Psychol.*, 1945, 35, 292-311.

MYER, J. S. Effects of punishing elements of a simple instrumental-consummatory response chain. *J. Exp. Anal. Behav.*, 1973, 19, 251-257.

NAPALKOV, A. V. Chains of motor conditioned reactions in pigeons. *Zh. Vyssh. Nervn. Deiatel.*, 1959, 9, 615-621.

NEURINGER, A. J., & SCHNEIDER, B. A. Separating the effects of interreinforcement time and number of interreinforcement responses. *J. Exp. Anal. Behav.*, 1968, 11, 661-667.

OVERMANN, S. R., & DENNY, M. R. The free-operant partial reinforcement effect: A discrimination analysis. *Learn. Motiv.*, 1974, 5, 248-257.

PLATT, J. R., & JOHNSON, D. M. Localization of position within a homogeneous behavior chain: Effects of error contingencies. *Learn. Motiv.*, 1971, 2, 386-414.

PLATT, J. R., & SENKOWSKI, P. C. Response-correlated stimulus functioning in homogeneous behavior chains. In J. H. Reynierse (Ed.), *Current Issues in Animal Learning*. Lincoln: University of Nebraska Press, 1970.

POULAS, C. X., SHEAFOR, P. J., & GORMEZANO, I. Classical appetitive conditioning of the rabbit's (Oryctolagus cuniculus) jaw-movement response with a single-alternation schedule. *J. Comp. Physiol. Psychol.*, 1971, 75, 231-238.

RASHOTTE, M. E., & AMSEL, A. Transfer of slow-response rituals to extinction of a continuously rewarded response. *J. Comp. Physiol. Psychol.*, 1968, 66, 432-443.

RICHARDS, R. W., & RILLING, M. Aversive aspects of a fixed-interval schedule of food reinforcement. *J. Exp. Anal. Behav.*, 1972, 17, 405-411.

RILLING, M. Number of responses as a stimulus in fixed interval and fixed ratio schedules. *J. Comp. Physiol. Psychol.*, 1967, 63, 60-65.

SCHNEIDER, B. A. A two-state analysis of fixed-interval responding in the pigeon. *J. Exp. Anal. Behav.*, 1969, 12, 677-687.

SIDMAN, M., & STEBBINS, W. C. Satiation effects under fixed-ratio schedules of reinforcement. *J. Comp. Physiol. Psychol.*, 1954, 47, 114-116.

SPIVEY, J. E., & HESS, D. T. Effect of partial reinforcement trial sequences on extinction performance. *Psychon. Sci.*, 1968, 10, 375-376.

SURRIDGE, C. T., & AMSEL, A. Acquisition and extinction under single alternation and random partial-reinforcement conditions with a 24-hour intertrial interval. *J. Exp. Psychol.*, 1966, 72, 361-368.

THOMAS, E., & WAGNER, A. R. Partial reinforcement of the classically conditioned eyelid response in the rabbit. *J. Comp. Physiol. Psychol.*, 1964, 58, 157-158.

THOMAS, J. R. Maintenance of behavior by conditioned reinforcement in the signaled absence of primary reinforcement. In D. P. Hendry (Ed.), *Conditioned Reinforcement*. Homewood, Ill.: Dorsey, 1969.

WAGNER, A. R., SIEGEL, S., THOMAS, E., & ELLISON, G. D. Reinforcement history and the extinction of a conditioned salivary response. *J. Comp. Physiol. Psychol.*, 1964, 58, 354-358.

WEINSTOCK, S. Acquisition and extinction of a partially reinforced running response at a 24-hour intertrial interval. *J. Exp. Psychol.*, 1958, 56, 151-158.

WEISS, R. F. Response speed, amplitude, and resistance to extinction as joint functions of work and length of behavior chain. *J. Exp. Psychol.*, 1961, 61, 245-256.

WILKIE, D. M. Stimulus control of responding during a fixed-interval reinforcement schedule. *J. Exp. Anal. Behav.*, 1974, 21, 425-432.

WOLACH, A. H., LATTA, K. II, MANSHIO, D., & ADERMAN, M. Determinants of rate of extinction in successive acquisitions and extinctions. *Psychon. Sci.*, 1972, 27, 257-259.

YOSHIOKA, J. G. Weber's law in the discrimination of maze distance by the white rat. *University of California Publications in Psychology*, 1929, 4, 155-184.

ZAMBLE, E. Conditioned motivational patterns in instrumental responding of rats. *J. Comp. Physiol. Psychol.*, 1969, 69, 536-543.

ZIMMERMAN, J. Meanwhile . . . back at the key: Maintenance of behavior by conditioned reinforcement and response-independent primary reinforcement. In D. P. Hendry (Ed.), *Conditioned Reinforcement*. Homewood, Ill.: Dorsey, 1969.

CHAPTER 7

Contrast Effects
and Other Topics

$\mathbb{A}$ contrast effect occurs when (a) the nature and/or strength of a response exhibited in situation 1 is altered when situation 2 occurs in sufficiently close physical and temporal proximity to situation 1; and (b) the effect of situation 2 on the response occurring in situation 1 is in a direction opposite (in contrast) to the nature and/or strength of the response taking place in situation 2. Contrast effects on responses to perceived stimuli and contrast effects on learned responses will be discussed. Topics not closely related to contrast effects will also be considered.

Contrast Effects on Responses to Perceived Stimuli

Contrast Effect: Response to Perceived No Particular Event. Previously discussed results indicate that, in general, the response to no particular event is altered when no particular event occurs in sufficiently close physical and temporal proximity to a reinforcer. These results are instances of a contrast effect on the response to the perceived stimulus of no particular event.

Adelman and Maatsch (1956) showed that rats were highly likely to escape from a box at the end of a runway during extinction of a reward-trained runway traversal response. The stimulus of food in the box can be thought of as stimulus 1, and the stimulus of the box in the absence of food, that is, in extinction, can be thought of as stimulus 2, the stimulus of no particular event. The two stimuli clearly occurred in just about the same physical location. In addition, they were at least somewhat temporally proximal to each other, because stimulus 2 followed stimulus 1 by a not very long time period. Because food, stimulus 1, is approached, the response of escaping from stimulus 2, the stimulus of no particular event, is obviously the opposite (contrast) of the approach response to stimulus 1. Thus, food, stimulus 1, occurring in relatively close physical and temporal proximity to no particular event, stimulus 2, apparently caused stimulus 2 to elicit a response opposite in direction to stimulus 1. Therefore, the reinforcer, food, appears to have been responsible for a contrast effect operating on the response to the perceived stimulus of no particular event.

Another study (Azrin, Hutchinson, & Hake, 1966) indicated that a reinforcer occurring in relatively close physical and temporal proximity to no particular event resulted in an altered emotional response to no particular event. Azrin et al. found that when a period of response-independent delivery of food alternated with a brief period of the absence of food, aggressive behavior occurred relatively frequently during the brief periods of absence of food. However, when an extended period of absence of food occurred, aggressive behavior occurred relatively infrequently. These findings indicate a contrast effect on the response to the perceived stimulus of no particular event. Only when the absence of food, that is, the stimulus of no particular event, occurred in relatively close temporal proximity to food was no particular event relatively likely to elicit aggressive behavior. Food and the absence of food occurred in the same physical location. The nature of the response to the absence of food, that is, no particular event, was in a direction opposite to the response to food; presenting food to a food-deprived animal would normally decrease rather than increase the frequency of aggressive behavior. It follows that the aggressive behavior elicited by no particular event when it occurred in relatively close physical and temporal proximity to food was a contrast effect on the response to the perceived stimulus of no particular event.

Contrast Effect: Response to Perceived Reinforcer. Contrast effects operate on responses to perceived reinforcers as well as on responses to perceived neutral stimuli.

Observations of Tinklepaugh (1932) suggest that when two positive reinforcers occur in relatively close physical and temporal proximity, the less positive reinforcer is at least temporarily escaped from and avoided, and elicits aggressive behavior. A banana was placed under a cup while subjects, monkeys, watched. Without the monkeys seeing, the banana was replaced with a piece of lettuce. When the monkeys picked up the cup and perceived the lettuce underneath it, they did not quickly eat the lettuce as they normally do when lettuce alone is used. They either did not eat the lettuce at all, or they delayed eating it; that is, they escaped from and then at least temporarily avoided the lettuce. In addition, when the banana was replaced with a piece of lettuce, they often exhibited aggressive behavior, such as shrieking at the observers.

The lettuce was placed under the same cup as the banana, and soon after the banana was placed there. The lettuce and banana therefore occurred in the same physical location and in relatively close temporal proximity. The escape and avoidance response elicited by the perceived lettuce was in a direction opposite (in contrast) to the relatively strong approach and continued perception response normally elicited by a banana. In addition, the aggressive responding elicited by the perceived lettuce was in a direction opposite to the presumed relatively strong positive emotional response normally elicited by a banana. The escape and avoidance and aggressive response to the perceived lettuce was therefore a contrast effect on responding to a perceived reinforcer.

Flaherty and Largen (1975) also obtained contrast effects on responding to perceived positive reinforcers. They showed that when a 32 percent sucrose solution and a 4 percent sucrose solution occurred in relatively close physical and temporal proximity, that the strength of the response to the perceived 32 percent sucrose solution was increased, and the strength of the response to the perceived 4 percent sucrose solution was decreased. The obtained results were contrast effects. The increase in the strength of responding to the 32 percent sucrose solution was in a direction opposite to the weaker strength of the drinking response elicited by the 4 percent sucrose solution.

On each test day, a tube containing sucrose solution was placed in a chamber in the left position and remained there until 1 minute after the first lick by subjects, rats. At the end of the 1-minute interval, the left tube was retracted and the right tube was put in place. The right tube remained in place until 1 minute after the occurrence of the first lick. Then the right tube was retracted and the left tube was put in place, and so on. In all, three presentations of the left and right tubes occurred per day. On some days the left tube contained 32 percent sucrose solution and the right tube contained 4 percent sucrose solution; on other days the left tube contained 4 percent sucrose solution and the right tube contained 32 percent sucrose solution; on other days both tubes contained 32 percent sucrose solution; and on other days both tubes contained 4 percent sucrose solution. The measures of the strength of responding to the perceived sucrose solutions were rate of licking and amount of solution consumed. The rate of licking and amount of solution consumed on days when only the 32 percent sucrose solution was available was greater than the rate of licking and amount of solution consumed on days when only the 4 percent sucrose solution was available. More importantly, both the lick rate and amount of solution consumed for the 32 percent sucrose solution was greater on days when the 32 percent sucrose solution alternated with the 4 percent sucrose solution than on days when only the 32 percent sucrose solution was available. In addition, both the lick rate and amount of solution consumed for the 4 percent sucrose solution was lower on days when the 4 percent sucrose solution alternated with the 32 percent sucrose solution than on days when only the 4 percent sucrose solution was available.

Consider the tube containing 32 percent sucrose solution as stimulus 1, and the tube containing 4 percent sucrose solution as stimulus 2. When the reinforcers occurred on the same day, that is, when they occurred in relatively close temporal proximity, the strength of responding to the 32 percent sucrose solution was enhanced, that is, affected in a direction opposite to the weaker responding elicited by stimulus 2. Likewise, when the reinforcers occurred on the same day, that is, when they occurred in relatively close temporal proximity, the strength of responding to the 4 percent sucrose solution was depressed, affected in a direction opposite to the stronger responding elicited by stimulus 1. Contrast effects on the responses to perceived (tasted) reinforcers therefore occurred. The obtained results were replicated using a between-groups experimental design and a rate of intake measure of strength of responding to a perceived reinforcer (Figure 7-1). Vogel, Mikulka, and Spear (1968) obtained a similar result.

Contrast effects on the responses to perceived positive reinforcers when these reinforcers occur in relatively close physical and temporal proximity to shock also appear to have been obtained. Amsel and Maltzman (1950) first permitted water-deprived rats to drink water. On subsequent days the rats were shocked immediately prior to being exposed to water. The shock increased the amount of water consumed. Sterritt (1962) shocked food-deprived rats for a 5-second period out of each 1 minute that elapsed. The shocked rats were more likely to eat food during the 5-second period in which they were shocked than rats that were not shocked.

Contrast Effect: Stimuli 1 and 2 Are Simultaneous. Except in the Sterritt (1962) study, the events that were referred to as stimuli 1 and 2 above occurred successively. For example, in the study in which lettuce was escaped from and avoided the lettuce and banana were presented at different times. A contrast effect most likely also operates on the response to a perceived stimulus that is simultaneously present with a second stimulus.

Consider an animal is deprived of food, food is present in the experimental chamber, and the animal can get very close to the food but cannot touch it because a wire screen is placed around it. The animal would certainly try to get past or through the screen. In addition, it is likely that it would exhibit aggressive behavior if an appropriate target for aggressive behavior were present. Also, responses indicating emotional distress, such as whining, would probably tend to occur as the animal continued to remain outside the wire screen. We may think of stimulus 1

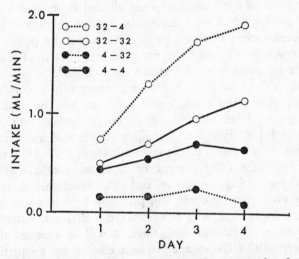

FIGURE 7-1. Contrast effect on the strength of responding to a perceived reinforcer. One group was given two tubes, each of which contained 32 percent sucrose solution. A second was given two tubes, each of which contained 4 percent sucrose solution. A third was given one tube containing the 32 percent solution and a second tube containing the 4 percent solution. The two tubes were presented alternately over the same day. (Adapted from Flaherty and Largen, 1975.)

as the stimuli outside the wire screen, that is, no particular event; and of stimulus 2 as the food inside the screen. Because the animal would probably continue to attempt to exit from stimulus 1 and because stimulus 1 would probably elicit aggressive responses and other responses indicative of emotional distress, the animal may be said to be trying to escape from stimulus 1. The animal would probably not ordinarily attempt to escape from stimulus 1, the stimulus complex outside the wire screen, the stimulus of no particular event. Therefore, the response of escaping from stimulus 1 should be viewed as the outcome of the fact that stimulus 1 and stimulus 2, the food, occur simultaneously. In addition, the response of escaping from stimulus 1 is in a direction opposite to the approach response that is elicited by food. Thus, the response of escaping from stimulus 1 appears to be a contrast effect resulting when no particular event and a reinforcer occur simultaneously. It will be assumed that, in general, contrast effects on responding to no particular event and a reinforcer occur when these two stimuli occur simultaneously.

The strength of the escape response elicited by no particular event is probably greater when an inaccessible positive reinforcer is simultaneously perceived, than when no particular event and a positive reinforcer occur successively. Consider the situation in which food has been made inaccessible by placing a wire screen around it. Most likely an animal that perceives food behind a screen will repeatedly make "determined" attempts to obtain the food, interpretable as making relatively strong exiting responses from the stimulus of no particular event. In addition, an animal that perceives food behind a screen will most likely aggress strongly against a suitable target (when it is not trying to get the food), and will otherwise exhibit signs of obvious emotional distress. The strength of the exiting, aggressive, and other emotional distress responses elicited by no particular event will probably be less when no particular event alternates in time with the occurrence of food, rather than when it is simultaneously present with food. It will be assumed that, in general, the strength of the escape response elicited by no particular event when it simultaneously occurs with a positive reinforcer is greater than when no particular event and a positive reinforcer alternate in time. The analogous assumption will be made for no particular event and a negative reinforcer.

Consider a similar situation. An animal is deprived of food; two kinds of food are present in the experimental situation; and a wire screen is placed around the "preferred" food. Repeated attempts to obtain the preferred food should occur, although certainly not as strongly as when the two relevant stimuli are no particular event and food. In addition, if the animal were forced to remain with the less preferred food outside of the wire screen, it may be relatively likely to aggress against a suitable target, and show some other signs of emotional distress. Therefore, perception of the less positive of two simultaneously present positive reinforcers may be viewed as eliciting escape. A perceived positive reinforcer is not ordinarily escaped from. In addition, escape from the less preferred positive reinforcer is a response in a direction opposite to the approach response that is made to the preferred positive reinforcer. Thus, the response of escaping from the less preferred positive reinforcer would be a contrast effect resulting when the less preferred positive reinforcer and the more preferred positive reinforcer occur simultaneously. It will be assumed that, in general, contrast effects on responding to perceived reinforcers occur when these reinforcers occur simultaneously, and one reinforcer is preferred over a second reinforcer. It will also be assumed that contrast effects on responding to perceived reinforcers that are simultaneously present are greater than contrast effects on responding to perceived reinforcers that are successively present.

Contrast Effects in Perception. Contrast effects in perception occur when stimuli occur successively in about the same physical location and in relatively close temporal proximity, and when stimuli occur simultaneously in about the same physical location (Helson, 1964).

As an example of the successive occurrence of stimuli resulting in a contrast effect on perception, consider two blocks that visually appear to be identical, but that differ in weight. Lifting the heavier block is known to reduce the perceived heaviness of the lighter block when the lighter block is lifted soon after the heavier block is lifted. Thus, the description of the heaviness of the lighter block is affected by previously lifting the heavier block in a direction opposite to the perceived heaviness of the heavy block. This outcome is therefore an instance of a contrast effect on the perception of the heaviness of the lighter block resulting from the heavier and lighter blocks occurring in relatively close physical and temporal proximity.

The magnitude of the contrast effect on perception increases with an increase in the temporal proximity of the relevant stimuli (Cohen, Hansel, & Sylvester, 1954; Needham, 1935). In the former study, three tones of different frequency were presented in succession. The frequencies of the tones varied from low to medium to high, or vice versa. The task for subjects was to judge the pitch of the middle tone by adjusting its frequency so that it appeared intermediate in pitch between the first and third tones. The frequency of the intermediate tone that the subjects determined moved closer to the frequency of the third tone as the time interval separating the occurrence of the first tone from the occurrence of the intermediate tone decreased. Therefore, as the length of the time interval between the first tone and the intermediate tone decreased, the effect on the perception of the pitch of the intermediate tone was increasingly in the direction opposite to the perceived pitch of the first tone. A contrast effect on the perceived pitch of the intermediate tone therefore occurred, and it increased as the length of the time interval separating the first tone and the intermediate tone decreased. The fact that temporal proximity between two stimuli similarly affects the magnitude of contrast effects on the responses of animals to stimuli of interest to learning psychologists, and human perceptions of stimuli suggests that the processes for these contrast effects are highly related.

Stimuli simultaneously occurring in about the same physical location produce contrast effects on perception (Helson, 1964). For example, if in a dark room a cone of light is made to fall on a disc that would ordinarily be perceived as black, the disc tends to be perceived as white. It therefore appears that the dark surround, stimulus 1, makes the disc, stimulus 2, look much less black than usual, an effect on the disc in the direction opposite (in contrast) to the perceived blackness of the surround.

The magnitude of the contrast effects on perception that result from simultaneously occurring stimuli is generally quite large. Consider the situation involving the disc just described. It is highly unlikely that the perceived brightness of the disc would have been as greatly affected if the dark surround were terminated just before the disc was illuminated with the cone of light.

Similarly, it was concluded above that the magnitude of a contrast effect on the strength of a response to a perceived stimulus is larger when the second relevant stimulus occurs simultaneously rather than successively. In addition, the finding that the magnitude of a contrast effect on both responses and perceptions increases with a decrease in the length of the time interval separating the two relevant stimuli supports the conclusion that the magnitude of a contrast effect on a response to a perceived stimulus is larger when this stimulus occurs simultaneously with the other relevant stimulus.

Analysis of Contrast Effects on Responses to Perceived Stimuli. Two simultaneously present stimuli can result in contrast effects on responses to perceived stimuli and on perceptions of stimuli. Other contrast effects, including contrast effects on learned responses, are viewed as derivative results.

In the discussion that follows we continue to speak of an image of a stimulus occurring, even though we cannot be sure that an animal experiences a stimulus when the temporary brain event that corresponds to it takes place. That contrast effects on responses to perceived stimuli and on perceptions of stimuli occur when the stimuli of interest, stimulus 1 and stimulus 2, are simultaneously present means that the temporary brain events corresponding to stimulus 1 and stimulus 2 somehow are responsible for these contrast effects. Suppose that the temporary brain event corresponding to one of the stimuli of interest occurred as the result of the existence of an image of this stimulus. Because images of stimuli and the effects of real stimuli are due to qualitatively identical temporary brain events, it follows that contrast effects should be obtained when the temporary brain event corresponding to stimulus 1 is stimulus-produced, and the temporary brain event corresponding to stimulus 2 exists because an image of stimulus 2 occurs. Therefore, a contrast effect on the response to a perceived stimulus that is the result of a second stimulus that is not simultaneously present is assumed to occur through the existence of an image of this second stimulus.

The magnitude of the contrast effect on a response to a perceived stimulus is greater when the relevant stimuli occur simultaneously rather than successively. Simultaneously present stimuli obviously result in very large amounts of their corresponding temporary brain events. Therefore, a maximal contrast effect on the response to a perceived stimulus occurs when the amounts of temporary brain events corresponding to the relevant stimuli are very large. A corollary is that the magnitude of the contrast effect on the response to a perceived stimulus increases with an increase in the amount of temporary brain event corresponding to the relevant stimulus not currently perceived. This last assumption means that the magnitude of the contrast effect on the response to a perceived stimulus should increase with the vividness of the image of the stimulus of interest not currently perceived.

The reason that it is necessary for stimulus 2 to occur in sufficiently close physical and temporal proximity to stimulus 1 in order for a contrast effect on responding to stimulus 1 to be obtained appears to be that a relatively close physical and temporal proximity of stimulus 1 to stimulus 2 facilitates the occurrence of an image of stimulus 2 when stimulus 1 is currently being perceived. Close physical proximity between stimulus 1 and stimulus 2—for example, stimuli 1 and 2 occurring in the same apparatus—should tend to result in an image of the stimulus not currently present. The effect of reminder stimuli on recall suggests that the stimuli of a learning apparatus can result in images of component stimuli of the acquired learning. Furthermore, it was reasoned that the stimuli of the learning apparatus result in images of the stimulus produced by the number of responses required for a reinforcement by a ratio schedule, the time-correlated stimulus corresponding to the length of the FI interval, and the stimuli stemming from consecutive N trials.

As for temporal proximity and an image of the stimulus not currently present, forgetting of the characteristics of stimuli tends to occur with the passage of time. In addition, the stimuli stemming from consecutive N trials are increasingly forgotten as the length of the intertrial interval increases. Recall of a stimulus is mediated by the occurrence of an image of this stimulus. The relatively incomplete recall of a stimulus that takes place because of forgetting may be due to the occurrence of a relatively faint image of this stimulus. Therefore, as the time separating the occurrence of the currently present stimulus from the occurrence of the other relevant stimulus decreases, vividness of the image of the other relevant stimulus may increase. The magnitude of the contrast effect on the response to a perceived stimulus increases with an increase in the vividness of the image of the relevant stimulus not currently perceived. It follows that as the time separating the occurrence of the currently perceived stimulus from the occurrence of the other relevant stimulus decreases, the magnitude of the contrast effect on the response to the currently perceived stimulus should increase, which it does.

Contrast Effects on Learned Responses

Contrast effects on learned responses are viewed as the outcome of factors correlated with the occurrence of contrast effects on responses to perceived stimuli.

Classical Conditioning and Instrumental Conditioning. When classical conditioning, instrumental conditioning, and discrimination learning were discussed, it was reasoned that (a) when no particular event occurs in sufficiently close physical and temporal proximity to a positive reinforcer, no particular event tends to be escaped from and continued to not be perceived; and (b) when no particular event occurs in sufficiently close physical and temporal proximity to a negative reinforcer, no particular event tends to be approached and continued to be perceived. Studies have indicated that no particular event is escaped from and elicits aggressive responses when it occurs in relatively close physical and temporal proximity to a positive reinforcer. These findings were viewed as a contrast effect on the response to the perceived stimulus of no particular event. Contrast effects on the responses to and perceptions of stimuli are widespread, and include (a) contrast effects on the response to a perceived reinforcer when it occurs in sufficiently close physical and temporal proximity to a second reinforcer; (b) contrast effects on the response to no particular event when it and a reinforcer occur simultaneously; (c) contrast effects on the response to a perceived reinforcer when it and another reinforcer occur simultaneously; (d) contrast effects on the perception of a stimulus when it occurs in sufficiently close physical and temporal proximity to a second stimulus; and (e) contrast effects on the perception of a stimulus when it and a second stimulus occur simultaneously. The fact that contrast effects are so widespread, so likely to occur, supports the assumption that no particular event is either approached and continued to be perceived or escaped from and avoided when it occurs in sufficiently close physical and temporal proximity to a reinforcer (as long as it is possible to make these responses), since these responses to no particular event should also occur through contrast.

Our analyses of basic classical conditioning, instrumental conditioning, and discrimination learning findings rest on the assumption that no particular event is either approached and continued to be perceived or escaped from and avoided when it occurs in sufficiently close physical and temporal proximity to a reinforcer. In regard to classical conditioning, consider, for example, the result that a CS paired with the absence of a positive UCS is escaped from and avoided. A stimulus paired with the absence of a positive UCS involves no particular event occurring in relatively close physical and temporal proximity to the positive UCS. No particular event should therefore tend to be escaped from and avoided through a contrast effect occurring on the response to the perceived stimulus of no particular event. A CS paired with this no particular event should then come to tend to be escaped from and avoided.

The classical conditioning result that a CS paired with the absence of a positive UCS comes to be escaped from and avoided is a contrast effect on a learned response. Escape from and avoidance of a CS, a learned response that results from a CS being paired with the absence of a positive UCS, is opposite in direction to the learned response of approaching and continuing to perceive a CS, the learned response that results when a CS is paired with the occurrence of a positive UCS. The finding that a CS paired with the absence of a positive UCS comes to be escaped from and avoided, a contrast effect on a learned response, is based on the assumption that a contrast effect operates on the response to the perceived stimulus of no particular event. All contrast effects on learned responses may be viewed as the outcome of factors correlated with the occurrence of contrast effects on responses to perceived stimuli.

The assumption that no particular event is either approached and continued to be perceived or escaped from and avoided when it occurs in sufficiently close physical and temporal proximity to a reinforcer is also critical for our analysis of the avoidance, escape, omission, and response-terminates-reward learning types of instrumental conditioning. Consider escape learning, for example. In escape learning, no particular event occurs in relatively close physical and temporal proximity to a negative reinforcer. It should therefore be approached and continued to be perceived through the operation of a contrast effect on the response to the perceived stimulus of no particular event. The stimulus produced by the instrumental response in escape learning is regularly followed by no particular event occurring in relatively close physical and temporal proximity to a negative reinforcer. A classically conditioned association should therefore occur between the response-produced stimulus and no particular event. An animal should thus attempt to approach the stimulus produced by the instrumental response in escape learning—which, in a sense, it may do by bringing it about, as image theory assumes.

In respect to discrimination learning, recall that the S— of a go/no-go successive discrimination and the stimulus produced by responding to the S— of a simultaneous discrimination are escaped from and avoided. Escape from and avoidance of a S— are learned responses that are in a direction opposite to the responses of approaching and continuing to perceive a S+ that occur in discrimination learning. Escape from and avoidance of S— are therefore contrast effects on learned responses. These contrast effects on learned responses were viewed as the outcome of no particular event tending to be escaped from and avoided. This is consistent with the fact that in go/no-go successive discrimination learning no particular event occurs in relatively close physical and temporal proximity to the positive reinforcer. Therefore, the learned tendency to escape from and avoid S— may be viewed as the outcome of factors correlated with the occurrence of a contrast effect on the response to no particular event.

Certain conditioned reinforcement results also bear on the assumption that no particular event tends to be either approached and continued to be perceived or escaped from and avoided when it occurs in relatively close physical and temporal proximity to a reinforcer. A stimulus paired with the absence of a positive reinforcer establishes escape learning; a CS paired with the absence of a negative reinforcer establishes reward and omission learning; and a CS paired with the termination of a negative reinforcer establishes reward learning. These results could not have been obtained unless the CSs employed tended to be approached and continued to be perceived or escaped from and avoided. And if such CSs tend to be responded to in this way, presumably the stimulus of no particular event with which they were paired tends to be either approached and continued to be perceived or escaped from and avoided through the operation of a contrast effect.

Multiple Schedules. Contrast effects on learned responses frequently involve multiple schedules of reinforcement. Multiple schedules are composed of component reinforcement schedules. The identities of the component schedules can vary widely, and there can be more than two component schedules. For all multiple schedules, a different stimulus is present while a particular component schedule is in effect. In addition, the experimenter determines when each of the component schedules is in effect, and more than one component schedule is never operative at the same time. Multiple schedules are usually employed with the free responding procedure.

A go/no-go successive discrimination is usually established using a multiple reinforcement schedule. A ratio or interval schedule is one component of the multiple schedule, and extinction is the second component of the multiple schedule. A stimulus (S+) is present when the positive reinforcement component schedule is in effect, and a different stimulus (S—) is present when the extinction component schedule is operative.

The predominant characteristics of responding on individual reinforcement schedules are exhibited when these schedules are components of multiple schedules. For example, in one study (Ferster & Skinner, 1957, p. 505), when a multiple (MULT) FR 50 FI 10 (minute) schedule was employed, response runs occurred at a fast rate when the FR 50 component schedule was in effect, and a scallop pattern of responding took place when the FI 10 component schedule was operative.

This finding indicates that the MULT FR 50 FI 10 schedule resulted in discrimination learning, because discrimination learning is defined as the exhibition of different learned responses in the presence of somewhat similar stimuli. Multiple schedules typically result in discrimination learning because the predominant characteristics of responding on individual reinforcement schedules are usually exhibited when these schedules are components of multiple schedules. Thus, the stimulus present while a component of a multiple schedule is in effect is called a *discriminative stimulus*. This practice is followed even when the components of the multiple schedule are identical, as, for instance, for a MULT VI 1 VI 1 schedule.

Two Positive Reinforcement Schedules and Nature of Learned Response. Basic results in classical and instrumental conditioning are due to factors correlated with the occurrence of a contrast effect on the response to the perceived stimulus of no particular event. A contrast effect alters the nature of the response to no particular event when it occurs in sufficiently close physical and temporal proximity to a reinforcer: through contrast, no particular event is likely rather than unlikely to be approached and continued to be perceived or escaped from and avoided. Contrast effects on learned responses occur that appear to involve contrast effects that alter the nature of the response to a perceived reinforcer. Naturally, this possibility supports the conclusion that basic classical and instrumental conditioning results are due to a contrast effect altering the nature of the response to the perceived stimulus of no particular event.

Cohen and Looney (1973) and Cole and Litchfield (1969) showed that a discriminative stimulus present when the larger of two FR components of a multiple schedule was in effect came to produce more aggressive responding than the discriminative stimulus present when the smaller of the two FR components of the multiple schedule was operative. In the former study, pigeons responded on a MULT FR 25 FR 100 schedule. Subsequently, the MULT FR 25 FR 100 schedule remained in effect, but the discriminative stimuli correlated with a component schedule were reversed. Originally, a green keylight was present when the FR 100 component schedule was in effect; subsequently it was present when the FR 25 component schedule was operative. Originally a white keylight was present when the FR 25 schedule was in effect; subsequently it was present when the FR 100 schedule was in effect. On the first reversal session, the discriminative stimulus previously correlated with the FR 100 component schedule continued to produce more aggressive responses; for two different pigeons 97 percent and 76 percent of the aggressive responses on the first reversal session occurred in the presence of the green keylight. The result that the discriminative stimulus correlated with the FR 100 component schedule came to produce aggressive responding is a contrast effect on a learned response. This aggressive responding is opposite in direction to the positive emotional response presumably produced by the discriminative stimulus correlated with the FR 25 component schedule.

The obtained result may seem surprising. Why should a stimulus present when food is being received on a FR component schedule come to produce aggressive responses? Recall that when two positive reinforcers, banana and lettuce, occurred in relatively close physical and temporal proximity, that the perceived less positive reinforcer, the lettuce, elicited aggressive responses. The FR 100 component schedule in the Cohen and Looney study may be viewed as the less positive reinforcement condition, because the FR 100 component schedule delivered food with a greater delay of reinforcement than the FR 25 component schedule. In addition, the FR 100 and FR 25 component reinforcement schedules occurred in the same physical location and in fairly close temporal proximity. Therefore, the possibility that the stimuli involved with the FR 100 component schedule elicited aggressive behavior through a contrast effect on the response to perceived stimuli is reasonable. The discriminative stimulus correlated with the FR 100 component schedule may have acquired the ability to produce aggressive responses through being paired with stimuli that elicit aggressive responses through the operation of a contrast effect. Note that this explanation of a contrast effect on a learned response is based on the assumption that a contrast effect on a learned response is the outcome of factors correlated with the occurrence of contrast effects on responses to perceived stimuli.

The discriminative stimulus correlated with the less positive of two component positive reinforcement schedules of a multiple schedule produces inhibitory effects on learned responding. The discriminative stimuli correlated with the less positive and more positive component reinforcement schedules will be referred to as S— and S+, respectively. The S— of a multiple schedule in which the two components were both positive reinforcement schedules reduced the rate of responding that the S+ produced when S— and S+ were simultaneously presented in a summation procedure (Adams & Allen, 1971; Weiss, 1972). The S— of a multiple schedule in which the two components were both positive reinforcement schedules resulted in an inhibitory stimulus generalization gradient (Weisman, 1969). In addition, the peak shift result was obtained when two unequal positive reinforcement schedules were employed as components of a multiple schedule (Guttman, 1959; Terrace, 1968).

The S— of a typical go/no-go successive discrimination is escaped from, produces inhibitory effects on learned responses, and produces aggressive responses. Because the S— of a multiple schedule in which the two components are positive reinforcement schedules produces learned aggressive responses and inhibitory effects on learned responses, it is likely that it is also escaped from. Escape from the S— of a multiple schedule with two positive reinforcement component schedules is clearly a contrast effect on a learned response. Escape from S— is a response in a direction opposite to the approach response that is made to the S+

of a multiple schedule with two positive reinforcement component schedules.

The inference that the S— of a multiple schedule in which the two components are positive reinforcement schedules is escaped from may also seem surprising. Why should a stimulus present when food is being delivered by a positive reinforcement schedule come to be escaped from? When two positive reinforcers, banana and lettuce, occurred in relatively close physical and temporal proximity, the perceived less positive reinforcer, the lettuce, was escaped from and at least temporarily avoided. In a multiple schedule, the less positive and more positive component reinforcement schedules occur in the same physical location and in fairly close temporal proximity. It follows that the stimuli involved with the less positive component reinforcement schedule may tend to at least temporarily be escaped from and avoided. S— is a stimulus paired with the less positive component reinforcement schedule, and therefore it too should be at least temporarily escaped from.

Basic results in classical and instrumental conditioning are the outcome of a contrast effect operating on the response to the perceived stimulus of no particular event. This conclusion was based on the assumption that no particular event can be either approached and continued to be perceived or escaped from and avoided through the operation of a contrast effect. It was indicated that the less positive of two positive reinforcement conditions tend to elicit escape and avoidance behavior and aggressive behavior through a contrast effect on the response to perceived stimuli. If the less positive of two positive reinforcement conditions tends to elicit these responses through contrast, then it certainly would appear that the perceived stimulus of no particular event can also elicit them through contrast.

Go/No-Go Discrimination Learning and Strength of Learned Response. Contrast effects on the nature of a learned response—whether or not a stimulus comes to be approached and continued to be perceived or escaped from and avoided and whether or not it comes to produce aggressive responses—have been described. Contrast effects on the strength of learned responses also occur. In particular, a go/no-go successive discrimination results in a contrast effect on the strength of a learned response.

Gutman, Sutterer, and Brush (1975) trained rats to press a lever on a MULT VI 30 (seconds) VI 30 (seconds) food reinforcement schedule. The stimulus, S_1, present when the first VI 30 component schedule was in effect, was a noise; the stimulus, S_2, present when the second VI 30 component schedule was in effect, was a light from a small lamp. Subsequently, the reinforcement schedule for one group of rats was changed to MULT VI 30 EXT; that is, this group received a typical go/no-go successive discrimination. S_1 continued to be present when the VI 30 component schedule was in effect, and S_2 was present when the extinction (EXT) component schedule was operative. A control group continued to respond on the original MULT VI 30 VI 30 schedule. The group that received the MULT VI 30 EXT schedule pressed the lever at a faster rate when the VI 30 component schedule with S_1 present was in effect than did the control group (Figure 7-2).

The rate of responding on one VI 30 component schedule increased as a result of replacing the other VI 30 component schedule with an extinction schedule. This result is a contrast effect on a learned response. Extinction decreases the strength of learned responding, so the increase in the rate of responding on the VI 30 component schedule is in a

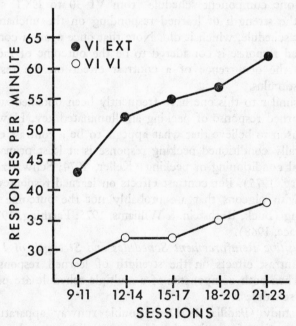

FIGURE 7-2. Contrast effect on the strength of learned responding on the VI component of MULT VI EXT. The switch for one group from MULT VI VI to MULT VI EXT began with session 9. (Adapted from Gutman, Sutterer, and Brush, 1975.)

direction opposite (in contrast) to the effect of extinction on learned responding. In addition, the VI 30 and extinction learning situations occurred in relatively close physical and temporal proximity. They occurred in the same location in the apparatus, and they followed one another every 3 minutes.

It is assumed that the switch in one component schedule from VI 30 to EXT increased the strength of the response to the perceived reinforcer delivered by the unchanged VI 30 component schedule. This assumption is supported by results described earlier that indicate that contrast effects operate on the responses to perceived stimuli. More specifically, cited studies indicate that a contrast effect alters the strength of a response to a perceived reinforcer. Both the classically conditioned and instrumentally conditioned response are quantitatively and qualitatively related to certain responses to a perceived stimulus that is the second member of the S_1-S_2 pairing resulting in conditioning. Therefore, the switch in one component schedule from VI 30 to EXT should have increased the strength of learned responding on the unchanged VI 30 component schedule, which it did. Note that once again a contrast effect on a learned response is considered to be the outcome of factors correlated with the occurrence of a contrast effect on the response to a perceived stimulus.

Results similar to this one have frequently been obtained with pigeons and the learned response of pecking an illuminated key. However, there is good reason to believe that what appears to be a contrast effect on an instrumentally conditioned pecking response is at least primarily due to the classical conditioning of pecking (Keller, 1974; Schwartz, Hamilton, & Silberberg, 1975). But contrast effects on learned responses have been obtained with pigeons that are probably not the outcome of classical conditioning (Buck, Rothstein, & Williams, 1975; Farthing, 1975; Malone, 1975; Terrace, 1968).

Two Positive Reinforcement Schedules and Strength of Learned Response. Contrast effects on the strength of learned responses are also obtained when both components of a multiple schedule are positive reinforcement schedules.

In one study (Padilla, 1971), a double runway apparatus was employed in conjunction with the free responding procedure typical of work with multiple schedules. The runways were parallel to each other; one was painted black and the other white. The subjects, rats, could move freely from one runway to the other. Through preliminary training rats learned to run down one runway, then run down it in the opposite direction, then run down it again, and so on, until food was obtained at one end of the runway. A VI component schedule was in effect for each runway. A response was defined as moving from the food cup down the length of the runway and then returning to the food cup. This response was followed by food delivered on a VI component schedule. As required by multiple schedules, only one of the component VI schedules was in effect at any one time. This was arranged for by signalling the runway with the currently operative VI component schedule by illuminating the runway with a light. Naturally, rats came to respond on only the runway in which the light was on.

At one point in the study, one group of rats responded on a multiple schedule in which the two VI component schedules were equal; each reinforcement provided by these component schedules was 2 pellets of food. Subsequently, one of the component VI schedules was changed; it delivered 5 rather than 2 pellets of food as a reinforcement. This change in one of the components of the multiple schedule decreased the response rate occurring on the unaltered VI component schedule, as Figure 7-3A indicates. The two component schedules can be viewed as two situations occurring in relatively close physical and temporal proximity. A change in response rate on the unaltered VI component schedule was caused by an increase in the amount of reinforcement delivered by the second component VI schedule. In addition, the change in response rate on the unaltered VI component schedule was in a direction opposite to the effect on learned responding resulting from an increase in amount of reinforcement. Therefore, the obtained result is a contrast effect on a learned response. The change in response rate on the unaltered VI component schedule is also referred to as a negative contrast effect, because the response rate on this component schedule decreased.

Padilla also obtained a positive contrast effect on a learned response. The procedures for another group were identical, except that at one point both component VI schedules delivered 5 pellets of food, and subsequently one of the component VI schedules delivered 2 rather than 5 pellets of food. This change in the multiple schedule increased the response rate occurring on the unaltered VI component schedule, as Figure 7-3B indicates. It is a positive contrast effect, because the rate of responding on the unchanged VI component schedule increased. The Gutman et al. (1975) result described above is also a positive contrast effect.

Figure 7-3B illustrates the frequently obtained result that the magnitude of the contrast effect on a learned response increases with continued training. Both figures 7-3A and 7-3B indicate that the contrast effect on a

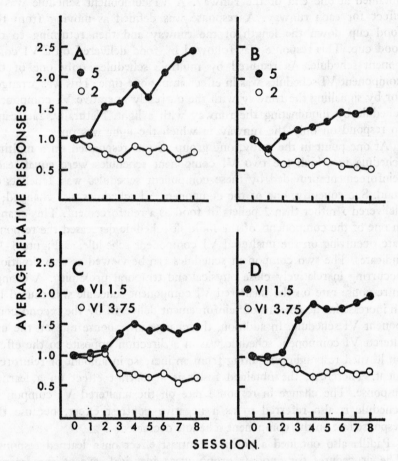

FIGURE 7-3. Contrast effect on the strength of learned responding on the constant component of a multiple schedule in which
both components are positive reinforcement schedules. Responding on both the altered and constant components is shown. For
A, the unaltered component is the one that delivered 2 pellets;
for B, 5 pellets. For C, the unaltered component is VI 1.5; for D,
VI 3.75. For session 0, the two components of a multiple schedule were identical, and starting with session 1 one of these
component schedules was changed. The ordinate indicates the
number of responses made in a session divided by the number
of responses made in session 0. (Adapted from Padilla, 1971.)

learned response may be quite durable. The duration of a session was 70 minutes.

Padilla also obtained a contrast effect on a learned response using VI component schedules that differed in the rate of reinforcement they delivered. One group of rats first responded on a MULT VI 1.5 (minute) VI 1.5 (minute) schedule. Subsequently, one component of the multiple schedule was switched to VI 3.75 (minutes), and the second component was left unchanged. The rate of reinforcement delivered by interval schedules is relatively insensitive to changes in response rate on these schedules. Consider, for example, that if responding on a VI 1 (minute) schedule occurred at the rate of 1 response per second, halving this response rate would mean that a reinforcement would be obtained on the average of 61.0 seconds since the last reinforcement was received, and doubling this rate would mean that a reinforcement would be obtained on the average of 60.25 seconds since the last reinforcement was received. A switch in one component schedule from VI 1.5 to VI 3.75 therefore surely resulted in a marked decrease in the rate of delivery of the reinforcer. The finding was that the switch from MULT VI 1.5 VI 1.5 to MULT VI 1.5 VI 3.75 resulted in an increase in the rate of responding on the unchanged VI 1.5 component schedule (Figure 7-3C). The rate of responding on the unchanged VI 1.5 component schedule was affected in a direction opposite to the effect of a decrease in the rate of reinforcement on learned response strength, and was increased; therefore this was a positive contrast effect on a learned response. Padilla also found that going from MULT VI 3.75 VI 3.75 to MULT VI 3.75 VI 1.5 decreased the response rate occurring on the unchanged VI 3.75 component schedule (Figure 7-3D), a negative contrast effect on a learned response.

A change in the rate that a reinforcer is delivered by a reinforcement schedule entails a change in the average delay of reinforcement. Rate of reinforcement affects reward learning through delay of reinforcement (Chapter 6). Richards (1973) obtained a contrast effect on a learned response when delay but not rate of reinforcement was changed in a second learning situation. This finding also indicates that the effects of changes in rate of reinforcement are mediated by changes in delay of reinforcement.

A contrast effect on a learned response has also been obtained with the addition of shock to one of the components of a multiple schedule (Coates, 1972; Terrace, 1968). In the Terrace study, pigeons responded on a MULT VI 1 (minute) VI 1 (minute) schedule. Subsequently, one of the component schedules was altered so that it delivered shock following each response that was made; however, it also continued to deliver positive reinforcement on the VI 1 schedule. The addition of shock to one component schedule did not noticeably reduce the rate with which food was obtained on this schedule, because the rate of reinforcement delivered by an interval schedule is relatively insensitive to a change in response rate that occurs on it. The addition of shock to this component schedule did result in a decrease in the rate of responding occurring on it, as expected. In addition, it resulted in an increase in the rate of responding occurring on the unaltered VI component schedule, a positive contrast effect on a learned response.

We assume that all the contrast effects on learned responses described thus far are due to factors correlated with the occurrence of contrast effects on the responses to perceived stimuli. One more account of a contrast effect on a learned response in terms of a contrast effect operating on the response to a perceived stimulus follows.

Padilla (1971) trained rats to respond on a MULT VI VI schedule in which both component schedules were identical and delivered 5 food pellets per reinforcement. The multiple schedule was then altered, so that one component VI schedule continued to deliver 5 food pellets per reinforcement. The rate of responding on the unchanged VI component schedule increased, a positive contrast effect on a learned response.

It is assumed that the switch in one VI component from 5 to 2 food pellets per reinforcement increased the strength of the response to the perceived stimulus of 5 food pellets that was delivered by the unchanged VI component schedule. A contrast effect on the response to a perceived reinforcer occurs when the reinforcer and a second reinforcer occur in relatively close physical and temporal proximity. Flaherty and Largen (1975) obtained a contrast effect on the response to a perceived reinforcer that is closely related to the contrast effect on a learned response under discussion. Rats were permitted access to 32 percent and 4 percent sucrose solutions. When these solutions were presented in relatively close temporal proximity, the strength of responding to the perceived 32 percent sucrose solution increased. This result provides relatively direct support for the assumption that the strength of the response to the perceived stimulus of 5 food pellets was increased when one component VI schedule delivered 2 food pellets. Both the classically and instrumentally conditioned response are quantitatively and qualitatively related to certain responses to a perceived stimulus that is the second member of the S_1-S_2 pairing resulting in conditioning. It follows that the rate of responding on the VI component schedule that continued to deliver 5 food pellets should have increased as a consequence of the second VI component schedule delivering 2 food pellets, which is the contrast effect on a learned response to be explained.

Contrast with the Discrete Trial Procedure. A study by Bower (1961) illustrates one procedure resulting in a contrast effect on discrete trial reward learning. For one group of rats, the reinforcer at the end of one runway (white or black) was 8 food pellets, and the reinforcer at the end of a second runway (the other color) was 1 food pellet. Another group received 1 food pellet in both the white and black runways. Four trials were run per day. For both groups half the trials per day were with one runway, and the remaining half were with the other runway. The group receiving the unequal number of food pellets ran slower in the runway in which 1 food pellet was received than the other group.

The obtained result indicates that a negative contrast effect on a discrete trial reward-trained response occurred. Eight pellets of food should establish a stronger runway response than 1 pellet of food, and receiving 8 pellets of food in one runway resulted in a weaker learned response in the runway in which 1 food pellet was received. Evidence of a positive contrast effect with fairly similar procedures has also been obtained (Calef, Calef, Maxwell, & McHewitt, 1975; Mellgren, Wrather, & Dyck, 1972).

A contrast effect on a reward-trained response with the two runway procedure described above was also obtained with immediate reinforcement in one runway and delayed reinforcement in the second runway (Mackintosh & Lord, 1973; Mellgren et al., 1972).

Another discrete trial procedure results in negative and positive contrast effects on reward learning (Benefield, Oscos, & Ehrenfreund, 1974; Zeaman, 1949). Yet another discrete trial procedure may be an instance of a contrast effect on reward learning (Amsel & Roussel, 1952).

Contrast in Escape Learning. Nation, Wrather, and Mellgren (1974) found that positive and negative contrast effects in escape learning occurred. One group of rats received a .2 mA. shock in all but the end of the runway on half the trials, and received a .4 mA. shock in all but the end of the same runway on the remaining trials. A second group received the same procedures, except that .2 mA. shock was received on all trials. A third group received the same procedures, except that .4 mA. shock was received on all trials. It was not necessary to employ two different runways because the two different shock intensities could function as discriminative stimuli (as well as reinforcers). Figure 7-4 indicates the obtained speeds of traversing the runway for the different groups. It is clear that both negative and positive contrast effects occurred.

Contrast in Classical Conditioning. Contrast effects on the nature of the CR in classical conditioning have already been discussed. Other contrast effects in classical conditioning have been found.

Pavlov (1927, pp. 188-196) established classically conditioned discriminations in dogs, and found that the occurrence of a CS+ trial following a CS— trial resulted in the CS+ producing a stronger CR than it did when the CS+ trial was preceded by a CS+ trial. Pavlov called this phenomenon *positive induction.* It probably should be considered to be a positive contrast effect on a CR. No particular event, which follows CS—, does not result in an excitatory CR. Therefore, the increased strength of the excitatory CR occurring on a CS+ trial that was preceded by a CS— trial is in a direction opposite to the failure of an excitatory CR to occur when a CS is followed by no particular event.

Another classical conditioning result (Wagner & Rescorla, 1972) ap-

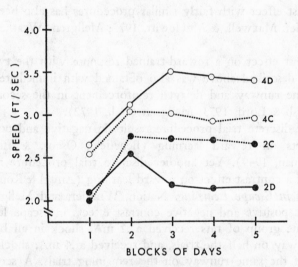

FIGURE 7-4. Contrast effect on escape learning. D refers to the group that received different, .4 and .2 mA., shocks. C refers to control groups; one received only .4 mA. shock, and the other only .2 mA. shock. There were two days to a block, and four trials to a day. (Adapted from Nation, Wrather, and Mellgren, 1974.)

pears to be an instance of a contrast effect on a CR. Conditioned suppression in rats was carried out, so preliminary procedures included establishing reward learning of bar pressing. In stage 1, shocks of 0.5 second and 5.0 seconds duration were employed as UCSs. The longer shock duration will be assumed to be a stronger reinforcer, much as a more intense shock is a stronger reinforcer. Three different treatments were employed in stage 1. The experimental group received pairings between a stimulus, A, and the 5.0 seconds shock. Intermixed with these trials were trials in which a compound stimulus, AX, was paired with the 0.5 second shock. (Recall that the offsets and onsets of the members of a compound stimulus occur simultaneously.) One control group received pairings between stimulus A and the 0.5 second shock. Intermixed with these trials were trials in which the compound stimulus, AX, was paired with the 0.5 second shock. A third group was employed to control for the use of the longer duration of shock with the experimental group; the procedures for this group need not be described.

In stage 2 the bar was made available, and responding on it was followed by food. In addition, while the bar was being made available, a new stimulus, B, was paired with the 0.5 second shock. Also, in the same stage a compound stimulus, BX (with X being the X stimulus used in stage 1), was presented, but shock did not follow it. Discrimination learning occurred; stimulus B produced conditioned suppression, and compound stimulus BX came to fail to produce conditioned suppression. The data of interest are the strengths of the conditioned suppression CR produced by BX as discrimination learning occurred for the groups receiving different treatments in stage 1.

The BX compound stimulus produced less suppression of bar pressing in the experimental group than in the two control groups. Because training with stimulus B was identical for all groups, this result was due to stimulus X producing a weaker CR in the experimental group than in the two control groups. In stage 1 the experimental group received pairings between stimulus A and the stronger reinforcer. In addition, in stage 1 the experimental group received pairings between stimulus X and the weaker reinforcer. Therefore, the relatively weak CR that stimulus X produced in the experimental group was in a direction opposite to the relatively strong CR that stimulus A presumably produced in the experimental group when it was presented alone. Thus, a negative contrast effect on the CR produced by stimulus X was obtained.

Wagner and Rescorla's (1972) theoretical explanation for this result is the same as for the blocking and overshadowing findings that are involved with attention. Evidence against this theory was discussed when attention was considered. In addition, contrast effects on learned responses and the blocking and overshadowing findings do not appear to involve the same process. It seems clear that contrast effects on learned responses are mediated by factors correlated with the occurrence of contrast effects on the responses to perceived stimuli. But blocking and overshadowing do not appear to be mediated by contrast effects on responses to perceived stimuli. Blocking and overshadowing in classical conditioning involve presenting two stimuli in compound, and pairing the compound with a UCS. Blocking or overshadowing occurs when one of the two stimuli produces a weaker CR than would occur if this stimulus was presented as a single CS (that is, not in compound with a second stimulus) and paired with the same UCS. This weaker CR could not be mediated by a change in the strength of the response to the UCS, because then the ability of the second member of the compound stimulus to produce a relatively strong CR could not be accounted for.

Analysis of Contrast Effects on Learned Responses

Simultaneous Occurrence of Images of Two Relevant Stimuli. Contrast effects on learned responses are due to factors correlated with the occurrence of contrast effects on responses to perceived stimlui. For learned responses, the contrast effect on the perceived stimulus of interest is the one on the second member of the S_1-S_2 pairing (in which S_2 is a reinforcer or no particular event) resulting in conditioning. But for learned responses, the S_2 of the S_1-S_2 pairing resulting in conditioning is not present when the learned response is executed. How can the contrast effect on the response to the S_2 of the S_1-S_2 pairing resulting in conditioning be involved with the occurrence of a contrast effect on a learned response, when this S_2 is not actually present when the learned response is executed?

Consider a multiple reinforcement schedule in which the two component schedules are identical, except that one delivers a larger amount of reinforcement than the other. The two stimuli relevant to the occurrence of a contrast effect on reward learning, stimulus 1 and stimulus 2, are the two different amounts of reinforcement. When component reinforcement schedule 1 is in effect, the general stimuli of the learning situation should result in an image of the reinforcer delivered by component reinforcement schedule 2. This assumption is analogous to the assumption made when a contrast effect on the response to a perceived stimulus that is not simultaneously present with the second relevant stimulus was discussed. It is supported in the same way.

In addition, when component reinforcement schedule 1 is in effect, it should result in an image of the reinforcer that it delivers. This assumption has been made for reward learning all along. But how can a contrast effect on the learned response for component reinforcement schedule 1 be mediated by factors correlated with the occurrence of a contrast effect on the response to the perceived reinforcer for this schedule, when only an image of this reinforcer occurs before the execution of the learned response?

This discussion indicates that images of the reinforcers delivered by both component reinforcement schedules should occur. In addition, contrast effects on the responses to perceived stimuli occur when the relevant stimuli are present simultaneously. Also, it has been assumed all along that images of stimuli and the effects of real stimuli on responding are due to qualitatively identical temporary brain events. It follows that a contrast effect on the learned responding on component reinforcement schedule 1 should occur even though the reinforcer delivered by this schedule is not currently present.

Physical Proximity, Stimulus Generalization, and Image of Second Stimulus. A contrast effect on the response to a perceived stimulus should not occur when the second relevant stimulus does not take place in sufficiently close physical proximity to the perceived stimulus. It was reasoned that this is because a relatively close physical proximity between the two relevant stimuli is necessary for the situation currently being perceived to result in an image of the relevant stimulus not currently present. Contrast effects on learned responses are due to factors correlated with the occurrence of contrast effects on responses to perceived stimuli. It follows that a contrast effect on a learned response occurring in learning situation 1 should not ordinarily occur when learning situation 2 does not take place in relatively close physical proximity to learning situation 1. This inference is supported.

For some contrast effects on learned responses, the relevant stimuli occur in the same apparatus, for example, contrast effects on reward learning obtained with the use of multiple schedules in which a bar is employed. When the same apparatus is used for the two learning situations, the stimuli of the learning situation currently in effect should result in an image of the relevant stimulus of the learning situation not currently operative.

Contrast effects on learned responses were described in which the two relevant stimuli—say, two different amounts of a reinforcer—occurred in different but similar runways. Stimulus generalization from one learning situation to the second learning situation should account for the occurrence of an image of the relevant stimulus of the learning situation not currently in effect. The stimuli of the learning situation currently in effect can be thought of as a test stimulus of a stimulus generalization determination. The stimuli of the learning situation not currently operative can be thought of as the training stimulus of this stimulus generalization determination. A test stimulus should result in an image of the training stimulus (Chapter 4). Therefore, the stimuli of the runway currently being perceived should result in an image of the stimuli of the runway learning situation not currently perceived, including an image of the reinforcer received in the runway not currently being perceived.

Studies support the idea that an image of the relevant stimulus of the learning situation not currently being perceived must occur while an animal is in the learning situation currently being perceived for a contrast effect on the learned response exhibited in the learning situation currently being perceived to take place. In work by Maxwell, Meyer, Calef, and McHewitt (1969), the group of rats of primary interest received one pellet of food at the end of a runway. It also received 12 pellets of food when placed in an open-top cage. Another group received one pellet of food at the end of the runway used for the first group. It also received 12 pellets of food at the end of another runway of a different brightness. This second group, the normal-contrast group, received a procedure that should result in a contrast effect on the speeds of traversing the runways. A third group received one pellet of food at the end of the runway used for the first group. It also received one pellet of food when placed in the open-top cage in which the first group received 12 pellets of food. The normal-contrast group ran slower in the runway in which it received one pellet of food than did the other two groups. The other two groups did not differ from each other in the speed of traversing the runway in which one pellet of food was received. Therefore, the normal-contrast group exhibited a negative contrast effect on a runway traversal response, and the group that received 12 pellets of food in the open-top cage did not.

The stimuli of the open-top cage were not similar to the stimuli of the runway. Therefore, little or no stimulus generalization between these two stimuli should have occurred. Therefore, while the group that received 12 pellets of food in the open-top cage was in the runway in which one pellet of food was received, an image of 12 pellets of food should not have occurred. It follows that this group should not have exhibited a negative contrast effect on reward learning in the runway in which it received 1 pellet of food, and it did not.

Suppose that a learned response was acquired in one apparatus, and a second relevant stimulus occurred in a different situation, but nevertheless an image of the second relevant stimulus occurred while an animal was in the first apparatus. A contrast effect on the learned response exhibited in the first apparatus should be obtained. A study by Harris, Collerain, Wolf, and Ludvigson (1970) confirms this expectation.

In this study, one group of rats received one pellet of food at the end of a runway, and 12 pellets of food on a steel surface outside the home cage. This group was taken from the home cage and placed directly on the steel surface on those trials in which 12 food pellets were received. A second group received the same treatment, except that on these trials in which 12 food pellets were received, rats were taken from the home cage, placed in the start box of the runway but not allowed to traverse it, removed from the start box after 3 seconds, and placed immediately on the surface with the 12 food pellets. A third group received the same treatment as the second group, except that it received one food pellet on the steel surface. The group that on some trials was placed in the runway and then put on the steel surface with the 12 food pellets, traversed the runway in which one food pellet was received at a lower rate than did the other two groups. The other two groups did not differ from each other in speed of traversing this runway. Therefore, the group that on some trials was placed in the runway and then put on the steel surface with 12 food pellets, exhibited a negative contrast effect on the rate of traversing the runway.

Placement of the group that exhibited the negative contrast effect in the start box of the runway before it was put on the steel surface with 12 food pellets should have made the start box a CS that came to be associated with 12 food pellets. Therefore, for this group the start box should have resulted in an image of 12 food pellets. Thus, while this group was in the start box, images of both one and 12 food pellets should have simultaneously occurred. These simultaneously occurring images should have resulted in the contrast effect on the learned runway traversal response that was obtained.

More on Stimulus Generalization. It was concluded that the magnitude of the contrast effect on the response to a perceived stimulus increases with an increase in the vividness of the image of the relevant stimulus not currently perceived. In addition, a contrast effect on a learned response is mediated by factors correlated with the occurrence of a contrast effect on the response to the perceived relevant stimulus of the learning situation currently in effect. It follows that the magnitude of a contrast effect on a learned response should increase with an increase in the vividness of the image of the relevant stimulus of the learning situation not currently in effect. Previous discussion supports the idea that as the amount of stimulus generalization occurring betwen two learning situations increases, the vividness of the image of the relevant stimulus of the learning situation not currently in effect increases. Therefore, the magnitude of a contrast effect on a learned response should increase with an increase in the amount of stimulus generalization occurring between the two relevant learning situations.

Contrast effects on learned responses have sometimes been found to disappear with continuing training (Nevin & Shettleworth, 1966; Pavlov, 1927, p. 193). This result may possibly occur because continued training reduces the amount of stimulus generalization that occurs between the two learning situations that are involved.

Increasing the similarity between discriminative stimuli results in an increase in the amount of stimulus generalization occurring between them. Increasing the similarity between discriminative stimuli should therefore increase the magnitude of a contrast effect on a learned response. A result in accord with this expectation was obtained by Pavlov (1927, p. 193). The positive induction result was first obtained. However, it disappeared with continued training. Subsequently, the CS— that had been employed was replaced by one more similar to the CS+. The induction result then reappeared. A similar finding is that conditions that should result in more difficult discrimination learning resulted in stronger contrast effects on learned responses (Hearst, 1969; Malone, 1975).

On the other hand, Mackintosh, Little, and Lord (1972) and Pierrel and Blue (1967) found that the magnitude of a contrast effect on a learned response decreased with an increase in the similarity of the discriminative stimuli signalling the different learning situations. This result will not be discussed except to suggest that it may be theoretically related to an outcome in perception called *assimilation* (Helson, 1964, pp. 282-286). An example of an assimilation outcome described by Helson is that under certain conditions white lines made adjacent gray areas appear whiter, and black lines made adjacent gray areas appear blacker.

Temporal Proximity. We inferred above that the magnitude of a contrast effect on a learned response should increase with an increase in the vividness of the image of the relevant stimulus of the learning situation not currently in effect. When we discussed the influence of temporal proximity between two relevant stimuli on the magnitude of the contrast effect on the response to a perceived stimulus, we asserted that as the time interval separating the occurrence of the currently present stimulus from the occurrence of the other relevant stimulus decreases, the vividness of the image of the other relevant stimulus should increase. It can be similarly reasoned that as the time interval separating the occurrence of the learning situation currently in effect from the other learning situation decreases, the vividness of the image of the relevant stimulus of the other learning situation increases. It follows that the magnitude of a contrast effect on a learned response should increase with a decrease in the time interval separating the occurrence of the learning situation in which this learned response occurs from the other learning situation.

Bernheim and Williams (1967) trained rats to run in a wheel on a multiple schedule. One component schedule delivered food after each time a rat ran above a criterion speed of 1 inch per second for 15 seconds on the average; a second component schedule delivered food each time a rat ran above the same criterion speed for 60 seconds on the average. When the component schedule delivering food at the higher rate was followed by the component schedule delivering food at the lower rate, the response rate on the component schedule delivering food at the lower rate was initially depressed. However, the response rate increased as the component schedule delivering food at the lower rate remained in effect. This temporary decrease in response rate is a negative contrast on a learned response. Because the contrast effect was limited to a portion of the component schedule, it is often called a *local contrast effect*. It was also found for some rats that when the component schedule delivering food at the lower rate was followed by the component schedule delivering food at the higher rate, the response rate on the component schedule delivering food at the higher rate was first elevated and then decreased. A local positive contrast effect was therefore also obtained.

The described results indicate that a contrast effect was obtained only for a relatively brief time period after the previous learning situation (component schedule) had terminated. Therefore, a contrast effect on a learned response was found only when the two learning situations occurred in relatively close temporal proximity. Thus, these findings support the expectation that the magnitude of a contrast effect on a learned response should increase with a decrease in the time interval separating the occurrence of the learning situation in which this learned response occurs from the other learning situation.

Pavlov (1927, p. 191) also found that a contrast effect on a learned response failed to occur when the time interval separating two learning situations was relatively long. He found that positive induction occurred only when the time interval separating the presentation of CS— from CS+ was less than 2 minutes.

Contrast Effects and Other Learning Results

Contrast Effect on Learned Response without Discrimination Learning. Except for the occurrence of contrast effects in classical conditioning in which a CS is paired with the absence of a UCS, and in the avoidance, escape, omission, and response-terminates-reward types of instrumental conditioning, our examples of contrast effects on learned responses have all involved discrimination learning. There is no reason to expect that contrast effects on learned responses require discrimination learning to occur. The role of discrimination learning in the mediation of contrast effects on learned responses most likely is only to provide two different learning situations occurring in relatively close physical and temporal proximity. Previous examples of contrast effects on responses to perceived stimuli did not involve the use of discrimination learning procedures. In addition, one type of learning result (Zeaman, 1949) indicates that a contrast effect on a learned response occurs although discrimination learning is not carried out. A study by Macphail (1975) also indicates that a contrast effect on a learned response occurred although discrimination learning was not carried out.

In Macphail's study, what will be referred to as "master" pigeons acquired a simultaneous discrimination between a stimulus projected on one response key and a different stimulus projected on a second response key. A second group received a successive discrimination between the same stimuli. In addition, the behavior of a master pigeon determined whether S+ or S— would be presented on a trial to a pigeon in the group receiving the successive discrimination. If a master pigeon pecked S+ on a trial, then S+ was presented to a pigeon in the successive group on the same trial. If a master pigeon pecked S— on a trial, then S— was presented to a pigeon in the successive group on the same trial. Also, a pigeon in the successive group received S+ or S— on the same key that it was on for a master pigeon. For example, if on a trial a master pigeon pecked the S+ key and the S+ key was on the right, a pigeon in the successive group received S+ on the right key on that trial. For the successive group, the key with S+ on it had to be pecked for the reinforcement to occur; naturally, pecking S— was not followed by the reinforcement. On a given trial a pigeon in a third group received the same discriminative stimulus, S+ or S— on the same key, the right or left one, that a pigeon in the successive group recevied. For this group, the key with a discriminative stimulus on it had to be pecked for the reinforcement to occur; however, even if this key was pecked, reinforcement did not always occur. In addition, delivery of the reinforcement following pecking a key with a discriminative stimulus on it was not correlated with whether or not the discriminative stimulus was S+ or S—. Thus, the third group did not receive discrimination training. The frequency with which a master pigeon obtained reinforcement determined the frequency with which pecking a key with a discriminative stimulus on it was followed by reinforcement for a pigeon in the third group.

Introduction of a new simultaneous discrimination decreased the latency to respond on the key carrying what was the S+ for groups 1 and 2 for all three groups to approximately equal extents. Introduction of a new simultaneous discrimination caused the master pigeons to make errors. Therefore, while the master pigeons were acquiring the new discrimination, reinforcements and nonreinforcements alternated fairly frequently for all three groups. Thus, a contrast effect on the response to the perceived reinforcer should have occurred for all three groups. It follows that a positive contrast effect on the reward-trained response causing the positive reinforcer to occur should have taken place for all three groups. This result was, in fact, obtained, as evidenced by the decreased latency to respond on the key with what was the S+ for groups 1 and 2 on it. Thus, the third group exhibited a contrast effect on a learned response even though this group did not receive training on a discrimination.

Evidence that contrast effects on learned responses occur in the absence of discrimination training supports the conclusion that contrast effects operate in a number of areas in conditioning, including classical conditioning in which a CS is paired with the absence or termination of a UCS, and the avoidance, escape, omission, and response-terminates-reward learning types of instrumental conditioning.

Instrumental Conditioning. Contrast effects are probably involved with all types of instrumental conditioning, not only with the types just mentioned. Reward learning will be considered as an example. The stimulus produced by the instrumental response in reward learning will always be followed by the positive reinforcer. The stimulus produced by not responding and by making other responses will always be followed by no particular event. Because at least early in training positive reinforcements and nonreinforcements occur in relatively close physical and temporal proximity, a contrast effect on the response to no particular event should take place; no particular event should tend to be escaped from and avoided. Because the stimuli produced by not responding and by making responses that are not the instrumental response are paired with no particular event, an animal should avoid bringing about these stimuli. Therefore, an animal should actively refrain from not making a response, and should actively refrain from exhibiting a response that is not the instrumental one. Thus, reward learning is probably not only a matter of bringing about the stimulus produced by the instrumental response; it probably also involves avoiding bringing about other response-produced stimuli. After reward learning, for example, was established, it would be of interest to force an animal to not exhibit the reward-trained response. The animal should struggle to avoid performing a response other than the reward-trained one; in addition, it should be relatively likely to aggress against an appropriate target.

Contrast effects are probably involved with all types of instrumental conditioning in another way as well. Reward learning of traversing a runway will be considered for illustrative purposes. At least early in training the rate of traversing the runway increases. Thus, the delay in reinforcement timed from the initiation of the runway traversal response decreases. Unequal delays of reinforcement in two different learning situations can result in contrast effects on learned responses. Therefore, the response to perceived stimuli involved with a longer delay of reinforcement of the runway traversal response should be affected through contrast by the previous occurrence of a shorter delay of reinforcement. Consequently, it may be that perceived stimuli involved with a longer delay of reinforcement tend to be escaped from and avoided. It follows that an animal may avoid bringing about the stimulus produced by traversing the runway more slowly; that is, an animal may actively refrain from executing a relatively slow runway traversal response.

Irrelevant Stimuli. An irrelevant stimulus is one that is as likely to occur when the positive discriminative stimulus is present as when the negative discriminative stimulus is present; in addition, the two discriminative stimuli must be equally likely to take place. The tendency to respond in the presence of or to irrelevant stimuli must be reduced if performance on a discrimination is to noticeably improve. Contrast effects provide help in understanding how the control of responding by irrelevant stimuli in discrimination learning decreases.

For a typical reward-learning discrimination, the rate with which positive reinforcement is delivered when responding occurs in the presence of or to an irrelevant stimulus is less than the rate with which positive reinforcement is delivered when responding occurs in the presence of or to a positive discriminative stimulus. The discriminative stimulus correlated with the component of a multiple schedule delivering the lesser of two rates of positive reinforcement acquires inhibitory properties. Therefore, while a typical reward-learning discrimination is in progress, a tendency for irrelevant stimuli to inhibit responding in their presence or to them may develop through a contrast process. Once this inhibition is strong enough attention to irrelevant stimuli should be decreased through a decrease in attention process operating on them.

Partial Reinforcement. Both the reinforcer and the absence of the reinforcer, no particular event, follow responses made on ratio schedules of reinforcement. In addition, for ratio schedules no particular event and the reinforcer occur in the same physical location and in fairly close temporal proximity. Therefore, a positive contrast effect on the response to the perceived reinforcer may occur. Thus, there may be a positive contrast effect on the rate of responding on ratio schedules. This possible positive contrast effect on a learned response may provide at least a partial explanation of why animals respond faster on ratio schedules than on the CRF schedule.

In Macphail's study (1975), the group that did not receive discrimination training responded on both a partial reinforcement schedule and a close approximation to a continuous reinforcement schedule. Its latency to respond on the partial reinforcement schedule was less. This finding is in accord with the account of faster responding on ratio schedules than on the CRF schedule.

Within-Group Procedure. Investigation of the effects of different amounts of positive reinforcement on simultaneous discrimination learning has shown that a larger amount of positive reinforcement is much more likely to result in fewer errors when the same animal receives both the larger and smaller amounts of positive reinforcement, than when one animal receives the larger and a second animal receives the smaller amount of reinforcement (Lawson, 1957). Receipt of both amounts of reinforcement by the same animal in simultaneous discrimination learning is arranged for by following correct responses on one simultaneous discrimination with the larger amount of positive reinforcement, and by following correct responses on a second simultaneous discrimination with the smaller amount of positive reinforcement. The same animal's receiving both amounts of positive reinforcement is referred to as a *within-group procedure.*

The same animal's receiving two different amounts of positive reinforcement in fairly similar apparatuses should result in a contrast effect on a learned response. We described above contrast effects on learned responses due to the same animal receiving different amounts of reinforcement from different component schedules of a multiple schedule or in different runways, and said also that a discriminative stimulus produces an inhibitory effect on responding when it is correlated with the component schedule delivering the lower rate of positive reinforcement. The discriminative stimuli present when an animal receives the lower of two amounts of positive reinforcement may therefore inhibit responding. This inhibition of responding should increase the frequency of errors on the simultaneous discrimination that delivers the lower amount of positive reinforcement. Therefore, the strong tendency for more errors to be made on the simultaneous discrimination that delivers the lower amount of reinforcement when the within-group procedure is employed appears to be due to the operation of a contrast effect.

A within-group procedure was also used to compare the strengths of conditioned reinforcers established with continuous and partial reinforcement (D'Amato, Lachman, & Kivy, 1958). The continuous reinforcement condition resulted in the stronger conditioned reinforcer. However, when one group of animals responds on a partial reinforcement schedule and a second group responds on a continuous reinforcement schedule, the partial reinforcement condition results in the stronger conditioned reinforcer. The result that the partial reinforcement condition fails to establish the stronger conditioned reinforcer when the within-group procedure is employed is most likely due to the operation of a contrast effect, a possibility supported by the finding that a stimulus produces an inhibitory effect on responding through operation of a contrast effect when it is present while a component of a multiple schedule delivering reinforcement at the lower, "more partial" of two rates is in effect.

Learning-Induced Polydipsia. When periods in which animals can receive food alternate in relatively close physical and temporal proximity with periods in which food cannot be obtained, they will tend to drink excessively during the absence-of-food periods. This phenomenon is called *learning-induced polydipsia.* In one study (Keehn & Colotla, 1971), rats could receive food in one time period by pressing a bar. A 30-second period immediately followed in which food could not be received. The food-present and food-absent periods continually alternated over an experimental session. The tube from which water was obtained was attached to the door of the experimental chamber 3.5 inches away from the wall containing the bar and food receptacle. The rats were deprived of food, but had free access to water in their home cages. The described procedures resulted in the rats drinking very large amounts of water in the food-absent periods. The amount of drinking that occurs in food-absent periods may be so great that the consequence may be some physiological stress on the animal (Stricker & Adair, 1966). When periods of absence of food did not alternate with periods in which food could be obtained, excessive drinking did not occur (Falk, 1966).

Periods of absence of food that alternate in relatively close physical and temporal proximity with periods in which food can be obtained should tend to elicit escape and avoidance and aggressive responses. Increased consumption of water during these periods of absence of food is in a direction opposite in nature to the escape and avoidance and aggressive responses that should tend to occur during periods of absence of food. Therefore, increased consumption of water during these periods of absence of food appears to be a contrast effect on the response to a perceived reinforcer. Amsel and Maltzman (1950) and Sterritt (1962) found that when shock occurred simultaneously with or in relatively close physical and temporal proximity to water or food, the consumption of water or food was increased. These results support this contrast interpretation of learning-induced polydipsia.

Concurrent Schedules

The first of the topics that are not closely related to contrast effects to be considered is the concurrent schedule of reinforcement. The distinguishing characteristic of a concurrent schedule is that an animal responding on this schedule is free to switch from responding on one component schedule to a second component schedule and back again, and so on. Both component schedules are usually positive reinforcement schedules. Because concurrent schedules provide a choice between responding on different positive reinforcement schedules, they are similar to simultaneous discriminations in which both choice responses may be followed by a positive reinforcer.

Simultaneous Discriminations: Both Choices Followed by Reinforcer. Let us consider simultaneous discriminations in which one response causes one positive reinforcement condition to be in effect, and a second response causes a different positive reinforcement condition to be operative. With continued training on such discriminations, an animal comes close to exclusively responding to the stimulus signalling the stronger reinforcement condition. This conclusion holds for simultaneous discriminations in which the two positive reinforcement conditions are unequal amounts of reinforcement (Hill & Spear, 1963); unequal delays of reinforcement (e.g., Anderson, 1932; Yoshioka, 1929); and unequal probabilities of reinforcement (Mackintosh, 1974, pp. 191-192). An illustrative result is Hill and Spear's. Rats were trained on a position discrimination in a T-maze. On every trial, 4 pellets of food were placed in one of the ends of the two arms of the T-maze, and 2 pellets of food were placed in the end of the other arm. Choice of the arm of the T-maze resulting in 4 food pellets by 16 rats reached 100 percent by trial 21.

Animals should acquire the response causing the stronger reinforcement condition to be in effect, because this response should be better learned than the other choice response. It is preferable to say that the acquired response is "better learned" than to talk in terms of an animal's "choosing" to make the response causing the stronger reinforcement condition to be in effect.

At least early in training on the type of simultaneous discrimination being considered, the stronger and weaker positive reinforcement conditions are followed by one another. When a stronger reinforcement condition occurs in relatively close physical and temporal proximity to a weaker reinforcement condition, the stimuli comprising the weaker reinforcement condition should at least temporarily tend to be escaped from and avoided through contrast. Therefore, for the type of simultaneous discrimination presently under consideration, the stimulus signalling the weaker reinforcement condition may tend to be escaped from and avoided. Such a possibility would increase the likelihood that an animal would almost exclusively exhibit the choice response putting the stronger reinforcement condition into effect, which is the result that is obtained.

The result that animals exclusively respond to the discriminative stimulus correlated with receiving the smaller delay of reinforcement is theoretically relevant, since it supports an earlier explanation of the finding that the strength of the instrumental response increases with continued training. The strength of the instrumental response was viewed as increasing with continued training because, in part, faster execution of this response decreases delay of reinforcement, which should increase the strength of the instrumental response, which should additionally increase the speed with which the instrumental response is executed, and so on. The result under consideration also supports an earlier account of the finding that the rate of responding on ratio schedules of reinforcement is usually greater than the rate of responding on interval schedules of reinforcement. The rate of responding on ratio schedules should usually be greater because faster responding on ratio schedules, but not interval schedules, leads to a decrease in delay of reinforcement. Most of the results involving concurrent schedules of reinforcement will also be viewed as the outcome of an animal's acquiring the response that causes a lesser delay of reinforcement to occur.

Concurrent Ratio Ratio Schedules. The distinguishing characteristic of concurrent schedules is that an animal responding on a concurrent schedule is free to switch from responding on one component schedule to a second component schedule and back again, and so on. Two operanda (for instance, bars or response keys) are typically employed with concurrent schedules. In one procedure for concurrent schedules, component reinforcement schedules are simultaneously in effect for responding on each operandum. For a concurrent ratio ratio schedule, this means that one ratio schedule is in effect for responding on one operandum, and a second ratio schedule is operative for responding on the other operandum. The component schedule in effect for responding on the same operandum remains constant. A component schedule is not alternated from right to left and vice-versa, as in a simultaneous visual discrimination in a T-maze or jumping stand apparatus. An animal is free to respond on either operandum, and therefore either component schedule. It does so by moving from one operandum to the other. It is obvious therefore that concurrent schedules employ the free responding procedure.

An important defining aspect of concurrent schedules is that the component schedules are independent. For a ratio component schedule, independence means that responses made on this component schedule do not affect the delivery of a reinforcer by the second component schedule in any way, and that responses made on the second component schedule do not affect delivery of the reinforcer by this ratio component schedule in any way. Suppose that a component schedule is FR 10, and that an animal makes 5 responses on this component schedule since delivery of the last reinforcement by this component schedule, and then switches to the second component schedule. Making 5 responses on the FR 10 component schedule does not affect the delivery of a reinforcement by the second component schedule, and when the animal switches back to the FR 10 component schedule it still must make 5 additional responses for this component schedule to deliver its next reinforcement.

The components of a concurrent FR FR (CONC FR FR) schedule are both FR schedules. For CONC FR FR schedules, responding on only the component schedule with the smaller ratio tends to occur (Herrnstein, 1958). Also, for concurrent schedules in which both components are VR schedules (CONC VR VR), responding on only the component with the smaller average ratio tends to occur (Herrnstein & Loveland, 1975).

These findings are readily explained by the assumption that an animal tends to acquire the response that causes a lesser delay of reinforcement to occur. Responding on the component schedule with the smaller ratio size will result in a smaller delay of reinforcement. Such responding should therefore be acquired, which it is. An animal may also actively refrain from responding on the component reinforcement schedule delivering reinforcement with the greater delay through contrast.

Concurrent FR FI Schedules. Concurrent schedules with an interval schedule component tend to result in responding on the component schedule that is at a given moment in time more likely to deliver its next reinforcer with the smaller delay.

The interval component schedule, like the ratio component schedule, is independent of the other component schedule. However, because of the different natures of ratio and interval schedules, a response on an interval component schedule should be followed by a smaller delay of reinforcement when the prior response was on the other component schedule, than when the prior response was on this interval component schedule. This is because the time elapsed since the moment the previous reinforcement was delivered by an interval component schedule lengthens while an animal responds on the other component schedule.

Catania (1966) and LaBounty and Reynolds (1973) employed concurrent FR FI (CONC FR FI) schedules. They found that as the time since delivery of the previous reinforcement by the FI component schedule increased, pigeons were increasingly likely to respond on the FI component schedule rather than to respond on the FR component schedule. Also, responding a short time after delivery of the previous reinforcement by the FI component schedule tended to be mainly on the FR component schedule.

The obtained results are understandable in terms of delay of reinforcement. Responding on the FR component schedule relatively soon after the last reinforcement delivered by the FI component schedule should be established because this responding causes a shorter delay of reinforcement to occur than responding on the FI component schedule. Responding on the FI component schedule when the FI interval is relatively close to elapsing should be established because this responding causes a shorter delay of reinforcement to occur than responding on the FR component schedule.

Concurrent VI VI Schedules. Concurrent VI VI (CONC VI VI) schedules are known to result in a high frequency of switching from one VI component to the other VI component. This result, like the switching result for CONC FR FI schedules described above, makes sense in terms of delay of reinforcement. While an animal responds on component VI schedule 1, the length of time that must pass for a response on component VI schedule 2 to be followed by a reinforcement delivered by this component VI schedule decreases. The response of switching to component VI schedule 2 should come to occur when this length of time decreases to a sufficient extent.

Another result obtained with CONC VI VI schedules is that when the VI component schedules are unequal, an animal responds on the component schedule delivering the greater rate of reinforcement more of the time than it responds on the component schedule delivering the lower rate of reinforcement. This result also makes sense in terms of delay of reinforcement. Responding on the VI component schedule delivering the greater rate of reinforcement will on the average cause a reinforcement to occur with a smaller time delay than responding on the VI component schedule delivering the lower rate of reinforcement. Therefore, responding on the VI component schedule delivering the greater rate of reinforcement should occur more of the time than responding on the VI component schedule delivering the lesser rate of reinforcement.

CONC VI VI Schedules and Local Reinforcement and Response Rates. CONC VI VI schedules are also of interest because of their effects on local response and reinforcement rates. The local response rate on a component schedule of a concurrent schedule equals the number of responses made on this component schedule divided by the time duration this component schedule is responded on by an ainmal—that is, by the time this component schedule is in effect. Let R_A and R_B equal the total number of responses made on component schedules A and B, respectively, in an experimental session. Also, let T_A and T_B equal the total time that an animal responds on component schedules A and B, respectively, in that session. The local response rates on component schedules A and B in a session then equal R_A/T_A and R_B/T_B, respectively.

The local reinforcement rate on a component schedule equals the number of reinforcements obtained from this component schedule divided by the time duration that this component schedule is responded on—that is, by the time duration that this component schedule is in effect. Let N_A and N_B equal the total number of reinforcements obtained on component schedules A and B, respectively, in an experimental session. The local reinforcement rates on component schedules A and B in a session then equal N_A/T_A and N_B/T_B, respectively, T_A and T_B being defined as above.

One result obtained with CONC VI VI schedules is that the local rates of reinforcement on the VI component schedules are approximately equal (Baum & Rachlin, 1969; Killeen, 1972). This result is obtained when the VI component schedules are far from being identical. This finding makes sense in terms of delay of reinforcement. Suppose that an animal initially "prefers" to respond on one of the two VI component schedules of a concurrent schedule to an "excessive" extent. By doing so, the average local delay of reinforcement following a response on the other VI component schedule would be less than the average local delay of reinforcement following a response on the preferred VI component schedule. The animal should therefore acquire the behavior of responding sufficiently frequently on the other VI component schedule for the average local delays of reinforcement following responses on both VI component schedules to be equal. The local rates of reinforcement provided by the VI component schedules would thereby be equal, as they are.

A second result obtained with CONC VI VI schedules is that the local rates of responding on the VI component schedules are approximately equal (Baum & Rachlin, 1969; Killeen, 1972). This result is obtained when the VI component schedules are far from being identical. This finding appears to have a simple explanation. The rates of responding on individual (independent) VI schedules do not differ that much. In addition, the local rates of reinforcement obtained from each VI component schedule should be equal. Obtaining equal local rates of reinforcement from VI component schedules should operate in the direction of making the rate of responding on these component schedules equal. Because the rates of responding on VI schedules are not that different to begin with, a factor operating in the direction of making the rates of responding on VI component schedules equal may result in these rates being equal.

A third effect of CONC VI VI schedules is that the total number of reinforcements obtained on a component schedule divided by the total number of responses made on this component schedule equals the total number of reinforcements obtained on the other component schedule divided by the total number of responses made on the other component schedule. Thus, three quantitative expressions describe the indicated effects of CONC VI VI schedules on responding. The local rates of reinforcement on component VI schedules A and B are equal, expressed as $N_A/T_A = N_B/T_B$ (equation 1). The local response rates on component schedules A and B are equal, expressed as $R_A/T_A = R_B/T_B$ (equation 2). The ratios of reinforcements to responses on component VI schedules A and B are equal, expressed as $N_A/R_A = N_B/R_B$ (equation 3).

Any one of these three equations can be obtained from the other two. Rachlin (1973) maintains that equation 3 is derivative, which appears to be the case. Equations 1 and 2 follow from established principles. In addition, equation 3 does not appear to be a generally valid description of responding on VI schedules. For individual VI schedules, the reinforcement rate decreases as the average length of the interval increases much more quickly than the response rate decreases, so that equation 3 is not valid for individual VI schedules.

Observing Responses

Responses are acquired that appear to be established with the reinforcer of information; these responses are called *observing responses*. However, it seems clear that conditioned reinforcers establish observing responses rather than the reinforcer of information.

Illustrative Study. In one study of observing responses (Wheling & Prokasy, 1962), the end of each arm of a T-maze contained a delay box and a goal box. Subjects, rats, were forced to choose each arm of the T-maze the same number of trials. This was accomplished by blocking entrance into the more preferred arm of the T-maze on some trials. The rats were detained in the delay boxes for 20 seconds across all conditions. They were then free to and did enter the goal box attached to the delay box in which they were detained. Food was present in each goal box on half the number of trials on which a rat entered the arm containing this goal box. The procedures for the two sides of the T-maze differed. For one side, both the delay and goal boxes were one color on trials when food was present, and both the delay and goal boxes were a second color on trials when food was absent. For the second side, the delay and goal boxes were one color on half the trials when food was present, and on half the trials when food was absent; the delay and goal boxes were the other color on the remaining half the trials when food was present, and the remaining half the trials when food was absent. For example, for some of the rats, white delay and goal boxes were on the left side of the T-maze on food trials; black delay and goal boxes were on the left side of the T-maze on food-absent trials; and delay and goal boxes of either color on the right side of the T-maze were not correlated with food or food-absent trials.

The finding was that rats were more likely to enter the side of the T-maze with one color correlated with food and a second color correlated with the absence of food, than they were to enter the other side of the T-maze. Thus, in a sense, information about whether or not food was forthcoming, which was provided by the colors of the delay box on one, but not the other, side of the T-maze appeared to serve as a reinforcer establishing the response of entering the side of the T-maze where the delay box provided this information. The response of entering the side of the T-maze with different colors correlated with the presence and absence of food is the observing response.

Conditioned Reinforcement Analysis. We may interpret Wheling and Prokasy's finding in terms of conditioned reinforcement. The color and position of the delay and goal boxes present on only food trials should have been a positive conditioned reinforcer, because these stimuli were regularly perceived just prior to obtaining food. The observing response caused the color and position of the delay and goal boxes present on only food trials to occur. Therefore, the observing response was acquired through reward learning established with the indicated positive conditioned reinforcer. An explanation based on primary reinforcement cannot account for the finding, because food was received in both the left and right goal boxes an equal number of times.

A problem with this interpretation is that the observing response caused a negative conditioned reinforcer to occur on half the trials the observing response was made. The negative conditioned reinforcer was the color and position of the delay box which were correlated with the absence of food. A similar result obtained with primary reinforcement is that rats were more likely to enter the side of a T-maze in which two or zero units of food were obtained equally frequently than the side of the T-maze in which one unit of food was always obtained (Leventhal, Morrel, Morgan, & Perkins, 1959). Therefore, it appears reasonable to conclude that the observing response was established with a positive conditioned reinforcer even though the observing response caused a negative conditioned reinforcer to occur equally often.

In general, in observing-response studies one or the other of two different reinforcement conditions involving primary reinforcement is in effect at any one time. In addition, the observing response causes one stimulus to occur if the first reinforcement condition is in effect, and causes a different stimulus to occur if the other reinforcement condition is operative. The stimulus signalling the more "positive" reinforcement condition should be a positive conditioned reinforcer. The stimulus signalling the less positive reinforcement condition should be (at least frequently) a negative conditioned reinforcer. Kendall's (1973) study supports the conclusion that the observing response is acquired through reward learning established with the positive conditioned reinforcer it causes to occur.

At the onset of a trial, the response key was dark. Trials terminated in two ways. On half the trials, food was provided independently of responding. On the other half the trials, no reinforcer and a blackout of the experimental chamber occurred. The duration of a trial was 32 seconds. Execution of a sufficient number of pecks by subjects, pigeons, on the dark key during a trial always resulted in illumination of this key with green light when food was programmed to be delivered. Also, execution of a sufficient number of pecks on the dark key during a trial always resulted in illumination of this key with red light when no reinforcer and a blackout were programmed to occur.

Two conditions were employed, as shown in Figure 7-5. In one condition, a single peck on the dark key caused this key to be illuminated with green light when food was to be delivered at the end of a trial, and six pecks on the dark key caused this key to be illuminated with red light when no reinforcer and a blackout were to occur at the end of a trial. In a second condition, six pecks on the dark key caused this key to be illuminated with green light when food was to be delivered at the end of a trial, and a single peck on the dark key caused this key to be illuminated with red light when no reinforcer and a blackout were to occur at the end of a trial.

1

1 PECK   ON (D) ⟶ (G) THEN FOOD

OR

6 PECKS ON (D) ⟶ (R) THEN BLACKOUT

2

6 PECKS ON (D) ⟶ (G) THEN FOOD

OR

1 PECK   ON (D) ⟶ (R) THEN BLACKOUT

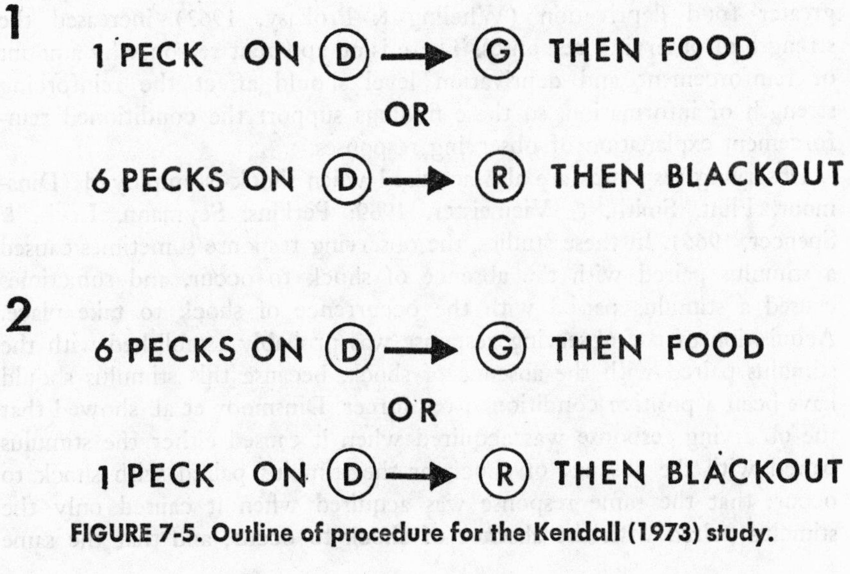

FIGURE 7-5. Outline of procedure for the Kendall (1973) study.

The results were that: (a) at least one peck on the dark key almost always occurred; (b) in the condition in which one peck was required to cause the green light to occur, additional pecks were not likely to be made on those trials terminating in no reinforcer and a blackout; and (c) in the condition in which one peck was required to cause the red light to occur, additional pecks were likely to take place on those trials terminating in food. A single peck on the dark key was the observing response, because in a sense it provided information about whether or not the trial would terminate in food. Result a indicates that the observing response was acquired. Results b and c suggest that the observing response was a reward-trained response established with the positive conditioned reinforcer of the green light. The green light should have been a positive conditioned reinforcer, because whenever it occurred it was followed by food. In addition, the pigeons pecked in order to cause the green light to occur: they pecked at the onset of a trial; they were not likely to peck when the green light had occurred; they were not likely to peck when the green light would not occur; and they were likely to exhibit more than a single peck when more than a single peck would cause the green light to occur.

The conditioned reinforcement explanation of observing responses is also supported by evidence indicating that the strength of observing responses is influenced by independent variables known to affect the strength of responses established with conditioned reinforcers. Larger amounts of reinforcement (Mitchell, Perkins, & Perkins, 1965) and greater food deprivation (Wheling & Prokasy, 1962) increased the strength of observing responses. There is no apparent reason why amount of reinforcement and deprivation level should affect the reinforcing strength of information, so these findings support the conditioned reinforcement explanation of observing responses.

Observing responses are also acquired when shock is employed (Dinsmoor, Flint, Smith, & Viemeister, 1969; Perkins, Seymann, Levis, & Spencer, 1966). In these studies, the observing response sometimes caused a stimulus paired with the absence of shock to occur, and sometimes caused a stimulus paired with the occurrence of shock to take place. Acquisition of the observing response was probably established with the stimulus paired with the absence of shock, because this stimulus should have been a positive conditioned reinforcer. Dinsmoor et al. showed that the observing response was acquired when it caused either the stimulus paired with the absence of shock or the stimulus paired with shock to occur; that the same response was acquired when it caused only the stimulus paired with the absence of shock to occur; and that the same response was not acquired when it caused only the stimulus paired with shock to occur. Therefore, it appears that the observing response was acquired because it was a reward-trained response established with the positive conditioned reinforcer of the stimulus paired with the absence of shock.

Adventitious Reinforcement

Suppose that a response does not cause a goal stimulus or negative-goal stimulus to occur, but that it is relatively likely to be followed by a stimulus that is more likely to be either approached and continued to be perceived or escaped from and avoided than are the stimuli present before this response is made. It would seem possible that such a response would be exhibited with a strength that would be greater than would otherwise occur. If the strength of the response is so altered, *adventitious reinforcement* of it has occurred. Responding that is affected by adventitious reinforcement is also called *superstitious behavior,* following Skinner (1948).

Adventitious Reinforcement with Response-Independent Reinforcement. The idea that the strength of a response is increased through adventitious reinforcement has been supported by delivering a reinforcer independently of responding. In a study of Lattal (1972), rats were first trained to respond on a multiple (MULT) FI VI schedule. Subsequently, the FI component schedule was replaced by a component schedule that delivered food independently of responding, at the same fixed-interval of time that the FI component schedule was programmed to provide food contingent upon the execution of the instrumental response. At the same time, the VI component schedule was replaced by a component schedule that delivered food independently of responding, at the same intervals of time that the VI component schedule was programmed to provide food contingent upon the execution of the instrumental response. The FI-like and VI-like schedules that delivered food independently of responding are called fixed-time (FT) and variable-time (VT) schedules, respectively. Thus, the MULT FI VI schedule was changed to a MULT FT VT schedule.

One result was that the rate of lever pressing on the FT and VT component schedules was less than the rate of responding on the FI and VI component schedules. This finding suggests that in general a response that causes a goal or negative-goal stimulus to occur maintains a stronger response than does the response-independent delivery of the same stimulus, an assumption that has been implicitly made all along.

The MULT FT VT schedule maintained responding at a not particularly low rate for the 25 and 50 experimental sessions (for different rats) that this schedule remained in effect. In addition, the rate of responding on the MULT FT VT schedule was considerably greater than the rate of responding on a MULT EXT EXT schedule that was subsequently introduced. The not particularly low rate of responding that occurred on the MULT FT VT schedule suggests that responding on this schedule was maintained by adventitious reinforcement. Lever pressing was originally acquired through response-dependent reinforcement provided by the FI and VI component schedules. Lever pressing therefore occurred when the MULT FT VT schedule was first introduced. Because response-independent food occurred on the MULT FT VT schedule, lever pressing was sometimes followed by food relatively quickly, even though lever pressing did not cause food to occur. Therefore, lever pressing on the MULT FT VT schedule may have been maintained through adventitious reinforcement.

A third result was that the extent of the reduction in the rate of lever pressing that occurred following the change from the FI component schedule to the FT component schedule was noticeably less than the extent of the reduction in the rate of lever pressing that occurred following the change from the VI component schedule to the VT component schedule. This result also suggests that responding on the MULT FT VT schedule was maintained by adventitious reinforcement. The scallop pattern of responding that is fairly typical of responding on FI schedules in general occurred on the FI component schedule. This means that when the FT component schedule was introduced, the rate of responding would be quite high just prior to the response-independent delivery of food by the FT schedule. Therefore, responding on the FT component schedule should have been relatively likely to be maintained through adventitious reinforcement. The rate of responding on the VI component schedule was steady, as is typical for VI schedules in general. Also, the response-independent delivery of food by the VT component schedule occurred by definition at variable intervals of time. Therefore, a high rate of responding on the VT component schedule was not particularly likely to be followed by the response-independent delivery of food. Thus, adventitious reinforcement of responding on the VT component schedule should have been less likely to occur than on the FT component schedule. This consideration probably accounts for the greater reduction in the rate of responding occurring for the VI to VT change than for the FI to FT change.

Adventitious Reinforcement in Multiple and Concurrent Schedules.

Adventitious reinforcement can maintain responding on components of multiple and concurrent schedules.

Morse (1955), as described in Kelleher (1966), first trained pigeons to respond on a MULT VI 3 (minute) FR 25 schedule. Subsequently, the FR 25 component schedule was changed to extinction; that is, the new schedule was MULT VI 3 EXT. The response rate on the EXT component schedule decreased, but not as much as it normally does when an individual (independent) extinction schedule is in effect. Later on, a 2-minute time-out was introduced between the EXT and VI 3 component schedules. During this 2-minute interval, responding had no programmed consequences, reinforcement was not delivered, and neither the S+ nor S— of the MULT VI EXT schedule was present. Introduction of the 2-minute time-out resulted in a further decrease in the response rate occurring on the EXT component schedule.

It appears that adventitious reinforcement maintained the responding on the EXT component of the MULT VI 3 EXT schedule that occurred prior to the introduction of the 2-minute time-out. Responding on the EXT component schedule when it was first introduced occurred at a relatively high rate due to the FR component schedule having previously been in effect. Thus, responding on the EXT component schedule when it was first introduced was followed by the S+ of the VI 3 component schedule, but did not cause this S+ to occur. The S+ of the VI 3 component schedule should have been a positive conditioned reinforcer. In addition, responding on the EXT component schedule when it was introduced was followed by food delivered by the VI 3 component schedule, but did not cause this food to occur. Therefore, the result that the rate of responding on the EXT component schedule was not particularly low was probably because responding had been maintained by adventitious conditioned reinforcement and/or primary reinforcement. Note that the S+ of the VI 3 component schedule immediately followed the EXT component schedule, and therefore may have contributed more than the food to the adventitious reinforcement of responding on the EXT component schedule. Introduction of the 2-minute time-out increased the delay between responding on the EXT component schedule and occurrence of positive reinforcement, and therefore should have decreased the rate of responding on the EXT component schedule, the obtained result.

Adventitious reinforcement of responding may occur on concurrent schedules as well. In a study of Catania and Cutts (1963), college students responded on a CONC VI 30 (seconds) EXT schedule. The operanda were two keys. Verbal instructions indicated that the reinforcer was to be a flash of green light. Thus, green light was delivered on a VI 30 (second) component schedule for responding on one key, and it was never delivered for responding on the second key. Almost all the students responded on the EXT component schedule to some extent, and many subjects responded on it at about the same rate as on the VI 30 component schedule.

Explanation of the obtained unusually high rate of responding on the EXT component schedule is like the explanation of maintained responding on the EXT component of a multiple schedule discussed above. The students responded on the VI 30 component schedule soon after responding on the EXT component schedule. Responding on the EXT component schedule was therefore followed by, but did not cause, reinforcements obtained by responding on the VI 30 component schedule. Thus, adventitious reinforcement of responding on the EXT component schedule probably occurred.

Summary

The nature of the response that no particular event elicits tends to be altered in a direction opposite to the response elicited by a perceived reinforcer when no particular event occurs in sufficiently close physical and temporal proximity to the reinforcer. A contrast effect on the response to a perceived reinforcer also occurs. The weaker of two perceived positive reinforcers that occurred in relatively close physical and temporal proximity elicited escape and avoidance and aggressive responses. In addition, the strength of a response to a perceived reinforcer is increased if the reinforcer occurs in relatively close physical and temporal proximity to a weaker reinforcer; an analogous result is obtained for the response elicited by the weaker of two perceived reinforcers. Contrast effects on the responses to perceived stimuli should also occur when the relevant stimuli take place simultaneously. In addition, it is likely that contrast effects on the responses to perceived stimuli will be maximal when the relevant stimuli occur simultaneously. Contrast effects on the perception of stimuli occur, both when the two relevant stimuli take place in relatively close physical and temporal proximity to each other, and when they occur simultaneously. The magnitude of contrast effects in perception is probably also maximal when the two relevant stimuli occur simultaneously. A contrast effect on a response to a perceived stimulus 1 that results because stimulus 2 occurs in sufficiently close physical and temporal proximity to stimulus 1 should be the consequence of an image of stimulus 2 taking place. The magnitude of the contrast effect on the response to a perceived stimulus should increase with an increase in the vividness of the image of the relevant stimulus not currently perceived. The extent of the physical and temporal proximity of one relevant stimulus to a second relevant stimulus should affect the vividness of the image of the not currently present relevant stimulus that occurs; therefore, the strength of the contrast effect on the response to the perceived relevant stimulus should be affected.

All contrast effects on learned responses are analyzed as the outcome of factors correlated with the occurrence of contrast effects on responses to perceived stimuli. That no particular event tends to be either approached and continued to be perceived or escaped from and avoided when it occurs in relatively close physical and temporal proximity to a reinforcer is a contrast effect that is basic to (a) the explanation of classical conditioning in which a CS is paired with the absence or termination of a UCS; and (b) the explanation of the avoidance, escape, omission, and response-terminates-reward learning types of instrumental conditioning. Multiple schedules and their effects on responding are described. The nature of a learned response can be affected when two positive reinforcement conditions occur in relatively close physical and temporal proximity. This supports the conclusion that the nature of the learned response can be affected through a contrast effect operating on the response to no particular event. A study is described in which the EXT component of a MULT VI EXT schedule was responsible for increasing the rate of responding on the VI component of the MULT VI EXT schedule. This and other contrast effects on the strength of a learned response are probably mediated by factors correlated with the occurrence of contrast effects on the strength of the response to the perceived reinforcer establishing the learned response. Studies are described in which multiple schedules with components delivering different amounts of reinforcement, different rates of reinforcement, different delays of reinforcement, and reinforcement plus shock resulted in contrast effects on learned responses. Contrast effects on discrete trial reward learning have frequently been obtained by putting unequal reinforcement conditions into effect for traversal of two similar runways. A contrast effect on an escape-trained response is described. The positive induction result and a second classical conditioning result appear to be contrast effects on the CR.

Contrast effects on learned responses should involve the simultaneous occurrence of images of both relevant stimuli. Relatively close physical proximity between two learning situations or the occurrence of a sufficiently large amount of stimulus generalization between two learning situations should permit an image of the relevant stimulus of the learning situation not currently in effect to occur, and thus should permit a contrast effect on a learned response to take place. Analyses of the effects of both the amount of stimulus generalization occurring between two learning situations and the length of the time interval separating two learning situations on the magnitude of a contrast effect on a learned response are based, in part, on the assumption that the magnitude of the contrast effect on the response to a perceived stimulus increases with an increase in the vividness of the image of the relevant stimulus not currently perceived. An increase in the amount of stimulus generalization occurring between two learning situations should result in a stronger contrast effect on a learned response; some, but not all, findings support this prediction. An increase in the temporal proximity between two learning situations should also result in a stronger contrast effect on a learned response, a prediction that has been well supported.

Contrast effects on learned responses are obtained even though discrimination learning is not carried out. In reward learning, an animal probably actively refrains from not responding and making responses other than the instrumental response because the nature of the response to no particular event is affected through contrast. Also, an animal probably actively refrains from responding more slowly in acquisition of reward learning because the nature of the response to stimuli involved with a more delayed reinforcer is affected through contrast. In a reward-learning discrimination, responding in the presence of or to irrelevant stimuli results in a lower rate of reinforcement than responding in the presence of or to S+. Responding in the presence of or to irrelevant stimuli should therefore be inhibited through contrast. A contrast effect operating on the reinforcer delivered by a ratio schedule may account for why the rate of responding on ratio schedules is greater than the rate of responding on the CRF schedule. Within-group procedures involve the same animal being exposed to two different reinforcement conditions, and thereby entail the occurrence of contrast effects. Learning-induced polydipsia may be the outcome of a contrast effect on the response to the perceived reinforcer of water.

Simultaneous discriminations between two stimuli signalling different positive reinforcement conditions result in almost exclusive responding to the stimulus correlated with the stronger positive reinforcement condition. This finding is the consequence of the exhibited choice response being the one that is better learned. Concurrent schedules permit an animal to respond on, and switch back and forth between, simultaneously available component schedules. The major effects on different concurrent schedules on the choice of responding between component schedules are due to the response that causes the shorter delay of reinforcement to occur being the one that is acquired. Exclusive responding on the smaller of two ratio component schedules usually occurs. Responding on the FR component schedule of a CONC FR FI schedule tends to occur soon after a reinforcer is delivered by the FI component schedule; later on in the FI interval, responding tends to occur on the FI component schedule. CONC VI VI schedules result in relatively frequent switching from one VI component schedule to the other, and proportionately more time spent on responding on the VI component schedule delivering the greater rate of reinforcement. The average local delay of reinforcement provided by the two VI component schedules of a CONC VI VI schedule should be equal, which probably accounts for or helps to account for the finding that local reinforcement and local response rates on the VI component schedules are equal.

Observing-response studies involve either of two different reinforcement conditions being in effect at any one time. An observing response causes one stimulus to occur if the first reinforcement condition is in effect, and it causes a second stimulus to occur if the other reinforcement condition is operative. The stimulus signalling the more "positive" reinforcement condition should be a positive conditioned reinforcer. Because the observing response causes a positive conditioned reinforcer to occur, it appears to be a reward-trained response established with this reinforcer. This possibility is supported by studies that show that the strength of responding decreases markedly when the instrumental response no longer causes the positive conditioned reinforcer for the observing response to occur.

Responding may be maintained by response-independent reinforcement, probably through the adventitious reinforcement of previously established learning. Responding may also be maintained on the EXT components of multiple and concurrent schedules by the positive reinforcement components of these schedules, again probably through adventitious reinforcement.

REFERENCES

Adams, D. L., & Allen, J. D. Compound stimulus control by discriminative stimuli associated with high and moderate response rates. *J. Exp. Anal. Behav.*, 1971, 16, 201-205.

Adelman, H. M., & Maatsch, J. L. Learning and extinction based upon frustration, food reward and exploratory tendency. *J. Exp. Psychol.*, 1956, 52, 311-315.

AMSEL, A., & MALTZMAN, I. The effect upon generalized drive strength of emotionality as inferred from the level of consummatory response. *J. Exp. Psychol.*, 1950, 40, 563-569.

AMSEL, A., & ROUSSEL, J. Motivational properties of frustration: I. Effect on a running response of the addition of frustration to the motivational complex. *J. Exp. Psychol.*, 1952, 43, 363-368.

ANDERSON, A. C. Time discrimination in the white rat. *J. Comp. Psychol.*, 1932, 13, 27-55.

AZRIN, N. H., HUTCHINSON, R. R., & HAKE, D. F. Extinction-induced aggression. *J. Exp. Anal. Behav.*, 1966, 9, 191-204.

BAUM, W. M., & RACHLIN, H. C. Choice as time allocation. *J. Exp. Anal. Behav.*, 1969, 12, 861-874.

BENEFIELD, R., OSCÓS, A., & EHRENFREUND, D. Role of frustration in successive positive contrast. *J. Comp. Physiol. Psychol.*, 1974, 86, 648-651.

BERNHEIM, J. W., & WILLIAMS, D. R. Time-dependent contrast effects in a multiple schedule of food reinforcement. *J. Exp. Anal. Behav.*, 1967, 10, 243-249.

BOWER, G. H. A contrast effect in differential conditioning. *J. Exp. Psychol.*, 1961, 62, 196-199.

BUCK, S. L., ROTHSTEIN, B., & WILLIAMS, B. A. A re-examination of local contrast in multiple schedules. *J. Exp. Anal. Behav.*, 1975, 24, 291-301.

CALEF, R. S., CALEF, R. A. B., MAXWELL, F. R., & McHEWITT, E. R. Positive discrimination contrast with delay of reward or low drive. *Bull. Psychon. Soc.*, 1975, 6, 120-122.

CATANIA, A. C. Concurrent operants. In W. K. Honig (Ed.), *Operant Behavior: Areas of Research and Application*. New York: Appleton-Century-Crofts, 1966.

CATANIA, A. C., & CUTTS, D. Experimental control of superstitious responding in humans. *J. Exp. Anal. Behav.*, 1963, 6, 203-208.

COATES, T. J. The differential effects of punishment and extinction on behavioral contrast. *Psychon. Sci.*, 1972, 27, 146-148.

COHEN, J., HANSEL, C. E. M., & SYLVESTER, J. D. Interdependence of temporal and auditory judgments. *Nature*, 1954, 174, 642-644.

COHEN, P. S., & LOONEY, T. A. Schedule-induced mirror responding in the pigeon. *J. Exp. Anal. Behav.*, 1973, 19, 395-408.

COLE, J. M., & LITCHFIELD, P. M. Stimulus control of schedule-induced aggression in the pigeon. *Psychon. Sci.*, 1969, 17, 152-153.

D'AMATO, M. R., LACHMAN, R., & KIVY, P. Secondary reinforcement as affected by reward schedule and the testing situation. *J. Comp. Physiol. Psychol.*, 1958, 51, 734-741.

DINSMOOR, J. A., FLINT, G. A., SMITH, R. F., & VIEMEISTER, N. F. Differential reinforcing effects of stimuli associated with the presence or absence of a schedule of punishment. In D. P. Hendry (Ed.), *Conditioned Reinforcement*. Homewood, Ill.: Dorsey Press, 1969.

FALK, J. L. The motivational properties of schedule-induced polydipsia. *J. Exp. Anal. Behav.*, 1966, 9, 19-25.

FARTHING, G. W. Behavioral contrast in pigeons learning an auditory discrimination. *Bull. Psychon. Soc.*, 1975, 6, 123-125.

FERSTER, C. B., & SKINNER, B. F. *Schedules of Reinforcement*. New York: Appleton-Century-Crofts, 1957.

FLAHERTY, C. F., & LARGEN, J. Within-subjects positive and negative contrast effects in rats. *J. Comp. Physiol. Psychol.*, 1975, 88, 653-664.

GUTMAN, A., SUTTERER, J. R., & BRUSH, F. R. Positive and negative behavioral contrast in the rat. *J. Exp. Anal. Behav.*, 1975, 23, 377-383.

GUTTMAN, N. Generalization gradients around stimuli associated with different reinforcement schedules. *J. Exp. Psychol.*, 1959, 58, 335-340.

HARRIS, D. R., COLLERAIN, I., WOLF, J. C., & LUDVIGSON, H. W. Negative S- contrast with minimally contingent large reward as a function of trial initiation procedure. *Psychon. Sci.*, 1970, 19, 189-190.

HEARST, E. Excitation, inhibition and discrimination learning. In N. J. Mackintosh and W. K. Honig (Eds.), *Fundamental Issues in Associative Learning*. Halifax: Dalhousie University Press, 1969.

HELSON, H. *Adaptation-level Theory: An Experimental and Systematic Approach to Behavior*. New York: Harper & Row, 1964.

HERRNSTEIN, R. J. Some factors influencing behavior in a two-response situation. *Trans. N. Y. Acad. Sci.*, 1958, 21, 35-45.

HERRNSTEIN, R. J., & LOVELAND, D. H. Maximizing and matching on concurrent ratio schedules. *J. Exp. Anal. Behav.*, 1975, 24, 107-116.

HILL, W. F., & SPEAR, N. E. Choice between magnitudes of reward in a T-maze. *J. Comp. Physiol. Psychol.*, 1963, 56, 723-726.

KEEHN, J. D., & COLOTLA, V. A. Stimulus and subject control of schedule-induced drinking. *J. Exp. Anal. Behav.*, 1971, 16, 257-262.

KELLEHER, R. T. Chaining and conditioned reinforcement. In W. K. Honig (Ed.), *Operant Behavior: Areas of Research and Application*. New York: Appleton-Century-Crofts, 1966.

KELLER, K. The role of elicited responding in behavioral contrast. *J. Exp. Anal. Behav.*, 1974, 21, 249-257.

KENDALL, S. B. Redundant information in an observing-response procedure. *J. Exp. Anal. Behav.*, 1973, 19, 81-92.

KILLEEN, P. A yoked-chamber comparison of concurrent and multiple schedules. *J. Exp. Anal. Behav.*, 1972, 18, 13-22.

LaBOUNTY, C. E., & REYNOLDS, G. S. An analysis of response and time matching to reinforcement in concurrent ratio-interval schedules. *J. Exp. Anal. Behav.*, 1973, 19, 155-166.

LATTAL, K. A. Response-reinforcer independence and conventional extinction after fixed-interval and variable-interval schedules. *J. Exp. Anal. Behav.*, 1972, 18, 133-140.

LAWSON, R. Brightness discrimination performance and secondary reward strength as a function of primary reward amount. *J. Comp. Physiol. Psychol.*, 1957, 50, 35-39.

LEVENTHAL, A. M., MORRELL, R. F., MORGAN, E. F., JR., & PERKINS, C. C., JR. The relation between mean reward and mean reinforcement. *J. Exp. Psychol.*, 1959, 57, 284-287.

MACKINTOSH, N. J. *The Psychology of Animal Learning*. London: Academic Press, 1974.

MACKINTOSH, N. J., LITTLE, L., & LORD, J. Some determinants of behavioral contrast in pigeons and rats. *Learn. Motiv.*, 1972, 3, 148-161.

MACKINTOSH, N. J., & LORD, J. Simultaneous and successive contrast with delay of reward. *Anim. Learn. Behav.*, 1973, 1, 283-286.

MACPHAIL, E. M. Behavioral-contrast in discrete-trial discriminations: Effects of non-reinforcement. *Q. J. Exp. Psychol.*, 1975, 27, 259-271.

MALONE, J. C., JR. Stimulus-specific contrast effects during operant discrimination learning. *J. Exp. Anal. Behav.*, 1975, 24, 281-289.

MAXWELL, F. R., JR., MEYER, P. A., CALEF, R. S., & McHEWITT, E. R. Discrimination contrast: Speeds to small reward as a function of locus and amount of inter-polated reinforcement. *Psychon. Sci.*, 1969, 14, 35-36.

MELLGREN, R. L., WRATHER, D. M., & DYCK, D. G. Differential conditioning and contrast effects in rats. *J. Comp. Physiol. Psychol.*, 1972, 80, 478-483.

MITCHELL, K. M., PERKINS, N. P., & PERKINS, C. C., JR. Conditions affecting acquisition of observing responses in the absence of differential reward. *J. Comp. Physiol. Psychol.*, 1965, 60, 435-437.

MORSE, W. H. *An Analysis of Responding in the Presence of a Stimulus Correlated with Periods of Non-reinforcement.* Unpublished Ph.D. dissertation, Harvard University, 1955.

NATION, J. R., WRATHER, D. M., & MELLGREN, R. L. Contrast effects in escape conditioning of rats. *J. Comp. Physiol. Psychol.*, 1974, 86, 69-73.

NEEDHAM, J. G. Rate of presentation in the method of single stimuli. *Am. J. Psychol.*, 1935, 47, 275-284.

NEVIN, J. A., & SHETTLEWORTH, S. J. An analysis of contrast effects in multiple schedules. *J. Exp. Anal. Behav.*, 1966, 9, 305-315.

PADILLA, A M. Analysis of incentive and behavioral contrast in the rat. *J. Comp. Physiol. Psychol.*, 1971, 75, 464-470.   .

PAVLOV, I. P. *Conditioned Reflexes* (G. V. Anrep, trans.). Oxford: Oxford University Press, 1927.

PERKINS, C. C., JR., SEYMANN, R. G., LEVIS, D. J., & SPENCER, H. R., JR. Factors affecting preference for signal-shock over shock-signal. *J. Exp. Psychol.*, 1966, 72, 190-196.

PIERREL, R., & BLUE, S. Antecedent reinforcement contingencies in the stimulus control of an auditory discrimination. *J. Exp. Anal. Behav.*, 1967, 10, 545-550.

RACHLIN, H. Contrast and matching. *Psychol. Rev.*, 1973, 80, 217-234.

RICHARDS, R. W. Stimulus generalization and delay of reinforcement during one component of a multiple schedule. *J. Exp. Anal. Behav.*, 1973, 19, 303-309.

SCHWARTZ, B., HAMILTON, B., & SILBERBERG, A. Behavioral contrast in the pigeon: A study of the duration of key pecking maintained on multiple schedules of reinforcement. *J. Exp. Anal. Behav.*, 1973, 24, 199-206.

SKINNER, B. F. "Superstition" in the pigeon. *J. Exp. Psychol.*, 1948, 38, 168-172.

STERRITT, G. M. Inhibition and facilitation of eating by electric shock. *J. Comp. Physiol. Psychol.*, 1962, 55, 226-229.

STRICKER, E. M., & ADAIR, E. R. Body fluid balance, taste, and postprandial factors in schedule-induced polydipsia. *J. Comp. Physiol. Psychol.*, 1966, 62, 449-454.

TERRACE, H. S. Discrimination learning, the peak shift, and behavioral contrast. *J. Exp. Anal. Behav.*, 1968, 11, 727-741.

TINKLEPAUGH, O. L. An experimental study of representative factors in monkeys. *J. Comp. Psychol.*, 1928, 8, 197-236.

VOGEL, J. R., MIKULKA, P. J., & SPEAR, N. E. Effects of shifts in sucrose and saccharine concentrations on licking behavior in the rat. *J. Comp. Physiol. Psychol.*, 1968, 66, 661-666.

WAGNER, A. R., & RESCORLA, R. A. Inhibition in Pavlovian conditioning: Application of a theory. In R. A. Boakes and M. S. Halliday (Eds.), *Inhibition and Learning*. New York: Academic Press, 1972.

WEISMAN, R. G. Some determinants of inhibitory stimulus control. *J. Exp. Anal. Behav.*, 1969, 12, 443-450.

WEISS, S. J. Stimulus compounding in free-operant and classical conditioning: A review and analysis. *Psychol. Bull.*, 1972, 78, 189-208.

WHELING, H. E., & PROKASY, W. F. Role of food deprivation in the acquisition of the observing response. *Psychol. Rep.*, 1962, 10, 399-407.

YOSHIOKA, J. G. Weber's law in the discrimination of maze distance by the white rat. *University of California Publications in Psychology*, 1929, 4, 155-184.

ZEAMAN, D. Response latency as a function of the amount of reinforcement. *J. Exp. Psychol.*, 1949, 39, 466-483.

CHAPTER 8

Conditioning
and Intelligence

Conditioning leads to intelligence behavior. We define intelligence behavior as the occurrence of relatively extensive positive transfer of learning. Positive transfer of learning occurs when the acquisition of a learned response facilitates acquisition of another learned response. Relatively extensive positive transfer of learning occurs when the acquisition of a learned response facilitates acquisition of a relatively different response, of a response in a relatively different situation. Discussion of human intelligence almost always includes the idea that intelligence is, at least in part, the successful application of previous learning to relatively different situations; that is, intelligence involves the occurrence of relatively extensive positive transfer of learning.

Intelligence behavior differs from learned behavior in simple conditioning situations, for instance, in straightforward classical conditioning, such as salivary conditioning; straightforward instrumental conditioning, such as reward learning of bar pressing; and straightforward discrimination learning, such as brightness discrimination learning in a T-maze. Learned behavior occurring in simple conditioning situations is not considered intelligence behavior because performance in simple conditioning situations does not involve the occurrence of relatively extensive positive transfer of learning.

Another approach to the definition of intelligence behavior is to consider that better performance on a learning task that species with high

433

phylogenetic statuses do well on indicates more intelligence. Monkeys and apes are closest to man in phylogenetic status—they are all primates —but the fact is that nonprimates may perform better than monkeys and apes on learning tasks that involve the occurrence of relatively extensive positive transfer of learning. Thus, we prefer to consider intelligence behavior in terms of the extent of transfer of learning that occurs.

Language in Chimpanzees

The most exciting research on intelligence behavior in nonhuman animals is the work on acquisition of language by chimpanzees. Premack's (1971) research is of particular interest, because it shows extensive positive transfer of language learning. The language of humans obviously involves extensive positive transfer, because even a young child can understand and speak words occurring in new combinations. Premack's research also undeniably demonstrates that the stimuli employed as words result in some sort of symbol, representation, or image of the events they are intended to refer to, which supports image theory. Premack's work and other research on language learning in chimpanzees employ small visual stimuli as words; chimpanzees perform well on straightforward discriminations between these kinds of stimuli.

Beginning of Object Language. Premack used pieces of magnetized plastic as words. Training frequently involved placing them on a metal board. Initially, a chimpanzee, Sarah, was taught to associate a specific plastic word, for example, a blue piece of plastic, with a specific fruit, for example, an apple, by requiring her to place the presented plastic word on the magnetic board while the fruit was present. She was then given the fruit by the experimenter. An experimenter remained in sight of and close to Sarah during all stages of testing. Plastic words for the experimenters were then introduced, each experimenter wearing the plastic object that signified him or herself around the neck. Then Sarah was required to place two plastic words on the magnetic board to obtain the apple or some other food placed in front of her—the plastic word for the experimenter, and the plastic word for the food. In addition, the two plastic words had to be placed on the magnetic board in the correct order for the food to be received. This order usually corresponded to the order of words in the English language. Thus, Sarah had to "write" the plastic word sentence, "Mary apple," (not "apple Mary") for Mary to give Sarah a piece of apple.

Sarah learned other words and longer sentences by much the same procedures. Verbs were used in the longer sentences. Training with them consisted of repeating the action a plastic word referred to with several objects. An example of a longer sentence that Sarah came to write is, "Mary give apple Gussie," which indicates that Mary is to give a piece of apple to Gussie (another chimpanzee).

Throughout Sarah's language learning program, new learning was based on previously acquired learning. In both the plastic-word sentences, "Mary apple," and "Mary give apple Gussie," the plastic word for Mary preceded the plastic word for apple. It is thought likely that Sarah's acquisition of longer plastic-word sentences was facilitated by previously acquired shorter word sentences, and Sarah's acquisition of the longer word sentences facilitated retention of the shorter word sentences, since words in the shorter and longer plastic-word sentences were in the same order. Language learning in human children appears similar. The acquisition of longer sentences is facilitated by prior acquisition of similar shorter sentences; and retention of previously learned shorter sentences is facilitated by acquisition of similar longer sentences. In other words, the structure of language appears to allow for transfer of learning from shorter to longer sentences, which simultaneously facilitates retention of shorter sentences.

Same, Different, and Question. To teach the meaning of the word, "same," Premack began by placing identical objects, for example, two cups, in front of Sarah. The plastic word for "same" was made available to Sarah, and she learned to place it between the identical objects placed before her. An analogous procedure was followed for the plastic word for "different," except that nonidentical pairs of objects were employed. Then Sarah was given both the plastic word for "same" and the plastic word for "different"; in addition, identical or nonidentical pairs of the objects previously used in training were placed before her, one pair at a time. The correct response was to place the correct plastic word, either "same" or "different," between each pair of objects. Subsequently, pairs of identical and nonidentical objects that had not been previously used were placed before Sarah, one pair at a time. Sarah placed the correct plastic word between these pairs of new objects. The use of new objects was a somewhat different learning situation. Sarah therefore exhibited relatively extensive positive transfer of learning, that is, intelligence behavior.

The plastic words for "same" and "different" were then used to introduce the plastic word for question, represented as "?". Four types of sentences asking questions are given in Figure 8-1. The plastic words for "same," "different," and "?" are the dark four-sided form; the light four-sided form with two equal marks on it; and the roundish object with a

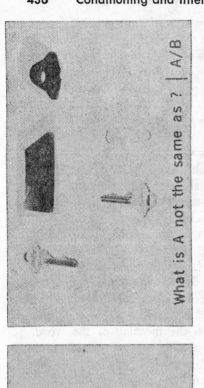

What is A the same as ? | A/B

What is A not the same as ? | A/B

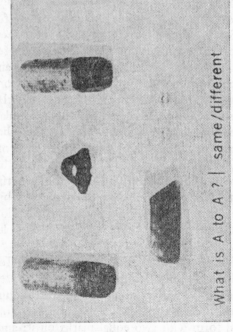

What is A to A ? | same/different

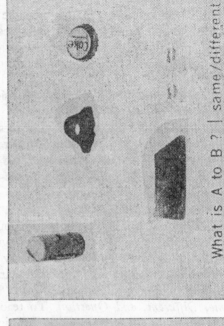

What is A to B ? | same/different

FIGURE 8-1. Sentences which include the plastic words for "same," "different," and "?" and real objects. (Premack, D. Language in chimpanzee? Science, May 21, 1971, 172, 808-822. Copyright 1971 by the American Association for the Advancement of Science.)

hole in it, respectively. The remainder of the items shown were real objects, that is, not plastic words. In the two sentences appearing in the top row of Figure 8-1, Sarah's task was to remove the plastic word for "?" and replace it with the correct object, either the one identical to or different from the one in the sentence, depending on whether the plastic word for "same" or "different" was employed in the sentence. In the two sentences appearing in the bottom row in Figure 8-1, Sarah's task was to remove the plastic word for "?" and replace it with the correct plastic word, either "same" or "different," depending on whether or not the two objects of the sentence were identical. An example of one of the sentences is "? same stamp." Placed before Sarah were a stamp and a paper clip. The correct response to this sentence was to replace the plastic word for "?" with the stamp rather than with the paper clip. Sarah successfully responded on the sentences in Figure 8-1 with a wide variety of objects.

Yes and No Questions. Initial training with the plastic words for "yes" and "no" was with sentences of the form "? object A same object B," where "?" and "same" were plastic words, and object A and object B were either identical or nonidentical real objects. When object A was identical to object B, Sarah was given the plastic word for "yes." She learned to replace the plastic word for "?" with it. Initial training with the plastic word for "no" was analogous, except that object A differed from object B.

Then both the plastic words for "yes" and "no" were made available to Sarah, and the correct response was to replace the plastic word for "?" appearing in the sentences in Figure 8-2 with either the plastic word for "yes" or "no." The daggerlike piece of plastic is the word for "yes," the piece of plastic adjacent to it is the word for "no," and the plastic words for "same," "different," and "?" are as described. The remainder of the components of the sentence were real objects. Consider the sentence in the bottom row, right column of Figure 8-2. It reads "? penny different penny." The correct response was to replace the plastic word for "?" with the plastic word for "no," rather than with the plastic word for "yes." With a little training, Sarah performed well on these sentences.

Name of and Not Name of. Training on the meaning of "name of" and "not name of" was undertaken. Sarah was taught to place the single plastic word for "name of" between the plastic word for "apple," which she previously had received training on, and a real apple. Analogous training was carried out with the plastic word for "name of," the plastic word for "banana," and a real banana. Sarah was also taught to insert

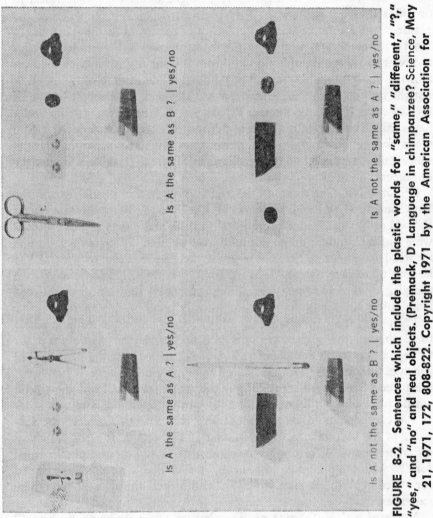

FIGURE 8-2. Sentences which include the plastic words for "same," "different," "?," "yes," and "no" and real objects. (Premack, D. Language in chimpanzee? Science, May 21, 1971, 172, 808-822. Copyright 1971 by the American Association for the Advancement of Science.)

the single plastic word for "not name of" between the plastic word for "banana" and a real apple, and to place the plastic word for "not name of" between the plastic word for "apple" and a real banana. Subsequently, the plastic words for "name of" and "not name of" were both placed before Sarah, and she had to insert one of these plastic words between pairs, one member of which was the plastic word for either "apple" or "banana," and the other member of which was a real apple or banana. She performed appropriately on this choice task. For example, when the plastic word for "apple" and a real banana were presented, she usually inserted the plastic word for "not name of" rather than the plastic word for "name of" between these two items.

Sarah was now given sentences which, if answered correctly, would indicate the occurrence of a considerable extent of positive transfer of learning, and therefore a relatively high level of intelligence behavior. She was given sentences such as "? banana name of apple," in which "?," "banana," and "name of" were plastic words, and apple was a real apple. In addition, she also had available the plastic words for "yes" and "no." These types of questions she answered correctly without further training. For example, for the sentence, "? banana name of apple," she replaced the plastic word for "?" with the plastic word for "no," rather than with the plastic word for "yes." Sarah's previous training with yes-no questions consisted of (a) using two real objects rather than a real object and a plastic word for an object; and (b) the plastic words for "same" and "different," rather than the plastic words for "name of" and "not name of." Therefore, her correct responses to this type of yes-no question shows positive transfer to a quite different situation.

This positive transfer supports the idea that the plastic words for "apple" and "banana" represented, symbolized, or resulted in an image of a real apple and banana, respectively. How else could transfer of the correct choice from questions containing two real objects (used in the training on yes-no questions) to questions containing a real object and a plastic word for the object (used in the transfer test) occur?

The described transfer also indicates that considerable understanding of the meanings of the plastic words for "yes" and "no" had been acquired. The "it is true" and "it is not true" meaning of yes and no were in evidence in the transfer tests, even though the plastic words for "name of" and "not name of" and the plastic words for objects appeared in the sentences used for the transfer tests; the stimuli present during training on "yes" and "no," that is, "same," "different," and two real objects in a sentence, did not appear in these sentences. The described transfer also indicates that understanding of the meanings of "name of" and "not name of" had been acquired. The meaning of the plastic word for "name of" is approximately "match between the plastic word for an object and the real object," and the meaning of the plastic word for "not name of" is approximately "no match between the plastic word for an object and a real object." These meanings were evidenced by Sarah's performance on the transfer tests, because they presented a choice between the plastic words for "yes" and "no," and training with the plastic words for "name of" and "not name of" did not involve the plastic words for "yes" and "no."

Another type of transfer test also indicated Sarah had acquired the meanings of the plastic words for "name of" and "not name of." Training on these plastic words involved using real bananas and apples and the plastic words for bananas and apples. The second type of transfer test employed sentences such as "? name of dish," in which "?" and "name of" were plastic words, and dish was a real dish. When Sarah received this sentence, the plastic words for "dish," "pail," "apple," and "raisin" were placed before her. She replaced the plastic word for "?" with the plastic word for "dish," and performed successfully on similar transfer tasks. This result indicates that the meanings of "name of" and "not name of" had been acquired to a considerable extent, because correct responding was not dependent on using the real objects and plastic words for these objects that were used in training.

Colors, Color of, and Not Color of. Training on the plastic words for "red" and "yellow" was undertaken. Training on the plastic word for "red" involved giving Sarah the plastic words for "Mary" (one of the experimenters), "give," "Sarah," and "red," the last word being the only one unfamiliar to Sarah. In addition, placed before Sarah were a variety of red objects, a ball, toy car, a Life Saver, and three other items. Sarah then wrote the sentence, "Mary give Sarah red," whereupon the experimenter (Mary) gave her one of the red objects. Analogous training was carried out with the plastic word for yellow. Subsequently, Sarah was given the plastic words for both "red" and "yellow," along with the plastic words for "Mary," "give," and "Sarah." Either a red or yellow object was placed before Sarah, and her task was to write the correct sentence, that is, the sentence that used the plastic word for the color that matched the color of the real object placed before her. She performed correctly on this task from the start. In addition, she established positive transfer to analogous tasks employing red and yellow objects that had not been used in training on the plastic words for "red" and "yellow."

Training on the plastic words for "color of" and "not color of" then ensued. One sentence used for this purpose was "red ? apple," in which all three items were plastic words. Sarah was also given the single plastic word for "color of," which she learned to insert in place of the plastic word for "?". Analogous training took place with the plastic words for "yellow" and "banana." Sentences such as "red ? banana," in which all three items were plastic words, were used to train Sarah with the single plastic word for "not color of." Subsequently, choice tests between the plastic words for "color of" and "not color of" were given. Sarah was presented with sentences, and she was supposed to replace the plastic word for "?" in these sentences with the correct plastic word, either "color of" or "not color of." Her initial performance on the choice tests was good.

Sarah was then presented with sentences such as "red ? cherry," in which all the items were plastic words. The plastic word for cherry had not previously been used with the plastic words for individual colors, or for "color of," and "not color of." Sarah responded correctly on this type of transfer task. For example, for the sentence, "red ? cherry," she replaced the plastic word for "?" with the plastic word for "color of," rather than the plastic word for "not color of."

Sarah's ability to respond correctly to this type of sentence indicates that the plastic words for objects in these sentences did represent, result in symbols of, or, as image theory maintains, lead to images of the real objects they correspond to. For example, Sarah in some sense matched the plastic word for "red" with the plastic word for "cherry," since she indicated that red was the color of cherry—but this matching could not have been accomplished unless the plastic word for "cherry" resulted in something approximating an image of a real cherry, because a real cherry is red, whereas the plastic word for "cherry" is not.

Words, Referents, and Classical Conditioning. The described results indicate that plastic words result in images of their referents. Classical conditioning between a plastic word and its referent should certainly be possible, according to image theory. In the initial training with plastic words, the plastic word and its referent were presented simultaneously. The simultaneous presentation of a plastic word and its referent should allow for focusing on first the plastic word and then the referent and vice versa. Thus, S_1-S_2 and S_2-S_1 acquired associations should be formed, where S_1 and S_2 are a plastic word and its referent. A plastic word and its referent are usually neutral stimuli, and we know that paired neutral stimuli become associated through the classical conditioning process. Therefore, viewing a plastic word should result in an image of its referent.

In human languages, words represent stimuli. A word and its referent probably become associated through classical conditioning, and the knowledge that a word represents a stimulus results from the word's functioning as a CS and producing an image of its referent. Thus, image theory provides an explanation for what is probably the most essential aspect of language, namely, that words represent stimuli.

Use of Language to Establish an Association between Word and Referent. Language itself is able to establish an association between a word and its referent. Training on the plastic word for "color of" involved using real red objects and the plastic word for "red," and real yellow objects and the plastic word for "yellow." Premack used the plastic word for "color of," rather than real brown objects to establish the referent for brown.

The sentence, "? color of chocolate," all plastic words, was given to Sarah. In addition, she was shown the plastic word for "brown," a word that had not been previously used. She replaced the plastic word for "?" with the plastic word for "brown." Knowledge of the referent for the plastic word for brown was then tested with the sentence, "Sarah take brown," all plastic words. Sarah was shown a number of objects, only one of which was brown, and took the brown object. She also performed well with analogous training and testing with the plastic word for "green."

This finding suggests that the plastic words, "color of chocolate," gave the plastic word for "brown" the appropriate referent, since the plastic word for "brown" had not previously been used. Sentence components in all languages probably contribute to the meaning of an individual word in a sentence. For example, the first five words, "The man went to the," of a six-word sentence contributes to the meaning of the sixth word: it is a place to go and occupies a position in space.

Language is an efficient means of teaching additional aspects of language. Many red and yellow objects had to be used to teach Sarah the referents for the plastic words for "red" and "yellow." Because of this training, only one sentence, "brown color of chocolate," was necessary for Sarah to acquire the referent for the plastic word for "brown."

Sarah's acquisition of this referent also indicates that the plastic word for "chocolate" resulted in an image of real chocolate, which is brown. Only the plastic word for "chocolate" was used in training with the plastic word for "brown"; if "chocolate" did not result in an image of real chocolate, how else could Sarah have chosen the real brown object when given the sentence, "Sarah take brown"?

Sarah's performance also suggests that she acquired associations between plastic words in two directions. Training on the plastic word for "color of" was based on sentences in which the plastic words for "red" and "yellow" appeared together with the plastic word for "color of." The referent for the plastic word for "brown" was acquired when this word appeared in the same sentence as the plastic word for "color of." Learning therefore probably occurred in two directions at different times —initially from plastic words for specific colors to the plastic word for "color of," and subsequently in the reverse direction. This reversability may have resulted from classical conditioning between the plastic word for a specific color and the plastic word for "color of" occurring in two directions. These two plastic words were presented simultaneously. If Sarah's eyes focused on them in different order, it would lead to classical conditioning between them in two directions.

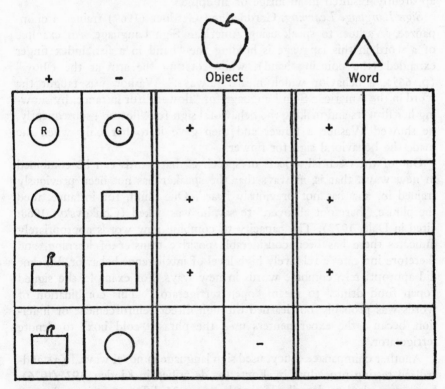

FIGURE 8-3. Choice of items that are more similar to a real apple and the plastic word for apple. (Premack, D. Language in chimpanzee? Science, May 21, 1971, 172, 808-822. Copyright 1971 by the American Association for the Advancement of Science.)

Words and Images of Their Referents. The idea that a plastic word leads to some kind of image of a real stimulus was investigated directly. First, Sarah chose which members of pairs of items were more similar to a real apple. These pairs were presented to her one at a time. The first two columns of Figure 8-3 indicate the pairs of items employed. For example, a red (R) circle and a green (G) circle were presented, and Sarah's task was to choose the member of this pair that more closely matched a real (red) apple. Sarah matched the red circle with the real apple, as indicated by the plus mark in the first row, third column of Figure 8-3. Subsequently, she was presented with the blue piece of plastic that was the word for apple. She continued to choose the member of the pair of items that more closely matched a real apple, as indicated in columns 5 and 6 of Figure 8-3. Therefore, the plastic word for "apple" apparently resulted in an image of an apple.

Sign Language Learning. Gardner and Gardner (1969) trained a chimpanzee, Washoe, to speak using American Sign Language. An example of a word in this language is holding the "hand in a fist, index finger extended (the pointing hand), while rotating the arm at the elbow" (p. 665), a behavior which means "always." Washoe was taught the word in the American Sign Language for "flower," for instance, by showing her flowers and making the behavioral sign for "flower"; subsequently, he showed Washoe a flower and then gave it to her only when she made the behavioral sign for flower.

One of the essential aspects of speech is that words can be combined in new ways, that is, in ways that the speaker has not been previously trained in, and has not previously heard. One child, for instance, used the phrase, "barefoot all over," to say he was naked (Chukovsky, 1968; cited in Dale, 1972). The capacity to combine new words appropriately indicates there has been considerable positive transfer of learning, and therefore indicates a relatively high level of intelligence behavior. Washoe did appropriately combine words in new ways. For example, she signed "open food drink" to mean, "open refrigerator." This combination of words was probably not learned through direct reinforcement or imitation, because the experimenters used the phrase "cold box" to denote refrigerator.

Another chimpanzee, Lucy, used sign language in novel ways. In a standardized testing procedure by Fouts (as described in Linden, 1975/1976), Lucy was asked to describe in sign language 24 different fruits and vegetables. Each fruit or vegetable was presented several times. After an individual fruit or vegetable was presented to Lucy, she answered by signing. At the time of testing, the words in her vocabulary included "food," "fruit," "drink," "candy," and "banana." One of her novel combinations was "drink fruit" for a piece of watermelon. Also, Linden (p. 106) reports, "For the first few days of the experiment Lucy referred to radishes as 'food.' Then she tasted one. Promptly spitting out the mouthful, she called it a 'cry hurt food'."

It may be that images of opening the refrigerator and food and drink within were responsible, in part, for Washoe's signing "open food drink." Related possibilities apply to the child's "barefoot all over," and Lucy's "cry hurt food." Thought consists, in part, of the occurrence of images of stimuli that have become associated; speech reflects these images.

In another study (Gardner & Gardner, 1975), Washoe was asked a number of questions. The relationship between the type of question asked and the grammatical category of her responses was correct. For example, one kind of question is the "who-pronoun" question—"Who you?" or "Who me?" This type of question always evoked answers that contained a proper noun or pronoun. Another kind of question is the "whose-demonstrative" question—"Whose that?", "Whose those?". Washoe's answers to this type always contained a possessive.

Premack's training conditions were much more controlled than the research with Washoe, so we can more clearly see that Sarah exhibited extensive positive transfer of language. Consider, for example, that Washoe answered a large number of who-pronoun questions with proper nouns and pronouns, but since her trainers spent hours day after day interacting with her in a relatively uncontrolled fashion, her answers may have been followed by food and attention behaviors from the experimenters prior to testing; she may therefore have been reward-trained to respond appropriately.

Imitation Learning, Matching, and Observation Learning

Imitation learning is the acquisition of behavior exhibited by a demonstrator by means of viewing the demonstrator's behavior, through a process related to the topography of the demonstrator's repsonse. Learning by the observer may be facilitated through other processes, for example, fear reduction; the demonstrator may reduce the observer's fear and thereby facilitate learning, but this would not be imitation learning.

Imitation Learning in a Chimpanzee. Imitation learning has been shown to occur in rats (Kohn & Dennis, 1972; Zentall & Levine, 1972) and in other species as well; but the most dramatic and informative study of imitation learning used a chimpanzee as a subject.

Hayes and Hayes (1952) gave Vicki, a home-reared chimpanzee, a series of 70 meaningless acts to imitate. Examples of these acts are spreading the mouth with two fingers (Figure 8-4), and twirling on one foot. These responses were sufficiently unusual that Vicki probably was not previously instrumentally conditioned to exhibit them. Early in training, Vicki had to be taught to perform the responses of the demonstrator by having her arms and legs molded into appropriate positions. When Vicki exhibited the act performed by the demonstrator, she received a piece of favorite food. The outcome of this training was that Vicki exhibited very quickly, without molding, and with excellent topography, 10 of the last 50 acts of the demonstrator. The topography of the other 40 acts was poorer, but the difficulties were due to lack of motor skill.

Vicki's acquiring the ability to imitate novel responses is an instance of positive transfer of learning. The training involved following a match between Vicki's response and the demonstrator's response by delivering food to Vicki. The matches came about early in training through molding, and subsequently through imitation. Positive transfer of learning occurred, because prior learning facilitated imitation of novel and relatively different responses of the demonstrator.

A relatively large amount of improvement over a series of tasks that are only somewhat related is often referred to as *learning to learn* or *acquisition of a learning set*. Vicki therefore learned to learn to imitate; she acquired an imitation learning set.

In order to imitate a response of the demonstrator, Vicki must have matched the stimuli produced by her own response to the stimuli provided by the demonstrator's response. This performance in of itself involves considerable transfer, because the stimuli produced by the imitated response are quite different from the stimuli provided by the demonstrator's response. In Figure 8-4, for instance, Vicki's hands are placed inside the lips of her own mouth, which is quite different from the way she sees the demonstrator's hands inside of his mouth.

Delayed Imitation. In the imitation learning set outcome previously described, Vicki imitated the demonstrator while the demonstrator continued to exhibit a response or immediately thereafter. Vicki also exhibited delayed imitation. For example, she watched windows being cleaned with a solution from a spray gun. About 15 minutes later she was admitted into the room with the spray gun, went directly to it, and sprayed the solution on the windows.

The delayed imitation result requires assuming that in some sense

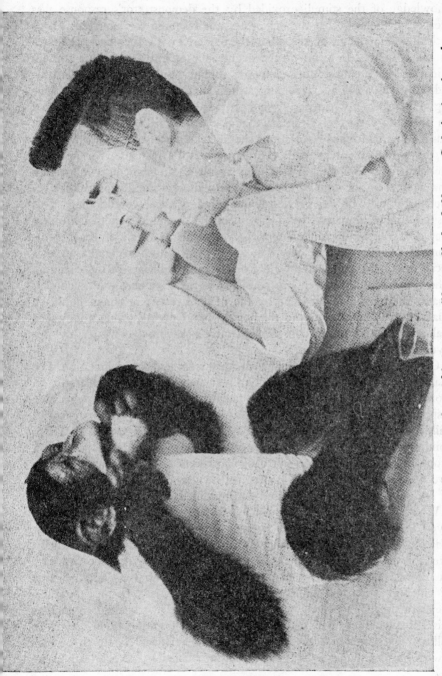

FIGURE 8-4. Imitation of a novel response by a chimpanzee. (Hayes, K. J., & Hayes, C. Imitation in a home-raised chimpanzee. Journal of Comparative and Physiological Psychology, 1952, 45, 450-459. Copyright 1952 by the American Psychological Association. Reprinted by permission.)

knowledge of the stimuli provided by the demonstrator's response was recalled at the time that the demonstrator's response was imitated. Theoretically, knowledge of the stimuli provided by the demonstrator's response is viewed in terms of the occurrence of images of these stimuli. Viewing the demonstrator's response should result in the stimuli provided by this response becoming associated through classical conditioning. The order in which the stimuli provided by this response are focused on probably varies, which means that S_1-S_2, S_2-S_1, S_1-S_3, S_3-S_1, and so on, classically conditioned associations should take place. Later, viewing some of the stimuli involved with the demonstrator's response, for instance, the spray gun and the window, may result in simultaneously occurring images of many or most of the stimuli provided by the demonstrator's response by way of the previously acquired classical conditioning. This assumption is supported by (a) previously discussed results indicating that components of a learning situation result in recall of other components of the learning situation; and (b) the earlier conclusion that recall of stimuli is mediated by the occurrence of images of these stimuli. The temporary brain events responsible for the simultaneously occurring images of the stimuli provided by the demonstrator's response should be qualitatively identical to the temporary brain events produced by the real stimuli provided by the demonstrator's response; consequently delayed imitation should occur.

Children (and of course adults) readily exhibit delayed imitation. For example, Bandura and Huston (1961) arranged for a demonstrator to work on a learning task, and at the same time make irrelevant aggressive responses toward dolls located on the learning apparatus. Subsequently, children who observed the demonstrator worked on the same task. These children exhibited more aggressive responses toward the dolls than a group of children who had not observed the demonstrator make aggressive responses. Bandura and Walters (1963) support the idea that much of our social behavior is acquired and modified through imitation.

Why are children relatively likely to imitate, including exhibiting delayed imitation? What is the purpose of imitating? It was previously indicated that appropriate behavior by children is probably relatively likely to be followed by a familiar person delivering contact comfort, attention behaviors, and other positive reinforcers as well. The behavior of older children and adults tends to be appropriate, because by then they are usually relatively well socialized. Thus, when children imitate this behavior they will usually be exhibiting appropriate behavior. It follows that imitated behavior by children is relatively likely to be followed by contact comfort and attention behaviors. Vicki learned to learn to imitate, that is, came to be relatively likely to imitate, because matches between her responses and those of a demonstrator were followed by Vicki's receiving food. It was just indicated that matches between a child's and other people's responses tend to be followed by the child's receiving contact comfort and attention behaviors. Consequently, the child should be relatively likely to imitate, which is what occurs.

Matching. In imitation learning, an observer matches the stimulus produced by his or her own response to the stimulus provided by the demonstrator's response. Similar matching is involved with another type of intelligence behavior and, in addition, occurs in straightforward instrumental conditioning.

Image theory explains straightforward instrumental conditioning, in part, by assuming that before the occurrence of the instrumental response, an image of the stimulus produced by this response occurs. Furthermore, for instrumental responses that come to increase in rate, an animal brings about the stimulus produced by the instrumental response and thereby executes it. In other words, because an image of the stimulus produced by an instrumental response occurs; and because an animal then brings about the stimulus produced by this response, the animal brings about a match between a response-produced stimulus and an image of the same stimulus.

The matching involved in delayed imitation appears to be quite similar to the matching that occurs in straightforward instrumental conditioning in which the instrumental response increases in rate. When an animal imitates a novel response, it must in some sense adjust its responding so that the response-produced stimulus that occurs approximately matches the stimulus provided by the demonstrator's response. In other words, in imitation learning an animal must in some sense bring about the stimulus produced by the response that matches the stimulus provided by the demonstrator's response. For delayed imitation, an animal brings about a response-produced stimulus that matches an image of the stimulus provided by the demonstrator's response. This matching corresponds relatively closely to an animal's bringing about the stimulus produced by the instrumental response that matches an image of this stimulus.

Imitation learning should be much more difficult than straightforward instrumental conditioning, because in imitation learning the stimuli produced by the observer's response and the stimuli provided by the demonstrator's response cannot be identical. Therefore, the occurrence of the indicated matching in delayed imitation definitely supports the possibility that the corresponding matching occurs in straightforward instrumental conditioning.

Imitation learning supports image theory in another important way. Recall that it is assumed that an animal brings about the stimulus produced by the instrumental response through a closed-loop process, and that closed-loop theory leads to the prediction that novel responding that is appropriate to the instrumental contingency of training will occur in straightforward instrumental conditioning. Vicki, the chimpanzee, came to immediately imitate a demonstrator's novel responses through training in which she received positive reinforcement following matches between her and the demonstrator's responses. This imitation learning is a clear example of novel responding that is appropriate to the instrumental contingency of training, because the demonstrator's novel responses were imitated, and because reinforcement was delivered following Vicki's approximating a match.

Another procedure appears to indicate that a nonhuman animal can bring about a stimulus that matches an image of a stimulus that is not currently present. Premack (1975) gave Sarah, the chimpanzee who acquired a plastic word language, pictures of four components of a chimpanzee's face—two eyes, nose, and mouth. Each of these pictures was mounted on a separate stiff backing. Sarah also was given a blank outline of a chimpanzee face. From the very beginning Sarah placed the four facial parts on the blank outline to approximate a chimpanzee's face; she placed the eyes above the nose, and the nose above the mouth. Sarah thus matched real stimuli, the blank outline and the four facial pieces, with what must in some sense be her knowledge of how a chimpanzee's face looks. Sarah's knowledge is probably based on the occurrence of images of the stimuli comprising a chimpanzee's face. Thus, her performance on this test supports the assumption that a nonhuman animal can bring about a stimulus that matches an image of a stimulus, as does the delayed imitation finding discussed above.

In construction tasks an animal matches a stimulus by appropriately assembling or combining its component parts. Sarah's completion of a construction task was the exhibition of a novel appropriate response— she had never been trained on constructing the chimpanzee's face. Of course, humans also make novel appropriate responses when they successfully complete construction tasks. For example, children who perceived a matrix of cylinders that increased in height along one dimension and increased in diameter along a second dimension constructed the matrix from memory from the outset (Bruner & Kenny, 1966).

Therefore, novel appropriate responding appears to occur in straightforward instrumental conditioning, delayed imitation learning, and construction task learning in which the stimulus to be made is no longer present. Moreover, for each type of learning, the novel appropriate responding seems to be due to an animal's matching stimulus consequences of its own responding with an image of a stimulus. In addition, for each type of learning, this matching is probably achieved through a closed-loop process—the stimulus consequences of responding are compared to the image of the stimulus to be matched, a response adjustment is made, a comparison is made again, and so on. For straightforward instrumental conditioning, the comparison is between the stimulus produced by the current response and an image of the stimulus produced by the instrumental response, and the animal reduces the discrepancy between this stimulus and image because by doing so it increases the vividness of the image of the goal stimulus.

Observation Learning. Observation learning is somewhat difficult to define precisely. It means approximately the occurrence of learning through perceiving stimuli, usually visual, that do not start and end in a relatively regular manner. Observation learning occurs in delayed imitation and language learning.

An apparatus called the Wisconsin General Test Apparatus is often employed in research with primates, including in one of the studies on observation learning. Figure 8-5 shows this apparatus. It is used to study discrimination learning between objects. Usually, two objects are simultaneously presented to a subject, as in Figure 8-5. One object is S+; displacing it with the hand or paw is the correct response. The second object is S—; displacing it with the hand or paw is the incorrect response. A piece of food is placed under the S+ object; displacing it is therefore almost immediately followed by a reinforcement. Nothing is placed under the S— object. Displacing it results in the termination of the trial; that is, a noncorrection procedure is used. The positions of the S+ and S— objects change from right to left and vice versa on an approximately random basis. A new trial is initiated by pushing the stimulus tray forward, and a trial is terminated by withdrawing it.

A study by Darby and Riopelle (1959) indicates that observation learning occurs. While demonstrator monkeys performed on a series of discriminations between objects in the Wisconsin General Test Apparatus, observer monkeys could watch the demonstrator monkeys. The series of object discriminations consisted of one object discrimination being followed by the next, with new objects being employed for each successive object discrimination. For the demonstrator monkeys, the probability of a correct response on the first trial of a new object discrimination was always .50, because there was no way of these monkeys "knowing" which object was correct. Observer monkeys were given the same object

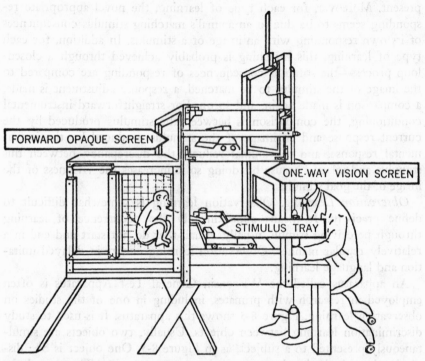

FORWARD OPAQUE SCREEN

ONE-WAY VISION SCREEN

STIMULUS TRAY

FIGURE 8-5. The Wisconsin General Test Apparatus. (Harlow, H. F. The formation of learning sets. Psychological Review, **1949, 56, 51-65. Copyright 1949 by the American Psychological Association. Reprinted by permission.)**

discriminations that the demonstrator monkeys performed on. In addition, observer monkeys received the first trial of a new object discrimination just after the opportunity to observe a demonstrator monkey respond on the first trial of the same object discrimination .Therefore, for observer monkeys it was possible for the probability of a correct response on the first trial of a new object discrimination to be one. This level of performance could be accomplished by choosing the object displaced by the demonstrator monkey when the demonstrator monkey's response was followed by food, and by choosing the object not displaced by the demonstrator monkey when the demonstrator monkey's response was not followed by food.

The proportions of correct responses made on the first trial of an object discrimination by the observer monkeys were initially close to .50, and then gradually increased as the number of discriminations that the monkeys received increased. The observer monkeys therefore acquired a tendency to make the correct response on the first trial of each new object discrimination, rather than to imitate the choice response made by the demonstrator monkeys on the first trial. Observing whether the object pushed aside by a demonstrator monkey was followed by the presence or absence of food led to the above chance performance of observer monkeys on trial 1 of the series of object discriminations. Thus, observation learning is said to have occurred.

A second observation learning study (Menzel, 1975) is of interest because it indicates that a relatively large amount of information can be acquired through observation learning. A chimpanzee was carried around a field by an experimenter while a second experimenter hid food in 18 different places in the field—in a clump of grass, for instance, or in a hole in the ground. Subsequently, the chimpanzee was released. Animals exposed to the food-baiting procedure found 12.5 pieces of food per trial. Control animals left in the field for the same length of time found only .2 pieces of food per trial. In addition, animals exposed to the food-baiting procedure usually ran directly to the precise locations of the hidden pieces of food. Thus, observation of the food baiting resulted in the chimpanzee's learning about the locations of a number of pieces of food.

In observation learning, stimuli that are viewed probably become associated with each other through classical conditioning as an animal focuses on one and then the other stimulus. In the described studies, the visual stimuli of objects—for example, the sight of a clump of grass—probably became associated through classical conditioning with the visual stimulus of food. Presumably the visual stimulus of food results in an image of the stimulus aspect of food responsible for its reinforcing strength. If so, the object choice and food finding responses in the described studies would be instances of a classically conditioned approach response to a CS that was previously paired with food.

Delayed imitation learning is a special case of observation learning, because acquired associations among the stimuli provided by the demonstrator's response occur through viewing them. In addition, much of Sarah's language learning occurred through observation learning. The simultaneous presentation of a plastic word and its referent resulted in an acquired association between these two stimuli through their being viewed, and therefore through observation learning. The assumption that focusing on simultaneously presented stimuli, S_1, S_2, and so on, in different orders leads to S_1-S_2, S_2-S_1, and additional stimulus-stimulus associations was previously used to explain aspects of language learning and the occurrence of delayed imitation; it applies to observation learning in general.

Observation learning does not necessarily involve the occurrence of a relatively large extent of positive transfer, and therefore should not be considered an intelligence behavior. But in the Darby and Riopelle study, positive transfer did occur from objects and reinforcers occurring in the situation in which the demonstrator performed to the situation in which the observer performed.

Because observation learning does occur, the possibility that observation learning typically contributes to the strength of the instrumental response (Chapter 3) has been supported.

Perceptual Learning. Observation and visual perceptual learning are obviously similar in that both types of learning involve viewing stimuli. One perceptual learning finding (Leeper, 1935) was that viewing an unambiguous figure of an old woman (Figure 8-6A) increases the likelihood that an ambiguous figure (Figure 8-6B), recognizable as either an old woman or a young woman, will be identified as an old woman. The analogous result was obtained when an unambiguous figure of a young woman (Figure 8-6C) is perceived first.

Perceptual learning may occur by way of observation learning. For example, if observation learning occurs when the unambiguous figure of an old woman or young woman is viewed, classical conditioning among the component stimuli of either unambiguous figure should occur and may be responsible for the perceptual effect occurring when the ambiguous figure is subsequently viewed.

To what extent and how conditioning affects perception is an important and longstanding problem. To support the idea that conditioning importantly contributes to perception, it is necessary to elaborate a means by which conditioning can affect what is reported as perceived. Viewing conditioning as mediated by images of stimuli brings the conditioning area closer to the perception area. King (1974) proposed a process by which images of stimuli occurring through classical conditioning affect what is reported as perceived.

Concept Learning

Concept Learning: Description. Concept learning refers to the control of a learned response by a constant substimulus of stimulus complexes despite relatively wide variation in other aspects of the stimulus complexes. If the substimulus we denote as a triangle, for example, controls

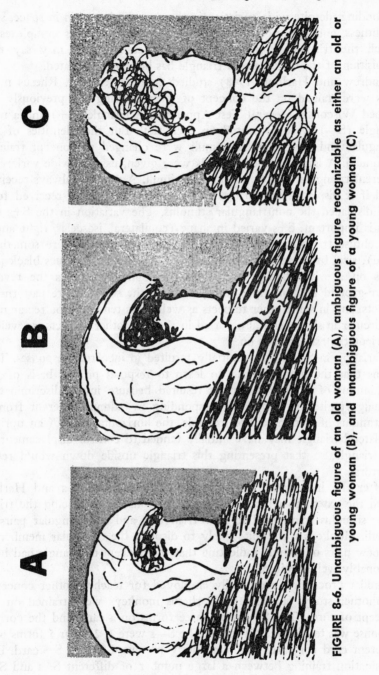

FIGURE 8-6. Unambiguous figure of an old woman (A), ambiguous figure recognizable as either an old or young woman (B), and unambiguous figure of a young woman (C).

responding, despite wide variation in the shape, orientation in space, size, brightness, and figure-ground relationship of the stimulus complexes of which the triangle substimulus is a member, then we may say that acquisition of the concept of a triangle has been approximated.

Andrew and Harlow (1948) studied concept learning. Rhesus monkeys were trained on the concept of triangle using the previously described Wisconsin General Test Apparatus. A triangle (S+) and a nontriangle (S—) were presented on each trial. But the identities of the triangular and nontriangular stimuli were changed as concept training continued. A large number of trials were given, using a wide variety of different triangular and nontriangular stimuli. A monkey always received food if it displaced the triangular stimulus, and it never received food if it displaced the nontriangular stimulus. The variation in the S+s and S—s is important. S+s varied in shape (equilateral, isosceles, right angle, and obtuse triangles were used); orientation (triangles were sometimes tilted); size; brightness; figure-ground relationship (sometimes black patterns on a white background were used, and sometimes the reverse figure-ground relationship); color; whether the stimuli were patterns or objects; and in some other respects as well. S—s tended to be rectangular or circular in shape, and also varied in shape in other respects, as well as in orientation, size, and so on.

Variation in S+ and S— initially resulted in incorrect responses. This means that the monkeys had to learn to respond on the basis of the substimulus of a triangle. Errors resulted because initial discrimination learning resulted in control of responding by stimuli different from a substimulus of a triangle. For example, the horizontal base of an upright equilateral triangle may have initially tended to control displacement of the triangle, so that presenting this triangle upside down would result in errors.

After the indicated training was terminated, Andrews and Harlow tested the extent to which the learned response of displacing the triangular stimulus transferred to new triangular and nontriangular pairs of stimuli. Monkeys were quite likely to displace the triangular member of the new pairs of stimuli, indicating that the concept of triangle had been reasonably well acquired.

Similar procedures are usually employed for teaching other concepts. In another study (Hicks, 1956), rhesus monkeys were trained on the concept of three. The S+s were three forms on a card, and the correct response was to displace this card. The S—s were 1, 2, 4, or 5 forms on a different card (or cards) simultaneously presented with a S+ card. Discrimination training between a large number of different S+s and S—s was carried out. Over the series of discriminations, the size, arrangement on the card, shape, and color of both the S+s and S—s were varied. Learning approximating acquisition of the concept of 3 occurred, because the monkeys were relatively likely to displace new cards with 3 forms on them when these cards and new cards with 1, 2, 4, or 5 forms on them were presented.

Procedures common to most demonstrations of concept learning in animals include (a) training on a number of discriminations between members of the concept (S+s) and other stimuli (S—s); (b) the use of S+s that vary widely in respects other than those defining the concept; and (c) the use of S—s that are quite similar to the S+s employed.

Concept learning involves the occurrence of relatively extensive positive transfer, and therefore is an instance of intelligence behavior. Relatively extensive positive transfer occurs because prior training facilitates acquisition of subsequent discriminations between new and relatively different S+s and S—s. Sometimes, in fact, responding to a new pair of discriminative stimuli is almost always correct the first time they are presented (Fields, 1932). When this occurs, the animal's acquisition of the concept can be considered to fairly closely approximate the concept learning of adult humans. Because performance on the discriminations employed in concept learning improves with an increase in the number of discriminations received, animals learn how to learn to discriminate between a stimulus that is a member of a concept and a second similar stimulus. Therefore, concept learning is a learning set result.

Concept Learning: Discussion. Analysis of concept learning involves understanding the stimuli that control responding in the discriminations between members of the concept (S+s) and other stimuli (S—s).

Why are S+s that vary in a number of respects (shape, orientation, and so forth) used to establish concept learning? Let us illustrate with acquisition of the concept of triangle. Lashley (1938) employed the jumping stand apparatus and discriminative stimuli like those shown in Figure 8-7A in a simultaneous discrimination. Reinforcement followed jumping toward the triangle but not the cross. After this discrimination was acquired, the rats were exposed to novel pairs of stimuli such as those indicated in Figures 8-7B and 8-7C, in what was essentially a stimulus generalization procedure. The rats were more likely to jump to the triangle for the pair of stimuli in Figure 8-7B, but were not more likely to jump to the triangle for the pair of stimuli in Figure 8-7C. The latter finding indicates that the discrimination between the triangle and cross of Figure 8-7A did not result in acquisition of the concept of triangle. It also gives some support to the possibility that the substimulus

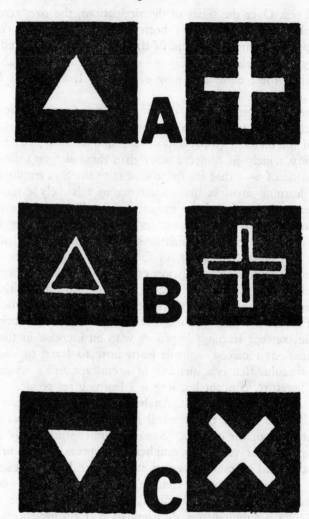

FIGURE 8-7. Stimuli for a discrimination (A) and stimuli for what was essentially a stimulus generalization determination (B and C). (Lashley, K. S. The mechanism of vision: XV. Preliminary studies of the rat's capacity for detail vision. Journal of General Psychology, 1938, 18, 123-193, Copyright 1938. Adapted by permission of The Journal Press.)

controlling responding on the acquired discrimination was the white base of the triangle used in this discrimination, because the triangle in Figure 8-7B but not in Figure 8-7C also had a white base.

Suppose that, in fact, the white base of the triangle did control responding. At the very least, then, the rats would have to learn to jump to a triangle but not jump to a white base for acquisition of the concept of triangle to occur. Not jumping to the white base might be accomplished by training rats on the pair of stimuli in Figure 8-7C. By carrying out this discrimination learning, jumping to the substimulus of a triangle would have been followed by a reinforcement more times than jumping to the white base would be followed by a reinforcement. This outcome should contribute to learning to jump to a triangle, but not to a white base. Of course, carrying out the discrimination illustrated in Figure 8-7C would involve exposing rats to a S+ that differed from the originally employed S+ of Figure 8-7A. That is at least one reason why it is necessary to use S+s that vary in a number of respects in establishing concept learning.

In general, a discrimination between S+ and S— may result in any number of substimuli of S+ other than the substimulus of the concept controlling responding. The use of S+s that vary in a number of respects assures that responding to the substimulus of the concept is more frequently followed by reinforcement than responding to other substimuli. The substimulus of the concept should therefore tend to acquire control over responding.

To establish concept learning, S—s that are similar to the S+s must ordinarily be used. Suppose that the S+ of the triangle in Figure 8-7A and the S— of a white rectangle were employed. These two stimuli are similar, in part because they both possess a white base. Responding to the white base of the rectangle will not be followed by reinforcement. Thus, the tendency for the white base of the triangle to control responding should be reduced, and acquisition of the concept of a triangle should thereby be facilitated. In general, S—s that are similar to S+s will share more substimuli in common; consequently, using such S—s reduces the probability that substimuli of the S+s that are not members of the concept acquire control over responding, and concept learning is thereby facilitated.

Concept Learning in Language. It will be seen that acquisition of the meaning of words by humans involves concept learning. So did Sarah's acquisition of a plastic word language.

Sarah acquired several concepts, for example, the concept of red. She was able to indicate that red was the color of, rather than not the color of, a wide variety of objects differing in shape, orientation, and so on that she had not previously received training on. Therefore, the color red controlled responding and was a constant substimulus of stimulus complexes varying relatively widely in other respects.

Her acquisition of the meaning of the plastic word for "yes" is also an instance of concept learning, although concept learning in this context no longer refers only to a substimulus of a single complex. Sarah used the plastic word for "yes" appropriately in sentences that also used the plastic word for "same" or "different"; for instance, in sentences composed of two identical real objects and the plastic word for "same." She used the plastic word for "yes" appropriately with sentences involving the plastic words for "color of" or "not color of"; as, for instance, in sentences composed of the plastic word for a specific color, the plastic word for an object of this color, and the plastic word for "color of." The constant substimulus in these sentences is a true relationship between the first and third items of the sentences, the nature of the relationship (same, color of) being referred to by the middle item. This constant substimulus of a true relationship between the first and third items controlled responding, as was shown by her choosing the plastic word for "yes" rather than the plastic word for "no" when responding to such sentences. In addition, she responded appropriately to such sentences with little or no training. Therefore, she did acquire the concept of a true relationship between the first and third items of such sentences.

Other Intelligence Tasks

Discrimination Reversal Intelligence Task. A study by Dufort, Guttman, and Kimble (1954) illustrates the discrimination reversal intelligence task. Rats received position discriminations in an apparatus similar to a T-maze. After a rat acquired one position discrimination, for example, left side correct, the other side, right, was made correct. After the second, reversed position discrimination was acquired, the original position discrimination was put into effect. After the original discrimination was reacquired, the discrimination was reversed once more, and so on. A reversal of the discrimination that was currently in effect was not given until a criterion of adequate performance on it was met. Figure 8-8 indicates that the rats improved over the series of discrimination reversals. A score of one error is a perfect score, because one error must be made to "find out" that a discrimination has been reversed. The extent of training required to satisfy a criterion of adequate performance on a

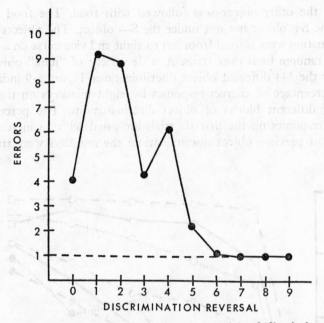

FIGURE 8-8. Improvement over a series of discrimination reversals. (Adapted from Dufort, Guttman, and Kimble, 1954.)

discrimination frequently decreases as the number of preceding discrimination reversals increases.

The just described discrimination reversal task can be employed with any discrimination. S+ and S— are simply reversed after a discrimination is acquired. Each reversal of a discrimination is at least a somewhat new learning situation. Therefore, improvement over a series of discrimination reversals can be considered an instance of intelligence behavior. Improvement on a discrimination over a series of reversals of this discrimination means that learning to learn discrimination reversals occurs; thus, improvement over a series of discrimination reversals is a learning set result.

Object Discrimination Intelligence Task. The object discrimination intelligence task consists of a series of discriminations between objects, each successive discrimination being between new objects. In one study (Harlow, 1949), rhesus monkeys received a series of 344 discriminations in which two new objects were employed for each of the 344 discriminations. The Wisconsin General Test Apparatus was employed. For each discrimination task, the same object was correct; displacing this object but not the other object was followed with food. The food appeared under the S+ object but not under the S— object. The objects for each discrimination were shifted from left to right and vice versa on an approximately random basis over trials. A wide variety of "junk" objects were used for the 344 different object discriminations. Figure 8-9 indicates the mean percentage of correct responses by eight monkeys on the first six trials of different blocks of object discriminations. The percentage of correct responses on the first six trials increased with an increase in the number of previous object discriminations the monkeys were trained on.

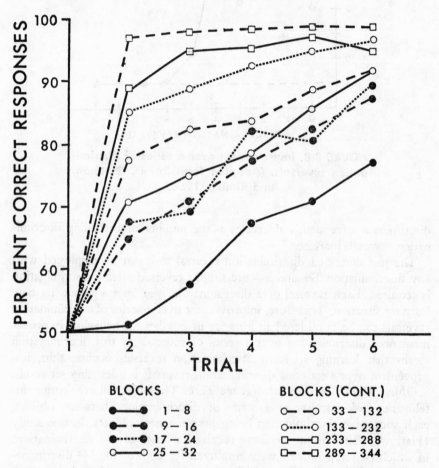

BLOCKS

●——● 1 – 8
●– –● 9 – 16
●······● 17 – 24
○——○ 25 – 32

BLOCKS (CONT.)

○– –○ 33 – 132
○······○ 133 – 232
□——□ 233 – 288
□– –□ 289 – 344

FIGURE 8-9. Improvement over a large number of object discriminations. (Adapted from Harlow, 1949.)

The response on trial 1 of each new object discrimination is necessarily correct on 50 percent of such discriminations, because an animal has no way of "knowing" which object is S+ on trial 1 of a new object discrimination. However, starting with trial 2 of each new object discrimination, perfect performance is possible. When the correct object is chosen on trial 1, perfect performance will result if an animal continues to choose this object on later trials, that is, if an animal stays with its initial choice. When the incorrect object is chosen on trial 1, perfect performance will occur if an animal continues to choose the object not chosen on trial 1 on later trials, that is, if an animal shifts to and then remains with the second object. Thus, when animals perform perfectly on trial 2 and the succeeding trials of each new object discrimination, their performance may be described as a win-stay lose-shift strategy. Figure 8-9 indicates that on the last block of object discriminations, monkeys performed almost perfectly starting with trial 2. Thus, after considerable training the monkeys performed in close accordance with a win-stay lose-shift strategy.

Each new object discrimination is a relatively new learning situation. Therefore, improvement over a series of new object discriminations means that relatively extensive positive transfer has occurred. Thus, this improvement signifies that learning to learn object discriminations occurs; the object discrimination intelligence task is therefore a learning set task.

Intelligence Behavior: Some Analysis

Discrimination Learning and Transfer. Intelligence behavior is the occurrence of relatively extensive positive transfer of learning. Why is it that the previously described intelligence behavior tasks result in the occurrence of relatively extensive positive transfer of learning?

All the previously described examples of intelligence tasks involved a series of discriminations between stimuli that differed along common dimensions. In addition, for all of these tasks, except the discrimination reversal task, the discriminative stimuli came from all portions of the common dimensions, for example, from the red, yellow, green, and blue portions of the wavelength dimension. Recall that a single discrimination between stimuli that differ along a common dimension greatly reduces the amount of stimulus generalization occurring between these stimuli. In addition, recall that there is evidence that nonlaboratory discriminations reduce the amount of stimulus generalization that occurs along a dimension. Therefore, it appears reasonable to expect that the acquisition of discriminations between stimuli that come from all portions of common dimensions will reduce the amount of stimulus generalization occurring along these dimensions.

As the amount of stimulus generalization occurring between two stimuli decreases, performance on a subsequent discrimination between these two stimuli improves. Moreover, carrying out discrimination learning between stimuli differing along a common dimension, which should reduce stimulus generalization along this dimension, facilitates subsequent discrimination learning between stimuli differing along the same dimension. It follows that acquiring a number of discriminations between stimuli that differ along all portions of common dimensions will facilitate acquisition of subsequent discriminations between stimuli along these dimensions, that is, will result in positive transfer. Therefore, it is possible that the relatively extensive positive transfer of learning that occurs on intelligence tasks is at least in part the consequence of the fact that these intelligence tasks involve a series of discriminations between stimuli that differ along common dimensions.

The previously described intelligence tasks do involve a series of discriminations between stimuli that differ along common dimensions. The acquisition of the meaning of words that are newly introduced into a language requires that these words be discriminated from previously introduced words. Although standard laboratory procedures for developing discrimination learning may not be employed in the acquisition of a language, acquisition of the meaning of words obviously requires that these words be discriminated from one another. In addition, the words of a language clearly differ along common dimensions—for Sarah's plastic word language, in size, color, and shape. Therefore, acquisition of a language, that is, successful performance on the language intelligence task, does involve a series of discriminations between stimuli that differ along common dimensions. Also, the referents for new words must be discriminated from the referents for previously introduced words, and these referents differ along common dimensions too.

In respect to imitation learning, the present response of a demonstrator must be discriminated from previous responses of the demonstrator for a successful imitation to occur. It is also clear that the different responses of a demonstrator differ along common dimensions—for example, the distance a limb is extended from the body differs from one response to another. Therefore, imitation of a series of responses of a demonstrator does involve a series of discriminations between stimuli that differ along common dimensions.

Concept learning obviously involves a series of discriminations. The substimulus equivalent to a concept varies along a number of common dimensions just as simpler stimuli may vary along common dimensions. For example, the lines that are part of the substimulus of a triangle will vary in orientation over the series of discriminations carried out to establish concept learning of a triangle.

The discrimination reversal and object discrimination intelligence tasks obviously involve a series of discriminations between stimuli that differ along at least a single common dimension.

Initial Discrimination Learning and Later Performance. It appears for intelligence tasks in general that performance on the initial discrimination of an intelligence task is positively related to performance on much later components of the intelligence task.

In a study by Miller, Hansen, and Thomas (1974), two groups of pigeons received a series of discrimination reversals in which the discriminative stimuli were lights of different wavelength that were otherwise identical. For one group the discriminative stimuli were relatively close together along the wavelength dimension, and for the second group the discriminative stimuli were relatively far apart along the wavelength dimension. Birds in both groups had to satisfy the same criterion of discrimination learning before receiving a reversal of the discrimination in effect. As the amount of stimulus generalization between discriminative stimuli decreases, performance on a subsequent discrimination between these stimuli improves. Thus, it was expected that the group receiving the discriminative stimuli that were relatively far apart along the wavelength dimension would reach criterion on the initial discrimination with less training than the other group. This result was, in fact, obtained. Of primary interest is that the group receiving the discriminative stimuli that were further apart along the wavelength dimension performed better over the entire series of discrimination reversals, even though both groups were trained to criterion on each discrimination before a reversal of it was given. Thus, the group that performed better on the initial discrimination also performed better on much later components of the discrimination reversal intelligence stask.

Blazek and Harlow (1955) obtained a similar result. The procedures typically employed with the object discrimination intelligence task were carried out, except that 2-dimensional colored squares rather than objects were the discriminative stimuli. The colored squares were mounted on a 3- by-3-inch square of white posterboard. For four different groups the colored squares covered 12.5, 25, 50, and 100 percent respectively, of the square of posterboard. Performance on the earlier discriminations between pairs of colors improved with an increase in the percentage of the posterboard that the colored square covered. The groups that performed better on the earlier discriminations continued to perform better on the later discriminations. Kay and Oldfield-Box (1965) used similar procedures, and found that performance on both the earlier and later of a series of discriminations was better when the discriminative stimuli were 3-dimensional objects rather than 2-dimensional forms.

Suppose that performance on the initial discrimination of an intelligence task can be improved by changing the training procedure used to establish discrimination learning. Will there be a corresponding improvement in performance on the later discriminations of the same intelligence task? The answer appears to be yes. Doty, Jones, and Doty (1967) employed a discrimination training procedure that probably facilitated acquisition of the initial discrimination between small objects by minks and ferrets. These species performed unusually well on the latter portion of a long series of discriminations between pairs of novel objects. Discrimination learning in fish usually entails some delay of positive reinforcement because the food is dropped on the surface of the water rather than placed close to the operandum. Mackintosh and Cauty (1971) reduced delay of reinforcement of a correct response by goldfish by delivering the food close to the operandum. This procedure should have facilitated acquisition of the initial discrimination. They found that the goldfish performed unusually well on the latter portion of a series of reversals of the discrimination.

Species Differences in Performance on Intelligence Tasks. The conclusion that performance on the initial discrimination of intelligence tasks is positively related to performance on much later components of intelligence tasks is further supported. Species differ in their performance on straightforward discriminations. For example, rats perform relatively well on discriminations between olfactory stimuli. The initial discrimination of an intelligence task is a straightforward discrimination. Therefore, if a species performs relatively well on the initial or straightforward discrimination of an intelligence task, it should also perform relatively well on the later discriminations of this intelligence task, which, it will be seen, is what occurs.

At least some monkeys and apes are more proficient than most nonprimate species on visual discriminations between small objects. For example, Warren (1966) found that cats made three times as many errors on an object discrimination as rhesus monkeys. Also, Gossette and Kraus (1968) found that squirrel monkeys were much superior to cacomistles (similar to raccoons), skunks, and kinkajous (also similar to raccoons) on a discrimination between small white and black blocks.

Thus, at least some monkeys and apes should perform better on the later discriminations of intelligence tasks in which small objects must be visually discriminated between than most nonprimate species. There is considerable support for this possibility. Probably most nonprimate species could not acquire the plastic-word and sign languages that were acquired by chimpanzees. In respect to the object discrimination intelligence task, monkeys and chimpanzees performed better than nonprimate species on the latter portion of a series of discriminations between small objects (Hayes, Thompson, & Hayes, 1953; Kay & Oldfield-Box, 1965; Meyers, McQuiston, & Miles, 1962; Miles, 1957; Shell & Riopelle, 1958). Gossette and Kraus (1968) provide strong support for the statement that a positive relation exists between performance on the initial discrimination of an intelligence task and performance on much later components of the intelligence task. Rhesus monkeys, caocmistles, skunks, and kinkajous were tested on the discrimination reversal intelligence task. The discriminative stimuli were a small white block and a small black block. The correlation between mean errors of the four species on the initial discrimination and mean errors of the four species on the 18th discrimination equaled .98 (calculated by the author from Figure 2 in Gossette & Kraus, 1968).

Rats probably acquire straightforward olfactory discriminations quite easily. They made a median of 1.5 errors on an olfactory discrimination between ethyl acetate and amyl acetate, while with similar training procedures they made a median of 124.5 errors on a discrimination between a flashing and steady light (Nigrosh, Slotnick, & Nevin, 1975). Positively related with the probably superior performance of rats on straightforward olfactory discriminations was their excellent performance on a discrimination reversal intelligence task in which olfactory discriminative stimuli were employed, and on an intelligence task in which a series of discriminations between pairs of novel olfactory stimuli were given. Nigrosh et al. found that rats given a series of reversals of an olfactory discrimination made not more than a few errors by the second reversal of the original discrimination. Slotnick and Katz (1974) gave rats a series of discriminations between olfactory stimuli. Each additional discrimination was between novel olfactory stimuli. The procedure employed is therefore analogous to the procedure for the object discrimination intelligence task. The rats performed better over the series of olfactory discriminations than the best nonhuman primate species over a series of object discriminations.

Dolphins are well known to respond differentially to auditory stimuli in nonlaboratory settings. Not surprisingly, they performed well over a series of discriminations between pairs of novel auditory stimuli. Their performance was about equivalent to that of apes and monkeys that perform relatively well on the analogous object discrimination intelligence task (Herman & Arbeit, 1973). However, the performance of dolphins over a series of visual discriminations between pairs of novel objects was inferior to that of at least some apes and monkeys on similar object discrimination intelligence tasks (Herman, Beach, Pepper, & Stalling, 1969).

Finally, species that perform well on a position discrimination perform well on the later position discriminations of the discrimination reversal task. Cats performed better than rhesus monkeys on a simple position discrimination, and over a series of reversals of this discrimination (Warren, 1966). Similarly, cacomistles performed better than squirrel monkeys on a simple position discrimination and over a series of reversals of this position discrimination (Gossette, Kraus, & Speiss, 1968). Rats made only a mean of 4.0 errors before reaching criterion on a position discrimination and then performed very well over a series of reversals of this discrimination (Dufort et al., 1954; see also Figure 8-8). Moreover, the correlation between mean errors made on the initial position discrimination and the accumulated mean errors made on the subsequent ten reversals of this discrimination by five avian species was .92 (calculated by the author from Table 1 in Gossette, 1969).

It is clear that the evidence supports the conclusion that, in general, performance on the initial discrimination of an intelligence task is positively related to performance on much later components of the intelligence task. The reviewed evidence also indicates that differences in the performance of various species on intelligence tasks are more related to the kind of stimuli employed for an intelligence task than to the phylogenetic status of the species. This consideration suggests that it is not appropriate to define intelligence behavior in terms of the tasks that species with relatively high phylogenetic statuses perform well on.

Human Differences in Performance on Intelligence Tasks. In general, performance on the initial discrimination of an intelligence task is positively related to performance on much later components of the intelligence task. Similarly, human performance on straightforward discriminations is positively related to intelligence behavior.

As children grow older, their intelligence increases. Older children are capable of solving more abstract problems, and so on. If it is true that performance on straightforward discriminations is positively related to intelligence behavior for humans, then older children should perform better on straightforward discriminations than younger children.

Rudel and Teuber (1963) found that younger children made more errors on straightforward discriminations between figures differing in their left-right orientation than older children. Hill (1965) found that younger children performed worse than older children on a straight-forward object discrimination; on two discriminations in which the correct response was to choose the odd object from a group of three objects; and on another discrimination as well. Younger children also perform worse than older children on a large number of perceptual tasks that do not employ standard discrimination learning procedures, but that do appear to involve discrimination learning (Gibson, 1969, Chs. 16-19).

The IQ test may be a rough measure of intelligence. Positive relations between performance on straightforward discriminations and IQ have also been obtained. Moderately-sized correlations between performance on maze tasks and IQ were found by Husband (1941) and Simrall (1947). Zeaman and House (1966) reviewed other studies that generally indicate that a positive relation exists between performance on straightforward discriminations and IQ.

Difficulty of Intelligence Tasks and Forgetting. Intelligence tasks are relatively difficult in the sense that even after the acquisition of a relatively large number of the discriminations that comprise them, there is often relatively little positive transfer of learning. Even with extensive training, nonprimate species probably could not acquire a plastic word or sign language. In addition, in respect to the discrimination reversal task, it is often found that perfect performance on trial 2 of each reversal of a discrimination is not approached after as many as 20 discrimination reversals, even though each discrimination is acquired to a satisfactory criterion level (Gossette & Kraus, 1968; Gossette et al., 1968). Also, in respect to the object discrimination intelligence task, many species do not approach perfect performance on discriminations between new objects. Meyers et al. (1962) found, for example, that cats made about only 70 percent correct choices on trial 2 of discriminations between new objects after receiving 1000 of these discriminations.

If animals can come to perform well on the individual discriminations comprising an intelligence task, why is it that they frequently do not come to exhibit fairly extensive positive transfer of learning to the later components of intelligence tasks? The answer to this question may be involved with the effects of proactive and retroactive inhibition on forgetting. Recall of verbal material may be impaired even though it is perfectly learned. Similarly, positive transfer to the later components of an intelligence task may be minimal, even though the prior discriminations of the intelligence task were perfectly learned. Also, forgetting of verbal material is well known to be due at least in part to proactive and retroactive inhibition, that is, to learning involved with somewhat similar stimuli that occur prior to and after acquisition of the verbal material that is tested for recall. Similarly, positive transfer of learning to the later components of an intelligence task may be minimal because previously acquired discriminations were forgotten, due to prior and subsequent acquisition of discriminations between similar stimuli, that is, proactive and retroactive inhibition.

In general, performance on the initial discrimination of an intelligence task is positively related with performance on much later components of the intelligence task. And as we have just said, intelligence tasks may be difficult, because previously acquired discriminations may be forgotten through proactive and retroactive inhibition. Therefore, if performance on the initial discrimination of an intelligence task is relatively good, perhaps there is relatively little forgetting of the acquired discriminations of an intelligence task. But why should relatively good performance on the initial discrimination of an intelligence task be positively related to little forgetting of the acquired discriminations of the intellgence task?

It is well-known that an increase in the similarity between learned verbal material and other verbal material acquired before and afterward tends to increase the amount of forgetting of this learned verbal material, that is, tends to increase proactive and retroactive inhibition. Therefore, the occurrence of a series of discriminations in which the members of a pair of discriminative stimuli are relatively similar to the members of other pairs of discriminative stimuli (or identical to them but with reversed valences, for the discrimination reversal intelligence task) should result in a relatively large amount of forgetting of previously acquired discriminations. In addition, suppose that the two members of pairs of discriminative stimuli are relatively similar to each other as well as relatively similar to the members of other pairs of discriminative stimuli. Discrimination learning is impaired when the two members of a pair of discriminative stimuli are relatively similar. It follows that when the two members of pairs of discriminative stimuli are relatively similar to each other, the initial discrimination of the intelligence task should be relatively difficult to acquire. Therefore, if the members of a pair of discriminative stimuli are relatively similar to the members of other pairs of discriminative stimuli, and if the two members of pairs of discriminative stimuli are relatively similar to each other, then both (a) a relatively large amount of forgetting of the acquired discriminations of an intelligence task should occur; and (b) performance on the initial discrimination of the intelligence task should be relatively poor. Therefore, the assumptions leading to *a* and *b* offer an answer to the question of why good performance on the initial discrimination of an intelligence task is positively related to little forgetting of the acquired discriminations of the intelligence task.

Consider Blazek and Harlow's study, in which the discriminative stimuli were colored squares covering different percentages of the area of 3-by-3-inch posterboard squares. The smaller colored squares should have been relatively similar to each other when they were the S+ and S— of a pair of discriminative stimuli, because they had a relatively large area of identically appearing posterboard as a surround. For the same reason, when the smaller colored squares were employed, the members of a pair of discriminative stimuli should have been relatively similar to the members of the other pairs of discriminative stimuli. Therefore, employing the smaller colored squares as discriminative stimuli should have resulted in both relatively poor performance on the initial discrimination of the intelligence task, and a relatively large amount of forgetting of the acquired discriminations of the intelligence task.

This discussion applies to species differences in performance on straightforward discriminations and species differences in performance on intelligence tasks. Species differences in performance on straightforward discriminations are a function of the type of discriminative stimuli employed. Stimuli of the same type are "functionally" more or less similar to each other, depending on the type of stimuli and the individual species being considered. Consider the performance of rats on a straightforward visual discrimination between two objects, and the performance of rats on the object discrimination intelligence task. Rats perform relatively poorly on a visual discrimination between two small objects. Two small objects can therefore be thought of as functionally relatively similar for rats. Because two small objects are functionally relatively similar for rats, the members of a pair of discriminative stimuli should be relatively similar to the members of the other pairs of discriminative stimuli used in an object discrimination intelligence task. A relatively large amount of forgetting of previously acquired object discriminations should therefore occur. Thus, rats should perform relatively poorly on the initial discrimination of the object discrimination intelligence task, and should also forget to a relatively large extent the object discriminations that they acquire. The occurrence of relatively extensive forgetting of previously acquired object discriminations by rats should be evidenced by their performing relatively poorly on the later discriminations of the object discrimination intelligence task, which is the obtained result (Warren, 1965).

More on Forgetting. Other results involve the relationship between performance on intelligence tasks and forgetting.

Mackintosh, McGonigle, Holgate, and Vanderver (1968) trained rats on a series of reversals of a black-white discrimination. Each discrimination was learned to a criterion of 18 correct responses out of 20 trials. In addition, the discrimination in effect was reversed only between days; that is, close to 24 hours always elapsed between a discrimination being in effect and a reversal of this discrimination being in effect. The percentages of correct responses made on the first trial for the first and second reversals of the initial discrimination, and the seventh and eighth reversals of the initial discrimination were about 20 and 50 percent, respectively. The result for discrimination reversals 1 and 2 is a negative transfer outcome; the rats had to learn not to respond in the way that was correct for the discrimination last in effect. The reason negative transfer failed to occur for discrimination reversals 7 and 8 is probably that by discrimination reversals 7 and 8 the rats at the beginning of a day's testing no longer remembered the discrimination last in effect. This forgetting probably resulted from proactive inhibition produced by acquiring previous reversals of discriminations. Negative transfer did not fail to occur because of the higher probability of obtaining reinforcement that would take place as a result. This was shown by a second experiment which found that the probability of a correct response on the first trial of a day's testing remained at about .50, even though performing at this level decreased the probability of obtaining reinforcement.

Proactive and retroactive inhibition may ultimately contribute to the acquisition of concept learning. Consider training on the concept of a triangle. An animal repeatedly obtains reinforcement by responding to the triangular member of pairs of stimuli, the triangles employed differing in a number of respects such as shape or orientation. Suppose that through proactive and retroactive inhibition almost complete forgetting of the specific triangles employed in training occurred. Perhaps then only the substimulus equivalent to a triangle could be recalled. Recall of this substimulus should be mediated by the occurrence of an image of this substimulus. Therefore, the ability to respond to the triangular member of a pair of novel stimuli may occur through a matching process: the triangular member of a pair of novel stimuli would more closely match the image of the substimulus equivalent to a triangle than would the other member of the pair. A similar result is that the conceptual memory of humans is more resistant to forgetting than their memory of the individual stimuli of learning (Bransford & Franks, 1971; Posner & Keele, 1970).

Both the discrimination reversal and object discrimination intelligence tasks probably involve recall of the events occurring on a preceding trial. For the former task, nonreinforcement following the occurrence of a correct response indicates that a discrimination reversal has just taken place. Obviously, if a nonreinforcement occurring under these circumstances were forgotten, performance on the discrimination reversal intelligence task would not be perfect. For the latter task, for each new object discrimination it would appear that an animal must recall the object chosen on trial 1, and must also recall whether or not this choice was followed by a reinforcement to exhibit perfect performance on trial 2. Recall of the events occurring on a preceding trial should be impaired by an increase in the length of the intertrial interval. Therefore, performance on both the discrimination reversal and object discrimination intelligence tasks should be noticeably impaired by lengthening the intertrial interval. Results in accord with this prediction have been obtained (Deets, Harlow, & Blomquist, 1970; North, 1959; Stretch, McGonigle, & Morton, 1964).

Relative Contribution of Factors to Intelligence Behavior. Recall that positive transfer of intelligence tasks occurs because carrying out discrimination learning between stimuli that differ along common dimensions will facilitate acquisition of other discriminations between stimuli that differ along the same common dimensions. However, other factors may contribute to the positive transfer that occurs on intelligence tasks. For the discrimination reversal and object discrimination intelligence tasks, an animal must remember certain events occurring on a preceding trial when the succeeding trial is in effect to achieve perfect performance on these intelligence tasks. Therefore, positive transfer on these tasks may occur because prior training improves an animal's ability to recall certain events that occurred on a preceding trial when the succeeding trial is in effect. Another consideration is that the probability of obtaining reinforcement following a correct response on each component task comprising an intelligence task is usually one. Animals may in some sense learn this. If they do, the occurrence of a nonreinforcement following a response on the discriminations of an intelligence task may increase the likelihood that a different stimulus will control responding on the next trial, with the outcome of a positive transfer of learning.

Findings of Bitterman, Wodinsky, and Candland (1958) and Mackintosh et al. (1968) support the conclusion that positive transfer on intelligence tasks occurs mainly because carrying out discrimination learning between stimuli that differ along common dimensions will facilitate acquisition of other discriminations between stimuli that differ along the same common dimensions. In the Mackintosh et al. study, one group of rats received an initial position discrimination and then 18 reversals of this discrimination in an apparatus similar to a T-maze. Then this group was given a black-white discrimination and six reversals of it in the same apparatus. A control group received the same treatment for the black-white discrimination, but did not receive any prior training. The group that received the prior reversals of the position discrimination made more errors on all six reversals of the black-white discrimination.

Prior training on reversals of a position discrimination should have increased control of responding by position stimuli. For the black-white discrimination, position stimuli are irrelevant stimuli. Performance on a discrimination is impaired when irrelevant stimuli control responding. It follows that prior training on reversals of a position discrimination should retard acquisition of a black-white discrimination and its reversals, the result that was obtained. Now suppose that the occurrence of positive transfer on intelligence tasks was mainly due to either: (a) prior training improving an animal's ability to remember certain events occurring on a preceding trial; or (b) prior training resulting in an animal's learning in some sense that the probability of obtaining reinforcement following a correct response on each discrimination comprising an intelligence task is usually one. Training on reversals of a position discrimination provides the opportunity for this learning. If possibilities a and b were valid, they should operate in the direction of facilitating the acquisition of the reversals of the black-white discrimination. However, acquisition of the reversals of the black-white discrimination was impaired rather than facilitated. Therefore, this result supports the conclusion that positive transfer on intelligence tasks occurs mainly because carrying out discrimination learning between stimuli that differ along common dimensions facilitates acquisition of subsequent discriminations between stimuli that differ along the same common dimensions.

Now suppose that training on reversals of a discrimination between two objects was first carried out, and then performance on the object discrimination intelligence task was determined. The discriminative stimuli for these two intelligence tasks should differ along common dimensions. Positive transfer on intelligence tasks occurs mainly because carrying out discrimination learning between stimuli that differ along common dimensions facilitates acquisition of subsequent discriminations between stimuli that differ along the same common dimensions. It follows that prior training on reversals of a discrimination between two objects should facilitate performance on the object discrimination task, the result that is, in fact, obtained (Schrier, 1966; Warren, 1966).

Intelligence Behavior and Stimulus Generalization. Positive transfer occurs on intelligence tasks because carrying out discrimination learning between stimuli that differ along common dimensions facilitates acquisition of subsequent discriminations between stimuli that differ along the same common dimensions. Acquiring the earlier discrimination problems should reduce the amount of stimulus generalization occurring along the dimensions of the stimuli used for the subsequent discriminations of the intelligence task. Another conclusion is that if the initial discrimination problem of an intelligence task is easy, then there is good performance on the later components of the intelligence task. And if the initial discrimination problem is easy, the amount of stimulus generalization occurring between the discriminative stimuli for this problem should be low. This expectation applies to species comparisons. For example, rats perform well on initial or straightforward olfactory discriminations, which means that they should exhibit a relatively low amount of stimulus generalization between two olfactory stimuli, and they also perform well on the later olfactory discriminations that are parts of intelligence tasks.

Therefore, the improvement that occurs on intelligence tasks and the factors predicting later performance on intelligence tasks are both importantly involved with the amount of stimulus generalization occurring between the discriminative stimuli for the early discrimination problems of intelligence tasks. Piaget assumes that children acquire rules and starting at a relatively specific age they successfully apply these rules to solve problems in which the types of stimuli that are used vary widely. His analysis of intelligence behavior in children does not relate to stimulus generalization at all. Moreover, performance on intelligence tasks depends on the type of discriminative stimuli that are used; children should not be able to apply the same rule to problems using different types of stimuli. In fact, children 18 months of age performed successfully on a problem that requires applying a certain rule (Bower, 1976), while children of about 9 years of age do not appropriately apply the same rule in different settings (Flavell, 1977). Piaget's assumption that only older children appropriately apply rules to problems that use representations of stimuli is consistent with the idea that successful rule application depends on the discriminative stimuli that are used.

Conditioning and Language in Humans

Types of Stimuli and Language. Performance on the initial discrimination of an intelligence task is positively related to performance on much later components of the intelligence task. This finding means that a species could hardly acquire a language unless it performed well on straightforward discriminations between the stimuli used as words for the language. Consequently, humans should be, and are, quite proficient at discriminating between small variations in speechlike sounds. Eimas, Siqueland, Juszyk, and Vigorito (1971) found that one-month-old infants discriminated between a "p" and "b" sound, which have physical characteristics more similar than most other pairs of sounds (phonemes) of English words.

Instrumental Conditioning Account of Language Acquisition. Language acquisition involves both comprehending someone else's speech and producing one's own speech. Both the child's comprehending and producing speech are viewed as essentially due to conditioning, because, in part, this comprehending and producing, providing they are suitable in other ways, is relatively likely to be followed by positive reinforcers, including attention behaviors and contact comfort. For example, the young child's obeying the mother when she tells the child to get out of the car is likely to be followed by the mother's talking to the chlid in a pleasant tone of voice; the child's comprehending what the mother said may therefore be instrumentally conditioned. An instance of the reinforcement of the child's producing speech is the child's correctly describing the color and size of an object; this speech is more likely to be followed by attention behaviors than an incorrect description, and thus it may be instrumentally conditioned. This account of the child's comprehension and production of speech is virtually identical to earlier accounts of the reward learning of appropriate behavior, and this is so because this comprehension and production are appropriate behaviors, as long as they are suitable in other respects.

Other reinforcers probably importantly contribute to the instrumental conditioning of the comprehension and production of speech by children. Brown, Cazden, and Bellugi-Klima (1969) found that semantically correct sentences were relatively likely to be followed by mothers' saying, for example, "That's right," to children. In addition, mothers expressed disapproval of semantically incorrect statements such as, "There's the animal farmhouse," when the building in question was a lighthouse.

The essence of language is to represent reality with words, so it is not surprising that Brown et al. also found that semantically incorrect sentences were more likely to meet disapproval than grammatically incorrect sentences. However, grammatically correct sentences are probably more likely to be followed by positive reinforcers than grammatically incorrect sentences, because grammatically correct speech is more appropriate behavior than grammatically incorrect speech. In addition, meaning and grammar are positively related. If a sentence contains a grammatical error, it will usually be more difficult to understand its meaning. Contrast the meaning of two sentences, one but not the other with the grammatical error of the article preceding the noun; for example, contrast the meaning of "The boy went to the store" and "Boy the went to the store." It therefore appears that the instrumental conditioning approach applies about as well to the acquisition of grammar as to the acquisition of meaning.

A child also acquires speech through imitating the speech of other people. However, it still appears that language is essentially acquired through conditioning, because it was reasoned earlier that the general tendency of the child to imitate other people's responses is due to instrumental conditioning.

The role of classical conditioning in the acquisition of language was discussed when language learning by chimpanzees was considered. It was indicated that a word results in an image of its referent through classical conditioning.

Transfer and Language Acquisition. Novel appropriate combinations of words are used both by the child and people around the child. Because these combinations are novel, their comprehension and production cannot be directly due to conditioning. The capacity to understand and use new speech is probably due to positive transfer from previous conditioning. After all, if nonhuman animals exhibit relatively extensive positive transfer of conditioning, then humans certainly can.

Of course the previously described result that most directly supports the assumption that comprehension and production of human speech occurs, in part, through positive transfer is the extensive positive transfer that took place as a result of training on a plastic word language.

Words refer to concepts as well as to individual stimuli. Consider that a child who understands the meaning of the word "dog" will respond similarly to real dogs, stuffed dogs, and pictures of dogs, and be able to distinguish them from similar stimuli such as real cats, stuffed cats, and pictures of cats. Thus, "dog" may not refer to a single dog; it may refer to the stimulus identifying dogs as a class, and this stimulus is a component of stimulus complexes that are similar to other stimulus complexes. Concept learning occurs when an animal responds appropriately to a constant substimulus of stimulus complexes. Therefore, the word "dog" refers to a concept as well as to an individual stimulus, and acquisition of the meaning of "dog" requires that the concept of dog be learned. The referents for most words may be concepts as well as individual stimuli, and these concepts must be acquired for these words to be understood.

Acquisition of the concept for an individual word by humans resembles the acquisition of a concept by nonhuman animals. Consider that a child is likely to receive positive reinforcement such as attention behaviors if he or she says "dog" to real dogs, stuffed dogs, and pictures of dogs; and the child is not likely to receive positive reinforcement if he or she says "dog" to real cats, stuffed cats, and pictures of cats. This training is analogous to that given to rhesus monkeys who acquired the concept of triangle. They got food when they responded to triangles and did not get food when they responded to similar stimuli.

The chimpanzee that acquired the plastic word language exhibited positive transfer when exposed to new relationships among the words of a sentence. Responding appropriately to a new relationship among the words of a sentence can be viewed as the acquisition of a concept. Humans may come to respond appropriately to new relationships among the words of a sentence through concept learning procedures.

The occurrence of positive transfer on intelligence tasks amounts to the acquisition of rules. For example, for concept learning, the rule is to respond on the basis of the constant substimulus of stimulus complexes, and for the object discrimination intelligence task, the rule is to adhere to a win-stay lose-shift strategy. Many aspects of human language are based on grammatical rules, such as adding "ed" to regular verbs to form the past tense. Children acquire this rule; often they will add "ed" to irregular verbs and to nonsense words to form the past tense. Prior conditioning results in animals acquiring rules, so it makes sense to assume that humans also acquire language rules through prior conditioning.

Summary

A chimpanzee received training on simple sentences of a plastic-word language. The plastic words for "same," "different," and "?" were introduced. Sarah came to respond appropriately to questions such as "? same stamp," in which "?" and "same" were plastic words and stamp was a real stamp, when provided with a choice between a second real stamp and a paper clip. The plastic words for "same," "different," and "?" were used to train Sarah on the plastic words for "yes" and "no." Eventually, Sarah could respond appropriately to questions such as "? penny different penny," in which "?" and "different" were plastic words and both pennies were real, when given a choice between the plastic words for "yes" and "no." Training on the plastic words for "name of" and "not name of" was accomplished with the plastic words for objects, either the corresponding real objects for these plastic words or different real objects, and the plastic word for "?." Subsequently, Sarah was able to respond appropriately to questions such as "? banana name of apple," in which "?," "banana," and "name of" were plastic words and apple was a real apple, when given a choice between the plastic words for "yes" and "no." This result indicates that Sarah achieved extensive transfer of learning; that an image of the object that the plastic word for an object in a sentence referred to occurred; and that she understood the meanings of the plastic words for "yes" and "no," and "name of" and "not name of." Training on the plastic words for specific colors and for "color of" and "not color of" was carried out. Subsequently, Sarah was able to answer such questions as "red ? cherry," in which all the items were plastic words, when given a choice between the plastic words for "yes" and "no." This indicates that plastic words for objects resulted in images of their referents. Because classical conditioning between a word and its referent should occur, image theory provides a straightforward explanation of the most essential aspect of language, which is that a word represents another stimulus. The referent for the plastic word for "brown" was taught using the plastic word sentence, "? color of chocolate." This result illustrates how language contributes to the meaning of words and indicates that the plastic word for chocolate resulted in an image of real chocolate. Real objects and the plastic words for these objects were both matched with component stimuli of the real object, again indicating that plastic words resulted in images of their referents. Other chimpanzees learned to communicate with humans in sign language. They were able to combine words in novel but appropriate ways, thereby indicating relatively extensive transfer of learning.

A chimpanzee received reinforcement each time her response matched the response of a demonstrator. She came to imitate novel responses of the demonstrator the first time they were exhibited, which indicates relatively extensive positive transfer. Delayed imitation appears to involve the occurrence of classically conditioned associations among the substimuli of the demonstrator's response and subsequent occurrences of images of these stimuli. In delayed imitation, an animal matches a stimulus produced by its response with an image of the stimulus provided by the demonstrator's response. An animal also matches stimulus consequences of its responding with an image of a stimulus, when it constructs a previously perceived stimulus from its components. This supports image theory, which assumes that an animal matches a response-produced stimulus with an image of the stimulus produced by the instrumental response. Novel appropriate responding occurs in both imitation and construction task learning, and supports the inference that in instrumental conditioning novel responding that is appropriate to the instrumental contingency of training occurs through a closed-loop process. Observation learning is described and analyzed in terms of classically conditioned associations occurring between viewed stimuli. Perceptual learning may occur through observation learning, and therefore the classical conditioning process may affect perception.

Concept learning is described. Reasons are indicated why the procedure for concept learning uses S+s that vary widely in ways other than in respect to the constant substimulus equivalent to the concept of interest, and uses S—s that are quite similar to the S+s. Sarah's acquisition of the plastic word language involved concept learning, including her appropriate response to certain relationships between items of a sentence.

The discrimination reversal and object discrimination intelligence tasks are described.

The acquisition of a number of discriminations between stimuli that differ along common dimensions facilitates acquisition of subsequent discriminations between stimuli that differ along these dimensions, and that is at least one reason why positive transfer occurs on intelligence tasks. Performance on the initial discrimination of an intelligence task is positively related to performance on much later components of the intelligence task. Similarly, when a species performs well on straightforward discriminations between certain kinds of stimuli, it also performs well on intelligence tasks using the same kinds of stimuli. Human performance on straightforward discriminations is also positively related to indicants of intelligence behavior. It may be difficult to perform well on intelligence tasks, because acquired discriminations are forgotten through proactive and retroactive inhibition. This idea is in accord with the conclusion that performance on the initial discrimination of an intelligence task is positively related to performance on much later components of the intelligence task; more similar discriminative stimuli should result in both poorer performance on the initial discrimination of an intelligence task and more proactive and retroactive inhibition. Forgetting may affect performance on intelligence tasks in other ways. Positive transfer occurs on intelligence tasks probably largely because the acquisition of a number of discriminations between stimuli that differ along common dimensions facilitates the acquisition of subsequent discriminations between stimuli that differ along these dimensions. The improvement that occurs on intelligence tasks and the factors predicting later performance on intelligence tasks are both importantly involved with the amount of stimulus generalization occurring between the discriminative stimuli for the early discrimination problems of intelligence tasks.

Human young are probably particularly skillful at discriminating between speech-like stimuli; this supports the conclusion that performance on the initial discrimination of an intelligence task is positively related to performance on much later components of the intelligence task. A child's comprehension and production of speech should be due in part to instrumental conditioning, since good comprehension and production of speech are likely to be followed by attention behaviors, contact comfort, and other reinforcers. Children are able to understand and use novel words, which should be due to positive transfer of conditioning.

REFERENCES

ANDREW, G., & HARLOW, H. F. Performance of macaque monkeys on a test of the concept of generalized triangularity. *Comp. Psychol. Monogr.*, 1948, 19 (3, Serial No. 100).

BANDURA, A., & HUSTON, A. C. Identification as a process of incidental learning. *J. Abnorm. Soc. Psychol.*, 1961, 63, 311-318.

BANDURA, A., & WALTERS, R. H. *Social Learning and Personality Development*. New York: Holt, Rinehart & Winston, 1963.

BITTERMAN, M. E., WODINSKY, J., & CANDLAND, D. K. Some comparative psychology. *Am. J. Psychol.*, 1958, 71, 94-110.

BLAZEK, N. C., & HARLOW, H. F. Persistence of performance differences on discriminations of varying difficulty. *J. Comp. Physiol. Psychol.*, 1955, 48, 86-89.

BOWER, T. G. R. Repetitive processes in child development. *Sci. Am.*, 1976, 235, 38-47.

BRANSFORD, J. D., & FRANKS, J. J. The abstraction of linguistic ideas. *Cogn. Psychol.*, 1971, 2, 331-350.

BROWN, R., CAZDEN, C., & BELLUGI-KLIMA, U. The child's grammar from I to III. In J. P. Hill (Ed.), *Minnesota Symposium on Child Psychology* (Vol. 2). Minneapolis: University of Minnesota Press, 1969.

BRUNER, J. S., & KENNY, H. J. On multiple ordering. In J. S. Bruner, R. R. Olver, and P. M. Greenfield (Eds.), *Studies in Cognitive Growth*. New York: Wiley, 1966.

CHUKOVSKY, K. *From Two to Five* (M. Morton, Ed. and trans.). Berkeley: University of California Press, 1968.

DALE, P. S. *Language Development: Structure and Function*. Hinsdale, Ill.: Dryden Press, 1972.

DARBY, C. L., & RIOPELLE, A. J. Observational learning in the rhesus monkey. *J. Comp. Physiol. Psychol.*, 1959, 52, 94-98.

DEETS, A. C., HARLOW, H. F., & BLOMQUIST, A. J. Effects of intertrial interval and trial 1 reward during acquisition of an object-discrimination learning set in monkeys. *J. Comp. Physiol. Psychol.*, 1970, 73, 501-505.

DOTY, B. A., JONES, C. N., & DOTY, L. A. Learning-set formation by mink, ferrets, skunks, and cats. *Science*, 1967, 155, 1579-1580.

DUFORT, R. H., GUTTMAN, N., & KIMBLE, G. A. One-trial discrimination reversal in the white rat. *J. Comp. Physiol. Psychol.*, 1954, 47, 248-249.

EIMAS, P. D., SIQUELAND, E. R., JUSCZYK, P., & VIGORITO, J. Speech perception in infants. *Science*, 1971, 171, 303-306.

FIELDS, P. E. Studies in concept formation. I. The development of the concept of triangularity by the white rat. *Comp. Psychol. Monogr.*, 1932, 9 (2).

FLAVELL, J. H. *Cognitive Development*. Englewood Cliffs, N.J.: Prentice-Hall, 1977.

GARDNER, B. T., & GARDNER, R. A. Evidence for sentence constituents in the early utterances of child and chimpanzee. *J. Exp. Psychol.: Gen.*, 1975, 104, 244-267.

GARDNER, R. A., & GARDNER, B. T. Teaching sign language to a chimpanzee. *Science*, 1969, 165, 664-672.

GIBSON, E. J. *Principles of Perceptual Learning and Development*. New York: Appleton-Century-Crofts, 1969.

GOSSETTE, R. L. Variation in magnitude of negative transfer on successive discrimination reversal (SDR) tasks across species. *Percept. Mot. Skills*, 1969, 29, 803-811.

GOSSETTE, R. L., & KRAUS, G. Successive discrimination reversal performance of mammalian species on a brightness task. *Percept. Mot. Skills*, 1968, 27, 675-678.

GOSSETTE, R. L., KRAUS, G., & SPEISS, J. Comparison of successive discrimination reversal (SDR) performances of seven mammalian species on a spatial task. *Psychon. Sci.*, 1968, 12, 193-194.

HARLOW, H. F. The formation of learning sets. *Psychol. Rev.*, 1949, 56, 51-65.

HAYES, K. J., & HAYES, C. Imitation in a home-raised chimpanzee. *J. Comp. Physiol. Psychol.*, 1952, 45, 450-459.

HAYES, K. J., THOMPSON, R., & HAYES, C. Discrimination learning set in chimpanzees. *J. Comp. Physiol. Psychol.*, 1953, 46, 99-104.

HERMAN, L. M., & ARBEIT, W. R. Stimulus control and auditory discrimination learning sets in the bottle-nose dolphin. *J. Exp. Anal. Behav.*, 1973, 19, 379-394.

HERMAN, L. M., BEACH, F. A., III, PEPPER, R. L., & STALLING, R. B. Learning set performance in the bottlenose dolphin. *Psychon. Sci.*, 1969, 14, 98-99.

HICKS, L. H. An analysis of number-concept formation in the rhesus monkey. *J. Comp. Physiol. Psychol.*, 1956, 49, 212-218.

HILL, S. D. The performance of young children on three discrimination-learning tasks. *Child. Dev.*, 1965, 36, 425-435.

HUSBAND, R. W. Intercorrelations among learning abilities: IV. The effects of age and spread of intelligence upon relationships. *J. Genet. Psychol.*, 1941, 58, 431-434.

KAY, H., & OLDFIELD-BOX, H. A study of learning-sets with an apparatus using 3-dimensional shapes. *Anim. Behav.*, 1965, 13, 19-24.

KING, D. L. Perception, binocular fusion, and an image theory of classical conditioning. *Percept. Mot. Skills*, 1974, 39, 531-537.

KOHN, B., & DENNIS, M. Observation and discrimination learning in the rat: Specific and nonspecific effects. *J. Comp. Physiol. Psychol.*, 1972, 78, 292-296.

LASHLEY, K. S. The mechanism of vision. XV. Preliminary studies of the rat's capacity for detail vision. *J. Gen. Psychol.*, 1938, 18, 123-193.

LEEPER, R. A. A study of a neglected portion of the field of learning: The development of sensory organization. *J. Genet. Psychol.*, 1935, 46, 42-75.

LINDEN, E. *Apes, Men, and Language*. New York: Penguin Books, 1976. (Originally published, 1975.)

MACKINTOSH, N. J., & CAUTY, A. Spatial reversal learning in rats, pigeons, and gold-fish. *Psychon. Sci.*, 1971, 22, 281-282.

MACKINTOSH, N. J., McGONIGLE, B., HOLGATE, V., & VANDERVER, V. Factors underlying improvement in serial reversal learning. *Can. J. Psychol.*, 1968, 22, 85-95.

MENZEL, E. W. Chimpanzee spatial memory organization. *Science*, 1973, 182, 943-945.

MEYERS, W. J., McQUISTON, M. D., & MILES, R. C. Delayed-response and learning-set performance of cats. *J. Comp. Physiol. Psychol.*, 1962, 55, 515-517.

MILES, R. C. Learning-set formation in the squirrel monkey. *J. Comp. Physiol. Psychol.*, 1957, 50, 356-357.

MILLER, J. T., HANSEN, G., & THOMAS, D. R. Effects of stimulus similarity and response criterion on successive discrimination reversal learning. *J. Comp. Physiol. Psychol.*, 1972, 81, 434-440.

NIGROSH, B. J., SLOTNICK, B. M., & NEVIN, J. A. Olfactory discrimination, reversal learning, and stimulus control in rats. *J. Comp. Physiol. Psychol.*, 1975, 89, 285-294.

NORTH, A. J. Discrimination reversal with spaced trials and distinctive cues. *J. Comp. Physiol. Psychol.*, 1959, 52, 426-429.

POSNER, M. I., & KEELE, S. W. Retention of abstract ideas. *J. Exp. Psychol.*, 1970, 83, 304-308.

PREMACK, D. Language in chimpanzee? *Science*, 1971, 172, 808-822.

PREMACK, D. Putting a face together. *Science*, 1975, 188, 228-236.

RUDEL, R. G., & TEUBER, H. Discrimination of direction of line in children. *J. Comp. Physiol. Psychol.*, 1963, 56, 892-898.

SCHRIER, A. M. Transfer by macaque monkeys between learning-set and repeated-reversal tasks. *Percept. Mot. Skills*, 1966, 23, 787-792.

SHELL, W. F., & RIOPELLE, A. J. Progressive discrimination learning in platyrrhine monkeys. *J. Comp. Physiol. Psychol.*, 1958, 51, 467-470.

SIMRALL, D. Intelligence and the ability to learn. *J. Psychol.*, 1947, 23, 27-43.

SLOTNICK, B. M., & KATZ, H. M. Olfactory learning-set formation in rats. *Science*, 1974, 185, 796-798.

STRETCH, R. G., McGONIGLE, B., & MORTON, A. Serial position-reversal learning in the rat: Trials/problem and intertrial interval. *J. Comp. Physiol. Psychol.*, 1964, 57, 461-463.

WARREN, J. M. Primate learning in comparative perspective. In A. M. Schrier, H. F. Harlow, and F. Stollnitz (Eds.), *Behavior of Nonhuman Primates: Modern Research Trends* (Vol. 1). New York: Academic Press, 1965.

WARREN, J. M. Reversal learning and the formation of learning sets by cats and rhesus monkeys. *J. Comp. Physiol. Psychol.*, 1966, 61, 421-428.

ZEAMAN, D., & HOUSE, B. J. The relation of IQ and learning. In R. M. Gagné (Ed.), *Learning and Individual Differences*. Columbus, Ohio: Merrill, 1967.

ZENTALL, T. R., & LEVINE, J. M. Observational learning and social facilitation in the rat. *Science*, 1972, 178, 1220-1221.

Author Index

485

Subject Index